CEMETERIES

OF

UPSTATE NEW YORK

CEMETERIES

OF

UPSTATE NEW YORK

Volume One

ROBERT M. SHEER

Cemeteries of Upstate New York: Volume One

Copyright © 2017 by Robert M. Sheer

Published 2017

For my wife, Rosemary,

with Love

CONTENTS

- Volume One -

Introduction

Cemeteries and Burial Locations: A-P

- Volume Two -

Cemeteries and Burial Locations: P-Z

Cremated

Remains Donated to Medical Science

Location of Remains Unknown

Buried Outside Upstate New York

INTRODUCTION

This project took shape as a profile of Oakwood-Morningside Cemetery, Syracuse's historic cemetery located in the heart of the city. Over time, its coverage was expanded to include other cemeteries in Syracuse, then Central New York and finally, all of Upstate New York, 55 of the state's 62 counties, those points north of the Tappan Zee Bridge. It serves as a companion to *The Cemeteries of Central New York,* published in 2016.

I never considered this work to be about death but rather the lives that were lead. Initially, the idea was to honor the history of the Syracuse community and those who first settled in the area, those who built the first mill, the first hardware store or brewery, founded the first bank and so on. The leaders from days past who deserve not to be forgotten. I didn't want this work to be simply a book of local celebrities but rather a book to include everyone who made a name for themselves, possibly your friend, family or neighbor. That initial premise was kept intact. The highest concentration of names and detail can be found in Central New York but great effort was made to capture those who made their mark in other communities throughout the state as well.

Genealogy plays a large part in many of the listings. Many familial references may seem obscure to some but interesting to others. With various television programs and websites dedicated to family history, I wanted to include the roots of those who left the state to find their way. Their parents, grandparents, aunts, uncles, cousins, and on up the line, I sought to connect as many families as I could.

The cemeteries are listed alphabetically and the entries within each cemetery list their dates of birth and death, birthplace and death location, and brief details of their life. This book was meant to be a walk through a cemetery and not a collection of names. But I did include others as many have chosen to be cremated, those numbers continue to grow, and some have chosen to donate their bodies to science. Others may have died a tragic or obscure death, their bodies never to be found. And lastly, there are those born and bred in Upstate New York, or have a passing reference to a certain area of New York State. They are included in the last chapter, buried outside the area. I did want to include these other sections to answer any lingering "whatever happened to" questions.

The Onondaga County Public Library proved to be an invaluable source of information. I would spend hour after hour, day after day, looking through the microfilm containing more than 100 years of newspaper. Now I can do that at home on their website. And much thanks to the many cemetery office staff who answered my questions and provided information. And thank you to my wife, Rosemary, for her wonderful painting for the cover of this book.

I did not attempt to make any judgements on those listed in the book or offer any personal opinion. Rather, I compiled the facts from as many sources as I could. Hopefully, they speak for themselves. Included in this first edition are those who died through March 2017.

Robert M. Sheer
Las Vegas, NV
April 2017

ACACIA PARK CEMETERY
4215 North Tonawanda Creek Road
North Tonawanda, NY 14120

MANTH, BURTON W. Jul 17, 1915 North Tonawanda, NY - Mar 7, 2005 North Tonawanda, NY
Founded Manth Manufacturing in Tonawanda, later merging with B.H. & N. Metal Products, co-founded by Vernon L. Brownell, to form Manth-Brownell, Inc., in Kirkville in 1951.

MONK (LeBlond)**, HELEN G.** Jul 8, 1919 Niagara Falls, NY - Oct 20, 2008 Lewiston, NY
Daughter of William LeBlond, operator of the Maid of the Mist tour boat on Niagara Falls, who discovered the body of baseball Hall of Famer, Ed Delahanty, one week after he went missing, falling from the Rainbow Bridge, and rescued Annie Edson Taylor, the first person to survive a trip over Niagara Falls in a barrel. Great-granddaughter of Frank LeBlond, co-founder of the Maid of the Mist Corporation, with R.F. Carter, in 1885.

ADAMS CORNERS CEMETERY
Peekskill Hollow Road
Putnam Valley, NY 10579

COO (Curry)**, EVA** Jun 17, 1889 Haliburton, ON, Canada - Jun 27, 1935 Ossining, NY
Bludgeoned Harry "Gimpy" Wright with a mallet, who was then run over in a car driven by her co-conspirator, Martha Clift, in an attempt to steal his insurance money, June 14, 1934 in Oneonta. Known as the "Mallet Murder." Convicted and sentenced to death in the electric chair in Sing Sing, Clift served 13 years, changed her name upon release and died in 1982. Buried in an unmarked grave, her family did not claim her body. Her husband, William James Coo, died May 7, 1963, age 89, White Rock, British Columbia, Canada, buried nearby, Ocean View Burial Park, Burnaby.

ADAMS STATE ROAD CEMETERY / HONEYVILLE CEMETERY
Route 177
Adams Center, NY 13606

DEWEY, DAVID Dec 31, 1776 Bromley, VT - Feb 7, 1827 Adams, NY
With **Polly Cole Dewey** (Feb 11, 1789 North Kingston, RI - Sept 22, 1859 Adams, NY), the grandparents of Melvil Dewey, creator of the Dewey Decimal System.

KEEP, HERMAN CHANDLER Aug 22, 1782 Longmeadow, MA - Oct 10, 1835 Adams, NY
With **Dorothy Kent Keep** (1790 Hartford County, CT - Jun 15, 1831 Adams, NY), the parents of financier and philanthropist, Henry Keep.

ADATH YESHURUN CEMETERY
Jamesville Avenue
Syracuse, NY 13210

ALDERMAN, BERNARD L. 1905 Syracuse, NY - May 15, 1955 Chicago, IL
Director for the New York senatorial campaign of Herbert H. Lehman, the first New York City mayoral race of Robert F. Wagner Jr., and the first Presidential campaign of Adlai E. Stevenson II. Father of actor, John Alderman. Husband of radio actress, Gertrude Fitzer Alderman, died May 12, 1990 in Los Angeles, age 88, buried there, Mount Sinai Memorial Park.

ARONSON, IRVING Oct 12, 1892 Syracuse, NY - Aug 7, 1967 Syracuse, NY
Owned and operated the Bond Baked Bean Company in Syracuse.

BIRNBAUM, HAROLD L. May 8, 1901 - May 6, 1967 Syracuse, NY
Founded the Birnbaum Funeral Service with his brother, Harvey Birnbaum, in Syracuse in 1934.

BURDICK, BERNARD 1910 Syracuse, NY - July 25, 1981 Syracuse, NY
Assistant New York State Attorney General, retiring in 1978. Brother of Arnie Burdick, Sports Editor for the *Syracuse Herald-Journal*, and Dr. Daniel Burdick, President of the Onondaga County Medical Society.

BYER, LOUIS May 12, 1896 Russia - Jun 11, 1963 Syracuse, NY
Owned and operated the Hollywood Theater in Mattydale until his death in 1963.

COMINSKY, JACOB ROBERT Apr 11, 1889 Rochester, NY - Aug 2, 1968 Asbury Park, NJ
Vice-President of McCall's Inc., publisher of McCall's magazine. Published the Saturday Review and programs for the Metropolitan Opera, the Vivian Beaumont Theater and the Philharmonic Hall at Lincoln Center in New York City.

FLAH, ALBERT Jun 21, 1889 Damascus, Syria - Jan 27, 1967 Syracuse, NY
Founded Flah & Company, with his brother, Paul Flah, in Syracuse in 1916.

FLAH, PAUL Mar 15, 1896 Damascus, Syria - Sept 29, 1966 Syracuse, NY
Founded Flah & Company, with his brother, Albert Flah, in Syracuse in 1916.

FLEISCHMAN, JACOB Nov 24, 1889 - Mar 25, 1974 Syracuse, NY
Co-founded the I. Fleischman & Sons Furniture Store and the Roy Furniture Company.

FRANK, WARREN H. Mar 8, 1925 NY - May 31, 2010 La Quinta, CA
Led the CNY Regional Transportation Authority for 20 years. Namesake of Centro's Syracuse campus. Inducted into the American Public Transit Association Hall of Fame in 1998.

FRANKEL, MAX 1869 Breslau, Germany - Dec 20, 1939 Syracuse, NY
Named one of the six greatest locksmiths in the United States by *Fortune* in 1938.

FREIMARK, FREDERICK Mar 18, 1918 Frankfurt, Germany - Aug 24, 1986 Syracuse, NY
Founded the Atlas Baking Company in Syracuse. Internationally-known culinary artist, whose work was requested by John Lennon, Mario Cuomo, Ed Koch and Senator Gary Hart.

FREIMARK (Bibring)**, GERTA** Sept 24, 1923 Vienna, Austria - Jul 28, 2001 Syracuse, NY
Survivor of the Holocaust. Co-owned and operated Atlas Bakery in Syracuse, with her husband, Fred Freimark. Took her oath of United States citizenship at the courthouse with her husband, while in labor, their daughter, Linda Sue Freimark, was born later that day, February 3, 1953.

GOLDBERG, ALBERT S. Dec 15, 1893 Russia - Sept 7, 1983 Miami, FL
Founded Goldberg's of Rome in 1922.

GOLDBERG, LEONARD Oct 26, 1920 Syracuse, NY - Oct 19, 1995 Syracuse, NY
Chairman of the Goldberg's Furniture Store from 1945-1992, founded by his grandfather, Meyer Goldberg, in Syracuse in 1910.

HART, EARL E. Sept 2, 1912 Syracuse, NY - Apr 9, 2005 Syracuse, NY
Owned and operated Hart's Jewelers in Syracuse and Manlius from 1957-1980.

HERR, DONALD M. May 5, 1913 Syracuse, NY - May 26, 1982 Syracuse, NY
Father of Michael Herr, Academy Award-nominated screenwriter for *Full Metal Jacket* in 1988.

KAMP, S. BERNARD (Sheldon) Apr 3, 1927 Syracuse, NY - Jun 2, 2006 Syracuse, NY
Founded, owned and operated Kamp Airport in Durhamville, from 1977-2002.

KAUFMAN, BARNET ASHER 1853 Poland - Jan 3, 1932 Syracuse, NY
Syracuse butcher. Father of singers and vaudeville performers, Irving Kaufman, Jack Kaufman and Phillip Kaufman. Great-grandfather of record producer and tour manager, Phil Kaufman, author of his autobiography, *Road Mangler Deluxe*.

KAUFMAN (Cohen)**, LENA** 1852 Poland - Jul 24, 1919 Syracuse, NY
Mother of singers and vaudeville performers, Irving Kaufman, Jack Kaufman and Phillip Kaufman. Great-grandmother of record producer and tour manager, Phil Kaufman, author of his autobiography, *Road Mangler Deluxe*. Died in Crouse Irving Hospital, spending 52 days in a coma, attracting the attention of the medical world who could not correctly diagnose her "sleeping sickness." Lost her ability to speak following a stroke in 1917, remained speechless until she let out a scream after seeing the body of her son, Phillip, who died six months prior to her death.

KAUFMAN, PHILLIP Jul 1883 Syracuse, NY - Jan 24, 1919 New York, NY
Professional singer. Performed with his brother, Jack Kaufman, on stage and in vaudeville as the
Kaufman Brothers. Brother of singer, Irving Kaufman. Granduncle of record producer and tour
manager, Phil Kaufman, author of his autobiography, *Road Mangler Deluxe*.

KUPPERMANN, HI (Hiram) Mar 4, 1898 Syracuse, NY - Jun 8, 1995 Syracuse, NY
Owned and operated Meyer's Brass Rail and Kuppermann's Restaurant in downtown Syracuse.

LERMAN (Sniderman)**, RHODA** Jan 18, 1936 Queens, NY - Aug 30, 2015 Port Crane, NY
Novelist. Wrote *Call Me Ishtar*, *The Girl That Marries*, *The Book of the Night*, *God's Ear* and *Eleanor*, a
biography of First Lady Eleanor Roosevelt, which became a one woman play starring Jean Stapleton.
Co-managed the Seven, a New York rock band in the 1960s, with her husband, Robert Lerman.

MARLEY, HARRY Jan 3, 1911 Syracuse, NY - Nov 21, 1989 Syracuse, NY
Central New York business executive. Republican civic leader. Husband of Lillian Cooper Marley, the
daughter of Abe Cooper, founder of Cooper Industries. She died two days after her husband,
November 23, 1989 in Syracuse, age 82. Father-in-law of Donald E. Newhouse, co-owner of the
Syracuse Newspapers.

MEYERS, JOSEPH B. Dec 22, 1900 Harrisburg, PA - Feb 28, 1953 Syracuse, NY
Owned and operated Meyers Brass Rail in Syracuse, from 1932-1953.

MICHAELS, MARTIN M. Mar 18, 1927 Brooklyn, NY - Dec 11, 2009 Syracuse, NY
Central New York attorney. Practiced law for 50 years, partner in Michaels & Michaels with his wife,
Beverly A. Kreisberg Michaels, and son, Edward Michaels. Father of Steven S. Michaels, first Deputy
Attorney General for the state of Hawaii.

NEIKRUG (Reich)**, MAY** Oct 30, 1899 New York, NY - Apr 12, 1989 Syracuse, NY
Wife of Lewis Morton Neikrug, European director of the Hebrew Sheltering and Immigrant Aid Society
(HIAS), located in Paris, from 1945-1953, helping relocate survivors of the Holocaust. He was born
February 23, 1898 in Slutzk, Russia, died April 8, 1953 in Paris, age 55,

POMERANZ, HERMAN A. Nov 13, 1903 Syracuse, NY - Aug 24, 1985 Syracuse, NY
Syracuse defense attorney.

ROTHSCHILD, GUSTAVE Sept 21, 1901 Syracuse, NY - Dec 23, 1989 Syracuse, NY
Owned and operated Rothschild Pharmacies and Rothschild Companies in Syracuse, from
1926-1979.

ROTHSCHILD, NORM Jul 24, 1919 - Jan 15, 1988 Syracuse, NY
Professional boxing promoter. Scheduled fights for Carmen Basilio, Sugar Ray Robinson and Tony
DeMarco. Brought *Friday Night Fights* to national television. Director of the New York State Fair in

1974. Onondaga County Republican Chairman from 1980-1985. Director of the Onondaga County War Memorial from 1984-1988.

RUBENSTEIN, JACOB H. 1903 - Nov 4, 1968 Syracuse, NY
Founded United Radio Service in Syracuse in 1923. Father of Milton J. Rubenstein, namesake of the Milton J. Rubenstein Museum of Science and Technology at the Syracuse Discovery Center.

RUDOLPH, MAX HYMAN Nov 2, 1882 Ithaca, NY - 1962 Syracuse, NY
Founded Rudolph Brothers, Inc. with his brother, Bernard G. Rudolph, in Syracuse in 1906.

SCHIFFER, LEWIS Jul 10, 1930 Bronx, NY - Aug 16, 1985 Golden, CO
National authority on cell kinetics. Chairman of the American Medical Center's Department of Experimental Therapeutics in Lakeland, CO. Authored more than 100 publications on the subject. Killed in a boating accident in Arapahoe County, CO.

SILVERMAN, SIMON J. Feb 1870 Russia - Dec 27, 1933 Syracuse, NY
Purchased the first automobile in Syracuse, a one-cylinder Cadillac. Founded the Syracuse Motor Car Company, with David Grody, in 1909 and the Syracuse Motor Marine Company in 1930. Founder and first President of the Syracuse Automobile Dealers Association.

SIMON, SEYMOUR B. Apr 24, 1927 Syracuse, NY - Jan 23, 2006 Syracuse, NY
Founded Seymour "Mr. Pens" Simon, Inc. in Syracuse in the 1950s, retiring in 1995.

SLUTZKER, MANNY (Emanuel) 1914 Rome, NY - Jun 13, 1985 Canandaigua, NY
Co-founded Manny's on the Syracuse University Hill, with his wife, Lillian Slutzker, in 1949. Donated 18,500 paperback books to the Onondaga Community College Library in 1965.

SLUTZKER (Ligeti)**, LILLIAN** Oct 7, 1917 Budapest, Hungary - Aug 18, 2016 Syracuse, NY
Co-founded Manny's on the Syracuse University Hill, with her husband, Emanuel "Manny" Slutzker, in 1949. Prominent Syracuse University benefactor, namesake of the Lillian and Emanuel Slutzker Center for International Services at the school.

SPECTOR, SOLOMON Apr 5, 1892 Russia - Jan 25, 1978 Miami, FL
Established Spector Cadillac in Syracuse in 1914, the first Cadillac dealer in Central New York and among the first in the United States.

TUCKER, HARVEY JOSEPH Feb 21, 1926 Albany, NY - Jun 19, 2006 West Palm Beach, FL
Founded, owned and operated Dy-Dee Diaper Service in Syracuse. President of the National Association of Diaper Services.

WEINSTEIN, SAMUEL Oct 2, 1895 Jerusalem, Israel - Apr 27, 1979 Syracuse, NY
Co-founded the City Electric Company in Syracuse.

WILSON, HENRY Sept 27, 1890 Warsaw, Poland - Nov 23, 1978 Syracuse, NY
Internationally-known jeweler. Founded Henry's Jewelry Store in Syracuse.

ZIEGLER, BENJAMIN Sept 5, 1911 New York, NY - Jul 3, 1995 Fayetteville, NY
Co-founded Snowflake Bakery in Syracuse in 1954. Founded Ziegler's Supply and Equipment Corporation.

AGEE FAMILY FARM
761 Rodman Road
Hillsdale, NY 12529

AGEE, JAMES Nov 27, 1909 Knoxville, TN - May 16, 1955 New York, NY
Author. Wrote the screenplays for *The African Queen*, *The Night of the Hunter* and *The Quiet One*. Posthumously awarded the Pulitzer Prize in 1958 for his autobiographical novel, *A Death in the Family*. Suffered a heart attack in a taxi, en route to a doctor's appointment. Buried on his farm, where he lived the last nine years of his life.

AGUDAS ACHIM CEMETERY
Old Route 17
Livingston Manor, NY 12758

SCHWARTZ, MAX Russia - Apr 3, 1920 Livingston Manor, NY
Butcher, owned a shop on Main Street, Livingston Manor. First Jewish resident of Livingston Manor, relocating his family from New York City in 1909. Congregation Agudas Achim, meaning a "gathering of brothers", organized in 1913, was placed on the National Register of Historic Places and New York State Register of Historic Places in 1999.

SORKIN, MAX (Mottel) Jun 7, 1878 Russia - Aug 24, 1938 Livingston Manor, NY
Owned and operated Sorkin's Department Store, Livingston Manor.

AGUDAT ACHIM CEMETERY
Schermerhorn Street
Schenectady, NY 12304

KREGER (Gold)**, MARJORIE RUTH** Jul 4, 1902 - May 30, 2001 Scotia, NY
Mother of pianist and composer, Robert Allen, co-writer of "Chances Are", It's Not for Me to Say",
"Everybody Loves a Lover" and "(There's No Place Like) Home for the Holidays", with lyricist, Al
Stillman.

AHAVATH ISRAEL CEMETERY
Hysana Road
Liberty, NY 12754

BROWN, CHARLES Mar 17, 1898 - Nov 29, 1978 Miami, FL
Owned and operated Brown's Hotel, a resort in Loch Sheldrake, the Borscht Belt region of the Catskill
Mountains, opened in 1944, with his wife, **Lillian Brown** (Oct 20, 1903 - May 30, 1997 Miami Beach, FL).
Employed Jerry Lewis as an emcee and teaboy at a previous resort, the Hotel Arthur, prior to his
Hollywood career. Built the Jerry Lewis Theatre Club at the resort, who would ask viewers to call "Aunt
Lillian and Uncle Charlie" to donate to the MDA during his Labor Day telethons. Lewis later arranged
for the hotel to premiere the latest Martin & Lewis film, *Living It Up*, without telling co-star, Dean
Martin, causing a rift that broke up the comedy team, in 1954.

GROSSINGER, HENRY Feb 16, 1899 Austria-Hungary - Jul 22, 1964 Liberty, NY
Co-owned and operated Grossinger's Catskill Resort Hotel, with his wife, Jennie Grossinger.

GROSSINGER (Grossinger)**, JENNIE** Jun 16, 1892 Baligrod, Austria - Nov 20, 1972 Liberty, NY
Hotelier. Owned and operated Grossinger's Catskill Resort Hotel, founded by her parents, Asher Selig
Grossinger and Malka Grumet Grossinger. First resort to use artificial snow during ski season, hosting
celebrities and notable guests in the Borscht Belt resort. Debbie Reynolds married Eddie Fisher at the
hotel, September 26, 1955. Married her first cousin, Henry Grossinger, in 1912.

SHAPIRO, IRVING Aug 27, 1917 Brooklyn, NY - Jan 22, 2001 New York, NY
Co-founded, owned and operated Sullivan's Department Store in Liberty and Middletown, with his
brother, Sidney Shapiro, from 1957-1994.

AIRMONT LUTHERAN CEMETERY
South Airmont Road
Suffern, NY 10901

JAEGERS, ALBERT Mar 28, 1868 Elberfeld, Germany - Jul 22, 1925 Suffern, NY
Sculptor. Created the Steuben Monument in Lafayette Park, Washington D.C., in 1910 and the Pastorius Monument in Philadelphia in 1917.

MCCONNELL, DAVID HALL Jul 18, 1858 Oswego, NY - Jan 20, 1937 Suffern, NY
Founder and president of the California Perfume Company in 1928, later to become Avon Allied Products.

RIPPON (Shannon), **ANNE JANE** 1865 Belfast, Ireland - Mar 28, 1940 Suffern, NY
Mother of Lillian Rippon Strait Rogers, the stepmother of William Pierce Rogers, United States Secretary of State from 1969-1973, under President Richard Nixon, and United States Attorney General from 1957-1961, under President Dwight D. Eisenhower.

ALBANY RURAL CEMETERY
48 Cemetery Avenue
Menands, NY 12204

ABEEL, JOHANNES Mar 23, 1667 Albany, NY - Jan 28, 1711 Albany, NY
Second Mayor of Albany, from 1709-1710. Grandfather of David Mathews, last Colonial Mayor of New York City, from 1776-1783. Great-grandfather of Johannes Abeel Jr., known as Cornplanter, a Seneca Chief and diplomat. Originally buried in the Second Dutch Reformed Churchyard on Beaver Street, Albany.

AMES, EZRA May 5, 1768 Framingham, MA - Feb 23, 1836 Albany, NY
Portrait artist. Painted portraits of President George Washington, Vice-President George Clinton, New York Governor, DeWitt Clinton and United States Senator, Gouverneur Morris.

ARTHUR, CHESTER ALAN Oct 5, 1829 Fairfield, VT - Nov 18, 1886 New York, NY
21st President of the United States, from 1881-1885. Vice-President of the United States in 1881. Ascended to the presidency following the assassination of James A. Garfield. Called the "Father of the American Navy." Dedicated the Washington Monument and Brooklyn Bridge during his presidency.

ARTHUR, CHESTER ALAN Jul 25, 1864 New York, NY - Jul 17, 1937 Colorado Springs, CO
Son of President Chester A. Arthur. Father of the President's only grandchild, Chester A. Arthur III, an astrologer, who died childless in 1972.

ARTHUR, CHESTER ALAN Mar 21, 1901 Colorado Springs, CO - Apr 28, 1972 San Francisco, CA
Bay Area astrologer. Won $32,000 on a television quiz show answering questions about Shakespeare, in 1957. Only grandchild of President Chester A. Arthur. Married three times, without children, leaving President Arthur without any remaining direct-descendants.

ARTHUR (Herndon)**, ELLEN LEWIS** Aug 30, 1837 Culpeper, VA - Jan 12, 1880 New York, NY
Wife of President Chester A. Arthur. Died of pneumonia, 18 months prior to her husband's presidency. Daughter of United States Naval Commander, William Lewis Herndon, who went down with his ship, *S.S. Central America*, in a hurricane off the coast of the Carolinas, September 9, 1857. Niece of United States Naval Commander, Matthew Fontaine Maury.

ARTHUR, JANE Mar 14, 1824 Fairfield, VT - Apr 15, 1842 NY
Sister of President Chester A. Arthur.

ARTHUR, WILLIAM Dec 5, 1796 Dreen, Antrim, Ireland - Oct 27, 1875 Newtonville, NY
Baptist preacher. With **Malvina Stone Arthur** (Apr 29, 1802 Berkshire, VT - Jan 16, 1869 Newtonville, NY), the parents of President Chester A. Arthur.

ARTHUR, WILLIAM LEWIS HERNDON Dec 10, 1860 New York, NY - Jul 7, 1863 Englewood, NJ
Oldest son of President Chester A. Arthur.

BARNARD, DANIEL DEWEY Jul 16, 1797 Sheffield, MA - Apr 24, 1861 Albany, NY
United States Representative-NY from 1827-1829 and 1839-1845. United States Minister to Prussia from 1850-1853, appointed by President Millard Fillmore.

BARNES, WILLIAM Nov 17, 1866 Albany, NY - Jun 25, 1930 Armonk, NY
New York State Republican leader for 30 years. Called the "maker of presidents and of governors." Sued former President, Theodore Roosevelt, for libel in 1915, losing the suit, following a five week trial, held at the Onondaga County Courthouse in Syracuse. Owner and publisher of *The Albany Evening Journal*, founded by his grandfather, Thurlow Weed.

BLEECKER, HARMANUS Oct 9, 1779 Albany, NY - Jul 19, 1849 Albany, NY
United States Representative-NY from 1811-1813.

CALVERLEY, CHARLES Nov 1, 1833 Albany, NY - Feb 25, 1914 Essex Falls, NJ
Sculptor. Created a bust for Senator Lafayette Foster in 1879, which is on permanent display at the United States Capitol in Washington D.C. Worked for sculptor, Erastus Dow Palmer, in his Albany studio from 1853-1868.

COCHRANE, JOHN Aug 27, 1813 Palatine, NY - Feb 7, 1898 New York, NY
United States Representative-NY from 1857-1861. Civil War Union Army General. One of two

brigadier generals to tell President Abraham Lincoln of General Ambrose Burnside's incompetence during the war. Nominated for vice-president in 1864, with presidential candidate, John C. Fremont, opposing incumbent president, Abraham Lincoln and his vice-president, Andrew Johnson, only to have Fremont withdraw prior to the election. Acting Mayor of New York City, following the resignation of A. Oakley Hall, during the investigation of Tammany Hall leader, William "Boss" Tweed. Grandson of John Cochran, Revolutionary War Continental Army Surgeon General, and Gertrude Schuyler Cochran, sister of Revolutionary War Continental Army Major General, Philip Schuyler.

CORNING, EDWIN Sept 30, 1883 Albany, NY - Aug 7, 1934 Bar Harbor, ME
Lieutenant Governor of New York from 1927-1928. Father of Erastus Corning II, Mayor of Albany from 1942-1983. Brother of Parker Corning, United States Representative-NY from 1923-1937. Grandson of Erastus Corning, United States Representative-NY from 1857-1859 and 1861-1863.

CORNING, ERASTUS Dec 14, 1794 Norwich, CT - Apr 9, 1872 Albany, NY
United States Representative-NY from 1857-1859 and 1861-1863. Founder and first President of the New York Central Railroad. Grandfather of Parker Corning, United States Representative-NY from 1923-1937 and Edwin Corning, Lieutenant Governor of New York from 1927-1928. Great-grandfather of Erastus Corning 2nd, Mayor of Albany from 1942-1983.

CORNING, ERASTUS Oct 7, 1909 Albany, NY - May 28, 1983 Boston, MA
Mayor of Albany from 1942-1983, longest-serving mayor in city history. Namesake of the Erastus Corning Tower in Albany. Son of Edwin Corning, Lieutenant Governor of New York from 1927-1928. Great-grandson of Erastus Corning, Mayor of Albany from 1834-1837. Nephew of Parker Corning, United States Representative-NY from 1923-1937.

CORNING, PARKER Jan 22, 1874 Albany, NY - May 24, 1943 Albany, NY
United States Representative-NY from 1923-1937. Brother of Edwin Corning, Lieutenant Governor of New York from 1927-1928. Grandson of Erastus Corning, United States Representative-NY from 1857-1859 and 1861-1863. Uncle of Erastus Corning 2nd, mayor of Albany from 1942-1983.

CROSBY, JOHN SCHUYLER Sept 19, 1839 Albany, NY - August 8, 1914 Newport, RI
Governor of Montana Territory from 1883-1884. Civil War Union Army officer. Served on the staff of General Philip Sheridan. United States Consul to France from 1876-1882, appointed by President Ulysses S. Grant. First Assistant Postmaster General of the United States, from 1883-1886. Survived an assault from his deranged Japanese valet, Iwa Mago, January 12, 1913.

DE PEYSTER, JOHANNES Jan 10, 1695 New Amsterdam, NY - Feb 27, 1789 Albany, NY
Mayor of Albany from 1729-1731 and 1732-1733. Son-in-law of Myndert Schuyler, Mayor of Albany from 1719-1721 and 1723-1725.

DIX, JOHN ALDEN Dec 25, 1860 Glens Falls, NY - Apr 9, 1928 New York, NY
Governor of New York from 1911-1912. Nephew of John Adams Dix, United States Senator-NY from 1845-1849, United States Secretary of the Treasury in 1861 and Governor of New York from 1873-1875.

DUDLEY, CHARLES EDWARD May 23, 1780 Staffordshire, England - Jan 23, 1841 Albany, NY
United States Senator-NY from 1829-1833. Mayor of Albany from 1821-1824 and 1828-1829.

EDSON, FRANKLIN Apr 5, 1832 Chester, VT - Sept 24, 1904 New York, NY
Mayor of New York City from 1883-1884. Husband of Fanny C. Wood, the granddaughter of Jethro Wood, inventor of the cast-iron plow.

ELLIS, CHESSELDEN 1808 New Windsor, VT - May 10, 1854 New York, NY
United States Representative-NY from 1843-1845.

FORT, CHARLES HOY Aug 6, 1874 Albany, NY - May 3, 1932 Bronx, NY
Writer and researcher. Studied anomalous phenomena. Wrote *The Book of the Damned* in 1919.

GANSEVOORT, LEONARD Jul 14, 1751 Albany, NY - Aug 26, 1810 Albany, NY
Delegate to the Continental Congress from New York in 1788.

GANSEVOORT, PETER Jul 17, 1749 Albany, NY - Jul 2, 1812 Albany, NY
Revolutionary War Continental Army Colonel. Defended Fort Stanwix in 1777. United States Army Brigadier General. Presided over the court-martial of General James Wilkinson, an accomplice in Aaron Burr's western conspiracy, in 1811. Grandfather of Herman Melville, author of *Moby-Dick*.

GANSEVOORT, PETER Dec 22, 1788 Albany, NY - Jan 4, 1876 Albany, NY
Member of the New York State Senate from 1833-1836. Son of United States Army Brigadier General, Peter Gansevoort Sr. Uncle of Herman Melville, author of *Moby-Dick*. Son-in-law of Nathan Sanford, United States Senator-NY from 1815-1821.

GRIGGS (Melville)**, HELEN** Aug 4, 1817 New York, NY – Dec 14, 1888 Albany, NY
Sister of Herman Melville, author of *Moby-Dick*. Granddaughter of United States Army Brigadier General, Peter Gansevoort, and Thomas Melvill, Revolutionary War Continental Army Major and close friend of John Hancock.

HAND, LEARNED (Billings) Jan 27, 1872 Albany, NY - Aug 14, 1961 NY
Associate Justice of the United States Court of Appeals, 2nd Circuit, from 1924-1951. Subject of the biography, *Learned Hand: The Man and the Judge*.

HARRIS, IRA May 31, 1802 Charleston, NY - Dec 2, 1875 Albany, NY
United States Senator-NY from 1861-1867. Father of Clara Hamilton Harris, who married his stepson,

Major Henry Reed Rathbone. They were invited guests of President Abraham Lincoln and First Lady Mary Todd Lincoln in the President's Box at Ford's Theater the night of Lincoln's assassination. Grandfather of Henry Riggs Rathbone, United States Representative-IL from 1923-1928.

HARRIS (Pinney)**, PAULINE** May 27, 1809 - Jan 15, 1894
Widow of Jared L. Rathbone, Mayor of Albany from 1838-1841. Remarried to Ira Harris, United States Senator-NY from 1861-1867. Mother of Major Henry Reed Rathbone, who married her stepdaughter, Clara Hamilton Harris. They were guests of President Abraham Lincoln and First Lady Mary Todd Lincoln in the President's Box at Ford's Theater the night of Lincoln's assassination. Grandmother of Henry Riggs Rathbone, United States Representative-IL from 1923-1928.

HAZEN, MOSES Jun 1, 1733 Haverhill, MA - Feb 5, 1803 Troy, NY
Revolutionary War Continental Army Brigadier General.

HOADLEY (Melville)**, CATHERINE G.** May 1825 New York, NY - Jan 17, 1905 Boston, MA
Sister of Herman Melville, author of *Moby-Dick*. Granddaughter of United States Army Brigadier General, Peter Gansevoort, and Thomas Melvill, Revolutionary War Continental Army Major and close friend of John Hancock.

HOOKER, PHILIP 1766 - Jan 31, 1836 Albany, NY
New York State architect.

JAMES, WILLIAM 1771 County Caven, Ireland - Sept 19, 1832 Albany, NY
Pioneer in the salt industry in Syracuse. Second wealthiest American at the time of his death, trailing John Jacob Astor. Namesake of James Street in Syracuse and Albany. Father of theologian, Henry James Sr. Grandfather of novelist, Henry James and philosopher, William James.

JENKINS, LEMUEL Oct 20, 1789 Bloomingburg, NY - Aug 18, 1862 Albany, NY
United States Representative-NY from 1823-1825.

LANSING, GERRIT YATES Aug 4, 1783 Albany, NY - Jan 3, 1862 Albany, NY
United States Representative-NY from 1831-1837.

LIVINGSTON, ROBERT Dec 13, 1664 Scotland - Apr 20, 1725 Albany, NY
Mayor of Albany from 1710-1719. "Robert Livingston the Younger." Suspected partner of the pirate, Captain Robert Kidd, who was using his ship, but later exonerated. Nephew of Robert Livingston the Elder, first Lord of Livingston Manor. Son-in-law of General Pieter Schuyler, first Mayor of Albany, from 1686-1694. Cousin of Philip Livingston, signer of the *Declaration of Independence*.

LYMAN (Hilton)**, MAY** (Anna) Sept 4, 1871 Lansing, MI - Jul 3, 1952 Albany, NY
Novelist. Wrote *The Trail of the Grand Seigneur*. Co-wrote the screenplay for the William S. Hart film, *The Whistle*, with her husband, Olin Lyman, in 1921.

LYMAN, OLIN LINUS Sept 22, 1873 Malone, NY - Jul 12, 1958 Albany, NY
Historical novelist. Sports editor for the *Post-Standard*. Called "the Bard." Co-wrote the screenplay for the William S. Hart film, *The Whistle*, with his wife, May Lyman, in 1921.

MANNING, DANIEL May 16, 1831 Albany, NY - Dec 24, 1887 Albany, NY
United States Secretary of Treasury from 1885-1887, under President Grover Cleveland. Appeared on $20 silver certificates in 1886.

MARCY, WILLIAM LEARNED Dec 12, 1786 Southbridge, MA - Jul 4, 1857 Ballston Spa, NY
United States Senator-NY from 1831-1833. Governor of New York from 1833-1839, following his resignation from the Senate. United States Secretary of State from 1853-1857, under President Franklin Pierce. United States Secretary of War from 1845-1849, under President James Polk.

MCAULIFFE, JACK Mar 24, 1866 Cork, Ireland - Nov 5, 1937 Queens (Forest Hills), NY
World champion lightweight boxer from 1886-1893. One of nine boxers to remain undefeated throughout his career. Boxed exhibitions against "The Nonpareil" Jack Dempsey in 1887 and future heavyweight champ, Jack Dempsey, in 1919. Inducted into the International Boxing Hall of Fame in 1995.

MCDONALD, ALTON P. 1855 Hartford, NY - Jul 11, 1911 Menands, NY
With **Katherine Elizabeth Farrell McDonald** (1866 Troy, NY - May 14, 1942 Menands, NY), the parents of Dorothy M. McDonald Balfe, the wife of Raymond A. Balfe, whose niece, actress, Veronica "Rocky" Balfe Cooper, was the wife of actor, Gary Cooper, from 1933-1961.

MCELROY (Arthur)**, MARY** Jul 5, 1841 Greenwich, NY - Jan 8, 1917 Albany, NY
Sister of President Chester A. Arthur. Served as White House hostess during his administration, assuming the role following the death or her sister-in-law, Ellen Herndon Arthur, 18 months prior to his presidency.

MCINTOSH, EZEKIEL C. 1806 Troy, NY - May 23, 1855 Albany, NY
President of the Schenectady and Troy Railroad. Purchased Schuyler Mansion in Albany in 1844 where his widow, Catherine Carmichael McIntosh, remarried to former President, Millard Fillmore, in 1858.

MCINTYRE, ARCHIBALD Jun 1, 1772 Kenmore, Perthshire, Scotland - May 6, 1858 Albany, NY
Iron ore miner and merchant. New York State Comptroller from 1806-1821. Namesake of the McIntyre Mountain Range in the Adirondacks.

MCKINNEY, LAURENCE Jun 2, 1891 - Apr 21, 1968 Loudonville, NY
Albany-area industrialist. Author of three books, *Garden Clubs & Spades*, *Lines of Least Resistance* and *People of Note*.

MELVILLE, ALLAN 1782 - 1832 Albany, NY
Clothing importer. Father of Herman Melville, author of *Moby-Dick*. Son of Thomas Melvill, Revolutionary War Continental Army Major and close friend of John Hancock. Son-in-law of United States Army Brigadier General, Peter Gansevoort.

MELVILLE, ALLAN Apr 7, 1823 New York, NY - Feb 9, 1872 Albany, NY
Brother of Herman Melville, author of *Moby-Dick*. Grandson of United States Army Brigadier General, Peter Gansevoort, and Thomas Melvill, Revolutionary War Continental Army Major and close friend of John Hancock.

MELVILLE, AUGUSTA Aug 24, 1821 New York, NY – Apr 4, 1876 Albany, NY
Sister of Herman Melville, author of *Moby-Dick*. Granddaughter of United States Army Brigadier General, Peter Gansevoort and Thomas Melvill, Revolutionary War Continental Army Major and close friend of John Hancock.

MELVILLE, GANSEVOORT Dec 6, 1816 New York, NY - May 12, 1846 London, England
Secretary to the American Legation in London, appointed by President James K. Polk. Brother of Herman Melville, author of *Moby-Dick*. Grandson of United States Army Brigadier General, Peter Gansevoort and Thomas Melvill, Revolutionary War Continental Major and close friend of John Hancock.

MELVILLE (Gansevoort)**, MARIA** Apr 6, 1791 Albany, NY - Apr 1, 1872 Bridgeton, RI
Mother of Herman Melville, author of *Moby-Dick*. Daughter of United States Army Brigadier General, Peter Gansevoort.

MELVILLE, PRISCILLA FRANCES Aug 26, 1827 New York, NY - Jul 9, 1885 Albany, NY
Sister of Herman Melville, author of *Moby-Dick*. Granddaughter of United States Army Brigadier General, Peter Gansevoort and Thomas Melvill, Revolutionary War Continental Army Major and close friend of John Hancock.

MILLARD, BRACE Mar 6, 1811 East Bloomfield, NY - Mar 14, 1907 Albany, NY
Cousin of President Millard Fillmore.

MILLER, MORRIS SMITH Jul 31, 1779 Utica, NY - Nov 17, 1824 Utica, NY
United States Representative-NY from 1813-1815. Father of Rutger Bleecker Miller, United States Representative-NY from 1836-1837.

PALMER, ERASTUS DOW Apr 2, 1817 Pompey, NY - Mar 9, 1904 Albany, NY
Sculptor. His work is included in Statutory Hall in the Capitol, Washington D.C. and in the Metropolitan Museum of Art in New York City. Father of artist, Walter Launt Palmer.

PARKER, AMASA JUNIUS Jun 2, 1807 Sharon, CT - May 13, 1890 Albany, NY
United States Representative-NY from 1837-1839. Associate Justice of the New York State Supreme Court from 1847-1855.

PARSONS, CORNELIUS R. May 22, 1842 York, NY - Jan 30, 1901 Rochester, NY
Mayor of Rochester from 1876-1890. Member of the New York State Senate from 1892-1901.

PATTERSON, WILLIAM Dec 24, 1745 Antrim, Ireland - Sept 9, 1806 Albany, NY
United States Senator-NJ from 1789-1790. Associate Justice of the United States Supreme Court from 1793-1806. Governor of New Jersey from 1790-1793. Delegate to the Continental Congress from New Jersey in 1780 and 1787. Father-in-law of Steven Van Rensselaer, United States Representative-NY from 1822-1829.

PECKHAM (Arnold)**, HARRIETTE M.** Dec 13, 1839 Brooklyn, NY - Jul 25, 1917 Albany, NY
Wife of Rufus Wheeler Peckham, Associate Justice of the United States Supreme Court from 1895-1909. Aunt of socialite, Dorothy Harriet Camille Arnold, who disappeared shopping on 5th Avenue in Manhattan, December 12, 1910, never seen again.

PECKHAM, RUFUS WHEELER Nov 8, 1838 Albany, NY - Oct 24, 1909 Altamont, NY
Associate Justice of the United States Supreme Court from 1895-1909. Son of Rufus Wheeler Peckham Sr., United States Representative-NY from 1853-1855. Brother of New York City prosecutor, Wheeler Hazard Peckham.

PECKHAM, WHEELER HAZARD Jan 1, 1833 Albany, NY - Sept 27, 1905 New York, NY
New York City attorney. Successfully prosecuted Tammany Hall leader, William "Boss" Tweed, for fraud and corruption in 1873. Nominated by President Grover Cleveland in 1894 to the United States Supreme Court, his confirmation blocked by the Senate. Brother of Rufus Wheeler Peckham Jr., Associate Justice of the United States Supreme Court from 1895-1909. Son of Rufus Wheeler Peckham Sr., United States Representative-NY from 1853-1855.

PERRY, ELI Dec 25, 1799 Cambridge, NY - May 17, 1881 Albany, NY
United States Representative-NY from 1871-1875. Mayor of Albany from 1851-1854, 1856-1860 and 1862-1866.

PHILLIPS, ETHEL CALVERT 1882 - Feb 6, 1947 Nutley, NJ
Children's novelist. Wrote the books, *Wee Ann*, *Black-Eyed Susan*, *The Santa Claus Brownies*, *Christmas Light*, *Little Rag Doll*, *Calico* and *A Story of Nancy Hanks*.

PINKERTON (Arthur)**, ELLEN HERNDON** Nov 21, 1871 New York, NY - Sept 6, 1915 Mount Kisco, NY
Daughter of President Chester A. Arthur.

PRUYN, JOHN VAN S. L. Jun 22, 1811 Albany, NY - Nov 21, 1877 Clifton Springs, NY
United States Representative-NY from 1863-1865 and 1867-1869.

PRUYN, ROBERT HEWSON Feb 14, 1815 Albany, NY - Feb 26, 1882 Albany, NY
United States Minister to Japan in 1861, appointed by President Abraham Lincoln. Father of banker
and toy manufacturer, Robert Clarence Pruyn.

RATHBONE, JARED LEWIS Aug 2, 1791 Colchester, CT - May 13, 1845 Albany, NY
First Mayor of Albany elected by popular vote, from 1838-1841. Father of Major Henry Reed
Rathbone, who, with his future wife, Clara Harris, were guests of President Abraham Lincoln and First
Lady Mary Todd Lincoln in the President's Box at Ford's Theater the night of Lincoln's assassination.
Grandfather of Henry Riggs Rathbone, United States Representative-IL from 1923-1928.

READ, JOHN MEREDITH Feb 21, 1837 Philadelphia, PA - 1896 Albany, NY
United States Minister to Greece from 1873-1877, appointed by President Ulysses S. Grant. Son of
John Meredith Read Sr., Chief Justice of the Pennsylvania Supreme Court from 1872-1873. Great-
grandson of George Read, signer of the *Declaration of Independence*, and Samuel Meredith, second
Treasurer of the United States, from 1789-1801.

REDFIELD, WILLIAM COX Jun 18, 1858 Albany, NY - Jun 13, 1932 New York, NY
United States Representative-NY from 1911-1913. First United States Secretary of Commerce, from
1913-1919, under President Woodrow Wilson.

REYNOLDS, MARCUS TULLIUS Dec 29, 1788 NY - Jul 11, 1864 NY
Associate Justice of the New York State Supreme Court. Railroad founder and president.

SANFORD, DAVID Dec 29, 1845 Glens Falls, NY - Dec 3, 1893 Syracuse, NY
Semi-pro baseball player. Catcher for the Central City Club of Syracuse. First catcher to stand up in
position behind the batter in a defensive strategy. Died falling down a flight of stairs at a tavern.

SANFORD, ROLLIN BREWSTER May 18, 1874 Nicholville, NY - May 16, 1857 Loudonville, NY
United States Representative-NY from 1915-1921. Great-grandson of Jonah Sanford, United States
Representative-NY from 1830-1831.

SCHOOLCRAFT, JOHN LAWRENCE 1804 Guilderland, NY - Jul 7, 1860 St. Catherines, ON, Canada
United States Representative-NY from 1849-1853. Died returning home from the Republican National
Convention, held in Chicago in 1860.

SCHUYLER (Van Rensselaer), **CATHERINE** 1734 Claverock, NY - Mar 1803 Albany, NY
Burned her crops during the Revolutionary War to prevent the British troops from consuming the food.
Wife of Philip John Schuyler, U.S. Senator-NY from 1789-1791 and 1797-1798. Mother of Philip
Jeremiah Schuyler, United States Representative-NY from 1817-1819. Mother-in-law of Founding
Father, Alexander Hamilton. 2nd great-granddaughter of Killian Van Rensselaer, the original founder
of Rensselaerswyck, the Dutch County in the Albany region of New York.

SCHUYLER, MYNDERT Jan 1672 Albany, NY - Oct 1755 Albany, NY
Mayor of Albany from 1719-1721 and 1723-1725. Father-in-law of Johannes de Peyster, Mayor of
Albany from 1729-1731 and 1732-1733.

SCHUYLER, PHILIP JOHN Nov 20, 1733 Albany, NY - Nov 18, 1804 Albany, NY
United States Senator-NY from 1789-1791 and 1797-1798. Revolutionary War Continental Army
General. Delegate to the Continental Congress from New York in 1775, 1777 and 1779-1780. Built the
first flax mill in the United States. Namesake of Schuyler County in New York and Illinois. Father of
Philip Jeremiah Schuyler, United States Representative-NY from 1817-1819. Father-in-law of
Founding Father, Alexander Hamilton.

SCHUYLER, PIETER P. Sept 17, 1657 Beverwyck, New Netherland - Feb 19, 1724 Albany, NY
First Mayor of Albany, from 1686-1694. Acting Governor of New York in 1709 and 1719-1720.
Commander of the British forces during King William's War. Father-in-law of Robert Livingston the
Younger, Mayor of Albany from 1710-1719. Brother-in-law of Stephanus Van Cortlandt, first   native-
born Mayor of New York City. Granduncle of General Philip Schuyler, United States Senator-NY from
1789-1791 and 1797-1798.

SEYMOUR, CY (James Bentley) Dec 9, 1872 Albany, NY - Sept 20, 1919 New York, NY
Left-handed starting pitcher and centerfielder for the New York Giants, Baltimore Orioles, Cincinnati
Reds and Boston Braves from 1896-1910 and 1913. Won 25 games for the Giants in 1898. Led   the
National League in batting average, hits, doubles, triples and RBI for the Reds in 1905. Retired with a
.303 batting average and 61 career wins.

SOUTHWICK, GEORGE NEWELL Mar 7, 1863 Albany, NY - Oct 17, 1912 Albany, NY
United States Representative-NY from 1895-1899 and 1901-1911.

SPENCER, AMBROSE Dec 13, 1765 Salisbury, CT - Mar 13, 1848 Lyons, NY
United States Representative-NY from 1829-1831. Mayor of Albany from 1824-1826. Husband of Mary
Clinton Norton and, following her death, Katharine Clinton Norton, sisters of New York Governor,
DeWitt Clinton. Father of John Canfield Spencer, United States Secretary of War from 1841-1843 and
Treasurer of the United States from 1843-1844.

SPENCER, JOHN CANFIELD Jan 8, 1788 Hudson, NY - May 18, 1855 Albany, NY
United States Secretary of War from 1841-1843, and Treasury of the United States from 1843-1844, under President John Tyler. United States Representative-NY from 1817-1819. Nominated by President Tyler to the United States Supreme Court in 1844, confirmation rejected by the Senate. Son of Ambrose Spencer, United States Representative-NY from 1829-1831. Father of Philip Spencer, midshipman hanged for mutiny aboard the *U.S.S. Somers* in 1842.

STAATS, ABRAM (Abraham) 1618 the Netherlands - Oct 1694 Albany, NY
Early settler, patriarch of the Staats family of Albany. Built the Staats House, the oldest building in Upstate New York, located where Henry Hudson landed at the mouth of the Stockport Creek, sailing up the Hudson River, September 17, 1609.

STREET, ALFRED BILLINGS Dec 18, 1811 Poughkeepsie, NY - Jun 2, 1881 Albany, NY
Author and poet. New York State Librarian from 1848-1881. Son of Randall Sanford Street, United States Representative-NY from 1819-1821.

STREWL, MANNY (Manning) Jul 6, 1903 Albany, NY - Dec 15, 1998 Albany, NY
Post-prohibition Albany-area gangster. Mastermind behind the kidnapping of John J. O'Connell Jr., nephew of Democratic Party Chairman, Daniel P. O'Connell, on July 7, 1933 in Albany. Settled for a ransom of $40,500 and freed O'Connell, following 23 days in captivity. Tried and convicted, along with John J. Oley, Percy Geary, Harold M. Crowley and three others, and served half of his 50-year federal prison sentence before his release in 1958. Oley, Geary and Crowley escaped from custody at the Onondaga County Penitentiary in Jamesville, November 1937, awaiting transfer to federal prison, captured within days and sent to Alcatraz Prison to serve their time.

SWINBURNE, JOHN May 30, 1820 Deer River, NY - Mar 28, 1889 Albany, NY
United States Representative-NY from 1885-1887. Mayor of Albany from 1883-1884. Medical officer during the Civil War.

TAYLOR, JOHN Jul 4, 1742 New York, NY - Apr 19, 1829 Albany, NY
Governor of New York in 1817. Hosted a dinner party in his home where Alexander Hamilton was quoted making disparaging remarks against his political rival, Vice-President Aaron Burr, leading to a duel, resulting in Hamilton's death, July 11, 1804 in Weehawken, NJ.

TEN EYCK, PETER GANSEVOORT Nov 7, 1873 Bethlehem, NY - Sept 2, 1944 Altamont, NY
United States Representative-NY from 1913-1915 and 1921-1923.

THATCHER, GEORGE HORNELL Jun 4, 1818 NY - Feb 5, 1887 Albany, NY
Mayor of Albany from 1860-1862, 1866-1868 and 1870-1874. Founded Thatcher Car Wheel Works, maker of railroad car wheels. Father of John Boyd Thatcher, Mayor of Albany from 1886-1888 and 1896-1897. Grandfather of John Boyd Thatcher II, Mayor of Albany from 1926-1940.

THATCHER, JOHN BOYD Sept 11, 1847 Ballston, NY - Feb 25, 1909 NY
Mayor of Albany from 1886-1888 and 1896-1897. Appointed by President Benjamin Harrison as a member of the World's Columbian Exposition in 1890. Son of George Hornell Thatcher, Mayor of Albany from 1860-1862, 1866-1868 and 1870-1874. Uncle of John Boyd Thatcher II, Mayor of Albany from 1926-1940.

THATCHER, JOHN BOYD Oct 26, 1882 Leadville, CO - Apr 25, 1957 Albany, NY
Mayor of Albany from 1926-1940, succeeding William S. Hackett, who was killed in a car accident in Cuba. Namesake of the John Boyd Thatcher State Park in Albany. Grandson of George Hornell Thatcher, Mayor of Albany from 1860-1862, 1866-1868 and 1870-1874. Nephew of John Boyd Thatcher II, Mayor of Albany from 1926-1940.

TRAVELL (Powell), **JANET G.** Dec 17, 1901 New York, NY - Aug 1, 1997 Northampton, MA
Physician for President John F. Kennedy, from 1955-1963. First woman to hold the position of White House physician, first civilian since the administration of President Warren G. Harding. Resigned in 1965 during the Lyndon B. Johnson administration, returning to private practice. Published her autobiography, *Office Hours: Day and Night*, in 1968.

TREMAIN, LYMAN Jun 14, 1819 Durham, NY - Nov 30, 1878 New York, NY
United States Representative-NY from 1873-1875.

WESTERLO, RENSSELAER Apr 29, 1776 Albany, NY - Apr 18, 1851 Albany, NY
United States Representative-NY from 1817-1819. Half-brother of Stephen Van Rensselaer, United States Representative-NY from 1822-1829. Grandson of Philip Livingston, signer of the *Declaration of Independence*. 2nd great-grandson of Robert Livingston the Elder, first Lord of Livingston Manor.

VAN ALSTYNE, THOMAS JEFFERSON Jul 25, 1827 Richmondville, NY - Oct 26, 1903 Albany, NY
United States Representative-NY from 1883-1885.

VAN BUREN, JOHN Feb 18, 1810 Hudson, NY - Oct 13, 1866 Atlantic Ocean
New York State Attorney General from 1845-1847. Died at sea, returning to New York City from Liverpool, England. Son of President Martin Van Buren.

VAN BRUGH, PIETER 1666 the Netherlands - Jul 1740 Albany, NY
Mayor of Albany from 1721-1723. Father of Catharina Van Brugh Livingston, the wife of Philip Livingston, second Lord of Livingston Manor. Grandfather of Philip Livingston, signor of the *Declaration of Independence*, Robert Livingston, third Lord of Livingston Manor and William Livingston, signor of the United States Constitution, and first Governor of New Jersey, from 1776-1790. Originally buried in the First Dutch Reformed Church, Albany.

VAN RENSSELAER, JEREMIAH Aug 27, 1738 New York, NY - Feb 19, 1810 Albany, NY
United States Representative-NY from 1789-1791. Lieutenant Governor of New York from 1801-1804.
Father of Solomon Van Vechten Van Rensselaer, United States Representative-NY from 1819-1822.
Cousin of Killian Van Rensselaer, United States Representative-NY from 1801-1811.

VAN RENSSELAER, SOLOMON V. Aug 6, 1774 East Greenbush, NY - Apr 23, 1852 Albany, NY
United States Representative-NY 1819-1822. Delegate from New York for the opening of the Erie
Canal in 1825. Son of Jeremiah Van Rensselaer, United States Representative-NY from 1789-1791.

VAN RENSSELAER, STEPHEN Nov 1, 1764 New York, NY - Jan 26, 1839 New York, NY
United States Representative-NY from 1822-1829. Cast the deciding vote in favor of John Quincy
Adams for president over Andrew Jackson, who later succeeded Adams. Lieutenant Governor of New
York from 1795-1801. Founded the Rensselaer Polytechnic Institute in Troy in 1824. Among the first
travelers on the first passenger train ride in the United States. Father of Henry Bell Van Rensselaer,
Civil War Union Army General and United States Representative-NY from 1841-1843. 2nd great-
grandfather of Jane Wyatt, actress and first wife of President Ronald Reagan, and Floyd Crosby,
Academy Award-winning cinematographer. 3rd great-grandfather of Rock and Roll Hall of Fame
singer, David Crosby. Great-grandson of Stephanus Van Cortlandt, Mayor of New York City from
1677-1678 and 1686-1688. Son-in-law of William Patterson, United States Senator-NJ from
1789-1790.

WEED, THURLOW Nov 15, 1797 Cairo, NY - Nov 22, 1882 New York, NY
Journalist and newspaper publisher. New York State Republican leader. Founded *The Albany Evening
Journal*. Grandfather of William Barnes, Jr., New York State Republican leader who sued former
President, Theodore Roosevelt, for libel in 1915, and lost.

WHITE, HUGH Dec 25, 1798 Whitestown, NY - Oct 6, 1870 Waterford, NY
United States Representative-NY from 1845-1851.

WOOD, BRADFORD RIPLEY Sept 3, 1800 Westport, CT - Sept 26, 1889 Albany, NY
United States Representative-NY from 1845-1847. United States Minister to Denmark from
1861-1865, appointed by President Abraham Lincoln.

YATES, ABRAHAM Aug 23, 1724 Albany, NY - Jun 30, 1796 Albany, NY
Mayor of Albany from 1790-1796. Delegate to the Continental Congress from New York from
1787-1788.

YOUNGLOVE, TRUMAN GILES Oct 31, 1815 Edinburg, NY - Sept 17, 1882 NY
Civil engineer. Speaker of the New York State Assembly in 1869.

ALEXANDER VILLAGE CEMETERY
Railroad Avenue
Alexander, NY 14005

CONABLE, BARBER BENJAMIN Nov 2, 1922 Warsaw, NY - Nov 30, 2003 Sarasota, FL
United States Representative-NY from 1965-1985. Longtime supporter of President Richard Nixon, he
was the first to use the term "smoking gun" in reference to the incriminating White House tapes that
would lead to Nixon's downfall. President of the World Bank Group from 1986-1991.

ALLEN'S HILL CEMETERY
Belcher Road
Bloomfield, NY 14469

ALLEN, NATHANIEL 1780 East Bloomfield, NY - Dec 22, 1832 Louisville, KY
United States Representative-NY from 1819-1821. Sheriff of Ontario County from 1814-1819. Died at
the Gault Hotel, during a business trip in Louisville.

BISSELL, DANIEL Dec 30, 1754 Windsor, CT - August 21, 1824 Bloomfield, NY
Revolutionary War Continental Army soldier. Honored by George Washington for his bravery with the
Badge of Military Merit, a precursor to the Purple Heart, one of only three issued personally by
Washington. The badge was destroyed in a house fire in 1813.

GARLINGHOUSE, JOSEPH Sept 14, 1784 Sussex County, NJ - Feb 22, 1862 LeRoy, NY
With **Submit Sheldon Garlinghouse** (1791 VT - Apr 16, 1861 Auburn, NY), the 2nd great-grandparents
of Academy Award-winning actress, Katharine Hepburn and Amory Houghton, United States
Ambassador to France from 1957-1961.

AMAWALK HILL (FRIENDS) CEMETERY
2445 Quaker Church Road
Amawalk, NY 10598

CAPA (Friedmann)**, CORNELL** Apr 10, 1918 Budapest, Hungary - May 23, 2008 New York, NY
Photographer. Staff photographer for *Life* magazine. Covered John F. Kennedy's 1960 presidential
campaign. Founded the International Center for Photography in New York City in 1974. Brother of
photographer, Robert Capa.

CAPA (Berkovits)**, JULIA HENRIETTA** May 1, 1888 Budapest, Hungary - 1961 NY
Mother of photographer, Cornell Capa, and photojournalist, Robert Capa, killed on assignment in
Vietnam, declining the offer of the United States Government to have her son buried in Arlington
National Cemetery.

CAPA (Friedmann)**, ROBERT** Oct 22, 1913 Budapest, Hungary - May 25, 1954 Thai Binh, Vietnam
Photographer. Photojournalist for *Life* magazine. Covered World War II, the Spanish Civil War and the 1948 Arab-Israeli War. Co-founded Magnum Photos in Paris in 1947. Stepped on a landmine, covering the First Indochina War. Brother of photographer, Cornell Capa.

CROCKETT, BRIAN Jan 4, 1983 White Plains, NY - Mar 27, 2009 Hackensack, NJ
Attackman for Syracuse University lacrosse from 2003-2006. Member of their 2004 NCAA national championship team, scoring three goals in the title game. Killed on the New Jersey Turnpike, returning home from dance lessons taken to surprise his girlfriend, when the car he was driving rear-ended a UPS tractor-trailer, in the early morning hours near Ridgefield Park, close to the George Washington Bridge.

WHELAN, RICHARD (David) Nov 12, 1946 NY - May 22, 2007 New York, NY
Historian. Curator of the Robert and Cornell Capa Archives at the International Center for Photography in New York City. Author of *Robert Capa: A Biography*, *Robert Capa: The Definitive Collection* and *Robert Capa at Work: This is War!*

AMITY DUTCH REFORMED CHURCH CEMETERY
335 Riverview Road
Rexford, NY 12148

FORT, NICHOLAS 1753 - Oct 24, 1821 Clifton Park, NY
Early settler in Clifton Park, established Fort's Ferry following the Revolutionary War. General George Washington ferried across the river, stopped at Fort's Tavern during his Northern tour in 1783.

VISCHER, ELDERT 1752 - 1840 Clifton Park, NY
Founded a rope ferry service on the Erie Canal following the Revolutionary War, becoming the hamlet of Vischer's Ferry in the town of Clifton Park.

ANSHE SFARD CEMETERY
Jamesville Road
Syracuse, NY 13210

ROCKFORD, ALLEN I. Apr 20, 1943 Syracuse, NY - Mar 27, 1979 Syracuse, NY
Radio announcer and newscaster for WONO-FM in Syracuse from 1966-1976. Hosted a classical music morning program for the station.

ANSHE TZAVDIK CEMETERY
Route 209
Wawarsing, NY 12489

REICHEL, EDWARD Apr 4, 1922 Brooklyn, NY - Aug 8, 1944 Reinickendorf, Germany
World War II United States Air Force pilot. B-17 bombardier, flew with the crew of pilot, Jay J. Hatfield, of the 487th Bomb Group, on a mission to bomb the Daimler-Benz plant outside of Berlin, the crew's 30th and final mission, August 6, 1944. Shot down, parachuted out, hit by flak fragments, taken prisoner by the Germans, moved to the German Air Force Hospital at Berlin-Reinickendorf-West where he died two days later from internal injuries. Originally buried in the German Military Cemetery, Elsgrund-Döberitz, west of Berlin.

ARCADE RURAL CEMETERY
249 Park Street
Arcade, NY 14009

STRIKER, FRAN (Francis Hamilton) Aug 19, 1903 Buffalo, NY - Sept 4, 1962 Elma, NY
Scriptwriter for radio and comics. Created the Lone Ranger and Green Hornet characters for radio, television and comics. Author of the young boys series of novels, *Tom Quest*. Created the Sgt. Preston of the Yukon character for the *Challenge of the Yukon*. Inducted into the Radio Hall of Fame in 1988. Killed in a two-car accident.

ARDEN HOUSE
Arden House Road
Harriman, NY 10926

HARRIMAN (Norton)**, MARIE** Apr 12, 1903 New York, NY - Sept 26, 1970 Washington D.C.
Owned and operated the Marie Harriman Gallery, 57th Street, Manhattan. Wife of W. Averell Harriman, Governor of New York from 1955-1958, and film producer and thoroughbred horse owner, Cornelius Vanderbilt "C.V." Whitney, the son of Gertrude Vanderbilt and Harry Payne Whitney.

HARRIMAN (Digby)**, PAMELA BERYL** Mar 20, 1920 Farnborough, England - Feb 5, 1997 Paris, France
United States Ambassador to France from 1993-1997, under President Bill Clinton. Wife of Randolph Churchill, the son of British Prime Minister, Winston Churchill, Hollywood agent and theatrical producer, Leland Hayward, and W. Earl Averell, Governor of New York from 1955-1958. Mother of Churchill's grandson, Winston Spencer-Churchill.

HARRIMAN, W. AVERELL (William) Nov 15, 1891 New York, NY - Jul 26, 1986 Yorktown Heights, NY
Governor of New York from 1955-1958. United States Secretary of Commerce from 1946-1948, under President Harry Truman. United States Ambassador to the United Kingdom in 1946. United States

Ambassador to the Soviet Union from 1943-1946. Son of railroad tycoon, Edward H. Harriman. Husband of Pamela Beryl Digby Harriman, United States Ambassador to France from 1993-1997, under President Bill Clinton.

ARMORY HILL CEMETERY
Benedict Avenue
Ilion, NY 13357

CLAYTON, FLOYD ASHTON Dec 7, 1881 Ilion, NY - Oct 15, 1956 Ilion, NY
Father-in-law of Edwin A. Link, inventor of the Link Flight Simulator, founder of Link Aviation, Inc. and namesake of the Binghamton airport, the Edwin A. Link Field. Grandfather of E. Clayton Link, who died June 18, 1973, off Key West, when his father's experimental Sea-Link became trapped underwater.

REMINGTON, ELIPHALET Oct 28, 1793 Suffield, CT - Jul 12, 1861 Ilion, NY
Inventor, gunsmith and arms manufacturer. Founded E. Remington and Sons, manufacturers of guns and typewriters, in 1816. Designed the Remington Rifle in 1816.

ARTISTS' CEMETERY
12 Mountainview Avenue
Woodstock, NY 12498

AVERY, MILTON Mar 7, 1885 Altmar, NY - Jan 3, 1965 New York, NY
Modern painter. His papers were donated to the Archives of American Art, located in the Smithsonian Institute.

BROUN, WOODY (Heywood Hale) Mar 10, 1918 New York, NY - Sept 5, 2001 Kingston, NY
Sportswriter, commentator and television character actor. CBS correspondent for 19 years. Son of Heywood C. Broun, columnist for *The New York World* and drama critic, Ruth Hale. Father of novelist, Hob Broun.

BROWN, BOLTON COIT Nov 27, 1865 Dresden, NY - Sept 15, 1936 Woodstock, NY
Painter, lithographer and outdoorsman. Co-founder of the Byrdcliffe Colony, commonly referred to as the Woodstock Artist Colony. Graduated from Syracuse University with a Master's Degree in Painting. Namesake of Mount Bolton Brown in the Sierra Nevada Mountains in California.

CHASE, FRANK SWIFT Mar 12, 1886 St. Louis, MO - Jul 3, 1958 Kingston, NY
Post-Impressionist landscape painter. Founder of the Woodstock Artists Association, the Sarasota School of Art in Longboat Key and the Art Association of Nantucket in Nantucket. Younger brother of painter, Ned Chase.

CHASE, NED (Edward Leigh) Aug 3, 1884 Elkhart Lake, WI - Feb 1965 Woodstock, NY
Painter and illustrator. Grandfather of actor, Chevy Chase, star of the original season of *Saturday Night Live!* and the *National Lampoon's Vacation* series of films. Older brother of artist, Frank Swift Chase.

COPELAND, PANSY DRAKE Feb 1, 1910 Philadelphia, PA - Mar 16, 1994 Woodstock, NY
Owned and operated Anne's Delicatessen, Tinker Street, Woodstock. Called the "Mother of Woodstock." Hosted a series of concerts on her farm off Glasco Turnpike, Saugerties, called Soundouts, between 1966-1968, prior to the Woodstock Festival. Mother of artist, Franklin Ross Drake.

DANZINGER, PAULA Aug 18, 1944 Washington D.C. - Jul 8, 2004 New York, NY
Children's book author. Published her first book, *The Cat Ate My Gymsuit*, in 1974 and the *Amber Brown* series of books.

DRAKE, FRANKLIN ROSS Nov 21, 1929 Philadelphia, PA - Jul 10, 2001 Woodstock, NY
Artist. Owned and operated the Café Espresso, Tinker Street, Woodstock. Bob Dylan rented a room above the café where he wrote his album, *Another Side of Bob Dylan*. Son of Pansy Drake Copeland.

DRAPER, PAUL Oct 25, 1909 Florence, Italy - Sept 20, 1996 Woodstock, NY
Tap dancer and choreographer. Teamed with harmonicist, Larry Adler, touring nationally in the late 1940s. Appeared in the film, *Colleen*, with Ruby Keeler in 1936. Nephew of actress, Ruth Draper.

GUSTON (Goldstein)**, PHILIP** Jun 27, 1913 Montréal, QC, Canada - Jun 7, 1980 Woodstock, NY
Abstract expressionist painter. Starred in the *Toonerville Trolley* silent film series.

HERALD, JOHN Sept 6, 1939 New York, NY - Jul 18, 2005 West Hurley, NY
Folk and bluegrass singer/songwriter. Lead guitarist, vocalist and co-founder of the Greenbriar Boys in 1959. Linda Ronstadt recorded his song, "High Muddy Water", in 1969. Police suspect he died from suicide although no official cause of death was listed.

KNIGHT, STEVE (Stephen Sanders) May 12, 1935 New York, NY - Jan 19, 2013 Riverdale, NY
Keyboardist for the rock band, Mountain. Wrote the official song for the town of Woodstock, "Valley Finale."

KOCH, HOWARD E. Dec 2, 1902 New York, NY - Aug 17, 1995 Kingston, NY
Screenwriter and playwright. Academy Award-winner for *Casablanca*, shared with Julius and Philip Epstein, in 1944. Academy Award-nominee for *Sergeant York* in 1942. Adapted H.G. Wells' sci-fi novel, *War of the Worlds*, for Orson Welles' CBS Mercury Theater on the Air radio program, *Invasion from Mars*, causing nationwide panic for many listeners in 1938.

MARTIN, FLETCHER Apr 19, 1904 Palisade, CO - May 30, 1979 New York, NY
Artist, illustrator, painter and muralist. Second husband of author, Jean Sigsbee Wexler.

MARVIN, LAMONT WALTMAN Dec 19, 1896 Elmira, NY - Apr 6, 1971 Boynton Beach, FL
Father of Academy Award-winning actor, Lee Marvin.

MARVIN, ROBERT DAVIDGE Jul 18, 1922 New York, NY - Aug 20, 1999 Woodstock, NY
Brother of Academy Award-winning actor, Lee Marvin.

ROBINSON, HENRY MORTON Sept 7, 1898 Boston, MA - Jan 13, 1961 New York, NY
Novelist. Author of *A Skeleton Key to Finnegans Wake*, *The Perfect Round* and *The Cardinal*. Died from second and third-degree burns, three weeks after taking a sedative, falling asleep during a hot bath.

SHECKLEY, ROBERT Jul 17, 1928 New York, NY - Dec 9, 2005 Poughkeepsie, NY
Hugo and Nebula Award-nominated science fiction novelist and short story writer.

TEE (Ten Ryk)**, RICHARD** Nov 24, 1943 Brooklyn, NY - Jul 21, 1993 Bronx, NY
Keyboardist, arranger and studio musician. Worked with George Harrison, Bee Gees, David Bowie, Peter Gabriel, George Benson, Paul Simon, Bob Marley, Quincy Jones, Lena Horne, Dizzy Gillespie, Grover Washington, Jr., Roberta Flack, Aretha Franklin, Joe Cocker, Hall & Oates, Billy Joel and Diana Ross among many others.

WATEROUS, ALLEN HUGH 1904 - Aug 2, 1965 Woodstock, NY
Baritone singer. Performed on Broadway, including many Gilbert and Sullivan operas. Performed on radio with Rudy Vallee. Son of operatic baritone, Herb Waterous.

WATEROUS, HERB (Herbert L.) 1868 Flint, MI - Aug 29, 1947 Woodstock, NY
Opera singer. Leading baritone for the Metropolitan Opera Company from 1908-1909. Performed in Gilbert and Sullivan operas for more than 30 years, including *The Mikado* and *The Pirates of Penzance*. Father of singer, Allen Hugh Waterous.

WEXLER (Small)**, JEAN SIGSBEE** Apr 15, 1921 Washington D.C. - Feb 20, 2010 Sarasota, FL
Author. Published *The Scissor Man*, under the pseudonym, Jean Arnold. *Stars & Stripes* correspondent in Germany, following the fall of Berlin in World War II. Granddaughter of U.S. Navy Rear Admiral, Charles D. Sigsbee, commander of the cruiser, *U.S.S. Maine*, when it was sunk in the Havana harbor in 1898. Married to violinist, Frank Mele, artist, Fletcher Martin and music producer and executive, Jerry Wexler.

WHITEHEAD, RALPH RADCLIFFE Nov 4, 1854 Glasgow, Scotland - Feb 23, 1929 Woodstock, NY
Founder and benefactor of the Byrdcliffe Arts and Crafts Colony in Woodstock, named from a

combination of his middle name and that of his wife's, Jane Byrd McCall.

WIDDOES (Browning), **CATHALENE P.** May 15, 1923 San Diego, CA - Jan 1, 2005 New York, NY
Mother of actor, Chevy Chase, star of the original season of *Saturday Night Live!* and the *National Lampoon's Vacation* series of films. Daughter of Miles Rutherford Browning, United States Navy Rear Admiral in World War I and II.

WILDE (Hervey), **WILNA** Oct 3, 1894 San Francisco, CA - Mar 6, 1979 Bradenton, FL
American silent film actress and artist.

ASCENSION CEMETERY
65 Saddle River Road
Monsey, NY 10952

BOSCO, RICHARD EDWARD Jan 19, 1967 Queens, NY - Sept 11, 2001 New York, NY
Citibank financial specialist, One World Trade Center, 105th floor, killed in the 9/11 terrorist attacks against the United States.

FAZIO, RONALD C. Jan 19, 1944 - Sept 11, 2001 New York, NY
Accountant with the AON Corporation, Two World Trade Center, 99th floor, killed in the 9/11 terrorist attacks against the United States.

GERMAIN, DENIS PATRICK 1968 - Sept 11, 2001 New York, NY
New York City firefighter killed in the 9/11 terrorist attacks against the United States.

MCCARTHY, ROBERT GARVIN Jun 29, 1968 - Sept 11, 2001 New York, NY
Bond Trader for Cantor Fitzgerald, One World Trade Center, 104th floor, killed in the 9/11 terrorist attacks against the United States.

MCPADDEN, ROBERT WILLIAM Oct 31, 1970 - Sept 11, 2001 New York, NY
New York City firefighter killed in the 9/11 terrorist attacks against the United States.

O'LEARY, JERRY (Gerald Thomas) May 26, 1967 - Sept 11, 2001 New York, NY
Head sous-chef for Forte Food Service, One World Trade Center, 101st floor, killed in the 9/11 terrorist attacks against the United States.

SIKORSKY, GREGORY R. Oct 5, 1966 - Sept 11, 2001 New York, NY
New York City firefighter killed in the 9/11 terrorist attacks against the United States.

WALKER, BENJAMIN JAMES Aug 2, 1960 England - Sept 11, 2001 New York, NY
Insurance broker for Marsh & McLennan, One World Trade Center, killed in the 9/11 terrorist attacks against the United States.

ZAMPIERI, ROBERT ALAN Oct 8, 1970 - Sept 11, 2001 New York, NY
Foreign exchange trader for Carr Futures, One World Trade Center, killed in the 9/11 terrorist attacks against the United States.

ASCENSION CHURCH CEMETERY
Route 9W
Esopus, NY 12429

DUMONT, JOHN IGNATIUS Nov 12, 1774 Kingston, NY - Apr 7, 1869 Esopus, NY
Ulster County landowner. Purchased slaves, John and Elizabeth Baumfree, from tavern keeper, Martinus Schryver, in 1810, which included their daughter, Sojourner Truth, 13-years old at the time, who later escaped to freedom in 1826, then successfully sued to regain custody of her son, the first black woman to win a court case against a white man, in 1828, later to become an influential orator and women's rights activist.

ASSUMPTION CEMETERY
Oregon Road
Cortlandt, NY 10567

LAGANA, MATTEO 1888 Calabria, Italy - 1969 Peekskill, NY
With **Agnes Lynch Laganà** (1888 County Louth, Ireland - 1973 Peekskill, NY), the grandparents of George E. Pataki, Governor of New York from 1995-2006.

PATAKI, JOHN JOSEPH (János Josef) Jun 15, 1884 Kopocsapati, Hungary - Jun 11, 1971 Peekskill, NY
With **Erzsébet (Elizabeth) Szanics Pataki** (Jan 26, 1888 Bacsaranyos, Hungary - Aug 16, 1975 Peekskill, NY), the grandparents of George E. Pataki, Governor of New York from 1995-2006.

PATAKI, LOUIS P. Oct 19, 1912 Peekskill, NY - Mar 23, 1996 Hudson, NY
Father of George E. Pataki, Governor of New York from 1995-2006.

ASSUMPTION CEMETERY
2401 Court Street
Syracuse, NY 13208

ABERT, JACK (John Edward) Aug 5, 1946 East Syracuse, NY - Aug 16, 2009 Largo, FL
Founding member and bass guitarist of the Central New York band, the Montereys, later led by his brother, lead singer, Dan Elliott.

ADRAGNA, BERNARD Mar 4, 1889 Italy - Mar 15, 1978 Syracuse, NY
Co-founded the Brothers Tire Company in Syracuse.

ALBANESE, THOMAS Aug 31, 1905 Syracuse, NY - Mar 1, 1981 Syracuse, NY
Self-employed building contractor and land developer. Built the Westvale Shopping Plaza, corner of Charles Avenue and West Genesee Street in Syracuse, in the 1950s.

ALLETZHAUSER, NORBERT 1913 Pittsburgh, PA - Oct 26, 1992 Syracuse, NY
Founded the Mattydale Sports Center in 1950. Co-founded the Sports-o-Rama in Mattydale, with Leonard Zimmer, in 1960.

BALDUZZI, MARIA D. Jun 19, 1888 Italy - Aug 7, 1978 Syracuse, NY
Founded Balduzzi's Big M Midstate Super Markets in Syracuse in 1929.

BALLARD, FRANK M. Aug 27, 1923 Syracuse, NY - Mar 11, 2008 Syracuse, NY
Owned and operated the Ballard Uniform Manufacturing Company in Syracuse.

BARBUTO, ABEL Aug 14, 1898 Italy - Jan 25, 1988 Syracuse, NY
Singer and vaudeville entertainer. Performed on Broadway with George White and the Ziegfeld Follies.

BARONE, NICK (Carmine Nicholas) Jun 12, 1926 Syracuse, NY - Mar 12, 2006 Syracuse, NY
Professional boxer. Nicknamed the "Fighting Marine." Fought heavyweight champion, Ezzard Charles, for the title, December 5, 1950, losing in the 11th round, Charles' first title defense after defeating former champion, Joe Louis.

BAUMER, EDMUND B. Jan 29, 1881 NY Syracuse, NY - May 1, 1922 Syracuse, NY
Vice-President and Director the Will & Baumer Candle Company, co-founded by his grandfather, Francis Baumer, in 1898 when he joined Eckermann & Will. Cousin of candlemaker, Francis A. Kreuzer.

BAUMER, FRANCIS X. Apr 15, 1826 Bavaria, Germany - Jul 28, 1897 Syracuse, NY
Founded the Francis Baumer Candle Company in Syracuse in 1855 and the Will & Baumer Candle Company. Founded the first Catholic bookstore in Syracuse. Grandfather of Francis A.

Kreuzer, co-founder of the Muench-Kreuzer Candle Company and candlemaker, Edmund B. Baumer.

BECKER, BOB Aug 15, 1875 Syracuse, NY - Oct 11, 1951 Syracuse, NY
Left-handed pitcher for the Philadelphia Phillies from 1897-1898. Teammate of Hall of Famers, Napoleon Lajoie and Ed Delahanty.

BELLO, MIKE Nov 21, 1912 NY - Aug 30, 1993 Syracuse, NY
Golf professional. Credited with teaching many of Central New York's outstanding golfers. Elected to the Greater Syracuse Sports Hall of Fame in 1993.

BERSANI, LEONARD F. Nov 21, 1932 Syracuse, NY - Apr 12, 2000 Syracuse, NY
Onondaga County Family Court Judge, from 1980-2000. Member of the New York State Assembly for ten years.

BIASONE, DANNY Feb 22, 1909 Miglianico, Chieto, Italy - May 25, 1992 Syracuse, NY
Founder and President of the Syracuse Nationals from 1946-1963, including their NBA championship season in 1955. Basketball pioneer, "father of the NBA's 24-second shot clock", introduced in the 1954-55 season. The Shot Clock Monument was dedicated in 2005 in Armory Square in Syracuse. Inducted into the National Basketball Hall of Fame, as a contributor, in 2000,

BISHOP, RAYMOND JOHN Jul 23, 1901 CT - Jan 8, 1967 Syracuse, NY
Saxophonist. Big band leader. Fronted the Ray Bishop Band in the 1940s.

BOMBARD, JOSEPH J. Feb 23, 1923 Syracuse, NY - Aug 6, 1988 Syracuse, NY
Owned and operated Joe Bombard's Used Cars and Joe Bombard Chevrolet in Phoenix.

BORIO, CHARLES Jan 3, 1927 Syracuse, NY - Dec 8, 1974 Syracuse, NY
Co-owned and operated Borio's Restaurant on Oneida Lake in Cicero.

BROWNING (Saumure)**, JOANNE M.** Feb 24, 1956 Massena, NY - Oct 25, 2007 Syracuse, NY
Mother of Jill-Lyn Euto, found stabbed to death, partially dressed, in her apartment at 600 James Street on Super Bowl Sunday, the victim of an unsolved homicide. She fought to keep her daughter's case in the public eye, appearing on such television shows as *America's Most Wanted* and *The Montel Williams Show*, until her accidental death from a fall from the roof of an auto repair shop on Erie Boulevard West in Syracuse.

BUTTARO, PETER JOSEPH Jul 21, 1934 - Jan 20, 2006 Syracuse, NY
Central New York drummer. Performed with Stan Colella's Orchestra and the Jimmy Cavallo Quintet. House drummer at the Three Rivers Inn in Phoenix.

CALO, FRANK Apr 12, 1924 Syracuse, NY - Jan 16, 1973 Syracuse, NY
Managed the Syracuse Chiefs from 1956-1957. Managed three years in the St. Louis Cardinals organization. Scouted for the Chicago Cubs for four years. Killed in a head-on crash on the New York State Thruway, near the Thompson Road interchange, mistaking the entrance and exit ramps leading to the highway.

CAMPBELL, RONALD P. Apr 16, 1943 Syracuse, NY - Dec 18, 2008 Syracuse, NY
Escaped an apartment fire in the Eastwood neighborhood, November 17, 1955, with his mother and sister, Dianne Campbell, who was rescued by their neighbor, Syracuse Nationals player, Jim Tucker, the same day the NBA awarded the team the 1954-1955 Championship trophy.

CASALE, ELIO S. Aug 23, 1922 Syracuse, NY - Oct 30, 1993 Syracuse, NY
World War II Army Air Corps pilot. Flew in an escort plane during the bombing of Hiroshima, August 6, 1945.

CASTAGNE (Panto)**, CATHERINE A.** Jul 25, 1928 Syracuse, NY - Oct 14, 1991 Syracuse, NY
With **Anthony Michael Castagne** (Aug 21, 1923 Syracuse, NY - May 23, 2000 Syracuse, NY), the parents of Rosemary Sheer, the artist who painted the covers of the books, *Cemeteries of Central New York* and *Cemeteries of Upstate New York*.

CASTRO, FRANCISCO 1890 the Philippines - Aug 25, 1966 Syracuse, NY
Bassist. Performed in the film, *George White's 1935 Scandals*. Appeared in vaudeville backing the Marx Brothers and mandolinist, Dave Apollon.

CAVALLO, NICK (Dominick R.) Mar 6, 1907 Syracuse, NY - Jul 20, 1992 Syracuse, NY
World War II veteran, captured by the German Army, spent 26 months as a prisoner-of-war, in North Africa. Father of Jimmy Cavallo, rock & roll, jazz and R&B saxophonist and bandleader, appeared with his band, Jimmy and the Houserockers in the film, *Rock, Rock, Rock*, in 1956, and were the first all-white band to play the Apollo Theater in Harlem.

CHARLES, PETER L. Jun 30, 1921 Syracuse, NY - Oct 15, 1967 Syracuse, NY
Owned and operated the Varsity Sports Shop in Syracuse from 1952-1967.

CHIOVITTI, PIETRA 1875 Italy - Aug 8, 1951 Syracuse, NY
Paid $250 to Fannie Pazullo to be "cured of evil spirits", July 1929. Pazullo, pregnant with her fifth child at the time, was arrested, charged with grand larceny in Onondaga County's first case of "witchcraft", accepting money to perform spiritual ceremonies for superstitious people, sentenced to one-to-three years in Auburn Prison.

CLARK, DAVID May 1, 1953 NY - Feb 11, 1987 Syracuse, NY
Onondaga County Deputy Sheriff, first on record to be killed in the line of duty. Fatally shot by William R. "Billy" Blake during Blake's failed escape attempt in the DeWitt Town Court. Sheriff's Deputy,

Bernard J. Meleski, was seriously wounded in the attack.

COLELLA, STANLEY M. Oct 9, 1932 Syracuse, NY - May 23, 2002 Syracuse, NY
Big band leader and trumpeter. Stage manager at the New York State Fair's Empire Court. Led the
Stan Colella Orchestra, backing performances by Tony Bennett, Rosemary Clooney, Natalie Cole, Vic
Damone and Jack Jones, among others. The Empire Court stage was renamed the Stan Colella
Stage in his honor. Performed with Liberace, Engelbert Humperdinck, Bob Hope, Lou Rawls, Ben
Vereen and Marvin Hamlisch during their stops in Syracuse.

COLLINS, EDWARD J. 1890 - Jan 9, 1961 Syracuse, NY
Owned and operated the Collins and Kesselring Luncheonette in Syracuse, from 1920-1956.

CORCORAN, THOMAS Sept 13, 1896 Syracuse, NY - Jan 10, 1956 Syracuse, NY
Mayor of Syracuse (D) from 1950-1954. First televised inauguration in city history, January 2, 1950.
War Manpower Director of Central New York in 1940, appointed by President Franklin Roosevelt.

CORSO (Russo), **WANDA A.** 1930 Naples, Italy - Sept 7, 1999 Chittenango, NY
Second cousin of Academy Award-winning actress, Sophia Loren, related through Loren's mother,
Romilda Villani.

COYE (Casciano), **MELANIE J.** Oct 3, 1956 Scarsdale, NY - Sept 4, 1994 San Diego, CA
Local singer and actress. Played small roles in the films, *Death Trap*, *Outrageous Fortune* and Woody
Allen's *Radio Days* and an episode of the TV series, *The Cosby Show*.

CUA, BUZ (Basilio N.) Feb 6, 1919 - May 19, 2009 Syracuse, NY
Elected to the Syracuse Area Music Awards Hall of Fame in 2006, for lifetime achievement in music,
with his sons, Rick Cua, former bassist for the Outlaws, and Nick Cua, country music producer and
manager, in 2006. Husband of Central New York women's golf champion, Rita Cua.

CUA (Rivoli), **RITA** Apr 28, 1921 Syracuse, NY - Jan 16, 1995 Syracuse, NY
Six-time women's golf champion at the Lakeshore Yacht and Country Club. Mother of Rick Cua,
former bassist for the Outlaws, and Nick Cua, country music producer and manager.

CULKIN (Mehlek), **GENEVIEVE** 1909 Syracuse, NY - Dec 18, 2005 Brewerton, NY
Grandmother of convicted serial killer, Herbert James Coddington, a 1976 graduate of Paull V. Moore
High School in Central Square, sentenced to death, January 20, 1989, for the kidnapping, rape and
strangulation deaths of two elderly women and a 12-year old girl, between 1981 and 1987. He is
serving his time in San Quentin State Prison in California.

D'AMICO, JAMES F. Apr 4, 1921 Syracuse, NY - Nov 5, 2004 Syracuse, NY
With **Melana Bertini D'Amico** (Oct 4, 1919 Cortland, NY - Mar 30, 1968 Syracuse, NY), the parents of

Janice D'Amico, guitarist for the 1970s Syracuse-area girl band, Sweet Jenny Grit. Janice died February 10, 2003 in a scuba diving accident in the Maldives Islands in the Indian Ocean.

DEAR, BILL (William) 1910 Syracuse, NY - Oct 30, 1966 Syracuse, NY
Semi-pro baseball player. Brother of semi-pro ballplayers, Oscar Dear and George Dear.

DEJOHN (Di Gianni)**, MICHAEL** 1892 Italy - Feb 13, 1970 Syracuse, NY
Father of five Syracuse-area professional boxers, Ralph, Carmen, Michael, Louis and most prominently, Joey DeJohn and John DeJohn, manager for world champion, Carmen Basilio.

DELL, SAMUEL R. Mar 14, 1917 Clearfield, PA - Apr 4, 1989 Syracuse, NY
Founded and owned Sam Dell Automotive Group in Syracuse, Auburn, Clifton Park and Richmond, VA, from 1938-1989.

DEMONG, JOHN Nov 23, 1833 - Mar 24, 1884 Syracuse, NY
Mayor of Syracuse (D) in 1882.

DEMORE, MICHAEL 1903 Syracuse, NY - Jun 28, 1936 Syracuse, NY
Central New York boxer. Fought under the name, "Young Coogan." Died from a fractured skull, ten days after falling down a flight of stairs at the Fern Café, 117 South Clinton Street, while in the midst of a very public divorce and custody battle with his wife, Pauline A. Macheda DeMore.

DENEVE (Standish)**, RITA ROSE** May 29, 1914 Fairport, NY - Oct 28, 2003 Charlotte, NC
10th great-granddaughter of Captain Myles Standish, one of 102 English settlers who sailed on the *Mayflower* in 1620, settling in New England.

DEREGIS, DOMINICK 1932 Syracuse, NY - Apr 10, 2010 Syracuse, NY
Owned and operated the DeRegis Monument Company in Syracuse, founded by his grandfather, Morris J. DeRegis. Co-owned and operated the Cabaret Restaurant in North Syracuse. Member of the New York State Softball Hall of Fame. Drafted by the Cincinnati Reds and Brooklyn Dodgers in the 1950s.

DEREGIS, MORRIS J. Feb 12, 1900 Italy - Dec 22, 1981 Syracuse, NY
Founded the DeRegis Monument Company in Syracuse.

DEYULIO, NICHOLAS Sept 11, 1895 Syracuse, NY - Jan 29, 1982 Syracuse, NY
Professional boxer. Minor league baseball player for the New York Giants. Scouted for the Giants for ten years. Oldest member of the New York State Republican Committee at the time of his death.

DIBELLA, ALFRED 1880 Italy - Sept 4, 1959 Syracuse, NY
Built the Palace Theater in Eastwood in 1924.

DIBELLA, FRANCES P. Apr 26, 1915 Syracuse, NY - May 10, 2004 Syracuse, NY
Owned and operated the Palace Theater in Eastwood for 45 years, following the death of her father, Alfred DiBella, in 1959.

DILAURO, NICHOLAS Oct 16, 1920 Syracuse, NY - May 27, 1972 Syracuse, NY
Owned and operated DiLauro's Bakery, founded by his father, John DiLauro, in Syracuse in 1908.

DINOLFI, ARMANDO 1929 Syracuse, NY - Mar 8, 1987 Liverpool, NY
Owned and operated the Onondaga Uniform Company. Disgruntled, in pain from an operation on his back, performed by Dr. Herbert Lourie in 1985, he knocked on the front door of the doctor's home in DeWitt and shot and killed him. Three days later, he shot his wife, 48-year old, Pasqualina Balestra DiNolfi, while she slept, then turned the gun on himself.

DONZE, MIKE (Mariano) Oct 28, 1888 Italy - Sept 10, 1966 Syracuse, NY
Founded, owned and operated Donze's Meat Market in Syracuse from 1925-1966.

DOTTERER, DUTCH (Henry John) Mar 15, 1904 Syracuse, NY - Jul 16, 1990 Syracuse, NY
Baseball scout for the Cincinnati Reds from 1949-1961, Cleveland Indians from 1961-1974 and New York Yankees from 1977-1985. Elected to the Syracuse Sports Hall of Fame in 1992. Father of catcher, Dutch Dotterer Jr.

DOTTERER, DUTCH (Henry John) Nov 11, 1931 Syracuse, NY - Oct 9, 1999 Syracuse, NY
Catcher for the Cincinnati Reds from 1957-1960 and the expansion Washington Senators in 1961. Only major league player to hit a grand slam off Hall of Famer, Sandy Koufax. Caught a baseball dropped from a helicopter, with his catcher's mitt, 585-feet over Crosley Field in Cincinnati. Finished his career playing two years for the Syracuse Chiefs, from 1962-1963. Elected to the Syracuse Sports Hall of Fame in 2005, thirteen years after his father, baseball scout Dutch Dotterer, Sr.

DOYLE, JAMES E. Dec 14, 1879 Syracuse, NY - Mar 13, 1925 Syracuse, NY
Managing Editor of the *Syracuse Herald*. Editor of the *Syracuse Courier* and *Syracuse Telegram*, from 1898-1905, one of the youngest editors in city history. Publicity advance man for minstrel entertainer, George "Honeyboy" Evans, from 1905-1906.

EASTERLY, HANK (G. Henry) Sept 1, 1905 Syracuse, NY - Oct 11, 1983 Syracuse, NY
With **Helen E. Slattery Easterly** (Nov 26, 1908 Syracuse, NY – Feb 18, 1996 Syracuse, NY), the parents of Richard P. "Dick" Easterly, quarterback, defensive back and punt returner for Syracuse University's 1959 National Championship team.

EASTERLY (Mautz)**, ROSALIE** 1899 Syracuse, NY - Nov 13, 1996 Syracuse, NY
Founded, owned and operated Jim's Fish Fry, 1248 Wolf Street, Syracuse, with her husband, **Frederick J. Easterly**, died in Syracuse in 1948, age 49.

EGLOFF (Korthas)**, MARY JANE** Sept 13, 1924 - Nov 18, 2012 Oswego, NY
Founded the Syracuse Women's Masters Bowling Tournament. Inducted into the USBCBA Hall of Fame in 1993.

EUTO, JILL-LYN Mar 20, 1982 Houston, TX - Jan 29, 2001 Syracuse, NY
Victim of an unsolved homicide. Found stabbed to death, partially dressed, in her apartment, 600 James Street, on Super Bowl Sunday. Her mother, Joanne M. Saumure Browning, 51, fought to keep her case in the public eye, appearing on the television shows, *America's Most Wanted* and *The Montel Williams Show*, until her accidental death, October 25, 2007, from a fall from the roof of an auto repair shop on Erie Boulevard West in Syracuse.

FABRIZIO, ANGELO 1918 Cortland, NY - Jun 1, 1959 Camillus, NY
Owned and operated Buttercup Bakery in Syracuse.

FALCONE, DOMINICK 1879 Italy - Mar 30, 1945 Syracuse, NY
Real estate and insurance broker. Founded the Dominick Falcone Agency in 1920.

FATTI, FRANK J. May 24, 1931 Syracuse, NY - Jun 8, 2006 Camillus, NY
Central New York homebuilder and developer. Co-founder and President of Camperlino & Fatti Builders.

FAZIO, CHARLES 1898 Syracuse, NY -Jul 10, 1962 Syracuse, NY
Local boxer. Boxed under the name "Cave Man Fisher." Brother of boxing referee, Richard Fazio.

FILICIA (Sardo)**, JANET K.** Jul 23, 1939 Syracuse, NY - Dec 1, 2001 San Diego, CA
Mother of interior designer Thom Filicia, co-star of *Queer Eye for the Straight Guy*, from 2003-2007.

FLOOK (Hofmann)**, ELIZABETH** Mar 1, 1918 Syracuse, NY - Dec 6, 1986 Syracuse, NY
President of the Hofmann Packing Company from 1957-1968, founded by her great-grandfather, Frank W. Hofmann. Wife of Walter E. Flook, who assumed control of the company in 1968, with John Kachmarik, and changed its name to the Hofmann Sausage Company. Mother of Rusty (Walter A.) Flook, President of Hofmann's from 1998-2012.

FORTINO, JOHN M. 1968 Syracuse, NY - Feb 28, 1988 Baldwinsville, NY
Captain of the 1987 Onondaga Community College baseball team. Stabbed four times, twice in the heart, defending his girlfriend and her family from James A. Matteson Jr., who broke into their home, dressed like a mummy, to burglarize the family, supporting his cocaine habit.

GANG, JOHN F. 1832 Baden, Germany - Oct 8, 1896 Syracuse, NY
Founded Gang Memorial Chapel in Syracuse.

GANG, JOHN F. Oct 1863 Syracuse, NY - Jul 23, 1932 Syracuse, NY
Owned and operated Gang Memorial Chapel in Syracuse, founded by his father, John F. Gang, Sr. Entered the funeral business with his father and brother, William Gang, remaining until his retirement in 1917.

GARZIO (Esce), MARY Apr 15, 1889 Syracuse, NY - May 27, 1980 Syracuse, NY
Last surviving member of the Garzio and Esce families, listed in *Ripley's Believe It or Not!* for having three brothers and two sisters from the Esce family marry two brothers and three sisters from the Garzio family. The Garzio family emigrated from Campobasso, Italy in 1882, followed shortly by the Esce family.

GENOVESE, TED (Samuel) Mar 16, 1922 Syracuse, NY - May 30, 1979 Syracuse, NY
Owned and operated the Casablanca Restaurant, Erie Boulevard in Syracuse, from 1949-1979. Brother of professional singer, Anna Marie Genovese.

GIBBONS, ROBERT May 24, 1942 Syracuse, NY - Dec 16, 2010 Syracuse, NY
Voice of the New York State Fair for twenty years. Performed throughout Central New York as "Skoopy the Clown" and for ten years as "Ronald McDonald"

GOSS, MASON A. 1922 Syracuse, NY - May 22, 1966 Erwin, PA
With **Antonetta C. Modafferi Goss** (1925 Syracuse, NY - Aug 13, 2013 Syracuse, NY), the parents of Chris Goss, lead singer of the rock band, Masters of Reality, and comedian, "Big Mike" Goss.

GRATZER, EDWARD Dec 1864 Syracuse, NY - Mar 12, 1931 Syracuse, NY
With **Carrie May Ahart Gratzer** (Apr 1872 Syracuse, NY - Aug 25, 1956 Syracuse, NY), the 2nd great-grandparents of Alan Gratzer, drummer and founding member of the rock band, R.E.O. Speedwagon.

GRAY, JOHN R. Mar 30, 1920 Hazelton, PA - Jan 24, 1997 Syracuse, NY
Local radio and television personality for WSYR-TV and radio from 1956-1986 and WFBL-AM radio. Host of *The John Gray Show*.

GREEN, JOHN E. 1928 Tully, NY - Nov 27, 1962 Syracuse, NY
Uncle of Tim Green, novelist, broadcaster, Syracuse University All-American lineman from 1982-1985 and the Atlanta Falcons, from 1986-1993.

GREENE, ARTHUR A. Dec 12, 1916 Syracuse, NY - Oct 7, 2004 Syracuse, NY
Owned and operated the Park Hill Tavern, 4623 James Street, East Syracuse, for 35 years.

GRETHEL, FREDERICK Sept 5, 1888 - Sept 11, 1967 Syracuse, NY
With **Mary Elizabeth Mellen Grethel** (Jul 3, 1893 Williamstown, NY - Jan 31, 1976 Syracuse, NY), the parents of fashion designer, Henry Grethel.

GROBOSKE, ALBERT J. Jul 7, 1903 Syracuse, NY - Dec 24, 1990 Syracuse, NY
Founded Albert's Jewelers in Syracuse in 1943.

GROSS, JOHNNY Oct 11, 1965 Syracuse, NY - Jan 28, 1990 Syracuse, NY
New York State Golden Gloves champion in 1986. Taught by Syracuse boxing legend, Billy Harris.
One hour after winning his super-middleweight fight with Michael Caminiti, at the Three Rivers Inn in
Phoenix, May 1, 1989, fell into a coma, died nine months later.

GRUEN, THEODORE Sept 26, 1907 Germany - Feb 17, 1980 Syracuse, NY
Founded and operated Gruen's Restaurant in Syracuse for 26 years.

HANNON, JIM (James) 1899 - Jun 13, 1929 Syracuse, NY
Syracuse police officer. Shot during a burglary at Walker Pharmacy on East Genesee Street in
Syracuse, May 1, 1929, died six weeks later of complications from his wound.

HARRIS (Svoboda), **MARY E.** Nov 13, 1918 Syracuse, NY - Nov 27, 2007 Liverpool, NY
Mother of Warren Anthony "Tony" Harris, killed with his wife, Dolores "Dodie" Lake Harris, and two
children, Shelby and Marc, in their home in Dryden, December 23, 1989, bound, tortured, shot in the
head and doused with gasoline, by Michael A. Kinge, later shot to death by troopers in a standoff,
February 7, 1990, in his Dryden home.

HEITZMAN, GEORGE C. May 22, 1923 East Syracuse, NY - Dec 29, 2016 Syracuse, NY
Thoracic surgeon. Implanted the first pacemaker in Syracuse in 1963 and performed the first coronary
bypass in 1970.

HOFMANN, AUGUST C. 1849 Bromberg, Germany - Oct 16, 1921 Syracuse, NY
Owned and operated the Hofmann Packing Company with his brother, John Hoffman, from
1879-1921. Son of Frank W. Hofmann, founder of the Hofmann Packing Company.

HOFMANN, FRANK WILLIAM Sept 17, 1819 Wurzburg, Germany - Aug 13, 1923 Syracuse, NY
Founded the Hofmann Meat Market in Syracuse in 1861. Died one month shy of his 104th birthday.

HOFMANN, JOSEPH A. 1829 Germany - Nov 26, 1911 Syracuse, NY
Editor of the German newspaper, *Central Democrat*, for many years. Among the oldest and most well-
known residents of the North side of Syracuse at the time of his death.

HUGHES, LEO VINCENT Apr 3, 1889 Syracuse, NY - Nov 26, 1955 New York, NY
Illuminating light designer and installation engineer. Consulted and installed systems in nearly every
state in the union.

HUNDSHAMER (Lutz)**, PAULINE** 1893 Rochester, NY - Jun 7, 1968 Syracuse, NY
Operatic soprano soloist. Performed on the vaudeville circuit. Opened at the Palace Theater in New York City. Performed for President Franklin Roosevelt and First Lady Eleanor Roosevelt at the White House on several occasions. Her only child, United States Army Private First Class, William F. Hundshamer, was killed in combat in World War II.

ITALIANO, GREGORY ANTHONY Aug 3, 1950 Syracuse, NY - May 17, 2010 Rochester, NY
Owned and operated the Syracuse rock club, the Lost Horizon.

KALLFELZ, JOHN B. 1876 Melz, Germany - Sept 10, 1916 Syracuse, NY
Founded, owned and operated Kallfelz Brothers Bakery in Syracuse with his brothers, Charles, Alois, Peter Kallfelz and Mathew J. Kallfelz.

KESEL, JOHN J. 1930 Fayetteville, NY - Nov 26, 1955 Syracuse, NY
United States Air National Guard Lieutenant. Killed during defense maneuvers, crashing his fighter jet into Onondaga Lake during a snowstorm. Grandson of John J. Kesel, former Postmaster of Syracuse.

KIRSCH, SAM (Bernard A.) Nov 15, 1912 Syracuse, NY - Jan 3, 1995 Syracuse, NY
Owned and operated Kirsch Dairy in Syracuse. His parents, John M. and Mary Kirsch, donated the land and were founding members of St. Margaret's Church in Mattydale.

KREUZER, FREDERICK A. Jun 29, 1902 Syracuse, NY - Feb 12, 1975 Syracuse, NY
Founded the Muench-Kreuzer Candle Company in Syracuse with his cousins, Norbert C.H. Muench and Alexis N. Muench. Cousin of pharmacist Albert A. Muench and Dr. Carl E. Muench, founder of Crouse-Irving Memorial Hospital in Syracuse. Grandson of Francis Baumer, co-founder of the Will & Baumer Candle Company. Cousin of candlemaker, Edmund B. Baumer.

KREUZER (Ahrens)**, MELANIE** 1908 Syracuse, NY - Jan 30, 1975 Syracuse, NY
Member of the Syracuse City Council from 1950-1958, President from 1954-1958. First woman in Syracuse history to be mayor, taking over for Donald H. Mead, January 28, 1954, while the mayor was out of town. Died thirteen days before her husband, Frederick A. Kreuzer, co-founder of the Muench-Kreuzer Candle Company.

LAMIRANDE, WILLIAM J. Dec 6, 1923 Syracuse, NY - Sept 3, 1996 Syracuse, NY
Local artist, mostly in water colors.

LARDEO, ALBERT Dec 13, 1926 Syracuse, NY - May 15, 1997 Syracuse, NY
Owned Big Al's Auto Shop, 413 S. West Street in Syracuse, where his son, Ronald A. Lardeo, 33, and friend, Michael D. Nappi, 43, were found beaten to death in the repair shop, February 12, 1991, murders that remain unsolved. Big Al's never re-opened, the site remaining vacant since that day. Both victims were buried in Assumption Cemetery.

LARUE, ARLENE May 5, 1912 Syracuse, NY - Aug 15, 1993 Syracuse, NY
Lifestyle Editor of the *Syracuse Herald-Journal* and *Herald American*, from 1947-1977. Continued to write her column, "All Those Yesterdays", until four months prior to her death.

LAURETTI, ANTHONY Oct 29, 1896 Italy - Apr 17, 1971 Syracuse, NY
Owned and operated the Roma Bakery in Syracuse, from 1938-1963.

LAVALLE, ANTHONY Jul 18, 1889 Sicily, Italy - Dec 24, 1982 Syracuse, NY
Founded the Anthony LaValle & Sons Paving Company in Syracuse in 1907.

LAZZARO, JOHN V. Nov 3, 1929 Syracuse, NY - Jun 12, 1968 Syracuse, NY
Owned the Syracuse Blazers of the EHL, from 1967-1968.

LESKOSKE, EDWARD JOSEPH Nov 2, 1915 Syracuse, NY - Oct 9, 2009 Syracuse, NY
Member of the first graduating class of Assumption Academy in Syracuse, in 1933, and last surviving graduate. Last employee of the Porter-Cable/Rockwell International plant in Syracuse, prior to the company leaving the city.

LINARES, MARIO May 8, 1902 Marsala, Sicily, Italy - Sept 12, 1984 Syracuse, NY
Called "the father of soccer in Central New York." Founded the Syracuse-Onondaga Inter-County Soccer Association, the oldest and largest soccer league in Syracuse.

LOMBARDI, ELVIRO Oct 10, 1907 Pogeroli, Amalfi, Italy - Jul 27, 1994 Syracuse, NY
Founded, owned and operated Lombardi's Fruits & Imports in Syracuse.

LOMBARDI, TARKY Jul 11, 1902 Italy - May 13, 1983 Syracuse, NY
Founded the Syracuse Tank and Manufacturing Company in Syracuse in 1951. Father of Tarky Lombardi Jr., New York State Senator from 1966-1992.

LOTITO, JOSEPH N. May 12, 1927 Syracuse, NY - Oct 25, 2009 Syracuse, NY
Central New York producer, director and actor. Executive Director of the Salt City Center for the Performing Arts, founded as the Salt City Playhouse in Syracuse, in 1968, with his wife, Patricia Montfort Lotito.

MAGLIONE (DeNiro)**, HELEN** Oct 23, 1901 Syracuse, NY - Jan 24, 1975 Syracuse, NY
Aunt of artist, Robert DeNiro Sr. Grandaunt of Academy Award-winning actor, Robert DeNiro. Resided at 1167 LeMoyne Avenue on the North side of Syracuse.

MAGNARELLI, ARMOND Sep 6, 1924 Syracuse, NY - Feb 8, 2008 Syracuse, NY
President of the Syracuse Common Council from 1979-1985. President of the Syracuse Board of Education. Director of the New York State Parks and Recreation Department. Host of *Armond's Music*

Italian Style, Sunday morning's on WFBL-AM radio. Performed with the Pompeian Players. Elected to the Syracuse Sports Hall of Fame as a three-sport scholastic and collegiate star. Father of jazz trumpeter, Joe Magnarelli.

MAHON (Fraser), **AMELIA** 1898 Syracuse, NY - Aug 9, 1954 Syracuse, NY
Mother of John Fraser Mahon, the husband of Susan Eisenhower Bradshaw, who was the granddaughter of President Dwight D. Eisenhower and First Lady Mamie Eisenhower. Grandmother of Amelia Eisenhower Mahon, the great-granddaughter of President Eisenhower.

MALFITANO, FRANK R. July 4, 1916 Syracuse, NY - May 31, 1967 Syracuse, NY
Father of Frank Malfitano, founder and director of the annual Syracuse Jazz Fest, in 1982.

MANZI, PAT Jul 31, 1927 Syracuse, NY - Aug 3, 1982 Syracuse, NY
Welterweight boxing contender. Lost to Tony DeMarco in a first round knockout, November 6, 1954, two fights before DeMarco won the world welterweight championship.

MARTIN (Secreti), **VIOLA** 1912 Syracuse, NY - Jan 10, 1998 Syracuse, NY
Mother of Shirley Anne Martin Hamlin, who kissed her mother's broken statue of Saint Ann as an 11-year old child, causing tears to flow from the eyes of the statue and continue to do so for many years. The statue had fallen from her windowsill, April 3, 1949, on Hawley Avenue in Syracuse. Her daughter's story made news around the world, her local Roman Catholic church calling it a "phenomenon."

MARTINEZ, JOSEPH May 25, 1904 Columbus, OH - Feb 10, 1977 Syracuse, NY
Father of Dolores Martinez Collard who, as a 12-year old in the 1950s, claimed she was in a car driven by her father on Cedarvale Road in Syracuse, known as "13 Curves", when the image of a woman in a white veil appeared, floating across the road at the 7th Curve. Their car drove through the figure, startling everyone in the vehicle, the most widely-known of the ghost stories at Dead Man's Curve. The legend stems from a story of a bride and groom whose car crashed at the site, with the ghostly bride's apparition lingering to this day.

MARTINO, JOHN Jul 8, 1897 Tiano, Italy - Sept 1985 Syracuse, NY
Bowling columnist for the *Post-Standard*. Co-founder and first President of the Bowling Writers Association of America. First Central New York bowler elected to the American Bowling Congress Hall of Fame.

MARZULLO, MARY ANNE 1953 Syracuse, NY - Aug 12, 1967 Cicero, NY
Murder victim. Last seen walking on Brewerton Road with her friend, Jacqueline Saunders, on their way home from the Mattydale Fire Department's Field Days, their bodies found the next morning, bound together by rope, strangled to death, off Oxbow Road, near Chittenango Creek, town of Cicero, murders that were never solved.

MARZULLO, SALVATORE May 31, 1918 Syracuse, NY - Jan 25, 1990 Syracuse, NY
Owned and operated the Pine Lounge Restaurant, Burnet Avenue in Syracuse. Father of Mary Anne
Marzullo, found strangled to death, August 12, 1967, the victim of an unsolved homicide.

MEIER, RUDOLF Jul 27, 1904 Germany - Dec 19, 1992 Syracuse, NY
Owned and operated Meier & Ranz Meat Company for more than 50 years in Syracuse.

MEOLA, FRANK M. Jul 15, 1909 Abruzzi, Italy - Feb 26, 1997 Syracuse, NY
Syracuse family physician. With **Sherie M. Perdue Meola** (1922 Ashland, KY - May 11, 1999 Wilmington,
DE), the parents of photographer, Eric Meola, best known for photographing the cover of Bruce
Springsteen's 1975 album, *Born to Run*.

MINALE, LOUIS J. Jun 9, 1925 Syracuse, NY - March 14, 2008 Syracuse, NY
Owned and operated the Minale Funeral Home on the North side of Syracuse for 30 years.

MIRBACH (Schucker)**, MARIE H.** Aug 11, 1895 Styer, Austria - Jun 26, 1989 Syracuse, NY
Owned and operated Mirbach's Restaurant in Syracuse from 1922-1982, with her husband, Henry J.
Mirbach, who died June 16, 1960 in Syracuse, age 67.

MONDO, CHRISTIAN N. Dec 25, 1914 - Dec 16, 2004 Syracuse, NY
Owned and operated Mondo's Bakery in Syracuse for 35 years. Brother-in-law of Dominick Tassone
Sr., owner of the Modern Bakery and Restaurant in Syracuse. Uncle of Dominick Tassone Jr., founder
and owner of Dominick's Restaurant in Syracuse and Samuel L. Tassone, owner and operator of
Sam's Lakeside Restaurant in Brewerton.

MONTANARO, FRANK J. Jul 22, 1921 Syracuse, NY - Dec 28, 2013 Syracuse, NY
Purchased the Liverpool estate of architect, Ward Wellington Ward, 629 Old Liverpool Road,
developing LeMoyne Manor, a banquet hall, lodge and restaurant.

MOORE (Muench)**, IRENE** Aug 26, 1906 Syracuse, NY - Jul 2, 1996 Syracuse, NY
Owned and operated the Catholic Shop in Syracuse with her husband, J. Edmund Moore. Daughter of
Alexis N. Muench, co-founder of the Muench-Kreuzer Candle Company.

MUENCH, ALBERT AUGUST Aug 4, 1891 NY - Apr 14, 1955 Syracuse, NY
Pharmacist. One of New York State's top druggists at the time of his death, known for his concoction
of "Muenchies", a prescription used to combat colds. Operated the Muench Pharmacy in Syracuse,
from 1925-1955, founded by his father, William G. Muench, in 1875. President of the New York State
Pharmaceutical Association. Brother of Dr. Carl E. Muench, founder of Crouse-Irving Memorial
Hospital in Syracuse and Alexis N. Muench and Norbert C.H. Muench, co-founders of the Muench-
Kreuzer Candle Company, with their cousin, Frederick Kreuzer.

MUENCH, ALEXIS N. Sept 30, 1881 NY - Nov 1965 Syracuse, NY
Founded the Muench-Kreuzer Candle Company in Syracuse with his brother, Norbert C.H. Muench and cousin, Fredrick Kreuzer, in 1925. Brother of pharmacist, Albert A. Muench and Dr. Carl E. Muench, founder of Crouse-Irving Memorial Hospital in Syracuse.

MUENCH, CARL EUGENE Mar 24, 1884 NY - Apr 13, 1976 Syracuse, NY
Founded Crouse-Irving Memorial Hospital in Syracuse. Brother of Alexis N. Muench and Norbert C.H. Muench, co-founders of the Muench-Kreuzer Candle Company, with their cousin, Frederick Kreuzer. Brother of pharmacist, Albert A. Muench. Brother-in-law of art critic, Robert W. Friedel.

MULHAUSER, LEONARD J. Mar 14, 1884 Syracuse, NY - Mar 29, 1981 Syracuse, NY
Owned the Leonard J. Mulhauser Florist Shop in Syracuse, founded by his parents, Joseph and Mary Mulhauser, in 1909. Oldest living member of the Pastime Athletic Club in Syracuse at the time of his death. He joined the club in 1902 as an 18-year old.

MYERS, MARGARET C. Jun 14, 1897 Syracuse, NY - Jun 26, 1991 Syracuse, NY
Nanny for the daughter of actress, Irene Dunn and for the children of actor, Phil Silvers, including actress Cathy Silvers, television scriptwriter, Nancey Silvers and producer, Tracey Silvers.

NICOLETTI (Fenu)**, VICTORIA L.** Sept 5, 1914 Syracuse, NY - Oct 16, 2002 Syracuse, NY
Mother of Joseph A. Nicoletti, New York State Assemblyman from 1991-1994. Rescued her   two-year-old niece, Paula Francine Fenu, from her burning bed, January 18, 1952, the child later dying from suffocation.

NILAND, TOM (Thomas James) Apr 28, 1920 Tonawanda, NY - Mar 16, 2004 Osterville, MA
LeMoyne College head basketball coach from 1948-1975 and Athletic Director from 1948-1990. First Division II athletic director named to the NCAA basketball rules committee. World War II veteran. Awarded a Silver Star and Purple Heart. Cousin of Frederick "Fritz" Niland, the inspiration for Private Ryan in the film, *Saving Private Ryan*, and his brothers, Robert Niland and Preston Niland, killed in the Allied invasion of Europe in 1944, and Edward Niland, shot down over Burma, thought to be killed in action, spent eleven months as a prisoner-of-war. Brother of Joe Niland, head basketball coach of Canisius from 1947-1953. Uncle of John Beilein, head basketball coach for LeMoyne College, Canisius, Richmond, West Virginia and Michigan.

OSBELT, HENRY Dec 17, 1885 Syracuse, NY - Mar 10, 1961 Syracuse, NY
Co-founded the Keegan and Osbelt Funeral Home in Syracuse.

PADUANO, DEBRA ANN 1954 Syracuse, NY - Jul 13, 1957 Syracuse, NY
Poster child for nephrosis, a disease which attacks the kidneys. Her photo was used in a campaign to raise funds for researching a cure for the disorder in December 1951. Lost her 18-month battle with the disease.

PASTERNACK, DAVID J. May 7, 1944 Syracuse, NY - Aug 3, 1999 Syracuse, NY
Local guitarist. Member of Carmen and the Vikings, Livin' Ennd and the Mercurys. Elected to the Syracuse Area Music Hall of Fame.

PELLICCIA, SANTO Nov 1, 1884 Gualdo Tadino, Umbria, Italy - Mar 21, 1962 Syracuse, NY
With **Filomena Castellani Pelliccia** (Jan 29, 1895 San Lorenzo, Italy - Dec 29, 1969 Syracuse, NY), the grandparents of Robert M. Sheer, author of *Cemeteries of Central New York* and *Cemeteries of Upstate New York*.

PETRAGNANI, MICHAEL J. Apr 1, 1951 Syracuse, NY - Apr 9, 1978 Syracuse, NY
One of four Syracuse firefighters killed in a house fire, 701 University Avenue, near the Syracuse University campus, succumbing to smoke poisoning, their air tanks ran out before they could escape the building, caused by two unattended candles left burning in a Styrofoam wig stand.

PIETRAFESA, ANTHONY JOSEPH Jan 19, 1893 Brooklyn, NY - Apr 8, 1940 Syracuse, NY
First Vice-President of the Joseph J. Pietrafesa Company, founded by his brother, Joseph J. Pietrafesa, in 1922, and the Learbury Clothes Company.

PIETRAFESA, JOSEPH J. May 30, 1885 New York, NY - Aug 14, 1968 Syracuse, NY
Founded the Joseph J. Pietrafesa Company in Syracuse in 1922. President of the Learbury Clothes Company from 1930-1968. Director of the Hotel Syracuse. Vice-President of WNDR-AM.

PIRAINO, THOMAS J. 1951 Syracuse, NY - Aug 30, 2005 Playa Del Rey, CA
Road manager for rock singer, Benny Mardones.

PIRRO, JOHN H. Mar 8, 1909 Syracuse, NY - Sept 7, 2005 Syracuse, NY
Co-founded the Deegan, Pirro, Edgecomb and Mead law firm in Syracuse, in 1948. Chairman of the Airport Committee in Syracuse, supervised construction of Hancock International Airport. Chairman of the Airport Dedication Ceremony, October 6, 1962. Vice-President and Secretary of the Syracuse Nationals from 1949-1963, the team's entire existence in the NBA. Elected to the Syracuse Bowling Hall of Fame in 1993. Son of funeral director, Joseph T. Pirro.

PIRRO, JOSEPH T. Nov 19, 1906 Syracuse, NY - Apr 22, 1985 Boca Raton, FL
Owned and operated Pirro & Sons Funeral Home in Syracuse, with his brother, Nicholas J. Pirro Sr.

PIRRO, JOSEPH T. Feb 20, 1875 Italy - Oct 25, 1937 Syracuse, NY
Founded Pirro & Sons Funeral Home in Syracuse. Grandfather of Nicholas J. Pirro Jr., Onondaga County Executive from 1987-2008.

PIRRO, NICHOLAS J. Feb 10, 1903 Syracuse, NY - Oct 4, 1965 Syracuse, NY
Owned and operated Pirro & Sons Funeral Home in Syracuse, with his brother, Joseph T. Pirro Jr. Father of Nicholas J. Pirro Jr., Onondaga County Executive from 1987-2008.

PIRRO, PAUL Aug 27, 1924 Syracuse, NY - Dec 12, 2009 Phoenix, NY
World War II infantryman. Earned five battle stars for each battle he participated, including Omaha Beach on D-Day. One of many D-Day participants interviewed by Universal/DreamWorks prior to filming *Saving Private Ryan*. Received a citation from President Bill Clinton for his bravery on the battlefield.

PORPIGLIO, FRANK Aug 22, 1953 Syracuse, NY - Apr 9, 1978 Syracuse, NY
One of four Syracuse firefighters killed in a house fire, 701 University Avenue, near the Syracuse University campus, succumbing to smoke poisoning, their air tanks ran out before they could escape the building, caused by two unattended candles left burning in a Styrofoam wig stand.

RAO, GEORGE S. Nov 28, 1915 Syracuse, NY - Aug 6, 1991 Syracuse, NY
Owned and operated George Rao Florist in Syracuse. Brother of florist, Sam Rao.

RISKO (Pelkowski)**, BABE** (Henry L.) Jul 15, 1910 Syracuse, NY - Mar 7, 1957 Syracuse, NY
Middleweight boxing champion, defeated Tommy Yarosz in September 1935, lost the title to Freddy Steele, in July 1936.

ROMEO, PAUL C. Dec 9, 1914 Syracuse, NY - Jul 14, 2006 Syracuse, NY
Physical Education Professor Emeritus at Syracuse University for 30 years. Coached Syracuse gymnastics to the 1959 NCAA national championship and 27 Eastern gymnastic titles. NCAA Coach of the Year in 1959. Coached five individual gymnasts to NCAA national championships.

ROTH, ARTHUR L. Mar 16, 1925 Syracuse, NY - Apr 14, 1988 Syracuse, NY
Employed with the Sheltered Workshop of the Onondaga County Association for Retarded Citizens.

SACKETT (Bell)**, BARBARA M.** May 20, 1924 Hackensack, NJ - Sept 22, 2005 Sarasota, NJ
Owned and operated Sackett's Restaurant in Brewerton with her husband, Frank L. Sackett, from 1950 to the 1980s.

SAMPERE, CHARLES R. Apr 6, 1913 Canastota, NY - Jul 29, 2005 Liverpool, NY
Owned and operated Buttercup Bakery in Syracuse.

SANTARO, MICHAEL A. Nov 2, 1911 - Jan 14, 1975 Syracuse, NY
Founded the Santaro Trucking Company in Syracuse in 1936.

SAUTER, JOSEPH M. Mar 27, 1932 - May 26, 2000 Syracuse, NY
Broadway playwright and composer. His song "You Are My Love" appeared in the Louis Prima film, *Hey Boy, Hey Girl*, in 1959.

SCANLAN, BRIDGET Syracuse, NY - May 21, 1919 Syracuse, NY
Mother of William D. "Doc" Scanlan, pitcher for the Pittsburgh Pirates, Brooklyn Superbas and Brooklyn Dodgers from 1903-1911.

SCHELL, LELAND F. Oct 2, 1934 Syracuse, NY - May 16, 1978 Syracuse, NY
Tow truck operator dispatched to recover a car left down an embankment when a youth attempted to steal it, crushed to death when the car slid off the blocks he used to hold it in place, pinning him underneath the vehicle as it moved.

SCHOTTHOEFER, GEORGE J. Mar 29, 1901 Syracuse, NY - Jan 3, 1989 Syracuse, NY
Owned and operated Shotty's Restaurant on Grant Boulevard in Syracuse, from 1933-1961.

SCIBILIA (Bottega), **GRACE** Feb 23, 1909 Italy - Apr 26, 1990 Syracuse, NY
Owned and operated Scibilia's Perennial Plants and Flowers in DeWitt for 50 years.

SCRO, SAM (Salvatore) 1892 Italy - Apr 25, 1962 New York, NY
Founder and President of the Darling Ice Cream Company, North State Street in Syracuse, from 1946-1962. Publicly identified by Robert F. Kennedy, Chief Counsel of the Senate Labor Rackets Committee, for having an association with Joseph Barbara, Stefano Magaddino and the Apalachin Mafia, in 1958. His wife, Mary J. Ludico Scro, died April 18, 2007, age 101.

SELLIN, LEN Feb 25, 1904 - Sept 4, 1991 Syracuse, NY
Local bowler. Elected to the Syracuse Bowling Association Hall of Fame in 1983.

SENSKA, ARLENE R. Jul 23, 1929 Syracuse, NY - May 19, 1996 Syracuse, NY
Murder victim. Stabbed twice in the back by Edward E. Williams, waiting for a bus to take her to Sunday Mass at Assumption Church. Williams told police, "I wanted to kill a senior citizen."

SIMS, JAMES F. Dec 31, 1941 Syracuse, NY - Aug 12, 1998 Syracuse, NY
Morning radio personality at WSEN-FM radio in Syracuse. Inducted into the Syracuse Area Music Awards Hall of Fame in 1997.

SMALL, SHEILA M. 1968 Syracuse, NY - May 22, 1984 Syracuse, NY
Murder victim. Beaten, strangled and sexually-molested, post-mortem, by Robin Rodney Murray, at Onondaga Park in Syracuse. Murray's arrest led to his being charged in the murder of store clerk, Kyle Heifferon, killed two months earlier.

SPEACH, MICHAEL May 8, 1882 Italy - Sept 25, 1961 Syracuse, NY
Founded M. Speach & Sons Candy Manufacturers in Syracuse in 1923. Father of Syracuse businessman, Victor A. Speach.

SPEACH, VICTOR A. Aug 14, 1909 Syracuse, NY - Feb 17, 1999 Tamarac, FL
Owned and operated Speach Limousine from 1942-1982. Musician, performed with Patti Page, Frankie Laine and Buddy Hackett. Son of Syracuse confectioner, Michael Speach.

SPINELLI, THOMAS May 27, 1894 Bari, Italy - Jul 7, 1969 East Orange, NJ
Opened a vegetable stand on the corner of Route 11 and Taft Road, North Syracuse in 1945, his son-in-law, George E. Gelsomin, opened Sweetheart Market on the site in 1952.

SPOSATO, JOHN F. Feb 14, 1900 Syracuse, NY - Jan 18, 1961 Hollywood, FL
Co-founder and president of the Sposato Brothers Paint Company.

STEBER, MICHAEL J. Aug 14, 1975 Syracuse, NY - Oct 14, 1989 Liverpool, NY
Victim of an accidental shooting by his 14-year old friend. His parents, Michael and Mary Steber, became outspoken advocates against gun violence as a result of his death, their story featured in the HBO documentary, *5 American Handguns, 5 American Families*, in 1995.

STEIGER, JIMMY (Daniel James) Apr 20, 1896 Syracuse, NY - Aug 5, 1930 New York, NY
Composer. Co-wrote the standards "Looking at the World with Rose-Colored Glasses" and "Stars are the Windows of Heaven" with lyricist, Tommy Malie. Malie, an orphan, lost both arms in a train accident as a toddler, earned $100,000 for his music, but died penniless, August 1, 1932 in Chicago, age 35, buried in Calvary Cemetery in Evanston.

STEIGERWALD, JACOB Mar 26, 1860 Bavaria, Germany - Feb 1, 1931 Syracuse, NY
Founded the Cathedral Candle Company in Syracuse in 1897.

STEIGERWALD, LUDWIG Feb 4, 1906 Germany - Oct 2, 1980 Syracuse, NY
Co-owned and operated the German butcher shop, Liehs & Steigerwald's, in Syracuse.

STODDARD (Dussing), **BERT** (Albert) 1885 Syracuse, NY - Oct 6, 1940 Syracuse, NY
Vaudeville headliner. Discovered in Syracuse in 1902 by vaudeville entertainer, Anna Eva Fay.

SULLIVAN, DENNY (Dennis J.) 1920 Oneonta, NY - Sept 17, 2003 Syracuse, NY
Central New York radio personality. Host of the *Musical Clock* on WFBL-AM and *Denny Sullivan and the Gang* on WSYR-AM, from 1951-1971.

TASSONE, DOMINICK Sept 24, 1918 Grotteria, Reggio Calabria, Italy - Feb 17, 1991 Syracuse, NY
Owned and operated the Modern Bakery and Restaurant in Syracuse from 1946-1981. Father of

Samuel L. Tassone, owner and operator of Sam's Lakeside Restaurant in Brewerton and Dominick Tassone Jr., owner and operator of Dominick's Restaurant in Syracuse. Brother-in-law of Christian N. Mondo, owner of Mondo's Bakery in Syracuse.

TOVERN, JOHN H. Nov 9, 1914 Syracuse, NY - Apr 19, 1991 Syracuse, NY
Owned and operated the Eastwood Dairy from 1940-1965. Piano player, performed locally as "Johnny Mills" with several area bands, including the Peanuts Hucko Orchestra.

TUCCI, MITZIE (Anthony) 1912 Syracuse, NY - Sept 28, 1964 Syracuse, NY
Syracuse gambler associated with organized crime. New York State Police bugged his home, 400 Brattle Road, overhearing arrangements to sell Cuban pesos for Meyer Lansky in 1959.

URCIUOLI (Alvino), **CONCETTA** 1879 Italy - Sept 16, 1963 Syracuse, NY
Grandmother of pianist, Vincent Falcone, musical director for Frank Sinatra from 1976-1982 and 1985-1986 and the 1980 Inaugural Gala for President Ronald Reagan.

VELLA, JOSEPH S. Apr 1, 1910 Sicily, Italy - Apr 29, 1988 Syracuse, NY
Estranged husband of murder victim, Alberta Mary Vella, whose body was unearthed, July 4, 1963, near an abandoned dump on Marsh Mill Road in Bridgeport, fourteen years after her disappearance. Kenneth E. Dudley, serving time in a Virginia penitentiary for the starvation death of his eight-year old daughter, was convicted of her murder in 1964.

VERONE, MICHAEL J. Oct 1, 1929 Carbondale, PA - May 1, 2009 Syracuse, NY
Bodyguard and chauffeur for Lee Alexander, Mayor of Syracuse from 1970-1985.

VITELLO, CARMEN J. Jan 28, 1928 Syracuse, NY - Dec 8, 2002 Baldwinsville, NY
Lost his wife, Sarah Raines Vitello, pregnant with their seventh child, and his six children, Carmen Jr., Michael, Francis, Harry, Joseph and James, January 25, 1961, victims of carbon monoxide poisoning, from a broken coal furnace. He survived, awoken nauseous, running from the house, yelling his family was dead, 14 hours after they died. He remarried and was survived by six stepchildren.

WALSER, JOHN F. 1850 Austria - Jan 29, 1920 Syracuse, NY
Founder and President of the Walser Brothers Monument Company in Syracuse, from 1900-1920.

WEINHEIMER, JACOB Jun 3, 1844 Bavaria, Germany - Jul 11, 1909 Syracuse, NY
Founded Jacob Weinheimer & Sons Furniture Store in 1872, one of the earliest furniture stores in Syracuse.

WHALEY, ROBERT 1931 Syracuse, NY - May 6, 1991 Syracuse, NY
Father of Hollywood film actor, Frank Whaley.

WHITE, H. PHILIP (Howard) Apr 5, 1921 Liverpool, NY - Mar 9, 1987 North Syracuse, NY
Right fielder for the "White Brothers Baseball Team" with his eight brothers, Benton Jr., Lewis, Earl, Thurlow, Robert, Richard, James and John, traveling throughout Central New York, competing against other semi-pro baseball clubs, managed by their father, Benton C. White. Sisters, Marie, Honora and Jeanne White, were cheerleaders for their brothers.

YEHLE, FRANK X. Dec 3, 1878 Syracuse, NY - Jun 23, 1969 Jonesboro, AR
Vaudeville showman. Performed on Broadway on the Keith circuit under the name, "Frank LaVell." Brother of Leo J. Yehle, Onondaga County Children's Court Judge.

YOUNG, ALBERT GOTTFRIED Jun 1, 1891 Syracuse, NY - Feb 3, 1939 Syracuse, NY
Syracuse Fire Department Lieutenant. One of eight firemen killed in the Collins Block fire, the deadliest fire in the history of the Syracuse Fire Department, 225 East Genesee Street in Syracuse, when flames swept thought the building, collapsing several floors crushing the firemen under tons of debris.

ZETT, GEORGE Aug 9, 1843 Syracuse, NY - Jul 4, 1911 Syracuse, NY
President of Zett's Brewery in Syracuse, founded by his father Xavier Zett in 1858.

ZETT, XAVIER 1822 Germany - Jun 3, 1881 Syracuse, NY
Founded, owned and operated Zett's Brewery in Syracuse from 1858-1888.

ZIMMER, MELVIN Oct 4, 1938 Syracuse, NY - Jan 4, 2002 Liverpool, NY
Democratic New York State Assemblyman, representing the 120th District, from 1975-1991. Secured funds for the Carrier Dome and the OnCenter and helped raise the legal drinking age to 21, before a stroke in 1989 ended his political career. Struck and killed by a car, walking near his home on Old Liverpool Road.

ATHENS RURAL CEMETERY
1st Street
Athens, NY 12015

DUNCAN, ANDREW JACKSON Oct 22, 1877 Marion, OH - Jul 13, 1955 Fort Worth, TX
President of the Fort Worth Power and Light Company. Nephew of President William McKinley, son of his sister, Sarah McKinley Duncan.

VAN SCHAICK, ISAAC WHITBECK Dec 7, 1817 Coxsackie, NY - Aug 22, 1901 Catonsville, MD
United States Representative-WI from 1885-1887 and 1889-1891.

ATTICA PRISON CEMETERY
Dunbar Road
Attica, NY 14011

LOBAGOLA, BATA KINDAI AMGOZA IBN 1877 Baltimore, MD - 1947 Attica, NY
Criminal imposter. Born Joseph Howard Lee. Claimed to be a West African savage, giving lectures and holding debates at public institutions, he was actually a poor American who committed a series of

crimes relating to his scandalous homosexual activities involving underage boys. Subject of the A.A. Knopf biography, *LoBagola: An African's Own Story*.

ATWATER CEMETERY
Route 41
Homer, NY 13077

ALVORD, THOMAS GOLD 1742 Farmington, CT - May 18, 1810 Homer, NY
Revolutionary War veteran. Grandfather of Thomas Gold Alvord, Lieutenant Governor of New York from 1865-1866.

MAYCUMBER (Bacon)**, ELSIE M.** 1902 Cortlandville, NY - Feb 16, 1968 Moravia, NY
Died from accidental asphyxiation. Fell asleep in her chair while smoking, igniting her clothing, suffering burns over 80 percent of her body.

BALDWINS CORNER CEMETERY
Route 247
Rushville, NY 14544

WHITMAN, BEZA May 13, 1773 Bridgewater, MA - Apr 7, 1810 Rushville, NY
With **Alice Green Loomis** (Dec 5, 1777 Thompson, CT - Sept 6, 1857 Rushville, NY), the parents of missionary, Dr. Marcus Whitman, who led the first party of wagon trains along the Oregon Trail heading West, in 1843, later attacked and killed with other members by Cayuse tribesmen in what became known as "the Whitman Massacre."

BALLARD-BARRETT CEMETERY
526 Route 6N
Mahopac, NY 10541

BALLARD, ENOS H. 1808 - Oct 25, 1861 Mahopac, NY
Pastor of the Red Mills Baptist Church, Route 6N, Mahopac, for 20 years.

BRADLEY (Broadhurst)**, LILLIAN TRIMBLE** Apr 23, 1879 Milton, KY - Jan 7, 1959 Santa Barbara, CA
Playwright, director and producer. First woman stage director on Broadway. Collaborated often with
her husband, playwright and theater owner, George H. Broadhurst.

BROADHURST, GEORGE HOWELLS Jun 3, 1866 Walsall, England - Jan 31, 1952 Santa Barbara, CA
Playwright, producer and theater manager. Co-owned and operated the Broadhurst Theatre in

Manhattan, with the Schubert Brothers, from 1917-1952. Wrote the plays, *The Wrong Mr. Wright* and
What Happened to Jones. Husband of Lillian Trimble Bradley, playwright and director.

BALLSTON SPA VILLAGE CEMETERY
Ballston Avenue
Ballston Spa, NY 12020

BROWN, ANSON 1800 Charlton, NY - Jun 14, 1840 Ballston Spa
United States Representative-NY from 1839-1840. Died during his first term in office.

JONES, REBECCA 1825 Gallupville, NY - Mar 19, 1905 Ballston Spa, NY
Known as "Obstinate Beckey." Employed by Manhattan banker, A. Gordon Hamersley, who died in
1883, four months later, his son, Louis C. Hamersley died, leaving a contested will. Refused to testify
at trial, upholding a promise to the Hamersley family never to discuss family matters, found in
contempt, spent 42 weeks in jail earning her nickname from the press. Louis C. Hamersley's widow,
Lady Lilian Warren Price Beresford, remarried to the Duke of Marlborough, George Charles Spencer-
Churchill, the uncle of Prime Minister Winston Churchill, and Lord William Leslie de la Poer Beresford,
British Army Lieutenant Colonel awarded the Victoria Cross for service in the Anglo-Zulu War, fought
in South Africa in 1879.

PALMER, BERIAH 1740 Bristol County, MA - May 20, 1812 Ballston Spa, NY
United States Representative-NY from 1803-1805.

ROONEY, WALTER SCOTT May 20, 1888 Holyoke, MA - Aug 23, 1959 Ballston Spa, NY
With **Ellinor Reynolds Rooney** (Aug 11, 1886 Milton, NY - Jun 1980 Norwalk, CT), the parents of
journalist and *60 Minutes* correspondent, Andy Rooney.

TAYLOR, JOHN W. Mar 26, 1784 Charlton, NY - Sept 18, 1854 Cleveland, OH
United States Representative-NY from 1813-1833. Speaker of the House of Representatives from
1820-1821 and 1825-1827. New York State Senator from 1840-1841, resigned following a paralytic
stroke.

WEST, GEORGE Feb 17, 1823 Bradninch, Devonshire, England - Sept 20, 1901 Ballston Spa, NY
United States Representative-NY from 1881-1883 and 1885-1889.

BANGOR CEMETERY
Route 11B
Bangor, NY 12966

GOTT, JESSE 1800 NH - Jun 11, 1861 Bangor, NY
Father of photographer, Calvin O. Gott, who took the first photograph of the Cardiff Giant as it was discovered on a Cardiff farm, later purchasing the hoax, storing it in his Fitchburg, MA home. He died, October 19, 1886 in Fitchburg, age 54, buried there, Forest Hill Cemetery.

BARKERSVILLE CEMETERY
South Line Road
Galway, NY 12074

CARPENTIER, HORACE WALPOLE Jul 1824 Galway, NY - Jan 31, 1918 New York, NY
Founder and first Mayor of Oakland, from 1854-1855. President of the Overland Telegraph Company in 1861. Sent the first transcontinental telegram to President Abraham Lincoln.

BARNES SETTLEMENT CEMETERY
Barnes Settlement Road
Alexandria Bay, NY 13607

PLIMPTON, WILLIAM H. May 26, 1909 Alexandria Bay, NY - Oct 31, 1999 Ogdensburg, NY
St. Lawrence boatbuilder. Father of educator, William H. Plimpton III, Ogdensburg Free Academy head football coach, where two of his players, future NFL players, brothers, Pete Gogolak and Charlie Gogolak, revolutionized the kicking game with their soccer-style placekicking.

BATAVIA CEMETERY
Harvester Avenue
Batavia, NY 14020

BERGEN, JOHN TUENIS 1786 Brooklyn, NY - Mar 9, 1855 Batavia, NY
United States Representative-NY from 1831-1833.

BRISBANE, ALBERT Aug 22, 1809 Batavia, NY - May 1, 1890 Richmond, VA
Utopian socialist and author. Popularized the theories of Charles Fourier in his book, *Social Destiny of Man*, in 1840. Father of Arthur Brisbane, American journalist and newspaper editor. Great-grandfather of Arthur S. Brisbane, public editor of *The New York Times*.

BRISBANE, ARTHUR Dec 12, 1864 Buffalo, NY - Dec 25, 1936 New York, NY
Journalist and newspaper editor. Called the "Patron Saint of Yellow Journalism." Editor of the *New York Evening Journal* from 1897-1921, owned by William Randolph Hearst. Son of Albert Brisbane, Utopian socialist and author. Grandfather of Arthur S. Brisbane, Public Editor of *The New York Times*.

CARY, TRUMBULL Apr 11, 1786 Mansfield, CT - Jun 20, 1869 Batavia, NY
New York State Senator from 1831-1834. Grandfather of architect, George Cary, and sculptor, Seward Cary. Great-grandfather of sculptor and polo player, Charles C. Rumsey, the brother-in-law of W. Averell Harriman, Governor of New York from 1955-1958.

ELLICOTT, BENJAMIN Apr 17, 1765 Ellicott's Mills, MD - Dec 10, 1827 Williamsville, NY
United States Representative-NY from 1817-1819. Originally buried in Williamsville Cemetery in Erie County. Brother of surveyors and city planners, Joseph Ellicott and Andrew Ellicott.

ELLICOTT, JOSEPH Nov 1, 1760 Bucks County, PA - Aug 19, 1826 New York, NY
Surveyor and city planner. Employed by the Holland Land Company. Founded the cities of Buffalo and Batavia. Namesake of Ellicottville in Chautauqua County. Spent his final years in Bellevue Hospital, an asylum in New York City, before ending his life by hanging. Brother of Benjamin Ellicott, United States Representative-NY from 1817-1819 and Andrew Ellicott, surveyor of the District of Columbia and areas west of the Appalachians.

EVANS, DAVID ELLICOTT Mar 19, 1788 Ellicott's Mills, MD - May 17, 1850 Batavia, NY
United States Representative-NY in 1827, resigning, May 2, 1827, after two months in office.

FISHER, JOHN Mar 13, 1806 Londonderry, NH - Mar 28, 1882 Batavia, NY
United States Representative-NY from 1869-1871.

LAY, GEORGE WASHINGTON Jul 26, 1798 Catskill, NY - Oct 21, 1860 Batavia, NY
United States Representative-NY from 1833-1837. United States Charge d'Affaires to Sweden from 1842-1845, under President John Tyler.

MARTINDALE, JOHN HENRY Mar 20, 1815 Sandy Hill, NY - Dec 13, 1881 Nice, France
Civil War Union Army Brevet Major General. New York State Attorney General from 1866-1867. Military Governor of Washington from 1862-1864. Son of Henry Clinton Martindale, United States Representative-NY from 1823-1831 and 1833-1835.

RAND (Rutland)**, ANGELINE** 1800 Fairfax, VT - Sept 26, 1882 Batavia, NY
Mother of Civil War Union Army Captain, Charles Franklin Rand, the first volunteer to enlist for war following President Abraham Lincoln's call to arms, awarded the Medal of Honor in 1897, died October 13, 1908 in Washington D.C., age 69, buried in Arlington National Cemetery.

RICHMOND, DEAN Mar 31, 1804 Barnard, VT - Aug 27, 1866 New York, NY
Railroad magnate. President of the New York Central Railroad from 1864-1866, first Vice-President, from 1853-1864. Namesake of *The Dean Richmond* locomotive engine, used by President-elect Abraham Lincoln on his journey to Washington D.C. in 1861, ate lunch with Lincoln and his family as the train traveled through Syracuse. Died at the New York City home of future New York State Governor, Samuel J. Tilden.

TRACY, PHINEAS LYMAN Dec 25, 1786 Norwich, CT - Dec 22, 1876 Batavia, NY
United States Representative-NY from 1827-1833. Brother of Albert Haller Tracy, United States Representative-NY from 1819-1825.

BATH NATIONAL CEMETERY
San Juan Avenue
Bath, NY 14810

ANDERSON (Craig), **EVELYN M.** Aug 15, 1943 Binghamton, NY - Sept 7, 2011 Hornell, NY
Aunt of David P. Sweat, convicted murderer, shot and killed Deputy Sheriff Kevin J. Tarsia, July 4, 2002 in Kirkwood, sentenced to life in prison. Sweat, with convicted murderer, Richard Matt, escaped from the Clinton Correctional Facility in Dannemora, June 6, 2015, reminiscent of the film, *The Shawshank Redemption*, the manhunt ending with Matt shot and killed by border agents on June 26th and Sweat shot twice, recaptured two days later.

BOUFFARD, EDMUND JOSEPH Mar 20, 1927 Waterbury, CT - Jun 21, 2014 Leeds, MA
First cousin, once removed, of Carolyn Bessette-Kennedy, the wife of John F. Kennedy Jr., killed, with her sister, Lauren Bessette, when the plane Kennedy was piloting crashed into the Atlantic Ocean, off Martha's Vineyard, July 16, 1999, their remains cremated and scattered in the ocean.

MUNSON, WILLIS WEBSTER Aug 13, 1841 Otisco, NY - Feb 28, 1920 Bath, NY
Town of Otisco physician for 40 years. Civil War veteran, assigned to the Peterson House in Washington D.C. from 1862-1865, present at the deathbed of President Abraham Lincoln after he was shot by John Wilkes Booth, across the street at Ford's Theater, dying the following morning.

RICHMOND, HORACE CULVER Apr 21, 1847 West Oneonta, NY - Jul 21, 1926 Bath, NY
Civil War veteran. Grandfather of actor, John Carradine. Great-grandfather of actors, David Carradine, Keith Carradine and Robert Carradine. 2nd great-grandfather of actresses, Martha Plimpton and Ever Carradine.

SNEDEN, ROBERT KNOX Jun 1832 Nova Scotia, Canada - Sept 18, 1918 Bath, NY
Civil War Union Army soldier. Captured, November 27, 1863, by "The Gray Ghost", Colonel John Singleton Mosby, spent thirteen months in Confederate prisons, leaving him permanently disabled.

Left behind a 5,000 page memoir and 1,000 watercolor drawings and maps, rediscovered a century later, published in 2000 as *Eye of the Storm: The Civil War Drawings of Robert Knox Sneden*.

BATTENVILLE CEMETERY
Route 61
Greenwich, NY 12834

READ, DANIEL Sept 10, 1754 Newton, MA - Feb 26, 1838 Greenwich, NY
Revolutionary War veteran. With **Susannah Richardson Read** (Dec 12, 1755 Newton, MA - Jan 1, 1839 Greenwich, NY), the grandparents of women's rights activist, Susan B. Anthony.

BAYSIDE CEMETERY
Clarkson Avenue
Potsdam, NY 13676

CRANE, JULIA ETTA May 19, 1855 Potsdam, NY - Jun 11, 1923 Potsdam, NY
Music educator. Founded the Crane School of Music at Potsdam Normal School, the first music education school in the United States.

PARKER, ABRAHAM X. Nov 14, 1831 Granville, VT - Aug 9, 1909 Potsdam, NY
United States Representative-NY from 1881-1889.

SISSON, RUFUS L. Sept 11, 1890 Potsdam, NY - Mar 9, 1977 Binghamton, NY
All-American basketball player for Dartmouth College, led the team in scoring during the 1911-1912 season. Died in Binghamton, traveling home after a trip to Florida.

SNELL, BERTRAND HOLLIS Dec 9, 1870 Colton, NY - Feb 2, 1958 Potsdam, NY
United States Representative-NY from 1915-1939. Chairman of the Republican National Convention in 1932 and 1936. Publisher of the *Potsdam Courier-Freeman* from 1934-1949.

BEARDSLEE'S (OLD CITY) CEMETERY
Route 5
Manheim, NY 13329

BEARDSLEE, JOHN KNICKERBOCKER Jun 1759 Sharon, CT - Oct 31, 1825 Manheim, NY
Began construction on Beardslee Castle, 123 Old State Road, Little Falls, in 1790, with his wife, **Lavina Pardee Beardslee** (Oct 30, 1770 Sharon, CT - Feb 27, 1855 Manheim, NY), completed in 1860 by their grandson, Guy Roosevelt Beardslee.

BEARSVILLE THEATER
291 Tinker Street
Woodstock, NY 12498

GROSSMAN, ALBERT B. May 21, 1926 Chicago, IL - Jan 25, 1986 London, England
Folk-rock music manager and entrepreneur. Managed the careers of Bob Dylan, Janis Joplin, the Band, Gordon Lightfoot, Todd Rundgren, John Lee Hooker and Phil Ochs. Formed Peter, Paul and Mary in 1961. Founded the Bearsville Recording Studio and Bearsville Theater, on the outskirts of Woodstock. Died of a heart attack, flying on the Concorde, traveling to London with plans to attend a music convention in Cannes, France, buried in a circle of ivy, behind the theater he owned.

BEAVERKILL CEMETERY
Craigie Clair Road
Roscoe, NY 12776

ATTELL, ABE (Abraham Washington) Feb 22, 1884 San Francisco, CA - Feb 7, 1970 New Paltz, NY
Professional boxer. Nicknamed the "Little Hebrew." World featherweight champion from 1906-1912. Charged with conspiring to fix the 1919 World Series, the "Black Sox Scandal", through his friendship with New York mob figure, Arnold Rothstein, later acquitted. Inducted into the International Boxing Hall of Fame in 1990. Brother of Monte Attell, bantamweight champion from 1909-1910, the first brothers to simultaneously hold world titles.

BEDDOE-ROSE FAMILY CEMETERY
West Bluff Drive
Keuka Park, NY 14478

MACOMB (Livingston), **CHRISTINA** Sept 25, 1774 New York, NY - Aug 24, 1841 Branchport, NY
Wife of New York City merchant, John Navarre Macomb, killed on the *Princess Charlotte* defending her against French buccaneers, May 10, 1810. Macomb was buried in Charles King and Martyr Parish Churchyard in Derbyshire, England. Granddaughter of Philip Livingston, signer of the *Declaration of Independence*. Daughter-in-law of Alexander Macomb, purchaser of three million acres on the St. Lawrence River, including all of the Thousand Islands, for the price of one shilling. Known at the time as "Macomb's Purchase", it is now Jefferson County.

BEEKMAN CEMETERY
Church Street
Poughquag, NY 12570

SHERMAN, BENJAMIN Nov 29, 1799 Wingdale, NY - Nov 10, 1862 Beekman, NY
With **Hannah Brill Sherman** (Jul 7, 1796 - Sept 20, 1884 Beekman, NY), the parents of John Brill Sherman, founder of the Union Stockyards in Chicago. Grandparents of Margaret Sebring Sherman Burnham, the wife of architect, Daniel Hudson Burnham, designer of New York City's Flatiron Building.

BELLE ISLE CEMETERY
Armstrong Road
Syracuse, NY 13209

DURLING, CLARENCE FREDERICK Nov 12, 1916 Syracuse, NY - Mar 30, 1991 Syracuse, NY
Owned and operated Atlantic Seafood in Syracuse.

GERE, JAMES BREWSTER Aug 14, 1867 Camillus, NY - Apr 25, 1933 Syracuse, NY
Co-founded the Onondaga Brick and Tile Company. Unsuccessful candidate for mayor of Syracuse in 1909. Grandson of William Stanton Gere, pioneer homesteader in the town of Camillus. 5th great-grandson of William Brewster, *Mayflower* passenger, the Reverend Elder of the Pilgrim's church in Plymouth and the oldest pilgrim to have participated in the first Thanksgiving.

GERE, WILLIAM STANTON Oct 28, 1785 Groton, CT - Oct 17, 1852 Syracuse, NY
Built Gere Lock Farm, along the Erie Canal in the town of Camillus, in 1823. Great-grandfather of William S. Gere, co-founder of O'Brien & Gere Engineers, Inc. Brother of salt manufacturer, Robert Gere. Husband of Louisa Brewster Gere, the 3rd great-granddaughter of William Brewster, *Mayflower* passenger, the Reverend Elder of the Pilgrim's church in Plymouth and the oldest pilgrim to have participated in the first Thanksgiving.

HARVEY, DANIEL 1774 Taghkanic, NY - Oct 24, 1853 Syracuse, NY
Belle Isle-area physician. Son of Rev. Benjamin Harvey, the country's oldest-active preacher at the time of his death in 1847, age 112.

PALUMBO, PETER EDWARD Jan 9, 1909 Palermo, Sicily, Italy - Feb 12, 1978 Syracuse, NY
Professional boxer. Fought under the name "Eddie Dempsey." Won the New York State lightweight championship in 1927.

SIDMAN, BARNEY B. Dec 18, 1821 NY - Jul 22, 1868 Camillus, NY
Uncle of vaudeville comedian and playwright, Arthur C. Sidman.

SIDNAM, IRVIN A. Nov 1876 Solvay, NY - Dec 22, 1928 Solvay, NY

With **Mary Louise Haas Sidnam** (1879 NS, Canada - Oct 13, 1969 Solvay, NY), the grandparents of Carol Martineau Baldwin, breast cancer survivor and founder of the Carol M. Baldwin Breast Cancer Research Fund, and the great-grandparents of Academy Award-nominated actor, Alec Baldwin, and his acting brothers, Daniel, Billy and Steven Baldwin.

BEMUS POINT CEMETERY
Center Street
Bemus Point, NY 14712

COLBY, BAINBRIDGE Dec 22, 1869 St. Louis, MO - Apr 11, 1950 Bemus Point, NY

United States Secretary of State from 1920-1921, under President Woodrow Wilson. Last surviving member of Wilson's presidential cabinet. Personal lawyer for author, Mark Twain.

BETH ABRAHAM-JACOB CEMETERY
Western Avenue / Route 20
Guilderland, NY 12084

DEMSKY (Sandler)**, BERTHA** (Bryna) 1887 Russia - Dec 12, 1958 Schenectady, NY

Mother of Academy Award-winning actor, Kirk Douglas. Grandmother of Academy Award-winning actor/producer, Michael Douglas. Lived at 1157 Parkwood Boulevard, Schenectady, following her divorce from her husband, Harry Demsky, died April 12, 1954 in Amsterdam, age 70, buried there, Sons of Israel Cemetery.

BETH ABRAHAM-JACOB CEMETERY #2
Fuller Road
Albany, NY 12203

WOLFSHEIMER, MOSES HIRSH Dec 25, 1800 Württemberg, Germany - Oct 15, 1873 Albany, NY

Husband of Caroline Wolfsheimer, died in 1891, buried next to him at her request, unearthed from her grave by her family the next day, reburied three days later in Beth Emeth Cemetery, five miles away, the family choosing a newer, better kept cemetery. The headline from the *New York Sun* read, "Grave Robbery Near Albany; The Body of a Jewess Surreptitiously Taken from One Cemetery and Buried in Another" followed with "the good old lady's husband, who died in 1873, and by whose side she was first buried, sleeps alone."

BETH EL CEMETERY
Jamesville Avenue
Syracuse, NY 13210

CHARNEY, HARRY Dec 15, 1893 - Feb 2, 1983 Syracuse, NY
Founded the Charney's Men's and Boys' Clothing Store in 1953, with his son and daughter-in-law, Jerome and Phyllis Hoffman Charney.

CHARNEY, JEROME F. Nov 19, 1922 Syracuse, NY - Nov 14, 1992 Syracuse, NY
Founded the Charney's Men's and Boys' Clothing Store in 1953, with his wife, Phyllis Hoffman Charney and father, Harry Charney.

CHARNEY (Hoffman)**, PHYLLIS** Aug 29, 1922 Haverhill, MA - Mar 24, 2016 Syracuse, NY
Founded the Charney's Men's and Boys' Clothing Store in 1953, with her husband, Jerome F. Charney and father-in-law, Harry Charney.

FINKELSTEIN, MORRIS Sept 21, 1901 Syracuse, NY - Sept 23, 1966 Syracuse, NY
Founded the Onondaga News Agency with his brother, Jack Finkelstein, in Syracuse in 1934.

HURWITZ, ALFRED 1918 Syracuse, NY - Dec 9, 2009 Syracuse, NY
Owned and operated DeWitt Cyclery from 1948-1983.

MARSHALL, DAVID Feb 3, 1913 NY - Apr 16, 2006 Syracuse, NY
First orthodontist in Central New York. Founded the Cleft Palate Clinic in Syracuse. World War II United States Army veteran, dentist to General George S. Patten during the war.

MILLER, HY (Hyman M.) Jul 20, 1922 Syracuse, NY - Mar 21, 2009 Syracuse, NY
New York State Assemblyman from 1970-1988. Member of the Board of Directors of the Syracuse Chiefs Baseball Club. The Chiefs wore his initials, "HM", on their sleeve in his honor during the 2009 season.

BETH EL CEMETERY
Woods Road
Whitesboro, NY 13492

COHEN, MOSES A. 1870 Lithuania - Dec 8, 1961 Utica, NY
Owned and operated the Old Forge Hardware and Furniture Company in Old Forge. Father of   A. Richard Cohen, co-founder of the Enchanted Forest Water Safari on July 7, 1956, located in the Adirondacks village of Old Forge.

BETH EMETH CEMETERY (NEW)
Cemetery Road
Albany, NY 12211

MANN, JOSEPH Jan 30, 1830 Bavaria, Germany - Jan 17, 1912 Albany, NY
Albany-area Jewish leader. Husband of **Dinah Wolfsheimer Mann** (1839 Albany, NY - Feb 2, 1910 Albany, NY), the daughter of Moses H. and Caroline Wolfsheimer. Created the headline from the *New York Sun*, "Grave Robbery Near Albany; The Body of a Jewess Surreptitiously Taken from One Cemetery and Buried in Another" followed with "the good old lady's husband, who died in 1873, and by whose side she was first buried, sleeps alone", when they removed her mother from her husband's gravesite and held a second service at Beth Emeth Cemetery five miles away.

WOLFSHEIMER, CAROLINE Apr 15, 1809 Württemberg, Germany - Oct 18, 1891 Albany, NY
Wife of Moses H. Wolfsheimer, died in 1873, initially buried next to her husband at her request, Beth Abraham-Jacob Cemetery #2, unearthed from her grave by her family the next day, reburied three days later in Beth Emeth Cemetery, five miles away, the family choosing a newer, better kept cemetery. The headline from the *New York Sun* read, "Grave Robbery Near Albany; The Body of a Jewess Surreptitiously Taken from One Cemetery and Buried in Another" followed with "the good old lady's husband, who died in 1873, and by whose side she was first buried, sleeps alone."

BETH ISRAEL CEMETERY UPPER
Utopia Street
Schenectady, NY 12304

SAHR, IMAN Jan 12, 1918 - Nov 14, 1991 Schenectady, NY
Husband of Ida Demsky Sahr, the sister of Academy Award-winning actor, Kirk Douglas, the aunt of Academy Award-winning actor/producer, Michael Douglas.

BETH SHOLOM-CHEVRA SHAS CEMETERY
Comstock Avenue
Syracuse, NY 13210

RUMANER, M. BRUCE (Merwin) Mar 19, 1931 Syracuse, NY - Nov 24, 1994 Syracuse, NY
President of Lund's Ski Shop in DeWitt, founded by Robert Lund in 1945, purchased by his father, Harvey Rumaner, in 1950.

SHANKMAN, NATHAN Aug 5, 1905 Russia - Jul 14, 2002 Jamesville, NY
With **Bertie Shankman** (Jun 15, 1905 Brooklyn, NY - Sept 8, 1995 Jamesville, NY), the parents of Rosemary Pooler, Associate Justice of the United States Court of Appeals, 2nd Circuit, appointed by President Bill Clinton in 1998.

BETHEL EVERGREEN CEMETERY
Route 17B
White Lake, NY 12786

WOOD, J. A. (John) Jun 11, 1837 Bethel, NY - Dec 18, 1910 Bethel, NY
Architect. Designed the Stuyvesant Hotel in Kingston, the Tampa Bay Hotel in Tampa, the Grand Hotel in Highmount, NY, and several buildings on the campus of Vassar College.

BETHLEHEM CEMETERY
286 Kenwood Avenue
Delmar, NY 12054

ANTONIO, SALVATORE F. 1894 NY - Mar 27, 1932 Schodack, NY
Murder victim. Shot him five times, stabbed him 15 more, on Albany-Castleton Road, Easter Sunday, by Vincent Saetta and Sam Ferraci, hitmen hired by his wife, Anna Capello "Little Anna" Antonio, who were arrested, convicted and sentenced to death in Sing Sing Prison. She is buried in St. Anthony Cemetery, Schenectady.

CANNIZZARO, JOSEPH R. Apr 27, 1954 Albany, NY - Jul 21, 2005 Albany, NY
Associate Justice of the New York State Supreme Court from 2000-2005. Delivered the eulogy at the funeral of his close friend, Peter R. Porco, eight months before his own death. Porco was bludgeoned to death with an ax by his son, Christopher Porco, which also left his wife, Joan M. Porco, severely disfigured.

BIXBY CEMETERY
Cemetery Road
Norfolk, NY 13667

ROGERS, HARRISON ALEXANDER Oct 23, 1879 Norfolk, NY - Sept 19, 1951 Norfolk, NY
With **Myra May Beswick Rogers** (Apr 10, 1889 - Aug 18, 1926 Norfolk, NY), the parents of William Pierce Rogers, United States Secretary of State from 1969-1973, under President Richard Nixon, and United States Attorney General from 1957-1961, under President Dwight D. Eisenhower.

BLACK CREEK CEMETERY
6172 Route 305
Black Creek, NY 14714

INGALLS, JOHN W. Dec 31, 1806 Bedford, QB, Canada - May 26, 1893 Cuba, NY
Brother of Samuel W. Ingalls, the great-grandfather of Laura Ingalls-Wilder, author of *Little House on the Prairie*.

BLOOMINGBURG RURAL CEMETERY
845 Bloomingburg Road
Bloomingburg, NY 12721

BODLE, CHARLES Jul 1, 1787 Poughkeepsie, NY - Oct 31, 1835 Bloomingburg, NY
United States Representative-NY from 1833-1835.

SAWARD, WAYNE C. Feb 9, 1957 Queens, NY - Mar 23, 2009 Middletown, NY
Designed and sculpted the Woodstock Monument, displayed at the site of the Woodstock Festival in Bethel.

B'NAI ISRAEL CEMETERY
Grocholl Road
Fleischmanns, NY 12430

BERG (Edelstein)**, GERTRUDE** (Tillie) Oct 3, 1899 New York, NY - Sept 14, 1966 New York, NY
Actress. Wrote, produced and starred in the radio serial, *The Rise of the Goldbergs*, in 1929. Won the Emmy Award for Lead Actress in a Comedy Series in 1951 for *The Goldbergs*, the first winner in that category. Tony Award-winner in 1959.

EDELSTEIN, JACOB Dec 15, 1878 Russia - Jun 12, 1944 NY
Operated a resort in the Catskill Mountains in Fleischmanns. Father of actress, Gertrude Berg.

B'NAI ISRAEL CEMETERY
Route 16
Olean, NY 14760

EVANS, PHILIP BERNARD 1886 Latvia - Apr 28, 1961 Salamanca, NY
With **Frances P. Lipsitz Evans** (Apr 29, 1891 - Nov 1972 Canandaigua, NY), the parents of three-time Academy Award-winning lyricist, Ray Evans, co-writer of "Que Sera, Sera (Whatever Will Be, Will

Be)", "Buttons and Bows", "Mona Lisa", "Tammy" and "Silver Bells", with songwriting partner, Jay Livingston, and member of the Songwriters Hall of Fame.

BOLTON RURAL CEMETERY
Lake Shore Drive / Route 9N
Bolton, NY 12814

HOMER (Beatty), **LOUISE DILWORTH** Apr 30, 1871 Pittsburgh, PA - May 6, 1947 Winter Park, FL
Opera singer. Contralto, sang opposite Enrico Caruso and Geraldine Farrar. Performed at the Metropolitan Opera House in New York City from 1900-1919 and 1927-1929. Listed as one of the "12 greatest living women" by the National League of Women voters in 1923 and 1924. Wife of composer, Sidney Homer. Mother of short story writer, Anne Homer. Aunt of composer, Samuel Barber, son of her sister, Marguerite McLeod Beatty Barber.

HOMER, SIDNEY Dec 9, 1864 Boston, MA - Jul 10, 1953 Winter Park, FL
Composer. Wrote "Requiem", "Casey at the Bat", "A Banjo Song" and "The House That Jack Built." Husband of opera singer, Louise Homer. Father of short story writer, Anne Homer.

BOONVILLE CEMETERY
Cemetery Street
Boonville, NY 13309

BENTLEY, HENRY WILBUR Sept 30, 1838 DeRuyter, NY - Jan 27, 1907 Boonville, NY
United States Representative-NY from 1891-1893.

HULBERT, RICHARD 1799 - Apr 15, 1869 Boonville, NY
Owned and operated Hulbert House, Main Street in Boonville, purchased in 1839 from Ephraim Owens, who built the hotel in 1812.

BORODINO CEMETERY
1984 Route 174
Skaneateles, NY 13152

EMMONS, GIDEON 1836 - Jul 3, 1908 Onondaga County, NY
Civil War Veteran, lost his left arm in the war. Hired by William C. "Stub" Newell, on the pretense to dig a well on his farm, to "discover" the Cardiff Giant, a ten-foot tall stone man, buried by his cousin, George Hull, creating the greatest hoax in 19th Century America.

SPERLING, HAROLD D. Nov 29, 1898 Oneida, NY - Jun 13, 1974 Skaneateles, NY
Saxophonist with the New York State Railway Band. Performed with the John Philip Sousa Band on several occasions.

UNCKLESS, CLARENCE Aug 8, 1885 Marietta, NY - Aug 21, 1971 Syracuse, NY
Two-term Onondaga County District Attorney, from 1926-1932.

BOTTSKILL BAPTIST CHURCH CEMETERY
32 Church Street
Greenwich, NY 12834

HEATH, JOSEPH May 22, 1754 Tolland County, CT - Jun 21, 1830 Greenwich, NY
With **Mabel Rising Heath** (Oct 19, 1756 Suffield, CT - Oct 29, 1820 Greenwich, NY), the great-grandparents of Sarah Palin, Governor of Alaska from 2006-2009.

BOXWOOD CEMETERY
North Gravel Road / Route 63
Medina, NY 14103

BURROUGHS, SILAS MAINVILLE Jul 16, 1810 Ovid, NY - Jun 3, 1860 Medina, NY
United States Representative-NY from 1857-1860. Died during his last year in office.

BRIDGEPORT CEMETERY
3091 East Bayard Street
Seneca Falls, NY 13148

FRENAY, ROBERT C. Jul 21, 1919 Oneida, NY - Feb 2, 1988 Syracuse, NY
Founder and president of Fremac Marine Sales, Inc. in Bridgeport. With **Doris Smith Frenay** (Nov 7, 1920 - Apr 10, 1998 Daytona Beach, FL), the parents of singer/songwriter Gary Frenay, founding member of the Flashcubes and Screen Test, and author, Robert C. Frenay.

HARRIS, JOHN Sept 26, 1760 Harrisburg, PA - Nov 1824 Bridgeport, NY
United States Representative-NY from 1807-1809.

SCHAD, THOMAS F. Jan 29, 1948 Auburn, NY – Mar 28, 1998 Syracuse, NY
Brother of murderer, Edward Harold Schad, sentenced to death, December 7, 1979, for the 1978 strangulation death of Lorimar Leroy Groves in Prescott, AZ. At the time of his execution in 2013, he was Arizona's oldest death row inmate.

BRIGGS CEMETERY
Brookline Road
Ballston Spa, NY 12020

BALL, ELIPHALET 1722 Bedford, NY - Apr 6, 1797 Ballston, NY
Presbyterian clergyman. Early settler and namesake of the town of Ballston and Ballston Spa.

GORDON, JAMES Oct 31, 1739 Killead, Antrim, Ireland - Jan 17, 1810 Ballston Spa, NY
United States Representative-NY from 1791-1795.

YOUNG, SAMUEL 1779 Lenox, MA - Nov 3, 1850 Ballston Spa, NY
Member of the New York State Assembly from 1814, 1814-1815 and 1826. Speaker of the New York
State Assembly from 1814-1815 and 1826. Member of the New York State Senate from   1818-1821
and 1846-1847. New York Secretary of State from 1842-1845. Unsuccessful candidate for United
States Senate in 1819, and governor of New York in 1824, losing to DeWitt Clinton.

BRIGHTON CEMETERY
Hoyt Place
Rochester, NY 14610

BLOSS, WILLIAM CLOUGH Jan 17, 1795 West Stockbridge, MA - Apr 18, 1863 Rochester, NY
Abolitionist and reformer. Published *The Rights of Man* anti-slavery paper. Member of the New York
State Assembly from 1844-1848.

HAGEN, WILLIAM M. Sept 1861 Rochester, NY - Jul 19, 1942 Rochester, NY
With **Louisa Balko Hagen** (Oct 1863 Germany - Oct 21, 1949 Rochester, NY), the parents of Hall of
Fame golfer, Walter Hagen.

BROOKSIDE CEMETERY
Cemetery Road
Gilbertsville, NY 13776

ELBRICK, CHARLES BURKE Mar 25, 1908 Louisville, KY - Apr 13, 1983 Washington D.C.
United States Ambassador to Portugal from 1958-1963, Yugoslavia in 1964 and Brazil from
1969-1970. Kidnapped by left-wing terrorists in broad daylight in Rio de Janeiro, September 1969,
released following a trade of fifteen prisoners. The event was the basis for the Academy   Award-
nominated Brazilian film, *Four Days in September*, in 1997.

GILBERT, ABIJAH Jun 18, 1806 Gilbertsville, NY - Nov 23, 1881 Gilbertsville, NY
United States Senator-FL from 1869-1875.

BROOKSIDE CEMETERY
Plank Road
Poestenkill, NY 12140

DREW, HAZEL I. Jun 3, 1888 Poestenkill, NY - Jul 7, 1908 Sand Lake, NY
Murder victim. Found dead in Teal's Pond, Taborton, from blunt force trauma to her head, her body
badly decomposed. Despite her mysterious death and no shortage of suspects, her murder remains
unsolved. Inspired the 1990s televison series, *Twin Peaks*.

BROOKSIDE CEMETERY
Fenton Street
Waddington, NY 13694

ARBUCKLE, MACLYN Jul 9, 1866 San Antonio, TX - Apr 1, 1931 Waddington, NY
Silent film actor. Starred in *The County Chairman* on Broadway and film. Brother of actor, Andrew
Arbuckle. Cousin of silent film comedian, Roscoe "Fatty" Arbuckle.

BROOKSIDE CEMETERY
Brookside Road
Watertown, NY 13601

ATKINSON, MARTIN GAY Jan 1860 Nova Scotia, Canada - Oct 1, 1928 Watertown, NY
Watertown eye, ear, nose & throat specialist. With **Emma Adelia Cutten Atkinson** (May 10, 1859
Canada - Mar 31, 1949 Watertown, NY), the great-grandparents of Academy Award-nominated actor,
Viggo Mortensen.

ATKINSON, WALTER SYDNEY Feb 3, 1891 Nova Scotia, Canada - Jan 9, 1978 Watertown, NY
Watertown ophthalmologist. Survived the crash-landing of an Eastern Airlines twin-engine plane at
Hancock Field in Syracuse, June 6, 1959, when it's landing gear failed. With **Mary Annie Gamble
Atkinson** (Aug 7, 1898 Watertown, NY - Nov 1, 1982 Watertown, NY), the grandparents of Academy
Award-nominated actor, Viggo Mortensen.

CLARK, AMBROSE WILLIAMS Feb 19, 1810 Cooperstown, NY - Oct 13, 1887 Watertown, NY
United States Representative-NY from 1861-1865. United States Consul to Valparaiso in 1865,
appointed by President Abraham Lincoln.

DEPHTEREOS, OTTO L. Jan 17, 1895 - Aug 20, 1981 Watertown, NY
Head chef for the Crystal Restaurant, 87 Public Square, Watertown, from 1928-1981, owned by his brother, Nicholas Dephtereos, who purchased the restaurant in 1943 from brothers, Dennis Valanos and Jerry Valanos, who founded the eatery in 1919.

EXLEY, FREDERICK Mar 28, 1929 Watertown, NY - Jun 17, 1992 Watertown, NY
Author of *A Fan's Notes* in 1968 and *Last Notes from Home* in 1988.

FLOWER, ROSWELL PETTIBONE Aug 7, 1835 Theresa, NY - May 12, 1899 Eastport, NY
United States Representative-NY from 1881-1883 and 1889-1891. Governor of New York from 1892-1895.

HUMES, NEALE C. Mar 30, 1920 Watertown, NY - Dec 16, 2010 Laguna Beach, CA
With **Rose Margaret "Peggy" Humes** (Aug 21, 1920 Harrisville, NY - Jul 26, 2003 Watertown, NY), the parents of Hollywood actress, Mary-Margaret Humes, crowned Miss Florida in 1975 and third runner-up in the Miss USA pageant, later that year.

KEEP, HENRY Jun 22, 1818 Adams, NY - Jul 31, 1869 New York, NY
Millionaire financier, railroad executive and philanthropist.

LANSING, FREDERICK Feb 16, 1838 Manheim, NY - Jan 31, 1894 Watertown, NY
United States Representative-NY from 1889-1891.

LANSING, ROBERT Oct 17, 1864 Watertown, NY - Oct 30, 1928 New York, NY
United States Secretary of State from 1915-1920, under President Woodrow Wilson. One of five United States delegates to attend the Paris Peace Conference in Versailles, France in 1919, signaling the end of World War I. Son-in-law of Gen. John Watson Foster, United States Secretary of State from 1892-1893, under President Benjamin Harrison.

MASSEY, LANCE EDWARD Sept 20, 1909 Syracuse, NY - Jun 4, 1942 Midway Islands
World War II United States Navy Lieutenant. Commanding officer of Torpedo Squadron III. Killed in action, leading aircraft from the *U.S.S. Yorktown* in an attack on the Japanese carrier force in the Battle of Midway. Portrayed by actor, Steve Kanaly, in the film, *Midway*, in 1976. Namesake of the destroyer, *U.S.S. Massey*.

NICHOLS (Stevens), **MARJORIE H.** Mar 21, 1890 Watertown, NY - Mar 26, 1976 Watertown, NY
Sister of Dr. Marvin Allen "Mal" Stevens, college football Hall of Fame running back and head football coach of Yale University from 1932-1942 and the Brooklyn Dodgers of the NFL in 1946.

PADDOCK, LOVELAND Mar 15, 1794 Middletown, CT - Jun 25, 1872 Watertown, NY
Built the Paddock Arcade in Watertown, the oldest continuously operating covered mall in the United States, in 1850.

PIERCE, CHARLES E. Feb 18, 1872 Limerick, NY - 1950 Watertown, NY
Physician. Grandfather of actor, Charles E. Pierce, celebrity female impersonator, called the "Master and Mistress of Surprise and Disguise."

PIERCE, GERALD SLOAT Jun 5, 1901 Watertown, NY - Jun 1973 Watertown, NY
With **Jessie Hickman Pierce** (Oct 27, 1903 - Oct 7, 1988 Watertown, NY), the parents of actor, Charles E. Pierce, celebrity female impersonator, called the "Master and Mistress of Surprise and Disguise."

TAYLOR, JOHN LOREEN Jun 22, 1835 NY - 1913 Watertown, NY
With **Lanah M. Fox Taylor** (Jun 23, 1836 - 1913 Watertown, NY), the grandparents of Hollywood socialite, Countess di Frasso, born Dorothy Caldwell Taylor, and Bertrand L. Taylor, member of the New York Stock Exchange from 1914-1940. 2nd great-grandparents of actress, Mary Taylor Zimbalist, wife of Academy Award-winning film producer, Sam Zimbalist.

WOODRUFF, THEODORE TUTTLE Apr 8, 1811 Watertown, NY - May 3, 1892 Gloucester City, NJ
Founded the Woodruff Sleeping Car Company, inventor of the railway sleeping car, later refined by George Mortimer Pullman. Died in an accident supervising construction of a railway car, struck as he stepped into the path of an oncoming train.

WRIGHT, GRAY (W. Graham) Mar 12, 1918 Rochester, NY - Jan 17, 2008 Sandpoint, ID
Published two volumes of poetry, *Journey* in 1989 and *Journey II* in 1991. Stepfather of Academy Award-nominated actor, Viggo Mortensen, married his mother, Grace Atkinson Mortensen Wright, January 12, 1971.

BROWNVILLE CEMETERY
West Main Street / Route 12
Brownsville, NY 13615

KIRBY, EDMUND Mar 11, 1840 Brownville, NY - May 28, 1863 Washington D.C.
Civil War Union Army Brigadier General. Wounded in battle at Chancellorsville, May 3, 1863, later died from infection following an amputation of his leg. President Abraham Lincoln visited him on his deathbed, raising his rank to brigadier general, assuring his family of a generous pension. Grandson of Major General Jacob Jennings Brown, Commander in Chief of the United States Army from 1815-1828, namesake of the town of Brownville in Jefferson County.

SHAWCROSS (Yerakes), **BESSIE** (Betty) Aug 4, 1926 Watertown, NY - Mar 2, 2011 Watertown, NY
Mother of serial killer, Arthur John Shawcross, known as "The Genesee River Killer."

SKINNER, ALANSON May 21, 1794 Westmoreland, NH - June 6, 1876 Watertown, NY
Member of the New York State Senate from 1850-1851. Brother of Avery Skinner, member of the New York State Senate from 1838-1841.

BRYANT CEMETERY
Quaker Road
Macedon, NY 14502

WILCOX, DAVID Jan 10, 1763 Bristol, MA - Aug 23, 1829 Macedon, NY
With **Anna Baker Wilcox** (May 29, 1761 NS, Canada - Dec 28, 1813 Macedon, NY), the great-grandparents of Jeanette Jerome, properly known as Lady Randolph Churchill, wife of Sir Randolph Henry Spencer-Churchill, married in 1874 at the British Embassy in Paris. 2nd great-grandparents of Sir Winston Churchill, Prime Minister of Great Britain from 1940-1945 and 1951-1955.

BUFFALO CEMETERY
Harlem Road / Route 240
Cheektowaga, NY 14225

BALL, JASPER CLINTON May 16, 1852 Pithole City, PA - May 24, 1933 Buffalo, NY
Grandfather of Emmy Award-winning actress, Lucille Ball. Great-grandfather of actress, Lucy Arnaz and actor, Desi Arnaz Jr. His wife, Mary Rebecca "Nellie" Durrell Ball, died in 1935 in Buffalo, buried in Holy Cross Cemetery, Lackawanna.

BURCH FARM CEMETERY
Meads Road
Johnsonville, NY 12094

HUNT, STEPHEN S. Mar 30, 1764 Pawling, NY - Apr 24, 1825 Schaghticoke, NY
3rd great-grandfather of Emmy Award-winning actress, Lucille Ball. 4th great-grandfather of actress, Lucy Arnaz and actor, Desi Arnaz Jr.

BURNHAM HOLLOW CEMETERY
Bard Road
Cassadaga, NY 14718

HORTON, BRADLEY A. June 9, 1981 NY - Jun 25, 2006 Erie, PA
Shot five times in the back by New York State trooper, Sean Pierce, attempting to flee a roadblock during their search for Ralph "Bucky" Phillips, a fugitive listed simultaneously on the FBI Ten Most Wanted Fugitives and the U.S. Marshal Service's Top 15 lists, for escaping prison and the shooting death of a state trooper in September 2006.

BUSTI CEMETERY
Mill Road
Jamestown, NY 14701

NYGREN (Mack)**, JANETTE E.** Aug 3, 1924 Chandlers Valley, PA - Dec 15, 2013 Jamestown, NY
Aunt of Robert Buck, founding member, guitarist and songwriter of the alternative rock band, 10,000
Maniacs. He died of liver cancer, December 19, 2000, age 42, and is buried in Mission Covenant
Church Cemetery in Sugar Grove, PA, 10 miles from Jamestown.

BUTLER-SAVANNAH CEMETERY
Route 89
Savannah, NY 13146

COLVIN, RAYMOND B. Dec 16, 1929 Syracuse, NY - Oct 31, 2000 Rochester, NY
Uncle of United States Army Four-Star General, Keith B. Alexander, Director of the National Security
Agency from 2005-2014, under President George W. Bush and President Barack Obama.

CALKINS CEMETERY
Calkins Cemetery Lane
Elizabethtown, NY 12932

POLETTI, CHARLES Jul 2, 1903 Barre, VT - Aug 8, 2002 Marco Island, FL
Governor of New York for 29 days, December 3-31, 1942, succeeding Herbert H. Lehman, who
resigned to take a post with the United States Department of State. First Italian-American Governor of
New York. Lieutenant Governor of New York from 1939-1942. Associate Justice of the New York State
Supreme Court from 1937-1938.

CALVARY CEMETERY
115 Clark Street
Canandaigua, NY 14424

GERKEN, DAVID M. Oct 6, 1986 Palmyra, NY - Nov 16, 2012 Buffalo, NY
Miami Dolphins fan, attended a Buffalo Bills game against the Dolphins, with his brother and a friend,
drank too much and ejected from the game. Later found dead, after the game, face down in Smoke's
Creek, outside Ralph Wilson Stadium, drowned, having fallen down a ravine. One of two fans to have
died that game, which included 94 ejections, 55 traffic tickets, 28 arrests and two DWI's.

CALVARY CEMETERY
481 Route 9W
Glenmont, NY 12077

KELLY, EDWARD F. May 19, 1940 Brooklyn, NY - Dec 15, Albany, NY
Professor at SUNY Albany. Father of journalist, Megyn Kelly, anchor of Fox News Channel's, *The Kelly File*.

CALVARY CEMETERY
West German Street
Herkimer, NY 13350

QUACKENBUSH, HENRY MARCUS Apr 27, 1847 Herkimer, NY - Sept 8, 1933 Herkimer, NY
Founded the H.M. Quackenbush Company in Herkimer in 1871, manufacturer of the first air pistol. Invented the extension ladder in 1867 and the nutpick and spring-jointed nutcracker in 1913.

CALVARY CEMETERY
5 Mile Drive / Route 13A
Ithaca, NY 14850

BARRA, MICHAEL JAMES Apr 5, 1932 Ithaca, NY - Feb 20, 1951 Pyokdong, North Korea
Korean War United States Army Sergeant. Captured by the Chinese People's Volunteer Army during the Battle of Wawon, Kunu-ri, North Korea, December 1, 1950, sent to a prisoner-of-war camp where he died 10 weeks later. Reported missing-in-action, his remains, along with more than 400 servicemen, were turned over to the United States government in 208 boxes by North Korea between 1991-1994, positively identified through the DNA of his brother and sister, and buried in his hometown, November 22, 2014.

FRICKE (Hines)**, JEANNE** 1924 Ithaca, NY - Jul 20, 1966 Waterloo, NY
Died in Taylor Brown Memorial Hospital from a broken neck suffered in a car accident, intersection of Routes 96 and 336, town of Fayette, driven by her husband, Richard I. Fricke, slightly injuring three of their children. Her husband later married Ruth Prince Byerly Fricke, the first wife of television executive, Grant Tinker, from 1950-1962, who co-founded MTM Enterprises, with his second wife, actress, Mary Tyler Moore, and served as CEO of NBC from 1981-1986.

FRICKE, RICHARD FELIX Jun 28, 1896 Buffalo, NY - Sept 21, 1976 Ithaca, NY

New York State agricultural pioneer. Professor Emeritus, Extension Service, New York State, from 1956-1973.

FRICKE, RICHARD IRVIN Mar 25, 1922 Buffalo, NY - Jan 17, 2003 Naples, FL

Banking and insurance executive. Involved in a car accident at the intersection of Routes 96 and 336, town of Fayette, July 20, 1966, the car he was driving colliding with another, killing his wife, Jeanne Hines Fricke, slightly injuring three of their children. Second husband of Ruth Prince Byerly Fricke, the first wife of television executive, Grant Tinker, from 1950-1962, who co-founded MTM Enterprises, with his second wife, actress, Mary Tyler Moore, and served as CEO of NBC from 1981-1986. Son of Richard F. Fricke, Professor Emeritus, Extension Service, New York State, from 1956-1973. Great-grandson of Richard von Fricke, Ballet Meister for German composer, Richard Wagner.

CALVARY CEMETERY
Windsor Highway
New Windsor, NY 12553

HUTTON (Winne)**, ROBERT** Jun 11, 1920 Kingston, NY - Aug 7, 1994 Kingston, NY

Hollywood film actor. Appeared in the films, *Tales from the Crypt*, *Destination Tokyo*, *Casanova's Big Night*, *And Baby Makes Three* and *The New Roof*. Related to Barbara Hutton, New York City socialite, dubbed the "Poor Little Rich Girl", married seven times, including third husband, actor, Cary Grant, through his grandmother, Matilda Jane Hutton More.

CALVARY CEMETERY
Dry Bridge Road
Norwood, NY 13638

MANFRED, FRANCIS H. 1906 - Mar 1, 1963 NY

Grandfather of Robert D. Manfred Jr., 10th Commissioner of Baseball, elected in 2015.

MANFRED, HENRY D. Mar 26, 1878 - Dec 21, 1959 NY

Great-grandfather of Robert D. Manfred Jr., 10th Commissioner of Baseball, elected in 2015.

CALVARY CEMETERY
Lagrange Avenue
Poughkeepsie, NY 12603

VIAFORE, VINCENT A. Aug 22, 1968 Bronxville, NY - Apr 19, 2015 Fishkill, NY
Murder victim. Kayaking the Hudson River, with his fiancé, Angelika Graswald, destination Bannerman's Island from Plum Point, when their kayak sinks, without a life vest, he drowns, his body found, May 23, 2015, near West Point. She was charged with second-degree murder and second-degree manslaughter, deliberately pulling the plug on the kayak and pushed his paddle away as he reached for help. The event was profiled on ABC's, *20/20*, in 2015.

CALVARY CEMETERY
Central Avenue
Salamanca, NY 14779

MERCHANT (Meyer)**, ANNE** Apr 11, 1941 Rochester, NY - Sept 5, 2010 Greenville, SC
Mother of singer/songwriter, Natalie Merchant, lead singer of the alternative rock band, 10,000 Maniacs, from 1981-1993.

MEYER, JEROME JOSEPH Jun 16, 1915 Rochester, NY - May 6, 2002 Olean, NY
Grandfather of singer/songwriter, Natalie Merchant, lead singer of the alternative rock band, 10,000 Maniacs, from 1981-1993.

WASS (Boesch)**, ELIZABETH C.** Mar 8, 1921 Syracuse, NY - Dec 17, 2007 Great Valley, NY
Grandmother of singer/songwriter, Natalie Merchant, lead singer of the alternative rock band, 10,000 Maniacs, from 1981-1993.

CALVARY CEMETERY
2407 Oneida Street
Utica, NY 13501

ALBANO, MICHAEL ANGELO Jan 6, 1882 - Aug 30, 1962 Utica, NY
With **Sarafina Fierro Albano** (1884 - 1939 Utica, NY), the grandparents of singer, actress and Mouseketeer, Annette Funicello.

BORGOVINI, JOSEPH Apr 16, 1892 Italy - May 9, 1972 Utica, NY
Co-founded the Florentine Bakery, 667 Bleecker Street, Utica, with Vincenzo Gennaro, in 1928.

BURLINE (Burlino)**, EUGENE** (Eugeno) Naples, Italy - 1958 Utica, NY
Founded, owned and operated O'Scugnizzo Pizzeria, Bleecker Street, Utica in 1914. Created his own of tomato pie, an upside-down pizza, placing the sauce and Romano cheese on top.

D'ALESSANDRO, DOMINICK Jan 5, 1923 - Sept 10, 1991 Utica, NY
With **Rosemary Pallaria D'Alessandro** (Feb 2, 1923 - Nov 15, 1986), the parents of corporate executive, David F. D'Alessandro, author of best-selling business books.

DETORE, GEORGE Nov 11, 1906 Utica, NY - Feb 7, 1991 Utica, NY
Reserve third basemen for the Cleveland Indians from 1930-1931. Made his major league debut the same day as future Hall of Famer, Hank Greenberg of the Detroit Tigers. Longtime minor league manager following his playing career.

DISPIRITO, HENRY R. (Erasmo Orazio) Jul 2, 1898 Castelforte, Italy - Feb 23, 1995 Utica, NY
Sculptor. Awarded a prize by the National Academy of Design in New York for his stone sculpture, "Ant", in 1982, age 84.

ELEFANTE, RUFUS P. Apr 11, 1903 - Nov 15, 1994 Utica, NY
Democratic Party leader in Utica for 70 years. Never elected to any public office, Utica's large Italian-American population would receive political favors from him and, in turn, vote according to his wishes, earning Utica the nickname, "Sin City", during this era.

FANELLI, JOSEPH L. Sept 18, 1923 - Apr 18, 2003 Utica, NY
Jazz trumpeter. Performed with the Tune Tones, throughout the United States in the 1940s and 50s. Husband of Cynthia Red Morreale, singer and played drums with the Tune Tones.

FUNICELLO, ANTHONY Jul 17, 1887 Italy - Nov 1977 Utica, NY
Grandfather of singer, actress and Mouseketeer, Annette Funicello.

KOGUT, ALEXANDRA GERACE Jan 19, 1994 New Hartford, NY - Sept 29, 2012 Brockport, NY
Murder victim. Beaten to death, blunt force trauma to her upper body, by high school boyfriend, Clayton S. Whittemore, in her dorm room, SUNY Brockport. Whittemore, high school hockey player named "Athlete of the Week" in Utica in 2010, was arrested on the New York State Thruway, convicted of second-degree murder and sentenced to 25-years-to-life in prison. The case was profiled on *Dateline* in 2015.

MURAD, KAISER Oct 25, 1922 - Sept 5, 2008 Utica, NY
Owned and operated Murad's Market in Utica.

SEBREGANDIO COUPLE Sept 21, 1994 Columbus, NY
Frank A. Sebregandio, born April 15, 1913, and his wife of 54 years, **Josephine R. Circelli Sebregandio**, born September 21, 1914, were reported missing by their family, August 1, 1994, one day after their Sunday drive for lunch, found dead seven weeks later, her body in the car, his a few feet away, in the town of Columbus, Chenango County, 35 miles south of their home, their car stuck in the mud, 200 yards off Route 8, unable to free themselves.

ZOGBY (Zogby), **CELIA ANN** (Salemi) 1906 Shenandoah, PA - Jan 1999 Utica, NY
With **Joseph (Yousef) Zogby** (Kfartay, Lebanon - 1961 Utica, NY), the parents of John Zogby, founding president of Zogby International, a leading polling firm, and James Zogby, founding president of the Arab American Institute. Both brothers graduated from LeMoyne College in Syracuse.

CALVARY CEMETERY
Route 52
Youngsville, NY 12791

OWENS, JAMES J. Dec 27, 1925 - Sept 1977 White Sulphur Springs, NY
Owned and operated the One Step Inn in Youngsville, Sullivan County. Recognized Patty Hearst, shooting pool in his bar with her former captor-turned-comrade, Wendy Yoshimura, in 1974, during the 19 months she was kidnapped by the SLA, held captive, later coerced into joining the terror group, becoming a fugitive from law. By the time he called the FBI, she was gone. She had been staying in a rented home on Creamery Road in nearby Jeffersonville.

CALVARY-ST. PATRICK CEMETERY
501 Fairview Street
Johnson City, NY 13790

BARBARA, JOSEPH M. Aug 9, 1905 Castellammare del Golfo, Italy - Jun 17, 1959 Johnson City, NY
Mafia figure known as "Joe, the Barber." Host of the Apalachin Mafia Conference, a summit of mafia leaders raided by authorities, November 17, 1957, among those apprehended, Vito Genovese, Carlo Gambino and Joseph Bonanno. High school football teammate and friend of longtime baseball umpire, Ron Luciano.

BIONDI, MICHAEL A. Jan 27, 1906 - Aug 29, 1978 Endicott, NY
With **Rose Biondi** (Sept 25, 1911 - Jan 28, 2005 Endicott, NY), the parents of disc jockey, Richard O. "Dick" Biondi, known as the "Wild I-tralian", one of the first national disc jockeys to play Elvis Presley, Jerry Lee Lewis and Gene Vincent, introduced the Beatles and the Rolling Stones at their Hollywood Bowl concerts.

CROWLEY, J.K. (James Kiernan) Oct 17, 1882 Poughkeepsie, NY - Dec 9, 1952 Binghamton, NY
Founded the Crowley Dairy Company in Poughkeepsie in 1904. Moved the business to Binghamton in 1915, later rebranded as Crowley Foods.

FARRELL, DOC (Edward Stephen) Dec 26, 1901 Johnson City, NY - Dec 20, 1966 Livingston, NJ
Infielder for the New York Giants, Boston Braves, St. Louis Cardinals, Chicago Cubs, New York Yankees and Boston Red Sox from 1925-1930, 1932-1933 and 1935. Played 26 games for the World Series champion Yankees in 1932.

FOLEY, HELEN M. Nov 12, 1912 Binghamton, NY - Dec 27, 2002 Binghamton, NY
Educator in the Binghamton City School District. Mentor to former student, Rod Serling, screenwriter and creator of *The Twilight Zone*. Serling named a character 'Helen Foley' in *Nightmare as a Child*, a season one episode of *The Twilight Zone*. Awarded a star on the Binghamton Walk of Fame in 1996.

HALLAHAN, BILL Aug 4, 1902 Binghamton - Jul 8, 1981 Binghamton, NY
All-Star pitcher for the St. Louis Cardinals, Cincinnati Reds and Philadelphia Phillies from 1925-1926 and 1929-1938. Nicknamed "Wild Bill." Led the National League in strikeouts in 1930 and 1931. Pitched for four National League pennant winners and three World Series championship teams for the Cardinals. Starting pitcher for the National League in the first-ever All-Star Game in 1933.

IACOVELLI, AGOSTINO Aug 3, 1898 Civitella, Abruzzo, Italy - Sept 24, 1987 Endicott, NY
Credited with inventing "Spiedies", a variation of shish-kabob, at his restaurant, Augie's, in 1939.

KANE (McManus), **MARY** May 1897 Choconut, PA - Jun 17, 1964 Binghamton, NY
Mother of three Roman Catholic priests, Rev. Joseph F. Kane, Rev. John W. Kane and Rev. James D. Kane. Her husband, Joseph J. Kane died December 20, 1965 in Binghamton, age 74.

LIBOUS, THOMAS W. Apr 14, 1953 Johnson City, NY - May 3, 2016 Binghamton, NY
New York State Senator from 1989-2015. Resigned, vacating his senate seat, when found guilty of lying to the FBI, fined and sentenced to six months house arrest.

LUCIANO, RON (Ronald Michael) Jun 28, 1937 Binghamton, NY - Jan 19, 1995 Endicott, NY
American League umpire from 1969-1980. Worked the 1974 World Series and the 1971 and 1975 American League Championship Series. President of the Major League Umpires Association. Wrote four books, including *The Umpire Strikes Back* and *The Fall of the Roman Umpire*. Syracuse University All-American tackle from 1956-1958. Selected by the Detroit Lions in the third round of the NFL Draft. Played briefly for the Buffalo Bills in the AFL. High school teammate and friend of Joseph Barbara, host of the Apalachin Mafia Conference raided by police in 1957. Committed suicide by carbon monoxide poisoning in his garage.

MELFI, LEONARD A. Feb 21, 1932 Binghamton, NY - Oct 28, 2001 New York, NY
Playwright and stage actor. Remembered for his play, *Birdbath*, first produced in 1965. Contributed to the 1969 Broadway musical, *Oh! Calcutta!* Wrote the screenplay to the film, *Lady Liberty*. Died at Mount Sinai Hospital from congestive heart failure, where his body remained for a month. Two months later, December 20th, his body was sent to Potter's Field on Hart's Island, unbeknownst to his family. In February 2002, the hospital error was uncovered and he was given a funeral and burial in the family plot, April 18, 2002.

MURPHY, MIKE Aug 19, 1888 Forestville, PA - Oct 26, 1952 Johnson City, NY
Played one game for the St. Louis Cardinals in 1912 and 14 games for the Philadelphia Athletics, managed by Hall of Famer Connie Mack, in 1916.

PAGLIA, PASQUALE J. Jun 12, 1925 Endicott, NY - Jan 22, 1991 Manlius, NY
Professor Emeritus at LeMoyne College in Syracuse from 1957-1987. Father of author, Camille Paglia.

WEST, JOHN H. Jul 25, 1934 NY - Jul 9, 2003 West Windsor, NY
Father of Barbara West Rogers, who, with her husband, Robert Rogers, sponsored six "Lost Boys of Sudan" in their home on Otisco Lake, including Joseph Lopepe "Lopez" Lomong, member of the 2008 United States Olympic Track and Field team.

ZANDY, EDWARD EUGENE Mar 27, 1920 Endicott, NY - Aug 23, 2003 Nassau, Bahamas
Trumpet player. Member of the Glenn Miller Orchestra, led by Ted Beneke, Ray McKinley and Buddy DeFranco. Played with Gene Krupa and Skitch Henderson.

CANAAN CEMETERY
Farm to Market Road / Route 5
Canaan, NY 12029

DOUGLAS, ASA Dec 24, 1739 Plainfield, CT - Apr 17, 1812 Canaan, NY
Revolutionary War Continental Army Major. Granduncle of Stephen A. Douglas, United States Senator-IL from 1847-1861, and Democratic Party candidate for president in 1860, losing to Abraham Lincoln.

CANAJOHARIE FALLS CEMETERY
6339 State Highway 10
Canajoharie, NY 13317

ARKELL, BARTLETT 1862 Canajoharie, NY - Oct 13, 1946 Bennington, VT
Industrialist. Noted art collector. Founder and first President of the Beech-Nut Packing Company in

Canajoharie, in 1891. Developed a vacuum packing technique and created packaging for food in glass containers. Brother of William J. Arkell, publisher of the periodicals, *Frank Leslie's* and *Judge* and founder of the George Washington Coffee Company.

ARKELL, JAMES Oct 16, 1829 Oxford, England - Aug 11, 1902 Canajoharie, NY
New York State Senator from 1884-1886. Co-founded Arkell & Smith's, an early manufacturer of paper and cotton bags. Father of William J. Arkell, publisher of the periodicals, *Frank Leslie's* and *Judge*, and Bartlett Arkell, first President of the Beech-Nut Packing Company.

ARKELL, WILLIAM JAMES 1858 Canajoharie, NY - Dec 29, 1930 New York, NY
Published the periodicals, *Frank Leslie's* and *Judge*. Founded the George Washington Coffee Company. Brother of Bartlett Arkell, first President of the Beech-Nut Packing Company.

BARBOUR (Arkell)**, BERTELLE** Jan 16, 1871 Canajoharie, NY - Jul 29, 1950 Canajoharie, NY
Wife of Francis Edward "Frank" Barbour, Yale University quarterback from 1890-1891 and executive for the Beech-Nut Packing Company, and political cartoonist, Bernhard Gillam. Sister of William J. Arkell, publisher of the periodicals, *Frank Leslie's* and *Judge*, and Bartlett Arkell, first President of the Beech-Nut Packing Company.

CARDIFF CEMETERY
Route 11A
Lafayette, NY 13084

SHETLER (Shute)**, RUTH IRENE** Dec 7, 1924 Lafayette, NY - Jan 14, 2002 Tully, NY
Mother of Cheryl Shetler Paccia, the wife of James Paccia, Tully High School track and field coach, who taught and trained Joseph Lopepe "Lopez" Lomong, one of the "Lost Boys of Sudan" and member of the 2008 United States Track and Field team.

CARLEY MILLS CEMETERY
Route 84
Hastings, NY 13076

STONE, BERYL G. Nov 2, 1937 Hastings, NY - Sept 7, 1998 Syracuse, NY
One of two people killed at the New York State Fair during the historic Labor Day Storm of 1998, when a tree fell on his camper, causing the cancellation of the last day of the fair. The other victim, John H. Perry III, born January 2, 1955, was killed when a section of roof flew off the Dairy Products Building landing on a concession stand where he slept. Perry was a fair worker from Silver Creek, Chautauqua County.

CARR CEMETERY
Route 291
Marcy, NY 13403

SIMON, KIMBERLY MICHELLE Jan 12, 1969 Utica, NY - Sept 19, 1985 Marcy, NY
Murder victim. Whitesboro High School student in Oneida County, found raped and murdered along the Mohawk River. Steven P. Barnes was convicted of the crime in 1989, spent 19 years in prison before his exoneration through DNA evidence. *America's Most Wanted* aired a segment in 2010, following Barnes' release, suspecting Satan worshipers in her murder.

CATHEDRAL OF THE IMMACULATE CONCEPTION
259 East Onondaga Street
Syracuse, NY 13202

CHAMPLIN, JOSEPH M. May 11, 1930 Hammondsport, NY - Jan 17, 2008 Syracuse, NY
Central New York priest from 1956-2008. Rector of the Cathedral of the Immaculate Conception in Syracuse from 1995-2005. Author of more than 50 books. Appeared regularly on radio with inspirational messages which concluded with "You may have tried everything else, why not try God." Founded the Guardian Angel's Society to help disadvantaged children with their education. Received the President's Volunteer Service Award from President George W. Bush in 2006. Brother of film critic and author, Charles D. Champlin. His body, donated to Upstate Medical Center in Syracuse after his death, was later cremated, interred beneath the alter of the Cathedral on St. Joseph's Day, March 19, 2009.

CURLEY, DANIEL JOSEPH Jun 16, 1869 New York, NY - Aug 3, 1932 Syracuse, NY
Third Roman Catholic Bishop of the Diocese of Syracuse, from 1923-1932. Presided at the benediction of the Loretto Rest Catholic Home for the Aged in Syracuse in 1927, the first diocesan home for the aged in North America.

GRIMES, JOHN Dec 18, 1852 Doughanmore, Limerick, Ireland - Jul 26, 1922 Syracuse, NY
Second Roman Catholic Bishop of the Diocese of Syracuse, from 1912-1922, succeeding Bishop Ludden. Namesake of Bishop Grimes High School in Syracuse.

LUDDEN, PATRICK Feb 4, 1836 County Mayo, Ireland - Aug 6, 1912 Syracuse, NY
First Roman Catholic Bishop of the Diocese of Syracuse, from 1886-1912, appointed by Pope Leo XIII. Namesake of Bishop Ludden High School in Syracuse.

MOYNIHAN, JAMES MICHAEL Jul 6, 1932 Rochester, NY - Mar 6, 2017 Syracuse, NY
Ninth Roman Catholic Bishop of the Diocese of Syracuse, from 1995-2009, appointed by Pope John Paul II.

CATSKILL TOWN CEMETERY
27 North Jefferson Avenue
Catskill, NY 12414

PENRAAT, JAAP Apr 11, 1918 Amsterdam, Netherlands - Jun 25, 2006 Catskill, NY
Architect. Designed the Dutch Mill Café at the 1964 World's Fair in New York. Dutch resistance fighter, forged identity papers for Jews, concealing their identities from Nazi's, saving hundreds of lives, during World War II. Subject of the Hudson Talbot children's book, *Forging Freedom: A True Story of Heroism During the Holocaust.*

CATSKILL VILLAGE CEMETERY
Thompson Street
Catskill, NY 12414

ADAMS, JOHN Aug 26, 1778 Durham, NY - Sept 25, 1874 Catskill, NY
United States Representative-NY from 1833-1835. Brother of Platt Adams, New York State Assemblyman from 1820-1821.

ASHLEY, HENRY Feb 19, 1778 Winchester, NH - Jan 14, 1829 Catskill, NY
United States Representative-NY from 1825-1827.

BAGLEY, JOHN HOLROYD Nov 26, 1832 Hudson, NY - Oct 23, 1902 Catskill, NY
United States Representative-NY from 1875-1877 and 1883-1885.

BRANDOW, PAULUS (Appolos) Feb 7, 1789 Coxsackie, NY - Oct 29, 1874 Catskill, NY
With **Catherine Van Orden Brandow** (Oct 4, 1797 Ulster County, NY - Mar 10, 1883 Catskill, NY), the 2nd great-grandparents of Academy Award-winning actor, Marlon Brando.

COLE, THOMAS Feb 1, 1801 Lancashire, England - Feb 11, 1848 Catskill, NY
Landscape artist. Founder of the Hudson River School art movement in the mid-1850s.

COOKE, THOMAS BURRAGE Nov 21, 1778 Wallingford, CT - Nov 20, 1853 Catskill, NY
United States Representative-NY from 1811-1813.

GRISWOLD, JOHN ASHLEY Nov 18, 1822 Cairo, NY - Feb 22, 1902 Catskill, NY
United States Representative-NY from 1869-1871.

KING, RUFUS H. Apr 20, 1820 Rensselaerville, NY - Sept 13, 1890 Catskill, NY
United States Representative-NY from 1855-1857.

CAUGHNAWAGA CEMETERY
Old Johnstown Road
Fonda, NY 12068

FONDA, GARRET TUNIS BREESE Apr 5, 1808 Fonda, NY - Sept 8, 1879 Fonda, NY
Great-grandfather of Academy Award-winning actor, Henry Fonda. 2nd great-grandfather of Academy Award-winning actress, Jane Fonda and actor, Peter Fonda. 3rd great-grandfather of actress, Bridget Fonda.

FONDA, JELLIS DOUW Mar 24, 1727 Schenectady, NY - Jun 23, 1791 Palatine, NY
New York State Senator from 1777-1778, 1779-1781 and 1787-1791.

FONDA (Bries), **NELLY** (Neeltje) Mar 18, 1738 NY - Dec 15, 1820 NY
2nd great-granddaughter of Anneke Jans Bogardus, who emigrated to New Amsterdam with her first husband, Roelof Janszen, in 1630. 4th great-granddaughter of William I, Prince of Orange, commonly known as "William the Silent." With **Adam Douw Fonda** (Dec 26, 1736 Schenectady, NY - Nov 2, 1808 Fonda, NY), the 3rd great-grandparents of Academy Award-winning actor, Henry Fonda, the 4th great-grandparents of Academy Award-winning actress, Jane Fonda and actor, Peter Fonda and the 5th great-grandparents of actress, Bridget Fonda.

CEDAR HILL CEMETERY
5468 Route 9W
Newburgh, NY 12550

BENNET, AUGUSTUS WITSCHIEF Oct 7, 1897 New York, NY - Jun 5, 1983 Concord, MA
United States Representative-NY from 1945-1947.

BROWN, JOHN W. Oct 11, 1796 Dundee. Scotland - Sept 6, 1875 Newburgh, NY
United States Representative-NY from 1833-1837.

CARR (Caravello), **ERIC** (Paul Charles) Jul 12, 1950 Brooklyn, NY - Nov 24, 1991 New York, NY
Drummer for the rock band, KISS, from 1980-1991, replacing original drummer, Peter Criss. Died from a rare form of heart cancer, the same day as Freddie Mercury, lead singer for Queen.

CASEY, KENNETH Jan 10, 1899 New York, NY - Aug 10, 1965 Cornwall, NY
Composer, author and child actor. Co-wrote "Sweet Georgia Brown", with Ben Bernie and Maceo Pinkard, in 1925. Appeared in the silent film, *We Must Do Our Best*, with Moe Howard, in 1909.

DOWNING, A. J. (Andrew Jackson) Oct 30, 1815 Newburgh, NY - Jul 28, 1852 Yonkers, NY
Landscape designer. Editor of *The Horticulturist* from 1846-1852. Killed traveling with family on the

steamboat, *Henry Clay*, when a boiler exploded causing a fire, killing dozens, in the deadliest Hudson River accident in its history. His wife, Caroline DeWindt Downing, the great-granddaughter of President John Adams, survived. Memorialized with an urn at the Enid A. Haupt Garden of the Smithsonian Institute, Washington D.C.

MONELL (DeWindt), **CAROLINE ELIZABETH** Aug 1815 - Jul 17, 1905 Newburgh, NY
Great-granddaughter of President John Adams and First Lady Abigail Adams. Great-grandniece of President John Quincy Adams and First Lady Louisa Adams. Survived the deadliest Hudson River accident in its history when a boiler on the steamboat, *Henry Clay*, exploded killing dozens, including her husband, landscape architect, A.J. Downing, and her mother, Caroline Amelia Smith DeWindt.

PENDINO, DOMINICK May 22, 1962 NY - Mar 3, 1999 Newburgh, NY
Murder victim. Beaten to death with a baseball bat in his driveway by Lawrence Weygant and Gregory Chrysler, defended by attorney, Bruce Cutler, both found guilty in the first case in Orange County history that prosecutors secured a guilty verdict without the victim's body. His family placed a cenotaph in the cemetery, hoping one day his remains are found.

CEDAR PARK CEMETERY
20 Columbia Turnpike
Hudson, NY 12534

CANNON, J. D. Apr 24, 1922 Salmon, ID - May 20, 2005 Hudson, NY
Film and television actor. Co-starred on the TV series, *McCloud* and in the series finale of *The Fugitive* in 1967. Appeared in the films, *Cool Hand Luke*, *Scorpio* and *Death Wish II*. Founding member of Joseph Papp's New York Shakespeare Festival. Husband of theater actress, Alice Cannon.

STOTT, ARTHUR CURTISS Oct 19, 1858 Esopus, NY - Jan 9, 1905 Hudson, NY
With **Harriet Elizabeth Evans Stott** (Apr 1858 Hudson, NY - Jun 20, 1914 Schenectady, NY), the grandparents of actress, Ann B. Davis, played Alice on *The Brady Bunch* from 1969-1974, born in Schenectady, died June 1, 2014 in San Antonio, age 88, buried there, St. Helena's Columbarium and Memorial Gardens.

TROWBRIDGE, BOB Jun 27, 1930 Hudson, NY - Apr 3, 1980 Hudson, NY
Pitcher for the Milwaukee Braves and Kansas City Athletics from 1956-1960. Member of the Braves' 1957 World Series championship team. Teammate of Hall of Famers, Hank Aaron, Eddie Matthews, Warren Spahn and Red Schoendienst.

CEDAR RIVER CEMETERY
West Main Street / Route 30
Indian Lake, NY 12842

BROOKS, ERNEST DOLAN Jan 7, 1872 NY - Jul 21, 1934 Indian Lake, NY
Owned and operated the Brooks Hotel in Speculator, where legendary Adirondack guide and hunter, "French Louie" Seymour died from Bright's Disease, February 28, 1915.

CEDARVILLE CEMETERY
Cedarville Road / Route 79
Ilion, NY 13357

BARTLE (Reynolds)**, NELLIE M.** Dec 2, 1923 Greenwich, England - Feb 15, 2011 Cooperstown, NY
Veteran of the British Woman's Land Army during World War II. Received a Commendation from British Prime Minister, Gordon Brown, in 2008 for her service in the British Army.

CEMETERY OF THE EVERGREENS
Cemetery Road / Route 5
New Lebanon, NY 12125

KING, JOHN 1775 Canaan, NY - Sept 1, 1836 New Lebanon, NY
United States Representative-NY from 1831-1833.

TILDEN, SAMUEL JOSEPH Feb 9, 1814 New Lebanon, NY - Aug 4, 1886 Yonkers, NY
Governor of New York from 1875-1876. New York City prosecutor, fought Tammany Hall. Democratic candidate for president in 1876, winning the popular vote, losing the election to Rutherford B. Hayes. His gravestones reads, "I still trust the people."

CEMETERY OF THE MAPLES
126 Black Bridge Road
Canaan, NY 12060

GATES COUPLE September 15, 1985 Canaan, NY
Dane Warren Gates, born June 30, 1960, and his wife, **Georgia Groudas Gates**, born May 20, 1961, were killed, with a friend, when their car crashed into several trees on Peaceful Valley Road, and burst into flames, leaving their two-year old son, Jason Warren Gates, an orphan. Fifteen months later, December 13, 1986, their son was shot and killed, with his guardian and uncle, Robert Gates Sr. and his uncle's live-in girlfriend, Cheryl Brahm, and his son, Robert Gates Jr. Honor student, Wyley Gates,

the son of Robert Gates Sr., and his friend, Damian Rossney, were tried separately, acquitted of murder, both convicted of conspiracy to commit murder, and released on parole, 12 months apart, in 2003 and 2004.

GATES, JASON WARREN Mar 6, 1983 - Dec 13, 1986 Canaan, NY
Murder victim. Orphaned at two-years old, shot to death, fifteen months later, with his uncle and guardian, Robert Gates Sr. and his uncle's live-in girlfriend, Cheryl Brahm, and his son, Robert Gates Jr. Honor student, Wyley Gates, his cousin and the son of Robert Gates Sr., and Damian Rossney, were tried separately, acquitted of murder, both convicted of conspiracy to commit murder, and released on parole, 12 months apart, in 2003 and 2004.

CHAPEL HILL CEMETERY
Chapel Hill Road
Parishville, NY 13672

PHILLIPS, GARRETT JOHN Aug 13, 1999 Potsdam, NY - Oct 24, 2011 Potsdam, NY
Murder victim. Found strangled and suffocated in his home, the victim of an unsolved homicide. Oral Nicholas "Nick" Hillary, Clarkson University head soccer coach and member of St. Lawrence University's undefeated 1999 NCAA championship team, and his mother's former live-in boyfriend, was arrested, charged with second-degree murder, and acquitted following his trial, prosecuted by Onondaga County District Attorney, William Fitzpatrick, September 28, 2016.

CHARLOTTE CEMETERY
28 River Street
Rochester, NY 14612

PATCH, SAM 1807 Pawtucket, RI - Nov 13, 1829 Rochester, NY
Stunt diver. First person to leap over Niagara Falls into the Niagara River and survive. Died one month later, diving into the Genesee River from atop the Genesee Falls, his body found frozen in ice four months later, March 1830.

CHATHAM RURAL CEMETERY
Cemetery Road
Chatham, NY 12037

BLUNT, JOHN W. May 18, 1840 Chatham, NY - Jan 21, 1910 Chatham, NY
Civil War Union Army Brevet Major. Awarded the Congressional Medal of Honor for action at Cedar Creek, VA, October 19, 1864.

CHENANGO VALLEY CEMETERY
120 Nowlan Road / Route 80
Binghamton, NY 13901

COLBY, FLICK (Felicity Isabelle) Mar 23, 1946 Hazleton, PA - May 26, 2011 Kirkland, NY
Founding member, dancer and choreographer for the British dance troupe, Pan's People. Appeared on *Top of the Pops* on BBC from 1968-1976. Owned and operated Paddywacks, a gift shop in Clinton. Married first to horror writer, Robert Marasco, died four months after the death of her third husband, George W. Bahlke, Professor of English at Hamilton College.

HULL, GEORGE 1821 - Oct 22, 1902 Binghamton, NY
Cigar manufacturer. Created the Cardiff Giant, a ten-foot tall stone man, made of gypsum, buried it on the Cardiff farm of his cousin, William C. "Stub" Newell, only to have the "petrified man" found a year later, October 16, 1869, creating the greatest hoax in 19th Century America. Sold his interest in the fake giant to David Hannum, who tried to lease it to showman, P.T. Barnum, for $60,000, who turned down his offer and built his own "giant", claiming his was the real giant and the Cardiff Giant a fake. Newspapers reported Barnum's version of his giant, and Hannum was quoted as saying "There's a sucker born every minute" in reference to Barnum's paying customers, the quotation has been misattributed to Barnum over the years. Hannum sued Barnum, a judge ruled that Barnum could not be sued for calling a "fake giant a fake."

ROGERS, JOHN PHELPS Jan 14, 1929 - Nov 19, 2001 Binghamton, NY
With **L. Lorraine Gardner Rogers** (1929 NY - Nov 20, 2011 Endwell, NY), the parents of Robert Rogers, who, with her husband, Barbara West Rogers, sponsored six "Lost Boys of Sudan" in their home on Otisco Lake, including Joseph Lopepe "Lopez" Lomong, member of the 2008 United States Olympic Track and Field team.

SKINNER, CHRISTOPHER GAIL Aug 15, 1971 Binghamton, NY - May 29, 2014 Chenango, NY
New York State trooper. Killed in the line of duty, purposely hit by a vehicle during a traffic stop, Exit 6 on I-81, Broome County. Almond Upton was convicted of first-degree murder, sentenced to life in prison.

CHERRY VALLEY CEMETERY
Alden Street
Cherry Valley, NY 13320

CAMPBELL, WILLIAM W. Jun 10, 1806 Cherry Valley, NY - Sept 7, 1881 Cherry Valley, NY
United States Representative-NY from 1845-1847. Associate Justice of the New York State Supreme Court from 1857-1865.

DARLING, CANDY Nov 24, 1944 Forest Hills (Queens), NY - May 21, 1974 New York, NY
Transgender actor, born James Lawrence Slattery. Closely associated with Andy Warhol, a Warhol
Superstar, appeared in the Warhol films, *Flesh* and *Women in Revolt*. Subject of the Velvet
Underground song, "Candy Says" in 1968 and referenced in the Lou Reed song, "Walk on the Wild
Side" in 1972. Subject of the documentary, *Beautiful Darling*, in 2010.

HAMMOND, JABEZ DELNO Aug 2, 1778 New Bedford, MA - Aug 18, 1855 Cherry Valley, NY
United States Representative-NY from 1815-1817. New York State Senator from 1817-1821.

MORSE, OLIVER ANDREW Mar 26, 1815 Cherry Valley, NY - Apr 20, 1870 New York, NY
United States Representative-NY from 1857-1859.

CHESTER RURAL CEMETERY
Main Street
Chestertown, NY 12817

FOSTER (Oliver)**, JEANNE ROBERT** Mar 10, 1879 Johnsburg, NY - Sept 22, 1970 Chestertown, NY
Poet, journalist and fashion model. Born Julia Elizabeth Oliver, married Matlack Foster, lived in
Rochester for a period of time. Close friend of artist, John Butler Yeats, who she was buried near, and
poets, Ezra Pound and Ford Madox Ford.

FOSTER, MATT (Matlack R.) 1850 Chester, NY - Aug 1933 Schenectady, NY
Husband of Jeanne Robert Foster, poet, journalist and fashion model.

YEATS, JOHN BUTLER Mar 16, 1839 County Down, Ireland - Feb 3, 1922 New York, NY
Artist. Associated with the Ashcan school of painters in New York City. Father of poet, William Butler
Yeats and painter, Jack Butler Yeats.

CHESTNUT HILL CEMETERY
Grove Street
Union Springs, NY 13160

BUSH, TIMOTHY Mar 4, 1795 VT - 1870 Springport, NY
Brother of Obadiah Newcomb Bush, the great-grandfather of Prescott Sheldon Bush, United States
Senator-CT from 1952-1963, the 2nd great-grandfather of President George Herbert Walker Bush,
and the 3rd great-grandfather of President George Walker Bush, John Ellis "Jeb" Bush, Governor of
Florida from 1999-2007, and entertainment reporter, Billy Bush.

CARR, GOTCH (Harlan B.) Apr 30, 1903 Union Springs, NY - Oct 24, 1970 Auburn, NY
Three-letter sports star at Syracuse University from 1925-1928. Assistant football coach for Syracuse University from 1930-1936, under head coach, Vic Hanson. Nephew of Syracuse University Hall of Fame baseball coach, Lew Carr.

DILORENZO, ALBERT M. Sept 23, 1913 Auburn, NY - Apr 30, 1992 Rochester, NY
Owned and operated the Albee Hotel in Auburn from 1950-1965.

CHICHESTER CEMETERY
Old Corner Road
Bedford, NY 10506

SEELEY (Speer), **JANE ETHEL** May 17, 1933 Mount Kisco, NY - Apr 28, 2004 Fayetteville, NC
Aunt of Scott R. Cantrell, part-time groundskeeper for the Rolling Stones' Keith Richards and his common-law wife, Anita Pallenberg, found dead in their bed from a self-inflicted gunshot.

SPEER, JIM (Walter L.) 1904 - 1980 Bedford, NY
With **Phebe Ethel Clark Speer** (Dec 15, 1908 Bedford, NY - 1972 Bedford, NY), the grandparents of Scott R. Cantrell, part-time groundskeeper for the Rolling Stones' Keith Richards and his common-law wife, Anita Pallenberg, found dead in their bed from a self-inflicted gunshot.

CHRIST CHURCH CEMETERY
River Street
Cooperstown, NY 13326

CARY, WILLIAM LUCIUS Nov 27, 1910 Columbus, OH - Feb 7, 1983 New York, NY
Chairman of the United States Security and Exchange Commission from 1961-1964, appointed by President John F. Kennedy. Husband of Katherine Lemoine Fenimore Cooper Cary, the 2nd great-granddaughter of author, James Fenimore Cooper. Father-in-law of author, Ved Mehta.

COOPER, JAMES FENIMORE Sept 15, 1789 Burlington, NJ - Sept 14, 1851 Cooperstown, NY
Author. Wrote the novels, *The Last of the Mohicans*, *The Pathfinder* and *The Deerslayer*. Son of William Cooper, United States Representative-NY from 1795-1797 and 1799-1801.

COOPER, WILLIAM Dec 2, 1754 Philadelphia, PA - Dec 22, 1809 Albany, NY
United States Representative-NY from 1795-1797 and 1799-1801. Settled in Otsego County in 1789, established the town of Cooperstown. First Judge in Otsego County, in 1791. Father of author, James Fenimore Cooper. Died of natural causes, though his family long thought he was killed from a blow to the head, by a political opponent following an argument.

RUSSELL, JOHN Sept 7, 1772 Branford, CT - Aug 2, 1842 Cooperstown, NY
United States Representative-NY from 1805-1809.

CHRIST CHURCH CEMETERY
Route 173
Manlius, NY 13104

EELLS, MOSES Mar 2, 1780 Coventry, CT - Apr 7, 1857 Manlius, NY
With **Anna C. Dimick Eells** (Aug 18, 1787 Tolland, CT - Aug 19, 1846 Manlius, NY), the grandparents of
Francis R. Bellamy, author of *The Pledge of Allegiance*.

FLEMING, JOHN 1752 MA - Oct 14, 1841 Syracuse, NY
Revolutionary War veteran. Settled in Manlius with his family, including slave, Isaac Wales, who
purchased his freedom in 1824, and moved to the hamlet of Syracuse, becoming the area's first black
resident. Father of John Fleming Jr., Onondaga County District Attorney in 1848.

PHILLIPS (Tousley)**, HARRIET** Sept 1808 Manlius, NY - Apr 10, 1827 Manlius, NY
First wife of Onondaga County Sheriff, Elihu Lyman Phillips, who conducted the first execution in the
county's history, November 19, 1840, at the Salina Street jail in Syracuse, hanging Zachariah
Freeman Jr. for the murder of his common-law wife, Sara Boyd. Phillips, born February 16, 1800 in
Manlius, died in 1889, Fond du Lac, WI.

TAYLOR, WILLIAM Oct 12, 1791 Suffield, CT - Sept 16, 1865 Manlius, NY
United States Representative-NY from 1833-1839.

CHRIST CHURCH CEMETERY
17 Church Road
Pawling, NY 12564

PEALE, NORMAN VINCENT May 31, 1898 Bowersville, OH - Dec 24, 1993 Pawling, NY
Clergyman, whose sermons were heard on radio and television. Author of *The Power of Positive
Thinking*. Co-founded *Guideposts Magazine* in 1945. Pastor of the University United Methodist
Church, 1085 East Genesee Street in Syracuse, from 1927-1932. Awarded the Presidential Medal of
Freedom in 1984.

THOMAS, LOWELL Aug 6, 1892 Woodington, OH - Aug 29, 1981 Pawling, NY
Journalist, author and broadcaster. Traveled with cameraman, Harry Chase, to the Western Front in
World War I, meeting British Army Captain, T.E. Lawrence, making Lawrence of Arabia a household
name throughout the world. Anchored radio and television programs for CBS and NBC. Elected to the
National Radio Hall of Fame in 1989.

CHRIST EPISCOPAL CHURCH
132 Duanesburg Churches Road
Duanesburg, NY 12056

DUANE, JAMES Feb 6, 1733 New York, NY - Feb 1, 1797 Schenectady, NY
Mayor of New York City from 1784-1789, the first post-colonial American mayor. Delegate to the Continental Congress in 1774. Associate Justice of the United States District Court for the District of New York, appointed by President George Washington.in 1789. Namesake of the town of Duanesburg.

DUANE (Livingston)**, MARY** Oct 29, 1738 New York, NY - May 6, 1821
Wife of James Duane, Mayor of New York City from 1784-1789. Daughter of Robert Livingston, third Lord of Livingston Manor. Granddaughter of Philip Livingston, second Lord of Livingston Manor. Great-granddaughter of Robert Livingston the Elder, first Lord of Livingston Manor. Niece of Philip Livingston, signer of the *Declaration of Independence*.

CHURCH STREET CEMETERY
Church Street
Little Falls, NY 13365

ALEXANDER, HENRY PORTEOUS Sept 13, 1801 Little Falls, NY - Feb 22, 1867 Little Falls, NY
United States Representative-NY from 1849-1851.

BEARDSLEE, GUY ROOSEVELT Oct 24, 1856 East Creek, NY - Jan 15, 1939 Miami, FL
Completed Beardslee Castle, 123 Old State Road, Little Falls, a project begun in 1790 by his grandparents, John Knickerbocker Beardslee and Lavina Pardee Beardslee.

JOUBEN, GREGORY May 4, 1955 - Oct 18, 1991 Little Falls, NY
Murder victim. Owned Gregg's Coin and Jewelry, shot to death in his store by serial killer, Gary Charles Evans, who jumped to his death from the Troy-Menands Bridge, briefly escaping custody being transported to Rensselaer County Jail from court, August 14, 1998, two days after being charged with his murder.

LOOMIS, ARPHAXED Apr 9, 1798 Litchfield, CT - Sept 15, 1885 Little Falls, NY
United States Representative-NY from 1837-1839.

PETRIE, GEORGE Sept 8, 1793 Little Falls, NY - May 8, 1879 Little Falls, NY
United States Representative-NY from 1847-1849.

SNYDER, HOMER PETER Dec 6, 1863 Amsterdam, NY - Dec 30, 1937 Little Falls, NY
United States Representative-NY from 1915-1925.

CICERO CEMETERY
Route 11
Cicero, NY 13039

CUSHING, SAMUEL 1772 VT - Mar 10, 1856 Cicero, NY
3rd great-grandson of Daniel Cushing, the brother of Colonel John Cushing, the great-grandfather of William Cushing, Associate Justice of the United States Supreme Court from 1789-1810, last remaining member of the original six justices appointed by President George Washington.

EASTWOOD, ASA Feb 20, 1781 Allentown, NJ - Feb 25, 1870 Cicero, NY
Early settler of Onondaga County. Democratic member of the New York State Assembly in the Tammany Hall Society in Manhattan. With **Mary Doxsey Eastwood** (Jun 30, 1782 Queens, NY - Apr 16, 1862 Cicero, NY), the 3rd great-grandparents of Academy Award-winning actor and director, Clint Eastwood.

EASTWOOD, NELSON PERRY Feb 4, 1822 - Jun 29, 1895 Cicero, NY
Brother of Lewis Washington Eastwood, the 2nd great-grandfather of Academy Award-winning actor and director, Clint Eastwood.

JOSLYN, HEZEKIAH 1797 MA - Oct 30, 1865 Fayetteville, NY
With **Helen Leslie Joslyn** (Oct 29, 1792 Aberdeenshire, Scotland - Nov 23, 1863 Cicero, NY), the parents of social reformer, Matilda Electa Joslyn Gage. Grandparents of Maud Gage Baum, the wife of L. Frank Baum, author of *The Wonderful Wizard of Oz* series of children's books.

PAGE, EPHRAIM JAMES May 22, 1867 Cicero, NY - Mar 1, 1950 Syracuse, NY
Onondaga County attorney for 60 years. Admitted to appear before the United States Supreme Court in 1908. Purchased Applecrest, a Baldwinsville mansion built by Ward Wellington Ward for Chicago businessman, George Day McBirney, in 1927.

PAGE, RUTH ABIGAIL Jul 22, 1899 Syracuse, NY - Dec 18, 1982 Auburn, NY
Award-winning potter, studied pottery under Adelaide Robineau at Syracuse University. Designed several chandeliers and lighting fixtures for Riverside Church in New York City. Daughter of attorney, Ephraim J. Page.

CICERO CENTER / STONE ARABIA CEMETERY
Route 31
Cicero, NY 13039

LUCE, ROSELL E. Dec 18, 1843 Cicero, NY - Oct 15, 1936 Syracuse, NY
Second-to-last surviving Civil War veteran from the town of Clay, fourteenth overall in Onondaga

County. Fought in the Battle of Gettysburg, wounded at Cold Harbor. Following his discharge, he was a guest at the home of Secretary of War, Edwin M. Stanton, and held personal conversations with President Abraham Lincoln.

CINCINNATUS CEMETERY
Cincinnatus Road
Cincinnatus, NY 13040

BABCOCK, JONATHAN 1764 Stonington, CT - Feb 10, 1849 Pitcher, NY
Great-grandfather of Grace M. Brown, murdered by her boyfriend, Chester E. Gillette, in 1906, events that inspired the Theodore Dreiser novel, *An American Tragedy,* and the film, *A Place in the Sun*, in 1951.

CLARENCE CENTRE CEMETERY
Goodrich Road
Clarence Center, NY 14032

DIVER (Barney), **JOAN LEE** Jun 29, 1961 Salt Lake City, UT - Sept 29, 2006 Newstead, NY
Murder victim. Mother of four, wife of a professor, raped and strangled on a bike path by Altemio Sanchez, known as the "Bike Path Killer" who committed rapes and murders over a 25-year period, including Linda Susan Yalem, killed September 29, 1990, buried in Mount Olive Memorial Park, Los Angeles and Majane Elizabeth McCauley Mazur, killed November 22, 1992, buried in Woodlawn Memorial Park, Greenville, SC. Anthony Capozzi served 22 years in prison for rapes committed by Sanchez before exonerated in through DNA evidence in 2007.

CLARENCE FILLMORE CEMETERY
Ransom Road
Clarence, NY 14031

DAWYDKO, PETER RONALD Jul 9, 1941 Buffalo, NY - Aug 25, 2007 Akron, NY
Owned and operated Anchor Farms in Akron. Tombstone is a replica of a lighthouse.

FICHTNER (Steitz), **PATRICIA A.** Nov 16, 1936 - Dec 24, 2009 Williamsville, NY
Mother of film and television actor, William Fichtner.

WIELINSKI, DOUGLAS C. Jul 13, 1947 Buffalo, NY - Feb 12, 2009 Clarence Center, NY
Died in the crash of Colgan Air, Continental Connection, Flight 3407, when the airplane, minutes from landing, plummeted into his home, 6038 Long Street, killing him as he sat in his dining room, and the

49 passengers on the plane. His wife, Karen Wielinski and daughter, Jill Wielinski, escaped the home and survived. The house is now the site of the Flight 3407 Memorial.

CLARYVILLE REFORMED CHURCH CEMETERY
946 Claryville Road
Claryville, NY 12725

CYPERT, PAUL ANTHONY Sept 20, 1919 Fallsburg, NY - May 3, 1991 Oliverea, NY
Carpenter. Employed by music manager, Albert Grossman, to do much of the woodwork for the Bearsville Theater and Studio, outside of Woodstock. Personally dug the grave for Grossman, following his death on the Concorde, January 25, 1986, behind the theater, within a circle of ivy, against the wishes of the town.

CLAUSLAND CEMETERY
South Greenbush Road
Orangeburg, NY 10962

SMITH, PETRUS (Peter) Nov 20, 1716 NY - Jan 24, 1797 Orangeburg, NY
Tappan farm owner, the site of the hanging of Major John André, executed as a spy during the Revolutionary War, marked by the Major John André Monument. Grandfather of Peter Smith, namesake of Peterboro. Great-grandfather of Gerrit Smith, United States Representative-NY from 1853-1854.

CLAVERACK REFORMED DUTCH CHURCHYARD
88 Route 9H
Claverack, NY 12513

DALE (Livingston)**, HARRIET** Dec 12, 1783 Clermont, NY - Mar 24, 1826 New York, NY
Widow of inventor, Robert Fulton, developer of *Clermont*, the first commercially successful steamboat, died February 24, 1815, age 49, buried in the Livingston family vault, Trinity Churchyard, New York City. Remarried to Charles Augustus Dale. Daughter of Walter Livingston, delegate to the Continental Congress in 1784. 2nd great-granddaughter of Robert Livingston the Elder, first Lord of Livingston Manor. Grandniece of Philip Livingston, signor of the *Declaration of Independence*.

LUDLOW (Fulton)**, MARY LIVINGSTON** Jul 19, 1813 New York, NY - Jun 3, 1861 Claverack, NY
Daughter of inventor, Robert Fulton, developer of *Clermont*, the first commercially successful steamboat. Mother of artist, Robert Fulton Ludlow. Granddaughter of Walter Livingston, delegate to the Continental Congress in 1784. 3rd great-granddaughter of Robert Livingston the Elder, first Lord of Livingston Manor.

LUDLOW, ROBERT FULTON Jun 25, 1846 New York, NY - May 20, 1930 Claverack, NY
Portrait and landscape artist. Grandson of inventor, Robert Fulton, developer of *Clermont*, the first commercially successful steamboat. Great-grandson of Walter Livingston, delegate to the Continental Congress in 1784. 4th great-grandson of Robert Livingston the Elder, first Lord of Livingston Manor.

WEBB, JAMES WATSON Feb 8, 1802 Claverack, NY - Jun 7, 1884 New York, NY
Newspaper publisher. Published the *New York Courier and Enquirer* from 1829-1859. Coined the name, Whig, for a new political party in 1834. Father of Civil War Union Army Major General, Alexander Stewart Webb, and railroad executives, H. Walter Webb and William Seward Webb. Son of Revolutionary War Continental Army General, Samuel Blatchley Webb.

WEBB, SAMUEL BLATCHLEY Dec 15, 1753 Wethersfield, CT - Dec 3, 1807 Claverack, NY
Revolutionary War Continental Army General. Secretary and aide-de-camp to General George Washington. Father of newspaper publisher, James Watson Webb.

CLAYTON VILLAGE CEMETERY
James Street / Route 12
Clayton, NY 13624

DAUGHEN (Robbins)**, PHOEBE J.** Feb 18, 1911 Clayton, NY - Jun 13, 2006 Alexandria Bay, NY
Wife of Ford E. Dodge, chauffeur for millionaire Syracuse industrialist, Willard Charles Lipe, and pilot of his speedboat, *The Giggle*, who was killed carrying Lipe, and his wife, Eloise Estelle Hoyt Lipe, when their boat collided with a passenger boat, *The Thousand Islander*, in the St. Lawrence River, between Wellesley and Cherry Islands, drowning all three on the boat. His body, thought to be trapped within the boat, was not recovered. They were married three weeks prior to the accident. She remarried twice, to Ross S. Wells and William J. Daughen.

CLEVELAND VILLAGE CEMETERY
North Street
Cleveland, NY 13042

LANDGRAFF, ANTHONY 1774 - Mar 25, 1867 Cleveland, NY
Owned and operated the first glass works company in Onondaga County. Founded Cleveland Glass Works in Cleveland, Oneida County, in 1840.

CLIFTON PARK BAPTIST CEMETERY
Clifton Park Center Road
Clifton Park, NY 12065

GROOM, JAMES 1790 NY - 1877 Clifton Park, NY
Early settler. Operated Grooms Tavern, Grooms Corners, in the town of Clifton Park, placed on the National Register of Historic Places in 2000. Clifton Park Town Clerk from 1832-1835. Clifton Park Town Supervisor from 1836-1837.

PECK, ABIJAH Apr 1758 Greenwich, CT - Nov 12, 1848 Clifton Park, NY
Revolutionary War veteran. Founder and pastor of the Clifton Park Baptist Church, in 1830. 3rd great-grandson of William Peck, founding father of New Haven, CT.

CLIFTON PARK VILLAGE CEMETERY
Cemetery Road
Clifton Park, NY 12065

CLUTE, JOHN H. - Jan 8, 1885 Clifton Park, NY
Early settler of the town of Clifton Park. Operated a dry dock. First Clifton Park Justice of the Peace, in 1830. Served in the New York Calvary.

CLIFTON SPRINGS CEMETERY
Pearl Street
Clifton Springs, NY 14432

MAXWELL, JOSEPH Mar 1833 Ireland - 1911 Clifton Springs, NY
Central New York clergyman. With **Elizabeth A. Holmes Maxwell** (Apr 1839 NY - 1922 Clifton Springs, NY), the parents of George Holmes Maxwell, prominent attorney, manufacturer, inventor and philanthropist and leading benefactor and founder of the Maxwell School of Citizenship and Public Affairs at Syracuse University, his alma mater.

STILES, ARTHUR Jul 25, 1835 Watkins Glen, NY - Nov 5, 1896 Clifton Springs, NY
Granduncle of Academy Award-winning actor, Humphrey Bogart.

CLOCKVILLE CEMETERY
Seeber Road
Clockville, NY 13043

CLOCK (Klock), **CONRAD** 1722 Palatine, NY - 1816 Clockville, NY
Founder and namesake of the town of Clockville.

WILCOX, ALANSON Sept 10, 1787 Simsbury, CT - Jun 30, 1849 Lenox, NY
Great-granduncle of Grafton Stiles Wilcox, managing editor of *The New York Herald-Tribune* from
1931-1941 and Frank Wilcox, stage actor and producer who appeared regularly in Syracuse.

CLOVESVILLE CEMETERY
Grocholl Road
Fleischmanns, NY 12430

TODD, SAMUEL H. Nov 19, 1752 Plymouth, CT - Mar 18, 1852 Clovesville, NY
Revolutionary War veteran. Great-grandson of Samuel Todd I, the brother of John "the Fox" Todd, the
3rd great-grandfather of First Lady Mary Todd Lincoln, the wife of President Abraham Lincoln. Their
common ancestor, Christopher William Todd, born January 11, 1617 in Pontefract, West Yorkshire,
England, died April 23, 1686 in New Haven, CT, buried there, Center Church on the Green
Churchyard.

COLD SPRING CEMETERY
33 Peekskill Road
Cold Spring, NY 10516

KEMBLE, GOUVERNEUR Jan 25, 1786 New York, NY - Sept 16, 1875 Cold Spring, NY
United States Representative-NY from 1837-1841. Founded the West Point Iron and Cannon Foundry
in Cold Spring, in 1817.

PARROTT, ROBERT PARKER Oct 5, 1804 Lee, NH - Dec 24, 1877 Cold Spring, NY
Superintendent of the West Point Iron and Cannon Foundry from 1836-1867, founded by his wife's
uncle, Gouverneur Kemble. Invented the Parrott rifle, an artillery weapon used in the Civil War, in
1860. Son of John Fabyan Parrott, United States Senator-NY from 1819-1825.

ROEBLING (Warren), **EMILY** Sept 23, 1843 Cold Spring, NY - Feb 28, 1903
Attended the coronation of Tsar Nicholas II of Russia. Presented to Queen Victoria in London in 1896.
Wife of Washington A. Roebling, Chief Engineer during the construction of the Brooklyn Bridge, and
son of John A. Roebling, designer of the Brooklyn Bridge. Sister of Civil War Union Army Major

General, Gouverneur Kemble Warren.

ROEBLING, WASHINGTON AUGUSTUS May 26, 1837 Saxonburg, PA - Jul 21, 1926 Trenton, NJ
Civil War Union Army Colonel. Chief Engineer during the construction of the Brooklyn Bridge. Son of
John A. Roebling, designer of the Brooklyn Bridge.

COLD SPRINGS CEMETERY
4849 Cold Springs Road
Lockport, NY 14094

BRANDT, ALLIE (Albert) Dec 14, 1902 Lockport, NY - Apr 17, 1982
Professional bowler. Bowled three successive games of 297, 289 and a perfect, 300, totaling 886 pins,
in 1939, a record for a three-game series that stood for 50 years. Elected to the American Bowling
Congress Hall of Fame in 1960.

HAWLEY, JESSE May 11, 1773 Bridgeport, CT - Jan 10, 1842 Cambria, NY
Flour merchant. Member of the New York State Assembly. Spent twenty months in debtors' prison,
publishing essays in the *Genesee Messenger* proposing the development of the Erie Canal.

MCVEIGH, EDWARD W. Dec 31, 1912 NY - Oct 16, 1994 Lockport, NY
With **Angela C. Litz McVeigh** (1915 NY - 1972 Lockport, NY), the grandparents of Timothy James
McVeigh, domestic terrorist, convicted of detonating a truck filled with explosives in front of the Alfred
P. Murrah Federal Building in Oklahoma City, April 19, 1995, killing 168 people, the largest act of
domestic terrorism in United States history, executed by lethal injection, June 11, 2001 in Terre Haute,
and cremated.

COLGATE UNIVERSITY CEMETERY
Chapel House Road
Hamilton, NY 13346

BRUEN, JACK (John F.) Mar 25, 1949 New York, NY - Dec 19, 1997 Hamilton, NY
Colgate University men's basketball coach from 1989-1997 and Catholic University from
1982-1989. Point guard and teammate of Lew Alcindor at Power Memorial High School in New York
City.

DES PRES, TERRANCE Dec 26, 1939 Effingham, IL - Nov 15, 1987 Hamilton, NY
Colgate University English professor. Author and authority on the Holocaust. Wrote *The Survivor: An
Anatomy of Life in the Death Camps"* in 1976. Appointed by President Jimmy Carter to the United
States Holocaust Memorial Council in 1980. Found dead in his campus apartment from accidental
asphyxiation.

COLLAMER CEMETERY
Fly Road
East Syracuse, NY 13057

BALDWIN, SPUD (Harold F.) 1920 Brookfield, NY - Jun 30, 1977 Syracuse, NY
With **Betty M. Spier Baldwin Graboske**, the great-grandparents of professional women's basketball player, Breanna Stewart, four-time NCAA champion and tournament MVP at the University of Connecticut from 2013-2016, three-time Naismith College Player of the Year and first overall pick of the WNBA's Seattle Storm in 2016.

FERREN, FRANCIS Sept 9, 1893 Batavia, NY - Jan 17, 1981 Auburn, NY
Chief of the Syracuse Fire Department from 1954-1957.

MILBACK, MARTHA LOUISE Jun 21, 1946 Syracuse, NY - Oct 5, 1949 Baltimore, MD
Born a "blue baby", a rare congenital heart defect that causes a bluish colorization of the skin. Operated on by Dr. Alfred Blalock, pioneer of "blue baby" surgery at Johns Hopkins Hospital in Baltimore, but did not survive. Daughter of Floyd L. and Katherine H. Milback.

SIMON, JOHN 1831 Germany - Feb 5, 1915 Dewitt, NY
With **Caroline C. Backer Simon** (1875 - Jul 29, 1909 Dewitt, NY), the 2nd great-grandparents of Alan Gratzer, drummer and founding member of the rock band, R.E.O. Speedwagon.

THOMAS, FRANCIS M. Feb 1934 Syracuse, NY - Sept 9, 1938 Syracuse, NY
Killed playing a game of hide-and-seek in First Ward Cemetery, when a 400-pound tombstone fell on top of him, crushing him to death. The abandoned cemetery, closed by the city in 1912, became a park and playground following his death.

CONSTANTIA RURAL CEMETERY / INGERSOLL CEMETERY
Cemetery Road
Constantia, NY 13044

WILLIS, ROBERT R. 1911 Constantia, NY - Jun 30, 1997 Utica, NY
Grandfather of convicted serial killer, Herbert James Coddington, a 1976 graduate of Paull V. Moore High School in Central Square, sentenced to death, January 20, 1989, for the kidnapping, rape and strangulation deaths of two elderly women and a 12-year old girl between 1981 and 1987. He is serving his time in San Quentin State Prison in California.

COOPERS PLAINS CEMETERY
Route 26 / Meads Creek Road
Painted Post, NY 14870

TAFT SISTERS May 22, 1957 Campbell, NY
Two sisters, **Kathleen Ina Taft**, born March 23, 1951, and **Marjorie Elaine Taft**, born March 10, 1953, were found dead in a refrigerator on the patio of their parents farm, suffocated when the refrigerator door swung shut while they were playing inside. The inside of the door showed signs of a struggle. Their parents, Norman J. Taft and Iris M. DeMonstoy Taft, died two months apart in the summer of 2005, Savona, Steuben County, survived by five children.

CORNWALL-TILDEN CEMETERY
Canaan Road
New Lebanon, NY 12125

TILDEN, ELAM Dec 31, 1781 Lebanon, CT - Apr 10, 1842 New Lebanon, NY
With **Polly Younglove Jones Tilden** (Mar 20, 1782 Cornwall, CT - Dec 11, 1860 New Lebanon, NY), the parents of Samuel J. Tilden, Governor of New York from 1875-1876 and Democratic candidate for president in 1876, winning the popular vote, losing the election to Rutherford B. Hayes.

CORTLAND RURAL CEMETERY
110 Tompkins Street
Cortland, NY 13045

CARR, DELMAR WILLIAM Nov 13, 1844 Cortlandville, NY - Dec 26, 1913 East Orange, NY
With **Anna Carson Carr** (1845 Armagh, County Armagh, Ireland - Nov 16, 1925 Cortland, NY), the grandparents of convicted murderer, Henry Judd Gray, involved in an affair with Ruth Brown Snyder, conspired to kill her husband, Albert Snyder, both convicted following a highly-publicized trial, executed minutes apart in the electric chair at Sing Sing Prison. Ruth Brown Snyder was photographed in the electric chair, minutes before death, and shown on the front page of the *New York Daily News*.

CHASE (Benedict)**, HARRIET PRICILLA** 1888 - 1944 Cortland, NY
Rumored to be the "other woman" in the sensational murder trial of Chester Gillette, who was executed for murdering his pregnant girlfriend, Grace M. Brown, she issued a press release denying the affair. Wife of Cortland attorney, Levi R. Chase Sr. Mother of United States Air Force Major General Levi R. Chase Jr.

CHASE, LEVI RICHARD Aug 15, 1876 Cortland, NY - Apr 3, 1948 Cortland, NY
Cortland attorney. Visited Chester Gillette in his jail cell to advise, following Gillette's arrest in the

murder of Grace M. Brown, prior to the sensational trial later that year. Married Harriet Benedict Chase, long rumored to be the "other woman" in the Gillette case. Father of United States Air Force Major General, Levi R. Chase Jr.

CHASE, LEVI RICHARD Dec 23, 1917 Cortland, NY - Sept 4, 1994 Cortland, NY
United States Air Force Major General. Flew missions in four combat tours, spanning World War II, the Korean War and the Vietnam War. Scored 12 air combat victories in World War II, one of three combat aces to have scored victories against all three Axis nations. Awarded three Silver Stars, the Distinguished Flying Cross six times, the Purple Heart, the Croix de Guerre and the British Distinguished Flying Cross. Cortland County Airport was renamed Chase Field in his honor, in 1972. Son of Cortland attorney, Levi R. Chase Sr.

CLARK, EDWARD H. Oct 8, 1885 Cortland, NY - Aug 28, 1973 Syracuse, NY
Publisher and President of the *Cortland Standard* from 1928-1973.

DUELL, RODOLPHUS HOLLAND Dec 20, 1824 Warren, NY - Feb 11, 1891 Cortland, NY
United States Representative-NY from 1859-1863 and 1871-1875. United States Commissioner of Patents from 1875-1877, appointed by President Ulysses S. Grant.

GOODWIN, ART May 1, 1926 Cortland, NY - Mar 8, 1983 Syracuse, NY
Newsman at WTVH-TV in Syracuse from 1951-1983. News Director for WTVH-TV, instituted the first noon newscast in Central New York, in 1971.

GROVER, ANDREW JACKSON Dec 22, 1830 Dryden, NY - Jul 1, 1863 Gettysburg, PA
Civil War Union Army Major. First Union regimental commander killed at the Battle of Gettysburg.

HULLAR, JACOB CASPER Jan 18, 1896 Cazenovia, NY - Apr 16, 1975 Syracuse, NY
Owned and operated Hullar's Restaurant in Fayetteville, from 1938-1955, founded by his father, Jacob C. Hullar, in 1908.

MILLER, NATHAN LEWIS Oct 10, 1868 Solon, NY - Jun 26, 1953 Cortland, NY
Governor of New York from 1921-1922, preceded and succeeded by Alfred E. Smith. Associate Justice of the New York State Supreme Court from 1903-1913. Associate Justice of the New York Court of Appeals from 1913-1915. New York State Comptroller from 1901-1903.

PANTAS, NICHOLAS Z. 1942 Cortland, NY - Feb 12, 1968 Winchester, CT
Guitarist for heavy metal singer, Ronnie James Dio, in various bands, beginning at Cortland High School in 1957. Killed in an automobile accident during a snowstorm, on tour with their latest band, the Electric Elves. Dio, who received 150 stitches to the head in the crash, went on to front Ritchie Blackmore's Rainbow, Black Sabbath, following the departure of Ozzy Osbourne, and his own band, Dio.

REYNOLDS, JOSEPH Sept 14, 1785 Easton, NY - Sept 24, 1864 Cortland, NY
United States Representative-NY from 1835-1837. First President of the village of Cortland, in 1864.
War of 1812 United States Army Brigadier General.

SKINNER, WESLEY R. Jul 10, 1917 Camden, NY - Jan 3, 2003 Lakeland, FL
Owned and operated Manth-Brownell, Inc. in Kirkville, from 1962-1990. Founded the Christian radio
station WMHR-FM. Founded the Sacred Melody Shop and Bookstore in Syracuse, with his wife,
Charlotte A. Smith Skinner (Oct 4, 1916 Cortland, NY - Mar 16, 2008 Jamesville, NY), in 1957.

SPERRY, STEPHEN DECATUR Mar 4, 1825 Cortland, NY - Feb 14, 1889 Cortland, NY
Father of Elmer Ambrose Sperry, inventor of the gyroscope.

WICKWIRE, THEODORE HARRY Mar 29, 1851 McGraw, NY - Aug 29, 1926 Buffalo, NY
Co-founded Wickwire Brothers, a wire cloth mill in Cortland, with his brother, Chester F. Wickwire.

WICKWIRE, CHESTER FRANKLIN May 31, 1843 McGraw, NY - Sept 14, 1910 Cortland, NY
Co-founded Wickwire Brothers, a wire cloth mill in Cortland, with his brother, Theodore H. Wickwire.

WILLCOX, SPIEGLE (Newell) May 2, 1903 Sherburne, NY - Aug 26, 1999 Cincinnatus, NY
Jazz trombonist. Performed with Tommy and Jimmy Dorsey, Bix Beiderbecke, Eddie Lang and with
Paul Whiteman's Collegians. Last surviving member of the Jean Goldkette Orchestra.

COWLESVILLE CEMETERY
Lapp Road
Alden, NY 14004

FOLSOM, JOHN BENNETT Jan 28, 1811 Warsaw, NY - May 19, 1886 Folsomdale, NY
With **Clarinda C. Harnden Folsom** (Jun 3, 1809 - Jan 19, 1873 Folsomdale, NY), the grandparents of
First Lady Frances Folsom Cleveland Preston, the wife of President Grover Cleveland, at age 21, the
youngest First Lady in United States history, remarried following Cleveland's death to Thomas Jex
Preston Jr., the first presidential widow to remarry. Great-grandparents of Ruth Cleveland, allegedly
the namesake of the Baby Ruth candy bar. Parents of Colonel Oscar Folsom, died July 23, 1875, age
37, thrown from a buggy in Buffalo, buried in Princeton Cemetery, Princeton, NJ.

MARTIN (Folsom)**, MARY AUGUSTA** Feb 20, 1849 Folsomdale, NY - Feb 3, 1873 Folsomdale, NY
Aunt of First Lady Frances Folsom Cleveland, the wife of President Grover Cleveland.

COYE CEMETERY
Route 21S
Naples, NY 14512

MORGAN (Canfield)**, CONSTANCE** 1922 Rochester, NY - 1964 NY
Wife of poet and publisher, George Frederick Morgan, founder and editor of the *Hudson Review* literary magazine. Mother of author, Seth David Morgan, who wrote the novel, *Homeboy*, following a prison sentence for robbery, while pinning a man's hand to the floor with a knife, and was the fiancé of singer, Janis Joplin, at the time of her death. He died in a motorcycle accident in New Orleans, October 17, 1990, age 41, and is buried in Seaside Cemetery, Blue Hill, ME, next to his brother, John Canfield Morgan, who committed suicide jumping off the Bay Bridge in Oakland, February 11, 1968, age 21. Sister of actress, Mary Grace Canfield.

CROWN HILL MEMORIAL PARK
3620 Route 12
Clinton, NY 13323

GREEN, LEICESTER G. Mar 1896 Sauquoit, NY - Feb 22, 1961 Tully, NY
Central New York educator. With **Hazel A. Evans Green** (1899 NY - Jun 9, 1967 Syracuse, NY), the grandparents of Tim Green, novelist, broadcaster, Syracuse University All-American lineman from 1982-1985 and the Atlanta Falcons, from 1986-1993.

HEMSTROUGHT, HARRY B. Jun 29, 1891 Franklin Forks, PA - Oct 1970 Utica, NY
Founded and owned Hemstrought Bakeries in Utica and Oneida County. Created the popular black and white cookie, better known as the "Half-Moon cookie", consisting of one half dark chocolate fondant and the other half vanilla fondant on a sponge-like cookie.

WALTER, GEORGE Jan 12, 1909 Little Falls, NY - Dec 26, 1972 Syracuse, NY
Local history author. City editor for the *Oneida Daily Dispatch*. Wrote *The Loomis Gang* and *Saints and Sinners*.

CRUM ELBOW RURAL CEMETERY
North Quaker Lane / Route 16
Hyde Park, NY 12538

SMITH, W. EUGENE (William) Dec 30, 1918 Wichita, KS - Oct 15, 1978 Tucson, AZ
Photojournalist. World War II correspondent, covering Iwo Jima. Photographed Dr. Albert Schweitzer in Africa, the city of Pittsburgh from 1955-1958 and New York City jazz musicians in   the 1950s.

CURRIERS RURAL CEMETERY
Route 22
Willsboro, NY 12996

THARNISH, MARTIN Nov 3, 1857 Bennington, NY – May 31, 1914 Sardinia, NY
Uncle of Al Tharnish, first person called "the World's Fastest Man", ran for Barnum & Bailey's Greatest
Show on Earth, never losing a race from 1884-1891.

DALE CEMETERY
104 Havell Street
Ossining, NY 10562

BOAS, FRANZ Jul 9, 1858 Minden, Germany - Dec 21, 1942 New York, NY
Anthropologist. Called "the Father of American Anthropology."

BRANDRETH (Holmes)**, BENJAMIN** Jun 23, 1809 Newtown, England - Feb 18, 1880 Ossining, NY
New York State Senator. Manufactured Brandreth Pills, laxative pills invented by his grandfather,
William Brandreth, mass-marketing the product throughout the county. 2nd great-grandfather of Gyles
Brandreth, English broadcaster and former Conservative member of Parliament.

HOFF, RED (Chester Cornelius) May 8, 1891 Ossining, NY - Sept 17, 1998 Daytona Beach, FL
Pitcher for the New York Highlanders and New York Yankees from 1911-1913 and the St. Louis
Browns in 1915. Struck out the first major league batter he faced, Hall of Famer, Ty Cobb. Longest-
lived major league player, longest-lived professional athlete. Last surviving player from baseball's
"dead-ball era." Died from an accidental fall.

HOFFMAN, JOHN THOMPSON Jan 10, 1828 Ossining, NY - Mar 24, 1888 Wiesbaden, Germany
Governor of New York from 1869-1872. Mayor of New York City from 1866-1868. The last New York
City mayor, to date, to be elected governor.

LOCKWOOD, MUNSON INGERSOLL Feb 13, 1806 Norwalk, CT - Feb 28, 1873 Ossining, NY
New York State Militia General. Warden of Sing Sing Prison from 1850-1855. Husband of Amelia Jane
Havell, the daughter of Robert Havell Jr., engraver for John James Audubon's, *The Birds of America*.

MOORE, BENJAMIN Aug 24, 1818 New York, NY - Sept 6, 1886 Boston, MA
Son of poet, Clement Clarke Moore, widely-accredited author of the Christmas poem, *A Visit from St.
Nicholas*.

SHARROCK, SONNY (Warren) Aug 27, 1940 Ossining, NY - May 26, 1994 Ossining, NY
Jazz guitarist. Appeared on the Miles Davis album, *A Tribute to Jack Johnson*. Husband of singer,
Lynda Sharrock.

WARD, AARON Jul 5, 1790 Sing Sing, NY - Mar 2, 1867 Washington D.C.
United States Representative-NY from 1825-1829, 1831-1837 and 1841-1843.

YOUNGS, SAMUEL Dec 4, 1760 Eastview, NY - Sept 12, 1839 NY
Revolutionary War Continental Army Lieutenant. Friend of author, Washington Irving, inspired Irving's "Ichabod Crane" character in *The Legend of Sleepy Hollow*. Originally buried in the Old Dutch Churchyard of Sleepy Hollow, reinterred in 1851, the first burial in Dale Cemetery.

DANSVILLE CEMETERY
Jefferson Street / Route 11
Pulaski, NY 13142

MOWRY, OLIVER BURRILL Nov 8, 1847 Oswego, NY - Oct 1940 Pulaski, NY
Last surviving Oswego County Civil War veteran. Father of Earle A. Mowry, Mayor of the village of Mexico for thirteen years.

DAW'S CORNERS CEMETERY
Route 98
Elba, NY 14058

SMILEY, FRANCIS Feb 21, 1759 Jaffrey, NH - Mar 23, 1844 Elba, NY
With **Eunice Mattison Smiley** (1777 NY - Jun 15, 1851 Elba, NY), the grandparents of Grace Greenwood Bedell, an 11-year old living in Westfield, who inspired Abraham Lincoln to grow his famous beard, sending Lincoln a letter weeks prior to his election as president, October 1860, encouraging him to improve his appearance. Lincoln responded and, making no promises, grew his beard within a month. Grace married George Newton Billings, and died November 2, 1936 in Delphos, KS, two days prior to her 88th birthday, buried in Delphos Cemetery.

DAYSVILLE CEMETERY
Route 3
Richland, NY 13144

BROWN, FLORANCE L. 1849 Richland, NY - 1914 Richland, NY
With **Emma Jane Loomis Brown** (Jan 22, 1853 Richland, NY - 1939 Richland, NY), the parents of Earl L. Brown, founder of Grandma Brown's Baked Beans with his wife, Lulu Manwaring "Grandma" Brown, in 1937.

COLE, LUCIUS B. Feb 11, 1808 VT - Dec 9, 1890 Richland, NY
Head keeper of the Selkirk Lighthouse, located at the mouth of the Salmon River, Lake Ontario, from 1849-1854. Lived at the lighthouse following its deactivation until his death.

DELEVAN CEMETERY
11077 Delevan-Elton Road
Delevan, NY 14042

KRIST, HOWIE (Howard) Feb 28, 1916 West Henrietta, NY - Apr 23, 1989 Buffalo, NY
Pitcher for the St. Louis Cardinals from 1937-1938, 1941-1943 and 1946. Member of the Cardinals' 1942 and 1946 World Series championship teams. Retired with a 37-11 lifetime record, including an undefeated, 10-0, season in 1941, his first full season.

DELPHI FALLS CEMETERY
Oran-Delphi Road
Delphi Falls, NY 13051

LITCHFIELD, ELISA Jul 12, 1785 Canterbury, CT - Aug 4, 1859 Cazenovia, NY
United States Representative-NY from 1821-1825. New York State Assemblyman from 1819, 1831-1833 and 1844. Speaker of the New York State Assembly in 1844.

SHANKLAND, WILLIAM Aug 15, 1762 Cherry Valley, NY - Apr 17, 1850 Cazenovia, NY
Revolutionary War veteran. Father of William H. Shankland, Associate Justice of the New York State Court of Appeals. Great-grandfather of William Shankland Andrews, Associate Justice of the New York Court of Appeals. 2nd great-grandfather of Ann Hyde Allen, the wife of author, Hervey Allen.

DEWITT COMMUNITY CEMETERY
3600 Erie Boulevard East
Syracuse, NY 13214

BOGARDUS, HENRY (Hendrick) Dec 11, 1763 - Jun 21, 1841 Syracuse, NY
Revolutionary War veteran. Purchased the first building lot in Syracuse, for $300 in 1805, operating the city's first inn and tavern, the Mansion House, at the location.

GIFFORD, ROSAMOND Sept 1873 - Apr 16, 1953 Jewell, NY
Philanthropist. Inherited her father's $1 million estate in 1917, invested wisely, leaving an estate of $5 million at the time of her death. In accordance with her will, a charitable foundation was established in her name with more than $30 million in grants given to various organizations and agencies in Central

New York. Namesake of the Rosamond Gifford Zoo at Burnet Park and the Rosamond Gifford Lecture Series.

GIFFORD, WILLIAM H. Oct 16, 1839 - May 2, 1917 Syracuse, NY
Syracuse District Attorney and wealthy stockholder. Left the majority of his $1 million estate to his only child, Rosamond Gifford.

KINNE, CYRUS Aug 11, 1746 New London, CT - Aug 8, 1808 Fayetteville, NY
Early settler and founder of Fayetteville and Manlius. Great-grandfather of Oscar F. Soule, co-founder of the Merrell-Soule Company, makers of "None Such" brand mincemeat and powdered milk, with G.L. Merrell, in 1869.

DEWITT FAMILY CEMETERY
Jamesville-Apulia Road
Lafayette, NY 13084

DEWITT, MOSES Oct 15, 1766 Machackemeck, NY - Aug 15, 1794 Onondaga County, NY
Revolutionary War Continental Army Major. Surveyed the Military Tract after the Revolutionary War. County Judge and Surrogate of Onondaga and Herkimer Counties, from 1791-1794. Namesake of the town of DeWitt. Nephew of George Clinton, first Governor of New York. Cousin of New York Governor, DeWitt Clinton. Uncle of early Syracuse landowner, Moses D. Burnet.

DEXTER CEMETERY
Cemetery Road
Dexter, NY 13634

HUBBARD, AMOS C. Mar 11, 1907 Fine, NY - May 28, 1989 Dexter, NY
Father of Marilyn Jean Hubbard-Herr, who played "Merrily" on the children's television program *The Magic Toyshop,* on WHEN-TV, later WTVH-TV in Syracuse, from 1955-1982.

VAADI (Fisher)**, CHRISTINE M.** Aug 11, 1957 Watertown, NY - Apr 2, 1994 Hounsfield, NY
Murder victim. Stabbed in the stomach and forehead by a customer, Daniel L. Dumas, cleaning up after hours at Tanner's Fireside Tavern, the bar then set on fire with her inside, dying 12 hours later from her injuries. He pled guilty to second-degree murder and first-degree arson, sentenced to 20-years-to-life in prison.

DISBROW GROUND
Church Hill Road
Carmel, NY 10512

FIXX, CALVIN HENRY Aug 1, 1906 Lyman, ID - Mar 3, 1950 Atlantic City, NJ
Journalist. Editor for *Time* magazine. Assistant to writer and editor, Whittaker Chambers. Father of Jim Fixx, author of *The Complete Book of Running* in 1977.

FIXX, JIM (James Fuller) Apr 23, 1932 New York, NY - Jul 20, 1984 Hardwick, VT
Author of the book, *The Complete Book of Running*, in 1977, promoting physical fitness through running and the health benefits of jogging. Died from a heart attack shortly after his daily jog. Son of journalist, Calvin H. Fixx, editor for *Time* magazine.

DOLGEVILLE CEMETERY
West State Street / County Road 83
Dolgeville, NY 13329

DOLGE, ALFRED Dec 22, 1848 Chemnitz, Germany - Jan 5, 1922 Milan, Italy
Felt manufacturer in Dolgeville and San Gabriel, CA. Namesake of the village of Dolgeville.

MCLAUGHLIN, EDWIN DELOS Feb 11, 1898 Dolgeville, NY - Mar 1960 Pinellas County, FL
Founded the Adirondack Bat Company in Dolgeville, owned by Rawlings since 1920.

SPOFFORD, JOHN PEMBROOKE Apr 10 1818 Herkimer, NY - Aug 27, 1884 Dolgeville, NY
Civil War Union Army Brevet Brigadier General. Fought at the Battle of Gettysburg.

DUESENBURY CEMETERY
Hunt Hill Road
Dryden, NY 13053

OVERACKER, ALBERT (Sebastian) Jul 31, 1789 Schaghticoke, NY - Apr 16, 1854 Ithaca, NY
With **Mary Avery Overacker** (Jan 23, 1794 - Apr 27, 1858 Ithaca, NY), the grandparents of Clara Louise Saltmarsh Westinghouse, the wife of inventor, Henry H. Westinghouse.

DUTCH HILL CEMETERY
Dutch Hill Road
West Monroe, NY 13167

HALL (Colvin)**, ALTHEA** Jul 7, 1926 Orwell, NY - Oct 1, 1992 Williamstown, NY
Aunt of United States Army Four-Star General, Keith B. Alexander, director of the National Security Agency from 2005-2014, under President George W. Bush and President Barack Obama.

EAST AURORA CEMETERY
Millard Fillmore Place
East Aurora, NY 14052

FILLMORE, ALMON HOPKINS Apr 13, 1806 Sempronius, NY - Jan 17, 1830 Aurora, NY
Brother of President Millard Fillmore.

FILLMORE, DARIUS INGRAHAM Nov 14, 1814 Sempronius, NY - Mar 9, 1837 Aurora, NY
Brother of President Millard Fillmore.

FILLMORE, NATHANIEL Apr 19, 1771 Bennington, VT - Mar 28, 1863 Aurora, NY
Father of President Millard Fillmore. First of four fathers to live through the entire presidency of a son, others being Dr. George T. Harding Sr., Joseph P. Kennedy Sr., and George H. W. Bush.

FILLMORE (Millard)**, PHOEBE** (Aug 12, 1781 Pittsford, VT - Apr 2, 1831 Aurora, NY
Mother of President Millard Fillmore.

EAST LAWN CEMETERY
Mitchell Street
Ithaca, NY 14850

NORTHUP, CLARK SUTHERLAND Jul 12, 1872 Edmeston, NY - May 18, 1952 Ithaca, NY
Professor of English Language and Literature at Cornell University. Published *A Register of Bibliographies of the English Language and Literature* in 1925.

REDDICK, DONALD Mar 1, 1883 Sheridan, MO - Apr 2, 1955 Gainesville, FL
Botanist. Professor of Plant Pathology at Cornell University, specializing in the potato.

EASTMAN BUSINESS PARK
1669 Lake Avenue
Rochester, NY 14652

EASTMAN, GEORGE Jul 12, 1854 Waterville, NY - Mar 14, 1932 Rochester, NY
Inventor, philanthropist and photography pioneer. Established the Eastman Kodak Company in
Rochester in 1892. Patented the first film in roll form, transforming photography into a popular hobby,
previously unaffordable. Committed suicide by gunshot following a long illness, leaving a note, "My
work is done. Why wait?" His ashes are buried on the grounds of the industrial complex, formerly
Kodak Park, renamed in 2008.

EASTMAN-SMITH CEMETERY
Route 5
Pulaski, NY 13142

BROWN, SYLVESTER 1792 - 1876 Port Ontario, NY
Sold 5,760 square feet of land to the government for $3000, September 1, 1837, to build the Selkirk
Lighthouse, located at the mouth of the Salmon River, Lake Ontario.

EDEN VALLEY CEMETERY
Route 62
Eden, NY 14057

STEBBINS, JOEL Dec 19, 1777 Wilbraham, MA - Mar 5, 1848 Eden, NY
With **Abigail Berry Stebbins** (Dec 23, 1784 Willington, CT - Aug 20, 1851 Eden, NY), the 2nd great-
grandparents of Academy Award-winning actor, Spencer Tracy.

ELBRIDGE RURAL CEMETERY
Route 5
Elbridge, NY 13060

MUNRO, SQUIRE Jun 27, 1758 Bristol, MA - Mar 31, 1835 Elbridge, NY
Early settler in the town of Elbridge. Constructed the Seneca Turnpike with his sons, including Judge
David Munro, early settler of Camillus. Great-grandfather of Baldwinsville banker, Otis Munro Bigelow.

ELMA CEMETERY
Cemetery Road
Elma, NY 14059

FRANK, JACKSON CAREY Mar 2, 1943 Buffalo, NY - Aug 3, 1999 Great Barrington, MA
Folk singer and songwriter. Released his only album, *Jackson C. Frank*, in 1965, produced by Paul
Simon. His songs have been recorded by Simon & Garfunkel, Nick Drake, Sandy Denny and John
Mayer. Survived a fire when a furnace exploded, as a student at Cleveland Hill Elementary School in
Cheektowaga, March 31, 1954, that killed 15 students. Wrote "Marlene" for his girlfriend, who died in
the explosion.

ELMLAWN MEMORIAL PARK
3939 Delaware Avenue
Kenmore, NY 14217

HERSHISER, OREL LEONARD 1856 - 1929 Buffalo, NY
Great-grandfather of Orel Hershiser, All-Star pitcher for the Los Angeles Dodgers, Cleveland Indians,
San Francisco Giants and New York Mets from 1983-2000.

RAND, BENJAMIN LONG Jun 22, 1855 North Tonawanda, NY - Feb 27, 1952 North Tonawanda, NY
Mayor of North Tonawanda from 1915-1918. Brother of James H. Rand Sr., founder of the Rand
Ledger Corporation. Uncle of James H. Rand Jr., founder of American Kardex. Both companies
merged into Rand Kardex in 1925, later merged with Remington to form, Remington Rand.

ROSE, TAM (Walter Sumner) Dec 5, 1888 Tonawanda, NY - Oct 2, 1961 Tonawanda, NY
Syracuse University football captain from 1913-1915. Two-time All-American. Player-coach of the
Tonawanda Kardex from 1916-1921, including its only NFL game, in 1921.

SCHULEFAND, SEYMOUR Aug 17, 1929 Buffalo, NY - Jan 15, 1991 Buffalo, NY
Brother of comedic actor, Dick Shawn, born Richard Schulefand in Buffalo, died from a heart attack
during a performance at Mandeville Hall, University of California, San Diego, April 17, 1987, San
Diego, buried in Hillside Memorial Park, Culver City. Uncle of Wendy Shawn Travolta, the wife of actor,
Joey Travolta, the brother of actor, John Travolta. Buried in the Temple Shaarey Zedek section of the
cemetery.

SJODEN, ERICK OLOF Jul 7, 1866 Stockholm, Sweden - Jan 31, 1939 Buffalo, NY
Superintendent and manager of the American Radiator Company in Buffalo from 1915-1930.
Designed and manufactured machinery for munitions in World War I.

SPILLMAN, ALBERT 1863 North Tonawanda, NY - Feb 1, 1949 North Tonawanda, NY
Co-founded the Herschell-Spillman Motor Company in 1901, with his brother, Edward Orton Spillman and brother-in-law, Allan Herschell, manufacturing auto and motorboat engines.

ELMWOOD CEMETERY
Elmwood Avenue
Adams, NY 13605

GROFF, SUSAN Nov 9, 1952 NY - Nov 21, 1987 Adams, NY
Murder victim. Sodomized, beaten and strangled by parolee, Philip J. Guinta, who she met through letters sent to him while incarcerated in an Oneida County prison, her body found sixty miles away, off Whiskey Hollow Road in Baldwinsville, a dark, tree-lined road urban legend claims is haunted. He was convicted, sentenced to 50 years in prison in 1988.

ELMWOOD CEMETERY
Harvester Avenue
Batavia, NY 14020

WAKEMAN, SETH Jan 15, 1811 Franklin, VT - Jan 4, 1880 Batavia, NY
United States Representative-NY from 1871-1873.

ELMWOOD CEMETERY
Route 281
Preble, NY 13141

MAYCUMBER, BRUCE S. - Apr 24, 1927 Belleville, NY
Drowned, fishing off Stony Point, Lake Ontario, with his brother-in-law, Garrett Nutting, when their boat capsized in a storm, their attempt to swim to shore failed, his body was recovered May 12, 1927.

NORTON, LLEWELLYN POWELL May 11, 1837 NY - Feb 16, 1914 Preble, NY
Civil War Union Army Sergeant Major. Awarded the Medal of Honor for action at Sailor's Creek, VA, April 6, 1865.

ELMWOOD (BETHLEHEM RURAL) CEMETERY
North Route 9W
Selkirk, NY 12158

MACDONALD, SEWARD WILBER Dec 6, 1920 Albany, NY - Jul 31, 2000 Albany, NY
Cousin of actor, Jack Briggs, married to Academy Award-winning actress, Ginger Rogers, from
1943-1949.

ELMWOOD HILL CEMETERY
51 Belle Avenue
Troy, NY 12180

GRATTO FAMILY Jun 2, 1978 Cohoes, NY
Victims of arson. **John Gratto**, 31, and his children, **Eleanor**, 9, **Evelyn**, 8, **Francis**, 5, **John Jr.**, 4,
Edward, 2 and four-month old twins, **Patricia** and **Sarah**, were killed in a house fire, 108-110 Ontario
Street, from asphyxiation. Virginia Bellerose Gratto, wife and mother of the seven children, and three-
months pregnant, managed to escape with minor injuries, locking the front door behind her, hindering
any chance of escape for the family, and hindering the firefighters rescue efforts. She moved to the
state of Washington two months later, married Norman Utigard, who she met through a personal ad,
remaining a person of interest.

EMERSON RURAL CEMETERY
O'Neil Road
Port Byron, NY 13140

JOHNSTON, ROBERT J. Jul 4, 1908 Norwich, NY - Jun 19, 1983 Auburn, NY
Local trumpet player and bandleader in the 1930s and 40s.

EMERSONS RURAL CEMETERY
Ballard Road / Route 33
Wilton, NY 12831

BRACKETT, JOHN ADAMS 1798 Ashfield, MA - Jan 4, 1871 Gurn Spring, NY
Grandfather of Edgar Truman Brackett, New York State Senator from 1896-1906 and 1909-1912.
Great-grandfather of Academy Award-winning screenwriter, Charles Brackett.

ENFIELD CEMETERY
Enfield Main Road / Route 327
Enfield, NY 14867

TEMPLE, ALEXANDER 1762 Aberdeen, Scotland - Feb 10, 1828 Enfield, NY
3rd great-grandfather of Shirley Temple Black, child movie star and United States Ambassador to Ghana from 1974-1976 and Czechoslovakia from 1989-1992.

ESPERANCE CEMETERY
Burtonsville Road
Esperance, NY 12066

LAWTON (Briggs)**, MARTHA LOUISE** Feb 3, 1919 Duanesburg, NY - Mar 30, 1976 Duanesburg, NY
Mother of Virginia Briggs Lawton, named after her godmother, Academy Award-winning actress, Ginger Rogers, born Virginia Katherine McMath, who was married at the time to her brother, actor, Jack Briggs. Her husband, Elwood D. Lawton, died May 4, 2016 in Niskayuna, age 98.

EVERGREEN CEMETERY
Levanna Road
Aurora, NY 13026

KELLOGG, BRUCE (Malcolm) Apr 12, 1948 Auburn, NY - Jun 9, 1991 Romulus, NY
Murder victim. Shot four times in the head, sleeping at his family's cottage on Vineyard Road. Teenager, Denver A. McDowell, pled guilty to the shooting in May 1992. Laurie Lee Kellogg, the victim's wife, was found guilty of conspiracy in July 1992, following a high-profile trial in Seneca County Court in Waterloo. The event was the basis for the made-for-TV movie, *Lies of the Heart: The Laurie Kellogg Story* in 1994, chronicling his murder and sensational trial.

EVERGREEN CEMETERY
Old Poland Road
Barneveld, NY 13304

GUITEAU, LUTHER Jun 3, 1778 Lanesborough, MA - Feb 12, 1850 Trenton, NY
Physician. Brother of Francis Guiteau Jr., the grandfather of Charles Julius Guiteau, assassin of President James Garfield, July 2, 1881, Washington D.C., hanged for his crime, June 30, 1882.

GUITEAU, LUTHER May 3, 1805 NY - Jun 13, 1885 Trenton, NY

Physician. Uncle of Charles Julius Guiteau, assassin of President James Garfield, July 2, 1881, Washington D.C., hanged for his crime, June 30, 1882.

MILLER, CHARLES ADDISON 1867 Utica, NY - 1944

President of the Reconstruction Finance Corporation from 1932-1933, appointed by President Herbert Hoover.

PENDER, ROBERT BEEBE Jul 16, 1920 Utica, NY - Jun 16, 1972 Clayton, NY

Medical Director of St. Luke's Memorial Hospital, New Hartford. Drowned off the dock of his summer cottage, Grindstone Island in the St. Lawrence River, Thousand Islands. Husband of Alice Culpepper Gordon O'Shea, who remarried to James Cornelius O'Shea, the first husband of Kathleen Corroon O'Shea, whose sister, Joan Patricia Corroon Skakel, married George Skakel, the brother of Ethel Skakel Kennedy, the wife of Senator Robert F. Kennedy.

EVERGREEN CEMETERY
East Main Street
Canton, NY 13617

BACHELLER, IRVING (Addison) Sept 26, 1859 Pierrepont, NY - Feb 24, 1950 White Plains, NY

Founded the Bacheller Syndicate, the first newspaper syndicate in the United States. Hired novelist, Stephen Crane, as a war correspondent in Cuba. Published the novel, *Eben Holden: A Tale of the North Country*, in 1900.

BESWICK, PIERCE ELISHA 1862 - 1929 Canton, NY

With **Lillian May Vebber Beswick** (1871 - 1947 Canton, NY), the grandparents of William Pierce Rogers, United States Secretary of State from 1969-1973, under President Richard Nixon, and United States Attorney General from 1957-1961, under President Dwight D. Eisenhower.

FREEMAN, MILTON HARVEY 1871 Canton, NY - Mar 24, 1925 Valhalla, NY

Chief Engineer of the Holland Tunnel, connecting New York City with New Jersey, succeeding Clifford Milburn Holland, who died during construction. Outlived Holland by five months.

REMINGTON, FREDERIC Oct 4, 1861 Canton, NY - Dec 26, 1909 Ridgefield, CT

Painter, sculptor and illustrator of the American West. Spanish-American War correspondent, illustrating scenes for publisher, William Randolph Hearst, including the Battle of San Juan Hill, led by Colonel Theodore Roosevelt and the Rough Riders.

RUSSELL, LESLIE W. Apr 15, 1840 Canton, NY - Feb 3, 1903 New York, NY

United States Representative-NY in 1891. Associate Justice of the New York State Supreme Court from 1891-1902. 3rd great-grandson of Samuel Russell, co-founder of Yale University.

EVERGREEN CEMETERY
Fenner Street
Cazenovia, NY 13035

ATWELL, ROY May 2, 1878 Syracuse, NY - Feb 6, 1962 New York, NY
Stuttering comedic actor. Appeared in vaudeville, Broadway musical comedies, film and radio. Voice of Doc in the Disney animated classic, *Snow White and the Seven Dwarfs*. Starred in the Broadway play, *How's Your Health?*, written by close friend, Booth Tarkington, and *The Firefly*. Composed the song "Some Little Bug is Going to Bite You."

BOND, GEORGE HOPKINS Oct 28, 1909 Syracuse, NY - Sept 27, 1973 Syracuse, NY
Attorney. Senior partner of the law firm, Bond, Schoeneck & King, since 1941.

COLGATE, ROBERT Jun 19, 1851 New York, NY - Jan 20, 1923 Cazenovia, NY
Grandson of William Colgate, soap manufacturer, philanthropist and founder of the Colgate-Palmolive Company.

DWINELL, JUSTIN Oct 28, 1785 Shaftsbury, VT - Sept 17, 1850 Cazenovia, NY
United States Representative-NY from 1823-1825. Madison County District Attorney from 1837-1845.

FAIRCHILD, CHARLES STEBBINS Apr 30, 1842 Cazenovia, NY - Nov 24, 1924
United States Secretary of Treasury from 1887-1889, under President Grover Cleveland. New York State Attorney General from 1876-1877.

HOLE, JAMES E. May 29, 1905 - Apr 15, 1977 Syracuse, NY
Founded the Theobald and Hole Drugstore in Cazenovia, with Frederick P. Theobald, in 1939.

HULLAR, JACOB CASPER 1851 - Dec 3, 1934 Cazenovia, NY
Operated hotels in Central New York. Founded Hullar's Restaurant in Fayetteville in 1908.

LINCKLAEN, JOHN Dec 24, 1768 Amsterdam, Holland - Feb 9, 1822 Cazenovia, NY
Early settler and founding father of the town of Cazenovia, named in honor of his Italian friend, Theophilus Cazenove.

MITCHELL, LUCIEN C. Jul 2, 1838 Cazenovia, NY - Jan 3, 1929 Syracuse, NY
Invented parachutes that opened more quickly and efficiently. Oldest man to fly in an airplane, age 83, when he flew over San Diego to test his parachutes in 1921. Granduncle of Donald M. Dey, Robert Dey and James G.S. Dey, founders of the Dey Brothers Department Store.

REMINGTON, ELIPHALET Sept 26, 1861 Ilion, NY - Nov 13, 1938 Cazenovia, NY
Grandson of Eliphalet Remington II, inventor, gunsmith and arms manufacturer.

STEBBINS, CHARLES Feb 9, 1789 Williamstown, MA - Mar 23, 1873 Cazenovia, NY
Lieutenant Governor of New York from 1829-1830, under Enos T. Throop. New York State Senator
from 1826-1829.

EVERGREEN CEMETERY
Kenney Settlement Road
Fabius, NY 13063

LAPE, WILLARD EVERETT Apr 24, 1930 Syracuse, NY - Sept 19, 2004 Syracuse, NY
Hosted children's programs on WSYR-TV in Syracuse. Known as "Bill Everett." Portrayed "Salty Sam"
on the *Saturday Popeye Theater*, *Popeye Playhouse* and *Salty Sam's Super Saturday*, from
1961-1980, "Epal" on the *Monster Movie Matinee*, from 1964-1980 and "Mr. Whitaker" on *Snuckleby
and Friends* in 1991.

MILLS (Adams)**, EMILY REXFORD** Sept 22, 1847 Syracuse, NY - Mar 13, 1904 Elmira, NY
Wife of Dr. Edmund Mead Mills, Central New York Minister in the Methodist Church and namesake of
the E.M. Mills Memorial Rose Garden in Thornden Park, Syracuse, dedicated in 1924.

PADDOCK, CLIFFORD Dec 25, 1918 Syracuse, NY - Aug 6, 1998 Syracuse, NY
Last surviving farmer in Woodchuck Hill, a town of DeWitt neighborhood. Suffered a broken hip and
deep gashes in his left arm and leg after a farming accident, dragged himself more than 100 yards,
climbed into his car and drove two miles to get help, at age 72, in 1991.

SKEELE, CHARLES WINSLOW Aug 14, 1899 Apulia Station, NY - Jul 13, 1992 Syracuse, NY
United States Army Colonel. Veteran of World War I, World War II and the Korean War. National
President of the Reserve Officers Association in 1950. Father of Charles W. Skeele Jr., unsuccessful
candidate for United States Representative-NY in 1994, losing to Sherwood L. Boehlert. Son of
Onondaga County homebuilder, Irving D. Skeele.

TEN EYCK, EDWARD G. Jan 23, 1864 Davenport, NY - Aug 30, 1943 Syracuse, NY
Onondaga County Sheriff from 1918-1921. New York State Assemblyman from 1897-1899.

UNDERWOOD, JAMES R. Jun 22, 1921 Cortland, NY - May 25, 1990 Liverpool, NY
Photographer for International School Studios in the 1960s. Covered World War II in Europe, Africa
and the Middle East.

EVERGREEN CEMETERY
Route 26N
Lee, NY 13363

BORGOVINI, ALICIA C. Sept 2, 1969 NY - Oct 30, 1988 Rome, NY
Granddaughter of Joseph Borgovini, co-founder of the Florentine Bakery in Utica in 1928. Killed in a car accident, the car she was driving striking several trees.

BROOKS (Pitcher)**, HARRIET** Jan 1, 1876 Exeter, ON, Canada - Apr 17, 1933 Montréal, QB, Canada
First Canadian nuclear physicist. Pioneer in the study of radioactivity. One of the first to discover radon. Worked for Marie Curie in Paris from 1906-1907.

RIGGS, JAMES 1758 CT - Sept 22, 1839 Rome, NY
Revolutionary War veteran. 3rd great-grandfather of First Lady Mamie (Marie Geneva) Doud Eisenhower, the wife of President Dwight D. Eisenhower.

FLEMING, BOB (Robert Gerard) Jul 25, 1952 Rome, NY - Sept 5, 2016 Camden, NY
Central New York musician. Guitarist and vocalist with the Moss Back Mule Band, formed in 1974. Opened for the Band, Lynyrd Skynyrd, the Charlie Daniels Band, Pure Prairie League and Hank Williams Jr. during his 40-year career.

EVERGREEN CEMETERY
East Avenue
Owego, NY 13827

DRAKE, JOHN REUBEN Nov 28, 1782 Pleasant Valley, NY - Mar 21, 1857 Owego, NY
United States Representative-NY from 1817-1819.

PARKER, JOHN MASON Jun 14, 1805 Granville, NY - Dec 16, 1873 Owego, NY
United States Representative-NY from 1855-1859.

PLATT, THOMAS COLLIER Jul 15, 1833 Owego, NY - Mar 6, 1910 New York, NY
United States Senator from 1881 and 1897-1909. United States Representative-NY from 1873-1877. Resigned from the Senate in 1881, after two months in office, following a dispute with President James Garfield. Republican leader in New York State, responsible for the election of Theodore Roosevelt as Governor of New York in 1898.

ROBISON, HOWARD WINFIELD Oct 30, 1915 Owego, NY - Sept 26, 1987 Rehoboth Beach, DE
United States Representative-NY from 1958-1975. Elected to Congress in a special election due to the resignation of W. Sterling Cole.

SA-SA-NA LOFT 1831 Canada - Feb 18, 1852 Deposit, NY
Mohawk Indian maiden from Western Canada. Lost her life in a train accident on tour, performing concerts to raise money translating books into the Mohawk language. Direct-descendant of Chief Joseph Brant, Mohawk leader during the Revolutionary War.

TAYLOR, JOHN JAMES Apr 27, 1808 Leominster, MA - Jul 1, 1892 Owego, NY
United States Representative-NY from 1853-1855.

EVERGREEN CEMETERY
North Main Street
Pine Plains, NY 12567

AMELIO, PHILIP JOHN Nov 3, 1977 Sharon, CT - Apr 1, 2005 Boston, MA
Child television actor. Played Lucille Ball's grandson on the TV series, *Life with Lucy*. Appeared on the soap opera, *All My Children*. Full-time teacher at Duanesburg High School in Delanson, Schenectady County, at the time of his death.

EVERGREEN CEMETERY
Cemetery Road
Salem, NY 12865

BLAIR, BERNARD May 24, 1801 Williamstown, MA - May 7, 1980 Salem, NY
United States Representative-NY from 1841-1843.

BOYD, JOHN HUGGINS Jul 31, 1799 Whitehall, NY - Jul 2, 1868 Salem, NY
United States Representative-NY from 1851-1853.

FITCH, ASA Nov 10, 1765 Groton, CT - Aug 24, 1843 Salem, NY
United States Representative-NY from 1811-1813. First entomologist of the New York State Agricultural Society.

HINDS, JAMES M. Dec 5, 1833 Hebron, NY - Oct 22, 1868 Indian Bay, AR
United States Representative-AR in 1868. First sitting member of Congress assassinated, campaigning for Ulysses S. Grant on the eve of the 1868 presidential election, shot in the head, knocked off his horse, by George Clark, a member of the Ku Klux Klan. A cenotaph in his memory was placed in Congressional Cemetery in Washington D.C.

PARKER, JAMES SOUTHWORTH Jun 3, 1867 Great Barrington, MA - Dec 19, 1933 Washington D.C.
United States Representative-NY from 1913-1933.

RUSSELL, DAVID ABEL 1780 Petersburg, NY - Nov 24, 1861 Salem, NY
United States Representative-NY from 1835-1841. Father of Civil War Union Army Brevet Major General, David Allen Russell.

RUSSELL, DAVID ALLEN Dec 10, 1820 Salem, NY - Sept 19, 1864 Winchester, VA
Civil War Union Army Brevet Major General. Killed in action in the Battle of Opequon, the Third Battle of Winchester. Son of David Abel Russell, United States Representative-NY from 1835-1841.

TANNER, ADOLPHUS HITCHCOCK May 23, 1833 Granville, NY - Jan 14, 1882 Whitehall, NY
United States Representative-NY from 1869-1871.

THOMAS, DAVID Jul 11, 1762 Pelham, MA - Nov 27, 1831 Providence, RI
United States representative-NY from 1801-1808. Resigned from Congress, becoming New York State Treasurer, from 1808-1810 and 1812-1813.

WILSON, MARALIE JEAN Jul 3, 1947 NY - Jul 22, 1977 Schenectady, NY
Murder victim. Found near train tracks in downtown Schenectady, strangled and mutilated, post-mortem, by serial killer, Lemuel Warren Smith, under police investigation for three additional murders at the time.

WILSON, NATHAN Dec 23, 1758 Bolton, MA - Jul 25, 1834 Salem, NY
United States Representative-NY from 1808-1809. Elected to Congress due to the resignation of David Thomas.

EVERGREEN HILL CEMETERY
Alleghany Road / Route 77
Corfu, NY 14036

SILLIMAN, MARY E. Jul 27, 1985 Rochester, NY - Feb 14, 2009 Brockport, NY
Murder victim. Lakeside Memorial Hospital nurse, shot and killed by Frank Garcia, a co-worker fired following sexual harassment complaints on the job. Randal Norman, a motorist who intervened, was also killed, while his girlfriend was wounded. Following those murders, Garcia drove to Canandaigua and killed, execution-style, a previous co-worker, Kimberly Glatz, who had also filed a sexual harassment complaint, and her husband, Christopher Glatz. Garcia was sentenced to five life sentences without parole in two separate trials.

EVERGREEN HILL CEMETERY
Poplar Hill Road One
Unadilla, NY 13849

FOREE, ROBERT E. Jan 2, 1933 Sidney, NY - Jul 25, 2003 Cooperstown, NY
Owned Foree's Used Cars in Unadilla. Collapsed from a heart attack in Section 315 of the Carrier Dome, clinically dead, his heart had stopped beating, just before halftime of Syracuse's 24-21 win over Cincinnati. Paramedics rushed to the scene, reviving the season ticket holder, who would live another ten years.

GOERLICH COUPLE Apr 6, 2006 Port Orange, FL
Robert F. Goerlich, 70, and his wife, **Shirley B. Goerlich**, 69, were shot and killed while watching television in their winter home by a neighbor, Linda Sue Anderson, who claimed the Goerlich's "tortured" her by feeding her "cookies with green mothballs in them." Robert Goerlich had just returned home from the hospital earlier that day, treated for a heart attack. Shirley Goerlich published the award-winning book, *Genealogy: A Practical Research Guide*, in 1994.

EVERGREEN LAWN CEMETERY
Bloomingdale Road
Akron, NY 14001

PERRY, MARLO H. Apr 3, 1915 Akron, NY - Mar 24, 1988 Akron, NY
Owned and operated Perry's Ice Cream, founded by his father, H. Morton Perry, in Akron, 1918.

EVERGREEN MEMORIAL PARK
2150 Central Avenue
Schenectady, NY 12304

VAN NESS, GORDON 1940 Albany, NY - Oct 19, 1990 Albany, NY
Founded the Albany civil rights group, the Brothers, in the 1960s. Interviewed by Pulitzer Prize-winning author, William Kennedy, for his book, *O Albany!: Improbable City of Political Wizards, Fearless Ethnics, Spectacular Aristocrats, Splendid Nobodies, and Underrated Scoundrels*, in 1983.

EVERSON MUSEUM OF ART
401 Harrison Street
Syracuse, NY 13202

ROBINEAU (Alsop)**, ADELAIDE BEERS** Apr 9, 1865 Middletown, CT - Feb 18, 1929 Syracuse, NY
Painter, potter and ceramist. Specialized in porcelain art. Awarded the Grand Prize in pottery at   the

Turin International Exhibition in 1911 for *The Scarab Vase*. Built her studio, Four Winds, next to her Robineau Road home in Syracuse. Founded the ceramics magazine, *Keramic Studio*, with her husband, Samuel E. Robineau. Fernando Carter, director of the Syracuse Museum of Fine Arts, purchased 31 of her porcelain art pieces, establishing the museum as one of the country's leaders in ceramic art.

ROBINEAU, SAMUEL EDOUARD Dec 20, 1856 - 1936 Syracuse, NY
Namesake of Robineau Road in Syracuse. Husband of porcelain artist, Adelaide Alsop Robineau.

EZRATH ISRAEL CEMETERY
Route 209
Napanoch, NY 12458

SLUTSKY, CHARLES 1861 Russia - May 31, 1931 Ellenville, NY
Purchased land in Wawarsing in 1901, and founded the Nevele Hotel and Country Club, established by his son, Joseph Slutsky. Grandfather of Milt Rosenstein, minor league baseball pitcher, killed in World War II.

SLUTSKY, JULIUS Feb 19, 1912 Ellenville, NY - Apr 7, 2006 West Palm Beach, FL
Owner and operator of the Nevele Grande Hotel in Wawarsing from 1955-1997, founded by his father, Joseph Slutsky in 1908. President Lyndon Johnson stayed one night at the resort, in town to dedicate a new hospital in Ellenville, in 1966. Spent one year in prison of tax evasion in 1973.

FACTORY VILLAGE CEMETERY
Northline Road
Ballston Spa, NY 12020

BLOTTO (Stephenson), CHEESE Jul 1, 1956 Ballston Spa, NY - Oct 3, 1999 Saratoga Springs, NY
Bass player for Blotto, an Albany-area rock band, toured throughout the United States and Europe. Born Keith A. Stephenson, members of the band assumed different "Blotto" stage names.

FAIRDALE CEMETERY
1279 Route 3
Hannibal, NY 13074

ULANOWSKI, CHRIS Jul 22, 1959 Buffalo, NY - May 29, 2011 Fulton, NY
News Director for WRVO-FM in Oswego from 1982-2009. Received the Syracuse Press Club's Career Achievement Award in 2008. Committed suicide weeks after purchasing a cemetery plot and

headstone with a symbol of the Grateful Dead.

FAIRFIELD CEMETERY
Route 259 / South Union Street
Spencerport, NY 14559

MARTIN, PAUL A. Jun 18, 1973 St. Johnsbury, VT - Dec 13, 2008 Spencerport, NY
Found dead, naked from the waist down with a homemade electrical contraption connected to his genitals and hand, the victim of auto-erotic electrocution. His widow sued their insurance company, The Hartford, who denied her claim, stating the electrician died from a deliberate act on his part, a decision backed by a federal judge in Rochester. The United States Second Circuit Court of Appeals ruled in her favor, awarding her accidental death benefits.

QUALE, MICHAEL J. Aug 20, 1950 Rochester, NY - Sept 25, 1994 Lancaster, NY
Hell's Angels President from 1984-1986, Rochester Chapter. Nicknamed "Mad Mike." Stabbed and beaten to death during a brawl by members of the rival Outlaws motorcycle club at a race track, attending drag races. Tombstone reflects a skull and the Hell's Angels of Rochester emblem.

FAIRVIEW CEMETERY
Upper Steadwell Avenue
Amsterdam, NY 12010

BREMER, RICHARD A. 1879 - 1920 Amsterdam, NY
Father of film actress and dancer, Lucille Bremer, co-star of the films, *Meet Me in St. Louis* and *Ziegfeld Follies*.

WATERSTREET (Overbaugh)**, DOROTHY F.** 1911 NY - Jan 21, 1958 Amsterdam, NY
Murder Victim. Wife of funeral director, Charles N. Waterstreet, robbed and bludgeoned to death, the first victim of serial killer, Lemuel Warren Smith.

FAIRVIEW CEMETERY
Miner Road
Canton, NY 13617

MCSORLEY, JOHN FRANCIS Jul 21, 1907 Spencerville, ON, Canada - Aug 11, 1993 Canton, NY
Brother of Ernest Michael McSorley, Captain of the Great Lakes freighter, *SS Edmund Fitzgerald*.

FAIRVIEW CEMETERY
Fairview Cemetery Lane
Stone Ridge, NY 12484

FITCH, EZRA HASBROUCK Sept 27, 1865 Coxsackie, NY - Jun 16, 1930 Santa Barbara, CA
Co-founded Abercrombie & Fitch in New York City, in 1892, with David Thomas Abercrombie, who died, August 29, 1931, age 64, buried in Green Mount Cemetery, Baltimore.

WOOD, EDWARD DAVIS Feb 23, 1895 - May 6, 1967 Poughkeepsie, NY
With **Lillian C. Phillips Wood** (Jul 5, 1903 - May 1989 Poughkeepsie, NY), the parents of director, writer and producer, Ed Wood, subject of the 1994 film, *Ed Wood*.

FANTINEKILL CEMETERY
State Road
Ellenville, NY 12428

COX, ISAAC NEWTON Aug 1, 1846 Fallsburg, NY - Sept 28, 1916 Ellenville, NY
United States Representative-NY from 1891-1893.

MEEHAN, CHICK (John) Jan 9, 1917 Brooklyn, NY - May 9, 2004 Kerhonkson, NY
Played for the Syracuse Nationals, their first two NBA seasons, from 1946-1948.

TUTHILL, JOSEPH HASBROUCK Feb 25, 1811 Blooming Grove, NY - Jul 27, 1877 Ellenville, NY
United States Representative-NY from 1871-1873.

FAYETTEVILLE CEMETERY
515 Orchard Street
Fayetteville, NY 13066

AUDI, ALFRED J. Apr 11, 1938 Brooklyn, NY - Sept 29, 2007 Fayetteville, NY
Furniture maker. Purchased L. & J.G. Stickley, Inc. in 1974, revitalizing the company after years of declining sales. Restored its popular Mission furniture line in 1989. Son of E.J. Audi, founder of E.J. Audi Furniture in New York City in 1928.

BEARD, HUNTINGTON 1826 - May 26, 1895 Fayetteville, NY
Founded Spring Roller Mill in Fayetteville in 1886. Son of Beach Beard, early settler in the town of Pompey. Uncle of Huntington Beard Crouse, co-founder of the Crouse-Hinds Company.

CALLENDER, FRANKLIN DYER Feb 27, 1817 Fayetteville, NY - Dec 13, 1882 Daysville, IL
Civil War Union Army Brevet Brigadier General.

COUGHLIN, ALLAN B. Apr 30, 1907 Syracuse, NY - Dec 26, 1973 Syracuse, NY
Member of the first Board of Trustees and second President of the Rosamond Gifford Charitable Foundation. Son of Patrick Coughlin, founder of the Coughlin Brothers Candy Factory in Syracuse.

CUSTER, CAL (Calvin H.) Jul 15, 1939 Atlantic City, NJ - Apr 21, 1998 Syracuse, NY
Conductor of the Syracuse Symphony Orchestra from 1976-1986.

ESTABROOK, WILLIAM SEAR Dec 12, 1877 Binghamton, NY - Feb 12, 1960 Syracuse, NY
Attorney. Senior member of the law firm Estabrook, Estabrook, Burns & Hancock.

GAGE (Joslyn)**, MATILDA ELECTA** Mar 25, 1826 Cicero, NY - Mar 18, 1898 Chicago, IL
Social reformer. Co-authored the first three volumes of *The History of Woman Suffrage*, with Susan B. Anthony and Elizabeth Cady Stanton. Mother of Maud Gage Baum, the wife of L. Frank Baum, author of *The Wonderful Wizard of Oz* series of children's books. Grandmother of Dorothy Louise Gage, namesake of "Dorothy" in *The Wizard of Oz*.

GILLETTE (Willett)**, HOLLY B.** 1958 Syracuse, NY - Jun 1, 1997 Hadley, NY
Niece of Grammy Award-winning gospel singer, George Beverly Shea.

HALE, CHARLOTTE C. Jan 21, 1925 Syracuse, NY - Dec 21, 1991 Syracuse, NY
Central New York jazz singer. Performed with the Stan Colella Orchestra at the New York State Fair. Recorded the Byrne Dairy Jingle on local radio.

HILDRETH, TRUMAN C. May 1862 NY - Apr 25, 1947 Syracuse, NY
Owned and operated Green Lakes Park for 50 years.

HUNT, EDWARD A. 1855 - Oct 2, 1931 Syracuse, NY
Founded, owned and operated Hunt Laundry in Syracuse, later Yale Laundry.

ROSEBOOM, WILLIAM F. Sept 8, 1920 Syracuse, NY - Sept 10, 1979 Syracuse, NY
Authored many books on the city of Syracuse including, *They Built a City* and *From Salt to Satellite*.

SMITH, JOHN F. Apr 1, 1914 Brooklyn, NY - Mar 7, 2009 Sarasota, FL
Union College Lacrosse All-American in 1936 and 1937. Captain of the United States National Lacrosse Team.

STICKLEY, LEOPOLD 1869 Osceola, WI - Nov 1, 1957 Ticonderoga, NY
President of L. & J.G. Stickley, Inc., from 1900-1950, with his brother, John George Stickley, the first to mass produce furniture made of cherry wood. Brother of Gustav Stickley, founder of the Craftsman Workshops and *Craftsman Magazine*.

TEALL, TIMOTHY May 27, 1754 Middletown, CT - Jun 11, 1820 Manlius, NY
Early Onondaga County settler. Father of Oliver Teall, a founding father of the city of Syracuse.

TIBBETTS, FRANK G. 1836 RI - Dec 24, 1924 Rochester, NY
Last surviving schoolmate of President Grover Cleveland, during his childhood years at the Fayetteville Academy.

WEBB, ALBERT R. Sept 12, 1917 Waltham, MA - Sept 12, 2000 Syracuse, NY
Co-owned and operated WPAW-AM radio in Syracuse, with Red Parton, from 1965-1970.

WILLETT, DANIEL S. 1942 Syracuse, NY - Sept 21, 1989 Syracuse, NY
Nephew of Grammy Award-winning gospel singer, George Beverly Shea.

FERNDALE CEMETERY
545 North Perry Street
Johnstown, NY 12095

BRODERICK (Crawford)**, HELEN** Aug 11, 1891 Philadelphia, PA -Sept 25, 1959 Los Angeles, CA
Character actress. Appeared in the films *Top Hat* and *Swing Time*, starring Fred Astaire and Ginger Rogers. Mother of Academy Award-winning actor, Broderick Crawford. Wife of actor, Lester Crawford.

CRAWFORD (Pendergast)**, LESTER** Dec 25, 1882 MA - Nov 24, 1962 Los Angeles, CA
Vaudeville actor. Appeared in small roles in films in the 1930s. Father of Academy Award-winning actor, Broderick Crawford. Husband of actress, Helen Broderick.

CRAWFORD, BRODERICK Dec 9, 1911 Philadelphia, PA - Apr 26, 1976 Rancho Mirage, CA
Academy Award-winning actor for the film, *All the King's Men*. Starred in the TV series, *Highway Patrol* and the film, *Born Yesterday*. Son of actress, Helen Broderick and actor, Lester Crawford.

MCNEAL, HARRY Aug 11, 1877 Iberia, OH - Jan 11, 1945 Cleveland, OH
Started ten games for the Cleveland Blues in 1901, splitting ten decisions. Committed suicide by gunshot in the Auditorium Hotel.

MORRIS, DEBRA L. 1967 Dolgeville, NY - Dec 22, 2007 Gloversville, NY
Killed in an apartment fire, intentionally set by owner, Jeffrey Alnutt, who was previously charged, but not convicted, in the 1974 murder of Damon Larrabee in Syracuse, a cold case that went unsolved for seventeen years, when Daniel H. Lohm was convicted in 1991.

PENDERGAST, DANIEL 1848 NY - 1904 Gloversville, NY
With **Fanny Crawford Pendergast** (1856 ME - 1945 Gloversville, NY), the grandparents of Academy Award-winning actor, Broderick Crawford. Parents of vaudeville actor, Lester Crawford.

PENDERGAST, HARDIE STEPHEN Jul 29, 1888 Merrimac, MA - Dec 28, 1958 NY
Uncle of Academy Award-winning actor, Broderick Crawford. Brother of actor, Lester Crawford.

FIRST BURYING GROUND CEMETERY
Brooks Avenue
Rushford, NY 14777

WYLIE, PHILIP GORDON May 12, 1902 Beverly, MA - Oct 25, 1971 Miami, FL
Author. Wrote *When Worlds Collide*, *The Savage Gentleman* and *Gladiator*, said to be an inspiration for the *Superman* comic book superhero. Father of author, Karen Wylie, the wife of Hawaii State Senator, Taylor Alderdyce "Tap" Pryor, and later, aquanaut, Jon Lindbergh, the son of aviator, Charles Lindbergh. Brother of writer, Max Wylie, co-creator of the television series, *The Flying Nun*. Uncle of Janice Wylie, a victim of the "Career Girls Murders" in New York City in 1963.

FIRST HEBREW CEMETERY
Oregon Road
Cortlandt, NY 10567

RUBENFELD, LEONARD May 7, 1916 Peekskill, NY - Dec 6, 2009 Peekskill, NY
Associate Justice of the New York State Supreme Court. New York State Assistant Attorney General. Westchester County District Attorney from 1962-1969. Brother of World War II United States Air Force and British Royal Air Force pilot, Milton Rubenfeld, one of five founding pilots of the Israeli Air Force in the 1948 Palestine War. Uncle of comedian, Paul "Pee Wee Herman" Reubens.

RUBENFELD, LOUIS 1886 - Mar 14, 1937 Peekskill, NY
With **Gussie Yormark Rubenfeld** (1892 - Dec 9, 1958 Peekskill, NY), the parents of World War II United States Air Force and British Royal Air Force pilot, Milton Rubenfeld, one of five founding pilots of the Israeli Air Force in the 1948 Palestine War. Grandparents of comedian, Paul "Pee Wee Herman" Reubens.

FIRST PRESBYTERIAN CHURCH CEMETERY
115 Union Street
Schenectady, NY 12308

EDWARDS, JONATHAN May 26, 1745 Northampton, MA - Aug 1, 1801 Schenectady, NY
Union College President from 1799-1801. Son of theologian, Jonathan Edwards Sr. Brother of Esther
Edwards Burr, the wife of Aaron Burr Sr., founder and President of Princeton University from
1747-1757. Uncle of United States Vice-President Aaron Burr.

FIRST REFORMED DUTCH CHURCHYARD (OLD DUTCH CHURCH)
272 Wall Street
Kingston, NY 12401

CLINTON, GEORGE Jul 26, 1739 Little Britain, NY - Apr 20, 1812 Washington D.C.
4th Vice-President of the United States, from 1805-1812. Served under Thomas Jefferson and James
Madison, one of two vice-presidents to serve under two different administrations. Governor of New
York from 1777-1795 and 1801-1805. Uncle of DeWitt Clinton, Governor of New York from 1817-1822
and 1822-1825. Namesake of Clinton County in New York and Ohio. Originally buried in
Congressional Cemetery, Washington D.C., reinterred in 1908.

DEWITT, JACOB HASBROUCK Oct 2, 1784 Marbletown, NY - Jan 30, 1857 Kingston, NY
United States Representative-NY from 1819-1821.

ELMENDORF, LUCAS CONRAD 1758 Kingston, NY - Aug 17, 1843 Kingston, NY
United States Representative-NY from 1797-1803.

GARDENIER, BARENT Jul 28, 1776 Kinderhook, NY - Jan 10, 1822 Kingston, NY
United States Representative-NY from 1807-1811.

SICKLES, NICHOLAS Sept 11, 1801 Kinderhook, NY - May 13, 1845 Kingston, NY
United States Representative-NY from 1835-1837.

VAN BUNSCHOTEN, THEUNIS E. Nov 11, 1643 Utrecht, Netherlands - Aug 1728 Kingston, NY
7th great-grandfather of Grammy Award-winning singer, Elvis Presley.

VAN BUREN, JOHN May 13, 1799 Kingston, NY - Jan 16, 1855 Kingston, NY
United States Representative-NY from 1841-1843.

VAN GAASBECK, PETER Sept 27, 1754 Kingston, NY - 1797 Kingston, NY
United States Representative-NY from 1793-1795.

FIRST WARD CEMETERY
Grant Boulevard (extinct)
Syracuse, NY 13208

ALVORD, DIOCLESIAN Feb 8, 1776 Farmington, CT - Mar 10, 1868 Syracuse, NY
Salt manufacturer. Established the largest salt business of his time, with his brother, Elisha Alvord.
Uncle of Thomas Gold Alvord, Lieutenant Governor of New York from 1865-1866.

ALVORD (Bush)**, POLLY** Jan 23, 1787 Chatham, CT - Oct 30, 1807 Manlius, NY
First wife of salt manufacturer, Elisha Alvord, the father of Thomas Gold Alvord, Lieutenant Governor
of New York from 1865-1866, with his second wife, Helen Lansing.

BAXTER, JOHN 1889 Syracuse, NY - July 29, 1815 Syracuse, NY
Notable for his grim tombstone which reads, "Fair and blooming yesterday, Now a loathsome corpse I
lie, History of First Ward Cemetery. See how beauty fades away, Oh! prepare, Prepare   to die."

BRACKETT, ICHABOD 1741 New Market, NH - Jan 1824 Syracuse, NY
Wealthy salt manufacturer.

CURTIS, FISHER 1779 Syracuse, NY - Apr 27, 1831 Syracuse, NY
First President of the village of Salina.

GILES, CHARLES Feb 1783 - Aug 30, 1867 Syracuse, NY
Methodist minister. Founded the First Ward Methodist Church. One of two remaining tombstones
visible on the surface of the now-defunct cemetery. The other, identified only as Mrs. Gamble, died
December 17, 1798, is the oldest tombstone in the cemetery.

RICHMOND (Dean)**, RACHEL** 1776 Taunton, MA - Apr 29, 1821 Syracuse, NY
Mother of railroad magnate, Dean Richmond. Her husband, Hathaway Richmond, died of yellow fever
in Mobile, AL, in 1790.

FISHKILL RURAL CEMETERY
801 Route 9
Fishkill, NY 12524

CASE, WALTER 1776 Pleasant Valley, NY - Oct 7, 1859 New York, NY
United States Representative-NY from 1819-1821.

KECK, CHARLES Sept 9, 1875 NY New York, NY - Apr 23, 1951 New York, NY
Sculptor. Created monuments and memorials of George Washington, Booker T. Washington, Lewis &
Clark and the *U.S.S. Maine*, located throughout the United States.

SANGER (Higgins), **MARGARET LOUISE** Sept 14, 1879 Corning, NY - Sept 6, 1966 Tucson, AZ
Social reformer, sex educator and nurse. Coined the term, "birth control", opening the first birth control
clinic in the United States, in 1916. Founded the American Birth Control League, later Planned
Parenthood, in 1921. Married to architect, William Sanger, from 1902-1921. Sister of Bob Higgins,
College Football Hall of Fame coach for Penn State.

SLEE, NOAH (James) Sept 12, 1861 Cape Town, South Africa - Jun 21, 1943 Tucson, AZ
Oil magnate. Husband of social reformer, Margaret Sanger.

TELLER, ISAAC Feb 7, 1799 Beacon, NY - Apr 30, 1868 Fishkill, NY
United States Representative-NY from 1854-1855. Elected to Congress due to the resignation of
Gilbert Dean. Nephew of Abraham H. Schenck, United States Representative-NY from 1815-1817.

FLORAL PARK CEMETERY
104 Burbank Avenue
Johnson City, NY 13790

JOHNSON, OTIS Nov 5, 1883 Fowler, IN - Nov 9, 1915 Johnson City, NY
Infielder for the New York Highlanders in 1911. Accidentally killed when he tripped and fell on his gun
during a foxhunt.

KILMER, JONAS M. Apr 11, 1843 Cobleskill, NY - May 13, 1912 Binghamton, NY
Purchased controlling interest in Dr. Kilmer & Company, the patent medicinal company founded by his
brother, S. Andral Kilmer, in 1892. President of the People's Bank of Binghamton from 1904-1912.
Father of Willis Sharpe Kilmer, President of Dr. Kilmer & Company.

KILMER, S. ANDRAL (Sylvester) Dec 19, 1840 Cobleskill, NY - Jan 14, 1924 Binghamton, NY
Homeopathic doctor. Founded Dr. Kilmer & Company. Invented the Dr. Kilmer's Swamp Root Kidney
Liver and Bladder Cure. Brother of Dr. Jonas M. Kilmer. Uncle of Willis Sharpe Kilmer, President of Dr.
Kilmer & Company.

KILMER, WILLIS SHARPE Oct 18, 1869 Brooklyn, NY - Jul 12, 1940 Windsor, NY
President of Dr. Kilmer & Company. Turned the patent medicinal company into a million dollar
business, following a national advertising campaign. Founded the *Binghamton Press* in 1904.
Successful race horse owner. Owned Exterminator, the 1918 Kentucky Derby winner, Sun Beau and
Genie, the son of Man O' War. Founded the Binghamton County Club. Son of Dr. Jonas M. Kilmer.
Nephew of Dr. S. Andral Kilmer, founder of Dr. Kilmer & Company.

LUMLEY, HARRY Sept 29, 1880 Forest City, PA - May 22, 1938 Binghamton, NY
Outfielder for the Brooklyn Superbas and Brooklyn Dodgers, from 1904-1910. Led the National
League in triples and home runs in 1904. Managed Brooklyn for one season in 1909.

FLORIDA CEMETERY
Bridge Street
Florida, NY 10921

SEWARD, SAMUEL SWEEZY Dec 5, 1768 Merits Island, NY - Aug 24, 1849 Florida, NY
New York State Assemblyman. Orange County Judge from 1815-1832. Father of William H. Seward,
United States Secretary of State from 1861-1869.

FLY CREEK CEMETERY
Cemetery Road
Fly Creek, NY 13337

BYARD, JAMES JACKSON Jan 15, 1872 Oaksville, NY - Jan 24, 1942 Albany, NY
Otsego County attorney. Lead defense attorney for Eva Coo, the notorious "Mallet Murderess",
executed for bludgeoning, Harry "Gimpy" Wright, with a mallet while her co-conspirator, Martha Clift,
ran him over in her car. Died in a car accident that left his wife, Lulu Grace Tarpenning, handicapped.

FOREST AVENUE CEMETERY
Forest Avenue
Angola, NY 14006

SCHWERT, PI (Pius Louis) Nov 22, 1892 Angola, NY - Mar 11, 1941 Washington D.C.
United States Representative-NY from 1939-1941. Died two months into his second term in Congress,
suffering a fatal heart attack, minutes after announcing his candidacy for mayor of Buffalo. Catcher for
the New York Yankees from 1914-1915, only former Yankee to have served in Congress.

FOREST HILL CEMETERY
40 High Street
Attica, NY 14011

ADAMS, PARMENIO Sept 9, 1776 Hartford, CT - Feb 19, 1832 Alexander, NY
United States Representative-NY from 1824-1827. Genesee County Sheriff from 1815-1816 and
1818-1821. War of 1812 United States Army Major.

BENEDICT, CHARLES BREWSTER Feb 7, 1828 Attica, NY - Oct 3, 1901 Attica, NY
United States Representative-NY from 1877-1879.

GODFREY (Schang), **HILDA M.** Feb 4, 1902 South Wales, NY - Jan 3, 1989 Attica, NY
Sister of Wally Schang, catcher for the Philadelphia Athletics, Boston Red Sox, New York Yankees, St. Louis Browns and Detroit Tigers from 1913-1931, winning four World Series championships, and Bobby Schang, catcher for the Pittsburgh Pirates, New York Giants and St. Louis Cardinals from 1914-1915 and 1927.

HOSKINS, GEORGE GILBERT Dec 24, 1824 Bennington, NY - Jun 12, 1893 Attica, NY
United States Representative-NY from 1873-1877. Lieutenant Governor of New York from 1880-1882. Speaker of the New York State Assembly in 1865.

JONES, HERBERT W. Jan 3, 1945 - Sept 13, 1971 Attica, NY
Industrial Account Clerk at Attica Correctional Facility. Civilian employee, killed in a prison riot at the prison, which left ten correctional officers and 33 prisoners dead.

KELLY, HUNTER JAMES Feb 14, 1997 Buffalo, NY - Aug 5, 2005 Buffalo, NY
Son of Jim Kelly, Hall of Fame quarterback for the Buffalo Bills from 1986-1996. Died from Krabbe disease, diagnosed shortly after his birth.

PUTNAM, HARVEY Jan 5, 1793 Brattleboro, VT - Sept 20, 1855 Attica, NY
United States Representative-NY from 1838-1839 and 1847-1851.

QUINN, WILLIAM E. Mar 25, 1943 - Sept 11, 1971 Attica, NY
New York State Correctional Officer. Stuck on the head and killed, the first day of a prison riot at Attica Correctional Facility, which left ten correctional officers and 33 prisoners dead.

STEVENS, ROBERT SMITH Mar 27, 1824 Attica, NY - Feb 23, 1893 Attica, NY
United States Representative-NY from 1883-1885.

URF, LORRIE J. 1957 Batavia, NY - May 13, 1976 Orlando, FL
Wyoming Central High School senior, planned and raised money with other students for their senior class trip to Florida, drowned in the student's motel swimming pool during the first night.

WATERMAN (Tharnish), **CATHARINE** 1851 Sheldon, NY - Jun 6, 1893 Attica, NY
Aunt of Al Tharnish, first person called "the World's Fastest Man", ran for Barnum & Bailey's Greatest Show on Earth, never losing a race from 1884-1891.

WERNER, ELON F. Sept 16, 1901 - Sept 13, 1971 Attica, NY
Industrial Account Clerk at Attica Correctional Facility. Civilian employee, killed in a prison riot at the prison, which left ten correctional officers and 33 prisoners dead. Uncle of New York State Correctional Officer, Ronald D. Werner, who also died in the prison uprising.

WERNER, RONALD D. Dec 3, 1936 - Sept 13, 1971 Attica, NY
New York State Correctional Officer. Held hostage, died from gunshot wounds, one of ten correctional officers killed in a prison riot at Attica Correctional Facility, which left 33 prisoners dead. Nephew of Elon F. Werner, a civilian employee at Attica, also killed in the prison uprising.

WHALEN, HARRISON W. Jul 9, 1934 - Oct 9, 1971 Attica, NY
New York State Correctional Officer. Held hostage, died from gunshot wounds, one month after a prison riot at Attica Correctional Facility, which left ten correctional officers and 33 prisoners dead.

FOREST HILL CEMETERY
East Main Street / Route 20
Fredonia, NY 14063

BALL, CLINTON MANROSS Jun 16, 1817 Wilmington, VT - Mar 27, 1893 Fredonia, NY
With **Cynthia E. Dale Ball** (Dec 30, 1823 Tionesta, PA - Apr 10, 1900 Fredonia, NY), the great-grandparents of Emmy Award-winning actress, Lucille Ball. 2nd great-grandparents of actress, Lucy Arnaz and actor, Desi Arnaz Jr.

DURRELL, GEORGE OSBORNE Apr 4, 1830 Newmarket, NH - Nov 2, 1922 Dunkirk, NY
Great-grandfather of Emmy Award-winning actress, Lucille Ball. 2nd great-grandfather of actress, Lucy Arnaz and actor, Desi Arnaz Jr.

EDWARDS, FRANCIS SMITH May 28, 1817 Windsor, NY - May 30, 1899 Dunkirk, NY
United States Representative-NY from 1855-1857.

HOOKER, WARREN BREWSTER Nov 24, 1856 Perrysburg, NY - Mar 5, 1920 Fredonia, NY
United States Representative-NY from 1891-1899.

PHILBRICK (Bastedo)**, MARGARET** Nov 13, 1875 Gowanda, NY - May 10, 1925 Alliance, OH
Great-grandmother of Ralph James "Bucky" Phillips, listed simultaneously on the FBI Ten Most Wanted Fugitives and the U.S. Marshal Service's Top 15 lists, for the shooting death of a New York State trooper and escape from prison in 2006, spending five months escaping justice.

RICHMOND (Smith)**, GRACE LOUISE** Mar 31, 1866 Pawtucket, RI - Nov 28, 1959 Fredonia, NY
Novelist. Wrote *Round the Corner in Gay Street*, *On Christmas Day in the Morning* and the *Red Pepper Burns* series of novels.

RISLEY, HANSON A. Jun 16, 1814 Fredonia, NY - Aug 23, 1893 West Newton, MA
Father of Olive Risley Seward, travel writer and adoptive daughter of William Henry Seward, United States Secretary of State under Abraham Lincoln and Andrew Johnson. His wife, Harriet Crosby Risley, died September 28, 1868.

SEWARD (Risley)**, OLIVE F.** Jul 15, 1844 Fredonia, NY - Nov 27, 1908 Washington D.C.
Travel writer and author. Adopted daughter and traveling companion of William Henry Seward, United States Secretary of State, under Abraham Lincoln and Andrew Johnson. Published *William H. Seward's Travels Around the World* in 1873.

WEBSTER (Moffett)**, ANNE** Jul 1, 1852 NY - Mar 25, 1950
Wife of publisher, Charles Luther Webster. Daughter of Pamela Ann Clemens Moffett, the older sister of author, Mark Twain. Mother of author, Jean Webster, who died giving birth to her first child, in 1916.

WEBSTER, CHARLES LUTHER Sept 24, 1851 Charlotte, NY - Apr 26, 1891 Fredonia, NY
Publisher. Business partner of Mark Twain, his wife's uncle, heading Twain's publishing company, Charles L. Webster and Co., from 1884 until a falling out between the two, in 1888. Published two volumes of President Ulysses S. Grant's memoirs, *Personal Memoirs of U.S. Grant*, in 1885 and 1886. Father of author, Jean Webster, who died giving birth to her first child, in 1916.

WEBSTER (McKinney)**, JEAN** (Alice Jane) Jul 24, 1876 Fredonia, NY - Jun 11, 1916 New York, NY
Author. Wrote *Daddy-Long-Legs* and *Dear Enemy*. Grandniece of author, Mark Twain. Daughter of publisher, Charles L. Webster. Died from complications of childbirth, one day after the birth of her first child, Jean McKinney.

FOREST HILL CEMETERY
2201 Oneida Street
Utica, NY 13501

ADAMS (Smith)**, SALLY** (Sarah) Nov 6, 1769 NY - Aug 3, 1828 Utica, NY
Wife of Charles Adams, the son of President John Adams and First Lady Abigail Adams. Sister of William Stephens Smith, United States Representative-NY from 1813-1815, and husband of her sister-in-law, Abigail Adams Smith. Sister-in-law of President John Quincy Adams.

BACON, EZEKIEL Sept 1, 1776 Boston, MA - Oct 18, 1870 Utica, NY
United States Representative-MA from 1807-1813. Oldest surviving member of Congress at the time of his death, and last from the administration of President James Madison. Father of William J. Bacon, United States Representative-NY from 1877-1879. Son of John Bacon, United States Representative-MA from 1801-1803.

BACON, WILLIAM JOHNSON Feb 18, 1803 Williamstown, MA - Jul 3, 1889 Utica, NY
United States Representative-NY from 1877-1879. Son of Ezekiel Bacon, United States Representative-MA from 1807-1813. Grandson of John Bacon, United States Representative-MA from 1801-1803.

BEARDSLEY, SAMUEL Feb 6, 1790 Hoosick, NY - May 6, 1860 Utica, NY
United States Representative-NY from 1831-1836 and 1843-1844. New York State Attorney General from 1836-1839. Associate Justice of the New York State Supreme Court from 1844-1847, and Chief Justice in 1847.

BREESE, ARTHUR Sept 11, 1770 Shrewsbury, NJ - Aug 13, 1825 New York, NY
Father of Sidney Morse, United States Senator-IL from 1843-1849. Uncle of Samuel F.B. Morse, inventor of the Morse Code.

BREESE, SAMUEL LIVINGSTON Aug 6, 1794 Utica, NY - Dec 17, 1870 Mount Airy, PA
United States Naval Rear Admiral. Brother of Sidney Morse, United States Senator-IL from 1843-1849. Cousin of Samuel F.B. Morse, inventor of the Morse Code.

BREITENSTEIN, ALONZO Nov 9, 1857 Utica, NY - Jun 19, 1932 Utica, NY
Pitched one game in his major league career, and lost, for the Philadelphia Quakers in 1883.

BUTTERFIELD, JOHN Nov 18, 1801 Berne, NY - Nov 14, 1869 Utica, NY
Founded the Overland Mail Company, the largest stagecoach company at the time. Personally carried mail on the first leg of the first official mail route, from St. Louis to San Francisco, in 1857. Mayor of Utica from 1865-1869. Formed the American Express Company, joining forces with Henry Wells and William Fargo. Father of Major General Daniel A. Butterfield, composer of "Taps", the music played at military funerals.

COCHRAN (Schuyler), **GERTRUDE** Aug 18, 1724 Albany, NY - Mar 1813 Palatine, NY
Only sister of Revolutionary War Continental Army Major General, Philip Schuyler. Mother of James Cochran, United States Representative-NY from 1797-1799. Wife of Revolutionary War Continental Army Surgeon, John Cochran.

COCHRAN, JOHN 1730 - Apr 6, 1807 Palatine, NY
Revolutionary War Continental Army Surgeon General, appointed by General George Washington. Director General of the Military Hospitals of the United States Army. Husband of Gertrude Schuyler Cochran, the wife of Revolutionary War Continental Army Major General, Philip Schuyler. Father of James Cochran, United States Representative-NY from 1797-1799.

CONKLING, ALFRED Oct 12, 1789 Amagansett, NY - Feb 5, 1874 Utica, NY
United States Representative-NY from 1821-1823. United States Minister to Mexico from 1852-1853. Father of Roscoe Conkling, United States Senator-NY from 1867 and 1869-1881,

and Frederick A. Conkling, United States Representative-NY from 1861-1863. Uncle of Judge, Alfred C. Conkling.

CONKLING, ROSCOE Oct 3, 1829 Albany, NY - Apr 18, 1888 New York, NY
United States Senator-NY in 1867 and 1869-1881. United States Representative-NY from 1859-1863 and 1865-1867. Mayor of Utica from 1858-1859. Son of Alfred Conklin, United States Representative-NY from 1821-1823. Brother of Frederick A. Conkling, United States Representative from 1861-1863. Cousin of Alfred C. Conkling, Associate Justice of the New York State Court of Appeals.

COXE, ALFRED CONKLING May 20, 1847 Auburn, NY - Apr 15, 1923 Utica, NY
Associate Justice of the New York State Court of Appeals from 1902-1917. Nephew of Alfred Conkling, United States Representative-NY from 1821-1823. Cousin of Roscoe Conkling, United States Senator-NY in 1867 and 1869-1881.

DOOLITTLE (Johnson), **MARY ADAMS** Apr 1, 1854 Washington D.C. - Dec 26, 1920 Utica, NY
Great-granddaughter of President John Quincy Adams and First Lady Louisa Adams. 2nd great-granddaughter of President John Adams and First Lady Abigail Adams. Daughter-in-law of Charles Hutchins Doolittle, Associate Justice of the New York State Supreme Court from 1869-1874.

FAXTON, THEODORE S. Jan 10, 1784 Conway, MA - Nov 30, 1881 Utica, NY
Financed Samuel F.B. Morse, inventor of the telegraph, and the Jason Parker & Company stagecoach line. Mayor of Utica in 1864. Founded and endowed Faxton Hospital in Utica.

HIND, ARTHUR Feb 4, 1856 Bradford, England - Mar 1, 1933 Palm Beach, FL
Philatelist. Rare stamp collector. Called the "Ferrary of America." Purchased the 1856 British Guiana 1c magenta for a world-record price.

HOGGATT, WILFORD BACON Sept 11, 1865 Paoli, IN - Feb 26, 1938 Bronx, NY
Governor of the Territory of Alaska from 1906-1909. Responsible for relocating Alaska's government to Juneau. Buried in the family plot of his second wife, Clarissa Eames Millard.

HOLROYD, LINCOLN May 9, 1881 Bradford, England - Feb 13, 1961 Utica, NY
Musician and band director. Cornet soloist. Performed with the John Philip Sousa Band

HUBBARD, THOMAS HILL Dec 5, 1781 New Haven, CT - May 21, 1857 Utica, NY
United States Representative-NY from 1817-1819 and 1821-1823. Co-founded Hamilton College in Clinton.

HUNT, WARD Jun 14, 1810 Utica, NY - Mar 24, 1886 Washington D.C.
Associate Justice of the United States Supreme Court from 1873-1878, appointed by President Ulysses S. Grant. Associate Justice of the New York State Circuit Court, presided over the trial of

Susan B. Anthony in 1873, fined her $100 when the jury found her guilty of knowingly voting without the lawful right to vote.

JOHNSON (Adams), **ABIGAIL LOUISA SMITH** Sept 8, 1798 New York, NY - Jul 4, 1836 Newark, NJ
Granddaughter of President John Adams and First Lady Abigail Adams. Daughter of Charles Adams and Sally Smith Adams. Wife of author, Alexander Bryan Johnson. Niece of President John Quincy Adams and William Stephens Smith, United States Representative-NY from 1813-1815.

JOHNSON, ALEXANDER BRYAN May 29, 1786 Gosport, England - Sept 9, 1867 Utica, NY
Author. Wrote several books on philosophy. Husband of Abigail Adams Johnson, the granddaughter of President John Adams and First Lady Abigail Adams. Father of William Clarkson Johnson, who married Mary Adams Johnson, the granddaughter of President John Quincy Adams and First Lady Louisa Adams, and the great-granddaughter of President John Adams and First Lady Abigail Adams.

JOHNSON (Adams), **MARY LOUISA** Dec 2, 1838 NY - Jul 16, 1859 Utica, NY
Granddaughter of President John Quincy Adams and First Lady Louisa Adams. Great-granddaughter of President John Adams and First Lady Abigail Adams. Daughter of John Adams II. Wife of William Clarkson Johnson, who was the son of writer, Alexander Bryan Johnson and Abigail Adams Johnson, her maternal aunt.

KIRKLAND, JOSEPH Jan 18, 1770 Lisbon, CT - Jan 26, 1844 Utica, NY
United States Representative-NY from 1821-1823. Mayor of Utica from 1832-1836.

LANSING, BARENT BLEECKER Jan 17, 1793 Argyle, NY - Dec 3, 1853 Brooklyn ,NY
Oneida County banker. Father of Manette Antill Lansing, the wife of Charles Walker Morse, the oldest son of Samuel F.B. Morse, inventor of the Morse Code. Son of Gerrit G. Lansing, Revolutionary War Continental Army Colonel. Nephew of John Lansing, Delegate to the Continental Congress from New York in 1785.

LEDLIE, JAMES HEWITT Apr 14, 1832 Utica, NY - Aug 15, 1882 Utica, NY
Civil War Union Army Brigadier General. Considered one of the worst generals in United States history, called 'inefficient' in the memoirs of Civil War Union Army General, Ulysses S. Grant.

MATTESON, ORSAMUS BENAJAH Aug 28, 1805 Verona, NY - Dec 22, 1889 Utica, NY
United States Representative-NY from 1849-1851 and 1853-1859.

MERKENT (Stevens), **VIOLA MAUDE** Jun 25, 1888 Boston, MA - Jul 1, 1977 Utica, NY
Sister of Academy Award-nominated actress, Barbara Stanwyck.

MILLER, RUTGER BLEECKER Jul 28, 1805 Lowville, NY - Nov 12, 1877 Utica, NY
United States Representative-NY from 1836-1837. Elected to Congress due to the resignation of
Samuel Beardsley. Son of Morris Smith Miller, United States Representative-NY from 1813-1815.

MILLS, ARTHUR GRANT Mar 2, 1903 Utica, NY - Jul 23, 1975 Utica, NY
Pitched for the Boston Braves from 1927-1928. Teammate of Hall of Famers, Rogers Hornsby, George
Sisler and Dave Bancroft. First base coach for the Detroit Tigers from 1944-1949. Son of Willie Mills,
pitcher for the New York Giants in 1901.

RICHARDSON, HARDY (Abram Harding) Apr 21, 1855 Clarksboro, NJ - Jan 14, 1931 Utica, NY
Played for the Buffalo Bisons, Detroit Wolverines, Boston Beaneaters, Washington Senators and
New York Giants from 1879-1892. Collected 1,688 hits in his major league career. Led the National
League in hits and home runs in 1886 and RBI in 1890.

ROBERTS, ELLIS HENRY Sept 30, 1827 Utica, NY - Jan 8, 1918 Utica, NY
United States Representative-NY from 1871-1875. Editor of the *Utica Morning Herald* from
1851-1889. Treasurer of the United States from 1897-1905.

SAVAGE, JOHN Feb 22, 1779 Salem, NY - Oct 19, 1863 Utica, NY
United States Representative-NY from 1815-1819. Chief Justice of the New York State Supreme Court
from 1823-1836.

SCHLITZER, BIFF (Victor J.) Dec 4, 1884 Rochester, NY - Jan 4, 1948 Wellesley Hills, MA
Pitched for the Philadelphia Athletics and Boston Red Sox from 1908-1909. Played for Hall of Fame
manager, Connie Mack and with Hall of Famers, Eddie Collins, Home Run Baker, Eddie Plank, Chief
Bender, Smokey Joe Wood, Tris Speaker, Harry Hooper and Jack Chesbro and with Shoeless Joe
Jackson in his brief playing career. Played with the Buffalo Buffeds in the short-lived Federal League
in 1914.

SEYMOUR, HORATIO May 31, 1810 Pompey, NY - Feb 12, 1886 Deerfield, NY
Governor of New York from 1853-1855 and 1863-1865. Known as the "Great Decliner." Defeated in
the New York State gubernatorial election in 1850, 1854 and 1864. Candidate for the United States
presidency in 1868. Mayor of Utica in 1843. Speaker of the New York State Assembly in 1845.
Brother-in-law of Roscoe Conkling, United States Senator-NY in 1867 and 1869-1881.

SHERMAN (Babcock), **CARRIE** Nov 16, 1856 Utica, NY - Oct 6, 1931 Utica, NY
Second Lady of the United States from 1909-1912. Wife of Vice-President James Schoolcraft
Sherman.

SHERMAN, JAMES SCHOOLCRAFT Oct 24, 1855 Utica, NY - Oct 30, 1912 Utica, NY
27th Vice-President of the United States, from 1909-1912. Served under President William H. Taft.

United States Representative-NY from 1887-1891 and 1893-1909. Mayor of Utica from 1884-1886. Seventh, and most recent, vice-president to die in office.

SHERMAN, RICHARD UPDIKE Jun 26, 1819 Vernon, NY - Feb 21, 1895 New Hartford, NY
New York State Assemblyman from 1857 and 1875-1876. Newspaper publisher. Father of James Schoolcraft Sherman, Vice-President of the United States from 1909-1912.

STROH, GEORGE J. May 1, 1881 Syracuse, NY - Dec 4, 1955 Syracuse, NY
Owned and operated the Stroh Clothing Company in Syracuse. Played for the Syracuse Stars in the Eastern League. Scouted for the Boston Red Sox for several years.

TALCOTT, CHARLES ANDREW Jun 10, 1857 Oswego, NY - Feb 27, 1920 Utica, NY
United States Representative-NY from 1911-1914. Mayor of Utica from 1902-1906.

TOWNSEND, EDWARD WATERMAN Feb 10, 1855 Cleveland, OH - Mar 15, 1942 New York, NY
United States Representative-NJ from 1911-1915. Short story writer. Published *Chimmie Fadden, Major Max and Other Stories* in 1895.

WALKER, BENJAMIN 1753 London, England - Jan 13, 1818 Utica, NY
United States Representative-NY from 1801-1803. Revolutionary War aide-de-camp to General George Washington and General Baron von Steuben. Originally buried in the Old Village Burying Ground on Water Street in Utica, reburied in Forest Hill Cemetery, June 17, 1875.

WILLIAMS, NATHAN Dec 19, 1773 Williamstown, MA - Sept 25, 1835 Geneva, NY
United States Representative-NY from 1805-1807. Originally buried in the Old Village Burying Ground on Water Street in Utica.

FOREST LAWN CEMETERY
1411 Delaware Avenue
Buffalo, NY 14209

ALEXANDER, DE ALVA STANWOOD Jul 17, 1846 Richmond, ME - Jan 30, 1925 Buffalo, NY
United States Representative-NY from 1897-1911. Lost reelection to Charles Bennett Smith by one vote in 1910. Published the *Political History of the United States* in 1923.

ALLEN (Cleveland)**, MARGARET** Jan 19, 1801 Norwich, CT - Sept 13, 1880 Buffalo, NY
Aunt of President Grover Cleveland and Rose Elizabeth "Libbie" Cleveland, First Lady from 1885-1886, during Cleveland's first presidency.

BASS, LYMON KIDDER Nov 13, 1836 Alden, NY - May 11, 1889 New York, NY
United States Representative-NY from 1873-1877. Defeated Grover Cleveland for district attorney of Erie County in 1865.

BELL, LARRY (Lawrence Dale) Apr 5, 1894 Mentone, IN - Oct 20, 1956 Buffalo, NY
Founded Bell Aircraft Corporation in 1935. Shared the 1947 Collier Trophy with pilot, Chuck Yeager, and NASA researcher, John Stack, for their role in the Bell X-1's first supersonic flight, which Yeager became the first pilot to exceed the speed of sound.

BERLIN (Goetz)**, DOROTHY** Feb 5, 1892 Buffalo, NY - Jul 17, 1912 New York, NY
Wife of composer, Irving Berlin. Married in February 1912, traveled to Havana for their honeymoon where an outbreak of typhoid occurred, died six months later. Sister of actor and composer, E. Ray Goetz.

BETHUNE (Blanchard)**, LOUISE** (Jennie) Jul 21, 1856 Waterloo, NY - Dec 18, 1913 Buffalo, NY
First American woman to work as a professional architect. Designed the Hotel Lafayette in Buffalo.

BISSELL, WILSON SHANNON Dec 31, 1847 New London, NY - Oct 6, 1903 Buffalo, NY
United States Postmaster General from 1893-1895. Close friend of President Grover Cleveland, best man for his wedding to First Lady Frances Folsom Cleveland in 1886. Campaign manager for Grover Cleveland.

BLOCHER, NELSON W. Feb 1, 1847 Buffalo, NY - Jan 24, 1884 Buffalo, NY
Notable for his tombstone, marble statues of him lying in his deathbed, clutching a bible left behind by the family maid, and his love interest, Katherine Sullivan, standing over him are his parents, **John Blocher** (Jul 22, 1825 Scipio, NY - Jun 30, 1911 Buffalo, NY) and **Elizabeth Neff Blocher** (Feb 1826 - Mar 31, 1904 Buffalo, NY), all encased in glass.

BOASBERG, AL (Albert) Dec 5, 1891 Buffalo, NY - Jun 18, 1937 Los Angeles, CA
Vaudeville, radio and film comedy writer and director. Help create the standup comedy format, teaming with Jack Benny on vaudeville. Wrote the Marx Brothers' films, *A Day at the Races* and *A Night at the Opera* and Buster Keaton's *The General*. The day before he died, scripted lines for the episode of the *Jack Benny Radio Show*, introducing the popular "Rochester" character, played by Eddie Anderson. Uncle of James W. Michaels, editor of *Forbes Magazine* from 1961-1999.

BUCHANAN, WILLIAM INSCO Sept 10, 1853 Covington, OH - Oct 17, 1909 London, England
United States Minister to Argentina from 1894-1899. United States Minister to Panama from 1903-1904. Director General of the Pan American Exposition in Buffalo in 1901, where President William McKinley was shot by Leon Czolgosz.

BUNTING, THOMAS LATHROP Apr 24, 1844 Eden, NY - Dec 27, 1898 Buffalo, NY
United States Representative-NY from 1891-1893.

BUTLER, JOHN CORNELIUS Jul 2, 1887 Buffalo, NY - Aug 13, 1953 Buffalo, NY
United States Representative-NY from 1941-1949 and 1951-1953.

CARLTON (Winslow)**, JOSEPHINE WOODRUFF** Apr 23, 1870 Buffalo, NY - 1929
Mother of Clifford Warren-Smith Jr., the husband of stage and film actress, Claire Luce.

CARNEVALE, DAN (Daniel J.) Feb 8, 1918 Buffalo, NY - Dec 29, 2005 Tonawanda, NY
Career minor league baseball player. Managed the International League's Buffalo Bisons in 1955,
including future Hall of Famer and United States Senator, Jim Bunning. Coach for the Kansas City
Royals in 1970. Cousin of baseball infielder, Sippy Sisti.

CARRIER, WILLIS HAVILAND Nov 26, 1876 Angola, NY - Oct 9, 1950 New York, NY
Engineer and inventor. Called the "father of the air conditioning industry." Founded the Carrier
Engineering Corporation in 1915. Carrier moved its company to Syracuse in the 1930s, becoming one
of Central New York's largest employers. 3rd great-grandson of Martha Allen Carrier, tried, convicted
and hanged, following the Salem Witch Trials in 1692.

CARY, GEORGE 1859 Buffalo, NY - May 5, 1945 Buffalo, NY
Architect. Designed the Ethnology Building and the New York State Pavilion for the Pan-American
Exposition in Buffalo, 1901. Grandson of Trumbull Cary, New York State Senator from 1831-1834.
Uncle of sculptor and polo player, Charles C. Rumsey, the husband of Mary Harriman Rumsey.

CARY, SEWARD 1862 Buffalo, NY - 1948 Buffalo, NY
Sculptor. Brother of architect, George Cary. Grandson of Trumbull Cary, New York State Senator from
1831-1834. Uncle of sculptor and polo player, Charles C. Rumsey, the husband of Mary Harriman
Rumsey.

CASS, WILLIAM ANDREW May 11, 1906 Buffalo, NY - Jun 13, 1934 Sullivan County, NY
Killed in the crash of an American Airlines, Curtiss Condor biplane, from Newark to Chicago, with
scheduled stops at Syracuse and Buffalo, killing seven. The burned wreckage was found on Last
Chance Mountain, near Mongaup Pond, in the Catskill Mountains. Two men, the first on the scene,
were charged with stealing money from his remains and sentenced to six months in prison. Husband
of Frances Fairbairn Cass, who remarried in 1949 to baseball Hall of Famer, Ty Cobb.

CHISHOLM (St. Hill)**, SHIRLEY** Nov 30, 1924 New York, NY - Jan 1, 2005 Ormond Beach, FL
United States Representative-NY from 1969-1983. First African-American woman elected to the
United States Congress. First African-American major-party candidate, and first woman in the
Democratic Party, to run for President of the United States, in 1972. Posthumously awarded the

Presidential Medal of Freedom in 2015.

CHRISTIAN, ARLESTER Jun 13, 1943 Buffalo, NY - Mar 13, 1971 Phoenix, AZ
R&B singer/musician nicknamed "Dyke." Lead singer and bassist of the funk band, Dyke & the Blazers. Recorded "Funky Broadway" in 1966. Shot to death on a Phoenix street by Clarence Daniels, who claimed self-defense and was not charged.

CLARK, STALEY NICHOLS May 24, 1794 MD - Oct 14, 1860 Ellicottville, NY
United States Representative-NY from 1841-1843. Brother of Archibald S. Clark, United States Representative-NY from 1816-1817. Originally buried in Jefferson Street Cemetery in Ellicottville.

CLEVELAND, WILLIAM Dec 20, 1769 Norwich, CT - Aug 18, 1837 Buffalo, NY
With **Margaret Falley Cleveland** (Nov 25, 1766 Westfield, MA – Aug 10, 1850 Buffalo, NY), the grandparents of President Grover Cleveland and Rose Elizabeth "Libbie" Cleveland, First Lady from 1885-1886, during Cleveland's first presidency.

COOK, FREDERICK ALBERT Jun 10, 1865 Callicoon, NY - Aug 5, 1940 New Rochelle, NY
Explorer and physician. Claimed to reach the North Pole on April 21, 1908, one year before Admiral Robert E. Peary, who is widely credited as the first to achieve the feat. His claim as the first to reach the summit of Mount Denali in 1906 was also disputed. Discovered the Meighan Island in 1908. Surgeon on Peary's 1891-1892 Arctic Expedition. Served seven years in prison for fraud, pardoned by President Franklin D. Roosevelt in 1940.

CORNELL, PETER CORTELYOU Jul 28, 1865 Buffalo, NY - 1948 Buffalo, NY
With **Alice Gardner Plimpton Cornell** (1870 - 1915), the parents of actress, Katharine Cornell.

CUMMINGS, C. DEFOREST (Charles) Jul 15, 1880 Springville, NY - Jun 25, 1957 Buffalo, NY
Syracuse University head football coach from 1911-1912. Played for Syracuse from 1898-1901.

DANIELS, CHARLES Mar 24, 1825 New York, NY - Dec 20, 1897 Buffalo, NY
United States Representative-NY from 1893-1897. Associate Justice of the New York State Supreme Court from 1863-1891.

DAY (Hodgeman)**, LUCILLE** Apr 11, 1915 Minneapolis, MN - Aug 15, 2010 Springville, NY
Hollywood dancer and choreographer. Worked for 20th Century Fox on more than twenty films including, *The Wizard of Oz*. Wife of Jack Yellen, composer of "Happy Days Are Here Again" and "Ain't She Sweet."

DENMAN (Welch)**, M. DOLORES** (Mary) Feb 16, 1931 Buffalo, NY - Jan 17, 2000 Naples, FL
Associate Justice of the Appellate Division of the New York State Supreme Court, appointed by Governor Hugh Carey, in 1977. First woman to serve as presiding justice, appointed by Governor

Mario Cuomo, in 1991. Heard the appeal of Cynthia Pugh, convicted of murdering Syracuse millionaire businessman, James Pipines, in 1984, upholding the conviction.

DIFRANCO, DANTE AMERICO Oct 3, 1921 Erie, PA - Jul 24, 2004 Buffalo, NY
Father of singer, songwriter and musician, Ani DiFranco.

DORSHEIMER, WILLIAM Feb 5, 1832 Lyons, NY - Mar 26, 1888 Savannah. GA
United States Representative-NY from 1883-1885. Lieutenant Governor of New York from 1875-1879, under Samuel J. Tilden and Lucius Robinson.

EATON, LEWIS Feb 17, 1790 Duanesburg, NY - Aug 22, 1857 Buffalo, NY
United States Representative-NY from 1823-1825.

ESENWEIN, AUGUST C. Nov 7, 1856 Esenwein-Virnsberg, Germany - Jun 29, 1926 Buffalo, NY
Architect. Partner in the firm, Esenwein & Johnson in Buffalo, with James A. Johnson. Designed the Public Library, the General Electric Building, the Niagara Mohawk Building, Lafayette High School, and the Temple of Music for the Pan-American Exposition, the building where President William McKinley was shot, in 1901.

ESPERSEN (Webb)**, DOROTHY H.** Jan 28, 1917 Buffalo, NY - Aug 21, 2009 Amherst, NY
Sister of Janet Webb Rich, the wife of Robert E. Rich, founder of Rich Products in Buffalo in 1945, inventor of the first frozen, non-dairy whipped topping, and namesake of Rich Stadium in Orchard Park, prior to its name change to Ralph Wilson Stadium in 1998.

FAIRCLOTH, WILLIAM WALLACE 1855 Fredonia, NY - Mar 15, 1934 Buffalo, NY
Uncle of Jean Marie Faircloth MacArthur, the wife of United States Army Five-Star General, Douglas MacArthur. She died January 22, 2000, age 101, in New York City, buried next to her husband in the rotunda of the MacArthur Memorial, Norfolk, VA.

FARGO, WILLIAM GEORGE May 20, 1818 Pompey, NY - Aug 3, 1981 Buffalo, NY
Mayor of Buffalo from 1862-1865. Founded the American Express Company and Wells Fargo & Company, with Henry Wells.

FELLOWS, ABRAHAM VAN BENSCHOTEN 1788 NY - Mar 24, 1851 Buffalo, NY
With **Harriet Chichester Fellows** (1793 - Mar 14, 1869 Buffalo, NY), the great-grandparents of Helen Lamar Grossman, the wife of Edwin Booth Grossman, the grandson of actor, Edwin Booth. They are buried in Mount Auburn Cemetery, Cambridge.

FIEDLER, LESLIE Mar 8, 1917 Newark, NJ - Jan 29, 2003 Buffalo, NY
Literary critic. Published *Come Back to the Raft Ag'in, Huck Honey!* in 1948 and *Love and Death in the American Novel* in 1960.

FILLMORE (Powers), **ABIGAIL** Mar 13, 1798 Stillwater, NY - Mar 30, 1853 Washington D.C.
First Lady of the United States from 1850-1853. Wife of President Millard Fillmore. Caught a cold at the inaugural ceremony for President Franklin Pierce, developed pneumonia, died 26 days later, the shortest post-presidential life of any First Lady.

FILLMORE (Carmichael)**, CAROLINE** Oct 21, 1813 Morristown, NJ - Aug 11, 1881 Buffalo, NY
Wife of President Millard Fillmore, marrying five years after he left office. Widow of Ezekiel C. McIntosh, President of the Schenectady and Troy Railroad.

FILLMORE, MARY ABIGAIL Mar 27, 1832 Buffalo, NY - Jul 26, 1854 East Aurora, NY
Daughter of President Millard Fillmore and First Lady Abigail Fillmore.

FILLMORE, MILLARD Jan 7, 1800 Moravia, NY - Mar 8, 1874 Buffalo, NY
13th president of the United States from 1850-1853. Vice-President of the United States from 1849-1850. Ascended to the presidency upon the death of Zachary Taylor. United States Representative-NY from 1833-1835 and 1837-1843. First president to spend the night in Syracuse. Opposed President Abraham Lincoln during the Civil War. The Fillmore Glen State Park in Moravia houses a replica of his birthplace, the Millard Fillmore Log Cabin, located four miles from the actual site, since demolished.

FILLMORE, MILLARD POWERS Apr 26, 1828 East Aurora, NY - Nov 15, 1889 Buffalo, NY
Son of President Millard Fillmore and First Lady Abigail Fillmore. Private secretary to his father during his presidency.

FUQUA, CHARLIE (Charles G.) Oct 20, 1910 New Haven, CT - Dec 21, 1971 New Haven, CT
Founding member of the doo-wop group, the Ink Spots. Elected to the Rock and Roll Hall of Fame in 1999. Uncle of R&B singer, songwriter and record executive, Harvey Fuqua.

GANSON, JOHN Jan 1, 1818 LeRoy, NY - Jan 28, 1874 Buffalo, NY
United States Representative-NY from 1863-1865.

GLADDEN (Sims), **BETTY** (Mabel) 1918 Cleveland, OH - Sept 21, 1991 Buffalo, NY
Mother of Grammy Award-winning singer/songwriter, Rick James.

GOETZ, E. RAY (Edward) Jun 12, 1886 Buffalo, NY - Jun 12, 1954 Greenwich, CT
Actor, producer and lyricist. Appeared in the films, *Somebody Loves Me*, *The Greatest Show on Earth* and *For Me and My Gal*. Wrote the songs, "For Me and My Gal" and " Toddling the Todalo." Founding member and director of ASCAP, from 1914-1917. Married to actress, Irene Bordoni, from 1918-1929. Former brother-in-law of composer, Irving Berlin.

GOODYEAR, ANSON CONGER Jun 20, 1877 Buffalo, NY - Apr 24, 1964 Old Westbury, NY
Founder and first President of the Museum of Modern Art in New York City. Son of railroad and lumber magnate, Charles W. Goodyear.

GOODYEAR, CHARLES WATERHOUSE Oct 15, 1846 Cortland, NY - Apr 16, 1911 Buffalo, NY
Co-founded the Great Southern Lumber Company, the Goodyear Lumber Company, the Buffalo and Susquehanna Railroad, the Buffalo & Susquehanna Coal and Coke Company, and the New Orleans Great Northern Railroad Company, with his brother, Frank Goodyear. Father of Anson C. Goodyear, founder and first President of the Museum of Modern Art in New York City.

GREEN (Rohlfs)**, ANNA KATHARINE** Nov 11, 1846 Brooklyn, NY - Apr 11, 1935 Buffalo, NY
Crime novelist. Called "the mother of the detective novel." Published *The Leavenworth Case* in 1878. Wife of furniture maker, Charles Rohlfs. Mother of aviator, Roland Rohlfs.

HALL, LAWRENCE WASHINGTON 1819 OH - Jan 18, 1863 Bucyrus, OH
United States Representative-OH from 1857-1859. Imprisoned during the Civil War for disloyalty to the Union, died less than a year later.

HALL, NATHAN KELSEY Mar 28, 1810 Marcellus, NY - Mar 3, 1874 Buffalo, NY
United States Representative-NY from 1847-1849. United States Post Master General from 1850-1852, appointed by President Millard Fillmore.

HARTER, JOHN FRANCIS Sept 1, 1897 Perry, NY - Dec 20, 1947 Eggertsville, NY
United States Representative-NY from 1939-1941.

HAVEN, SOLOMON GEORGE Nov 17, 1810 Guilford, NY - Dec 24, 1861 Buffalo, NY
United States Representative-NY from 1851-1857. Mayor of Buffalo from 1846-1847.

HAZEL, JOHN RAYMOND Oct 18, 1860 Buffalo, NY - Oct 31, 1951 Buffalo, NY
Associate Justice of the United States District Court of Western New York, from 1900-1931. Administered the oath of office to Theodore Roosevelt as President of the United States, who did not use a bible, in the home of Ansley Wilcox in Buffalo, September 14, 1901, following the assassination of President William McKinley at the Pan-American Exposition. Presided over the Wright Brothers lawsuit against Glenn Curtiss and the Henning-Curtiss Company, for patent infringement, from 1910-1913, ruling in favor the Wright Brothers.

HEINTZELMAN, SAMUEL PETER Sept 30, 1805 Manheim, PA - May 1, 1880 Washington D.C.
United States Army General. Civil War and Mexican-American War veteran. Led the Yuma Expedition, establishing Fort Yuma in 1852. First President of the Sonora Exploring and Mining Company in Arizona. Grandfather of Major General Stuart Heintzelman, highly decorated World War I officer.

HENGERER, WILLIAM GOTTLIEB Mar 2, 1839 Württemberg, Germany - Dec 3, 1905 Buffalo, NY
Founded the department store chain, Hengerer's, in Buffalo, in 1876.

HINSON, SARAH M. Feb 25, 1841 Buffalo, NY - Mar 20, 1886 Buffalo, NY
Buffalo educator. Founded Flag Day, officially becoming a holiday under President Woodrow Wilson in 1916.

HORTON (Pratt)**, KATHARINE LORENZ** 1848 - Aug 28, 1931 Buffalo, NY
President of the City Federation of Women's Clubs in Buffalo, from 1901-1930.

HOWARD, KATHLEEN Jul 27, 1884 Clifton, ON, Canada - Apr 15, 1956 Hollywood, CA
Opera singer and actress. Mezzo soprano, performed at the Metropolitan Opera House in New York City. Appeared in the W.C. Fields' films, *It's a Gift*, *Man on the Flying Trapeze* and *You're Telling Me!* Published her autobiography, *Confessions of an Opera Singer*, in 1918.

HUBBARD, SILAS D. May 9, 1821 Mayville, NY - May 18, 1917 Buffalo, NY
With **Juliana Frances Read Hubbard** (Nov 16, 1829 New York, NY - Dec 28, 1924 Buffalo, NY), the parents of author, Elbert Green Hubbard, publisher of the Roycroft Press, who died with his wife, author, Alice Moore Hubbard, on the *Lusitania*, torpedoed and sunk off the coast of Ireland by a German U-boat, May 7, 1915, en route to interview Kaiser Wilhelm II of Germany during World War I. Their bodies were not recovered.

HUGHES, ISAIAH HARRIS Dec 25, 1813 Essex, England - May 24, 1891 Buffalo, NY
Magician. Commonly known as "Fakir of Ava", billed himself as "The Fakir of Ava, Chief of Staff of Conjurors to His Sublime Greatness the Nanka of Aristaphae." Teacher of Harry Keller, the "Dean of American Magicians" in the 19th Century.

HUMPHREY, JAMES MORGAN Sept 21, 1819 Holland, NY - Feb 9, 1899 Buffalo, NY
United States Representative-NY from 1865-1869.

JAMES (Johnson)**, RICK** (James A.) Feb 1, 1948 Buffalo, NY - Aug 6, 2004 Los Angeles, CA
R&B singer/songwriter. Grammy Award-winner. Wrote and recorded the 1980s hits "The Freak", "Give It to Me Baby" and "You and I." Wrote and produced the Eddie Murphy hit, "Party All the Time", in 1981. Invited to a party at Roman Polanski's house by hairstylist, Jay Sebring, in August 1969, the night of the Manson Family murders, missing due to a hangover. Godfather of Marvin Gaye's daughter, Nona Gaye.

KENT, EDWARD AUSTIN Feb 19, 1854 Bangor, ME - Apr 15, 1912 Atlantic Ocean
Architect. Junior partner in the Syracuse firm, Silsbee and Kent, with Joseph Lyman Silsbee. Drowned in the sinking of *Titanic*. His body was recovered by the *CS Mackay-Bennett*.

KLEINHANS, EDWARD LIVINGSTON 1864 Pontiac, MI - Feb 2, 1934 Buffalo, NY
Co-founded Kleinhans Clothing Store in Buffalo, with his brother, Horace Kleinhans, in 1893.
Namesake of Kleinhans Music Hall in Buffalo, opened in 1940.

KNOX, NORTHRUP RAND Dec 24, 1928 Buffalo, NY - Jul 23, 1998 East Aurora, NY
Co-founded and owned the Buffalo Sabres, with his brother, Seymour H. Knox III, from 1970-1998.
Grandson of businessman, Seymour H. Knox I, co-owner of the F.W. Woolworth Company.

KNOX, SEYMOUR HORACE Apr 11, 1861 Russell, NY - May 17, 1915 Buffalo, NY
Businessman. Founded S.H. Knox & Company in Buffalo in 1888. Merged his stores with those of his
first cousins, Frank Winfield Woolworth and Charles Woolworth, to form the F.W. Woolworth Company.
Grandfather of Seymour H. Knox III and Northrup R. Knox, co-founders of the Buffalo Sabres, in 1970.

KNOX, SEYMOUR HORACE Sept 1, 1898 Buffalo, NY - Sept 27, 1990 Buffalo, NY
Banker, philanthropist and art patron. First chairman of the New York State Council on the Arts.
Subject of an Andy Warhol painting, "Portrait of Seymour H. Knox" in 1985. Awarded the National
Medal of Arts by President Ronald Reagan in 1986. Father of Seymour H. Knox III and Northrup R.
Knox, co-founders of the Buffalo Sabres, in 1970. Son of businessman, Seymour H. Knox I, co-owner
of the F.W. Woolworth Company.

KNOX, SEYMOUR HORACE Mar 9, 1926 Buffalo, NY - May 27, 1996 Buffalo, NY
Principal owner of the Buffalo Sabres from 1970-1996, co-founded with his brother, Northrup R. Knox
III. Named the Hockey News Executive of the Year in 1975. Inducted into the Hockey Hall of Fame in
1993. Grandson of businessman, Seymour H. Knox I, co-owner of the F.W. Woolworth Company.

KUEHN, JOHANN CARL GOTTHOLD Jan 13, 1857 South Euclid, OH - Oct 9, 1940 Buffalo, NY
With **Sophia Meyer Kuehn** (1863 - Dec 16, 1947 Buffalo, NY), the grandparents of "Buffalo Bob" Smith,
host and creator of *The Hoody Doody Show* from 1947-1960.

KURTZ, PAUL Dec 21, 1925 Newark, NJ - Oct 20, 2012 Amherst, NY
Humorist and educator. Called the "father of secular humourism." Founded the publishing house,
Prometheus Books, in 1969.

LARKIN (Hubbard)**, FRANCES HANNAH** Jun 10, 1853 Buffalo, NY - Apr 15, 1922 Buffalo, NY
Wife of John D. Larkin, founder of the Larkin Soap Company. Sister of author, Elbert Hubbard,
publisher of the Roycroft Press, who died with his wife, author, Alice Moore Hubbard, on the *Lusitania*,
torpedoed and sunk off the coast of Ireland by a German U-boat, May 7, 1915, en route to interview
Kaiser Wilhelm II of Germany during World War I. Their bodies were not recovered.

LARKIN, JOHN DURRANT Sept 29, 1845 Buffalo, NY - Feb 15, 1926 Buffalo, NY
Founded the Larkin Soap Company in Buffalo in 1875. Pioneered the selling of merchandise through

mail-order, with his wife's brother, Elbert Hubbard, later an author who died with his wife, Alice Moore Hubbard on the *Lusitania*, torpedoed and sunk off the coast of Ireland by a German U-boat, May 7, 1915.

LEBLOND, FRANK 1847 - Nov 13, 1916 Buffalo, NY
Co-founded the Maid of the Mist Corporation, with R.F. Carter, in 1885, a steamboat tour company taking tourists to the foot of Niagara Falls.

LETCHWORTH, WILLIAM PRYOR May 26, 1923 Brownville, NY - Dec 1, 1910 Castile, NY
Businessman, humanitarian and philanthropist. Donated his estate, Glen Iris, and the surrounding 1,000 acres along the Genesee River gorge, to the state of New York, forming Letchworth State Park.

LINDEMAN (Westcott)**, HELEN ELIZABETH** Dec 13, 1910 NY - Aug 21, 1948 Kenmore, NY
Murder victim. Wife of a Buffalo-area dentist, disappeared running errands, her body parts were found five weeks later, on Hunter's Creek Road, near Goodleburg Cemetery, Erie County, where urban legend claims a "woman in white" haunts the cemetery.

LOCKWOOD, DANIEL NEWTON Jun 1, 1841 Hamburg, NY - Jun 1, 1906 Buffalo, NY
United States Representative-NY from 1877-1879 and 1891-1895.

LOVE, THOMAS CUTTING Nov 30, 1789 Cambridge, NY - Sept 17, 1853 Buffalo, NY
United States Representative-NY from 1835-1837.

MACGREGOR, CLARENCE Sept 16, 1872 Newark, NY - Feb 18, 1952 Buffalo, NY
United States Representative-NY from 1919-1929.

MARCHAND, RAYMOND L. Jan 26, 1902 - Mar 20, 1981 Boynton Beach, FL
With **Marjorie E. Freeman Marchand** (Feb 13, 1902 - Apr 28, 1987 Bridgeport, CT), the parents of Emmy Award-winning actress, Nancy Marchand.

MARTIN, DARWIN DENICE Oct 25, 1865 Bouckville, NY - Dec 17, 1935 Buffalo, NY
Corporate Secretary of the Larkin Soap Company in Buffalo. Commissioned architect, Frank Lloyd Wright, to design the Larkin Administration Building and his summer home, Graycliff.

MAZZARA, FILIPPO Oct 16, 1889 Castellammare del Golfo, Sicily, Italy - Dec 22, 1927 Buffalo, NY
Buffalo prohibition-era Mafia figure killed in response to the Cleveland "Sugar Wars", when driving on the West side of Buffalo, two cars forced him off the road and six gunmen opened fire.

MILCH, ELMER Jun 15, 1909 - Mar 20, 1979 Buffalo, NY
Buffalo-area gastrointestinal surgeon. Committed suicide by gunshot. Father of writer and producer, David Milch, creator of the television series, *NYPD Blue* and *Deadwood*.

MOSELEY, WILLIAM ABBOTT Oct 20, 1798 Whitesboro, NY - Nov 19, 1873 New York, NY
United States Representative-NY from 1843-1847.

MYER, ALBERT JAMES Sept 20, 1828 Newburgh, NY - Aug 24, 1880 Buffalo, NY
Civil War Union Army Brevet Brigadier General. First Chief Signal Officer for the United States Army
Signal Corps. Called the "Father of the National Weather Service." Son-in-law of Ebenezer Walden,
Mayor of Buffalo from 1838-1839.

PARKER, ELY SAMUEL 1828 Indian Falls, NY - Aug 30, 1895 Fairfield, NY
Native American, Seneca tribe, born Ha-sa-no-an-da. Civil War Union Army Brevet Brigadier General.
Drafted and handwrote the Confederate surrender papers, signed at Appomattox Courthouse by
General Robert E. Lee and General Ulysses S. Grant. Commissioner of Indian Affairs, appointed by
President Ulysses S. Grant in 1869. Studied civil engineering at Rensselaer Polytechnic Institute in
Troy.

PATERSON, WILLIAM Jul 7, 1919 Buffalo, NY - Sept 3, 2003 San Francisco, CA
Award-winning theater actor at the American Conservatory Theater in San Francisco and the
Cleveland Play House. Appeared in the Clint Eastwood film, *Dirty Harry*.

PFAFF, KRISTEN MARIE May 26, 1967 Buffalo, NY - Jun 15, 1994 Seattle, WA
Bass guitarist for the rock band, Hole, fronted by lead singer, Courtney Love, and the Minneapolis
band, Janitor Joe. Died from a drug overdose, two months after the suicide of Kurt Cobain, husband
of Courtney Love.

PIERCE, GEORGE NORMAN Jan 9, 1846 Friendsville, PA - Mar 23, 1910 Buffalo, NY
Founded the Pierce Arrow Motor Car Company in Buffalo, in 1901.

PIERCE, RAY VAUGHN Aug 1840 Stark, NY - Feb 4, 1914 St. Vincent Island, FL
United States Representative-NY from 1879-1880. Practiced medicine in Titusville, PA, selling more
than one million bottles of Dr. Pierce's Smart Weed.

PRICE, IRVING LANOUETTE Sept 21, 1884 Worcester, MA - Nov 23, 1976 Buffalo, NY
Founded the children's toy company, Fisher-Price, with his wife, Margaret Evans Price, Herman G.
Fisher, and Helen Schelle, in East Aurora in 1930. Mayor of East Aurora from 1929-1932.

PRICE (Evans), **MARGARET** Mar 20, 1888 New York, NY - Nov 20, 1973 Buffalo, NY
Children's book illustrator. Founded the children's toy company, Fisher-Price, with her husband, Irving
L. Price, Herman G. Fisher, and Helen Schelle, in East Aurora in 1930. Cousin of Charles Evans
Hughes, Chief Justice of the United States Supreme Court from 1930-1941.

RANDALL, EDWARD CALEB Jul 19, 1860 Ripley, NY - Jul 3, 1935 Buffalo, NY
Author. Wrote *The Dead Have Never Died*, *Life's Progression* and *The Living Dead*.

RATHBUN, MARY JANE Jun 11, 1860 Buffalo, NY - Apr 14, 1943 Washington D.C.
Marine zoologist. Specialized in the study of crustaceans. Worked at the Smithsonian Institute from 1884-1943. Brother of Richard Rathbun, biologist and administrator of the Natural History building at the Smithsonian Institute.

RED JACKET (Sa-go-ye-wa-tha) 1752 Geneva, NY - Jan 20, 1830 Buffalo, NY
Native American orator. Chief of the Seneca Indian tribe. Fought for the British during the Revolutionary War, and named for the British red coats used in battle. Presented the Silver Peace Medal by President George Washington in 1792, for mediating relations between the United States Government and the Seneca tribe.

REIDPATH, CHARLES DECKER Sept 20, 1889 Buffalo, NY - Oct 21, 1975 Lockport, NY
Olympic track & field sprinter. Won two gold medals at the 1912 Games. Set an Olympic record for in the 400m in 1912, broken in 1924 by Scottish Olympian, Eric Henry Liddle, whose story was depicted in the 1981 Academy Award-winning film, *Chariots of Fire*. Graduated from Syracuse University in 1912.

RICHARDSON, ALVIN LOUIS May 18, 1907 Buffalo, NY - Mar 10, 1963 Syracuse, NY
Built the Brewerton Speedway in 1948, originally a 1/4 mile dirt track.

ROGERS, WILLIAM FINDLAY Mar 1, 1820 Forks Township, PA - Dec 16, 1899 Buffalo, NY
United States Representative-NY from 1883-1885. Mayor of Buffalo from 1868-1869. Hired landscape architect, Frederick Law Olmstead, to design Delaware Park in Buffalo.

ROHLFS, CHARLES Feb 15, 1853 New York, NY - Jun 30, 1936 Buffalo, NY
Furniture maker. Showcased his work at the 1901 Pan American Exhibition in Buffalo. Husband of novelist, Anna Katharine Green. Father of aviator, Roland Rohlfs.

ROHLFS, ROLAND Feb 10, 1892 Buffalo, NY - Mar 22, 1974 Manhasset, NY
Aviator. Flew a hydroplane, the "Dunkirk Fighter", for Curtiss Aeroplane. Set the flight airspeed record flying a Curtiss Wasp in 1918 and an altitude record the flowing year in a Curtiss L-3. Son of novelist, Anna Katharine Green, and furniture maker, Charles Rohlfs.

RUMSEY, CHARLES CARY Aug 29, 1879 Buffalo, NY - Sept 21, 1922 Floral Park, NY
Sculptor and polo player. Husband of Mary Harriman Rumsey, the sister W. Averell Harriman, Governor of New York from 1955-1958. Great-grandson of Trumbull Cary, New York State Senator from 1831-1834. Died in a car accident on the Jericho Turnpike.

SCHERBATOW, KYRIL Nov 23, 1902 St. Petersburg, Russia - Apr 13, 1993 Buffalo, NY
Russian Prince. Son of Prince Pavel Scherbatow, Russian Colonel and aide-de-camp for Tsar
Nicholas II, and Princess Anna Bariatinskaya, lady-in-waiting for Empress Alexandra. Godson of Tsar
Nicholas II.

SCHMIDT, EMIL H. Dec 5, 1882 IL - Oct 23, 1933 Buffalo, NY
With **Emma J. Kuehn Schmidt** (1883 TX - Aug 30, 1966 Buffalo, NY), the parents of "Buffalo Bob"
Smith, host and creator of *The Hoody Doody Show* from 1947-1960. He was born Robert Emil
Schmidt, November 27, 1917 in Buffalo, died July 30, 1998 in Hendersonville, NC, and was cremated.

SHEPHERD, ELVIN J. 1923 Alexandria, VA - Jun 2, 1995 Buffalo, NY
Saxophonist. Nicknamed "Shep." Toured with Bill Doggett and Billy Ekstine. Performed with Gladys
Knight, Ray Price, Della Reese and Aretha Franklin. Taught saxophonist, Grover Washington Jr.

SOUTHWICK, ALFRED P. May 18, 1826 Buffalo, NY - 1898 Buffalo, NY
Buffalo-area dentist. Invented the electric chair, intended to replace hanging as a method of legal
execution. Attended the first execution by electric chair, convicted murderer, William Francis Kemmler,
in Auburn, August 6, 1890.

SPAULDING, ELBRIDGE GERRY Feb 24, 1809 Summer Hill, NY - May 5, 1897 Buffalo, NY
United States Representative-NY from 1849-1851 and 1859-1863. Mayor of Buffalo from
1847-1848. Known as the "Father of the Greenback." Introduced the Legal Tender Act and the
National Currency Bank Bill during the Civil War, designed to replace gold and silver as a primary
source of U.S. currency.

SPILLMAN, EDWARD ORTON Oct 7, 1875 North Tonawanda, NY - Oct 28, 1959 Buffalo, NY
Co-founded the Herschell-Spillman Motor Company in 1901, with his brother, Albert Spillman and
brother-in-law, Allan Herschell, manufacturing auto and motorboat engines.

SPILLMAN, JOHN 1833 Frankfort, Germany - May 17, 1905 North Tonawanda, NY
Father of Edward O. Spillman, co-founder of the Herschell-Spillman Motor Company. Father-in-law of
Allan Herschell, innovative amusement park ride creator. Struck and killed by a New York Central train
at the Tremont Street crossing, mutilating his body.

STONE, ALFRED PARISH Jun 28, 1813 Worthington, MA - Aug 2, 1865 Columbus, OH
United States Representative-OH from 1844-1845. Ohio State Treasurer from 1857-1862. Deep in
debt, he committed suicide at the graves of his two children, Green Lawn Cemetery in Columbus.

STREETER, EDWARD Aug 1, 1891 Buffalo, NY - Mar 31, 1976 New York, NY
Novelist and journalist. Wrote *Mr. Hobbs' Vacation* and *Father of the Bride*, the basis for the Spencer
Tracy and Elizabeth Taylor film of the same name. Wrote the *Dere Mable* letters during World War I.

SUTHERLAND, VICTORIA 1849 Lockport, NY - May 25, 1902 Buffalo, NY
Vaudeville singer. Appeared on stage with her sisters, Dora, Mary, Sarah, Isabella, Grace and Naomi, as the Seven Sutherland Sisters, famous for their very long hair, five feet in length. Her sisters, with their parents, Fletcher and Mary Brink Sutherland, are buried in Glenwood Cemetery in Lockport.

SWADOS, ROBERT ORVILLE Feb 27, 1919 Buffalo, NY - Nov 23, 2012 Buffalo, NY
Buffalo attorney. Co-founded the Buffalo Sabres with the Knox Brothers. Father of writer, compser and theatre director, Elizabeth Swados. Husband of poet and actress, **Sylvia Maisel Swados** (1921 - Apr 4, 1974 Buffalo, NY), who committed suicide.

THOMAS, EDWIN ROSS Nov 3, 1850 Webster, PA - Sept 13, 1936 Buffalo, NY
Founded the E.R. Ross Motor Company in Buffalo in 1900. Designer of the Thomas Flyer automobile, driven by George N. Schuster, winner of the 1908 New York to Paris Race.

TILDEN, DANIEL ROSE Nov 6, 1805 Lebanon, CT - Mar 4, 1890 Cleveland, OH
United States Representative-OH from 1843-1847.

TOLLEY, HAROLD SUMNER Jan 16, 1894 Honesdale, PA - May 20, 1956 Kenmore, NY
United States Representative-NY from 1925-1927. Graduated from Syracuse University in 1916.

WALDOW, WILLIAM FREDERICK Aug 26, 1882 Buffalo, NY - Apr 16, 1930 Snyder, NY
United States Representative-NY from 1917-1919.

WASHINGTON, GROVER Jun 7, 1926 - Feb 17, 1993 Buffalo, NY
Father of Grammy Award-winning saxophonist, Grover Washington, Jr.

WEBER, JOHN BAPTISTE Sept 21, 1842 Buffalo, NY - Dec 18, 1926 Lackawanna, NY
United States Representative-NY from 1885-1889. First Commissioner of Immigration at the Port of New York. Opening day of Ellis Island, January 1, 1892, he gave a $10 Liberty coin to Annie Moore in celebration of her being the first foreigner to pass U.S. federal immigration inspection. Commissioner General of the Pan American Exhibition in Buffalo in 1901.

WHITE, RUSSELL JESSE Apr 9, 1814 Buffalo, NY - Feb 19, 1886
Physician. With **Helena Anne Boynton White** (Apr 20, 1824 - Jan 11, 1894), the great-grandparents of actor, Vincent Price. Father-in-law of Dr. Vincent Clarence Price, inventor of "Dr. Price's Baking Powder", the first cream of tartar baking powder.

WHITE, WILL (William Henry) Oct 11, 1854 Caton, NY - Aug 31, 1911 Port Carling, ON, Canada
Pitcher for the Boston Red Caps, Cincinnati Reds and Detroit Wolverines from 1877-1886, winning 229 games. Holds the major league single season records for most games started, complete games and inning pitched. First major leaguer to wear eyeglasses on the field. Died from an accidental

drowning. Brother of Deacon White, star catcher and third baseman for eight major league teams from 1871-1890. Cousin of Elmer White, outfielder for the Cleveland Forest Citys in 1871 and the first active major leaguer in history to die.

WILKESON, SAMUEL Mar 9, 1817 Buffalo, NY - Dec 2, 1889 New York, NY
Journalist and editor. Covered the Civil War as a war correspondent for *The New York Times*. Purchased the *Albany Evening Journal* from Thurlow Weed in 1865. Namesake of the town of Wilkerson, WA. Husband of Catherine Cady Wilkeson, the sister of social reformer, Elizabeth Cady Stanton. Father of Samuel Wilkeson, Jr., a prominent settler of Tacoma, and Bayard Wilkeson, a Civil War Union Army officer killed in the Battle of Gettysburg.

WILCOX, ANSLEY Jan 27, 1856 Augusta, GA - Jan 26, 1930 Buffalo, NY
Commissioner of Civil Service Reform, appointed by President Grover Cleveland. Close friend of Theodore Roosevelt, who took the oath of office as President of the United States in the library of his home, 641 Delaware Avenue in Buffalo, September 14, 1901, following the assassination of President William McKinley at the Pan-American Exposition in Buffalo.

WILLIAMS, WILLIAM Sept 6, 1815 Bolton, CT - Sept 10, 1876 Buffalo, NY
United States Representative-NY from 1871-1873.

FOREST PARK CEMETERY
Harden Boulevard / Route 13
Camden, NY 13316

BABCOCK, OGDEN F. 1827 Amboy, NY - Dec 23, 1913 Hillsboro, NY
With **Charlotte R. Foster Babcock** (1830 - Jun 19, 1904 Camden, NY), the great-grandparents of songwriter, Jimmy Van Heusen, born Edward Chester Babcock in Syracuse.

BABCOCK, SETH ALBERT 1863 NY - Aug 26, 1941 Syracuse, NY
With **Martha Myers Babcock** (1864 NY - May 1921 Syracuse, NY), the grandparents of songwriter, Jimmy Van Heusen, born in Edward Chester Babcock in Syracuse.

FOREST PARK CEMETERY
387 Pinewoods Avenue (extinct)
Troy, NY 12180

CHRISTIAN, WILLIAM J. 1883 - Jan 5, 1962 Troy, NY
Caretaker for Forest Park Cemetery, formally Pinewoods Cemetery, town of Brunswick, designed by Garnet Baltimore, the first African-American engineer and graduate of RPI. Urban legend claims the

cemetery is haunted, and rumored to have been listed by *LIFE* magazine as one of the "Top Ten Most Haunted Places in the Country."

FORESTVILLE CEMETERY
Prospect Road
Forestville, NY 14062

ABBOTT (McLaury)**, HANNAH MAY** 1869 - Jun 20, 1940 Hamburg, NY
Mother of George Abbott, five-time Tony Award-winning playwright, producer and director, died January 31, 1995, age 107, and cremated.

PHILLIPS, ADRIAN May 28, 1963 Dunkirk, NY - May 7, 2004 Jamestown, NY
Brother of Ralph James "Bucky" Phillips, listed simultaneously on the FBI Ten Most Wanted Fugitives and the U.S. Marshal Service's Top 15 lists, for the shooting death of a New York State trooper and escape from prison in 2006, spending five months escaping justice.

PHILLIPS, RALPH JAMES Jul 11, 1901 NY - Sept 1975 Jamestown, NY
With **April Pearl Philbrick Phillips** (Apr 6, 1943 Gowanda, NY - Nov 26, 1996 Dunkirk, NY), the parents of Ralph James "Bucky" Phillips, a fugitive who gained folk hero status for a time, escaping from the Erie County Correctional Facility in Alden, April 2006, later listed simultaneously on the FBI Ten Most Wanted Fugitives and the U.S. Marshal Service's Top 15 lists, for the shooting death of a state trooper in September 2006, and the wounding of two others, captured September 8, 2006 by Pennsylvania State Police, near the community of Russell.

FORT HILL CEMETERY
19 Fort Street
Auburn, NY 13021

ALLEN, LLOYD SEWARD Feb 15, 1889 Auburn, NY - May 1, 1918 Fairfield, OH
World War I cadet. Killed in a flying accident at Wilbur Wright Field. Grandson of Civil War Union Army Brigadier General, William H. Seward, Jr. Great-grandson of William H. Seward, United States Secretary of State from 1861-1869.

BARNEY, FRANK A. Dec 7, 1862 Union Springs, NY - Dec 12, 1954 Auburn, NY
Artist. Painted more than 3,000 works of art in his lifetime.

BEARDSLEY, JOHN Nov 9, 1783 Southbury, CT - Mar 11, 1857 Auburn, NY
New York State Assemblyman from 1832-1833. New York State Senator in 1835. Associate Judge of Cayuga County from 1820-1823. Patriarch of a family of Cayuga County business and civic leaders.

BUNDY, WILLARD DOUGLAS Nov 9, 1815 Auburn, NY - Dec 25, 1889 Auburn, NY
Father of Willard L. Bundy, inventor of the first time clock machine and Harlow E. Bundy, brothers who formed the Bundy Manufacturing Company in Binghamton in 1889, consolidated years after their deaths with two additional companies, forming IBM.

CASE, THEODORE WILLARD Dec 12, 1888 Auburn, NY - May 13, 1944 Auburn, NY
Invented the first commercial soundtrack for motion pictures in 1922. Formed Movietone with William Fox. Debuted a short film of Charles Lindbergh's historic transatlantic flight in 1927, the first time the public could see and hear newsmakers.

CLAPP, E. D. (Emerous Donaldson) Nov 12, 1829 Ira, NY - Jun 10, 1889 Auburn, NY
Founded the E.D. Clapp Manufacturing Company and the E.D. Clapp Wagon Company.

CLOUGH, GEORGE LAFAYETTE 1824 Auburn, NY - Feb 20, 1901 Auburn, NY
New York State landscape painter. Trained under portrait artist, Charles Loring Elliot.

COLLIER, WILLIAM MILLER Oct 11, 1867 Lodi, NY - Apr 15, 1956 Auburn, NY
United States Minister to Spain from 1905-1909. United States Ambassador to Chile from 1921-1928. President of George Washington University from 1917-1921. Authored many treatises on bankruptcy.

CRAWFORD, HUGH D. 1856 Auburn, NY - May 19, 1907 Auburn, NY
Born the same day, died virtually the same time on the same day, and buried the same day as his lifelong, next-door neighbor, Marie Dates, the coincidence ending there, his neighbor was buried in St. Joseph's Cemetery, Auburn.

DAPPING, WILLIAM O. Jun 15, 1880 NY - Aug 1, 1969 Auburn, NY
Managing editor of the *Auburn Citizen-Advertiser* from 1916-1960. Awarded a Pulitzer Prize in 1930 for his coverage of the 1929 Auburn Prison riot. President of the New York Press Association from 1930-1943. Last surviving presidential elector who voted for Franklin D. Roosevelt in each of his four elections.

DAVIS, NELSON CHARLES 1844 Elizabeth City, NC - Oct 14, 1888 Auburn, NY
Civil War veteran. Married Harriet Tubman, Underground Railroad conductor, at Central Presbyterian Church in Auburn in 1869.

DENNIS, CYRUS C. 1806 Auburn, NY - May 31, 1866 Auburn, NY
First Mayor in the history of Auburn, in 1848.

DULLES, ALLEN MACY Aug 19, 1854 Philadelphia, PA - Nov 13, 1930 Auburn, NY
Presbyterian minister, theologian and professor at the Auburn Theological Seminary. Father of John

Foster Dulles, United States Secretary of State, under President Dwight D. Eisenhower, Allen Welsh Dulles, first civilian Director of the CIA from 1953-1961 and a member of the Warren Commission, and Eleanor Lansing Dulles, United States State Department official for 26 years. Grandfather of Avery Robert Cardinal Dulles, S.J., elevated to Cardinal by Pope John Paul II in 2001.

DULLES (Foster)**, EDITH** 1854 Evansville, IN - Jun 8, 1941 Auburn, NY
Mother of John Foster Dulles, United States Secretary of State, under President Dwight D. Eisenhower, Allen Welsh Dulles, first civilian Director of the CIA from 1953-1961 and a member of the Warren Commission, and Eleanor Lansing Dulles, United States State Department official for 26 years. Grandmother of Avery Robert Cardinal Dulles, S.J., elevated to Cardinal by Pope John Paul II in 2001. Daughter of John Watson Foster, United States Secretary of State, under President Benjamin Harrison. Sister-in-law of Robert Lansing, United Secretary of State, under President Woodrow Wilson.

DURNFORD, GEORGE A. 1885 - Dec 11, 1929 Auburn, NY
Principal keeper for Auburn Prison at the time of the prison's second major riot. Killed in the uprising, with eight convicts. Inmate Max Becker was acquitted of his murder in 1930.

DURSTON, CHARLES F. 1840 NY - Oct 12, 1894 Auburn, NY
Warden at the Auburn Prison in 1876 and 1887-1892. Convicted murderer, William Francis Kemmler, was executed, August 6, 1890, the country's first electrocution in the electric chair, during his tenure as warden.

EMERSON, FREDERICK L. 1876 Auburn, NY - Sept 11, 1948 Auburn, NY
President of Dunn & McCarthy Shoes. First to mass produce size-marked shoes.

FAY, EDWIN REED May 27, 1829 Aurelius, NY - Jan 1, 1930 Auburn, NY
Founded the Edwin R. Fay & Sons banking house with his sons, Fred H. Fay and Charles R. Fay.

FOSGATE, BLANCHARD 1809 - Sept 11, 1887 Auburn, NY
Physician at Auburn Prison in 1834. First customer at Auburn Savings Bank, opening day, May 19, 1949, depositing $50 into a savings account.

FOWLER, JOHN S. Nov 1, 1821 NY - Dec 8, 1902 Auburn, NY
Mayor of Auburn from 1866-1867.

GARROW, NATHANIEL Apr 25, 1780 Barnstable, MA - Mar 3, 1841 Auburn, NY
United States Representative-NY from 1885-1889. Cayuga County Sheriff from 1815-1819 and 1821-1825.

GREEN, WHARTON Dec 19, 1910 East Orange, NJ - May 6, 1969 Fort Lauderdale, FL
Owned and operated the Nye Wait Carpet Company in Auburn. Installed carpeting at the White House in 1948 and in the *U.S.S. Constitution* in 1950. Invented nylon carpet during World War II. Son of New York City-based architect, Wharton Green Sr., who designed the World's Fair in 1939, JFK (formally Idyllwild) International Airport and the IRT Subway system.

HALL, BENJAMIN FRANKLIN Jul 25, 1814 Hartford, NY - Sept 5, 1891 Auburn, NY
Chief Justice of the Colorado Territorial Supreme Court from 1861-1863. Mayor of Auburn in 1852. Author of the *Fort Hill Cemetery Handbook*.

HARDENBERGH, JOHN L. 1746 Ulster, NY - Apr 23, 1806 Auburn, NY
Founder of the city of Auburn in 1793. Revolutionary War commander and surveyor.

HEWSON, DANIEL Aug 14, 1796 Auburn, NY - Jul 16, 1881 Auburn, NY
Mayor of Auburn in 1849.

HIPPISLEY, GEORGE W. Oct 9, 1913 Rutherford, NJ - Jun 21, 1980 Buffalo, NY
Magician. Known by his stage name "Karlin." Personal friend of magician, Harry Blackstone, storing much of his act in a Weedsport storage unit in 1955, ten years before Blackstone's death. The memorabilia is displayed in the American Museum of Magic in Marshall, MI, founded by Robert and Elaine Lund.

HOLLAND, BRUD (Jerome) Jan 9, 1916 Auburn, NY - Jan 13, 1985 New York, NY
United States Ambassador to Sweden from 1970-1972, appointed by President Richard Nixon. First African-American Director of the New York Stock Exchange. First African-American football player at Cornell University. All-American in 1937. Elected to the College Football Hall of Fame in 1965. Father of Joe Holland, the first African-American to rush for 1,000 yards in an Ivy League season, in 1978.

HOWE (How)**, THOMAS** 1801 Auburn, NY - Jul 15, 1860 Auburn, NY
United States Representative-NY from 1851-1853. Mayor of Auburn from 1853-1854. Donated land for Fort Hill Cemetery, one of eight founders of the cemetery.

HUMPHREYS, FREDERICK Mar 11, 1816 Marcellus, NY - Jul 8, 1900 Monmouth Beach, NJ
Founded the Humphreys Homeopathic Medicine Company in Auburn in 1844.

HUMPHREYS, GEORGE Mar 18, 1812 Buffalo, NY - Jun 9, 1885 Cambridge, MA
Mayor of Auburn from 1861-1862 and 1865.

HUMPHREYS, SUZANNE Apr 2, 1915 Far Hills, NJ - Jul 25, 2001 Grandview-on-Hudson, NY
World War II Royal Air Force pilot. President of Humphreys Pharmaceutical, Inc. from 1952-2001,

founded by her great-grandfather, Dr. Frederick Humphreys. Married to Peter deFlorez, son of aviation pioneer, Admiral Louis deFlorez, until their divorce in 1974.

HUNTER, ROBERT NEAL Jan 26, 1914 Auburn, NY - Aug 19, 1991 Winter Haven, FL
Owned and operated the Hunter Diner in Auburn from 1951-1968. With **Louise Basl Hunter** (Oct 29, 1915 Dryden, NY - Feb 23, 1993 Haines City, FL), the parents of Neilia Hunter Biden, the wife of Vice-President Joe Biden, killed in a car accident, along with her one-year old daughter, Naomi (Amy) Christina Biden, in 1972, one month after Biden's election to the Senate. Grandparents of Joseph R. "Beau" Biden III, Delaware State Attorney General from 2007-2015.

JENNINGS, EDGAR STILLSON Aug 25, 1871 Auburn, NY - Jun 10, 1956 St. Petersburg, FL
Spanish-American War veteran. World War I United States Army Brigadier General. Warden at Auburn Prison from 1919-1930, taken captive by prisoners during the prison riot in 1929, rescued by the New York State Police.

KEOGH, MYLES WALTER Mar 25, 1840 Leighlinbridge, Carlow, Ireland - Jun 25, 1876 Bighorn, MT
Civil War Union Army Captain. Veteran of the Papal Wars. Joined the 7th Calvary, led by General George A. Custer, killed by the Sioux at the Battle of Little Bighorn. His horse, Comanche, the only survivor of the battle, was badly wounded, lived until 1891.

LAWTON, LOUIS B. Mar 13, 1872 Independence, IA - Jul 9, 1949 Skaneateles, NY
Awarded the Medal of Honor for his service during the Boxer Rebellion in Tientson, China in July 1900.

LONG, WALTER K. Feb 2, 1904 NY - Jan 4, 1986 Auburn, NY
Founding director and art instructor at the Cayuga Museum in 1936.

MEAD, J. WARREN Nov 2, 1845 Auburn, NY - May 17, 1913 Auburn, NY
Warden at the Auburn Prison from 1897-1905. Signed the death sentence for Leon Czolgosz, assassin of President William F. McKinley, and gave the signal to the executioner to pull the lever to electrocute Czolgosz in the electric chair in 1901.

MELONE, HARRY L. 1894 NY - Jan 11, 1949 Auburn, NY
Local editor and author. Published *150 Years of Progress* in 1929 and *History of Central New York: Embracing Cayuga, Seneca, Wayne, Ontario, Tompkins, Cortland, Schuyler, Yates, Chemung, Steuben, and Tioga Counties* in 1932.

MERRIMAN, TRUMAN Sept 5, 1839 Auburn, NY - Apr 16, 1892 New York, NY
United States Representative-NY from 1885-1889. President of the New York Press Club from 1882-1884.

METCALF, EDWIN DICKINSON Mar 14, 1848 Smithfield, RI - Dec 31, 1915 Auburn, NY
Founded the Columbian Rope Company in 1903. Mayor of Springfield, MA in 1886.

METCALF, EDWIN FLINT Aug 21, 1876 Springfield, IL - Sept 30, 1949 Auburn, NY
President of the Columbian Rope Company from 1916-1928, founded by his father, Edwin D. Metcalf.
Father of New York State Senator, George R. Metcalf. Brother of industrialist, Stanley W. Metcalf.

METCALF, GEORGE RICH Feb 5, 1914 Auburn, NY - May 30, 2002 Auburn, NY
New York State Senator from 1950-1965. Columnist for the *Auburn Citizen-Advertiser*. Founded the
Auburn Press in 1938. Awarded the Silver Star in World War II. Grandson of Edwin D. Metcalf, founder
of the Columbian Rope Company, and Adelbert P. Rich, Associate Justice of the New York State
Supreme Court.

METCALF, STANLEY WARREN Jan 1, 1893 - Sept 11, 1980 Auburn, NY
Executive with the Columbian Rope Company from 1916-1975, founded by his father, Edwin D.
Metcalf. World War II United States Army Colonel. Brother of industrialist, Edwin F. Metcalf. Uncle of
New York State Senator, George R. Metcalf.

MICHAELS, GEORGE M. Sept 15, 1910 College Point (Queens), NY - Dec 3, 1992 Auburn, NY
New York State Assemblyman. Cast the deciding vote to legalize abortion in New York on April 9,
1970, essentially ending his political career. New York was the first state in the country to legalize
abortion prior to the landmark *Roe v. Wade* United States Supreme Court decision.

MILLER, ELIJAH 1772 - Nov 13, 1851 Auburn, NY
Cayuga County Judge. Father-in-law of William H. Seward, United States Secretary of State from
1861-1869, under presidents, Abraham Lincoln and Andrew Johnson.

MILMINE (Adams)**, GEORGINE** Mar 1872 Oxford, ON, Canada - Aug 27, 1950 Falmouth, MA
Newspaper journalist. Extensively researched, and contributed a manuscript for *The Life of Mary
Baker G. Eddy and the History of Christian Science*, published in the February 1908 issue of
McClure's Magazine, later adapted to book form. Wife of journalist, Benjamin E. Welles, at the time of
his death.

MORGAN, CHRISTOPHER Jun 4, 1808 Aurora, NY - Apr 3, 1877 Auburn, NY
United States Representative-NY from 1839-1843. Mayor of Auburn from 1860-1862. Brother of
Edwin Barber Morgan, United States Representative-NY from 1853-1859. Nephew of Noyes Barber,
United States Representative-CT from 1821-1835.

NELSON, ROBERT A. Jan 30, 1900 NY - Apr 17, 1984 Auburn, NY
Mayor of Auburn from 1952-1956.

NYE, GEORGE HYATT Dec 2, 1854 Auburn, NY - Nov 23, 1916 Auburn, NY
President and Treasurer of the Nye & Wait Carpet Company, founded by his father, Lorenzo W. Nye, and William F. Wait in 1871. Grandson of Judge John Beardsley, New York State Senator in 1835.

OSBORNE, CHARLES DEVENS 1889 Auburn, NY - Jun 1, 1961 Auburn, NY
Mayor of Auburn in 1931 and 1937-1939. Publisher of the *Auburn Citizen-Advertiser*. Son of Thomas Mott Osborne, Mayor of Auburn from 1903-1905. Brother of Lithgow Osborne, United States Ambassador to Norway. Grandson of David Munson Osborne, Mayor of Auburn from 1879-1880. Great-grandson of suffragist, Martha Coffin Pelham Wright.

OSBORNE, DAVID MUNSON Dec 16, 1822 Rye, NY - Jul 6, 1886 Auburn, NY
Mayor of Auburn from 1879-1880. Father of Thomas Mott Osborne, Mayor of Auburn from 1903-1905. Grandfather of Lithgow Osborne, United States Ambassador to Norway and Charles Devens Osborne, Mayor of Auburn in 1931 and 1937-1939.

OSBORNE, ELIZA WRIGHT Sept 5, 1822 Aurora, NY - Jul 18, 1911 Auburn, NY
Feminist. Wife of David Munson Osborne, Mayor of Auburn from 1879-1880. Mother of Thomas Mott Osborne, Mayor of Auburn from 1903-1905. Grandmother of Lithgow Osborne, United States Ambassador to Norway and Charles Devens Osborne, Mayor of Auburn in 1931 and 1937-1939. Daughter of abolitionist and feminist, Martha Coffin Pelham Wright. Niece of feminist, Lucretia Coffin Mott. Sister-in-law of William Lloyd Garrison, Jr., the son of social reformer, William Lloyd Garrison.

OSBORNE, LITHGOW Apr 2, 1892 Auburn, NY - Mar 10, 1980 Auburn, NY
United States Ambassador to Norway, appointed by President Franklin D. Roosevelt in 1944. Vice-President and editorial writer of the *Auburn Citizen-Advertiser*. Husband of Countess Lillie Raben-Levetzau of Denmark. Son of Thomas Mott Osborne, Mayor of Auburn from 1903-1905. Brother of Charles Devens Osborne, Mayor of Auburn in 1931 and 1937-1939. Grandson of David Munson Osborne, Mayor of Auburn from 1879-1880. Great-grandson of suffragist, Martha Coffin Pelham Wright.

OSBORNE, THOMAS MOTT Sept 23, 1859 Auburn, NY - Oct 20, 1926 Auburn, NY
Mayor of Auburn from 1903-1905. Warden of Sing Sing Prison in Ossining from 1914-1916. Commander of the U.S. Naval Prison in Portsmouth, NH from 1917-1920. Spent much of his career working to reform prison conditions, disguising himself as an inmate, most notably in Auburn Prison. Son of David Munson Osborne, Mayor of Auburn from 1879-1880. Father of Lithgow Osborne, United States Ambassador to Norway and Charles Devens Osborne, Mayor of Auburn in 1931 and 1937-1939.

PAYNE, SERENO ELISHA Jun 26, 1843 Hamilton, NY - Dec 10, 1914 Washington D.C.
United States Representative-NY from 1883-1887 and 1889-1914. First House Majority Leader, from

1899-1911. Chairman of the Committee on Ways and Means. Helped draft the McKinley Tariff Act in 1890. Died in office, one month after his reelection to Congress in 1914.

PEARCE, CHARLES May 29, 1842 Whitesboro, NY - Jan 30, 1902 St. Louis, MO
United States Representative-MO from 1897-1901. Head of the Indian Commission, under President Benjamin Harrison, at the time of the Battle of Wounded Knee, attempting a treaty with the Sioux Indians.

POMEROY, THEODORE Dec 31, 1824 Cayuga, NY - Mar 23, 1905 Auburn, NY
United States Representative-NY from 1861-1869. Speaker of the House for one day in 1869, declined to seek re-nomination. Mayor of Auburn from 1875-1876. Named first Vice-President and General Counsel of American Express in 1868.

RATHBUN, GEORGE (Oscar) 1803 Scipioville, NY - Jan 5, 1870 Auburn, NY
United States Representative-NY from 1843-1847.

REDDICK, MAXWELL ARLINGTON Nov 28, 1914 Syracuse, NY - Jul 17, 1989 Auburn, NY
Auburn-area basketball star. Nicknamed "Sugar." Former member of the Harlem Globetrotters.

SCHWARTZ, MAURICE Jun 5, 1901 Rochester, NY - Dec 8, 1967 Auburn, NY
Mayor of Auburn from 1960-1967.

SELOVER, ISAAC Mar 18, 1801 NY - 1858 Auburn, NY
First cousin, once removed, of John Davison Rockefeller, co-founder of Standard Oil, first American billionaire.

SEWARD, AUGUSTUS HENRY Oct 1, 1826 Auburn, NY - Sept 11, 1876 Montrose, NY
United States Army Brevet Colonel. Son of William Henry Seward, United States Secretary of State from 1861-1869. Injured, stabbed seven times, in the assassination attempt on his father's life, April 14, 1865, by Lewis (Payne) Powell, the night President Abraham Lincoln was assassinated. His brother, Frederick William Seward and sister, Frances Adeline "Fanny" Seward, were also injured in the attack. Namesake of Augustus Street in Auburn.

SEWARD, CORNELIA (Frances Adeline) 1836 Auburn, NY - Jan 14, 1837 Auburn, NY
Daughter of William Henry Seward, United States Secretary of State from 1861-1869. Originally buried in St. Peter's Churchyard, Auburn, reinterred following the deaths of mother and sister.

SEWARD, FANNY (Frances Adeline) Dec 9, 1844 Auburn, NY - Oct 29, 1866 Washington D.C.
Daughter of William Henry Seward, United States Secretary of State from 1861-1869. Witnessed the assassination attempt on her father's life by Lewis (Payne) Powell, who threw her aside as he repeatedly stabbed her father, helping to save his life after Powell fled, the night President Abraham Lincoln was shot by John Wilkes Booth, April 14, 1865.

SEWARD (Miller), **FRANCES ADELINE** Sept 25, 1805 Auburn, NY - Jun 21, 1865 Washington D.C.
Wife of William Henry Seward, United States Secretary of State from 1861-1869. First Lady of New York from 1839-1842 during her husband's term as governor. Three of her children, Frederick, Augustus and Fanny, were injured in an assassination attempt on her husband in their Washington home by Lewis (Payne) Powell, a conspirator of John Wilkes Booth, who shot President Abraham Lincoln the same night, April 14, 1865. Died two months after the attack from a heart attack, Powell was executed 16 days later. Mother of Frederick W. Seward, United States Assistant Secretary of State from 1861-1869 and 1877-1879 and William H. Seward Jr., Civil War Union Army Brigadier General

SEWARD, FREDERICK WILLIAM Jul 8, 1830 Auburn, NY - Apr 25, 1915 New York, NY
United States Assistant Secretary of State from 1861-1869 and 1877-1879. Son of William H. Seward, United States Secretary of State from 1861-1869. Injured in the assassination attempt on his father's life, April 14, 1865, by Lewis (Payne) Powell, the night President Abraham Lincoln was assassinated. His brother, Augustus Henry Seward and sister, Frances Adeline "Fanny" Seward, were also injured in the attack.

SEWARD, WILLIAM HENRY May 16, 1801 Florida, NY - Oct 15, 1872 Auburn, NY
United States Secretary of State from 1861-1869, under President Abraham Lincoln and President Andrew Johnson. United States Senator-NY from 1849-1861. Governor of New York from 1839-1843. Negotiated the purchase of Alaska from Russia in 1867, mocked at the time as "Seward's Folly." Appeared on the $50 bill in the 1891 series. Recovering from a carriage accident, survived an assassination attempt on his life, April 14, 1865, the night President Lincoln was assassinated, when Lewis (Payne) Powell, an accomplice of John Wilkes Booth, burst into his bedroom stabbing him repeatedly. Powell was hanged for his crime, with other co-conspirators. His wife, Frances Adeline Miller Seward, died two months after the attack, June 21st, suspected heart attack.

SEWARD, WILLIAM HENRY Jun 18, 1839 Auburn, NY - Apr 26, 1920 Auburn, NY
Civil War Union Army Brigadier General. Youngest son of William H. Seward, United States Secretary of State from 1861-1869.

SEYMOUR, JAMES A. 1864 Auburn, NY - Jun 28, 1943 New York, NY
Co-founded the Seymour & McIntosh Corporation, later ALCO, makers of high-speed stationary steam and oil diesel engines for powering factories and ships, with John E. McIntosh, in 1886.

SEYMOUR, JAMES S. Apr 15, 1791 NY - Dec 3, 1875 Auburn, NY
Banker and philanthropist. Founded the Seymour Library and Auburn City Hospital.

SEYMOUR (Dulles), **NATALIE** Jan 22, 1898 - May 31, 1988 Henderson Harbor, NY
Wife of James Sayre Seymour, the son of industrialist James A. Seymour. Daughter of Rev. Allen Macy Dulles. Sister of John Foster Dulles, United States Secretary of State, under President Dwight

D. Eisenhower, Allen Welsh Dulles, first civilian Director of the CIA and member of the Warren Commission, and Eleanor Lansing Dulles, United States State Department official for 26 years. Granddaughter of John Watson Foster, United States Secretary of State, under President Benjamin Harrison. Cousin of Avery Robert Cardinal Dulles, S.J., elevated to Cardinal by Pope John Paul II in 2001. Niece of Robert Lansing, United States Secretary of State, under President Woodrow Wilson.

SHIMER, ANTHONY 1819 NY - Oct 8, 1896 Auburn, NY
Real estate entrepreneur. Owned much of downtown Auburn in the 1880s.

STORKE, ALAN Sept 27, 1884 Auburn, NY - Mar 19, 1910 Newton, MA
Infielder for the Pittsburgh Pirates, managed by Hall of Fame player/manager, Fred Clarke, and St. Louis Cardinals from 1906-1909. Starting third baseman for the 1907 Pirates, teammate of Hall of Fame shortstop, Honus Wagner.

TABER, JOHN May 5, 1880 Auburn, NY - Nov 22, 1965 Auburn, NY
United States Representative-NY from 1923-1963. Won twenty consecutive elections to Congress, before retiring in 1962. Chairman on the Committee on Appropriations.

TALLMAN, J. K. (John) 1825 NY - May 10, 1893 Auburn, NY
Founded the Searles & Tallman Company in Auburn, with Theodore J. Searles. Father of undertaker, S.C. Tallman.

TALLMAN, S. C. (Selah Cornwell) Dec 20, 1855 Scipio, NY - May 6, 1925 Auburn, NY
Owned and operated the S.C. Tallman & Company in Auburn, founded by his father, John K. Tallman, in 1880.

TUBMAN (Davis)**, HARRIET** 1820 Bucktown, MD - Mar 10, 1913 Auburn, NY
Conductor of the Underground Railroad. Called "the Moses of Her People." Born a slave named Araminta Ross in Dorchester County, MD. Married John Tubman, a free black man, in 1844, changed her name to Harriet, to honor her mother. Conducted more than 20 trips to the South, in the years prior to and during the Civil War, to escort slaves to the North, with a bounty of $40,000 for her capture. Selected by the United States Treasury Department in 2016 to replace Andrew Jackson on the $20 bill, the first woman whose portrait appears on U.S. paper currency. First husband, John Tubman, was killed during an argument in Maryland in 1867. She remarried to Nelson Davis in Auburn in 1869.

UPTON, EMORY Aug 27, 1839 Batavia, NY - Mar 15, 1881 San Francisco, CA
Civil War Union Army Major General. Military strategist. West Point graduate. Committed suicide by gunshot at his post at the Presidio.

WAIT, WILLIAM F. Mar 1, 1846 Amsterdam, NY - Jan 15, 1915 Auburn, NY
Co-founded the Nye & Wait Carpet Company, with George S. Nye, in 1871.

WATROUS, JOHN LUCIAN Mar 1, 1801 Colchester, CT - Mar 14, 1862 Auburn, NY
Mayor of Auburn in 1855. One of eight founders of Fort Hill Cemetery.

WEGMAN, HENRY 1845 - Oct 1894 Auburn, NY
Founded, owned and operated the Wegman Piano Company, from 1882 until his death in 1894.

WHEELER, CYRENUS 1817 NY - Mar 24, 1899 Auburn, NY
Mayor of Auburn from 1881-1886 and 1889-1890. Invented and manufactured the Cayuga Chief drop reaper. Founded the Cayuga Chief Manufacturing Company in Auburn.

WILDER, DAVID Apr 19, 1809 Leominster, MA - Jan 16, 1891 Boston, MA
Father of Burt Green Wilder, Professor of Neurology and Vertebrate Zoölogy at Cornell University, founder of the Wilder Brain Collection, first to use the term, "neuron", in 1884.

WILLARD, SYLVESTER D. Dec 24, 1798 Saybrook, CT - Mar 1886 Auburn, NY
Cayuga County physician. President of the Oswego Starch Factory from 1848-1886. Namesake, with his wife, Jane Frances Case Willard, of the Willard Memorial Chapel on Nelson Street in Auburn, built in their memory by their daughters, Georgiana and Caroline Willard. Designated a National Historic Landmark in 2005, it's the last remaining complete structure built by Louis Comfort Tiffany.

WRIGHT, DAVID Apr 18, 1806 - Feb 24, 1887 Auburn, NY
Lawyer. Husband of abolitionist and feminist, Martha Coffin Wright. Father of Eliza Wright Osborne. Grandfather of Thomas Mott Osborne, Mayor of Auburn from 1903-1905. Great-grandfather of Charles Devens Osborne, Mayor of Auburn in 1931 and 1937-1939, and Lithgow Osborne, United States Ambassador to Norway.

WRIGHT, MARTHA COFFIN Dec 25, 1806 Boston, MA - Jan 4, 1875 Auburn, NY
Feminist. Abolitionist. President of the National Women's Suffrage Association in 1874. Mother of Eliza Wright Osborne. Grandmother of Thomas Mott Osborne, Mayor of Auburn from 1903-1905. Great-grandmother of Charles Devens Osborne, Mayor of Auburn in 1931 and 1937-1939, and Lithgow Osborne, United States Ambassador to Norway. Sister of abolitionist and feminist, Lucretia Coffin Mott.

YATES, HORATIO H. 1842 - Mar 3, 1912 Cortland, NY
Auburn Prison Protestant Chaplain from 1888-1897. Provided spiritual counseling for condemned killer, William Francis Kemmler, executed August 6, 1890, the world's first execution by electric chair.

FORT HILL CEMETERY
Parmalee Road / Route 17
LeRoy, NY 14482

LEBARON, DAVID Feb 21, 1775 Killingworth, CT - Aug 6, 1829 LeRoy, NY
With **Azubah L.H. King LeBaron** (Jun 1, 1786 Rupert, VT - Aug 23, 1817 LeRoy, NY), the parents of Naomi Roxania LeBaron Holman, who traveled with her husband, James Sawyer Holman, in the Brigham Young "Pioneer Company" in 1848, and the 5th great-grandparents of Elizabeth Ann Smart-Gilmour, abducted from her Salt Lake City home in 2002 as a 14-year old child, and held captive for nine months until her rescue.

FORT PLAIN CEMETERY
29 Clyde Street
Fort Plain, NY 13339

WAGNER, PETER JOSEPH Aug 14, 1795 Palatine, NY - Sept 13, 1884 Fort Plain, NY
United States Representative-NY from 1839-1841.

FOXWOOD MEMORIAL PARK
5969 Route 812
Ogdensburg, NY 13669

GORDON, NANETTE R. 1955 Ogdensburg, NY - Aug 17, 1985 Syracuse, NY
Victim of an unsolved homicide. Resident pathologist at University Hospital, found dead in her bed in her home, 115 Croyden Lane in DeWitt. It took four years for the Onondaga County coroner to list her death a homicide, a victim of asphyxiation.

FRANCISCAN MOTHERHOUSE CHAPEL
2500 Grant Boulevard
Syracuse, NY 13208

COPE (Koob)**, MARIANNE** Jan 23, 1838 Hessen, Germany - Aug 9, 1918 Kalaupapa, HI
Roman Catholic Saint. Born Maria Anna Barbara Koob, raised in Utica. Member of the Sisters of St. Francis of Syracuse. Canonized for her work with leprosy patients in Hawaii. Beautified by Pope Benedict XVI, May 14, 2005, canonized, October 21, 2012. Took her vows as a Franciscan sister at Assumption Church, Syracuse, in 1863, established as the Provincial Mother of Syracuse before leaving for Hawaii in 1883. Established Maui's first hospital in Wailuku in 1884. Exhumed from her grave at the Convent of the Bishop Home, Kalaupapa, Molokai, January 2005, returned to Syracuse.

FRANKLIN D. ROOSEVELT NATIONAL HISTORIC SITE
4079 Albany Post Road
Hyde Park, NY 12538

ROOSEVELT (Roosevelt), **ELEANOR** (Anna) Oct 11, 1884 New York, NY - Nov 7, 1962 New York, NY
First Lady of the United States. Longest-served first lady in history. Called the "First Lady of the World"
by President Harry S Truman. United States Representative to the United Nations from 1946-1953.
Married her distant cousin, Franklin D. Roosevelt, March 17, 1905. Human Rights and Civil Rights
activist. Niece of President Theodore Roosevelt.

ROOSEVELT, FRANKLIN DELANO Jan 30, 1882 Hyde Park, NY - Apr 12, 1945 Warm Springs, GA
32nd President of the United States. Only president to win four presidential elections. Longest-served
president in history. Led the country out of the Great Depression with his New Deal program. Led the
United States into World War II, following the Japanese attack on Pearl Harbor. Suffered from polio,
spent the better part of his presidency in a wheelchair. Governor of New York from 1929-1932. Distant
cousin of President Theodore Roosevelt.

FRIENDS CEMETERY
East Quaker Street / Route 20A
Orchard Park, NY 14127

THORN, FRANK MANLY Dec 7, 1837 Collins, NY - Apr 17, 1907 Orchard Park, NY
Superintendent of the United States Coast and Geodetic Survey from 1885-1889, first non-scientist,
appointed by President Grover Cleveland. Columnist for the *Buffalo Express*, co-owned by Mark
Twain, writing under the pseudonyms, Hy Slocum and Carl Byng. Namesake of Thorne Bay in Alaska.

FRUMAH PACKARD CEMETERY
Jamesville Avenue
Syracuse, NY 13210

ABERSON, ELLIS Jan 15, 1894 Syracuse, NY - Apr 7, 1946 Syracuse, NY
Owned the State Siding and Roofing Company in Syracuse. Brother of Helen Aberson, author of the
children's book, *Dumbo, the Flying Elephant*, illustrated by her first husband, Harold Pearl.

ABERSON, J. BELLE Apr 1900 Syracuse, NY - Jul 25, 1922 Auburn, NY
Drowned on Owasco Lake, when the canoe she was riding with a friend, Bernard Simon of Pine Bluff,
AR, capsized. Despite an extensive search, her body was not found until August 2, 1922. Simon
survived, found clinging to the canoe. Sister of Helen Aberson, author of the children's book, *Dumbo,
the Flying Elephant*, illustrated by her first husband, Harold Pearl.

MARKSON, ABRAHAM 1861 Poland - Apr 2, 1923 Syracuse, NY
Co-founded the chain of Markson Brothers Furniture Stores.

NEWER, BERNARD S. 1913 Syracuse, NY - Apr 13, 1963 Syracuse, NY
Business Editor and columnist for the *Post-Standard* from 1954-1963.

PRINSTEIN, JACOB 1850 Poland - Feb 10, 1922 Syracuse, NY
Father of United States Olympian and Syracuse University track & field star, Myer Prinstein. Died ten months prior to his wife, Julia Prinstein, who died December 2, 1922 in Syracuse.

SERLING, PHIL May 21, 1931 Syracuse, NY - Jan 6, 2002 Fayetteville, NY
Founder and President of the Syracuse Cinephile Society, from 1968-2002. Boxing trainer and voting member of the International Boxing Hall of Fame. Died two days after suffering injuries in a single car accident.

SERLING, SAMUEL LAWRENCE Jun 21, 1891 Detroit, MI - Sept 1, 1945 Bridgewater, NY
With **Esther L. Cooper Serling** (1893 - Mar 5, 1958 Miami, FL), the parents of screenwriter and producer, Rod Serling, creator of *The Twilight Zone* and *Night Gallery*, and novelist, Robert J. Serling.

FULTONVILLE CEMETERY
Upper Mohawk Street
Fultonville, NY 12072

HORTON, THOMAS RAYMOND Apr 18, 1823 Fultonville, NY - Jul 26, 1894 Fultonville, NY
United States Representative-NY from 1855-1857.

STARIN, JOHN HENRY Aug 27, 1825 Sammonsville, NY - Mar 21, 1909 New York, NY
United States Representative-NY from 1877-1881. Grandson of Thomas Sammons, United States Representative-NY from 1803-1807 and 1809-1813.

FYLER SETTLEMENT CEMETERY
Fyler Road
Kirkville, NY 13082

BROWNELL, VERNON L. Jul 14, 1917 Kirkville, NY - Sept 25, 1988 Pensacola, FL
Co-founded B. H. & N. Metal Products, later to merge with Manth Manufacturing, founded by Burton W. Manth, to form Manth-Brownell, Inc. in Kirkville in 1951.

FYLER, SILAS Mar 31, 1782 Windsor, CT - Apr 16, 1841 Kirkville, NY
First settler and founder of the Fyler Settlement, town of Sullivan, Madison County.

HOWARD, FRANK J. Feb 9, 1906 Sherburne, NY - Jun 27, 1995 Kirkville, NY
Co-founder of B. H. & N. Metal Products in Kirkville, later to merge into Manth-Brownell, Inc.

GALLUPVILLE RURAL CEMETERY
515 Route 443
Schoharie, NY 12157

GALLUP (Hinckley)**, REBECCA** Oct 6, 1766 Stonington, CT - Aug 10, 1843 Gallupville, NY
Sister of Abel Hinckley Jr., the 3rd great-grandfather of John W. Hinckley Jr., attempted assassin of President Ronald Reagan, shooting the President and three others, March 30, 1981, in Washington D.C., also, the grandfather of Francis Edward Hinckley, co-founder of the University of Chicago, and the 3rd great-grandson of Samuel Hinckley, who was the 10th great-grandfather of President Barack Obama.

GARBUTTSVILLE CEMETERY
Union Street
Scottsville, NY 14546

BLACKMER (Harmon)**, LYDIA** Dec 30, 1800 Eaton, NY - Feb 11, 1875 Wheatland, NY
Sister of Clarinda C. Harmon Folsom, the grandmother of First Lady Frances Folsom Cleveland, the wife of President Grover Cleveland.

GARBUTT, JOHN 1779 Northumberland, England - 1855 Garbutt, NY
New York State Assemblyman in 1829. Namesake of the village of Garbutt.

GARLAND CEMETERY
7743 West Ridge Road
Brockport, NY 14420

PARKER, EVAN JENKINS Feb 1, 1885 Hornell, NY - May 28, 1966 Rochester, NY
Dirigible pilot. Awarded an "early bird certificate" in Washington D.C. in 1955, given to aviators who flew before pilot licenses were needed. Left his scrapbook to the Air and Space Museum of the Smithsonian Institute. Brother of Captain Jack Dallas, who piloted dirigibles. Son of playwright, producer and actor, Dan Darleigh.

GARNSEY CEMETERY
Route 146
Clifton Park, NY 12065

GARNSEY, NATHAN 1740 - Dec 3, 1822 Clifton Park, NY
Early settler of the town of Clifton Park. Town supervisor in 1829. Namesake of Garnsey Park, off Route 146, town of Rexford.

GATE OF HEAVEN CEMETERY
500 Riverdale Avenue
Lewiston, NY 14092

BIRO, GUY (Wayne) Jun 2, 1945 Niagara Falls, NY - Mar 9, 2006 Lewiston, NY
Uncle of John Wayne Bobbitt, who made national news, June 23, 1993, when his wife, Lorena Gallo Bobbitt, cut off his penis with a knife, as he lay sleeping in bed, drove from the house and threw it out the window of her car. She was found not guilty by reason of insanity. After an extensive search, his penis was found and reattached. He later starred in two adult movies, *John Wayne Bobbitt: Uncut* and *Frankenpenis*.

CAZEN (Kaczynski)**, WALTER** Sept 29, 1911 NY - May 7, 1946 Lockport, NY
Syracuse Chiefs outfielder from 1936-1937 and 1942-1945. Played on three Governor's Cup championship teams with the Chiefs. Broke the International League single-season stolen base record with 74 in 1945. Holds the Chiefs single-season records with 204 hits, 74 stolen bases and 620 at-bats, all during the 1945 season. Inducted into the International League Hall of Fame in 2009. Contracted tuberculosis in December 1945, died six months later.

JACKSON (Murray)**, MARIE K.** Dec 18, 1926 Niagara Falls, NY - May 28, 1999 Niagara Falls, NY
Girlfriend of Mafia informant, Joseph M. Valachi, continuing their relationship through the rest of his life spent in prison in Texas. Claimed his body when his wife, Mildred, would not, paid to have him sent to Niagara Falls, buried side-by-side in the cemetery upon her death.

PILEGGI, PHILOMENA Sept 14, 1895 Canada - Dec 6, 1990 Lewiston, NY
Mother-in-law of Sal Maglie, pitcher for the New York Giants, Cleveland Indians, Brooklyn Dodgers, New York Yankees and St. Louis Cardinals from 1945 and 1950-1958.

VALACHI, JOSEPH MICHAEL Sept 22, 1904 New York, NY - Apr 3, 1971 El Paso, TX
Mafia informant. Testified before the United States Senate in 1963, the first Mafia member to publicly acknowledge the true existence of the Mafia, making "Cosa Nostra", meaning "Our Thing", a household phrase. Previously worked for mob boss, Lucky Luciano, and the Genovese crime family. Peter Maas published the *Valachi Papers* in 1968, based on Valachi's memoirs and a series of interviews between the two. Died of a heart attack in prison, Vito Genovese's $100,000 bounty he

placed on him following his testimony went uncollected. Son-in-law of Gaetano Reina, New York Mafia boss, shot to death at the start of the Castellammarese War in 1930.

GATES OF HEAVEN CEMETERY
Watt Street
Schenectady, NY 12304

GERSHON, IRVING Dec 10, 1913 - May 14, 1990 Schenectady, NY
Founded, owned and operated Gershon's Deli, 1600 Union Street, Schenectady, with his wife, **Lena Kosatzky Gershon** (Jul 26, 1914 - Jan 23, 1996 Schenectady, NY), from 1954-1978, when the business was sold to Antonio Lauria, who owned the deli until his death, September 9, 2016.

GERALD B. H. SOLOMON NATIONAL CEMETERY
200 Duell Road
Schuylerville, NY 12871

ABRAMS, IRVING Jan 30, 1922 - Mar 15, 2003 Plattsburgh, NY
With **Adelaide J. Abrams** (May 10, 1926 New York, NY - Feb 14, 2006 Plattsburgh, NY), the step-grandparents of Tony Award-winning actor, John Lloyd Young.

ALASKEY, JOSEPH FRANCIS Nov 15, 1918 Troy, NY - Sept 30, 2006 Cohoes, NY
Father of Emmy Award-winning voice actor and cartoonist, Joe Alaskey.

BRIGGS, JACK (John Calvin) Aug 1, 1920 Schenectady, NY - Aug 22, 1998
Actor. Played small roles in films in the 1940s. Married to Academy Award-winning actress, Ginger Rogers, from 1943-1949.

CRIMMINS, JACK (John Paul) Sept 25, 1919 Worcester, MA - Nov 9, 2005 Rochester, NY
Uncle of political satirist and comedian, Barry "Bearcat" Crimmins.

DALESSANDRO, PETER JOSEPH May 18, 1919 Watervliet, NY - Oct 15, 1997
New York State Senator from 1947-1957. World War II United States Army Technical Sergeant. Award the Medal of Honor, presented by President Harry Truman in 1945. Second-most decorated World War II veteran, including three Purple Hearts and the Silver Star.

LONGOBARDO, JOSEPH ANTHONY May 24, 1974 Amsterdam, NY - Sept 3, 2006 Buffalo, NY
New York State trooper. Shot by Ralph James "Bucky" Phillips in Pomfret, Chautauqua County, dying two days later. Phillips, listed simultaneously on the FBI Ten Most Wanted Fugitives and the U.S. Marshal Service's Top 15 lists, was wanted for his murder, and the shooting of two additional troopers,

following his escape from the Erie County Correctional Facility in Alden, April 2006, captured September 8, 2006 by Pennsylvania State Police, near the community of Russell.

OSWALD, RUSSELL GEORGE Aug 4, 1908 Racine, WI - Mar 8, 1991 Albany, NY
Commissioner of the New York State Department of Correctional Services from 1970-1973. Attempted to negotiate a settlement during the prison rebellion at Attica Correctional Facility in 1971, between the state, led by Governor Nelson A. Rockefeller, and the rioting prisoners, which led to the deaths of ten correctional officers and 33 prisoners.

PERSICO, JOSEPH EDWARD Jul 19, 1930 Gloversville, NY - Aug 30, 2014 Guilderland, NY
Author. Wrote, *Nuremberg: Infamy on Trial*, *The Imperial Rockefeller* and *My Enemy, My Brother: Men and Days of Gettysburg*. Chief speechwriter for Vice-President Nelson Rockefeller from   1974-1977.

QUINLAN, JOHN P. Jun 13, 1919 - Dec 18, 2000 Peekskill, NY
World War II United States Army Air Corps veteran. Tail gunner of the *Memphis Belle* B-17 bomber, the first to complete its combat tour of 25 missions and return to the United States without a casualty.

ROSENFELS, PAUL Mar 21, 1909 Chicago, IL - Aug 12, 1985 New York, NY
Psychiatrist. Author of *Homosexuality: The Psychology of the Creative Process*, published in 1971.

SMITH, W. SNOWDON (Walter) Feb 18, 1916 Syracuse, NY - May 12, 2006 Saratoga Springs, NY
World War II United States Army Air Corps pilot. Awarded the Purple Heart, lost his leg in the Japanese attack on Pearl Harbor. Among a group of disabled veterans who stripped to their underwear in the Oval Office in 1947, helping President Harry S Truman understand the inadequacies of their artificial limbs. Grandson of Syracuse real estate magnate, W. Snowdon Smith. Great-grandson of Syracuse drama critic, S. Gurney Lapham.

SOLOMON, GERALD B. H. Aug 14, 1930 Okeechobee, FL - Oct 26, 2001 Glens Falls, NY
United States Representative-NY from 1979-1999. Namesake of the Gerald Brooks Hunt Solomon National Cemetery, renamed following his death, formerly the Saratoga National Cemetery.

WILSON, ALMON C. Jul 13, 1924 Hudson Falls, NY - Jun 30, 2003 Silverdale, WA
United States Navy Rear Admiral. Architect of the Navy's Fleet Hospital Program in 1981. Personal physician to Admiral Thomas H. Moorer, Chairman of the Joint Chiefs of Staff from 1970-1974.

GETHSEMANE CEMETERY
Rockland Lake Road
Valley Cottage, NY 10989

KELLY, RAY (Raymond) May 12, 1918 New York, NY - Nov 11, 2001 Valley Cottage, NY
Nicknamed "Little Ray." Babe Ruth's personal mascot with the New York Yankees, from 1921-1932, appearing in uniform in the Yankee's dugout most games.

GIDEON PUTNAM BURYING GROUND
South Franklin Street
Saratoga Springs, NY 12866

PUTNAM, GIDEON Apr 17, 1763 Sutton, MA - Dec 1, 1812 Saratoga Springs, NY
Founder of Saratoga Springs. Built the Congress and Grand Union Hotels. Namesake of the Gideon Putnam Hotel in Saratoga Spa State Park. Nephew of Revolutionary War Generals, Rufus Putnam and Israel Putnam.

GILBERT CEMETERY
Pleasant Valley Road
Marcellus, NY 13108

BARNARD, GEORGE N. Dec 23, 1819 Coventry, CT - Feb 4, 1902 Marcellus, NY
Photographer. Photographed battlefields during the Civil War, as an associate of photographer, Mathew Brady. Accompanied General William Sherman on his famous March to Atlanta, publishing *Photographic Views with Sherman's Campaign* in 1866. Photographed the famous Chicago Fire in 1871. Credited with photographing one of the earliest actions news pictures, of an Oswego grain elevator fire in 1853.

GILEAD BURYING GROUND
Mechanic Street
Carmel, NY 10512

CROSBY, ENOCH Jan 4, 1750 Harwich, MA - Jun 26, 1835 Southeast, NY
Revolutionary War Continental Army Spy. Counter-intelligence agent. Basis for the "Harvey Birch" character in the James Fenimore Cooper novel, *The Spy*.

GLEN WILD CEMETERY
Marsh Road
Glen Wild, NY 12738

ABRAMSON, SHERI Apr 8, 1961 Brooklyn, NY - Oct 15, 2011 Liberty, NY
Sister of Jeryl Abramson Howard, co-owner of Yasgur's Farm, town of Bethel, with her husband, Roy Howard, the location of the Woodstock Festival, August 15-17, 1969.

HOWARD, ROY Apr 14, 1934 Brooklyn, NY - Jan 29, 2013 Bethel, NY
Co-owned Yasgur's Farm, town of Bethel, with his wife, Jeryl Abramson Howard, the location of the Woodstock Festival, August 15-17, 1969, purchased from Max Yasgur's widow, Miriam Yasgur Mass, in 1985, leaving one square foot of the farm in the Yasgur family.

GLENS FALLS CEMETERY
38 Ogden Street
Glens Falls, NY 12801

BISHOP, SAMUEL Dec 19, 1798 Caldwell, NY - Oct 16, 1827 Caldwell, NY
With **Maria Reed Bishop** (1801 - Feb 14, 1821 Glens Falls, NY), the parents of Charles Reed Bishop, founder of Hawaii's first bank, the First Hawaiian Bank, and husband of Bernice Pauahi Pâkî, of the Royal House of Kamehameha.

COOL, CHARLES WILLIS Aug 19, 1858 Glens Falls, NY - Sept 24, 1932 Glens Falls, NY
First Mayor of Glens Falls, from 1908-1910, and again, from 1922-1924. Founded the Cool Insurance Agency in 1879.

COWLES (Benton), **JOANN AMZELLE** May 5, 1920 Spokane, WA - Feb 25, 2013 Charleston, SC
Mother of Douglas S. Luke Jr., married to Anne Sturgis Roosevelt, the granddaughter of President Franklin D. Roosevelt and First Lady Eleanor Roosevelt, in 1964. Grandmother of Haven Roosevelt Luke, David Russell Luke and Lindsay Hall Luke, the great-grandchildren of President Roosevelt. Predeceased by her husbands, Douglas S. Luke Sr. and Frank Little Cowles.

ELKES, HARRY D. Feb 28, 1878 Port Henry, NY - May 30, 1903 Cambridge, MA
Bicycle racer. Won the USA National Paced Championship in 1900. World record-holder in 5, 10, and 15 mile races. Killed in a bicycle accident when his rear tire blew, somersaulting over his handlebars, crushing his head during the Charles River Race.

FERRIS, ORANGE Nov 26, 1814 Glens Falls, NY - Apr 11, 1894 Glen Falls, NY
United States Representative-NY from 1867-1871.

FOLSOM, JOHN May 17, 1756 Stratford, CT - Aug 4, 1839 Glens Falls, NY
With **Elizabeth File Folsom** (May 10, 1761 Albany, NY - Apr 12, 1840 Glens Falls, NY), the 5th great-grandparents of two-time Academy Award-winning actress, Sally Field.

GOODRICH, SOLOMON P. Feb 1757 Albany, NY - Sept 1831 Glens Falls, NY
With **Anne Folsom Goodrich** (Aug 26, 1782 Albany, NY - Dec 6, 1854 Glens Falls, NY), the 4th great-grandparents of two-time Academy Award-winning actress, Sally Field.

JOHNSON, FREDERICK AVERY Jan 2, 1833 Fort Edward, NY - Jul 17, 1893 Glens Falls, NY
United States Representative-NY from 1883-1887.

LEERET, GEORGE A. 1866 Syracuse, NY - Jan 1, 1942 Syracuse, NY
Owned the Leeret and Blasdel Box Factory in Syracuse. Son-in-law of publisher, Andrew Boyd.

LUKE, DOUGLAS SIGLER Jul 3, 1918 Luke, Maryland - Aug 1984 Glens Falls, NY
Selected the National Christmas Tree, a 72-foot tall white spruce, planted by Buel Robinson in the 1880s, from the town of Chestertown, delivered to Washington D.C. in 1964. Grandson of William Luke, founder of the West Virginia Pulp and Paper Company in Luke, MD, 1888. Father of Douglas S. Luke Jr., married to Anne Sturgis Roosevelt, the granddaughter of President Franklin D. Roosevelt and First Lady Eleanor Roosevelt, in 1964. Grandfather of Haven Roosevelt Luke, David Russell Luke and Lindsay Hall Luke, the great-grandchildren of President Roosevelt.

MCGREGOR, DUNCAN 1808 Wilton, NY - Mar 19, 1895 Wilton, NY
Namesake of Mount McGregor in Wilton. Built the first hotel and restaurant atop the mountain, in 1874. Sold the property to Philadelphia banker, Joseph William Drexel, who built the Hotel Balmoral on the summit. Drexel offered his cabin to terminally ill, President Ulysses S. Grant, to finish his memoirs, died there, six weeks later of throat cancer, Grant's Cottage, July 23, 1885.

MILLER (Mortimer), **CHARLIE** (Julius) Jan 1, 1850 New York, NY - Jan 15, 1955 Glens Falls, NY
Last surviving Pony Express rider, started in 1861, age 11. Performed at Queen Victoria's Golden Jubilee in 1887 at Windsor Castle, England, as part of Buffalo Bill's Wild West shows.

RUSSELL, JOSEPH 1800 Warrensburg, NY - Apr 24, 1875 Glens Falls, NY
United States Representative-NY from 1851-1853.

GLENWOOD CEMETERY
Rixle Drive
Afton, NY 13730

LORD, BERT Dec 4, 1869 Sanford, NY - May 24, 1939 Washington D.C.
United States Representative-NY from 1935-1939. Died four months into his third term in office.

GLENWOOD CEMETERY
La Grange Street
Binghamton, NY 13905

BOOTH (Henderson)**, OGARITA** Oct 23, 1859 Providence, RI - Apr 12, 1892 Binghamton, NY
Off-off Broadway touring actress. Claimed to be the only child of John Wilkes Booth, assassin of President Abraham Lincoln. Daughter of Martha Lizola Mills. Wife of stage actor, Alexander Henderson. Mother of author, Izola Louise (Wallingford) Forrester. Died from acute indigestion at the Crandall Hotel, originally buried in a pauper's grave in Binghamton Cemetery, reburied in 1907.

HOGG, DAVID Jan 10, 1773 Ettrick, County Selkirk, Scotland - Nov 5, 1852 East Maine, NY
Brother of novelist, James Hogg, called the "Ettrick Shepherd", attended the flock of novelist, Sir Walter Scott as a young farmhand.

RULLOFF, EDWARD H. 1820 Saint John, NB, Canada - May 18, 1871 Binghamton, NY
Studied the origins of language, publishing "The Methods of Languages" to the American Philological Association in 1869. Suspected seral killer. Accused of beating his wife, Harriett Schutt Rulloff, and three-month old daughter, Priscilla, to death, June 24, 1845, convicted despite the absence of their bodies, later reversed by the New York State Court of Appeals due to the "no body, no conviction" law. Murdered Frederick Merrick in 1870, convicted and hanged, the last public hanging in New York State. His brain, the second-largest recorded on record, is held in the Wilder Brain Collection in the Psychology Department at Cornell University. Buried in the Potter's Field. Brother of photographer, William Herman Rulofson, who fell off the roof of his studio in San Francisco, heard to say, "I am killed!", as he tumbled to his death, November 2, 1878.

SEYMOUR, WILLIAM Feb 22, 1775 Waterbury, CT - Dec 28, 1848 Binghamton, NY
United States Representative-NY from 1835-1837.

GLENWOOD CEMETERY
Route 14
Geneva, NY 14456

CHATTERTON, TOM Feb 12, 1881 Geneva, NY - Aug 17, 1952 Hollywood, CA
Hollywood character actor. Silent film director. Played a small, uncredited role in the classic Christmas movie, *It's a Wonderful Life*.

FISHER, LOUIS Sept 23, 1824 Saxony, Germany - Aug 26, 1881 Geneva, NY
With **Catherine Kau Fisher** (Mar 18, 1830 Germany - Feb 1, 1926 Geneva, NY), the great-grandparents of Walter L. Farley, best-selling author of the children's book, *The Black Stallion*.

FOLGER, CHARLES JAMES Apr 16, 1818 Nantucket, MA - Sept 4, 1884 Geneva, NY
United States Secretary of Treasury from 1881-1884, under James Garfield and Chester Arthur. Defeated by Grover Cleveland in the 1882 New York gubernatorial election.

GAYLORD (Buchanan)**, ELIZABETH** 1812 Hammondsport, NY - Aug 18, 1902 Geneva, NY
Sister, last surviving sibling, of President James Buchanan.

JOHNSTON, JOHN Apr 11, 1791 Moffat, County Dumfries, Scotland - Nov 24, 1880 Geneva, NY
Yates County farmer. Called "the Father of Tile Drainage in America." The Mike Weaver Drain Tile Museum is located down the road from his home, Rose Hill Mansion.

LAFARO, SCOTT Apr 3, 1936 Newark, NJ - Jul 6, 1961 Flint, NY
Jazz bassist. Performed with the Bill Evans Trio. Recorded with Ornette Coleman, Stan Getz, Chet Baker and Miles Davis. Killed in an automobile accident in Flint, two days after accompanying Stan Getz at the Newport Jazz Festival.

NICHOLAS, JOHN 1757 Williamsburg, VA - Dec 31, 1819 Geneva, NY
United States Representative-NY from 1793-1801. Brother of Wilson Cary Nicholas, United States Senator-VA from 1799-1804. Uncle of Robert Carter Nicholas, United States Senator-LA from 1836-1841. Grandfather of Peter Myndert Dox, United States Representative-AL from 1869-1873.

O'HANLON (Niland)**, INABELLE** Sept 8, 1916 Tonawanda, NY - May 15, 2009 Geneva, NY
Sister of Tom Niland, LeMoyne College head basketball coach from 1948-1975. Cousin of Frederick "Fritz" Niland, the inspiration for Private Ryan in the film, *Saving Private Ryan*, and his brothers, Robert Niland and Preston Niland, killed in the Allied invasion of Europe in 1944, and Edward Niland, shot down over Burma, thought to be killed in action, spent eleven months as a prisoner-of-war. Aunt of John Beilein, head basketball coach for LeMoyne College, Canisius, Richmond, West Virginia and Michigan.

ROSE, ROBERT SELDEN Feb 24, 1774 Amherst County, VA - Nov 24, 1835 Waterloo, NY
United States Representative-NY from 1823-1827 and 1829-1831. Father of Robert Lawson Rose, United States Representative-NY from 1847-1851. Originally buried in the now-defunct Old Pulteney Street Cemetery in Geneva.

VAN SLYKE, DONALD DEXTER Mar 29, 1883 Pike, NY - May 4, 1971 Garden City, NY
Biochemist. Associated with the Brookhaven National Laboratory from 1948-1971. Awarded the President's National Medal of Science by President Lyndon Johnson in 1965.

GLENWOOD CEMETERY
31 North Main Street
Homer, NY 13077

ALLEN (Crandall)**, BEATRICE A.** Jun 2, 1925 Taylor, NY - May 1, 2016 Cortland, NY
Aunt of Gary Wood, quarterback for Cornell University and the New York Giants and New Orleans
Saints from 1964-1969.

CARPENTER, FRANCIS BICKNELL Aug 8, 1830 Homer, NY - Mar 23, 1900 New York, NY
Portrait artist. Painted a 1864 hand-tinted lithograph, *President Lincoln and His Cabinet, Reading the
Emancipation Proclamation*. Wrote of his experience with Lincoln, *The Inner Life of Abraham Lincoln:
Six Months at the White House*, published in 1866. Painted portraits of presidents, Millard Fillmore,
Abraham Lincoln, John Tyler and Franklin Pierce.

CREAL, CAP (Harold L.) Jul 31, 1896 Homer, NY - Feb 6, 1987 Englewood, FL
Agriculturist. Member of the New York State Assembly from 1939-1950. Director of the New York State
Fair. Died from injuries suffered when he was struck by a car in Sarasota County, January 20, 1987.

FITTS, SHARI A. 1975 Syracuse, NY - May 1, 1991 Cortland, NY
Homer High School Honor Society student. Committed suicide while dating Jonathan P. Merchant.
Merchant later dated the daughter of Dryden High School teacher and coach, Stephen A. Starr. Starr's
daughter broke up with Merchant, who did not accept the end of the relationship, and gets a
restraining order. Merchant is angry, breaks into the Starr house and kills Stephen as he defends his
daughter, a Dryden High School cheerleader. He then drives to the cemetery and commits suicide by
gunshot at Shari's grave. This event is one of a series of tragedies involving Dryden High School in
the mid-to-late 1990s, chronicled in the May 2001 issue of *Spin* magazine, written by E. Jean Carroll.

HANNUM, DAVID H. Feb 6, 1822 Homer, NY - Jan 1, 1892 Homer, NY
Inspiration for the fictional title character in the Edward Noyes Westcott novel, *David Harum*.
Purchased the Cardiff Giant, a ten-foot tall stone man, one of the most famous hoaxes in American
history, and tried to lease it to showman, P.T. Barnum, for $60,000, who turned down his offer and built
his own "giant", claiming his was the real giant and the Cardiff Giant a fake. Newspapers reported
Barnum's version of his giant, and Hannum was quoted as saying "There's a sucker born every
minute" in reference to Barnum's paying customers, the quotation has been misattributed to Barnum
over the years. Hannum sued Barnum, a judge ruled that Barnum could not be sued for calling a "fake
giant a fake."

MONTGOMERY, WILLIAM OWEN Feb 26, 1865 Adana, Turkey - Aug 2, 1885 Homer, NY
Brother of Mary Montgomery Williams Borglum, the wife of Danish-born American sculptor, Gutzon
Borglum, creator of Mount Rushmore and Stone Mountain, near Atlanta.

REED, EDWARD CAMBRIDGE Mar 8, 1793 Fitzwilliam, NH - May 1, 1883 Ithaca, NY
United States Representative-NY from 1831-1833. Cortland County District Attorney from 1827-1836.

RIGGS, LEWIS Jan 16, 1789 Norfolk, CT - Nov 6, 1870 Homer, NY
United States Representative-NY from 1841-1843. Postmaster of Homer from 1829-1839, appointed by President Andrew Jackson.

ROBINSON (Washburn)**, SEMANTHA** Jan 5, 1807 Greensboro, VT - Sept 15, 1882 Homer, NY
Direct-descendant of multiple *Mayflower* passengers. Adopted her orphaned niece, Emily Ruth Redington, whose only daughter, Mary Montgomery Williams Borglum, married Danish-born American sculptor, Gutzon Borglum, creator of Mount Rushmore and Stone Mountain, near Atlanta.

SIDMAN, PETER Apr 4, 1826 Rochester, NY - Dec 12, 1884 Homer, NY
With **Elvira M. Todd Sidman** (Oct 16, 1832 Pompey, NY -Jan 11, 1887 Tully, NY), the parents of vaudeville comedian and playwright, Arthur C. Sidman.

TANNER (Abbott)**, ELIZABETH** Apr 29, 1870 Trenton, NJ - Sept 24, 1949 Syracuse, NY
Mother of Wilbur Crisp, Syracuse University basketball star and innovative high school coach.

GLENWOOD CEMETERY
325 Glenwood Avenue
Lockport, NY 14094

CROWLEY, RICHARD Dec 14, 1836 Pendleton, NY - Jul 22, 1908 Olcott Beach, NY
United States Representative-NY from 1879-1883. United States District Attorney for the Northern District of New York from 1871-1879, appointed by President Ulysses S. Grant. Successfully prosecuted Susan B. Anthony, arrested for illegally voting in the 1872 election.

FLAGLER, THOMAS THORN Oct 12, 1811 Pleasant Valley, NY - Sept 5, 1897 Lockport, NY
United States Representative-NY from 1853-1857.

HOLLY, BIRDSILL Nov 8, 1820 Auburn, NY - Apr 27, 1894 Lockport, NY
Invented the modern day fire hydrant, rotary pump and district heating for residential and commercial units. Ostracized for divorcing his wife and marrying his teenage ward in 1860. Died at his home, 31 Chestnut Street, the first building to be heated by steam heat. Granted more than 150 patents at the time of his death, second only to Thomas Edison. Six hours after his death, the city of Gasport, NY burned, ironically, one of the few cities not to have purchased his fire protection system.

HUNT, WASHINGTON Aug 5, 1811 Windham, NY - Feb 2, 1867 New York, NY
Governor of New York from 1851-1852.

MILLARD, ALMON HOPKINS Apr 19, 1787 Pittsford, VT - May 6, 1838 Lockport, NY
First Sheriff of Niagara County. Uncle of President Millard Fillmore.

MORGAN, WILLIAM GEORGE Jan 23, 1870 Lockport, NY - Dec 27, 1942 Lockport, NY
Invented Volleyball, originally called, "Mintonette", in Holyoke, MA in 1895.

SUTHERLAND, FLETCHER Mar 1, 1816 Pittsford, VT - Sept 6, 1888 Cambria, NY
Methodist minister. With **Mary Brink Sutherland** (1824 Lyons, NY - Sept 24, 1867 Lockport, NY), the parents of the Seven Sutherland Sisters, vaudeville singing performers, famous for their very long hair, five feet in length.

SUTHERLAND SISTERS
Seven sisters from Sutherland Farm, Cambria, Niagara County, singers, performed in vaudeville as the Seven Sutherland Sisters, famous for their very long hair, five feet in length. **Dora**, died December 12, 1926 in Los Angeles, car accident, age 62, **Mary**, died May 12, 1939 in Buffalo, age 93, **Sarah**, died September 9, 1919 in Newfane, age 74, **Isabella**, died December 1, 1914 in Lockport, age 62, **Grace**, January 13, 1946 in Lockport, age 91 and **Naomi Sutherland**, died July 13, 1893 in Lockport, age 35. Seventh sister, Victoria Sutherland, died May 25, 1902 in Buffalo, age 53, buried there in Forest Lawn Cemetery.

VAN HORN, BURT Oct 28, 1823 Newfane, NY - Apr 1, 1896 Lockport, NY
United States Representative-NY from 1861-1863 and 1865-1869.

GLENWOOD CEMETERY
Glenwood Avenue / Route 46
Oneida, NY 13421

GOLDSTEIN, JULIUS M. 1865 Germany - Jan 16, 1938 Oneida, NY
Cigar manufacturer. First Mayor of the city of Oneida, served one term in 1901. Father of Mae Goldstein Oberdorfer, the wife of theatrical manager, Jesse L. Oberdorfer.

MILLER, FRANCIS CHARLES 1830 NY - Aug 17, 1878 Oneida, NY
Civil War Union Army Colonel. Led the 147th New York Volunteer Infantry at the Battle of Gettysburg, July 1863, wounded in the head during battle. Spent time in five Confederate prison camps before his parole in December 1864.

OBERDORFER, JESSE LIGHT 1875 Syracuse, NY - Aug 19, 1935 Syracuse, NY
Syracuse haberdasher, later theatrical manager. Associated with Sam Shubert and Lee Shubert, traveled to New York City with the brothers in 1900 to start their theatrical career, building theaters on Broadway. Managed the career of actress, Edna May, during her appearance in *The Belle of New*

York. Son of Moses L. Oberdorfer, founder of Oberdorfer Foundries in Syracuse in 1890. Husband of Mae Goldstein Oberdorfer, the daughter of Julius M. Goldstein, the first Mayor of Oneida. Committed suicide, drinking poison in his home, 1600 James Street.

GLENWOOD CEMETERY
Main Street / Route 7
Oneonta, NY 13820

EDGARTON, H. VINCENT Nov 21, 1901 Fulton, NY - May 9, 1969 Syracuse, NY
Owned and operated Edgarton & Edgarton Architecture and Engineer Associates with his twin brother, W. Dexter Edgarton. Designed the Onondaga County War Memorial in Syracuse.

FAIRCHILD, GEORGE WINTHROP May 6, 1854 Oneonta, NY - Dec 31, 1924 New York, NY
United States Representative-NY from 1907-1919. Father of aviation inventor, Sherman M. Fairchild.

FAIRCHILD, SHERMAN MILLS Apr 7, 1896 Oneonta, NY - Mar 28, 1971 New York, NY
Invented aerial mapping photography. Designed the first airplane to have a closed cockpit. Son of George W. Fairchild, United States Representative-NY from 1907-1919.

MYATT COUPLE Apr 27, 2014 Verona, NY
Earl L. Myatt, born July 25, 1954 in Oneida, and his wife, **Mary M. Bellinger Myatt**, born June 4, 1954 in Oneida, married 42 years, were killed in a train accident on Fox Road, in what was officially ruled a murder-suicide, by intentionally leading his wife, who suffered a brain aneurysm earlier in the year, in front of an oncoming train shortly after phoning his son telling him what he was intending to do. Buried next to their two-day old daughter, Karen C. Myatt, died January 26, 1976 in Syracuse.

WILBER, DAVID Oct 5, 1820 Schenectady, NY - Apr 1, 1890 Oneonta, NY
United States Representative-NY from 1873-1875, 1879-1881 and 1887-1890. President of the Wilber National Bank in Oneonta from 1874-1890. Father of David Forrest Wilber, United States Representative-NY from 1895-1899.

WILBER, DAVID FORREST Dec 7, 1859 Milford, NY - Aug 14, 1928 Upper Dam, ME
United States Representative-NY from 1895-1899. United States Consul in Barbados, Singapore, Halifax, Kobe, Vancouver, Zurich, Genoa and Wellington from 1903-1922. Son of David Wilber, United States Representative-NY from 1873-1875, 1879-1881 and 1887-1890.

GLENWOOD CEMETERY
Handley Street
Perry, NY 14530

BOWLES, KAREN L. Mar 30, 1949 - Jan 1, 2009 Castile, NY
Widow, found dead in her home from natural causes on March 2, 2010, more than a year after her death. Two sisters who live in the area declined to comment on why there was no contact between them, stating their reasons were personal. Officials believe she died between January 6, 2009 and February 6, 2009. Her husband, John N. Bowles, died April 26, 2001, age 66.

GLENWOOD CEMETERY
Old Main Road
Silver Creek, NY 14136

EHMKE, CHARLES G. Feb 1855 Germany - Mar 25, 1918 Silver Creek, NY
With **Julia Green Ehmke** (Feb 7, 1856 NY - Feb 24, 1940 Silver Creek, NY), the parents of Howard Ehmke, pitcher for the Buffalo Blues, Detroit Tigers, Boston Red Sox and Philadelphia Athletics from 1915-1930, and the inventor of tarpaulin, used to cover baseball fields when it rains.

GLENWOOD CEMETERY
23348 Route 67
Watertown, NY 13601

AMEDEO (Benedetto)**, ANTONETTA** Nov 6, 1891 Italy - Jan 1969 Ogdensburg, NY
Aunt of Grammy Award-winning singer, Tony Bennett, sister of his father, Giovanni Benedetto.

AMEDEO (Amedeo)**, ROSE MARIE** Mar 11, 1911 New York, NY - July 26, 1997 Watertown, NY
Cousin of Grammy Award-winning singer, Tony Bennett. Lost her granddaughter, Jenelle J. Amedeo Berry, two-months pregnant, and her 4-year old great-granddaughter, Christina McKenzie Berry, July 2, 1997, four weeks before her death, when their car was struck by a logging truck on Route 177, town of Rodman. They are buried in Brookside Cemetery, Watertown.

ANZALONE, SAMUEL F. Oct 15, 1915 Gouverneur, NY - Nov 25, 2000 Watertown, NY
With **Lillian M Rosenberg Anzalone** (Dec 20, 1927 Canton, NY - Apr 2011 Watertown, NY), the grandparents of singer, Eric Anzalone, the leather-clad biker of the disco band, the Village People, replacing Glenn Hughes in 1995.

BENEDETTO, DOMINICK Aug 24, 1893 Reggio Calabria, Italy - Aug 3, 1975 Watertown, NY
Uncle and namesake of Grammy Award-winning singer, Tony Bennett, born Anthony Dominick Benedetto in New York City in 1926 to Giovanni and Anna Suraci Benedetto. Anna died in Hackensack

on November 26, 1977, Giovanni from a heart attack, stricken boarding a bus on Welfare Island, now Roosevelt Island, to visit his Watertown relatives, August 7, 1936.

CANALE, LEO P. Aug 11, 1919 Watertown, NY - Feb 24, 2013 Sackets Harbor, NY
Syracuse University halfback from 1938-1941. Captain of Syracuse's tennis team. Played three games for Syracuse basketball in 1939-1940. Cousin of NFL player, Rocco Canale.

CANALE, ROCCO May 1, 1917 Watertown, NY - Nov 1, 1995 Watertown, NY
Offensive lineman for the Philadelphia Eagles, Pittsburgh Steelers and Boston Yanks from 1943-1947. All-American at Boston College from 1941-1943. Briefly a Boston College teammate of Ed McMahon, referenced by Johnny Carson's sidekick on *The Tonight Show*, in 1969. World War II United States Army Corporal, listed on a plaque in the Pro Football Hall of Fame, for NFL veterans.

DUFFY, ALEXANDER THOMAS Jan 7, 1899 Watertown, NY - Aug 31, 1999 Watertown, NY
Watertown historian. Poultry breeder. President of the Jefferson County Agricultural Society for 30 years. Namesake of the Alex T. Duffy Fairgrounds in Jefferson County.

FINNERTY, HANNAH M. Jun 25, 1981 Denver, CO - Jun 1, 2004 Syracuse, NY
Murder victim. Watertown High School honor student, five-months pregnant, found stabbed to death, stuffed in a trash bin, 732 West Onondaga Street, killed by serial killer, Nicholas Lee Wiley, who murdered two other girls, Lottie Thompson and Tammy Passineau, following his release from prison for sexual assault and battery.

GRANT, TIMOTHY J. Sept 15, 1953 Watertown, NY - Nov 26, 2001 Watertown, NY
Associate pastor of the Faith Fellowship Church in Watertown. Local musician. Opening act for the Beach Boys in 1994. Uncle of musician, Sean Paddock, musical director and drummer for country singer, Kenny Chesney.

GRIECO (O'Reilly), **CAROLYN ANNE** Jul 25, 1944 Watertown, NY - October 20, 2001 Pamelia, NY
Mother of Hollywood actor, Richard Grieco.

NIMS, THOMAS E. Dec 25, 1961 Syracuse, NY - Nov 16, 1993 Syracuse, NY
Syracuse University All-American lacrosse goaltender from 1982-1985. Member of Syracuse's 1983 NCAA Championship team. Father of attackman, Kenny Nims, member of Syracuse University's 2008 and 2009 NCAA Championship team.

SIRIANNI, PAUL J. Aug 10, 1931 Old Forge, PA - Jul 30, 2004 Montezuma, NY
With **Gloria M. Caruso Sirianni** (January 8, 1932 Buffalo, NY - Jul 30, 2004 Montezuma, NY), the parents of operatic tenor, Craig P. Sirianni. Killed on the New York State Thruway in a single-car accident, driven by their son-in-law, Randy F. Demar, who survived with their daughter, Amy Sirianni Demar, returning from a Rochester hospital, where he received news that he did not have cancer the family

had feared. His wife died from heart failure, en route to Auburn Memorial Hospital, from the scene of the accident.

WOOL (Lucas), **CLAUDINE** Jul 5, 1909 Watertown, NY - Jun 8, 1997 Watertown, NY
Concert pianist. Mother of singer/songwriter, Ed Wool, who performed with his band, Ed Wool & the Nomads, opening for the Rolling Stones at the War Memorial in Syracuse, October 30, 1965.

GLENWOOD CEMETERY
Cemetery Road
Watkins Glen, NY 14891

BOGART (Stiles), **JULIA A.** Aug 7, 1832 Watkins Glen, NY - Nov 2, 1868 Watkins Glen, NY
Mother of New York City physician, Belmont DeForest Bogart. Grandmother of Academy Award-winning actor, Humphrey Bogart. Lost her first born son to a head injury in her home, sliding down a bannister and striking his head. Her husband, Adam Welty Bogart, died May 7, 1892 in Watkins Glen, cremated.

HUNGERFORD, JOHN NEWTON Dec 31, 1825 Vernon, NY - Apr 2, 1883 Watkins Glen, NY
United States Representative-NY from 1877-1879.

KRESS, CHARLES W. 1896 Watkins Glen, NY - Feb 27, 1964 Binghamton, NY
Mayor of Binghamton from 1938-1941. Investigator for the Kefauver Committee, a United States Senate Committee, chaired by Senator Estes Kefauver in 1950, examining organized crime. Indicted in 1939 for conspiracy and obstruction of justice, acquitted the following year in a trial held in the New York State Supreme Court.

MAGEE, JOHN Sept 3, 1794 Easton, PA - Apr 5, 1868 Watkins Glen, NY
United States Representative-NY from 1827-1831.

GOODLEBURG CEMETERY
12119 Goodleburg Road
South Wales, NY 14139

DOSTER, MARY AGNES Oct 2, 1894 South Wales, NY - Sept 12, 1895 South Wales, NY
Eleven month-old baby, daughter of John Phillip Doster and Mary Margaret Auer Doster, buried in a cemetery listed among the most haunted in the United States, visited often by those interested in paranormal activity. Attempts were made by overzealous vandals, to dig up her grave due to the belief that a neighboring abortion doctor, Albert Speaker, would dispose of unborn babies in the graveyard, possibly linking her remains to the doctor, who committed suicide, hanged from a tree in his yard,

October 3, 1948, buried in New Montefiore Cemetery, West Babylon, Long Island. Robert Edward Carr, a member of the Paranormal and Ghost Society, was struck and killed by a drunk driver, Debra Saddleson, June 21, 2003, age 19, researching the cemetery, buried in Village View Cemetery, Sarahsville, OH.

GRACELAND CEMETERY
680 Delaware Avenue
Albany, NY 12209

GEARY, PERCY 1905 New York, NY - Jul 16, 1959 Atlanta, GA
Post-prohibition Albany-area gangster. Nicknamed "Angel Face." Kidnapped John J. O'Connell Jr., nephew of Democratic Party Chairman, Daniel P. O'Connell, with co-conspirators, Manny Strewl, John J. Oley, Harold M. Crowley and three others, July 7, 1933 in Albany. Settled for a ransom of $40,500 and freed O'Connell, following 23 days in captivity. Escaped from custody, with Oley and Crowley, at the Onondaga County Penitentiary in Jamesville, November 1937, awaiting transfer to federal prison, captured within days and sent to Alcatraz Prison to serve their time. Committed suicide throwing himself under a prison truck.

JEFFERSON, FATS (William) Jun 6, 1901 Waco, TX - Feb 26, 1988 Albany, NY
Albany-area jazz pianist and singer. Protégé of jazz legend, Thomas "Fats" Waller, adopting Waller's nickname when he died in 1943. Performed in New York City from the 1920s to the 1940s.

JOHNSON, ALBERT L. 1958 Schenectady, NY - Feb 28, 1994 Albany, NY
High School basketball star for Mount Pleasant in Schenectady. Won the 1975-76 Schoolboy Basketball Player-of-the-Year Award. Played three seasons at the University of Connecticut for coaches, Dee Rowe and Dom Perno. Committed suicide, stuck by a truck, walking into the westbound lane of I-90.

KEYES (Mumma)**, MARTHA** Oct 6, 1907 Des Moines, IA - Feb 22, 1992 Albany, NY
Actress, drama teacher and former Revlon model. Appeared in episodes of *Perry Mason*, *Rawhide* and *From These Roots*.

LEIGH, CHARLIE (Charles I.) Oct 29, 1945 Halifax, VA - Oct 26, 2006 Albany, NY
Kick returner and running back for the Cleveland Browns, Miami Dolphins and Green Bay Packers from 1968-1969 and 1971-1974. Two-time Super Bowl champion with the Dolphins, including their undefeated 17-0 season in 1972. Played behind Hall of Fame running backs, Larry Csonka and Leroy Kelly and All-Pro's, Mercury Morris and Jim Kiick. Fourth player in NFL history to sign a professional contract directly out of high school, bypassing college.

GRANBY CENTER CEMETERY
Granby Center Road
Hannibal, NY 13074

HANCOCK, FREEMAN 1807 MA - Jul 12, 1872 Granby, NY
With **Mary Williams Hancock** (1816 Providence, RI - Jul 13, 1880 Granby, NY), the parents of Theodore E. Hancock, New York State Attorney General from 1893-1898. Grandparents of Clarence E. Hancock, United States Representative-NY from 1927-1947, and attorney, Stewart F. Hancock Sr. Great-grandparents of Judge Stewart F. Hancock Jr.

GRAND VIEW CEMETERY
West Street
Whitesboro, NY 13492

BARNARD, MOSES Dec 12, 1750 Simsbury, CT - Jan 3, 1811 Whitesboro, NY
Revolutionary War veteran. Fought at Bunker Hill. Great-grandfather of Olivia Louise Langdon Clemens, the wife of author, Mark Twain. Married his cousin, Hannah Barnard, who died June 19, 1848 in Lenox, NY, three months shy of her 103rd birthday.

GOLD, THOMAS RUGGLES Nov 4, 1764 Cornwall, CT - Oct 24, 1827 Whitesboro, NY
United States Representative-NY from 1809-1813 and 1815-1817.

KAISER, FRANK (Francis John) 1842 Steinheim, Germany - Oct 18, 1929 Daytona Beach, FL
With **Mary (Anna Marie) Yops Kaiser** (1847 Nordrhein-Westfalen, Germany - Dec 1, 1899 Whitesboro, NY), the parents of industrialist, Henry J. Kaiser, called "the father of modern shipbuilding" and founder of Kaiser Permanente health care. Great-grandparents of Edgar Kaiser, Jr., owner of the Denver Broncos from 1981-1984, and musician, Henry Kaiser.

SPRIGGS, JOHN THOMAS Apr 5, 1825 Peterborough, England - Dec 23, 1888 Utica, NY
United States Representative-NY from 1883-1887. Mayor of Utica from 1868-1880.

GRANDVIEW CEMETERY
Clinton Street
Batavia, NY 14020

ANDERSON, GLENN RICHARD Oct 16, 1916 OH - Feb 15, 1986 De Leon Springs, FL
Father of Terry A. Anderson, American journalist held hostage in Lebanon from March 16, 1985 until his release on December 4, 1991, the longest held American hostage, captured by Shiite Hezbollah militants during the Lebanese Civil War. Died of cancer, eleven months after his son's abduction.

ANDERSON, GLENN RICHARD Mar 21, 1940 Lorain, OH - Jun 7, 1986 NY
Brother of Terry A. Anderson, American journalist held hostage in Lebanon from March 16, 1985 until his release, December 4, 1991, the longest held American hostage, captured by Shiite Hezbollah militants during the Lebanese Civil War. Died on an airplane returning home from New York City, receiving treatment for lung cancer. Delivered an impassioned plea to his brother's kidnappers to release him in the weeks prior to his death.

GARDNER, JOHN CHAMPLIN Jul 21, 1933 Batavia, NY - Sept 14, 1982 Susquehanna, PA
Novelist and critic. Author of *Grendel, The Sunset Dialogues* and *October Light*. Husband of poet, Liz Rosenberg, from 1980-1982. Killed in a motorcycle accident on Route 92, near Oakland, Susquehanna County, PA, days before he was to marry a third time.

LEWIS, RICHARD J. Aug 1, 1929 - Sept 13, 1971 Attica, NY
New York State Correctional Officer. Held hostage, died from gunshot wounds, one of ten correctional officers killed in a prison riot at Attica Correctional Facility, which left 33 prisoners dead.

ROWELL, E.N. (Edward Newton) 1847 Utica, NY - Dec 21, 1929 Batavia, NY
Owner and operator of the E.N. Rowell Company, manufacturers of paper boxes. On October 29, 1883, thinking his wife, Jennie Abigail Luce Rowell, was having an affair, he hid in the closet of his home, 123 Bank Street in Batavia, and shot and killed, Johnson Lynch, of Utica. He was arrested and charged with second-degree manslaughter, found not guilty in January 1884.

GREEN HILL CEMETERY
Market Street
Amsterdam, NY 12010

ARNOLD, BENEDICT Oct 5, 1780 Amsterdam, NY - Mar 3, 1849 Amsterdam, NY
United States Representative-NY from 1829-1831. Namesake, though no relation, of General Benedict Arnold, Revolutionary War hero-turned-traitor. Brother-in-law of Matthias Jacob Bovee, United States Representative-NY from 1835-1837.

CHARLES, WILLIAM BARCLAY Apr 3, 1861 Glasgow, Scotland - Nov 25, 1950 Amsterdam, NY
United States Representative-NY from 1915-1917.

COCHRANE, CLARK BETTON May 31, 1815 New Boston, NH - Mar 5, 1867 Albany, NY
United States Representative-NY from 1857-1861.

DUNCAN, MARY Aug 13, 1895 Luttrellville, VA - May 9, 1993 Palm Beach. FL
Film and theater actress. Appeared on Broadway. Wife of international polo star, Stephen "Laddie" Sanford. Daughter-in-law of John Sanford, United States Representative-NY from 1889-1893. Close friend and neighbor of Rose Fitzgerald Kennedy, the mother of President John F. Kennedy.

SANFORD, JOHN Jun 3, 1803 Roxbury, CT - Oct 4, 1857 Amsterdam, NY
United States Representative-NY from 1841-1843. Father of Stephen Sanford, United States Representative-NY from 1869-1871. Grandfather of John Sanford II, United States Representative-NY from 1889-1893. Uncle of Henry Shelton Sanford, United States Minister to Belgium, under President Abraham Lincoln, and founder of Sanford, FL.

SANFORD, JOHN Jan 18, 1851 Amsterdam, NY - Sept 26, 1939 Saratoga, NY
United States Representative-NY from 1889-1893. Prominent thoroughbred racehorse breeder. Owned the Sanford Racing Stable in Saratoga. Won the 1916 Kentucky Derby with his colt, George Smith. Father of international polo star, Stephen "Laddie" Sanford and World War II spy, explorer and environmentalist, Gertrude Sanford Legendre. Son of Stephen Sanford, United States Representative-NY from 1869-1871. Grandson of John Sanford, United States Representative-NY from 1841-1843.

SANFORD, LADDIE (Stephen) Sept 14, 1898 Amsterdam, NY - May 1977
International polo star. Husband of actress, Mary Duncan. Son of John Sanford II, United States Representative-NY from 1889-1893. Sister of World War II spy, explorer and environmentalist, Gertrude Sanford Legendre. Grandson of Stephen Sanford, United States Representative-NY from 1869-1871. Great-grandson of John Sanford, United States Representative-NY from 1841-1843.

SANFORD, STEPHEN May 26, 1826 Mayfield, NY - Feb 13, 1913 Amsterdam, NY
United States Representative-NY from 1869-1871. Thoroughbred racehorse breeder. Founded Hurricana Stock Farms in Amsterdam. Namesake of the Sanford Stakes at the Saratoga Racetrack. Father of John Sanford II, United States Representative-NY from 1841-1843. Son of John Sanford, United States Representative-NY from 1841-1843. Cousin of Henry Shelton Sanford, United States Minister to Belgium, under President Abraham Lincoln, and founder of Sanford, FL.

STEWART, JOHN KNOX Oct 20, 1853 Perth, NY - Jun 27, 1919 Amsterdam, NY
United States Representative-NY from 1899-1903.

WALLIN, SAMUEL Jul 31, 1856 Easton, PA - Dec 1, 1917 Amsterdam, NY
United States Representative-NY from 1913-1915. Mayor of Amsterdam from 1901-1902.

GREEN HILL CEMETERY
Mill Street
Dryden, NY 13053

SWEETLAND, EDWIN R. Jan 10, 1875 - Oct 21, 1951 Dryden, NY
Syracuse University head football coach from 1900-1902, and Ohio State, Colgate, Kentucky, Miami University, West Virginia, Tulane and Alfred from 1904-1905 and 1908-1918. Founder and first coach

for the Syracuse University crew. First paid coach for the University of Kentucky basketball team, in 1909. Played collegiate football for Cornell University, under head coach, Pop Warner, in 1898.

GREENBUSH REFORMED CHURCH CEMETERY
688 Columbia Turnpike
East Greenbush, NY 12061

GENET, EDMOND-CHARLES Jan 8, 1763 Versailles, France - Jul 14, 1834 Rensselaer County, NY
French Ambassador to the United States, during the French Revolution. Known as "Citizen Genet." Granted political asylum by President George Washington, sparing him the guillotine in France. Sister of Jeanne-Louise-Henriette Campan, lady-in-waiting to Queen Marie Antoinette. Son-in-law of Vice-President George Clinton.

HERRICK, RICHARD PLATT Mar 23, 1791 East Greenbush, NY - Jun 20, 1846 Washington D.C.
United States Representative-NY from 1845-1846. Died during his first term in office. A cenotaph in his memory was placed in Congressional Cemetery in Washington D.C.

PHELPS, ED Mar 3, 1879 Albany, NY - Jan 31, 1942 East Greenbush, NY
Catcher for the Pittsburgh Pirates, Cincinnati Reds, St. Louis Cardinals and Brooklyn Dodgers from 1902-1910 and 1912-1913. Appeared in the first World Series, 1903 for Pittsburgh, collecting a base hit of Hall of Famer, Cy Young.

GREENLAWN CEMETERY
Greenlawn Avenue
Bainbridge, NY 13733

IVES, IRVING MCNEIL Jan 24, 1896 Bainbridge, NY - Feb 24, 1962 Norwich, NY
United States Senator-NY from 1947-1959. Lost the 1954 New York gubernatorial race to Averell Harriman. Speaker of the New York State Assembly in 1936. Namesake of Ives Hall in the Cornell University School of Industrial and Labor Relations.

GREENLAWN MEMORIAL PARK
2932 Warners Road
Warners, NY 13164

BEARE, KATHRYN M. Nov 7, 1917 Syracuse, NY - Jan 27, 1997 Syracuse, NY
Catcher for the Fort Wayne Daisies in the All-American Girl's Professional Baseball League in 1946.

Enshrined in the Baseball Hall of Fame in Cooperstown in 1988 as part of their *Women in Baseball* display.

BRUNDIDGE, EMILY MAY May 2, 1908 Manchester, England - January 13, 2010 East Syracuse, NY
Traveled to the United States on the *Lusitania*, arriving in New York City, April 24, 1915. *Lusitania* was torpedoed and sunk, on its return voyage, off the coast of Ireland by a German U-boat, May 7, 1915, killing 1,198 of its 1,959 passengers.

CHARLES, BILL Mar 30, 1923 Solvay, NY - Feb 20, 2002 Syracuse, NY
Co-owner and general manager of the Syracuse Blazers from 1969-1974. Named Minor League Executive-of-the-Year by *The Hockey News*, following the Blazers' Walker Cup championship in 1972.

CORRENTE, JAMES Jul 4, 1923 Syracuse, NY - Sept 5, 1997 Syracuse, NY
With **Pauline Diana Shoff Corrente** (Apr 16, 1925 VT - Apr 8, 2011 Sebastian, FL), the parents of Syracuse University honor student, James E. Corrente, who shot his 17-year old girlfriend, Nancy Marie Greco, three times, May 28, 1966 in Syracuse, drove to the Solvay police station and told officers "There's a girl in the car." He was found not guilty by reason of insanity, released from Marcy State Hospital in 1973.

DEJOHN (Di Gianni)**, JOHN** Oct 4, 1913 Clyde, NY - Apr 21, 2001 Syracuse, NY
Co-manager of two-time, world champion boxer, Carmen Basilio. He was in Basilio's corner when he won the welterweight title in 1955 against Tony DeMarco and in 1957 at Yankee Stadium when he beat Sugar Ray Robinson for the middleweight crown. Father of Jacqueline DeJohn, author of the novel, *Antonio's Wife*.

DOELL (Klim)**, M. CHRISTINE** (Mary) Nov 2, 1950 Niskayuna, NY - Jul 13, 2002 Syracuse, NY
Landscape preservation planner and garden historian. Sister of David G. Klim, Onondaga County Family Court Judge from 1995 until his death in 2006.

FLANDERS, JEREMY PHILIP Nov 9, 1980 Richmond, VA - Jul 25, 2008 New Tampa, FL
Budding photographer and artist. His work could be found on his website, Crazed Incorporated, as well as his quote, "For those who wish to know. This is it. This is what you are looking for. You may realize this now, or you may come to an understanding later. Your future is yours, this time is yours. What you do is up to you. What you are looking for will forever be in front of you. This will soon be the past. If you are wondering what I am talking about, don't worry, you will find out. When you find out is up to you. Sooner or later, it is all the same."

GRIESHABER (Honis)**, JENNA CHRISTINE** Jun 14, 1975 Camillus, NY - Nov 6, 1997 Albany, NY
Murder victim. Russell Sage College nursing student, choked to death by Nicholas Eugene Pryor, a paroled ex-convict, who was released from prison against the recommendation of the New York State Parole Board. Gov. George Pataki signed "Jenna's Law", August 6, 1998, requiring convicted felons to serve at least six-sevenths of their prison sentence.

HACHEY, TAMMARA KAY May 1, 1961 Syracuse, NY - Oct 25, 2009 Albany, NY
Educator. On-set teacher for the Tom Cruise and Dakota Fanning film, *War of the Worlds*, in 2005.

INGERSOLL, MERWIN 1917 Syracuse, NY - Apr 26, 1931 Syracuse, NY
Killed in his home when the dirt walls of an excavation under his house collapsed, crushing him, Oakley Road, Fairmount.

KLIM, DAVID G. Oct 18, 1952 Niskayuna, NY - Jul 13, 2006 Syracuse, NY
Onondaga County Family Court Judge from 1995-2006. Born with a hereditary disorder called osteogenesis imperfect. Brother of M. Christine Doell, landscape preservation planner and garden historian.

LITCHISON, PAUL CHARLES May 19, 1926 Syracuse, NY - Feb 28, 2015 Syracuse, NY
After his retirement, handmade and played a wash-tub bass, performed locally at social events with Chuckles 'n' Tunes for 20 years. Nicknamed "Hot Tub Paul" by his friend, radio personality, Phil Markert.

MICHELS, PAUL J. Dec 28, 1899 - Feb 25, 1974 Baldwinsville, NY
Owned and operated Michels Marina on the Seneca River in Baldwinsville for 25 years. Owned the original Syracuse Radio Supply Company, with John Sullivan. Comptroller for the Circus Hall of Fame in Sarasota.

MURPHY, RICHARD D. Nov 3, 1869 Stamford, CT - May 14, 1936 Syracuse, NY
Grandfather of jazz singer, Mark Murphy.

RAO, SAMUEL Apr 30, 1918 Syracuse, NY - Apr 1, 1994 Syracuse, NY
Owned and operated Sam Rao Florist and Greenhouses in Fairmount from 1949-1994. Brother of florist, George S. Rao.

REDDICK, RUTH RICHARD Oct 24, 1877 Southport, NY - Jul 23, 1979 Baldwinsville, NY
Direct descendant of John Robinson, pastor for the Pilgrim fathers, prior to their voyage on the *Mayflower*.

RICHARDSON, ALICE M. Jun 7, 1937 Syracuse, NY - Jun 10, 1952 Syracuse, NY
Victim of an unsolved homicide. Reported missing from her East Syracuse home, June 7, 1952, her body was found face down in a swamp, off Route 5 near Green Lakes State Park. Nine weeks later, 54-year old, Beatrice Grace Dain, was found nude and beaten in Syracuse, a similar murder that also remains unsolved.

SEARLES, GLENN MATTHEW Aug 5, 1972 Rochester, NY - Nov 29, 2003 Syracuse, NY
Onondaga County Deputy Sheriff, second to be killed in the line of duty, struck by a van on Interstate

481 in DeWitt, as he stopped to help a stranded motorist. Namesake of the Ambrose-Searles Move Over Act, signed into New York State law in 2010.

TRAINO, SAM C. Sept 16, 1919 Syracuse, NY - Apr 6, 2006 Syracuse, NY
Co-owned and operated the Coda Restaurant in Syracuse, with Norm Coleman, for 20 years.

WOODWORTH, SAMUEL Sept 10, 1896 Manlius, NY - Oct 22, 1954 Syracuse, NY
Central New York radio pioneer. Founded WFBL-AM, Syracuse's first radio station, in the Onondaga Hotel, November 19, 1924.

GREENMOUNT CEMETERY
Cemetery Road
Dansville, NY 14437

ALEXANDER, TAMMY JO Nov 2, 1963 Atlanta, GA - Nov 9, 1979 Caledonia, NY
Victim of an unsolved homicide. Known as "Caledonia Jane Doe." She was shot twice, and left in a rain-soaked cornfield off Route 20, near the Genesee River, remained unidentified for 35 years, until she was identified through a DNA match with her sisters. Despite being raised in Brooksville, FL, her family decided to keep her buried in the cemetery, with a new headstone, replacing the "Jane Doe" marker.

WALL, JERRY C. Jul 1, 1841 Geneva, NY - Apr 8, 1923 Dansville, NY
Civil War Medal of Honor recipient, for his capture of a Confederate Army flag at the Battle of Gettysburg, July 3, 1863.

GREENMOUNT CEMETERY
56 Greenmount Cemetery Lane
Whitehall, NY 12887

TEFFT, LAWRENCE M. Jan 20, 1914 Whitehall, NY - Apr 2, 1991 Syracuse, NY
Central New York radio personality, known professionally as "Larry Lawrence."

GREENRIDGE CEMETERY
17 Greenridge Place
Saratoga Springs, NY 12866

BATCHELLER, GEORGE SHERMAN Jul 25, 1837 Batchellerville, NY - Jul 2, 1908 Paris, France
United States Minister to Portugal from 1890-1892. Civil War Union Army Colonel. 4th great-grandson

of John Batcheller, Jurist for the Salem Witch Trials. Grandnephew of Roger Sherman, signer of the *Declaration of Independence* and United States Senator-CT from 1791-1793.

BRACKETT, CHARLES WILLIAM Nov 26, 1892 Saratoga Springs, NY - Mar 9, 1969 Bel Air, CA
Novelist, screenwriter and film producer. Collaborated with Billy Wilder on 13 films, including the Academy Award-winning films, *Sunset Boulevard*, *The Lost Weekend* and *Titanic*. Received an honorary Oscar for Lifetime Achievement in 1959. President of the Screen Writers Guild from 1938-1939 and the Academy of Motion Picture Arts and Sciences from 1949-1955. Drama Critic for *The New Yorker* from 1925-1929.

BRACKETT, EDGAR TRUMAN Jul 30, 1853 Wilton, NY - Feb 27, 1924 Saratoga Springs, NY
New York State Senator from 1896-1906 and 1909-1912. Built McGregor Links, a Saratoga County golf course, in 1921. Father of Academy Award-winning screenwriter, Charles Brackett.

BRACKETT (Fletcher)**, ELIZABETH BARROWS** Apr 7, 1890 Indianapolis, IN - Jun 7, 1948
Descendant of *Mayflower* passenger, Stephen Hopkins. First wife of Academy Award-winning screenwriter and producer, Charles Brackett. Five years after her death, Brackett married her sister, Lillian Fletcher Brackett. Niece of photographer, Kate Matthews.

BRACKETT (Fletcher)**, LILLIAN** Aug 14, 1894 Indianapolis, IN - May 5, 1984
Descendant of *Mayflower* passenger, Stephen Hopkins. Married her brother-in-law, Academy Award-winning screenwriter and producer, Charles Brackett, December 26, 1953, five years after the death of her sister, Elizabeth Barrows Fletcher Brackett. Niece of photographer, Kate Matthews.

CLARKE, JOHN May 12, 1773 England - May 6, 1846 Saratoga Springs, NY
Developed Congress Park in Saratoga. Bottled and sold Congress Water, turning Saratoga Spring water into an international brand.

DOE, NICHOLAS BARTLETT Jun 16, 1786 New York, NY - Dec 6, 1856 Saratoga Springs, NY
United States Representative-NY from 1840-1841.

HATHORN, HENRY HARRISON Nov 28, 1813 Greenfield, NY - Feb 20, 1887 Saratoga Springs, NY
United States Representative-NY from 1873-1877.

MARVIN, JAMES MADISON Feb 27, 1809 Ballston, NY - Apr 25, 1901 Saratoga Springs, NY
United States Representative-NY from 1863-1869.

MCMENOMY, JOHN 1816 - Jul 13, 1892 Saratoga, NY
First pastor of St. John the Evangelist Church, founded on the North side of Syracuse in 1852, celebrated the first mass at the church, on Easter Sunday in 1855. Pastor of St. Peter's Church in Saratoga at the time of his death.

PIERCE, GEORGE HYDE Jul 29, 1910 Richfield Springs, NY - Feb 25, 1998 Burlington, VT
With **Laura Marie Hughes Pierce** (Jun 15, 1922 NY - May 16, 1955 Saratoga Springs, NY), the parents of Emmy Award-winning actor, David Hyde Pierce.

SACKETT, WILLIAM AUGUSTUS Nov 18, 1811 Aurelius, NY - Sept 6, 1895 Saratoga Springs, NY
United States Representative-NY from 1849-1853.

WALWORTH (Hardin)**, ELLEN** Oct 20 1832 Jacksonville, IL - Jun 23, 1915 Washington, D.C.
Author, educator and poet. Co-founder of the National Society of the Daughters of the American Revolution. Daughter-in-law of Reuben Hyde Walworth, United States Representative-NY from 1821-1823. Her tumultuous marriage to Mansfield Tracy Walworth resulted in his murder, by their son, Frank Hardin Walworth, after his discovery of a series of threatening letters his father wrote to his mother. He was convicted of second-degree murder, sentenced to life in prison, pardoned by Gov. Lucius Robinson in 1877.

WALWORTH, FRANK HARDIN Aug 17, 1853 Saratoga, NY - Oct 19,1886 Saratoga, NY
Shot and killed his father, Mansfield Tracy Walworth, at Sturtevant House in Manhattan, June 3, 1873, after he discovered threatening letters his father wrote to his mother, author, Ellen Hardin Walworth. Convicted of second-degree murder, sentenced to life in prison, including Sing Sing and Auburn Prison, before his pardon by Gov. Lucius Robinson in 1877. Subject of the book, *The Fall of the House of Walworth: A Tale of Madness and Murder in Gilded Age America*, published in 2010. Grandson of Reuben Hyde Walworth, United States Representative-NY from 1821-1823.

WALWORTH, MANSFIELD TRACY Dec 3, 1830 Albany, NY - Jun 3, 1873 New York, NY
Author. Spent three months in Old Capitol Prison in Washington D.C. following his arrest in the company of Confederate spy, Augusta Morris, in 1862, paroled, sent to the custody of his father, Reuben Hyde Walworth, United States Representative-NY from 1821-1823. Married his stepsister, Ellen Hardin Walworth, the daughter of his father's second wife, Sarah Ellen Smith Walworth. Shot and killed by his son, Frank Hardin Walworth, at Sturtevant House in Manhattan, following his son's discovery of threatening he letters sent to his estranged wife. His son was convicted of second-degree murder, sentenced to life in prison, pardoned by Governor Lucius Robinson in 1877.

WALWORTH, REUBEN HYDE Oct 26, 1788 Bozrah, CT - Nov 27, 1867 Saratoga Springs, NY
United States Representative-NY from 1821-1823. Nominated by President James Tyler to the United States Supreme Court in 1844, not confirmed by the Senate.

WHITNEY, C.V. (Cornelius Vanderbilt) Feb 20, 1899 Roslyn, NY - Dec 13, 1992 Saratoga Springs, NY
Hollywood film producer. Founded C.V. Whitney Productions. Three-time winner of the U.S. Open Polo Championship. Thoroughbred horse race owner. Son of Harry Payne Whitney and Gertrude Vanderbilt. Grandson of William C. Whitney, United States Secretary of the Navy from 1885-1889, and Cornelius Vanderbilt II. 2nd great-grandson of Commodore Cornelius Vanderbilt. Cousin of John Hay

"Jock" Whitney, United States Ambassador to the United Kingdom, and Joan Whitney Payson, owner and President of the New York Mets from 1968-1975.

WOOLLEY, MONTY (Edgar Montillion) Aug 17, 1888 New York, NY - May 6, 1963 Albany, NY
Film and stage actor. Nicknamed "The Beard." Played Sheridan Whiteside in the 1941 film, *The Man Who Came to Dinner*, reciting the now classic line, "My, How Time Flies When You're Having Fun." English and drama professor at Yale University teaching, Cole Porter, Thornton Wilder and Stephen Vincent Benet, among others.

GREENWICH CEMETERY
Cottage Street / Route 52
Greenwich, NY 12834

CULVER, ERASTUS DEAN Mar 15, 1803 Champlain, NY - Oct 13, 1889 Greenwich, NY
U.S. Representative-NY from 1845-1847. United States Minister to Venezuela from 1862-1866, appointed by President Abraham Lincoln.

DON (Fish), **LAURA** (Anna) Feb 20, 1852 Glens Falls, NY - Feb 10, 1886 Greenwich, NY
Theater actress and playwright. Wrote the play, *A Daughter of the Nile*. Mother of writer and lyricist, Glen MacDonough, co-writer of the operetta, *Babes in Toyland*.

GANNON, KIM (James Kimball) Nov 18, 1900 Brooklyn, NY - Apr 29, 1974 Lake Worth, FL
Lyricist. Co-wrote "Moonlight Cocktail" with Luckey Roberts, recorded by the Glenn Miller Orchestra in 1942, "Angel in Disguise" with Paul Mann and Stefan Weiß, for the movie, *It All Came True*, and the Christmas standard, "I'll Be Home for Christmas", with Walter Kent, originally recorded by Bing Crosby in 1943. Inscription on his tombstone reads, "The Song is Forever."

POTTER, JOSEPH H. 1821 Easton, NY - Mar 31, 1902 Greenwich, NY
Associate Justice of the New York State Supreme Court from 1871-1885. Built Skene Manor in Whitehall in 1875, called the "Castle on the Mountain", listed on the National Register of Historic Places in 1974. Father of United States Navy Rear Admiral, William P. Potter, who served on the Sampson Board's Court of Inquiry investigating the *U.S.S. Maine* in 1898, and sailed with the Great White Fleet, 16 battleships sent around the world by President Theodore Roosevelt in 1907.

GREENWOOD CEMETERY
Roosevelt Highway / Route 18
Kendall, NY 14476

AUGUR, AMMON Nov 1789 - May 6, 1830 Kendall, NY
With **Annis Wellman Augur** (Feb 2, 1795 Jamaica, VT - Sept 24, 1872 Kendall, NY), the parents of Civil War Union Army Major General, Christopher Columbus Augur, present when President Abraham Lincoln died at Peterson's House, detailed to escort the President's body to the White House. He died January 16, 1898 in Washington D.C., age 76, buried in Arlington National Cemetery.

GROTON RURAL CEMETERY
Clark Street
Groton, NY 13073

DICK (Shumway)**, SARAH** Mar 13, 1820 Stockbridge, MA - Feb 19, 1914 Syracuse, NY
As a five-year old child in Stockbridge, had the distinction of being kissed on the hand by Marquis de Lafayette, French General and Revolutionary War hero, under General George Washington.

LOVE (Stewart)**, MARY ANN** Apr 7, 1760 NY - Aug 14, 1818 Groton, NY
First wife of Samuel Love, the second husband of Eunice Smith Fillmore, who married Nathaniel Fillmore, the widowed father of President Millard Fillmore.

WILLOUGHBY, FRANKLIN Oct 30, 1800 MA - May 29, 1867 Groton, NY
With **Keziah Delano Willoughby** (Jul 19, 1797 Kent, CT - Dec 17, 1848 Groton, NY), the parents of Westel Willoughby, Associate Justice of the Virginia Supreme Court of Appeals, presided over *Lee v. Chase*, in which the estate of Robert E. Lee and his wife, Mary Anna Custis Lee, was awarded to the United States Government for the formation of Arlington National Cemetery. Grandparents of political science academics, Westel Woodbury Willoughby and his twin brother, William Franklin Willoughby.

GROVE CEMETERY
East Morris Street
Bath, NY 14810

AVERELL, WILLIAM WOODS Nov 5, 1832 Cameron, NY - Feb 3, 1900 Bath, NY
Civil War Union Army Brevet Major General. United States Consul to British North America from 1866-1869, under President Andrew Johnson.

HOWELL, EDWARD Oct 16, 1792 Newburgh, NY - Jan 30, 1871 Bath, NY
U.S. Representative-NY from 1833-1835.

HUBBELL, WILLIAM SPRING Jan 17, 1801 Painted Post, NY - Nov 16, 1873 Bath, NY
U.S. Representative-NY from 1843-1845.

NELLIS (Brundage)**, ELIZA M.** Sept 11, 1839 Bath, NY - Aug 8, 1883 Bath, NY
Tombstone is a large sphere with a banner wrapped around its center that reads, "Perfection to Eternity", designed and patented by her husband, Aaron J. Nellis.

ROBIE, REUBEN Jul 15, 1799 Corinth, VT - Jan 21, 1872 Bath, NY
U.S. Representative-NY from 1851-1853. His home, the Reuben Robie House in Bath, was listed on the National Register of Historic Places in 1983.

RUMSEY, DAVID Dec 25, 1810 Salem, NY - Mar 12, 1883 Bath, NY
U.S. Representative-NY from 1847-1851. Associate Justice of the New York State Supreme Court from 1873-1880.

UNDERHILL, EDWIN STEWART Oct 7, 1861 Bath, NY - Feb 7, 1929 Cooper Plains, NY
United States Representative-NY from 1911-1915.

WOODS, WILLIAM 1790 Washington County, NY - Aug 7, 1837 Bath, NY
U.S. Representative-NY from 1823-1825. Elected to Congress due to the resignation of William B. Rochester.

GROVE CEMETERY
Main Street / Route 395
Delanson, NY 12053

BRIGGS, JOHN CALVIN May 10, 1863 Duanesburg, NY - Mar 21, 1953 Duanesburg, NY
Quaker Street homesteader. With **Bertha Wemple Briggs** (Dec 7, 1867 NY – Apr 27, 1949 Duanesburg, NY), the grandparents of actor, Jack Briggs, the husband of Academy Award-winning actress, Ginger Rogers, from 1943-1949.

BRIGGS, WALTER W. 1891 Duanesburg, NY - Mar 28, 1960 Albany, NY
Father of actor, Jack Briggs, the husband of Academy Award-winning actress, Ginger Rogers, from 1943-1949.

GURN SPRINGS CEMETERY
Ballard Road / Route 33
Wilton, NY 12831

GOGOLAK, JOHN E. (Janos) Sept 11, 1910 Budapest, Hungary - Apr 1988 Wilton, NY
Physician. Father of NFL placekickers, Pete Gogolak, of the Buffalo Bills and New York Giants from 1964-1974, and Charlie Gogolak, of the Washington Redskins, Boston Patriots and New England Patriots from 1966-1968 and 1970-1972. Grandfather of restauranteur, David P. Gogolak, co-founder of Asqew Grill in San Francisco, killed in an avalanche, skiing with his brother-in-law on Whitefish Mountain Resort, January 13, 2008, age 36.

HAGUE CEMETERY
Cemetery Road
Hague, NY 12836

BENNETT, LEROY D. Dec 18, 1888 Warrensburg, NY - Nov 13, 1966 Schenectady, NY
Brother of aviator, Floyd Bennett, pilot for Admiral Richard E. Byrd on the first-ever flight over the North Pole, in 1926, died of influenza, April 25, 1928, Quebec City, age 37, buried in Arlington National Cemetery.

HAILESBORO CEMETERY
Old Route 58
Hailesboro, NY 13642

ABSALON, JOHN J. Feb 5, 1934 Gouverneur, NY - Jan 24, 2004 Hailesboro, NY
Father of Krista Absalon, who accused five men of gang-rape at the Casablanca Bar in Gouverneur, October 1991, catching the attention of the national media. Jodie Foster won an Academy Award for the film, *The Accused*, based on the event, in 1988.

HALSEY VALLEY CEMETERY
Halsey Valley Road
Barton, NY 13734

PIIPARI (Viljanen)**, EMILY** (Emilia) Jan 21, 1879 Helsinki, Finland - May 21, 1954 Sayre, PA
Mother of Greta Konen Peck, died January 19, 2008 in Beverly Hills, age 96, the wife of Academy Award-winning actor, Gregory Peck, from 1942-1955. Buried with her second husband, Olli Piipari, who died in 1962.

HAMIL CEMETERY
Old Oneida Road / Route 83
Rome, NY 13440

LIVINGSTON, GILBERT JAMES Oct 14, 1758 Poughkeepsie, NY - Apr 7, 1833 Rome, NY
3rd great-grandfather of Prescott Sheldon Bush, United States Senator-CT from 1952-1963. 4th great-grandfather of President George Herbert Walker Bush. 5th great-grandfather of President George Walker Bush, John Ellis "Jeb" Bush, Governor of Florida from 1999-2007, and entertainment reporter, Billy Bush. Husband of Susannah Lewis Livingston, buried in Prospect Hill Cemetery, Schuylerville.

HAMILTON COLLEGE CEMETERY
Hamilton College
Clinton, NY 13323

BATT, GREGORY JOSEPH Jan 7, 1920 Buffalo, NY - Mar 22, 1993 Clinton, NY
Hockey player-head coach for Colgate University, including its undefeated season in 1943. Center for the Clinton Comets from 1949-1956. Professor of Physical Education at Hamilton College from 1948-1985. Son of Paul J. Batt, Associate Justice of the New York State Supreme Court.

ERHARDT, JOHN GEORGE Nov 1, 1889 Brooklyn, NY - Feb 18, 1951 Cape Town, South Africa
United States Minister to Austria from 1946-1950. United States Ambassador to South Africa from 1950-1951.

GRANT, ULYSSES SIMPSON Jul 4, 1881 Chicago, IL - Aug 29, 1968 Clinton, NY
World War II General. Civil Defense Planner. Graduated from West Point Academy, sixth in his class, which included General Douglas MacArthur. Grandson of President Ulysses S. Grant and First Lady Julia Dent Grant. Son of General Frederick Dent Grant. Son-in-law of Elihu Root, United States Secretary of War from 1899-1904 and United States Secretary of State from 1905-1909. Father-in-law of John S. Dietz, President of the R.E. Dietz Company from 1967-1977.

KIRKLAND, SAMUEL Dec 1, 1741 Norwich, CT - Feb 28, 1808 Clinton, NY
Founded Hamilton College in 1793. Congregational Minister to the Iroquois Confederacy. Negotiated the Oneida Alliance between the Colonists and Oneida Indians during the American Revolution. Originally buried in the garden of his home, Harding Street in Clinton.

ROOT, ELIHU Feb 15, 1845 Clinton, NY - Feb 7, 1937 New York, NY
United States Secretary of War from 1899-1904, under President William McKinley and President Theodore Roosevelt. United States Secretary of State from 1905-1909, during President Roosevelt's second term in office. United States Senator-NY from 1909-1915. Awarded the Nobel Peace Prize in 1912. Father-in-law of General Ulysses S. Grant III.

SKENANDOA (Shenandoah) 1716 Conestoga, ON, Canada - Mar 11, 1816 Oneida County, NY
Oneida Indian Chief. Supported the Colonists in the Revolutionary War. Converted to Christianity by
Rev. Samuel Kirkland and, per his request, was buried next to Kirkland.

WOOLLCOTT, ALEXANDER Jan 19, 1887 Phalanx, NJ - Jan 23, 1943 New York, NY
Drama critic. Commentator for *The New York Times*, *New York Herald* and *The New Yorker* magazine.
His positive review of the Marx Brothers' Broadway play, *I'll Say She Is*, helped launch their film
career. Founding member of the Algonquin Round Table. Inspiration for Sheridan Whiteside, the lead
character in the play, *The Man Who Came to Dinner*, written by George S. Kaufman and Moss Hart.

HANNACROIX RURAL CEMETERY
Newry Road / Route 411
Westerlo, NY 12193

TYRON (Garrow)**, FLORENCE M.** Mar 22, 1934 Dannemora, NY - Feb 8, 2014 Schenectady, NY
Sister of spree killer, Robert Garrow, who killed four people in 1973, shot dead during a prison escape
in 1978. Mother of Suzanne Margaret Burns Basso, convicted in the 1998 murder of Louis Charles
"Buddy" Musso, outside of Houston, executed by lethal injection, February 5, 2014, at the Texas State
Penitentiary in Huntsville, buried in the Captain Joe Byrd Cemetery, the prison graveyard.

HANNIBAL CENTER CEMETERY
Cemetery Drive
Hannibal, NY 13074

BRACKETT (Flower)**, ANNA WATSON** Mar 29, 1777 Ashfield, MA - Feb 11, 1866 Hannibal, NY
Great-grandmother of Edgar Truman Brackett, New York State Senator from 1896-1906 and
1909-1912. 2nd great-grandmother of Academy Award-winning screenwriter, Charles Brackett.

HARFORD MILLS CEMETERY
Route 200
Harford Mills, NY 13835

ROCKEFELLER, GODFREY LEWIS Sept 24, 1783 Albany, NY - Sept 28, 1857 Richford, NY
With **Lucy Avery Rockefeller** (Feb 11, 1786 Great Barrington, MA - Apr 6, 1867 Richford, NY), the
grandparents of John Davison Rockefeller, co-founder of Standard Oil, first American billionaire.
Great-grandparents of John D. Rockefeller Jr., founder of Rockefeller Center in New York City. 2nd
great-grandparents of Vice-President Nelson A. Rockefeller and Winthrop Rockefeller, Governor of

Arkansas from 1967-1971. 3rd great-grandparents of John Davison "Jay" Rockefeller IV, United States Senator-WV from 1985-2015.

HARRIS HILL CEMETERY
8401 Main Street
Williamsville, NY 14221

FILLMORE, SIMEON Dec 13, 1768 Bennington, VT - Apr 30, 1848 Clarence, NY
Uncle of President Millard Fillmore, brother of the President's father, Nathaniel Fillmore.

HEBREW AID SOCIETY CEMETERY
Route 209
Napanoch, NY 12458

RESNICK, JOSEPH YALE Jul 13, 1924 Ellenville, NY - Oct 6, 1969 Las Vegas, NV
United States Representative-NY from 1965-1969. Co-founded Channel Master, after his invention of an inexpensive, easy to install, television antenna. Namesake of the Joseph Y. Resnick Airport in Ellenville.

ROSENSTEIN, MILT (Milton) Jun 20, 1920 Hunter, NY – Nov 28, 1944 Leyte, the Philippines
Minor League pitcher for the Miami Beach Flamingos of the Florida East Coast League in 1941, winning 20 games his only professional season. Killed in combat during World War II. Grandson of Charles Slutsky, founder of the Nevele Hotel and Country Club in Wawarsing, in 1901.

SLUTSKY, CHARLES A. Feb 20, 1940 New York, NY - Apr 17, 1984 Poughkeepsie, NY
Co-owned and operated the Nevele Grande Hotel in Wawarsing. Owner and breeder of champion harness race horses, including Incredible Nevele.

HEBREW TAILORS CEMETERY
Western Avenue
Guilderland, NY 12084

SIMON (Demsky)**, BETTY** Dec 26, 1910 Amsterdam, NY - Jul 1980 Albany, NY
Sister of Academy Award-winning actor, Kirk Douglas. Aunt of Academy Award-winning actor/producer, Michael Douglas.

HECTOR UNION CEMETERY
Route 79
Burdett, NY 14818

ARGETSINGER, CAMERON REYNOLDS Mar 1, 1921 Youngstown, OH - Apr 22, 1908 Burdett, NY
Founded road-racing at Watkins Glen, introducing Formula 1 racing to the area. Inaugurated the U.S.
Grand Prix at Watkins Glen in 1961. President of the International Motor Racing Research Center
from 2002-2007. Inducted into the Sports Car Club of America Hall of Fame in 2005.

WOOD (Van Etten), **LOIS SHIRLEY** Aug 5, 1930 Ithaca, NY - Sept 2, 2008 Seagrove, NC
Mother of child killer, Lewis Stephen Lent Jr., sentenced to life in prison for the murders of Sarah Anne
Wood, of Frankfort, and Jimmy Bernardo, of Pittsfield, MA. Wife of **Alfred George Wood** (Sept 13,
1925 Sayre, PA - Feb 25, 2008 Seagrove, NC). Former wife of Lewis Stephen Lent Sr., died May 17, 1992
in Deland, FL, age 67.

HERKIMER HOME STATE HISTORIC SITE
200 State Route 169
Little Falls, NY 13365

HERKIMER, NICHOLAS 1728 German Flatts, NY - Aug 17, 1777 Danube, NY
Revolutionary War New York Militia General. Mortally wounded leading his command into an ambush
in the Battle of Oriskany, in an effort to relieve Fort Stanwix. Namesake of Herkimer County.

HERMON CEMETERY
Route 17
Hermon, NY 13652

CUYLER (Smith), **FRANCES E.** Jun 1873 De Kalb, NY - Sept 20, 1948 Syracuse, NY
Operated a boarding house on Burnet Avenue in Syracuse where escaped convicts, John J. Oley,
Percy Geary and Harold M. Crowley, were captured following their escape from the Onondaga County
Penitentiary in Jamesville, November 1937. The prisoners, awaiting transfer to federal prison, were
captured within days, sent to Alcatraz Prison to serve their time. They were convicted of kidnapping
John J. O'Connell, nephew of Daniel P. O'Connell, chairman of the Albany Democratic Party, in July
1933.

GOINGS, HORACE Jun 1850 NY - Mar 14, 1919 Hermon, NY
Great-grandfather of Hollywood actor, Peter Breck, co-star in the TV series, *The Big Valley* and son of
jazz musician, Joseph "Jobie" Breck.

GOINGS, WINDSOR A. Apr 1876 Fowler, NY - 1937 Hermon, NY
Grandfather of Hollywood actor, Peter Breck, co-star in the TV series, *The Big Valley*. Father-in-law of jazz musician, Joseph "Jobie" Breck.

MASTON, JOSEPH Nov 2, 1945 Massena - Jun 8, 1987 Watertown, NY
Syracuse weekend radio personality for WHEN-AM, known as "Jay Walker."

WHITEFORD, IVAN Apr 1893 De Kalb, NY - 1957 Syracuse, NY
Convicted of first-degree perjury in the divorce trial of Bert and Lillian Sanderson in 1944, sent to Attica Prison for two-to-four years. Janitor at a boarding house on Burnet Avenue in Syracuse, operated by his mother, Frances E. Cuyler. Offered a tip to the FBI leading to the capture of escaped convicts, John J. Oley, Percy Geary and Harold M. Crowley, hiding in the boarding house after their escape from the Onondaga County Penitentiary in Jamesville, November 1937. The prisoners, awaiting transfer to federal prison, were captured within days, sent to Alcatraz Prison after their convictions in the kidnapping John J. O'Connell, nephew of Daniel P. O'Donnell, chairman of the Albany Democratic Party, July 1933.

HICKS CEMETERY
Wyncoop Creek Road / Route 3
Van Etten, NY 14889

BODINE, ELI H. Jun 18, 1887 Hurley, WI - Feb 24, 1975 Chemung, NY
Co-owner and founder of the Chemung Speedrome with his son, Eli H. Bodine, Jr. With **Edith E. Bodine** (Jul 27, 1880 Lambs Creek, PA - Jun 12, 1973 Chemung, NY), the grandparents of motorsport drivers, Geoff Bodine, winner of the 1986 Daytona 500, and Brett and Todd Bodine.

HIGGINSVILLE CEMETERY
Germany Road
Verona, NY 13478

LOOMIS, WILLIAM WALTER 1819 Sangerfield, NY - Jul 3, 1896 Higginsville, NY
Brother of Wash, Grove and Plumb Loomis, outlaws who terrorized Oneida and Madison Counties in the mid-1800s.

HIGHLAND CEMETERY
Vineyard Avenue / Route 44
Highland, NY 12528

PRATT, HARCOURT JOSEPH Oct 23, 1866 Highland, NY - May 21, 1934 Highland, NY
United States Representative-NY from 1925-1933. Died in a car accident.

HIGHLAND CEMETERY
13 1/2 Main Street
Marcellus, NY 13108

ATKINSON, ROBERT C. Oct 10, 1928 NY - Jan 2, 2011 Marcellus, NY
Editor of the *Post-Standard* from 1965-1993.

COLES, ALICE Aug 28, 1865 Eastham, VA - Nov 5, 1978 Syracuse, NY
Onondaga County's oldest resident, unofficially, with no official documents to confirm her birthdate. The 1978 *Guinness Book of World Records* lists only two people who have been authenticated to have lived longer. President Lyndon Johnson sent her a birthday card in 1965 to commemorate her 100th birthday.

CUMMINGS (Reed)**, RUTH** Mar 26, 1900 Marcellus, NY - Jan 23, 1975 Syracuse, NY
Nationally-known painter of primates. Did not begin painting until 1963, age 63.

DEJOHN (DiGianni)**, JOEY** (Joseph J.) Nov 21, 1926 Syracuse, NY - May 9, 2008 Oswego, NY
Professional boxer. Nicknamed "Golden Boy." Top-ranked middleweight contender from 1947-1955. His fight with Pete Mead in 1949, a seventh round loss, was ranked by *Ring Magazine* in 1999, one of the Top Ten fights in Madison Square Garden history. Lost to Jake LaMotta in the eighth round at the State Fair Coliseum in Syracuse in 1949. Brother of professional boxers, Ralph, Carmen, Michael and Louis DeJohn and John DeJohn, manager of world champion boxer, Carmen Basilio.

GALLINGER, JOHN M. Aug 12, 1918 Syracuse, NY - Dec 27, 2009 Marcellus, NY
Real estate executive. Founded Gallinger Real Estate in Syracuse in 1959.

LUCHSINGER, JOHN Y. 1882 Schwanden, Switzerland - Oct 19, 1959 Syracuse, NY
Jersey cattle breeder for 50 years. Six time-winner of a ribbon at the New York State Fair for offering the "best of the breed."

STONE, HORACE M. Jan 6, 1890 Marcellus, NY - Mar 7, 1944 Syracuse, NY
New York State Assemblyman from 1923-1936. Law partner of Syracuse mayor, Roland Marvin. Husband of Republican leader, Norma Stone. Stricken with a heart attack near the end of his speech to the Republican City Campaign Committee at the Hotel Syracuse.

STONE (Walsh), **NORMA** Aug 24, 1895 Marcellus, NY - Jul 4, 1981 Syracuse, NY
Known as "Mrs. Republican." Member of the first-ever edition of *Who's Who of American Woman*. Daughter of Thomas F. Walsh, first Sheriff in Onondaga County history. Wife of New York State Assemblyman, Horace Stone.

WALSH, THOMAS F. Feb 1862 Marcellus, NY - Dec 5, 1919 Marcellus, NY
First Sheriff in Onondaga County history, serving from 1907-1909. Father of Central New York Republican leader, Norma Stone.

WILSON, ARTHUR W. Jan 25, 1902 Marcellus, NY - Sept 8, 1988 Marcellus, NY
Two-term Onondaga County District Attorney, from 1954-1958.

HIGHLAND CEMETERY
Route 79
Richford, NY 13835

HOYT (Nixon), **WANETA ETHEL** May 13, 1946 Richford, NY - Aug 9, 1998 Bedford Hills, NY
Smothered to death her five children, Erik, James, Julie, Molly and Noah, ages one month to two years, between 1965-1971, long thought to have died from sudden infant death syndrome. Dr. Alfred Steinschneider cited the deaths as evidence that SIDS ran in families in his landmark study, published in the medical journal, *Pediatrics*, in 1972. Onondaga County District Attorney, William Fitzpatrick, prosecuting a similar case, tracked down the family in 1992, handing his case over to Tioga County district attorney, Robert Simpson, for prosecution. Convicted in 1995, sentenced to 75-years-to-life in prison, 15 years for each child. After the death of her last child, she and her husband, Tim Hoyt, adopted a boy, Jay Hoyt, who survives. Died from pancreatic cancer in prison, buried near her five children.

HOYT CHILDREN
Murder victims. Siblings, **Erik Hoyt**, October 17, 1964 - January 26, 1965, **James Avery Hoyt**, May 31, 1966 - September 26, 1968, **Julie Marie Hoyt**, July 19, 1968 - September 5, 1968, **Molly Hoyt**, March 18, 1970 - June 5, 1970, and **Noah Timothy Hoyt**, March 9, 1971 - July 28, 1971, victims of infanticide, killed by their mother, Waneta E. Hoyt, convicted and sentenced to 75 years-to-life in prison in 1995.

NIXON, ALBERT E. Sept 1, 1919 Richford, NY - Sept 8, 2000 Richford, NY
With **Dorothy I. Hutchings Nixon** (Nov 29, 1920 - Sept 1, 1989 Binghamton, NY), the parents of Waneta Ethel Nixon Hoyt, convicted of infanticide, smothering her five children, Erik, James, Julie, Molly and Noah to death, between 1965-1971. Involved in a car accident on Route 13, Tompkins County, August 30, 1989, rear-ended when driving, pushing his car into the path of another, suffered a broken arm, his wife dying two days later from a fractured skull.

HILLCREST CEMETERY
Cemetery Road
DeRuyter, NY 13052

CRAFT (Brown), **HAZEL MADELENE** Mar 19, 1891 South Otselic, NY - Feb 10, 1956 Norwich, NY
Sister of Grace M. Brown, murdered by her boyfriend, Chester E. Gillette, in 1906, events that inspired
the Theodore Dreiser novel, *An American Tragedy,* and the film, *A Place in the Sun*, in 1951.

JOHNSON (Brown), **RUBY** Mar 18, 1895 South Otselic, NY - Feb 18, 1985 Norwich, NY
Sister, last surviving sibling, of Grace M. Brown, murdered by her boyfriend, Chester E. Gillette, in
1906, events that inspired the Theodore Dreiser novel, *An American Tragedy,* and the film, *A Place in
the Sun*, in 1951.

MILKS, GRANT S. Apr 18, 1892 Great Valley, NY - Apr 8, 1978 Cortland, NY
Mayor of DeRuyter for 20 years. Owned and operated the Taber House in DeRuyter.

HILLCREST CEMETERY
Route 12
Sauquoit, NY 13456

KILBOURN (Ballard), **MARY** Aug 28, 1786 Plainfield, NH - Jan 1, 1831 Paris, NY
With **Thomas Kilbourn** (Aug 22, 1771 East Hartford, CT – Jan 8, 1837 Paris, NY), the grandparents of
George Eastman, founder of the Eastman Kodak Company and the Eastman School of Music. Sister
of Jonathan Ballard, the great-grandfather of Helen Geneva Baughman Thomas, who married Jason
Ray Thomas, the great-grandson of Jacob Driver Sr., whose brother, Benjamin Driver, was the
grandfather of comedian, Phyllis Diller.

HILLINGTON CEMETERY
Route 23
Morris, NY 13808

GODLEY, GEORGE MCMURTRIE Aug 23, 1917 New York, NY - Nov 7, 1999 Oneonta, NY
United States Ambassador to Congo from 1964-1966, Laos from 1969-1973 and Lebanon from
1974-1976.

FRANCHOT, NICHOLAS VAN VRANKEN Aug 21, 1855 Morris, NY - May 6, 1943 Olean, NY
President of the Mid-Continent Oil and Gas Producers from 1907-1908. Son of Richard Hanson
Franchot, United States Representative-NY from 1861-1863. Grandfather of actor, Franchot Tone,
husband of actresses, Joan Crawford, Jean Wallace, Barbara Payton and Dolores Dorn.

HILLSIDE CEMETERY
Van Buren Street
Antwerp, 13608

COOLIDGE, CASSIUS MARCELLUS Sept 18, 1844 Antwerp, NY - Jan 13, 1934 New York, NY
Painter, printer and inventor. Painted *Dogs Playing Poker* and other oil paintings depicting dogs in a
variety of human activities. Created carnival cut-outs, painted-wood props with holes to stick your face
through, generally seen at carnivals and fairs.

HILLSIDE CEMETERY
43 North Broad Street
Carthage, NY 13619

FLICK (Woolworth)**, FLORA M.** 1870 Champion, NY - 1943 Champion, NY
Sister of Frank Winfield Woolworth, founder of F.W. Woolworth's, the original "five & dime" store.

HILLSIDE CEMETERY
41 Jackson Road
Central Square, NY 13036

BURDICK, JEFFERSON R. 1900 Central Square, NY - Mar 13, 1963 Syracuse, NY
The "father of baseball card collecting." Created the *American Card Catalog* in 1937, using checklists
and card designations, some of which are still in use today. Donated his baseball collection, 306,353
cards, to the Metropolitan Museum of Art in New York City. Employed by Crouse-Hinds in Syracuse,
prior to his retirement due to arthritis.

COBLE, JOHN A. Dec 12, 1855 Fayetteville, NY - Feb 13, 1931 Syracuse, NY
Drove the team that turned the first furrow during the construction of the R.W. & O. Railroad at
Johnson's Cut, near Brewerton.

OTTOWAY, FLOYD W. Jul 3, 1917 Meridian, NY - Nov 11, 1984 Syracuse, NY
Central New York radio personality. Hosted the *Quiz Kids Show* and after the death of Jim DeLine,
hosted *Floyd Ottoway and the WSYR Gang* on WSYR-AM in Syracuse from 1962-1964.

VITELLO FAMILY January 25, 1961 Hastings, NY
Sarah Raines Vitello, age 25, expecting her seventh child momentarily, her six children, **Carmen Jr.**,
age 9, **Michael**, age 8, **Francis**, age 7, **Harry**, age 5, **Joseph**, age 3, and **James**, age 1, and their
dog, Lassie, victims of carbon monoxide poisoning, from a broken coal furnace. Her husband, Carmen
J. Vitello, the children's father, awoke nauseous, running from the house, yelling his family was dead,
14 hours after they died.

HILLSIDE CEMETERY
1033 Oregon Road East
Cortlandt, NY 10567

BALDWIN, ELEANOR L. Nov 11, 1897 NY - Jan 30, 1973 Syracuse, NY
Called the "First Lady of Fashion" in Central New York. Fashion Designer for Addis Company from 1946-1971. Host of the *Fashion at Luncheons* specials on WTVH-TV in Syracuse.

BOSWELL (Lloyd)**, MARTHA** Jun 9, 1905 Kansas City, MO - Jul 2, 1958 Peekskill, NY
Performed with her sisters, Connee and Vet Boswell, as the Boswell Sisters, recording and appearing in films in the 1930s. Performed regularly on Bing Crosby's radio program. Inducted into the Vocal Group Hall of Fame in 1998.

BOSWELL (Foore)**, MELDANIA GEORGE** Nov 1871 Randolph County, MO - Jul 6, 1947 Peekskill, NY
Mother of the Boswell Sisters, Connee, Vet and Martha, popular recording trio of the 1930s. Buried with two of her daughters, Vet and Marta, third daughter, Connee Boswell Leedy, lead singer of the trio, performed in a wheelchair, paralyzed from the waist down, died October 11, 1976 in New York City, age 68. buried in Ferncliff Cemetery, Hartsdale. Her husband, Alfred Clyde Boswell Sr., died September 1, 1944 in New Orleans, age 66, buried there, Carrollton Cemetery, next to their son, Alfred Clyde Boswell Jr., died October 22, 1918, age 18.

BOSWELL (Jones)**, VET** (Helvetia) May 20, 1911 Birmingham, AL - Nov 12, 1988 Peekskill, NY
Performed with her sisters, Connee and Martha Boswell, as the Boswell Sisters, recording and appearing in films in the 1930s. Performed regularly on Bing Crosby's radio program. Inducted into the Vocal Group Hall of Fame in 1998. Last surviving sister.

DEPEW, CHAUNCEY MITCHELL Apr 23, 1834 Peekskill, NY - Apr 5, 1928 New York, NY
United States Senator-NY from 1899-1911. President of the New York Central & Hudson River Railroad from 1885-1898. Attorney for railroad and shipping magnate, Cornelius Vanderbilt. Namesake of the village of Depew, NY and the town of Depew, OK.

HUSTED, JAMES WILLIAM Oct 31, 1833 Bedford, NY - Sept 25, 1892 Peekskill, NY
Speaker of the New York State Assembly from 1874-1890. Called "the Bald Eagle of Westchester." Father of James W. Husted II, United States Representative-NY from 1915-1923.

HUSTED, JAMES WILLIAM Mar 16, 1870 Peekskill, NY - Jan 2, 1925 New York, NY
United States Representative-NY from 1915-1923.

MACK (McNair)**, JIMMY** (James D.) May 9, 1952 Peekskill, NY - Jun 7, 2014 Cranbury, NJ
Comedian. Sketch writer, contributed material for *Saturday Night Live!* Killed in a six-vehicle accident on the New Jersey Turnpike, returning home from the Dover Downs Hotel & Casino in Delaware,

where his friend, comedian, Tracey Morgan, was performing, when their minibus was struck by a Walmart tractor-trailer driver, Kevin Roper, who fell asleep at the wheel. Morgan survived, suffering traumatic brain injuries and broken bones. Morgan, and other passengers in the minibus, sued Walmart, settling out of court, the driver was charged with first-degree manslaughter.

NELSON, WILLIAM Jun 29, 1784 Hyde Park, NY - Oct 3, 1869 Peekskill, NY
United States Representative-NY from 1847-1851.

TRIMPE, MICHAEL RICHARD Apr 29, 1946 Peekskill, NY - Mar 19, 2001 Arlington, VA
Brother of comic book artist, Herb Trimpe, first to draw the character, Wolverine, of the X-Men.

VAN CORTLANDT (Clinton)**, CATHERINE** Nov 5, 1770 - Jan 10, 1811 Cortlandt Manor, NY
Wife of Pierre Van Cortlandt, United States Representative-NY from 1811-1813. Daughter of   Vice-President George Clinton. Sister-in-law of French diplomat, Edmond-Charles "Citizen" Genet.

VAN CORTLANDT, PHILIP Aug 21, 1749 New York, NY - Nov 21, 1831 Cortlandt Manor, NY
United States Representative-NY from 1793-1809. Revolutionary War Continental Army Brigadier General. Accompanied General Marquis de Lafayette, on his tour of the United States in 1824. Son of Pierre Van Cortlandt Sr., Lieutenant Governor of New York from 1777-1795. Brother of Pierre Van Cortlandt Jr., United States Representative-NY from 1811-1813.

VAN CORTLANDT, PIERRE Jan 10, 1721 Cortlandt Manor, NY - May 1, 1814 Cortlandt Manor, NY
Lieutenant Governor of New York from 1777-1795. Grandson of Stephanus Van Cortlandt, Mayor of New York City from 1677-1678. Inherited the Van Cortlandt Manor House in 1748. Father of Philip Van Cortlandt, United States Representative-NY from 1793-1809.

VAN CORTLANDT, PIERRE Aug 29, 1762 Cortlandt Manor, NY - Jul 13, 1848 Cortlandt Manor, NY
United States Representative-NY from 1811-1813. Husband of Catherine Clinton Van Cortlandt, the daughter of Vice-President George Clinton. Son of Pierre Van Cortlandt Sr., Lieutenant Governor of New York from 1777-1795. Brother of Philip Van Cortlandt, United States Representative-NY from 1793-1809.

HILLSIDE CEMETERY
50 Mulberry Street
Middletown, NY 10940

POWELSON, JOHN ABRAHAM Nov 18, 1883 Somerset, NJ - Aug 6, 1933 Syracuse, NY
Founded the Powelson Institute of Accounting, Inc. in Syracuse in 1926, purchased by Bryant & Stratton in 1976. Son of two-term Orange County district attorney, Abraham Van Nest Powelson. Brother of United States Navy ensign, Wilfred Van Nest Powelson, who gained notoriety for his

participation in the investigation of the loss of the battleship, *Maine*, died in Fort Lauderdale, May 20, 1960, age 87, buried in Arlington National Cemetery.

HINSDALE CEMETERY
4227 Route 16
Hinsdale, NY 14743

CHAMBERLIN SIBLINGS
Siblings **Earl W. Chamberlin** (Jun 9, 1875 - Jan 1, 1885 Maplehurst, NY) and his sister, **Susan M. Chamberlin** (Aug 4, 1881 - Jan 31, 1885 Maplehurst, NY) died one month apart, the epitaph on their shared tombstone reads "Their last words." Earl's side reads "I am going home", Susan's "I am where Earl is."

GIFFORD, BENJAMIN Sept 13, 1833 German Flatts, NY - Jul 14, 1901 Cuba, NY
Civil War Union Army Private. Awarded the Medal of Honor for capturing the flag at Sailor's Creek, VA, April 6, 1865.

JONES, AMASA 1790 - 1885 Hinsdale, NY
Buried twice in the same cemetery. Reburied in the back of the cemetery to accommodate the construction of Route 17, now Route 86.

NORTON, NELSON IRA Mar 30, 1820 Great Valley, NY - Oct 28, 1887 Hinsdale, NY
U.S. Representative-NY from 1875-1877. Elected to Congress due to the death of Augustus F. Allen. New York State Assemblyman from 1861-1862.

HOLLAND PATENT CEMETERY
9600 Powell Road
Holland Patent, NY 13354

BACON (Cleveland)**, MARGARET FALLEY** Oct 28, 1838 Caldwell, NJ - Mar 5, 1932 Toledo, OH
Sister, and last surviving sibling, of President Grover Cleveland, Sister of Rose Elizabeth "Libbie" Cleveland, First Lady from 1885-1886, during Cleveland's first presidency.

CLEVELAND (Neal)**, ANN** Feb 4, 1806 Baltimore, MD - Jul 13, 1882 Holland Patent, NY
Mother of President Grover Cleveland and Rose Elizabeth "Libbie" Cleveland, First Lady from 1885-1886, during Cleveland's first presidency, prior to his marriage to Frances Folsom Cleveland.

CLEVELAND, RICHARD FALLEY Jun 19, 1804 Norwich, CT - Oct 1, 1853 Holland Patent, NY
Father of President Grover Cleveland and Rose Elizabeth "Libbie" Cleveland, First Lady from

1885-1886, during Cleveland's first presidency, prior to his marriage to Frances Folsom Cleveland. Moved his family from New Jersey, where the president was born, to 109 Academy Street in Fayetteville, where he served as pastor of the Presbyterian Church. President Cleveland's three youngest siblings were born in Fayetteville, the family later moved to Oneida County.

CLEVELAND, WILLIAM NEAL Apr 7, 1832 Windham, CT - 1906
Brother of President Grover Cleveland and Rose Elizabeth "Libbie" Cleveland, First Lady from 1885-1886, during Cleveland's first presidency.

GUITEAU, FRANCIS Aug 12, 1736 Woodbury, CT - Jul 21, 1814 Whitesboro, NY
Physician. With **Anne Hodge Guiteau** (Mar 12, 1757 Woodbury, CT - Jan 17, 1851 Holland Patent, NY) , the great-grandparents of Charles Julius Guiteau, assassin of President James Garfield, July 2, 1881, Washington D.C., hanged for his crime, June 30, 1882.

HASTINGS (Cleveland), **ANNE NEAL** Jul 30, 1830 Windham, CT - Jun 1909
Sister of President Grover Cleveland and Rose Elizabeth "Libbie" Cleveland, First Lady from 1885-1886, during Cleveland's first presidency.

YEOMANS (Cleveland)**, SUSAN SOPHIA** Sept 2, 1843 Fayetteville, NY - Nov 4, 1930 Brooklyn, NY
Sister of President Grover Cleveland and Rose Elizabeth "Libbie" Cleveland, First Lady from 1885-1886, during Cleveland's first presidency.

HOLMESVILLE BURYING GROUND
Route 8
New Berlin, NY 13411

BURLINGAME, DANIEL May 11, 1778 Scituate, RI - May 10, 1824 Utica, NY
Methodist Church preacher. Son of Silas Burlingame, early settler of the village of New Berlin. With **Betsy Ludlow Burlingame** (Mar 25, 1782 New Berlin, NY - Sept 19, 1865 New Berlin, NY), the grandparents of Anson Burlingame, United States Representative-MA from 1855-1861. 4th great-grandparents of actor, Christopher Reeve.

BURLINGAME, SILAS May 20, 1741 Cranston, RI - Mar 5, 1829 New Berlin, NY
Early settler of the village of New Berlin. Participated in the Boston Tea Party, December 16, 1773. Father of Methodist preacher, Daniel Burlingame. Great-grandfather of Anson Burlingame, United States Representative-MA from 1855-1861. 5th great-grandfather of actor, Christopher Reeve.

HOLY CROSS CEMETERY
West Oak Hill Road / Route 120
Jamestown, NY 14701

BENENATI, BARTOLO 1870 Italy - 1955 Jamestown, NY
Great-grandfather of singer/songwriter, Natalie Merchant, lead singer of the alternative rock band, 10,000 Maniacs from 1981-1993.

MERCHANT, ANTHONY J. Feb 16, 1940 Jamestown, NY - Sept 5, 2015 Jamestown, NY
Father of singer/songwriter, Natalie Merchant, lead singer of the alternative rock band, 10,000 Maniacs from 1981-1993. Died five years to the day, after the death of his first wife, Anne Meyer Merchant.

MERCHANT (Mercante)**, TONY** (Anthony) Nov 8, 1900 Sicily, Italy - Feb 1983 Jamestown, NY
With **Ada R. Benenati Merchant** (Oct 21, 1903 Italy - Jan 1983 Jamestown, NY), the grandparents of singer/songwriter, Natalie Merchant, lead singer of the alternative rock band, 10,000 Maniacs from 1981-1993.

SMITH (Sweeney)**, AGNES** Jul 29, 1874 Jamestown, NY - Apr 14, 1959 Jamestown, NY
Sister of Catherine "Kitty" Sweeney Hershey, the wife of confectioner, Milton S. Hershey.

HOLY CROSS CEMETERY
2900 South Park Avenue
Lackawanna, NY 14218

ASHE, JOHN GREGORY Sept 23, 1826 Minard, County Kerry, Ireland - Aug 9, 1892 NY
With **Catherine Mary Prendiville Ashe** (Feb 20, 1847 Minard, County Kerry, Ireland - Dec 19, 1918 NY), the great-grandparents of Academy Award-winning actor, Gregory Peck.

BALL (Durrell)**, NELLIE** (Mary Rebecca) Oct 9, 1856 Dunkirk, NY - 1935 Buffalo, NY
Grandmother of Emmy Award-winning actress, Lucille Ball. Great-grandmother of actress, Lucy Arnaz and actor, Desi Arnaz Jr. Her husband, Jasper Clinton Ball, died May 24, 1933 in Buffalo, buried in Buffalo Cemetery, Lackawanna.

COLLINS, JIMMY (James Joseph) Jan 16, 1870 Buffalo, NY - Mar 6, 1943 Buffalo, NY
Third baseman for the Boston Beaneaters, Louisville Colonels, Boston Americans and Philadelphia Athletics from 1895-1908. Player-manager for the Americans from 1901-1906, winning the first-ever World Series in 1903. Led the National League in home runs in 1898. Elected to the Baseball Hall of Fame in 1945.

DRISCOLL, DANIEL ANGELUS Mar 6, 1875 Buffalo, NY - Jun 5, 1955 Buffalo, NY
United States Representative-NY from 1909-1917.

GOETZ, AUGUSTUS OTTO Feb 1865 Buffalo, NY - Oct 11, 1924 Atlantic City, NJ
With Marie **Blanche McGowan Goetz** (Mar 11, 1868 Buffalo, NY - Jun 14, 1941 Buffalo, NY), the parents of Augustus Goetz, playwright and screenwriter, collaborated with his wife, Ruth Goodman Goetz. They are buried in Kellers Church Union Cemetery, Perkasie, PA.

MADONIA, BENEDETTO - Apr 14, 1903 New York, NY
Counterfeiter associated with the mob. Killed in the "Barrel Murder", his body cut to pieces, his throat cut ear-to-ear and his testicles placed in his mouth, remains placed in a barrel and left on the corner of 11th Street and Avenue D, allegedly killed by the Morello crime family in Manhattan, a tactic used to make example of "squealers." New York City Police Lieutenant, Joseph Petrosino, who investigated the murder, was assassinated in Palermo, Sicily, Italy, March 12, 1909, age 48.

ROSS, CHET (Chester James) Apr 1, 1917 Buffalo, NY - Feb 21, 1989 Buffalo, NY
Outfielder for the Boston Bees and Boston Braves from 1939-1944. Played for Hall of Fame manager, Casey Stengel from 1939-1943. Teammate of Jackie Robinson with the Montreal Royals of the International League in 1946.

WILLIAMS, CY (Edwin Joseph) Jul 24, 1913 Buffalo, NY - May 8, 2006 Buffalo, NY
Scout for the Detroit Tigers from 1945-1987, including their World Series championship teams in 1945 and 1968. Signed Pat Dobson, Mark Lemke, Dick McAuliffe, John Hiller and Mel Hall to professional contracts. Elected to the Western New York Baseball Hall of Fame in 1996.

HOLY SEPULCHRE CEMETERY
3063 Harlem Road
Buffalo, NY 14225

CACI, JIMMY (Vincent Dominic) Aug 1, 1925 Westfield, NY - Aug 16, 2011 Rancho Mirage, CA
Captain in a Los Angeles crime syndicate, under mob boss, Peter Milano, briefly leading the family when Milano was sentenced to prison in 1988. Spent eight years in the Attica Correctional Facility for armed robbery. Brother of singer, Bobby Milano, the husband of singer, Keely Smith.

MILANO (Caci), **BOBBY** (Charles J.) Oct 16, 1936 Buffalo, NY - Jan 17, 2006 Rancho Mirage, CA
Nightclub singer. Won a *Ted Mack Amateur Hour* as a 12-year old. Recorded "Life Begins at Four O'Clock." Called the "Crooning Crybaby", following his conviction in a jewel heist in 1968, from his association with his brother, Jimmy Caci, a captain in the Los Angeles crime family. Married singer, Keely Smith, in 1975, with Frank Sinatra giving the bride away.

TATA, MICHAEL JOHN May 23, 1971 Buffalo, NY - Jul 6, 2004 Henderson, NV
Nevada casino executive. Vice-President of Hotel Operations at the Green Valley Ranch Resort and Casino in Henderson from 2001-2004. Appeared on the Discovery Channel series, *American Casino*, in 2004. Died from an accidental overdose of painkillers and alcohol.

HOLY SEPULCHRE CEMETERY
3rd Avenue Extension
East Greenbush, NY 12061

ELLIOTT, ROBERT GREENE Jan 27, 1874 Hamlin, NY - Oct 10, 1939 Ossining, NY
State electrician for New York from 1926-1939, credited with perfecting electrocutions as a form of capital punishment. Executed 387 convicts, including Sacco and Vanzetti, Ruth Brown Snyder and Bruno Hauptmann. Published his memoir, *Agent of Death: The Memoirs of an Executioner*.

KENESTON (Cody)**, ISABELLE H.** Mar 3, 1923 Peekskill, NY - Jan 11, 2002 Albany, NY
Epitaph on her grave marker reads, "I'd rather be at the mall."

HOLY SEPULCHRE CEMETERY
West Oak Hill Road / Route 120
Jamestown, NY 14701

MCCUSKER, JIM (James Brian) May 19, 1936 Jamestown, NY - Feb 13, 2015 Jamestown, NY
Defensive tackle for the Chicago Cardinals, Philadelphia Eagles, Cleveland Browns and New York Jets from 1958-1964. Member of the Eagles 1960 NFL Championship team.

MIANO (Merchant)**, ROSE MARY** Aug 6, 1926 Jamestown, NY - May 10, 2007 Jamestown, NY
Aunt of singer/songwriter, Natalie Merchant, lead singer of the alternative rock band, 10,000 Maniacs from 1981-1993.

HOLY SEPULCHRE CEMETERY
2461 Lake Avenue
Rochester, NY 14612

BABUSCI, MASSIMO Aug 1884 Italy - Apr 16, 1976 Rochester, NY
With **Bernice Ippolito Babusci** (1888 Italy - Apr 26, 1963 Rochester, NY), the grandparents of singer/songwriter, Jim Croce. Great-grandparents of singer/songwriter, A. J. Croce.

BARRY, JAMES CORBETT 1855 - Sept 9, 1897 Rochester, NY
With **Mary Agnes Quinn Barry** (1859 - Mar 9, 1927 Rochester, NY), the parents of playwright, Philip Barry. Grandparents of film and television producer, Philip Barry Jr.

BARRY, PATRICK May 24, 1816 Ireland - Jun 23, 1890 Rochester, NY
Horticulturist. Founded the Ellwanger & Barry Nursery in Rochester, with George Ellwanger, in 1840. Grandfather of Peter Barry, Mayor of Rochester from 1955-1961.

BIANCHI, NICHOLAS EDWARD 1919 NY - Jul 25, 1965 Rochester, NY
Adoptive father of Kenneth Alessio Bianchi, serial killer who terrorized the Los Angeles-area with his cousin, Angelo Buono Jr., as the "Hillside Strangler", from 1977-1979. Their victims, ten young women and children aged 12 to 28, were kidnapped, raped and tortured before their bodies were dumped in the wooded hillside.

BOESCH, AUGUST H. 1889 Austria - Oct 10, 1956 Rochester, NY
With **Clara W. Boesch** (Dec 5, 1901 Austria - Apr 3, 2003 Rochester, NY), the parents of Rudy Boesch, oldest contestant in the history of *Survivor*. The ex-Navy Seal finished in third place on the premier season, *Survivor: Borneo*, age 72, and the second voted out on *Survivor: All-Stars*, age 76.

BROOKS, LOUISE (Mary) Nov 14, 1906 Cherryvale, KS - Aug 8, 1985 Rochester, NY
Hollywood silent film star. Starred in *Pandora's Box*, *Diary of a Lost Girl* and *Beggars of Life*. Performed with the Ziegfeld Follies in 1925.

BOYLAN, MARY ELIZABETH Feb 23, 1913 Plattsburgh, NY - Feb 18, 1984 New York, NY
Actress. Appeared in the films, *Annie Hall*, *The Night of the Iguana*, *Heartland*, *Alice Sweet Alice* and Andy Warhol's *Bad*.

CANTISANO (Masiello)**, ASSUNTA** Jul 29, 1892 Italy - Dec 1980 Rochester, NY
Founded Ragu Foods with her husband, Giovanni Cantisano, in Rochester in 1937.

CAREY, TOM Oct 11, 1906 Hoboken, NJ - Feb 21, 1970 Rochester, NY
Infielder for the St. Louis Browns from 1935-1937 and Boston Red Sox from 1939-1942 and 1946. Oldest player in major league baseball in 1946, age 39 years and 10 months.

COLL (Wheelwright)**, KATE** (Catherine) 1858 Bruree, Limerick, Ireland - Jun 12, 1932 Rochester, NY
Mother of Eamon de Valera, President of the Republic of Ireland and 20th century Irish political leader from 1917-1973, born in New York City, died August 29, 1975 in Blackrock, Dublin, Ireland, age 92, buried in Glasnevin Cemetery, Dublin.

COLON, CARMEN G. 1961 Rochester, NY - Nov 16, 1971 Churchville, NY
Victim of an unsolved homicide. Strangled and sexually assaulted, the first victim of the Alphabet

Killer, named for the double initials of his young victims, including Michelle Maenza, found in Macedon, and Wanda Walkowicz, found in Webster, between 1971-1973 in the Rochester-area. The 2008 film, *The Alphabet Killer*, was loosely based on the murders.

CONSIDINE, JOHN J. Oct 28, 1930 Rochester, NY - Oct 16, 2016 Rochester, NY
Rochester attorney whose opening line of his obituary read, "Born in Rochester on October 28, 1930, and passed away in Rochester, October 16, 2016 at age 85 - narrowly escaping the 2016 election", highlighting the tumultuous presidential contest between Hillary Clinton and Donald Trump.

COOK, PAUL May 5, 1863 Caledonia, NY - May 25, 1905 Rochester, NY
Catcher for the Philadelphia Quakers of the National League in 1884. Played for the Louisville Colonels and St. Louis Browns of the American Association from 1886-1889 and 1891 and with Brooklyn, in the Players League, in 1890.

CROCE (Babusci), **FLORA MARY** May 28, 1913 Rochester, NY - Dec 22, 2000 Rochester, NY
Mother of singer/songwriter, Jim Croce, killed in an airplane crash following a concert, September 20, 1973. Grandmother of singer/songwriter, A.J. Croce. Wife of James Albert Croce, died March 1972 in Drexel Hill, PA, buried nearby, Saints Peter and Paul Cemetery, Springfield.

DOOIN, RED (Charles Sebastian) Jun 12, 1879 Cincinnati, OH - May 14, 1952 Rochester, NY
Catcher for the Philadelphia Phillies, Cincinnati Reds and New York Giants from 1902-1916. Player-manager for the Phillies from 1910-1914. Managed, and caught, Hall of Famers, Grover Cleveland Alexander and Eppa Rixey.

DUFFY, JAMES PATRICK BERNARD Nov 25, 1878 Rochester, NY - Jan 8, 1969 Rochester, NY
United States Representative-NY from 1935-1937. Associate Justice of the New York State Supreme Court from 1936-1937.

ERWIN, TEX (Ross) Dec 22, 1885 Forney, TX - Apr 5, 1953 Rochester, NY
Backup catcher for the Detroit Tigers, Brooklyn Superbas and Cincinnati Reds in 1907 and 1910-1914.

FOERY (O'Brien), **AGNES** 1864 NY - Feb 15, 1951 Rochester, NY
Mother of Bishop Walter A. Foery, the fifth Roman Catholic Bishop of the Diocese of Syracuse, from 1937-1970.

GADD, KENDALL F. Apr 25, 1916 Rochester, NY - Sept 19, 1976 Rochester, NY
Father of drummer, Steve Gadd, inducted into the Modern Drummer Hall of Fame in 1984.

GINGELLO, SAMMY (Salvatore) Oct 24, 1939 Rochester, NY - Apr 23, 1978 Rochester, NY
Rochester crime family capo. Known as "Sammy G." Killed by a car bomb, detonated by remote control outside Ben's Café Society, Stillson Street. Survived five previous attempts on his life.

GRUBER, PETER P. 1857 Oil City, PA - Oct 11, 1932 Rochester, NY
Rattlesnake curator. Known as "Rattlesnake Pete." Louis Pasteur, among other scientists, ordered samples of his rattlesnake venom for use in their experiments.

HILL, KAREN ANN 1964 Rochester, NY - Sept 2, 1972 Watertown, NY
Murder victim. Second victim of serial killer, Arthur John Shawcross, known as "the Genesee River Killer." Four-months prior, Shawcross murdered ten-year old, Jack Owen Blake. He plea bargained with prosecutors a charge of manslaughter after his arrest, served 15-years of a 25-year sentence. Shawcross moved to Rochester following his parole in 1987, raped and murdered eleven women, eating the genital flesh of his victims. He was found guilty of murder, sentenced to 250 years in state prison.

HOWE, JOHN BENEDICT Mar 21, 1859 Utica, NY - May 16, 1943 Syracuse, NY
Chief editorial writer for the *Syracuse Herald-Journal* for 50 years.

HRYWNAK, OREST 1956 Rochester, NY - Jun 2, 2016 Rochester, NY
Rochester radio promoter. Known as "Captain Cash" on WBBF-AM. Owner and President of the Rochester RazorSharks, professional basketball team, from 2005-2016, winners of six PBL championships.

KACZOWKA, TOMASZ May 16, 1993 Rochester, NY - Dec 24, 2012 Webster, NY
Murder victim. One of two firefighters shot and killed by William H. Spengler Jr., who set fire to his house on Lake Road, off Lake Ontario, ambushing the responding firefighters, killing two, wounding two others, before taking his own life. Spengler's sister, Cheryl Spengler, was found dead among the ruins of the fire, which spread to seven homes. He previously was convicted of first-degree manslaughter in 1981 for the bludgeoning death of his grandmother, 92-year old Rose H. Hames Spengler, July 18, 1980, released on parole in 1998.

KEEGAN, BOB (Robert Charles) Aug 4, 1920 Rochester, NY - Jun 20, 2001 Rochester, NY
Right-handed pitcher for the Chicago White Sox from 1953-1958. Originally drafted by the New York Yankees in 1946. American League All-Star in 1954. Pitched a no-hitter against the Washington Senators in 1957. Pitched for the Syracuse Chiefs from 1951-1952 and the Rochester Red Wings from 1958-1959. Won 20 games for the Chiefs in 1952. Father of Robert J. Keegan, CEO and President of the Goodyear Tire & Rubber Company, from 2003-2009.

KLIMM, MICHAEL Dec 1831 Germany - Feb 4, 1918 Rochester, NY
With **Elizabeth Ehrmantraut Klimm** (Aug 1834 Germany - May 9, 1920 Rochester, NY), the parents of Hall of Fame umpire, Bill Klem

KONDOLF, MATHIAS ANTHONY Jul 21, 1885 Rochester, NY - Mar 16, 1925 Rochester, NY
Purchased the Reisky & Spies Brewery in Rochester in 1878, rebranded the Genesee Brewery.

LEONARDO, ANTHONY F. Feb 3, 1925 Rochester, NY - Apr 27, 2011 Rochester, NY
Rochester Police Department Captain. Decorated World War II veteran. Awarded a medal from U.S.S.R. president, Mikhail Gorbachev, in 1991 for his service on the Murmansk Run in 1942-1943. Father of lawyer, Anthony Leonardo Jr., who was imprisoned for thirteen years for money laundering in connection with the 1993 Brinks and 2000 AMSA armored car heists, and setting up his business partner, Anthony Vaccaro, for murder in 2000.

MAENZA, MICHELLE Nov 28, 1962 Rochester, NY - Nov 26, 1973 Macedon, NY
Victim of an unsolved homicide. Strangled and sexually assaulted, the third victim of the Alphabet Killer, named for the double initials of his young victims, including Wanda Walkowicz, found in Webster, and Carmen Colon, found in Churchville, between 1971-1973 in the Rochester-area. The 2008 film, *The Alphabet Killer*, was loosely based on the murders.

MANGIONE, FRANK C. Jul 2, 1910 Rochester, NY - Aug 20, 2001 Rochester, NY
Father of Grammy Award-winning jazz flugelhornist, Chuck Mangione, and jazz pianist, Gap Mangione. Subject of the Chuck Mangione songs, *Papa Mangione* and *60 Miles Young*. Brother of author, Jerre Mangione.

MCAVOY, WICKEY (James E.) Oct 22, 1894 Rochester, NY - Jul 6, 1973 Rochester, NY
Backup catcher for the Philadelphia Athletics from 1913-1919, managed by Hall of Fame manager, Connie Mack.

MOGRIDGE, GEORGE Feb 18, 1889 Rochester, NY - Mar 4, 1962 Rochester, NY
Pitcher for the Chicago White Sox, New York Yankees, Washington Senators, St. Louis Browns and Boston Braves from 1911-1912 and 1915-1927. Won Game Four and pitched five crucial innings in Game Seven of the 1924 World Series for the champion Washington Senators. Pitched the first no-hitter in Yankees history, April 24, 1917, against the Boston Red Sox in Fenway Park. Played for Hall of Fame managers, Hugh Duffy and Miller Huggins. Teammate of Hall of Famers, Babe Ruth, Ed Walsh, Home Run Baker, Sam Rice, Goose Goslin, Bucky Harris, George Sisler and Walter Johnson.

O'BRIEN, JOSEPH JOHN Oct 9, 1897 Rochester, NY - Jan 23, 1953 Rochester, NY
United States Representative-NY from 1939-1945. Professional football player and heavyweight wrester from 1919-1926.

O'GRADY, JAMES MARY EARLY Mar 31, 1863 Rochester, NY - Nov 3, 1928 Rochester, NY
United States Representative-NY from 1899-1901. Speaker of the New York State Assembly from
1897-1898.

O'RORKE, PATRICK H. Mar 25, 1837 Drumbess, Cornafean, Ireland - Jul 2, 1863 Gettysburg, PA
Civil War Union Army Colonel. Led the 140th New York Infantry Regiment into the Battles of
Fredericksburg, Chancellorsville and Gettysburg. Shot in the neck and killed at Little Round Top at
Gettysburg, during the battle's second day. Classmate of General George A. Custer at the United
States Military Academy at West Point. Graduated first in his class in 1861, the only class member
born outside the United States. Originally buried in St. Patrick's Cemetery on Pinnacle Hill in
Rochester.

RICHARDSON, ARLINE M. Jun 30, 1920 NY - Nov 23, 2010 Rochester, NY
Great-grandmother of 17-year old, Brittanee Marie Drexel, who disappeared April 25, 2009, during a
spring break trip to Myrtle Beach, without her parents knowledge, officially declared a victim of a
homicide by the FBI in 2016.

ROBER (Rauber)**, RICHARD** May 14, 1910 Rochester, NY - May 26, 1952 Santa Monica, CA
Broadway musical comedy star. Killed in an automobile accident as his film career was developing.

SANTAMARIA (Ruscio)**, CECILIA** 1866 Italy - Jun 9, 1934 Rochester, NY
Mother of Blessed Grimoaldo of the Purification, beautified by Pope John Paul II on January 29, 1995.
Relocated to Rochester in 1920, following the death of her husband, Pietro Paolo Santamaria, to live
with her daughter, Vincenzina Panella at 55 Stonewood Street. Blessed Grimoaldo, a seminarian of
the Passionist Order, was born Ferdinando Santamaria, May 4, 1883, died November 18, 1902 of
meningitis, age 19. His Feast Day is celebrated on November 18.

SARGENT, JOE Sept 24, 1893 Rochester, NY - Jul 5, 1950 Rochester, NY
Reserve infielder for the Detroit Tigers in 1921, managed by Hall of Famer, Ty Cobb.

SIGL, AL (Alphonse Joseph) Mar 18, 1883 Rochester, NY - Aug 13, 1966 Rochester, NY
Rochester radio personality and humanitarian.

SYPNIER, EDWARD Mar 13, 1888 Russia - Sept 11, 1962 Rochester, NY
Father of convicted pedophile, Theodore A. Sypnier, New York State's oldest prison inmate at the time
of his death, December 7, 2010, age 101, at the Coxsackie Correctional Facility.

TUMBLETY (Tumuelty)**, FRANCIS J.** 1833 Ireland - May 28, 1903 St. Louis, MO
Considered a suspect in the "Jack the Ripper" slayings in London in 1888, murders that remain
unsolved. Arrested in St. Louis, May 5, 1865, on orders from United States Secretary of War, Edwin
Stanton, for his alleged involvement in the assassination of President Abraham Lincoln, due to his

acquaintance, David Herold, a conspirator captured with John Wilkes Booth, though released without charge, May 30, 1865.

VACCARO, ANTHONY Nov 2, 1956 Rochester, NY - May 1, 2000 Greece, NY
Co-owned and operated Club Titanic in Charlotte, with Anthony Leonardo Jr. Shot and killed, execution-style, by Albert M. Ranieri, following accusations by Leonardo that he was embezzling from the club. Leonardo and Ranieri also served time in connection with the 1993 Brinks and 2000 AMSA armored car heists.

VALENTI, JOHN A. May 26, 1919 Rochester, NY - May 25, 2014 Rochester, NY
Brother of Rochester crime family bosses, Frank J. Valenti and Constenze P. "Stanley" Valenti.

VALENTI, JOSEPH (Giuseppe) Jun 13, 1878 Italy - Nov 21, 1969 Rochester, NY
With **Rosalie Inserra Valenti** (1889 Italy - Apr 8, 1966 Rochester, NY), the parents of Frank J. Valenti, Rochester crime family mob boss from 1964-1972, one of the last remaining survivors who attended the Apalachin Mafia Conference, an historic gathering of American Mafia leaders, November 14, 1957, and Constenze P. "Stanley" Valenti, Rochester's first well-known mob boss.

WALKOWICZ, WANDA LEE Aug 4, 1961 NY - Apr 2, 1973 Webster, NY
Victim of an unsolved homicide. Strangled and sexually assaulted, the second victim of the Alphabet Killer, named for the double initials of his young victims, including Michelle Maenza, found in Macedon, and Carmen Colon, found in Churchville, between 1971-1973 in the Rochester-area. The 2008 film, *The Alphabet Killer*, was loosely based on the murders.

WEAVER, HARRY Feb 26, 1892 Clarendon, PA - May 30, 1983 Rochester, NY
Pitched for the Philadelphia Athletics, managed by Hall of Famer, Connie Mack and Chicago Cubs from 1915-1919. Teammate of Hall of Famers, Grover Cleveland Alexander and Napoleon Lajoie.

WEGMAN, ROBERT B. Oct 14, 1918 Rochester, NY - Apr 20, 2006 Rochester, NY
President and CEO of Wegmans Food Markets from 1950-2005, founded by his father, Walter E. Wegman, and uncle, John Wegman, in Rochester in 1916.

WEGMAN, WALTER E. Jul 3, 1891 Rochester, NY - Dec 17, 1935 Rochester, NY
President of Wegmans Food Markets from 1916-1935, founded with his brother, John Wegman, in Rochester in 1916. Buried with his wife, Anna Frankenstein Wegman, died August 11, 1978 in Rochester, age 88.

WIEDMAN, STUMP (George E.) Feb 17, 1861 Rochester, NY - Mar 2, 1905 New York, NY
Pitched for the Buffalo Bisons, Detroit Wolverines, Kansas City Cowboys and New York Giants of the National League from 1880-1888.

WIIG, GUNNAR ARNA Apr 1903 Norway - Apr 13, 1970 Rochester, NY
With **Frances McCue Wiig** (Nov 27, 1902 Kingston, ON, Canada - Jun 29, 1985 Lancaster, PA), the grandparents of actress, Kristin Wiig.

WILKIN (Burns)**, ELOISE MARGARET** Mar 30, 1904 Rochester, NY - Oct 4, 1987 Brighton, NY
Children's book illustrator. Illustrated more than 50 books in the Little Golden Book series.

HOLY SPIRIT CEMETERY
Front Street
Chenango Forks, NY 13746

KACHMARIK, JOHN W. Feb 5, 1916 Elmira Heights, NY - Nov 4, 2000 Hollywood, FL
Acquired control of the Hofmann Packing Company in 1968, with Walter E. Flook, husband of Elizabeth Hofmann Flook, the great-granddaughter of founder, Frank W. Hofmann, and changed its name to the Hofmann Sausage Company. Owned Karcher's Meat Market in Syracuse from 1968-1998.

HOLY SPIRIT CEMETERY
Shirley Road
North Collins, NY 14111

FRICANO, MARION J. Jul 15, 1923 Brant, NY - May 18, 1976 Tijuana, Mexico
Knuckleball pitcher for the Philadelphia Athletics and Kansas City Athletics from 1952-1955. Died from pneumonia, vacationing with relatives.

HOLY TRINITY CEMETERY
1500 Champlin Avenue
Utica, NY 13502

KANTOR, ADOLPH A. October 26, 1914 New York Mills, NY - Jul 21, 2013 Utica, NY
Pastor of the Basilica of the Sacred Heart in Syracuse from 1970-1989, retiring following a 50-year career in the Syracuse and Utica dioceses. Elevated to Monsignor by Pope Paul VI in 1971.

MIAZGA, SUZANNE MARIE Jul 31, 1966 Marcy, NY - Dec 21, 1988 Lockerbie, Scotland
Syracuse University graduate student. Victim of the terrorist bombing of PanAm Flight 103 over Lockerbie, Scotland, killing 270 people, including 35 Syracuse University students.

HOPE CEMETERY
34 East Mill Street
Castile, NY 14427

LUTHER, DARIUS W. 1839 NY - 1872 Castile, NY
With **Mary Ann Chittenden Luther** (1839 - 1907 Castile, NY), the grandparents of actress, Irene Rich, born Irene Frances Luther in Buffalo. Great-grandparents of sculptor, Frances Rich.

HOPE CEMETERY
101 Park Avenue
Corning, NY 14830

DAVIS (White), **PHOEBE M.** May 15, 1855 Caton, NY - Feb 8,1902 Caton, NY
Sister of Deacon White, star catcher and third baseman for eight major league teams from 1871-1890 and Will White, pitcher for the Boston Red Caps, Cincinnati Reds and Detroit Wolverines from 1877-1886. Cousin of Elmer White, outfielder for the Cleveland Forest Citys in 1871, and the first active major leaguer in history to die.

HILL, DELLA 1870 - 1901 Corning, NY
Wife of Pacy Hill, convicted murderer who shot and killed his cousin, Chloe Hancock in 1908, executed in the electric chair in 1909. He is buried in Soule Cemetery in Auburn.

HOUGHTON, AMORY Oct 30, 1837 Cambridge, MA - Nov 5, 1909 Corning, NY
President of Corning Glass Works from 1875-1909, founded by his father, Amory Houghton Sr. Developed the glass for Thomas Edison's first light bulb. Father of Alanson Bigelow Houghton, United States Representative-NY from 1919-1922. Grandfather of Amory Houghton, United States Ambassador to France from 1957-1961. Great-grandfather of Amory Houghton Jr., United States Representative-NY from 1987-2005. Granduncle of Academy Award-winning actress, Katharine Hepburn. Great-granduncle of actress, Katharine Houghton.

PRATT, HARRY HAYT Nov 11, 1864 Corning, NY - Nov 13, 1932 Corning, NY
United States Representative-NY from 1915-1919.

SOUSA, ALFRED R. 1897 Madeira, Portugal - May 7, 1947 Corning, NY
Grandnephew of composer and musician, John Philip Sousa.

HOPE CEMETERY
East Mill Street
Perry, NY 14530

HANLEY, JOSEPH RHODES May 30, 1876 Davenport, IA - Sept 4, 1961 Perry, NY
Lieutenant Governor of New York from 1943-1950, under Thomas E. Dewey. Majority Leader of the
New York State Senate from 1939-1943. Republican nominee for United States Senator-NY in 1950,
losing to Herbert H. Lehman.

HOPE CEMETERY ANNEX
101 Park Avenue
Corning, NY 14830

CARDER, FREDERICK Sept 18, 1863 Dudley, West Midlands, England - Dec 10, 1963 Corning, NY
Co-founded the Steuben Glass Works, Corning, with Thomas J. Hawkes, in 1903.

HOUGHTON, ALANSON BIGELOW Oct 10, 1863 Cambridge, MA - Sept 15, 1941 Dartmouth, MA
United States Representative-NY from 1919-1922. United States Ambassador to Germany from
1922-1925 and Great Britain from 1925-1929. President of Corning Glass Works from 1910-1918,
founded by his grandfather, Amory Houghton Sr. Appeared on the cover of *Time* on April 5, 1926.
Father of Amory Houghton, United States Ambassador to France from 1957-1961. Grandfather of
Amory Houghton Jr., United States Representative-NY from 1987-2005. Second-cousin of Academy
Award-winning actress, Katharine Hepburn.

HOUGHTON, AMORY Jul 27, 1899 Corning, NY - Feb 21, 1981 Charleston, SC
United States Ambassador to France from 1957-1961. President of the Boy Scouts of America from
1946-1951. President of Corning Glass Works, founded by his 2nd great-grandfather, Amory
Houghton Sr. Father of Amory Houghton Jr., United States Representative-NY from 1987-2005. Son
of Alanson Bigelow Houghton, United States Representative-NY from 1919-1922.

HOPKINTON-FORT JACKSON CEMETERY
County Road 49
Hopkinton, NY 12965

ASHLAW, JOHN J. 1958 - May 14, 1976 Atlanta, GA
Shot and killed by Atlanta police detectives, acting on a tip a drugstore was to be robbed, they staked
out the store, when he broke in, the detectives identified themselves and he turned a .38 revolver in
the direction of the detectives, who fired, hitting him on the left side, killing him instantly.

BRUSH, ELIPHALET Nov 12, 1781 Bennington, VT - Jan 11, 1872 Hopkinton, NY
Grandfather of baseball executive, John Tomlinson Brush, owner of the New York Giants, Cincinnati Reds and Indianapolis Hoosiers from 1886-1912, who he raised when orphaned at four years old. Widowed twice, first from Polly Tomlinson Brush, died April 26, 1810, giving birth to their first child, John Tomlinson Brush Sr., and second, Malinda Pier, died September 15, 1862.

CHITTENDEN, SOLOMON Sept 14, 1761 Killingworth, CT - Feb 9, 1855 Hopkington, NY
Revolutionary War soldier. Grandson of Thomas Chittenden, first Governor and founding father of Vermont. Uncle of Lucius E. Chittenden, Register of the United States Treasury, from 1861-1864, under President Abraham Lincoln.

HORNELLSVILLE RURAL CEMETERY
Almond Road
Hornell, NY 14843

BLAAS, ALBERT G. 1881 Holland - Dec 31, 1956 Hornell, NY
With **Helena Rookus Blaas** (1883 - Jan 3, 1953 Hornell, NY), the grandparents of Hollywood film actor, Bill Pullman.

PULLMAN, JAMES Aug 11, 1914 - Sept 15, 1992 Hornell, NY
With **Johanna Blaas Pullman** (Jul 28, 1911 Rochester, NY - Mar 30, 1993 Hornell, NY), the parents of Hollywood film actor, Bill Pullman.

ROCKWELL, ROBERT FAY Feb 11, 1886 Cortland, NY - Sept 29, 1950 Maher, CO
United States Representative-CO from 1941-1949. Lieutenant Governor of Colorado from 1923-1925.

HORTONVILLE CEMETERY
North Branch Road
Hortonville, NY 12745

COOK (Koch), THEODORE ALBERT L. Jun 8, 1822 Germany - May 10, 1870 Callicoon, NY
With **Magdalena Helena Long Cook** (Jun 24, 1836 Germany - Dec 8, 1906 Toms River, NJ), the parents of explorer, Frederick A. Cook, who claimed to have been the first to reach the North Pole.

COOK, THEODORE ALBERT 1858 Jeffersonville, NY - May 20, 1923 Callicoon, NY
Worked in a creamery in Hortonville, died from pneumonia when accidentally locked in the icebox for an extended period of time. Brother of explorer, Frederick A. Cook, who claimed to have been the first to reach the North Pole.

HOUSE OF ISRAEL CEMETERY
Woods Road
Whitesboro, NY 13492

COMINSKY, MANUEL Oct 5, 1905 Russia - Jun 6, 1971 Palm Beach, FL
Founded the Chicago Markets food chain in Central New York.

HOWLETT HILL CEMETERY
3209 Howlett Hill Road
Syracuse, NY 13215

BACON, LEONARD 1771 Woodstock, CT - Mar 27, 1849 Syracuse, NY
With **Elizabeth Clift Bacon** (1776 - May 24, 1823 Syracuse, NY), the parents of Judge Daniel Stanton Bacon of Monroe County, MI. Grandparents of Elizabeth "Libbie" Clift Bacon Custer, the wife of General George A. Custer.

HOWLETT, PARLEY Jun 4, 1754 Shaftsbury, VT - Jul 29, 1803 Onondaga County, NY
Revolutionary War veteran. Founder of Howlett Hill, an early Onondaga County settlement. Father of salt manufacturer, Parley L. Howlett. Great-grandfather of Alfred H. Durston, President of the Durston Gear Corporation in Syracuse.

HOWLETT, PARLEY LEWIS Jun 1, 1784 Shaftsbury, VT - May 18, 1861 Syracuse, NY
Central New York salt manufacturer. First to initiate shipment of salt westward. Son of Parley Howlett, founder of Howlett Hill in Onondaga County. Grandfather of Alfred H. Durston, President of the Durston Gear Corporation in Syracuse.

SPACK, CHRISTOPHER JON Sept 10, 1968 Syracuse, NY - Nov 20, 2009 Cato, NY
Victim of a random act of road rage, killed when his pickup truck was repeatedly rammed from behind by drunk driver, William L. LeVea, on Route 370, colliding head-on with another vehicle, ten minutes after placing a 911 call reporting he was being harassed. LeVea was sentenced to 6-18 years in prison.

HUDSON CITY CEMETERY
20 Columbia Turnpike
Hudson, NY 12534

MILLER, KILLIAN Jul 30, 1785 Claverack, NY - Jan 11, 1859 Hudson, NY
United States Representative-NY from 1855-1857.

SIMPSON, KENNETH FARRAND May 4, 1895 New York, NY - Jan 25, 1941 New York, NY
United States Representative-NY in 1941. Sworn into Congress on January 3, 1941, died of a heart attack 22 days later.

THOMPSON, SMITH Feb 14, 1843 Poughkeepsie, NY - Jul 5, 1909 Hudson, NY
Son of Smith Thompson, Associate Justice of the U.S. Supreme Court from 1823-1843. 3rd great-grandson of Colonial politician, Robert Livingston the Elder, the first Lord of Livingston Manor.

HUDSON VIEW CEMETERY
Harris Avenue
Mechanicville, NY 12118

ANDERSON, BARRY Jan 25, 1950 Mechanicville, NY - Oct 4, 1961 Mechanicville, NY
Tombstone is a statue of a young boy in a baseball cap, smiling with his hands clasped together.

ELLSWORTH, ELMER EPHRAIM Apr 11, 1837 Malta, NY - May 24, 1861 Alexandria, VA
Civil War Union Army Colonel. Close friend of President Abraham Lincoln, who called him "the greatest little man I ever met" due to his 5'6" height. First casualty of the Civil War, shot retrieving a Confederate flag for Lincoln, who ordered an Honor Guard to retrieve his body, return it to the White House, where he lay in state in the East Room.

HUGHES, LORADO T. Jul 26, 1902 MI - Jun 8, 1992 Mechanicville, NY
With **Mildred Sherman Hughes** (Feb 8, 1901 NY - May 30, 1991 Mechanicville, NY), the grandparents of Emmy Award-winning actor, David Hyde Pierce.

IMMACULATE CONCEPTION CEMETERY
Cemetery Road
Fabius, NY 13063

BYRNE, RICHARD PAUL Oct 27, 1880 Pompey, NY - Jul 18, 1958 Syracuse, NY
New York State Senator. Personal attorney for J. Myer Schine, President of Schine theaters and hotels.

CONNORS, MARTIN J. Jul 2, 1893 Mayo, Ireland - Aug 12, 1984 Syracuse, NY
Founded the Commander Food Company, one of the first supermarket chains in Syracuse, later merged into P&C Foods, Inc.

DRUMMOND, NONIE ANNE 1988 Syracuse, NY - Aug 11, 2002 Fabius, NY
Murder victim. Killed by Spencer Lee King, a 17-year old, Oswego County resident, who she met

following a nine-month Internet romance, stabbed multiple times with a knife, beaten repeatedly with furniture and set fire to her home. King claimed he snapped when he found out she lied about her age.

GRABOSKY, GENE (Harry Eugene) Sept 1, 1936 Syracuse, NY - May 4, 2001 Liverpool, NY
Syracuse University defensive tackle. Member of their undefeated 1959 National Championship team. Drafted by the Washington Redskins, he played one season for the Buffalo Bills in 1960.

OLEY (Joyce)**, THERESA MARIE** 1869 Peterborough, ON, Canada - Aug 26, 1939 Syracuse, NY
Sister of Rev. Francis P. Joyce, decorated World War I Army Chaplain, served under General John J. Pershing in World War I and the Mexican Revolution in pursuit of Pancho Villa.

IMMACULATE CONCEPTION CEMETERY
400 Salt Springs Street
Fayetteville, NY 13066

COSTELLO, FRANK Mar 9, 1902 Syracuse, NY - Jun 1, 1980 Syracuse, NY
Mayor of Syracuse (R) from 1945-1949.

GAYNOR, EDWARD Mar 12, 1824 County Kerry, Ireland - Apr 26, 1890 Fayetteville, NY
Early settler in the town of Fayetteville. Owned and operated Bangs & Gaynor, with Reuben Bangs, a limestone quarry and plaster business. Father of Colonel John F. Gaynor.

GAYNOR, JOHN F. Apr 6, 1850 Fayetteville, NY - Oct 1, 1915 Washington D.C.
New York State Colonel. Democratic Party leader. Held contracts with the United States Government to build jetty and harbor work along the Atlantic Coast. Indicted in 1899 with conspiracy to defraud the government in contract work in Savannah Harbor in Georgia. Former Syracuse Mayor, William B. Kirk, posted a $20,000 bond for Gaynor in 1902, he promptly fled to Canada as a fugitive from justice, Marshals placed a levy placed against Kirk's property in 1903. Gaynor was extradited in 1905, convicted in 1906, sentenced to four years in federal prison. The United States Supreme Court heard his appeal in 1907, and upheld the lower court ruling. Son of town of Fayetteville settler, Edward Gaynor.

GRIFFIN, SANDY (Tobias) Oct 24, 1858 Fayetteville, NY - Jun 4, 1926 Syracuse, NY
Outfielder for the New York Giants, Rochester Broncos, Washington Senators and St. Louis Browns from 1884, 1890-1891 and 1893. Managed the Senators for six games in 1891. Player, manager and owner of the Syracuse Stars for 16 years, following his major league career.

JOYCE, FRANCIS P. Mar 17, 1875 Peterborough, ON, Canada - Jun 26, 1952 Syracuse, NY
Decorated Army Chaplain. Served with the United States Army, under General John J. Pershing in World War I and in pursuit of Mexican General, Pancho Villa, during the Mexican Revolution in

1916-1917. Received an apostolic blessing from Pope Pius XI, helping several hundred priests and nuns during the Veracruz incident in Mexico in 1914.

MAHON, GEORGE S. Feb 1, 1860 Syracuse, NY - Jun 27, 1930 Syracuse, NY
Pastor and founder of the Church of the Most Holy Rosary in Syracuse. Last surviving member of the clergy from the formation of the Syracuse Roman Catholic Diocese.

O'NEILL, BUCK (Frank J.) Mar 6, 1875 Syracuse, NY - Apr 21, 1958 Hamilton, NY
Syracuse University football coach from 1906-1907, 1913-1915 and 1917-1919 and Colgate University from 1902 and 1904-1905. Columbia University head coach from 1920-1922, coaching future New York Yankees' Hall of Famer, Lou Gehrig, who played tackle on the team. Inducted into the College Football Hall of Fame in 1951.

OOT, EARL L. Sept 10, 1921 Minoa, NY - Jan 14, 2004 Syracuse, NY
Attorney. Real estate developer. Co-founder and president of Oot Bros., Inc.

SEARLE, FRED W. May 15, 1898 Syracuse, NY - Aug 30, 1967 Fayetteville, NY
Owned and operated Suburban Park, off Route 92 in Manlius, from 1925-1955. The amusement park closed in 1973.

INDIAN MOUND CEMETERY
Route 38A
Moravia, NY 13118

CARR, LEW Aug 15, 1872 Union Springs, NY - Jun 15, 1954 Moravia, NY
Head baseball coach for Syracuse University from 1910-1947. Played for the Toronto Maple Leafs of the International League for manager, Edward Barrow. Played nine games behind starting shortstop, Honus Wagner, for the 1901 Pittsburgh Pirates. Uncle of Harlan "Gotch" Carr, three-sport star at Syracuse.

DAY, ROWLAND Mar 6, 1779 Chester, MA - Dec 23, 1853 Moravia, NY
United States Representative-NY from 1823-1825 and 1833-1835.

SELOVER, PERRY HAZARD Jul 8, 1825 Cayuga, NY - Sept 5, 1887 Moravia, NY
Father-in-law of William Seward Burroughs, inventor of the adding machine. Great-grandfather of "Beat Generation" author, William Seward Burroughs II. 2nd great-grandfather of author, William Seward Burroughs III. His wife, Mary Ann Allen Selover, died August 27, 1888, age 63.

INDIAN OPENING CEMETERY
Indian Opening Road
Madison, NY 13402

RICHARDSON (Woodward)**, MARY** Feb 28, 1732 Newton, MA - Dec 21, 1823 Schuyler, NY
Great-grandmother of suffragist, Susan B. Anthony.

IONIA CEMETERY
West Dead Creek Road
Memphis, NY 13112

TAPPAN, JOHN Feb 4, 1756 Morristown, NJ - Nov 29, 1818 Baldwinsville, NY
Revolutionary War veteran. Early settler in the town of Van Buren. Father of Colonel Gabriel Tappan.

IRISH-COOK-SHAW CEMETERY
Foster Road / Route 508
Gowanda, NY 14070

WARNER, SAMUEL HARMON 1808 - 1883 Collins Center, NY
With **Mary P. Saunders Warner** (1810 - 1864 Collins Center, NY), the grandparents of College Football
Hall of Fame coaches, Glenn S. "Pop" Warner and William J. "Bill" Warner.

IRISH HILL CEMETERY
245 Main Street
Cooperstown, NY 13326

RICHMOND (Ryan)**, WINIFRED** 1855 NY - Feb 19, 1888 Otsego County, NY
Grandmother of actor, John Carradine. Great-grandmother of actors, David Carradine, Keith
Carradine and Robert Carradine. 2nd great-grandmother of actresses, Martha Plimpton and Ever
Carradine.

IRONDEQUOIT CEMETERY
Culver Road
Irondequoit, NY 14617

BREMIGAN, NICK (Nicholas Gregory) Apr 4, 1945 Philadelphia, PA - Mar 28, 1989 Garland, TX
American League umpire from 1974-1989. Worked the 1980 World Series and the 1979 and 1985 All-
Star Games.

KIRCHER (Kerscher), **MIKE** (Wolfgang) Sept 30, 1897 Rochester, NY - Jun 26, 1972 Rochester, NY
Pitched two games for the Philadelphia Athletics, managed by Connie Mack, and 12 games for the St. Louis Cardinals, managed by Branch Rickey, from 1919-1921.

LOW, HUNTER (William) Jun 12, 1933 New Orleans, LA - Sept 18, 2008 Irondequoit, NY
Called "the Father of the All-American Team." Managed Eastman Kodak's United States Sports Program. Created the Eastman Award for the NCAA college basketball player of the year. Elected to the Woman's Basketball Hall of Fame.

SPENGLER (Hames), **ROSE HANNAH** Feb 22, 1888 Ontario, Canada - Jul 18, 1980 Webster, NY
Murder victim. Bludgeoned to death by her grandson, William H. Spengler Jr., convicted of first-degree manslaughter in 1981, released on parole in 1998. 14 years later, Christmas Eve, Spengler set fire to his house on Lake Road, off Lake Ontario, town of Webster, ambushing the responding firefighters, killing two, wounding two others, before taking his own life. His sister, Cheryl Spengler, was found dead, among the ruins of the fire, which spread to seven homes.

IROQUOIS FARM
Susquehanna Avenue / County Road 52
Cooperstown, NY 13326

CLARK, F. AMBROSE (Frederick) Aug 1, 1880 Cooperstown, NY - Feb 26, 1964 New York, NY
Equestrian. Namesake of the F. Ambrose Clark Award, the highest honor given by the National Steeplechase Association. Buried on his 5,000-acre estate beside his beloved horse, Kellsboro Jack and dog, Buttons. Grandson of Edward S. Clark, co-founder of the Singer Sewing Machine Company. Brother of Stephen Carlton Clark, founder of the National Baseball Hall of Fame in Cooperstown.

IVANDELL CEMETERY
Route 202
Somers, NY 10589

BAILEY, HACHALIAH LYMAN Jul 31, 1775 Somers, NY - Sept 2, 1845 Somers, NY
Formed the Bailey's Circus in 1808, purchased an elephant he named, "Old Bet", that became the first circus elephant in the country. Built the Elephant Hotel in Somers, designated a National Historic Landmark in 2005. Namesake of Bailey's Crossroads, VA. Uncle of Frederic Harrison Bailey, who hired teenage orphan, James Anthony McGinnis, as his assistant, later to take the Bailey surname and join with P.T. Barnum to form Barnum and Bailey's Circus.

BIRCH, WYRLEY (Ernest W.) May 7, 1883 Montréal, QB, Canada - Feb 7, 1959 Mount Kisco, NY
Broadway and Hollywood film and television actor. Appeared in the films, *The Last Days of Pompeii*, *Air Hawks* and *Grand Exit*.

JACKSON STREET CEMETERY
Jackson Street
Lowville, NY 13367

COLLINS, ELA Feb 14, 1786 Meriden, CT - Nov 23, 1848 Lowville, NY
United States Representative-NY from 1823-1825. Father of William Collins, United States Representative-NY from 1847-1849. Grandfather of First Lady Helen Herron Taft, the wife of President William H. Taft. Great-grandfather of Robert A. Taft, U.S. Senator-OH from 1939-1953. 2nd great-grandfather of Robert A. Taft Jr., U.S. Senator-OH from 1971-1976 and William Howard Taft III, United States Ambassador to Ireland. 3rd great-grandfather of Robert A. Taft III, Governor of Ohio from 1999-2007.

JACKSONVILLE RURAL CEMETERY
Fenner Road
Lysander, NY 13094

DEBOTTIS, JAMES L. Mar 22, 1910 Mentz, NY - May 25, 1991 Auburn, NY
Ira Town Justice from 1961-1964. With **Vera M. Johnson DeBottis** (1909 Fulton, NY - Jan 26, 1964 Syracuse, NY), the parents of Theda DeBottis Shue, shot and bayonetted to death by her husband, James Shue, in a murder-suicide, January 5, 1938.

POST, LEWIS NIXON Jul 17, 1903 Staten Island, NY - Sept 12, 1992 Syracuse, NY
Atlantic Division canoe racing champion in singles from 1930-1934. United States National Tandem champion in 1930 with Jack Lenihan.

JAKWAY BURIAL GROUNDS
13164 South Street
Cato, NY 13033

JAKWAY, JOHN 1782 VT - Apr 30, 1845 Cato, NY
First permanent resident and physician for the village of Cato, originally named Jakway's Corners, in 1809. Buried standing straight up, with the top of his skull exposed, so that passersby could crack nuts upon his head. Location of his grave is behind the Jewel Funeral Home within an iron picket fence with no gate.

JAMESVILLE CEMETERY
Route 173
Jamesville, NY 13078

GARDNER (Morris), **ADELAIDE** Jan 11, 1898 Brooklyn, NY - Sept 21, 1983 Crockett, TX
Artist. Painted historical scenes and subjects, displayed in the Brooklyn Museum, the Onondaga Historical Museum and the Smithsonian Museum, Washington D.C.

HEATH, TIMOTHY B. May 22, 1962 Syracuse, NY - Apr 15, 1997 Manlius, NY
Killed in a car accident near 240 West Seneca Street in Manlius. Jumped out of the passenger seat of his 1995 Dodge pickup truck following a disagreement with his wife, Catherine Zarczynski Dodge, fell to the road and driven over by a car traveling west, on the other side of the road.

JEFFERSONVILLE PRESBYTERIAN CEMETERY
Willy Avenue
Jeffersonville, NY 12748

LEHMANN-HAUPT, SANDY (H. Alexander) Mar 22, 1942 New York, NY - Oct 28, 2001 Callicoon, NY
One of the "Merry Pranksters" on author, Ken Kesey's, psychedelic bus in the 1960s, and primary source for Tom Wolfe's book, *The Electric Kool-Aid Acid Test*, in 1968. Brother of journalist, Christopher Lehmann-Haupt.

SCHADT, FREDERICK W. V. Jan 28, 1911 NY - Nov 19, 1992 Jeffersonville, NY
Mayor of Jeffersonville from 1945-1987, winning 22 consecutive elections.

JERUSALEM CORNERS CEMETERY
Erie Road / Route 5
Derby, NY 14047

SALISBURY, AARON 1786 - 1861 Evans, NY
First permanent settler in the town of Evans, in 1809. Grandfather of Broadway and silent film actor, Morgan Salisbury.

JOHN BROWN FARM STATE HISTORIC SITE
John Brown Road
Lake Placid, NY 12946

BROWN, JOHN May 9, 1800 Torrington, CT - Dec 2, 1859 Charles Town, VA
Abolitionist. Called "the Liberator." Commanded anti-slavery forces in the Battle of Black Jack and the

Battle of Osawatomie in Kansas in 1856. Led John Brown's Raiders on a slave revolt, raiding an armory in Harpers Ferry in 1859, capturing Colonel Lewis W. Washington, the great-grandnephew of George Washington. Defeated by United States Marines, led by Colonel Robert E. Lee, and hanged for treason, an execution witnessed by John Wilkes Booth, six years before he assassinated President Abraham Lincoln. Two sons, Oliver and Watson Brown, were killed in the raid, a third son, Owen Brown, escaped captured, died January 8, 1889 in Pasadena, age 64. His wife, Mary Ann Day Brown, mother of 11 of his 16 children, died February 29, 1884 in San Francisco, age 67, and is buried in Madronia Cemetery in Saratoga, CA.

BROWN, OLIVER May 9, 1839 Portage County, OH - Oct 18, 1859 Harpers Ferry, VA
Son of abolitionist, John Brown. Killed by United States Marines, fighting with John Brown's Raiders, in a slave revolt on the Harpers Valley Armory.

BROWN, WATSON Oct 7, 1835 Ross County, OH - Oct 17, 1859 Harpers Valley, VA
Son of abolitionist, John Brown. Killed by United States Marines, fighting with John Brown's Raiders, in a slave revolt on the Harpers Valley Armory. His body was claimed by Winchester Medical College as a teacher cadaver for students, reburied in 1882.

NEWBY, DANGERFIELD 1815 Warrenton, VA - Oct 16, 1859 Harpers Ferry, VA
Born a slave, joined with abolitionist, John Brown, fighting with John Brown's Raiders, in an attack on the Harpers Valley Armory, first to be killed by United States Marines defending the armory. John Brown was hanged for treason following his capture.

JOHN RICHARDS CEMETERY
87 Old Military Road
Lake George, NY 12845

RICHARDS, JOHN Apr 13, 1765 Gwynedd, Wales, UK - Apr 18, 1850 Lake George, NY
United States Representative-NY from 1823-1825. New York State Surveyor from 1810-1812.

JOHNSONBURG CEMETERY
Centerline Road
Varysburg, NY 14167

MONTELEONE, JOHN G. Nov 21, 1929 - Sept 13, 1971 Attica, NY
Industrial Training Supervisor at Attica Correctional Facility. Civilian employee, killed in a prison riot at the prison, which left ten correctional officers and 33 prisoners dead.

JOHNSTOWN CEMETERY
Cemetery Road
Johnstown, NY 12095

CADY, DANIEL Apr 29, 1773 Canaan, NY - Oct 31, 1859 Johnstown, NY
United States Representative-NY from 1815-1817. Associate Justice of the New York State Supreme Court from 1847-1854. Montgomery County attorney, worked a case with Abraham Lincoln, representing clients in a land dispute with Beloit College. Father of social reformer, Elizabeth Cady Stanton. Uncle of John Watts Cady, United States Representative-NY from 1823-1825.

CADY, JOHN WATTS Jun 28, 1790 Florida, NY - Jan 5, 1854 Johnstown, NY
United States Representative-NY from 1823-1825. Nephew of Daniel Cady, United States Representative-NY from 1815-1817. Cousin of social reformer, Elizabeth Cady Stanton.

CADY (Livingston)**, MARGARET CHINN** 1784 - Sept 15, 1871 Johnstown, NY
Wife of Daniel Cady, United States Representative-NY from 1815-1817. Mother of social reformer, Elizabeth Cady Stanton. Daughter of Revolutionary War General, James Livingston. Granddaughter of Robert Livingston the Younger, Mayor of Albany from 1710-1719. Great-granddaughter of General Pieter Schuyler, first Mayor of Albany, from 1686-1694.

CARROLL, JOHN MICHAEL Apr 27, 1823 Springfield, NY - May 8, 1901 Johnstown, NY
United States Representative-NY from 1871-1873.

EDWARDS, JOHN Aug 6, 1781 Dutchess County, NY - Dec 28, 1850 Johnstown, NY
United States Representative-NY from 1837-1839.

HILL (Livingston)**, GRACE** Apr 16, 1865 Watertown, NY - Feb 23, 1947 Philadelphia, PA
Novelist and short story writer. Wrote under the pseudonym, "Marcia Macdonald." Niece of author, Isabella Macdonald Alden, who wrote under the pseudonym, "Pansy."

KNOX, CHARLES BRIGGS Oct 8, 1855 Johnstown, NY - Jan 17, 1908 Quebec City, QB, Canada
Founded the Knox Gelatine Company, the first easy-to-use granulated gelatin for home cooks. Called "the Napoleon of Advertising" for marketing his product.

KNOX (Markward)**, ROSE** Nov 18, 1857 Mansfield, OH - Sept 27, 1950 Johnstown, NY
Owned and operated the Knox Gelatine Company, following the death of her husband, Charles B. Knox, in 1908, becoming one of the country's first successful business woman.

WELLS, JOHN Jul 1, 1817 Johnstown, NY - May 30, 1877 Johnstown, NY
United States Representative-NY from 1851-1853.

JONESVILLE CEMETERY
Ushers Road
Clifton Park, NY 12065

GARNSEY, ISAAC 1757 - Jun 24, 1824 Halfmoon, NY
With **Elizabeth Spicer Garnsey** (Dec 6, 1754 - Mar 14, 1838 Halfmoon, NY), the parents of Daniel G. Garnsey, U.S. Representative-NY from 1825-1829.

JONES, JAMES 1765 Halfmoon, NY - May 5, 1850 Clifton Park, NY
Namesake of the hamlet of Jonesville, town of Clifton Park. Owned and operated the Jonesville Hotel, on the Waterford-Saratoga Turnpike, in 1820

KENNEDY, ROSCIUS R. 1804 Saratoga Springs, NY - May 17, 1874 Clifton Park, NY
Founded Jonesville Academy, a private boarding school in Clifton Park, in 1836.

VAN PATTEN, ROBERT WILLIAM Dec 8, 1918 Ballston Spa, NY - Feb 28, 1990 Clifton Park, NY
Clifton Park builder. Built the Clifton Knolls housing development and the Van Patten Golf Club. His tombstone claims him to be "the Father of Clifton Park."

VAN VRANKEN, GARRET Sept 23, 1783 Clifton Park, NY - May 24, 1834 Clifton Park, NY
Local undertaker. Descended from the Van Vranken family, early settlers in Saratoga County.

JORDAN VILLAGE CEMETERY
Quince Street
Jordan, NY 13080

WOOLSEY, LUTHER SMITH Aug 16, 1798 Ulster, NY - Jan 9, 1842 Elbridge, NY
3rd great-grandfather of actor, Christopher Reeve.

KELLOGGSVILLE CEMETERY
5725 Mack Road
Skaneateles, NY 13152

FILLMORE (Smith)**, EUNICE** 1779 VT - Jun 20, 1866 Aurora, NY
Stepmother of President Millard Fillmore. Married her third husband, Nathaniel Fillmore, May 2, 1834, the third anniversary of the death of Phoebe Millard Fillmore, Nathaniel's first wife and the President's mother. She is buried beside her second husband, Samuel Love.

LOVE, SAMUEL Dec 9, 1766 Coventry, RI - Aug 18, 1831 Sempronius, NY
Third husband of Eunice Smith Bassett Fillmore, the stepmother of President Millard Fillmore.

POWERS, CYRUS 1879 Croydon, NH - Oct 10, 1841 Kelloggsville, NY
Brother-in-law of President Millard Fillmore. Brother of First Lady Abigail Powers Fillmore.

KINDERHOOK REFORMED CHURCH CEMETERY
Albany Avenue / Route 21
Kinderhook, NY 12106

BEALE, CHARLES LEWIS Mar 5, 1824 Canaan, NY - Jan 29, 1899 Hudson, NY
United States Representative-NY from 1859-1861.

BEEKMAN, THOMAS Jul 4, 1790 Kinderhook, NY - Feb 2, 1870 Kinderhook, NY
United States Representative-NY from 1829-1831.

HOES, JOHN DIRCKSEN May 25, 1753 Kinderhook, NY - Jan 25, 1789 Kinderhook, NY
Revolutionary War veteran. With **Maria Quackenbush Hoes** (Jan 26, 1754 Kinderhook, NY - Dec 5, 1852 Kinderhook, NY), the parents of Hannah Hoes Van Buren, the wife of President Martin Van Buren, died of tuberculosis 18 years prior to his presidency.

REYNOLDS, JOHN H. Jun 21, 1819 Moriah, NY - Sept 24, 1875 Kinderhook, NY
United States Representative-NY from 1859-1861.

ROCKEFELLER, LEWIS KIRBY Nov 25, 1875 Schenectady, NY - Sept 18, 1948 Chatham, NY
United States Representative-NY from 1837-1843.

SILVESTER, PETER 1734 Shelter Island, NY - Oct 15, 1808 Kinderhook, NY
United States Representative-NY from 1789-1793. Grandfather of Peter Henry Silvester, United States Representative-NY from 1847-1851.

SILVESTER, PETER HENRY Feb 17, 1807 Kinderhook, NY - Nov 29, 1882 Coxsackie, NY
United States Representative-NY from 1847-1851. Grandson of Peter Silvester, United States Representative-NY from 1789-1793.

VAN ALEN, JAMES I. Dec 31, 1772 Kinderhook, NY - May 18, 1822 Kinderhook, NY
United States Representative-NY from 1807-1809. Half-brother of President Martin Van Buren.

VAN ALEN, JOHANNES Oct 21, 1744 Albany, NY - 1773 Kinderhook, NY
First husband of Maria Hoes Van Buren, mother of President Martin Van Buren, who remarried to Abraham Van Buren in 1776, giving birth to the future president in 1782. Father of James I. Van Alen, United States Representative-NY from 1807-1809.

VAN BUREN, ABRAHAM 1737 Albany, NY - Apr 4, 1817 Kinderhook, NY
Father of President Martin Van Buren.

VAN BUREN (Hoes), **HANNAH** Mar 8, 1783 Kinderhook, NY - Feb 5, 1819 Kinderhook, NY
Wife of Martin Van Buren. Died of tuberculosis, eighteen years prior to his presidency. He never
remarried, his daughter-in-law, Angelica Singleton Van Buren, served as First Lady and official hostess
of the White House. She died, December 29, 1877 in New York City, age 59, and is buried in
Woodlawn Cemetery, the Bronx, next to her husband, Abraham Van Buren Jr.

VAN BUREN (Hoes), **MARIA** Jan 16, 1747 Claverack, NY - Dec 16, 1817 Kinderhook, NY
Mother of President Martin Van Buren. Mother of James I. Van Alen, United States Representative-
NY from 1807-1809.

VAN BUREN, MARTIN Dec 5, 1782 Kinderhook, NY - Jul 24, 1862 Kinderhook, NY
8th President of the United States from 1837-1841. Vice-President of the United States from
1833-1837, under President Andrew Jackson. United States Senator-NY from 1821-1828. Governor of
New York in 1829, for nine weeks, resigned to become United States Secretary of State, from
1829-1831. His supporters popularized the phrase "OK" during his unsuccessful presidential
reelection campaign in 1840.

VAN BUREN, MARTIN Dec 20, 1812 Hudson, NY - Mar 19, 1855 France
Son of President Martin Van Buren.

KING DAVID CEMETERY
101 Mill Street
Putnam Valley, NY 10579

CREIGHTON (Avery), **MARY FRANCES** Jul 29, 1899 Rahway, NJ - Jul 16, 1936 Ossining, NY
Convicted murderer. Conspired with Everett C. Applegate in the poisoning death of his wife, Ada
Johnson Applegate, in Baldwin, Nassau County, September 27, 1935, both convicted and sentenced
to death. Despite passing out prior to her execution, she was put to death in an unconscious state.
Previously arrested for the poisoning death of her brother, Raymond Avery, acquitted following a trial,
days later arrested in the death of her father-in-law, acquitted again. Ada Johnson Applegate is buried
in Rockville Cemetery, Lynbrook, her husband, Greenville Cemetery, Uniondale.

KIRKVILLE CEMETERY
Poolsbrook Road
Kirkville, NY 13082

SMITH, ORSON Aug 20, 1800 - Dec 5, 1886 Manlius, NY
Owned a farm on a large portion of what became Green Lakes State Park. Buried a chain link, six feet deep, across a road separating the farms of his sons, Orson Duane Smith and Anson Smith, leaving two feet of each end above ground, for the two bickering boys to pull, to work out their frustration. The chain was buried across Route 290, near the entrance to the park.

SMITH, ORSON DUANE Apr 24, 1849 Manlius, NY - Jan 2, 1949 Manlius, NY
Oldest-living Manlius resident at the time of his death, just over 100 days short of his 100th birthday.

STEINAKER, WERNER J. Jan 21, 1853 Switzerland - Jun 7, 1934 Syracuse, NY
Owned and operated the Steinaker Grocery on the South side of Syracuse for 40 years.

KNESSETH ISRAEL CEMETERY
Clyde Street
Gloversville, NY 12078

SCHINE (Feldman)**, HILDEGARDE** Mar 23, 1903 Johnstown, NY - Sept 7, 1994 Gloversville, NY
Namesake of the Hildegarde and J. Myer Schine Student Center at Syracuse University, with her husband, theater magnate, J. Myer Schine. Mother of G. David Schine, film producer and key figure in the 1954 Army-McCarthy Senate Hearings. He was killed in a plane crash with his wife, Hillevi Rombin Schine, the 1955 Miss Universe, and their son, F. Berndt Schine, who piloted the plane, June 19, 1996 in Burbank. They are buried in Westwood Village Memorial Park, Los Angeles.

SCHINE, J. MYER (Junius) Feb 28, 1889 Latvia - May 8, 1971 New York, NY
Theater and hotel magnate. Founded Schine Enterprises with his brother, Louis W. Schine. Namesake of the Hildegarde and J. Myer Schine Student Center at Syracuse University, with his wife, Hildegarde Feldman Schine. Father of G. David Schine, film producer and key figure in the 1954 Army-McCarthy Senate Hearings. He was killed in a plane crash with his wife, Hillevi Rombin Schine, the 1955 Miss Universe, and their son, F. Berndt Schine, who piloted the plane, June 19, 1996 in Burbank. They are buried in Westwood Village Memorial Park, Los Angeles.

SCHINE, LOUIS WILLIAM Dec 24, 1897 Latvia - Nov 6, 1956 New York, NY
Theater and hotel magnate. Founded Schine Enterprises with his brother, J. Myer Schine.

SCHINE (Rubin), **MARTHA** Dec 1, 1894 Syracuse, NY - Mar 21, 1984 Gloversville, NY
Wife of theater and hotel magnate, Louis W. Schine, founder of Schine Enterprises with his brother, J. Myer Schine.

SENATOR, JACOB Aug 24, 1900 Warsaw, Russia - Jun 23, 1969 Gloversville, NY
Owned and operated Senator's Restaurant in Gloversville. Brother of George Senator, roommate of Jack Ruby at 223 South Ewing Street #207 in Dallas, at the time of President John F. Kennedy's assassination and Ruby's shooting of Lee Harvey Oswald, later testified before the Warren Commission in 1964. He died April 21, 1992, age 78.

LAFAYETTE RURAL CEMETERY
Route 11
LaFayette, NY 13084

AUNGIER, BERNARD L. Mar 23, 1919 Syracuse, NY - Jan 10, 2006 Syracuse, NY
Town of LaFayette Tax Assessor, longest-serving in Onondaga County, retiring in 2005. With **Mabel Louise Schaeffer Aungier** (Jan 11, 1916 Spafford, NY - May 24, 1996 LaFayette, NY), the step-grandparents of "Craigslist Killer" Philip H. Markoff.

BAKER, BYRON W. Dec 15, 1842 LaFayette, NY - Aug 27, 1866 LaFayette, NY
Semi-pro baseball player. Pitched for the Central City Club of Syracuse before his death from typhoid fever.

HAMMERSTEIN (Miller), **MARY EMMA** 1883 LaFayette, NY - Jan 14, 1946 Syracuse, NY
Widow of theater impresario, Oscar Hammerstein I, died August 1, 1919, age 73, buried Woodlawn Cemetery, Bronx. Stepmother of Broadway producer, Arthur Hammerstein, who built the Ed Sullivan Theater on Broadway, New York City, in 1927, originally Hammerstein's Theatre, and theater manager, Willie Hammerstein, the father of composer, Oscar Hammerstein II. Previously married into the family of Gustavus Franklin Swift of Chicago, founder of Swift & Company, first meatpacking business to use refrigerated railroad cars. Resided on Comstock Avenue the last three years of her life.

SIGNOR (Smith), **ANNA LUCINDA** 1884 LaFayette, NY - Nov 1, 1964 Syracuse, NY
Sole beneficiary in the will of her friend, Mary Miller Swift Hammerstein, the widow of theater impresario, Oscar Hammerstein I, who passed away in 1946, leaving an estate worth $5000.

LAKE DELAWARE CEMETERY
Lake Delaware Drive
Delhi, NY 13753

GERRY (Dresser)**, EDITH STUYVESANT** Jan 17, 1873 Newport, RI - Dec 21, 1958 Providence, RI
Widow of George Washington Vanderbilt, the son of financier, William Henry Vanderbilt, grandson of
shipping and railroad tycoon, Cornelius Vanderbilt, and brother of Cornelius Vanderbilt II, the
grandfather of socialite, Gloria Vanderbilt. Remarried, Peter G. Gerry, United States Senator-RI from
1935-1947, in October 1925. Grandniece of Hamilton Fish, Secretary of State from 1869-1877 and
Governor of New York from 1849-1850.

GERRY, PETER GOELET Sept 18, 1879 New York, NY - Oct 31, 1957 Providence, RI
United States Senator-RI from 1935-1947. United States Representative-RI from 1913-1915. Great-
grandson of Vice-President Elbridge Gerry, signer of the *Declaration of Independence*.

GERRY, ROBERT LIVINGSTON May 31, 1877 New York, NY - Oct 31, 1957 Delhi, NY
Thoroughbred racehorse owner and breeder. Died the same day, hours apart, as his brother, Peter G.
Gerry, United States Senator-RI from 1935-1947. Great-grandson of Vice-President Elbridge Gerry,
signer of the *Declaration of Independence*. Brother-in-law of W. Averell Harriman, Governor of New
York from 1955-1959.

LAKE GEORGE BATTLEFIELD PARK
2224 Route 9 / Fort George Park Road
Lake George, NY 12845

DE WOEDTKE, BARON (Frederick William) 1740 Prussia - Jul 28, 1776 Lake George, NY
Revolutionary War Continental Army Brigadier General. Accompanied Benjamin Franklin, Samuel
Chase and Charles Carroll on a diplomatic mission to Montréal at the beginning of the American
Revolution. Major in the Prussian Army of Frederick the Great, King Frederick II of Prussia. Buried in
an unmarked grave, near the Fort George military post.

LAKE VIEW CEMETERY
907 Lakeview Avenue
Jamestown, NY 14701

BALL, FRED (Frederick Henry) Jul 17, 1915 Jamestown, NY - Feb 5, 2007 Cottonwood, AZ
Television studio executive. Served on the Board of Directors for Desilu Productions, a company
formed by his sister, actress, Lucille Ball and brother-in-law, actor and bandleader, Desi Arnaz.

BALL, HENRY DURRELL Sept 16, 1887 Sheridan, NY - Feb 28, 1915 Jamestown, NY
With **Desiree Eveline Hunt Ball** (Sept 21, 1892 Jamestown, NY - Jul 20, 1977 Los Angeles, CA), the parents of Emmy Award-winning actress, Lucille Ball. Grandparents of actress, Lucy Arnaz and actor, Desi Arnaz Jr.

BALL, LUCILLE Aug 6, 1911 Jamestown, NY - Apr 26. 1989 Beverly Hills, CA
Comedic actress. Four-time Emmy Award winner. Star of the sitcoms, *I Love Lucy*, *The Lucy-Desi Comedy Hour*, *The Lucy Show* and *Here's Lucy*. Teamed with husband, Desi Arnaz, to form Desilu Productions, producer of the classic TV programs, *Star Trek, Mission: Impossible*, *The Untouchables* and her own series, *I Love Lucy*. Appeared in the films, *Stage Door*, *The Fuller Brush Girl*, *Yours, Mine and Ours* and the Marx Brothers' film, *Room Service*. Awarded two stars on the Hollywood Walk of Fame. Mother of actress, Lucy Arnaz and actor, Desi Arnaz Jr. Cremated, originally buried in Forest Lawn Memorial Park-Hollywood Hills, Los Angeles, reinterred by her children in 2002.

FENTON, REUBEN EATON Jul 4, 1819 Carroll, NY - Aug 25, 1889 Jamestown, NY
U.S. Senator-NY from 1869-1875. United States Representative-NY from 1853-1855 and 1857-1865. Governor of New York from 1865-1869.

GALLOWAY, GRACE LAVERNE Oct 5, 1871 Jamestown, NY - Nov 2, 1898 Jamestown, NY
Local opera singer known for her monument, commissioned by her parents, John and Sarah Calhoun Galloway, a life-size replica depicting her in a dress, sculpted of marble from Florence, Italy.

GOODELL, CHARLES ELLSWORTH Mar 16, 1926 Jamestown, NY - Jan 21, 1987 Washington D.C.
U.S. Senator-NY from 1968-1971. United States Representative-NY from 1959-1968. Appointed by Governor Nelson A. Rockefeller to fill the Senate seat due to the assassination of Robert F. Kennedy, killed June 5, 1968 in Los Angeles, while campaigning for the Democratic Party nomination for president. Father of NFL Commissioner, Roger Goodell.

GOODRICH, B.F. (Benjamin Franklin) Nov 4, 1841 Ripley, NY - Aug 3, 1888 Akron, OH
Rubber and tire manufacturer. Founded the B.F. Goodrich Company in Akron in 1870. Battlefront surgeon for the Union Army during the Civil War. First man in Ohio to own a telephone, receiving one as a gift from its inventor, Alexander Graham Bell, in 1877. Grandfather of photojournalist and cinematographer, Marvin (Mary) Breckinridge Patterson. Son-in-law of Richard Pratt Marvin, United States Representative-NY from 1837-1841.

HALL, CHAPIN Jul 12, 1816 Busti, NY - Sept 12, 1879 Jamestown, NY
United States Representative-PA from 1859-1861.

HAZELTINE, ABNER Jul 10, 1793 Wardsboro, VT - Dec 20, 1879 Jamestown, NY
United States Representative-NY from 1833-1837.

HUNT, FRED CHARLES Jul 25, 1865 Jamestown, NY - Jan 9, 1944 Los Angeles, CA
With **Flora Belle Orcutt Hunt** (Jun 19, 1867 Pomfret, NY - Jul 1, 1922 Celeron, NY), the grandparents of Emmy Award-winning actress, Lucille Ball. Great-grandparents of actress, Lucy Arnaz and actor, Desi Arnaz Jr.

LENNA, REGINALD A. Dec 3, 1912 Jamestown, NY - Feb 6, 2000 Jamestown, NY
President of the Blackstone Manufacturing Company. Namesake of the Reg Lenna Civic Center in Jamestown. Knighted by the King of Sweden, Carl XVI Gustaf, in 1976.

MARVIN, RICHARD PRATT Dec 23, 1803 Fairfield, NY - Jan 11, 1892 Jamestown, NY
United States Representative-NY from 1837-1841. Father-in-law of rubber manufacturer, B.F. Goodrich. Great-grandfather of photojournalist and cinematographer, Marvin (Mary) Breckinridge Patterson.

PETERSON, KARL Jan 17, 1866 Malmö, Sweden - Jun 20, 1933 Jamestown, NY
Founded the Crescent Tool Company in Jamestown in 1902, maker of the first adjustable wrench.

PHILBRICK, ORLAND WILLIAM Aug 14, 1945 Gowanda, NY - May 31, 2006 Jamestown, NY
Uncle of Ralph James "Bucky" Phillips, listed simultaneously on the FBI Ten Most Wanted Fugitives and the U.S. Marshal Service's Top 15 lists, for the shooting death of a New York State trooper and escape from prison in 2006, spending five months escaping justice.

SHELDON, PORTER Sept 29, 1831 Victor, NY - Aug 15, 1908 Jamestown, NY
United States Representative-NY from 1869-1871.

TEW, HARVEY WILLIAM Sept 23, 1832 Jamestown, NY - Nov 14, 1911 Jamestown, NY
Co-founded the B.F. Goodrich Company, with his brother-in-law, B.F. Goodrich, in Akron in 1870. With **Susan D. Goodrich Tew** (Mar 22, 1837 Jamestown, NY - Feb 25, 1921 Jamestown, NY), the 2nd great-grandparents of actress, Paget Brewster.

WORK, A.D. (Aaron) 1848 Millersburg, OH - Apr 12, 1928 Jamestown, NY
Owned A.D. Work's Confectionary in Jamestown. Employed Catherine "Kitty" Sweeney in his candy shop, where she met Milton S. Hershey in 1897, traveling through town promoting his own candy product, they married the next year, May 25, 1898 in St. Patrick's Cathedral, New York City.

LAKE VIEW CEMETERY
Court Street
Penn Yan, NY 14527

DEPEW, ISAAC PURDY Aug 4, 1834 Montgomery, NY - Dec 19, 1932 Syracuse, NY
Onondaga County's oldest Civil War veteran at the time of his death. Gold rush-seeker in California. Survived the Panama Fever epidemic in the 1850s. Friend of President Abraham Lincoln in Washington, he marched as one of the honor guard, beside Lincoln's body as it was removed from the Capital, to the funeral train en route to Springfield. Oldest subscriber to the *Syracuse Herald*, reading the paper since its inception, January 15, 1877.

ELLSWORTH, SAMUEL STEWART Oct 13, 1790 Pownal, VT - Jun 4, 1863 Penn Yan, NY
United States Representative-NY from 1845-1847.

LEE, JOSHUA 1783 Hudson, NY - Dec 29, 1842 Penn Yan, NY
United States Representative-NY from 1835-1837. War of 1812 surgeon, commissioned by New York Governor, Daniel D. Tompkins.

MORSE, HARRY C. 1866 Penn Yan, NY - Jan 3, 1936 Penn Yan, NY
Steamboat Captain for the *Mary Bell* on Keuka Lake. Manager of the Elmwood Theatre in Penn Yan. In 1873, age 7, he peered too close into Keuka Lake from his mother's rowboat when a trout jumped up and bit his nose. The story made the local papers and a local legend was born.

MORSE, OSCAR Mar 19, 1845 Penn Yan, NY - Apr 9, 1927 Geneva, NY
Steamboat Captain from 1883-1891. Civil War veteran. Attended the funeral of President Abraham Lincoln in Washington D.C. Uncle of Harry C. Morse, Captain of the *Mary Bell* on Keuka Lake.

MORRIS, DANIEL Jan 4, 1812 Fayette, NY - Apr 22, 1889 Penn Yan, NY
United States Representative-NY from 1863-1867. Yates County District Attorney from 1847-1850.

OLIVER, ANDREW Jan 16, 1815 Springfield, NY - Mar 6, 1889 Penn Yan, NY
United States Representative-NY from 1853-1857.

OLIVER, WILLIAM MORRISON Oct 15, 1792 Londonderry, NH - Jul 21, 1863 Penn Yan, NY
United States Representative-NY from 1841-1843. Lieutenant Governor of New York, under Enos T. Throop in 1830.

REMER, WILLIAM AARON Jul 27, 1855 Penn Yan, NY - Jul 31, 1943 Gayville, SD
Black Hills pioneer. Sheriff of Deadwood, Lawrence County, from 1892-1896. First husband of Marguerite N. "Madge" Bullock Mackall, the daughter of Seth Bullock, Western folk figure, United States Marshal and close friend of President Theodore Roosevelt.

SPENCER, ELIJAH 1775 Columbia County, NY - Dec 15, 1852 Benton, NY
United States Representative-NY from 1821-1823.

LAKE VIEW CEMETERY
West Genesee Street / Route 20
Skaneateles, NY 13152

ALLYN, WILLIAM G. Feb 23, 1908 NY - Jun 24, 2006 Skaneateles, NY
President of Welch Allyn, Inc. from 1947-1971. Son of Welch Allyn co-founder and first President,
William N. Allyn.

ALLYN, WILLIAM NOAH Dec 3, 1874 Whitesboro, NY - Oct 7, 1964 Skaneateles, NY
Founded Welch Allyn, Inc., a leading global manufacturer of frontline medical products, with Dr.
Francis A. Welch, in Skaneateles Falls in 1915. Welch died later that same year.

ANGYAL, JOHN 1940 Auburn, NY - May 9, 2010 Skaneateles, NY
Owned and operated Johnny Angel's Heavenly Burgers in Skaneateles. Skaneateles Town Supervisor
and Town Justice.

BARNES, GEORGE R. 1910 - Apr 9, 1961 Auburn, NY
Builder and skipper of small-craft sailboats. Won the International Lightning class championship in
1945.

BARROW, JOHN DODGSON 1824 New York, NY - December 7, 1906 Skaneateles, NY
Landscape painter and portrait artist. Created the John D. Barrow Art Gallery in Skaneateles in 1900.
Designed the Soldiers and Sailors Monument in Lake View Cemetery in 1893.

BARTLETT, EDWARD THEODORE Jun 14, 1841 Skaneateles, NY - May 3, 1910 Albany, NY
Associate Justice of the New York State Court of Appeals from 1894-1910.

BATES, PAUL R. Feb 14, 1920 Far Rockaway, NY - Apr 23, 1990 Syracuse, NY
Raised and raced homing pigeons. Member of the Finger Lakes Racing Pigeon Club. Husband of Lia
Van den Ancker Bates, childhood classmate and friend of Anne Frank in Montessori, Amsterdam, the
Netherlands, in the late 1930s, prior to the Frank family going into hiding for two years, and their arrest
by German police. Anne Frank died in the Bergen-Belsen concentration camp, March 1945, days prior
to its liberation by Allied forces, her father Otto Frank, the only surviving family member, published
Anne Frank's diary in 1947.

BEAUCHAMP, WILLIAM MARTIN Mar 25, 1830 Coldenham, NY - Dec 13, 1925 Syracuse, NY
Episcopal priest. Archeologist for the New York State Museum from 1884-1910. Studied the Iroquois

Indians, surveyed Iroquois territory in New York and Canada.

BESSE (Starkweather), **JANET KENT** Oct 2, 1925 Philadelphia, PA - Dec 9, 2004 Skaneateles, NY
Co-founded Concerned Citizens Against Drunk Driving in 1975, in response to being struck by a drunk
driver in 1966, who only received a $10 fine for the accident. Received the *Post-Standard* Woman of
Achievement Award for citizenship in 1977. Inducted into the National Women's Hall of Fame Book of
Lives and Legacies in 2001. Co-founded the Skaneateles Sailing Club and the Sailboat Shop with her
husband, Richard Waterman Besse.

BESSE, RICHARD WATERMAN Dec 27, 1920 - Sept 17, 2004 Skaneateles, NY
Award-winning sailor and boatman. Qualified as an alternate Finn class skipper for the 1952 Olympics.
Co-founded the Skaneateles Sailing Club and the Sailboat Shop with his wife, Janet Starkweather
Besse.

CHASE, DAVID O. Jan 13, 1930 Syracuse, NY - Mar 7, 1995 Lake Worth, FL
Captain of the 1976 United States Olympic Polo Team. Chairman of Chase Design, Inc., named one
of the country's top ten industrial design firms by the Association of Professional Design.

CUDDEBACK, ABRAHAM A. 1754 Minisink, NY - Aug 23, 1855 Skaneateles, NY
First settler of the town of Skaneateles, arriving June 14, 1794. Brother-in-law of Simeon DeWitt,
Surveyor-General for the State of New York.

DAY, WINSTON 1767 - Sept 11, 1831 Skaneateles, NY
First merchant in the town of Skaneateles. Founded the Sherwood Inn in Skaneateles in 1807, with
his brother-in-law, Isaac Sherwood.

DIETZ, GERRY JOHNSON Mar 17, 1917 Albuquerque, NM - May 27, 1993 Syracuse, NY
President of the R.E. Dietz Company in Syracuse from 1950-1967, founded by his great-grandfather,
Robert E. Dietz. Brother-in-law of Julia Grant Dietz, the great-granddaughter of President Ulysses S.
Grant.

DODGE, FRED (Frederick A.) Nov 22, 1844 Skaneateles, NY - Sept 5, 1886 Skaneateles, NY
Semi-pro baseball player. Pitched for the Central City Club of Syracuse from 1867-1868. Editor of the
Skaneateles Democrat.

FELDMANN, LESLIE KAREN Feb 9, 1964 Syracuse, NY - Dec 15, 1997 Littleton, CO
AirLife flight team nurse. Worked in burn units throughout the country. Killed in a helicopter accident,
attempting to save a car accident victim, when it struck electrical wires and crashed. The pilot, a flight
nurse and the patient also died. Daughter of Robert Curtis Feldmann, founder of Bob's True Value
Hardware in Syracuse.

FELDMANN, ROBERT CURTIS Nov 11, 1924 - Feb 22, 2011 Longboat Key, FL
Founder and namesake of Bob's True Value Hardware in Syracuse.

HALL, DEACON (David) 1786 - Jun 4, 1865 Skaneateles, NY
Early Skaneateles landowner. Built the tavern which houses the Sherwood Inn, the Methodist
Church on Jordan Street and a house which became the home of the Glen Haven Hotel.

HARPER, WILLIAM B. Jun 17, 1923 Amber, NY - Jun 12, 1988 Pittsburgh, PA
Two-term President of the National Campers and Hikers Association, from 1986-1988.

HARRIS, LINDSAY MARIE Sept 3, 1983 Smithtown, NY - May 4, 2005 Henderson, NV
Victim of an unsolved homicide. Last seen May 4, 2005 in Henderson, NV at an ATM, mailing a
Mother's Day card. Three weeks later, May 23, 2005, two severed legs were discovered on the
shoulder of an exit ramp off Interstate 55 in Divernon, IL. Three years later, May 2008, they were
positively identified through DNA as her legs. Her murder has been featured on *America's Most
Wanted* and *Anderson Cooper's 360*.

JEWETT, FREEBORN GARRETTSON Aug 4, 1791 Sharon, CT - Jan 27, 1858 Skaneateles, NY
United States Representative-NY from 1831-1833. First Chief Justice of the New York State Court of
Appeals, from 1847-1850. Onondaga County District Attorney in 1839. Father-in-law of William Marvin,
Governor of Florida in 1865.

KELLOGG (Bartlett)**, MARY** Jun 29, 1842 Skaneateles, NY - Sept 13, 1915 Skaneateles, NY
Great-granddaughter of Josiah Bartlett, signer of the *Declaration of Independence*.

KREBS (Horsington)**, CORA** 1869 Skaneateles, NY - Aug 3, 1936 Skaneateles, NY
Restauranteur. Co-founded Krebs' Restaurant, with her husband, Fred Krebs on West Genesee Street
in Skaneateles. Provided dinners for her neighbors and vacationers for 50 cents a meal, with her
sister, Anna, in 1899, gaining a national reputation, the restaurant became a local landmark.

KREBS, FRED Jul 15, 1868 Skaneateles, NY - Jun 17, 1938 Skaneateles, NY
Restaurateur. Co-founded Krebs' Restaurant in Skaneateles, with his wife, Cora Krebs.

LEGG, JOHN May 3, 1783 Northampton, MA - Dec 19, 1857 Skaneateles, NY
Prominent carriage manufacturer. Father-in-law of banker, Joel Thayer.

LONEY (Norton)**, MARY HISE** 1876 New York, NY - Mar 17, 1900 Asheville, NC
New York City socialite, notable for her tomb, designed by American architect, Cass Gilbert.
Reinterred to Moravian Cemetery, Staten Island, in 1934. Granddaughter of Mary Hise Norton, a
quilter whose work, in possession of the Smithsonian, hangs in the United States Embassy in Oslo.

MARVIN, WILLIAM Apr 14, 1808 Fairfield, NY - Jul 9, 1902 Skaneateles, NY
Provisional Governor of Florida in 1865, appointed by President Andrew Johnson. Associate Justice of the United States District Court for the Southern District of Florida in 1840. Son-in-law of Freeborn Garrettson Jewett, United States Representative-NY from 1831-1833.

MCLENNAN, FRED 1866 Canandaigua, NY - Jul 18, 1945 Willard, NY
Self-proclaimed "Mac-O-the-Mystic", claimed to predict the future through electricity within his body, attaching a copper wire to himself, which connects to a coin on a dish, "ringing" three times for yes, twice for no, to a question he raises.

MENEGUZZO, SILVIO 1877 Valdagno, Italy - Feb 19, 1962 Fayetteville, NY
Oboist and eighth horn with John Philip Sousa, the Syracuse Symphony Orchestra and the NBC Orchestra.

MESSENGER, JAMES H. Jul 16, 1925 Lackawanna, NY - Dec 15, 2011 Skaneateles, NY
President and CEO of Sair Aviation, Inc. in Syracuse, from 1978-1999.

PIRRO, DAVID Jul 3, 1965 Syracuse, NY - Apr 8, 2005 Bonita Springs, FL
Owner and president of Dave Pirro Ford in Skaneateles from 1991-2005. Struck and killed by lightening, golfing near his parents' home in Florida.

RICHARDS, LOUIS C. Jun 8, 1885 Marcellus, NY - May 5, 1977 Syracuse, NY
First electrician in the village of Marcellus. Wired Howe Caverns in the 1920s, discovered by Lester Howe in 1842 in Howes Cave, near Cobleskill.

ROOSEVELT, FREDERICK Feb 27, 1850 New York, NY - Jun 18, 1916 New York, NY
Son of James John Roosevelt, United States Representative-NY from 1841-1843. 2nd great-grandson of Archibald Bulloch, Governor of Georgia from 1776-1777. Cousin of President Theodore Roosevelt.

ROOSEVELT, HENRY LATROBE Oct 30, 1811 Louisville, KY - Jan 10, 1884 Skaneateles, NY
Son of engineer, Nicholas J. Roosevelt and Lydia Latrobe Roosevelt. Born on his father's steamboat, the *New Orleans*, during a stopover on the Mississippi River, the historic maiden voyage of the boat. Grandson of architect, Benjamin Henry Latrobe, designer of the United States Capitol Building and the cenotaphs in Congressional Cemetery in Washington D.C.

ROOSEVELT (Latrobe)**, LYDIA MARY** Mar 23, 1791 London, England - Mar 2, 1878 Skaneateles, NY
Wife of engineer, Nicholas J. Roosevelt. Daughter of architect, Benjamin Henry Latrobe, designer of the United States Capitol Building and the cenotaphs in Congressional Cemetery, Washington D.C.

ROOSEVELT, NICHOLAS JAMES Oct 27, 1767 New York, NY - Jul 30, 1854 Skaneateles, NY
Inventor and engineer. Built the first steamboat, *New Orleans*, to navigate the Mississippi and Ohio

Rivers. Great-granduncle of President Theodore Roosevelt. 2nd great-granduncle of First Lady, Eleanor Roosevelt. Son-in-law of architect, Benjamin Henry Latrobe, designer of the United States Capitol Building and the cenotaphs in Congressional Cemetery in Washington D.C.

ROOSEVELT, NICHOLAS LATROBE Jun 11, 1847 Skaneateles, NY - Dec 13, 1892 New York, NY
Father of Henry Latrobe Roosevelt, Assistant Secretary of the Navy, appointed by President Franklin D. Roosevelt in 1933. Grandson of engineer, Nicholas J. Roosevelt and Lydia Latrobe Roosevelt. Great-grandson of architect, Benjamin Henry Latrobe, designer of the United States Capitol Building and the cenotaphs in Congressional Cemetery in Washington D.C.. Brother of artist, Samuel M. Roosevelt.

ROOSEVELT, SAMUEL MONTGOMERY Feb 20, 1857 NY - Aug 19, 1920 New York, NY
Portrait artist. Painted President Theodore Roosevelt and Oliver Hazard Perry Belmont. Purchased a 25-room mansion on Skaneateles Lake, named it Roosevelt Hall. Died from a brain hemorrhage at the Knickerbocker Hotel in New York City. Grandson of engineer, Nicholas J. Roosevelt and Lydia Latrobe Roosevelt. Great-grandson of architect, Benjamin Henry Latrobe, designer of the United States Capitol Building and the cenotaphs in Congressional Cemetery in Washington D.C.

SHAW, BILLY 1902 Hoboken, NJ - May 8, 1958 Syracuse, NY
Central New York fight promoter, amateur boxer and columnist for *Ring Magazine*.

SHERWOOD, ISAAC Oct 12, 1769 Williamston, MA - Apr 24, 1840 Skaneateles, NY
Owned and operated a stagecoach business, delivering mail from Buffalo to Albany. Founded the Sherwood Inn in Skaneateles in 1807, with his brother-in-law, Winston Day.

SHOTWELL, WILLIAM J. 1864 Skaneateles, NY - Sept 11, 1922 Skaneateles, NY
Namesake and benefactor of Shotwell Park, on the shore of Skaneateles Lake, adjoining Clift Park.

SHULTZ, SEARLES G. Apr 29, 1897 Skaneateles, NY - Dec 31, 1975 Skaneateles, NY
New York State Senator from 1955-1958. New York State Assemblyman from 1947-1954.

THAYER, JOEL Jul 18, 1812 Ontario, NY - May 16, 1881 Skaneateles, NY
Postmaster of Skaneateles. Founder and President of the Bank of Skaneateles. Director of the American Steamboat Company. Founder and President of the Skaneateles Railroad Company. Donated the St. James Tower Clock in the village of Skaneateles in honor of his wife's parents, carriage-maker, John Legg and Emma Colvin Legg, on Christmas Day, 1873.

LAKEMONT CEMETERY
Hayes Road
Dundee, NY 14837

BOWLES, CLAUDE DIETZ Mar 24, 1878 Waukesha, WI - Jun 15, 1966 St. Petersburg, FL
With **Rena Frances Winnewisser Bowles** (Oct 2, 1884 Bellows Falls, VT - Jun 8, 1966 St. Petersburg, FL), the parents of author and composer, Paul Bowles.

BOWLES, PAUL Dec 30, 1910 Jamaica (Queens), NY - Nov 18, 1999 Tangier, Morocco
Author and composer. Wrote the novels, *The Sheltering Sky, Let It Come Down* and *Up Above the World*. Composed music for Orson Welles and John Houseman from 1936-1938. Lived in Tangier, Morocco, from 1947 until his death. Husband of playwright, Jane Auer Bowles, died in Andalucia, Spain, May 4, 1973, age 56, buried there in Cementerio de San Miguel, though her name appears on his tombstone.

LAKESIDE CEMETERY
4810 Camp Road / Route 75
Hamburg, NY 14075

BROST, WILLIAM A. 1871 - 1932 Buffalo, NY
Father of composer, Ray Henderson, co-writer of "Bye Bye Blackbird", "The Birth of the Blues", "Five Foot Two, Eyes of Blue (Has Anybody Seen My Girl?)", "The Best Things in Life Are Free" and "I'm Sitting on Top of the World", with songwriting partners, Lew Brown and Buddy DeSylva. He died December 31, 1970, Greenwich, CT, age 74.

HOLMES, EDWARD L. Jul 15, 1920 NY - Nov 21, 1998 Farnham, NY
With **Audrey F. Holmes** (Nov 21, 1915 Kenilworth, Warwickshire, England - Oct 12, 2011 Las Vegas, NV), the parents of singer/songwriter and Las Vegas nightclub performer, Clint Holmes, who scored a hit with "Playground In My Mind" in 1973.

PILLION, JOHN RAYMOND Aug 10, 1904 Conneaut, OH - Dec 31, 1978 Eden, NY
United States Representative-NY from 1953-1965.

SADLER, BILL (William J.) Jun 12, 1923 Erie, NY - Mar 13, 2011 Buffalo, NY
Founded Sadler's Wells, creator and producer of Coffee Break, one of the first non-dairy coffee creamers. Father of actor, William T. Sadler.

LAKESIDE CEMETERY
Dodge Avenue
Sackets Harbor, NY 13685

GUTHRIE, SAMUEL 1782 Brimfield, MA - Oct 19, 1848 Jewettville, NY
Chemist. Invented chloroform in 1830, first used in Madison Barracks Hospital in Sackets Harbor.

SACKET, AUGUSTUS Nov 10, 1769 New York, NY - Apr 11, 1827 Albany, NY
Founder and namesake of the village of Sackets Harbor, Jefferson County, in 1801.

LAKEVIEW CEMETERY
40 White Road
Brockport, NY 14420

SEYMOUR, WILLIAM HENRY Jul 21, 1834 Brockport, NY - Apr 7, 1906 Washington D.C.
United States Representative-MI from 1888-1889. Member of the Michigan State House of Representatives from 1880-1882 and the Michigan State Senate from 1882-1884 and 1886-1888.

SHANNON, RICHARD CUTTS Feb 12, 1839 New London, CT - Oct 5, 1920 Brockport, NY
U. S. Representative-NY from 1895-1899. United States Minister to Nicaragua, Salvador and Costa Rica, from 1891-1893.

LAKEVIEW CEMETERY
West Lake Road / Route 36
Honeoye, NY 14471

PITTS, GIDEON 1807 Honeoye, NY - Jun 18, 1888 Honeoye, NY
With **Jane Wells Pitts** (May 4, 1811 - Mar 26, 1892 Washington D.C.), the parents of Helen Pitts Douglass, the wife of social reformer, Frederick Douglass.

LAKEVIEW CEMETERY
3685 Skillet Road
Interlaken, NY 14847

SERLING (Arone), **PRISCILLA ELAINE** Apr 23, 1943 Boston, MA - Jun 5, 2000 Tucson, AZ
Wife of novelist, Robert J. Serling. Sister-in-law of screenwriter, Rod Serling, creator of *The Twilight Zone* and *Night Gallery*.

SERLING, ROBERT J. (Jerome) Mar 28, 1918 Cortland, NY - May 6, 2010 Tucson, AZ
Author and aviation journalist. Wrote the novels, *The President's Plane is Missing*, *The Probable Cause*, *Something's Alive on the Titanic* and *Character and Characters*. Co-wrote *The Twilight Zone* episode, *The Odyssey of Flight 33*, with his brother, Rod Serling, creator of *The Twilight Zone*. Cremated, a portion of his ashes reside in the Community Church of the Rockies, Estes Park, CO.

SERLING, ROD (Edwin) Dec 25, 1924 Syracuse, NY - Jun 28, 1974 Rochester, NY
Television screenwriter and producer. Created *The Twilight Zone* and *Night Gallery*. Won six Emmy Awards, one Golden Globe and a Peabody Award. Wrote screenplays for the films, *Requiem for a Heavyweight, The Planet of the Apes* and *Seven Days in May*. Highly decorated World War II paratrooper. Brother of novelist, Robert J. Serling.

LAKEVIEW CEMETERY
605 Eastshore Drive
Ithaca, NY 14850

BAILEY, LIBERTY HYDE Mar 14, 1858 South Haven MI - Dec 25, 1954 Ithaca, NY
Botanist and horticulturist. Organized the United States' first school of horticulture, at Michigan State University in 1882. Instrumental in the formation of the 4-H Movement.

DOBIE, GILMOUR Jan 21, 1879 Hastings, MN - Dec 23, 1948 Hartford, CT
Head football coach for North Dakota State University, University of Washington, Navy, Cornell and Boston College from 1906-1938. Nicknamed "Gloomy Gil." Won three national champions at Cornell from 1921-1923. Inducted into College Football Hall of Fame in 1951.

SAGAN, CARL EDWARD Nov 9, 1934 New York, NY - Dec 20, 1996 Seattle, WA
Cornell University professor of astronomy and space sciences. Consultant and advisor for NASA. Briefed Apollo astronauts before their flights to the moon. Experimenter on the Mariner, Viking, Voyager and Galileo expeditions. Co-produced and narrated the TV series, *Cosmos*, based on his Pulitzer Prize-winning book. Founder and first president of the Planetary Society.

LAKEVIEW CEMETERY
Cemetery Road
Richfield Springs, NY 13439

BRUCE, LOU (Louis R.) Jan 16, 1877 St. Regis, NY - Feb 9, 1968 Ilion, NY
Played 30 games for the Philadelphia Athletics in 1904, managed by Hall of Famer, Connie Mack. Attended the University of Pennsylvania Dental School and the Syracuse University School of Theology. Father of Louis R. Bruce Jr., United States Commissioner of Indian Affairs from 1969-1973.

CHASE, SAMUEL 1789 Cooperstown, NY - Aug 3, 1838 Richfield Springs, NY
United States Representative-NY from 1827-1829. Otsego County District Attorney from 1821-1829.

HEWES, GEORGE ROBERT TWELVES Aug 25, 1742 Boston, MA - Nov 5, 1840 Richfield, NY
Political protester during the American Revolution. Played key roles in the Boston Tea Party and Boston Massacre, one of the last surviving participants. Subject of the biography, *A Retrospective of the Boston Tea-Party*. Joseph Cole painted his portrait, *The Centenarian,* which hangs in the Old State House in Boston. Died four months after an accident, boarding a carriage to attend Fourth of July festivities.

LAKEVIEW CEMETERY
Lake Road / Route 101
Williamson, NY 14589

ORBAKER, ADRIAN Apr 9, 1862 the Netherlands - Jul 22, 1937 Pultneyville, NY
Owned and operated Orbaker's Farm, just off the shores of Lake Ontario, now a New York State Century Farm, a continuously operated farm on the same land, owned by the same family for more than 100 years.

LAKEWOOD CEMETERY
East Lake Road
Cooperstown, NY 13326

ASHFORD, EMMETT LITTLETON Nov 23, 1914 Los Angeles, CA - Mar 1, 1980 Marina del Rey, CA
American League umpire from 1966-1970. First African-American to umpire a major league baseball game. Worked the 1967 All-Star Game and the 1970 World Series between the Baltimore Orioles and the Cincinnati Reds. Appeared in the Richard Pryor film, *The Bingo Long Traveling All-Stars & Motor Kings*, and the 1977 TV series, *The Jacksons*.

BEADLE, ERASTUS FLAVEL Sept 11, 1821 Pierstown, NY - Dec 21, 1894 Cooperstown, NY
Author. Published "dime novels", with his brother, Irwin Beadle, in 1860.

BOWERS, JOHN MYER Sept 25, 1772 Boston, MA - Feb 24, 1846 Cooperstown, NY
United States Representative-NY in 1813. Elected to Congress due to the death of Representative-elect, William Dowse, served seven months, replaced by Isaac William, who contested the election. Grandfather of John M. Bowers, Chief Counsel for former President, Theodore Roosevelt, in his libel defense, sued by William Barnes Jr., in Syracuse in 1915.

BOWERS, JOHN MYER Nov 1849 Cooperstown, NY - Mar 8, 1918 Lakewood, NJ
Chief Counsel for former President, Theodore Roosevelt, in his libel defense, sued by New York State

Republican leader, William Barnes Jr., in 1915, held at the Onondaga County Courthouse in Syracuse, won by Roosevelt. Grandson of John Myer Bowers, United States Representative-NY in 1813.

CLARK, ALFRED CORNING Nov 14, 1844 Cooperstown, NY - Apr 8, 1896 New York, NY
Built the first gymnasium in Cooperstown, on the future site of the National Baseball Hall of Fame. His widow, Elizabeth Scriven Clark, married Henry Codman Potter, seventh Bishop of the Episcopal Church of New York, in 1902. Son of Edward S. Clark, co-founder of the Singer Sewing Machine Company. Father of Stephen Carlton Clark, founder of the National Baseball Hall of Fame in Cooperstown, Robert Sterling Clark, founder of the Sterling and Francine Clark Art Institute, and equestrian, F. Ambrose Clark.

CLARK, EDWARD S. Dec 19, 1811 Athens, NY - Oct 14, 1882 Cooperstown, NY
New York City lawyer. Co-founded the Singer Sewing Machine Company, with Isaac Merritt Singer, in 1851. Hired the firm of Henry Janeway Hardenberg, designer of the Plaza Hotel in New York City, to build the Dakota, 72nd Street, Manhattan, completed in 1884, the site of John Lennon's murder, December 8, 1980, nearly a century later. Grandfather of Stephen Carlton Clark, founder of the National Baseball Hall of Fame in Cooperstown, Robert Sterling Clark, founder of the Sterling and Francine Clark Art Institute, and equestrian, F. Ambrose Clark.

CLARK, STEPHEN CARLTON Aug 29, 1882 Cooperstown, NY - Sept 17, 1960 New York, NY
Publisher and art collector. Member of the New York State Assembly. Founder and president of the National Baseball Hall of Fame in Cooperstown, in 1939. Built the Otesaga Resort Hotel in Cooperstown, with his brother, Edward Severin Clark, in 1909. Brother of equestrian, F. Ambrose Clark, and Robert Sterling Clark, founder of the Sterling and Francine Clark Art Institute.

HYDE (Lewis)**, MOLLIE** (Mary Annie) Jan 10, 1868 NY - Jun 28, 1921 Richfield Springs, NY
Great-grandmother of Emmy Award-winning actor, David Hyde Pierce.

NELSON, SAMUEL Nov 10, 1792 Hebron, NY - Dec 13, 1873 Cooperstown, NY
Associate Justice of the United States Supreme Court, nominated by President John Tyler, from 1845-1872. Chief Justice of the New York State Supreme Court from 1837-1845.

PHINNEY (Cooper)**, CAROLINE M.** Jan 26, 1815 Cooperstown, NY - Jan 10, 1892 Cooperstown, NY
Daughter of author, James Fenimore Cooper. Daughter-in-law of publisher, Elihu Phinney Jr.

PHINNEY, ELIHU Jul 1, 1785 New Canaan, NY - Jan 26, 1863 NY
Owned and operated the H. & E. Phinney Publishing Company, with his brother, Henry Phinney. Published 138 editions of the Bible, including an edition used by Mormon founder, Joseph Smith, for his translation. Owned a farm in Cooperstown where Abner Doubleday, the historically accepted inventor of baseball, regularly played the game, dedicated in 1920 as Doubleday Field, the site of the

Baseball Hall of Fame Game from 1940-1944 and 1946-2007. Supervisor for the town of Otsego from 1833-1840.

PRENTISS, JOHN HOLMES Apr 17, 1784 Worcester, MA - Jun 26, 1861 Cooperstown, NY
United States Representative-NY from 1837-1841. Brother of Samuel Prentiss, United States Senator-VT from 1831-1842.

SCHNEIDER, HENRY HERMAN May 6, 1870 New York, NY - Jul 20, 1918 Cooperstown, NY
Owned and operated Schneider's Bakery, 157 Main Street, Cooperstown, founded by his father, Frederick Schneider, in 1887.

SMITH (Sampson), **MARGARET ALDRICH** Oct 15, 1863 Palmyra, NY - May 21, 1929 Newport, RI
Daughter of United States Navy Admiral, William Thomas Sampson. Collapsed and died, walking with her daughter, Marjorie Sampson Smith Bowers, the wife of attorney, Spotswood Dandridge Bowers, whose father, John M. Bowers, represented former President, Theodore Roosevelt, in his libel suit in Syracuse.

STARKWEATHER, GEORGE ANSON May 19, 1794 Preston, CT - Oct 15, 1879 Cooperstown, NY
United States Representative-NY from 1847-1849.

VAN HORN, GEORGE Feb 5, 1850 Otsego, NY - May 3, 1904 Cooperstown, NY
United States Representative-NY from 1891-1893.

WALSH, EDWARD J. Apr 9, 1913 Schuyler, NY - Aug 14, 2009 Cooperstown, NY
Head football coach at Manhasset High School, Long Island, from 1948-1978, where he coached and mentored Hall of Fame running back, Jim Brown, as well as Olympian, Jim Thorpe.

WEBB, ROBERT STEWART Aug 12, 1824 New York, NY - Aug 27, 1899 Pomfret Center, CT
Son of newspaper publisher, James Watson Webb. Brother of Civil War Union Army Major General, Alexander Stewart Webb, and railroad executives, H. Walter Webb and William Seward Webb. Grandson of Revolutionary War Continental Army General, Samuel Blatchley Webb.

WILSHERE, WHITEY (Vernon S.) Aug 3, 1912 Popular Ridge, NY - May 23, 1985 Cooperstown, NY
Pitcher for the Philadelphia A's from 1934-1936, managed by Hall of Famer, Connie Mack. Only former major league ballplayer buried in Cooperstown, home of the Baseball Hall of Fame.

LANCASTER RURAL CEMETERY
70 Cemetery Road
Lancaster, NY 14086

DAVIS, GEORGE ALLEN May 9, 1890 Lancaster, NY - Jun 4, 1961 Buffalo, NY
Pitcher for the Boston Braves and New York Highlanders from 1912-1915. Nicknamed "Iron." Pitched a no-hitter for the Braves in 1914, defeating the Philadelphia Phillies. Retired from baseball following his graduation from law school. Taught astronomy at the University of Buffalo. Attended St. John's Military Academy in Syracuse. Committed suicide, hanging himself in his home.

LANDFIELD AVENUE SYNAGOGUE CEMETERY
Thompsonville Road
Monticello, NY 12701

ELSTON (Yasgur)**, LOIS** Dec 4, 1944 NY - Dec 4, 1977 Champaign, IL
Daughter of Max Yasgur, who leased his dairy farm in Bethel to concert promoters who staged the Woodstock Music and Art Fair from August 15-18, 1969. Killed in a car accident on her 33rd birthday.

KUTSHER (Wasser)**, HELEN** Jul 11, 1923 New York, NY - Mar 19, 2013 Philadelphia, PA
Owned and operated Kutsher's Hotel and Country Club in Thompson, Sullivan County, a popular Catskills Borscht Belt resort, following the death of her husband, Milton Kutsher in 1988.

KUTSHER, MILTON M. Feb 9, 1916 Monticello, NY - Nov 16, 1988 Monticello, NY
Owned and operated Kutsher's Hotel and Country Club in Thompson, Sullivan County, a popular Catskills Borscht Belt resort, founded by his father, Max Kutsher, and uncle, Louis Kutsher, in 1907. Heavyweight champion, Rocky Marciano, trained at the club, Wilt Chamberlain was a bellhop in the 1950s.

YASGUR, MAX B. Dec 15, 1919 New York, NY - Feb 9, 1973 Marathon, FL
Dairy farmer. Leased one of his farms in Bethel to concert promoters for $10,000 who staged the Woodstock Music and Art Fair from August 15-18, 1969. Addressed the massive crowd on day three of the festival. Second cousin of actor, Sorrell Booke.

YASGUR, SAMUEL Jan 9, 1942 Monticello, NY - Jun 23, 2016 Charles County, MD
Assistant District Attorney in Manhattan for 27 years. Son of dairy farmer, Max Yasgur. Wrote a book about his father, *Max B. Yasgur: The Woodstock Festival's Famous Farmer* in 2009.

LANSINGVILLE CEMETERY
Lansingville Road / Route 155
Lansing, NY 14882

BUSH, ALIZA MAY Feb 19, 1988 NY - Feb 2, 1990 Lansing, NY
Murder victim. Her mother, Christine Lane, reported to police on February 2nd, her daughter was missing from their apartment. Hundreds of volunteers searched wooded, snowy areas for four days when, on February 7th, her mother reported receiving a package in the mail containing her pink mitten, leading police to think she was kidnapped. On February 15th, her mother confessed, led police to her body, and was convicted of manslaughter.

LEE-OATMAN CEMETERY
Route 149
Granville, NY 12832

HAYNES, LEMUEL Jul 18, 1753 West Hartford, CT - Sept 28, 1833 Granville, NY
Calvinist minister and abolitionist. First African-American pastor to serve an all-white congregation. Granted an Honorary Master of Arts from Middlebury College in 1804, the first advanced degree awarded to an African-American.

PARKER, ASA Nov 18, 1790 Granville, NY - Nov 24, 1878 Granville, NY
With **Laura Whitney Parker** (Mar 17, 1797 - Aug 21, 1887 Granville, NY), the great-grandparents of gunsmith, P.O. Ackley, maker of Wildcat cartridges.

LEICESTER CEMETERY
U.S. Route 20A
Leicester, NY 14481

REDINGTON, JOHN HARRIS Sept 23, 1801 Madrid, NY - Sept 23, 1841 Leicester, NY
Presbyterian Minister. Died from cholera, assisting an African-American family on their way to Canada, via the underground railroad. Grandfather of Mary Montgomery Williams Borglum, the wife of Danish-born American sculptor, Gutzon Borglum, creator of Mount Rushmore and Stone Mountain, near Atlanta. Great-grandfather of sculptor, Lincoln Borglum, who completed Mount Rushmore following his father's death in 1941.

REDINGTON (Washburn), **RUTH EMILY** May 31, 1813 Greensboro, VT - Dec 5, 1839 Moscow, NY
Wife of Presbyterian Minister, John Harris Redington. Direct-descendant of *Mayflower* passenger Resolved White. Grandmother of Mary Montgomery Williams Borglum, the wife of Danish-born American sculptor, Gutzon Borglum, creator of Mount Rushmore and Stone Mountain, near Atlanta.

Great-grandfather of sculptor, Lincoln Borglum, who completed Mount Rushmore following his father's death in 1941.

LENOX RURAL CEMETERY
Nelson Road
Canastota, NY 13032

BARNARD (Barnard)**, HANNAH** Sept 4, 1745 Windsor, CT - Jun 19, 1848 Lenox, NY
Great-grandmother of Olivia Louise Langdon Clemens, the wife of author, Mark Twain. Wife of Moses Barnard, Revolutionary War Continental soldier who fought at Bunker Hill, died January 3, 1811, buried in Grandview Cemetery, Whitesboro.

CHAPMAN, NOYES PALMER Jan 14, 1811 Stonington, CT - Apr 28, 1889 Canastota, NY
Postmaster of Canastota. Invented the Fifteen Puzzle, a 4x4 sliding puzzle consisting of numbered squares, 1-15, with one number missing, the goal of which is to unjumble the numbers.

LEWIS, EDWARD EDMOND Jul 6, 1726 Guilford, CT - Jul 13, 1810 Lenox, NY
Grandfather of Olivia Langdon Clemens, the wife of author, Mark Twain. His wife, Olive Barnard Lewis, died March 1, 1812, age 40.

MULFORD, CASS EDWARD Sept 20, 1935 Syracuse, NY - Dec 12, 1990 Canastota, NY
Canastota developer, civic leader and entrepreneur. Owned and operated the Madison Lumber and Block Company, New Yorker Construction Company and the Lincoln Stone Company. Committed suicide by gunshot, shooting himself twice, the first shot was not fatal.

LEVANT CEMETERY
Lindquist Drive
Falconer, NY 14733

BEDIENT, HUGH CARPENTER Oct 23, 1889 Gerry, NY - Jul 21, 1965 Jamestown, NY
Pitcher for the Boston Red Sox from 1912-1914. Pitched for the Buffalo Blues of the Federal League in 1915. Won 20 games for the Red Sox in 1912, outpitching Hall of Famer, Christy Mathewson, in Game Five of the World Series that year, won by the Red Sox. Struck out 42 batters in a 23-inning semi-pro game, pitching for Falconer in 1908, mentioned in *Ripley's Believe It or Not!* In 1931.

LICKVILLE CEMETERY
Lick Street
Locke, NY 13092

LICK, GEORGE Oct 16, 1797 NY - May 9, 1865 Summerhill, NY
Early Cayuga County settler. Namesake of Lick Street, through the towns of Locke and Groton.

STORRS, STEPHEN RENSLAER Apr 16, 1847 Oswego, NY - Nov 19, 1929 Montville, NY
Distant-relative of Seth Storrs, primary founder of Middlebury College, Middlebury, VT and namesake of Storrs, CT.

LIVERPOOL VILLAGE CEMETERY
North Tulip Street
Liverpool, NY 13088

BAHN, PHILIP 1835 Darmstadt, Germany - Mar 12, 1918 Liverpool, NY
Basket maker. Designed the first oval clothes basket in the United States, while employed with Jacox & Green in Syracuse. Grandfather of film critic and editor, Chester B. Bahn.

GASS, EDWARD WILLIAM 1937 Syracuse, NY - Feb 21, 1989 Arlington, VA
Washington D.C. attorney. Deputy Solicitor with the United States Department of Energy.

HEID, WILLIAM P. Nov 4, 1896 NY - May 8, 1968 Syracuse, NY
Co-owned and operated Heid's Grocery Store in Liverpool. Brother of Liverpool Mayor, Michael Heid and restaurateur, Valentine Heid.

LEE, THOMAS H. 1865 Syracuse, NY - Sept 5, 1930 Syracuse, NY
American stage actor. Performed with actor, Maurice Costello. Killed, struck by a truck as he stepped of a curb on Erie Boulevard.

TARBY, RUSSELL Nov 28, 1922 Auburn, NY - Aug 6, 1991 Syracuse, NY
Co-owned and operated Hotel Tarbe, a Liverpool restaurant and bar, opened in 1964.

LOCUSTS-ON-HUDSON
135 Old Post Road
Staatsburg, NY 12580

KEETON (Guccione), **KATHY** (Kathryn) Feb 17, 1939 South Africa - Sept 17, 1997 New York, NY
Magazine publisher. Founded the magazines *Viva*, *Longevity* and *Omni*. Wife of *Penthouse* magazine founder and publisher, Bob Guccione. Buried on the Guccione estate, The Willows, a 76-acre estate

dating back to 1792, owned by United States Supreme Court Justice, Henry B. Livingston, foreclosed in 2003 by Guccione, sold to hotelier, André Balazs and his wife, actress, Uma Thurman, who renamed the estate. Guccione died October 20, 2010 in Plano, TX, age 79.

LOOMIS HILL CEMETERY
4069 Howlett Hill Road
Syracuse, NY 13215

GRANT, LIONEL D. May 11, 1910 Schenectady, NY - Mar 1986 Syracuse, NY
Strangled his friend, Ernest Uhlig, November 11, 1939, at his apartment, 161 East Onondaga Street in Syracuse, placed him in a trunk, moved the trunk to the attic of a house he was renting, 705 Bellevue Avenue. He was released on parole from Attica State Prison in 1964, serving 24 years of his 40-year sentence.

GROBSMITH, STANLEY E. Dec 12, 1960 Syracuse, NY - Feb 21, 1996 Syracuse, NY
Murdered Qiana Dickerson, a 12-year old girl, missing since April 3, 1991, dismembered her body, undiscovered until found by three boys playing near his property, 555 Columbus Avenue in Syracuse. Police searched his home, 227 Charles Avenue in Solvay, and found her leg and torso wrapped in plastic, sealed in cardboard boxes. He hanged himself with an extension cord the following day in a police interview room at the Public Safety Building. Competed in the Empire State Games, winning medals in wrestling, judo and boxing.

HOWARD STREET FIRE VICTIMS Jul 6, 1981 Syracuse, NY
Lee M. Hanks, upset he was locked out of the house of his father-in-law, **Walter Allen**, 411 Howard Street in Syracuse, where his nine-months pregnant wife, **Patricia Hanks**, was staying, intentionally set fire to the house, killing seven people. Walter Allen, age 63, Patricia Hanks, age 23, her mother, **Martha Allen**, age 55, brother, **Leonard Allen**, age 31, sister, **Nancy Allen**, age 12, nephew, **Francis Allen**, age 5, and the father of her brother-in-law, **Charles Nitzke**, age 60, died in the fire. He was convicted of seven counts of second-degree murder.

JACKSON, CHRISTOPHER H. 1972 - Mar 3, 2008 Syracuse, NY
Victim of Central New York's first Taser-related death. Police responded to a 911 domestic disturbance call at the Norstar Apartments in Clay, placed by his mother, Verna M. Gordon, forced to fire the Taser in an effort to control Jackson. He died from cardiac arrest en route to the hospital.

NGUYEN, QUAN DAVID MICHAEL Jun 21, 2004 Syracuse, NY - Aug 28, 2004 Baldwinsville, NY
Nine-week old baby found starved to death, abandoned by his parents, Quan David Nguyen and Jade Marie Beiter, who phoned police to notify them of his death, then fled town. They were arrested in an Anaheim hotel, fourteen months later, October 14, 2005, and charged with manslaughter. On November 4, 2005, the baby's mother, Jade Marie, born November 19, 1982 in Akron, died of malnutrition, age 22, in a California hospital, cremated, her ashes divided between her parents.

REOME (Burton), **MARGARET ROSZELLE** May 29, 1958 Seneca Falls, NY - Feb 1990 Syracuse, NY
Murder victim. Missing for fourteen years, until her skeletal remains were discovered, April 1, 2004, in a storage trunk, room B032 at the U-Haul Self Storage Facility in Cicero. George William Geddes Jr., her live-in boyfriend, had been renting the facility since her murder, which included time he spent in prison for raping her 13-year old daughter. Police believe she was killed between January 17 and February 28, at the homes she shared with Geddes, 304A Raphael Avenue. Geddes was convicted of second-degree murder for bludgeoning her to death, sentenced to 25-years-to-life in state prison.

WITHEREL, CARL R. Sept 6, 1947 Buffalo, NY - Mar 6, 1991 Syracuse, NY
Paid $600 to illegally dump seven drums loaded with industrial waste, renting a U-Haul truck, driving 200 miles round-trip from Syracuse to Rochester, when he was found dead, behind a barn, 6026 McKinley Road in Cicero, from inhaling fumes from the hazardous chemicals. James R. Povino, a Rochester construction company owner, pled guilty to criminally negligent homicide, was fined $60,000, without probation or prison time.

LOWER CEMETERY
Hylan Boulevard / Route 7
Prattsville, NY 12468

PRATT, ZADOCK Oct 30, 1790 Stephentown, NY - Apr 5, 1871 Bergenfield, NJ
United States Representative-NY from 1837-1839 and 1843-1845. Built the world's largest tannery on the banks of Schoharie Creek. Commissioned Pratt's Rock, a series of stone carvings depicting his life, called "New York's Mount Rushmore" by *Ripley's Believe It or Not!* Namesake of the town of Prattsville.

LOWVILLE RURAL CEMETERY
Park Avenue
Lowville, NY 13367

DAYAN, CHARLES Jul 8, 1792 Amsterdam, NY - Dec 25, 1877 Lowville, NY
United States Representative-NY from 1831-1833. Lieutenant Governor of NY for three months in 1828, under Nathaniel Pitcher.

DOIG, ANDREW WHEELER Jul 24, 1799 Salem, NY - Jul 11, 1875 Brooklyn, NY
United States Representative-NY from 1839-1843.

KNAPP, CHARLES LUMAN Jul 4, 1847 Harrisburg, NY - Jan 3, 1929 Lowville, NY
United States Representative-NY from 1901-1911. Elected to Congress following the death of Albert D. Shaw.

LYONS RURAL CEMETERY
Spencer Street
Lyons, NY 14489

BOEHEIM, FREDERICK WILHELM Oct 30, 1825 Württemberg, Germany - 1905 Lyons, NY
Founded the Frederick Boeheim & Sons Funeral Home and furniture store in Lyons, in 1854, succeeded by his son, Frederick W. Boeheim II, in 1905. 2nd great-grandfather of Syracuse University Hall of Fame men's basketball coach, Jim Boeheim.

BOEHEIM, JAMES ARTHUR Sept 10, 1917 Lyons, NY - Feb 6, 1986 Lyons, NY
Funeral director for Frederick Boeheim & Sons Funeral Home in Lyons, founded by his great-grandfather, Frederick W. Boeheim, in 1854. Father of Syracuse University Hall of Fame men's basketball coach, Jim Boeheim.

HANNETT, WILLIAM Oct 1844 Welland, ON, Canada - 1930 Lyons, NY
With **Mary Emily McCarthy Hannett** (Jan 1843 Syracuse, NY - 1916 Lyons, NY), the parents of Arthur Thomas Hannett, Governor of New Mexico from 1925-1927.

HOLLEY, JOHN MILTON Nov 10, 1802 Salisbury, CT - Mar 8, 1848 Jacksonville, FL
United States Representative-NY from 1847-1848. Died during his first term in office. A cenotaph was constructed in Congressional Cemetery in Washington D.C. in his honor.

RICHMOND, VAN RENSSELAER Jan 12, 1812 Preston, NY - Nov 20, 1883 Lyons, NY
New York State Engineer and Surveyor from 1858-1861 and 1868-1871. Chief Engineer of construction of portions of the Erie Canal.

LYONSBURG CEMETERY
Route 39
Bliss, NY 14024

ALMETER, RYAN R. Nov 6, 1981 Warsaw, NY - Jun 10, 2016 Nunda, NY
Livingston and Monroe County educator. Crew member for Balloons Over Letchworth, a hot-air balloon company offering scenic rides over Letchworth State Park. Died helping passengers out of the balloon's basket, when wind pulled the balloon into the air, failing to let go, he fell 100 feet to his death.

MACHPELAH CEMETERY
71 North Street
LeRoy, NY 14482

SKINNER, SCOTT W. Jun 24, 1920 Rochester, NY - May 20, 1990 Litchfield Park, AZ
Founded Eisenhower College in Seneca Falls in 1968, closed in 1982 after fourteen years. Former President Dwight Eisenhower and entertainer, Bob Hope, attended the ground-breaking ceremony in 1965.

WAIT, PEARL BIXBY 1873 LeRoy, NY - Jul 28, 1915 Buffalo, NY
Cough syrup manufacturer. Invented Jell-O in 1897, named by his wife, May M. Davis Wait. Sold the business to his neighbor, Orator Francis Woodward, for $450 in 1899.

WOODWARD, ORATOR FRANCIS Jul 26, 1856 Bergen, NJ - Jan 21, 1906 Hot Springs, AR
Purchased the Jell-O formula from his neighbor, and creator of the dessert, Pearl B. Wait, in 1899, marketed the product through his company, Genesee Pure Food Company.

MADISON STREET CEMETERY
Madison Street
Hamilton, NY 13346

COOK, R. C. (Ramson) Jul 9, 1849 Smithfield, NY - 1928 Hamilton, NY
Notable for his tombstone, a bas-relief of his beloved trotter, "Husky Harry."

GOODWIN, HENRY CHARLES Jun 25, 1824 DeRuyter, NY - Nov 12, 1860 Hamilton, NY
United States Representative-NY from 1854-1855 and 1857-1859. Elected to Congress due to the resignation of Gerrit Smith in 1854.

JUDSON (Chubbuck)**, EMILY** Aug 22, 1817 Eaton, NY - Jun 1, 1854 Hamilton, NY
Author. Wrote under the pen name, "Fanny Forrester." Third wife of Abraham Forrester, American Baptist Missionary to Burma.

STOWER, JOHN G. 1791 Madison, NY - Dec 20, 1850 Sullivan, NY
United States Representative-NY from 1827-1829.

MALTA RIDGE CEMETERY
Route 9
Malta, NY 12020

CRUM (Speck), **GEORGE W.** Jul 1828 Malta, NY - Jul 22, 1914 Malta, NY
African-American, Native American head chef at Moon's Lake House in Saratoga Springs. Invented potato chips at the resort, on August 24, 1853, a result of a customer complaint that his French fries were "too thick." Opened Crumb's House in 1860, selling his now-popular "Saratoga Chips."

MANLIUS MILITARY SCHOOL (VERBECK FAMILY CEMETERY)
Military Drive
Manlius, NY 13104

PEER (Halcomb), **MURIEL VERBECK** May 27, 1889 NY - Apr 30, 1970 Tampa, FL
Wife of Colonel Guido Fridolin Verbeck II, following his death, remarried to Cornell law professor, Sherman Peer. Daughter of Charles H. Halcomb, founder of the Halcomb Steel Company in Syracuse. Granddaughter of Syracuse banker, William W. Teall. Great-granddaughter of Civil War General, Edwin Vose Sumner and Oliver Teall, founding father of Syracuse. Daughter-in-law of William Verbeck, Adjunct-General of New York State and President of the Manlius Military School from 1888-1930.

VERBECK, GUIDO FRIDOLIN May 2, 1887 Aurora, NY - Jul 27, 1940 Manlius, NY
United States Army Colonel. Superintendent of the Manlius Military School from 1926-1940. Son of William Verbeck, Adjunct-General of New York State and President of the Manlius Military School from 1888-1930. Grandson of Guido F. Verbeck, founder of the Kyushu Imperial University in Fukuoka, Japan. Nephew of cartoonist, Gustav Verbeck. Son-n-law of Charles H. Halcomb, founder of the Halcomb Steel Company in Syracuse.

VERBECK, WILLIAM Jan 18, 1861 Nagasaki, Japan - Aug 24, 1930 Manlius, NY
Adjunct-General for New York State National Guard. President, Headmaster and Superintendent of the Manlius Military Academy for 42 years. Past students of the Academy include casino mogul, Steve Wynn, and actor, Tab Hunter. National Commander of the Boy Scouts of America from   1910-1911. Son of Guido F. Verbeck, founder of the Kyushu Imperial University in Fukuoka, Japan. Brother of cartoonist, Gustav Verbeck.

MANLIUS VILLAGE CEMETERY
East Seneca Street
Manlius, NY 13104

BOLAND, FREDERICK ANSON Nov 4, 1844 Cortland, NY - Dec 27, 1940 Syracuse, NY
Last surviving Civil War veteran from Syracuse. Served under Admiral David Farragut in the Battle of Mobile Bay, August 5, 1864. Stood in the presence of President Abraham Lincoln on several occasions.

LYMAN, LESLIE OLIN Jun 16, 1908 Syracuse, NY - Dec 16, 1959 San Jose, CA
Son of novelist, May Hilton Lyman and Olin Lyman, sports editor for the *Post-Standard*.

MAPLE AVENUE CEMETERY
Maple Avenue
Fultonville, NY 12072

WEMPLE, EDWARD Oct 23, 1843 Fultonville, NY - Dec 18, 1920 Fultonville, NY
United States Representative-NY from 1883-1885.

MAPLE GROVE CEMETERY
Owego Road / Route 968
Candor, NY 13743

SNOVER, JOHN F. Feb 1829 NJ - 1904 Candor, NY
Tombstone is 20-foot square, 18-foot tall granite monument with a life-sized statue of a man wearing an apron, holding a wood plane and a saw.

MAPLE GROVE CEMETERY
10505 Turnpike Road
Clyde, NY 14433

COWLES, GEORGE WASHINGTON Dec 6, 1823 Otisco, NY - Jan 20, 1901 Clyde, NY
United States Representative-NY from 1869-1871.

ELLIS, WILLIAM A. Oct 30, 1850 - May 19, 1884 Cape Sabine, Ellesmere Island, Canada
One of 25 members of the ill-fated Greely Expedition, under Adolphus W. Greely, who sailed the Arctic, July 1881, only to find themselves stranded, starving for three years. The expedition set the record for achieving the farthest point north toward the North Pole, seven men, including Greely, survived.

MAPLE GROVE CEMETERY
54 Falconer Street
Frewsburg, NY 14738

JACKSON, ROBERT HOUGHWOUT Feb 13, 1892 Spring Creek, PA - Oct 9, 1954 Washington D.C.
Associate Justice of the United States Supreme Court from 1941-1954. United States Attorney
General from 1940-1941. United States Chief Counsel, prosecuting Nazi war criminals at Nuremberg
from 1945-1946, taking a leave of absence from the Supreme Court.

MAPLE GROVE CEMETERY
484 Hill Road
Hoosick Falls, NY 12090

MOSES (Robertson), **GRANDMA** (Anna) Sept 7, 1860 Greenwich, NY - Dec 13, 1961 Hoosick Falls, NY
Folk artist. Widowed, following the death of her husband, Thomas Salmon Moses, Jr. in 1927, began
painting ten years later, age 78. Three of her paintings were exhibited at the Museum of Modern Art in
New York City the following year, in 1939. Hallmark licensed her paintings for greeting cards in 1945.
Her painting, *Fourth of July* was honored on a U.S. postage stamp in 1969.

THOMAS, WILLIAM DAVID Mar 22, 1880 Granville, NY - May 17, 1936 Washington D.C.
United States Representative-NY from 1934-1936. Elected to Congress due to the death of James
Southworth Parker.

MAPLE GROVE CEMETERY
715 West Broad Street
Horseheads, NY 14845

TODD, AL (Alfred Chester) Jan 7, 1902 Troy, NY - Mar 8, 1985 Elmira, NY
Catcher for the Philadelphia Phillies, Pittsburgh Pirates, Brooklyn Dodgers and Chicago Cubs from
1932-1941 and 1943. Caught Hall of Fame pitcher, Dizzy Dean, with the Cubs in 1940.

TUTTLE, WILLIAM EDGAR Dec 10, 1870 Horseheads, NY - Feb 11, 1923 Westfield, NJ
United States Representative-NY from 1911-1915. United States Commissioner to the Panama
Expedition in 1916.

MAPLE GROVE CEMETERY
660 Cooper Road
Jordan, NY 13080

ARNOLD, JAMES IRZA Jun 26, 1887 Warners, NY - February 18, 1965 Hudson, NY
Architectural designer in New York City. Specialized in early American interiors. Produced two series of etchings, the "New York" series and "Vanishing America" series, in the 1930s and 1940s.

DAGGETT (Potter)**, MABEL** 1870 Syracuse, NY - Nov 13, 1927 New York, NY
Journalist. World War I correspondent, reported from France. Editor of *The Delineator* and *Hampton's Magazine*. Wrote a biography of Queen Marie of Romania, "A Close-Up of a Queen", for *Good Housekeeping* in 1926.

DOMAN, LEWIS B. 1867 England - Apr 3, 1935 Jordan, NY
Inventor. Manufacturer of the player piano. Founded the Amphion Piano Player Company and the L.B. Doman Corporation.

DUNK, WILLIAM Jul 4, 1878 Rovenden, Kent, England - Oct 4, 1966 Cleveland, NY
Co-founded Dunk & Bright Furniture, with William H. Bright, in Syracuse in 1927.

HARE BROTHERS
Brothers, **Thomas Duane Hare Jr.**, died March 7, 1964, 7-months old, and **William L. Hare**, Died June 26, 1967, age 3, thought to have died from sudden infant death syndrome for three decades until their brother, Leonard Hare, pursued the truth following the highly-publicized trial of Waneta Hoyt in 1995, convicted of infanticide, killing five of her children in the 1960s. Dorothy Mae King of Auburn, the mother of the boys, pled guilty to manslaughter in 1995, sentenced to six years in prison. Originally buried in Loomis Hills Cemetery in Syracuse, reburied in the family plot in Jordan. Thomas D. Hare Sr., father of the children, was arrested in 1999, at a Greyhound bus station in Cleveland, for the murder of his girlfriend, Louann Roberts, in Pompano Beach.

KNOBLOCH (Sharp)**, EUNICE JEAN** 1921 Jordan, NY - Apr 27, 2009 Auburn, NY
Co-authored the *History of Christ Church 1840-1990*, with her mother, Bessie Sharp.

LAW, CHARLES BLAKESLEE Feb 5, 1872 Hannibal, NY - Sept 15, 1929 Kattskill Bay, NY
United States Representative-NY from 1905-1911. Drowned, swimming at his summer home, near Lake George.

SPERRY, DWIGHT ANDREW Nov 18, 1851 Woodbridge, CT - Apr 6, 1924 Syracuse, NY
President of Sperry & Rockwell, manufacturer of wheelbarrows. Seventh descendant of Richard Sperry, pioneer settler of New Haven, CT.

MAPLE GROVE CEMETERY
Route 11
Richville, NY 13681

MCSORLEY (Rohrmoser)**, GRACE ALMINA** Mar 22, 1910 Theresa, NY - Apr 20, 1998 Potsdam, NY
Married John Francis McSorley, the brother of Ernest Michael McSorley, Captain of the Great Lakes
freighter, *SS Edmund Fitzgerald*, following the death of her first husband, Levi Hitchman.

MAPLE GROVE CEMETERY
63 Stark Street
Waterloo, NY 13165

BIRDSALL, SAMUEL May 14, 1791 Hillsdale, NY - Feb 8, 1792 Waterloo, NY
United States Representative-NY from 1837-1839.

CHAPIN, EDWARD PAYSON Aug 16, 1831 Waterloo, NY - May 27, 1863 Port Hudson, LA
Civil War Union Army Brigadier General. Wounded in battle, Hanover Court House, VA, May 1862,
killed one year later, leading a charge against Confederate forces, Plain Store, LA.

JENKS, ANANIAS May 26, 1786 Homer, NY - Jun 30 1859 Waterloo, NY
Father of temperance leader, Amelia Jenks Bloomer, remembered for her unique style of dress.

LOUCKS, AVERY MOSES Mar 14, 1876 Waterloo, NY - Sept 25, 1965 Waterloo, NY
With **Nellie E. Darling Loucks** (Sept 1886 Sodus, NY - 1930 Waterloo, NY), the great-grandparents of
Academy Award-winning actor, Philip Seymour Hoffman.

SCHAFFER, LYNN E. Mar 2, 1897 Fayette, NY - Jun 2, 1967 Geneva, NY
Placed his scythe in a tree, with his brother, Raymond Schaffer, on the farm of their father, C.L.
Schaffer, 841 Waterloo Geneva Road, prior to their service in World War I, following Wyman James
Johnson, who placed his scythe in the tree in 1861 prior to leaving for the Civil War, stating, "Leave
the scythe in the tree until I return", only to be killed in battle, May 22, 1864. The Scythe Tree was one
of 11 trees selected by the New York State Department of Environmental Conservation to be of
extraordinary historic significance, in 1990.

WELLES, HENRY CARTER May 13, 1821 Glastonbury, CT - Jul 1868 Waterloo, NY
Official founder of Memorial Day. He suggested that all shops in town close for one day to honor
soldiers who lost their lives in the Civil War, citizens placing flowers and wreaths on their graves.
President Lyndon Johnson proclaimed Waterloo the birthplace of Memorial Day in 1966, in
observance of the 100th anniversary of the first commemoration.

MAPLE GROVE CEMETERY
Cook Street
Worcester, NY 12197

KONSTANTY, JIM Mar 2, 1917 Strykersville, NY - Jun 11, 1976 Oneonta, NY
Right-handed pitcher for the Cincinnati Reds, Boston Braves, Philadelphia Phillies, New York Yankees and St. Louis Cardinals in 1944, 1946 and 1948-1956. Won the 1950 National League MVP Award. National League All-Star in 1950. Pitched for Syracuse University from 1937-1939.

MAPLE HILL CEMETERY
Coal Hill Road
Taberg, NY 13471

SEXTON (Morton)**, SUSAN** 1808 Oneida County, NY - Sept 11, 1892 Taberg, NY
Great-granddaughter of John Morton, signer of the *Declaration of Independence*. Sister of Eunice Morton Stanford, the 3rd great-grandmother of actress and model, Raquel Welch.

MAPLE LAWN CEMETERY
Route 417W
Bolivar, NY 14715

INGALLS, SAMUEL WORTHEN Jul 11, 1771 Sandown, NH - Feb 15, 1841 Bolivar, NY
Great-grandfather of Laura Ingalls-Wilder, author of *Little House on the Prairie*. His wife, Margaret Delano Ingalls, died May 6, 1836, age 61, buried North Cuba Cemetery, Cuba, NY.

MAPLE VIEW CEMETERY
Route 11
Mexico, NY 13114

HITCHCOCK, SETH Apr 22, 1781 New Lebanon, NY - Feb 12, 1856 Mexico, NY
Executor of the estate of his half-brother, Alpheus Hitchcock, Madison Center music teacher, who murdered his wife, Belinda Hitchcock, poisoning her dinner with arsenic, April 6, 1807. He proclaimed his innocence in trial, claiming her death an accident, stating, "I thought I could live more agreeably with some other woman than my wife", convicted and hanged, September 11, 1807, the first public execution in Madison County.

SKINNER, AVERY Jun 9, 1796 Westmoreland, NH - Nov 24, 1876 Mexico, NY
Member of the New York State Senate from 1838-1841. Brother of Alanson Skinner, member of the New York State Senate from 1850-1851.

MAPLEWOOD CEMETERY
West Genesee Street
Camillus, NY 13031

BOWKER (McGraw), **MARGARET** Aug 28, 1879 Truxton, NY - Feb 10, 1924 Auburn, NY
Sister of John McGraw, Hall of Fame manager for the New York Giants from 1902-1932.

CAPPUCCILLI, J. ANTHONY Apr 26, 1920 - Aug 22, 1995 Syracuse, NY
Architect. Studied under architect, Frank Lloyd Wright. Designed the Onondaga County Correctional
Facility in Jamesville, St. Joseph's Church in Camillus, Our Lady of Pompeii rectory, convent and
school in Syracuse and Village Green a housing complex in Baldwinsville.

DONNELLY (McGraw), **HELEN** Jul 29, 1883 Truxton, NY - Jul 12, 1978 Hamilton, NY
Youngest sister of John McGraw, Hall of Fame manager for the New York Giants from 1902-1932.

MCGRAW, JAMES MICHAEL 1881 Truxton, NY - Feb 12, 1930 Toledo, OH
Club Secretary of the Buffalo Bisons, Executive Secretary of the Toledo Mud Hens of the International
League. Managed A.G. Spaulding Company, a sporting goods store in Syracuse. Brother of John
McGraw, Hall of Fame manager for the New York Giants from 1902-1932.

MUNRO, DAVID Dec 8, 1784 Lanesboro, MA - May 10, 1866 Camillus, NY
Early settler. First Postmaster and Judge in Camillus, in 1811. Constructed the Seneca Turnpike, with
his brothers and father, Squire Munro, early settler in the town of Elbridge. Grandfather of
Baldwinsville banker, Otis Munro Bigelow.

MUNRO, DAVID ALLEN Aug 18, 1818 Camillus, NY - Aug 30, 1897 Elbridge, NY
Elected Republican Supervisor by the Free Soil Party in 1852, considered the first Republican
Party meeting to take place in the country. Built the Green Gate Inn in Camillus in 1861. Son of David
Munro, early settler of the town of Camillus.

MUNRO, THOMAS HILL Mar 22, 1876 Camillus, NY - Feb 19, 1939 Camillus, NY
Onondaga County Sheriff from 1934-1937.

NAPIER, PETE (Donald) Aug 21, 1924 Syracuse, NY - Mar 16, 2008 Boynton Beach, FL
Director of the Onondaga County War Memorial from 1964-1985. Hosted the Rolling Stones in 1966,
Led Zeppelin, Janis Joplin, Jimi Hendrix, Elton John, the Grateful Dead, Herb Alpert & the Tijuana
Brass, Blood, Sweat & Tears and Elvis Presley, among many others, at the arena.

QUINLIVAN, JOHN D. Jan 12, 1921 Binghamton, NY - May 5, 1993 Syracuse, NY
Architect. Designed several military installations in the Northeast, including West Point. Designed
Christian Brothers Academy in Syracuse.

SHOVE, BENJAMIN E. Mar 23, 1892 Syracuse, NY - Jul 18, 1977 Camillus, NY
Syracuse attorney and civic leader. Donated land to the town of Camillus in 1960, developing Shove Park.

SWIFT, NOLAN Jan 31, 1923 Taylorville, IL - Mar 27, 2004 Camillus, NY
New York State stock car champion at the Oswego Motor Speedway. Won more than 250 races in his career. Developed the first steel-tube space frame modified race car, with partner, Bill Wright.

MAPLEWOOD CEMETERY
Middle Road
Henrietta, NY 14467

BROWN, JOSEPH 1784 Thompson, CT - Mar 7, 1877 Henrietta, NY
With **Abby M. Morse Brown** (1793 Douglass, MA - Aug 30, 1873 Henrietta, NY), the parents of Antoinette Louisa Brown Blackwell, first woman to be ordained as a Protestant minister in the United States, died November 6, 1921age 96, in Elizabeth, NJ, cremated.

MAPLEWOOD CEMETERY
Route 11
Mannsville, NY 13661

WOOLWORTH, JASPER Feb 8, 1789 Granville, MA - Oct 8, 1873 Adams, NY
Grandfather of Frank Winfield Woolworth, founder of F.W. Woolworth's, the original "five & dime" store. 2nd great-grandfather of Barbara Hutton, New York City socialite, dubbed the "Poor Little Rich Girl", married seven times, including third husband, actor, Cary Grant.

MAPLEWOOD CEMETERY
West Main Street / Route 39
Springville, NY 14141

DYGERT, ROBERT Mar 19, 1814 - Jun 11, 1891 Springville, NY
Founded Dygert Farm, Elk Street, Springville, which hosted the Erie County Fair from 1866-1867, and where Pop Warner trained Jim Thorpe for the 1912 Summer Olympics in Stockholm. Great-grandfather of Belgian Horse importer, Erwin F. Dygert.

SCHUSTER, GEORGE N. Feb 4, 1873 Buffalo, NY - Jul 4, 1972 Springville, NY
Race driver. Drove a 1907 Thomas Flyer around the world, more than 22,000 miles in 169 days, to win the 1908 New York to Paris Race, started February 12, 1908 in Times Square, New York City, finished July 30, 1908 in Paris, 26 days ahead of the second place German team. Only three of the six cars to

start the race finished, which was the basis for the film, *The Great Race*, in 1965. Inducted into the Automotive Hall of Fame in 2010. Died eight months shy of his 100th birthday.

STRUNK, JUD (Justin Roderick) Jun 11, 1936 Jamestown, NY - Oct 5, 1981 Carrabassett, ME
Singer/songwriter. Recorded the Top 20 hit, "Daisy a Day" in 1973, the first recorded song played on the moon, during the Apollo 17 mission. Appeared on the final season of TV's *Rowan & Martin's Laugh In*. Suffered a heart attack in a plane he was piloting, killing him and his passenger, Richard Ayotte.

WARNER, POP (Glenn Scobey) Apr 5, 1971 Springville, NY - Sept 7, 1954 Palo Alto, CA
College football coach. Head coach for the Georgia, Iowa State, Cornell, Pittsburgh, Stanford and Temple. Won national championships with Pittsburgh in 1915, 1916 and 1918 and Stanford in 1926. Retired with the most career wins in college football. Inducted into the College Football Hall of Fame in 1951. Founded the Pop Warner Little Scholars youth football program in 1929. Brother of College Football Hall of Fame coach, William J. "Bill" Warner.

YELLEN, JACK (Jacob Selig) Jul 6, 1892 Raczki, Poland - Apr 17, 1991 Springville, NY
Composer and screenwriter. Collaborated frequently with Milton Ager. Wrote the lyrics to "Happy Days Are Here Again" and "Ain't She Sweet. Husband of actress and dancer, Lucille Day.

MARATHON CEMETERY
Albro Road
Marathon, NY 13803

GRAY, JERRY C. 1832 Cortland, NY - Apr 28, 1916 Marathon, NY
Grandfather of convicted murderer, Henry Judd Gray, involved in an affair with Ruth Brown Snyder, conspired to kill her husband, Albert Snyder, both convicted following a highly-publicized trial, executed minutes apart in the electric chair at Sing Sing Prison. Ruth Brown Snyder was photographed in the electric chair, minutes before death, and shown on the front page of the *New York Daily News*. His wife, Fanny A. Judd Gray, died in 1890, age 52.

MARCELLUS VILLAGE CEMETERY
33 North Street
Marcellus, NY 13108

HUMPHREY, REUBEN Sept 2, 1757 West Simsbury, CT - Aug 12, 1831 Marcellus, NY
United States Representative-NY from 1807-1809. Revolutionary War Army Captain.

RICE, DEACON SAMUEL Oct 28, 1751 Wallingford, CT - Aug 13, 1834 Marcellus, NY
Revolutionary War veteran. Founding father of the town of Marcellus. Owned the first tavern, built the first saw mill in Onondaga County.

MARTVILLE CEMETERY
15129 Route 104
Sterling, NY 13156

RICHARDSON (Keeling)**, PAMELA F.** Aug 2, 1952 Sodus, NY - Sept 11, 1991 Syracuse, NY
Murder victim. Found strangled in her bed, 1002 Butternut Street in Syracuse, unsolved for two years, when Mark J. Denslow was arrested and convicted of criminally negligent homicide, breaking her voice box and crushing her airway during rough sex. He was sentenced to 1 1/3-to-4 years in prison.

MAYVILLE CEMETERY
East Chautauqua Street / Route 430
Mayville, NY 14757

BROOKS, JESSE Sept 1, 1788 Ashford, CT - Jun 30, 1877 Mayville, NY
With **Olivia Lyon Brooks** (Jul 29, 1795 Hamilton, NY - Mar 16, 1842 Mayville, NY), the grandparents of short story writer, Walter R. Brooks, author of the *Freddy the Pig* and *Mr. Ed* series.

ORCUTT, WILLIAM CYRUS 1840 Oneida County, NY - May 18, 1882 Dunkirk, NY
Great-grandfather of Emmy Award-winning actress, Lucille Ball. 2nd great-grandfather of actress, Lucy Arnaz and actor, Desi Arnaz Jr.

TOURGEE, ALBION WINEGAR May 2, 1838 Williamsfield, OH - May 21, 1905 Aquitaine, France
United States Consul to France from 1897-1905, appointed by President William McKinley. Civil War Union Army Lieutenant. Wounded twice, captured and held as a prisoner-of-war in Libby Prison, Richmond. Author of the novels, *A Fool's Errand, by One of the Fools* and its sequel, *Bricks Without Straw*. Civil Rights lawyer, lead attorney for Homer Plessy in the *Plessy v. Ferguson* case regarding racial segregation in 1896.

MCCONNELLSVILLE (VIENNA) CEMETERY
Route 13
McConnellsville, NY 13401

HARDEN, CHARLES HERBERT Nov 7, 1828 Verona, NY - Feb 5, 1915 McConnellsville, NY
Founded Harden Furniture with his son, Frank S. Harden, in McConnellsville.

HARDEN, FRANK SYLVESTER Sept 1, 1858 IL - Jul 17, 1938 McConnellsville, NY
Founded Harden Furniture with his father, Charles H. Harden, in McConnellsville.

MCLEAN CEMETERY
Lafayette Road
Groton, NY 13073

DRYDEN CHEERLEADERS Oct 4, 1996 Otselic, NY
Murder victims. Dryden High School cheerleaders, **Sarah Ann Hajney**, born September 5, 1980, and **Jennifer Lynn Bolduc**, born June 21, 1980, were abducted from Sarah's home by next-door neighbor, John Benjamin Andrews, taken to a cabin in Muller Hill State Forest, Chenango County, and killed, dismembering their bodies, scattering them 30 miles away. Andrews hanged himself with his shoelaces in the Tompkins County jail, two days after his arrest, November 2, 1996.

SAVINO, KATIE ELIZABETH Apr 28, 1980 Ithaca, NY - Jun 11, 1999 Cortlandville, NY
Former Dryden High School cheerleader, best friend of murder victim, Sarah Ann Hajney. Killed in a drunk driving accident three years after Sarah's murder, the last in a series of tragic events marring Dryden High School in the mid-to-late 1990s, chronicled in the May 2001 issue of *Spin* magazine by writer, E. Jean Carroll.

MEADOW LAWN-PLEASANT VALLEY CEMETERY
Hewitt Road
Petersburgh, NY 12138

BAUM (Tassini), **CYNTHIA** Jun 9, 1909 NY - Feb 10, 2005 Jamesville, NY
Niece of L. Frank Baum, author of *The Wonderful Wizard of Oz* series of children's books. Last member of the Baum family to have personally known the author.

MELROSE CEMETERY
Melrose Road / Route 72
Auburn, NY 13021

EDSON, MERRICK May 3, 1802 - Mar 23, 1850 Auburn, NY
Owned a flour mill. Father of Annie Edson Taylor, first person to go over Niagara Falls in a wooden barrel and survive, October 24, 1901, her 63rd birthday.

MEMORY'S GARDEN
983 Watervliet Shaker Road
Colonie, NY 12205

HARTUNIAN, LYNNE CAROL Mar 13, 1967 Schenectady, NY - Dec 22, 1988 Lockerbie, Scotland
SUNY Oswego student. Victim of the terrorist bombing of PanAm Flight 103 over Lockerbie, Scotland, killing 270 people, including 35 Syracuse University students.

VAWTER, ELTON LEE Jul 4, 1925 Garland, AR - Sept 14, 1972 San Francisco, CA
World War II United States Army Lieutenant Colonel. With **Matilda B. Bottoni Vawter** (Mar 30, 1924 Whitehall, NY - Jan 9, 2010 Niskayuna, NY), the parents of actor, Ron Vawter, co-founder of the Wooster Group, an experimental theater group in New York City.

MERIDIAN (MONUMENTAL GROVE) CEMETERY
Main Street / Route 370
Cato, NY 13033

LANGWORTHY (Davis), **ELSIE** 1911 Cato, NY - Apr 9, 1964 Auburn, NY
Mother of Sarah Raines Vitello, expecting her seventh child momentarily, and grandmother of her six children, Carmen Jr., Michael, Francis, Harry, Joseph and James, victims of carbon monoxide poisoning, from a broken coal furnace. Her son-in-law, Carmen J. Vitello, the children's father, awoke nauseous, running from the house, yelling his family was dead, 14 hours after they died.

MERRITT CEMETERY
Merritt Road
Fulton, NY 13069

FELT, BENJAMIN Jul 31, 1780 Packersfield, NH - Sept 19, 1827 Granby, NY
Great-grandfather of Wright Lafayette Felt, Nevada Public Works Administrator at the time the Hoover Dam was built. 2nd great-grandfather of child actress, Joan Carroll, who appeared in the films, *Meet Me in St. Louis* and *The Bells of St. Mary's*.

METTOWEE VALLEY CEMETERY
North Street
Granville, NY 12832

PARKER, FRANK (Franklin Fish) Mar 29, 1836 Granville, NY - 1928 Granville, NY
With **Anna Peckham Norton Parker** (Mar 9, 1842 Granville, NY - Jun 19, 1915 Granville, NY), the grandparents of gunsmith, P.O. Ackley, maker of Wildcat cartridges.

MEXICO PRIMITIVE CEMETERY
Tubbs Road
Mexico, NY 13114

BROWN (Manwaring)**, LULU** Apr 4, 1875 Richland, NY - Nov 25, 1950 Sodus, NY
Grandma Brown of Grandma Brown's Baked Beans. Co-founded the Brown-Whitney-Brown
Company, with her husband, Earl L. Brown, and Richard G. Whitney, in 1937, selling baked beans
based on her recipe.

BROWN, EARL L. Jan 30, 1875 Daysville, NY - Dec 25, 1938 Mexico, NY
Co-founded the Brown-Whitney-Brown Company, maker of Grandma Brown's Baked Beans, with
Richard G. Whitney, and his wife, Lulu Manwaring "Grandma" Brown, in 1937.

BROWN, ROBERT EARL Jun 18, 1916 Mexico, NY - May 15, 1974 Syracuse, NY
Developed a canning system used to mass-market Grandma Brown's Baked Beans, founded by his
father and mother, Earl L. and Lulu "Grandma" Brown, and Richard G. Whitney.

MEXICO VILLAGE CEMETERY
3678 Route 104
Mexico, NY 13114

COBB, GEORGE LINUS Aug 31, 1886 Mexico, NY - Dec 25, 1942 Brookline, MA
Ragtime composer. Collaborated with lyricist, Jack Yellen. Co-wrote "The Russian Rag", "All Aboard
for Dixieland" and "Are You from Dixie?", an early hit for Al Jolson. Columnist for the music magazines,
The Truthful Yankee and *Melody*.

COBB, LINUS B. 1847 Mexico, NY - Jan 24, 1925 Boston, MA
Merchant and entrepreneur. With **Janette S. Mains Cobb** (1848 Mexico, NY - Apr 1, 1938 Newtonville,
MA), the parents of ragtime composer, George L. Cobb.

COLLINS, RIPPER (James) Mar 30, 1904 Altoona, PA - Apr 15, 1970 New Haven, NY
First baseman for the St. Louis Cardinals, Chicago Cubs and Pittsburgh Pirates from 1931-1938 and
1941. Led the National League in home runs in 1934 with 35. Member of the National League   All-
Star team from 1935-1937. Appeared in three World Series for the Cardinals "Gas House Gang"
teams, winning twice, 1931 and 1934.

MOWRY, EARLE A. 1876 Mexico, NY - Oct 12, 1942 Mexico, NY
Mayor of the village of Mexico from 1929-1942. Graduated from the Syracuse University School of
Medicine. Son of Oliver B. Mowry, last surviving Oswego County Civil War veteran.

NICKLUS, PATRICIA A. Aug 28, 1946 Syracuse, NY - Aug 29, 1993 Syracuse, NY
Murder victim. Shot and killed during a lovers quarrel by Laymon Herring, publisher of the *Syracuse Banner*.

PAYNE, FRED Sept 2, 1880 Camden, NY - Jan 16, 1954 Camden, NY
Catcher for the Detroit Tigers and Chicago White Sox from 1906-1911. Only batter to pinch-hit for Ty Cobb during the Hall of Famer's career.

SACHEL, GEORGE C. Jul 23, 1924 New Haven, NY - Dec 23, 2002 Boynton Beach, FL
Founded, owned and operated Mimi's Drive Inn, Route 481 in Fulton, in 1960.

WHITNEY, RICHARD GARY Jul 3, 1916 Mexico, NY - Mar 19, 1990 Mexico, NY
Co-founder and owner, with Earl L. Brown and his wife Lulu "Grandma" Brown, of Grandma Brown's Baked Beans, originally the Brown-Whitney-Brown Food Company, in 1937.

MIDDLE PATENT RURAL CEMETERY
Middle Patent Road
Bedford, NY 10506

GIFFORD, WALTER SHERMAN Jan 10, 1885 Salem, MA - May 7, 1966 New York, NY
United States Ambassador to Great Britain from 1950-1953, appointed by President Dwight D. Eisenhower. President of AT&T from 1925-1948. Hosted the first video telephone conference, with United States Secretary of Commerce, Herbert Hoover, in 1927.

MARSHALL (Grunz), **E. G.** (Everett Eugene) Jun 18, 1914 Owatonna, MN - Aug 24, 1998 Bedford, NY
Actor. Two-time Emmy Award-winner. Starred in the TV series, *The Defenders*. Appeared in the films, *12 Angry Men*, *Superman II*, *Tora! Tora! Tora!*, *The Caine Mutiny*, *Creepshow*, *Nixon*, *Absolute Power* and *National Lampoon's Christmas Vacation*. Hosted the *CBS Radio Mystery Theater* from 1974-1982. Portrayed four United States Presidents in films.

MIDDLEBURGH CEMETERY
Huntersland Road
Middleburgh, NY 12122

BORST, PETER I. Apr 24, 1797 Middleburgh, NY - Nov 14, 1848 Middleburgh, NY
United States Representative-NY from 1829-1831.

BOUCK, JOSEPH Jul 22, 1788 Schoharie, NY - Mar 30, 1858 Middleburgh, NY
United States Representative-NY from 1831-1833. Brother of William C. Bouck, Governor of New York from 1843-1844.

BOUCK, WILLIAM CHRISTIAN Jan 7, 1786 Schoharie, NY - Apr 19, 1859 Schoharie, NY
Governor of New York from 1843-1844. Father of Gabriel Bouck, United States Representative-WI from 1877-1881. Brother of Joseph Bouck, United States Representative-NY from 1831-1833. Namesake of the town of Bouckville.

MURPHY, TIMOTHY 1751 PA - Jun 27, 1818 Middleburgh, NY
Revolutionary War Continental Army sniper. Fired the shot that killed British General, Simon Fraser, at the Battle of Saratoga, October 7, 1777, considered a turning point in the war. Subject of the John Brick novel, *The Rifleman*, in 1953.

MILLER CEMETERY
Miller Street
Big Flats, NY 14814

EACKER (Acker)**, JACOB I.** Mar 18, 1785 Palatine, NY - Mar 8, 1873 Big Flats, NY
Husband of Gertrude Herkimer Eacker, the niece of Revolutionary War New York Militia General, Nicholas Herkimer. Brother of George I. Eacker, who shot and killed Philip Hamilton in a duel, November 23, 1801, two-and-a-half years before Hamilton's father, Alexander Hamilton, was killed in a duel with Vice-President Aaron Burr on the same dueling grounds in Weehawken, NJ.

MILLPORT CEMETERY
Cemetery Hill Road
Millport, NY 14864

BABCOCK, ALBERT FRANKLIN Jan 22, 1814 South New Berlin, NY - Jul 15, 1881 Millport, NY
With **Ann Almira Crandall Babcock** (Sept 20, 1813 South New Berlin, NY - Jan 19, 1895 Millport, NY), the grandparents of Carrie Babcock Sherman, Second Lady of the United States from 1909-1912, the wife of Vice-President James Schoolcraft Sherman.

MOHAWK CEMETERY
Columbia Street / Route 28
Mohawk, NY 13407

JARVIS, ALEXANDER BRUCE Oct 30, 1917 Utica, NY - Jan 6, 2003 Orlando, FL
Father of NASA astronaut, Gregory Bruce Jarvis, payload specialist on the Challenger space shuttle that exploded 73 seconds after takeoff from the Kennedy Space Center in Florida, January 28, 1986. Mohawk Cemetery placed a cenotaph for him following his cremation, his ashes were scattered in the Pacific Ocean. Unidentified remains from the seven shuttle astronauts were buried beneath a memorial in Arlington National Cemetery.

SPINNER, FRANCIS ELIAS Jan 21, 1802 Mohawk, NY - Dec 31, 1890 Jacksonville, FL
United States Representative-NY from 1855-1861. Treasurer of the United States, appointed by President Abraham Lincoln, from 1861-1875.

MONTREPOSE CEMETERY
75 Montrepose Avenue
Kingston, NY 12401

AMACHER, MARYANNE Feb 25, 1938 Kane, PA - Oct 22, 2009 Rhinebeck, NY
Avant-garde composer. Installation artist of three-dimensional work.

CORNELL, THOMAS C. Jan 23, 1814 White Plains, NY - Mar 30, 1894 Kingston, NY
United States Representative-NY from 1867-1869 and 1881-1883.

FISCHER, ANTON OTTO Feb 23, 1882 Regensburg, Germany - Mar 26, 1962 Woodstock, NY
Illustrator for *The Saturday Evening Post* for 48 years. Illustrated the books, *Moby-Dick*, *Treasure Island* and *20,000 Leagues Under the Sea*.

FLEMMING, ARTHUR SHERWOOD Jun 12, 1905 Kingston, NY - Sept 7, 1996 Alexandria, VA
Secretary of Health, Education and Welfare from 1958-1961, under President Dwight D. Eisenhower. Awarded two Presidential Medals of Freedom, from Dwight D. Eisenhower and Bill Clinton.

LINDSLEY, JAMES GIRARD Mar 19, 1819 Orange, NY - Dec 4, 1898 Kingston, NY
United States Representative-NY from 1885-1887.

MCENTEE, JERVIS Jul 14, 1828 Rondout, NY - Jan 27, 1891 Rondout, NY
Landscape painter. Associated with the Hudson River School of artists. Brother-in-law of landscape architect, Calvert Vaux.

MORA, F. LUIS (Francis) Jul 27, 1874 Montevideo, Uruguay - Jun 5, 1940 New York, NY
Artist. Painted in watercolor and oils, depicting American life in the 20th century. His works is held in the Museum of Modern Art in New York City and the Smithsonian American Art Museum.

VAUX, CALVERT Dec 20, 1824 London, England - Nov 19, 1895 Brooklyn, NY
Landscape architect. Co-designed Central Park in New York City and Prospect Park in Brooklyn, with his protégé, Frederick Law Olmstead. Designed the grounds of the White House and Smithsonian Institute, with Andrew Jackson Downing. Husband of Mary McEntee Vaux, sister of landscape painter, Jervis McEntee. Drowned by accident in Gravesend Bay, Brooklyn.

WEBER, GEORGE Mar 17, 1834 - Jul 4, 1882 Kingston, NY
Chief Engineer. Tombstone is a marble replica of a fireman standing next to a fire hydrant.

MORGAN MEETING HOUSE CEMETERY
Wetzel Road
Clay, NY 13041

MORGAN, ABRAHAM Sept 5, 1794 - May 21, 1872 Onondaga County, NY
Methodist minister. Built the Morgan Meeting House, off Wetzel Road, town of Clay. Son of Revolutionary War spy, Charles Morgan.

MORGAN, CHARLES 1745 Monmouth County, NJ - 1803 Onondaga County, NY
Revolutionary War Veteran. Possibly buried in an unmarked grave off Old Liverpool Road, though there is a tombstone next to his wife, **Rachel Prest Morgan** (Apr 3, 1765 - Mar 14, 1846 Clay, NY), which reads, "Revolty Spy, One of the Captors of Major Andre, Capt. Wm. Gifford's Co., Col. Dayton's 3rd N.J. Reg., 1745-1803." Served as a spy for General Marquis de Lafayette during the Yorktown campaign in the Revolution.

MORRISVILLE RURAL CEMETERY
Cedar Street
Morrisville, NY 13408

ARMOUR, LUCIEN BONAPARTE Dec 11, 1823 Stockbridge, NY - Jun 19, 1896 Morrisville, NY
Cousin of Philip D. Armour and Herman O. Armour, co-founders of Armour & Company, a meatpacking business, in Chicago in 1867. Fell from an apple tree, suffering critical injuries.

BICKNELL, BENNET Nov 14, 1781 Mansfield, CT - Sept 15, 1841 Morrisville, NY
United States Representative-NY from 1837-1839. His son, James Madison Bicknell, died March 19, 1814, eleven months old, the first known burial in Morrisville Rural Cemetery.

HOLMES, SIDNEY TRACY Aug 14, 1815 Schaghticoke, NY - Jan 18, 1890 Morrisville, NY
United States Representative-NY from 1865-1867.

HOWLETT (DePree)**, KATHY M.** 1954 Syracuse, NY - Jan 1, 2009 Lee, MA
Associate professor of English and co-director of the Cinema Studies Program at Northeastern
University. Author of *Framing Shakespeare on Film* in 2000.

SENN, JOSEPH D. 1860 Verona, NY - 1936 Oneida, NY
Associate Justice of the New York State Supreme Court.

MOSCOW CEMETERY
Main Street / Route 20A
Leicester, NY 14481

HORSFORD, JEREDIAH Mar 8, 1791 Charlotte, VA - Jan 14, 1875 Livonia, NY
United States Representative-NY from 1851-1853.

LEHR, NORM (Norman Carl Michael) May 28, 1901 Rochester, NY - Jul 17, 1968 Conesus, NY
Right-handed pitcher for the Cleveland Indians for four games in 1926, managed by Hall of Famer,
Tris Speaker.

MOST HOLY REDEEMER CEMETERY
2501 Troy Schenectady Road
Schenectady, NY 12309

BLATNICK, JEFF (Jeffrey Carl) Jul 26, 1957 Schenectady, NY - Oct 24, 2012 Schenectady, NY
United States Olympic wrestler. Won the gold medal, heavyweight division, in Los Angeles in 1984,
following a battle with Hodgkin's Disease. Two-time NCAA Division II heavyweight wrestling champion,
in 1978 and 1979.

CUSHING, JAMES EDWARD Aug 19, 1885 Niskayuna, NY - Nov 1, 1971 Niskayuna, NY
Founding president of the Cushing Stone Company, Inc. Chairman of the Schenectady County
Republican Party from 1939-1942. Father of James E. Cushing, Jr., the husband of actress, Maureen
O'Sullivan.

CUSHING, JAMES EDWARD 1921 Niskayuna, NY - Jun 17, 2011 Phoenix, AZ
Husband of actress, Maureen O'Sullivan, from August 22, 1983 until her death, June 23, 1998.
Namesake of the Cushing Center in the Ellis Health Center, Schenectady.

MOUNTAIN, FRANK HENRY May 17, 1860 Fort Edward, NY - Nov 19, 1939 Schenectady, NY
Right-handed pitcher for the Troy Trojans, Detroit Wolverines, Worcester Ruby Legs, Philadelphia Athletics, Columbus Buckeyes and Pittsburgh Alleghenys from 1880-1886. Pitched a no-hitter for Columbus in 1884, against the Washington Nationals.

O'SULLIVAN (Cushing)**, MAUREEN** May 17, 1911 Boyle, Ireland - Jun 23, 1998 Scottsdale, AZ
Hollywood film actress. Starred as Jane, opposite Johnny Weissmuller, in *Tarzan* films, from 1932-1942. Wife of filmmaker, John Farrow, from 1936-1963. Mother of actress, Mia Farrow and Prudence Farrow, immortalized in the Beatles' song "Dear Prudence", from the *White Album*. Grandmother of Soon-Yi Previn Allen, wife of screenwriter/director, Woody Allen. Married James E. Cushing Jr., August 22, 1983, at the St. Mary of the Angel Chapel, Siena College in Albany, also the location of her funeral.

PLAKAS, DEAN THOMAS 1980 New Haven, CT - Dec 6, 2016 Schenectady, NY
Co-owned and operated Peter Pause Restaurant, Nott Street, Schenectady with his fiancé, Amie Marie Phillips. Found dead three days before they were due to be married.

RILEY, LEE (Leon Francis) Aug 20, 1906 Princeton, NE - Sept 13, 1970 Schenectady, NY
Minor league outfielder. Retired with 2,418 hits. Appeared in four games with the Philadelphia Phillies in 1944. Played for the Rochester Red Wings in 1932. Father of Pat Riley, forward for the San Diego Rockets, Los Angeles Lakers and Phoenix Suns from 1967-1976 and Hall of Fame coach for the Lakers, New York Knicks and Miami Heat, and Lee Riley Jr., defensive back for the Detroit Lions, Philadelphia Eagles and New York Giants and the New York Titans of the AFL.

RILEY, LEE (Leon Francis) Aug 24, 1932 Omaha, NE - Jun 9, 2011 Chicago, IL
Defensive back for the Detroit Lions, Philadelphia Eagles and New York Giants from 1955-1956 and 1958-1960 and the New York Titans of the AFL from 1961-1962. Led the AFL in interceptions in 1962, his final year of professional football. Son of Lee Riley, outfielder for the Philadelphia Phillies in 1944. Brother of Pat Riley, forward for the San Diego Rockets, Los Angeles Lakers and Phoenix Suns from 1967-1976 and Hall of Fame coach for the Lakers, New York Knicks and Miami Heat.

ROE, ALTON LEWIS May 12, 1917 Schenectady, NY - Oct 16, 1971
Father of Marybeth Roe Tinning, convicted of infanticide, July 17, 1987, killing nine of her children, covering a 14-year period. Subject of the book, *From Cradle to Grave: The Short Lives and Strange Deaths of Marybeth Tinning's Nine Children*.

TINNING CHILDREN
Victims of infanticide. **Barbara Ann** (May, 31, 1967 - March 2, 1972), **Joseph Jr.** (January 10, 1970 - January 20, 1970), **Jennifer** (December 26, 1971 - January 3, 1972), **Nathan** (March 30, 1973 - September 2, 1975), **Timothy** (November 21, 1973 - December 10, 1973), **Mary Frances** (October 29, 1978 - February 22, 1979) and **Jonathan** (November 19, 1979 - March 24, 1980), seven of nine

children killed by their mother, Marybeth Roe Tinning, convicted on July 17, 1987, sentenced to 20 years-to-life in prison. Under suspicion for years, it was thought the children died from SIDS, or possibly a genetic condition. Subject of the book, *From Cradle to Grave: The Short Lives and Strange Deaths of Marybeth Tinning's Nine Children*. The two other children, Michael (adopted 1978 - March 2, 1981) and Tami Lynne (August 22, 1985 - December 19, 1985), were buried in Schenectady Memorial Park.

WALLACE, THOMAS W. 1900 - Jul 17, 1943 Schenectady, NY
Lieutenant Governor of New York, under Thomas E. Dewey, from January 1, 1943 until his death, six months later, from pneumonia.

MOTTVILLE CEMETERY
81 Jordan Street
Mottville, NY 13119

EARLL, DANIEL 1729 Whitehall, NY - Mar 29, 1817 Skaneateles, NY
Grandfather of Jonas Earll Jr., United States Representative-NY from 1827-1831. Great-grandfather of Nehemiah Hezekiah Earll, United States Representative-NY from 1839-1841.

MOUNT ADNAH CEMETERY
706 East Broadway Street
Fulton, NY 13069

BALLOU, BUD (Dudley J.) Dec 11, 1942 Fulton, NY - Apr 15, 1977 South Natick, MA
Syracuse disc jockey. Interviewed the Beatles on WOLF-AM radio, February 8, 1964, one day before their first appearance on *The Ed Sullivan Show*. Hosted a television dance show on WNYS-TV in Syracuse.

BRANDO, MARLON Aug 14, 1843 Parish, NY - 1900 Fulton, NY
Brother of Eugene Everet Brando, the grandfather of Academy Award-winning actor, Marlon Brando.

DEFOREST, HENRY PELOUZE 1864 Fulton, NY - Jun 13, 1948 New York, NY
New York City Police Department surgeon, from 1902-1912. Established the first fingerprint file in the United States. Wrote the *Text Book for First Aid Classes of the American Red Cross*, at the request of Clara Barton.

EDGARTON, LEE E. 1868 Oswego County, NY - Feb 20, 1952 Fulton, NY
Father of architects, W. Dexter Edgarton and H. Vincent Edgarton, co-designers of the Onondaga County War Memorial.

EMERICK, JOHN H. Nov 7, 1843 Fulton, NY – May 11, 1902 Brooklyn, NY
Civil War Union Army Telegrapher. Superintendent of the Postal Telegraph Company of New York.

HAVENS, DONALD Apr 6, 1964 New York, NY - Jan 1, 1993 Fulton, NY
Shot twice in the chest, in his home, Whitaker Road in Fulton, by Elizabeth Ann Wirth, who claimed to be protecting her friend, Charlotte Havens, from her violent husband. Charged with second-degree murder in 1994, her first trial was declared a mistrial due to prosecutorial misconduct, murder charges dismissed altogether in 1995. Following an appeal and reinstatement of charges in 1996, she reached a plea bargain, second-degree manslaughter and one year in jail.

LEE, ALBERT LINDLEY Jan 16, 1834 Fulton, NY - Dec 31, 1907 New York, NY
Civil War Union Army Brigadier General. Associate Justice of the Kansas State Supreme Court in 1861. Namesake of A.L. Lee Memorial Hospital in Fulton. Son of Moses Lindley Lee, United States Representative-NY from 1859-1861.

LEE, MOSES LINDLEY May 29, 1805 Minisink, NY - May 19, 1876 Petersburg, VA
United States Representative-NY from 1859-1861. Father of Albert Lindley Lee, Associate Justice of the Kansas State Supreme Court.

MURPHY, DWIGHT LOUIS 1898 Worcester, MA - Sept 21, 1957 Syracuse, NY
Central New York attorney. Died from an accidental gunshot wound to his head. With **Margaret Howe Murphy** (1901 - Oct 17, 1972 Fulton, NY), the parents of jazz singer, Mark Murphy.

RYAN (Paul)**, CAROL M.** Jul 4, 1954 Boylston, NY - Sept 1, 1996 Syracuse, NY
Victim of an unsolved homicide. Spent her last night at the East Room bar in Eastwood, died five hours after she was discovered by a fisherman, badly beaten, lying naked near the Jamesville Reservoir, off Route 91, due to injuries sustained when an explosive device was inserted into her vagina and detonated.

MOUNT ALBION CEMETERY
14925 Route 31
Albion, NY 14411

BULLOCK, RUFUS BROWN Mar 28, 1834 Bethlehem, NY - Apr 27, 1907 Albion, NY
Governor of Georgia from 1868-1871, first Republican governor of Georgia. Referenced in the novel, *Gone With the Wind*, by Georgia-native, Margaret Mitchell. Master of Ceremonies for the Cotton States and International Exposition in 1895, introducing Booker T. Washington, who gave his "Atlanta Compromise" speech.

BURROWS, LORENZO Mar 15, 1805 Groton, CT - Mar 6, 1885 Albion, NY
United States Representative-NY from 1849-1853. Nephew of Daniel Burrows, United States Representative-CT from 1821-1823.

CHAMBERLAIN, JOHN CURTIS Jun 5, 1772 Worcester, MA - Dec 8, 1834 Utica, NY
United States Representative-NH from 1809-1811.

CHURCH, SANFORD ELIAS Apr 18, 1815 Milford, NY - May 13, 1880 Albion, NY
Lieutenant Governor of New York, under Washington Hunt and Horatio Seymour, from 1851-1854.

DAVIS, NOAH Sept 10, 1818 Haverhill, NH - Mar 20, 1902 New York, NY
United States Representative-NY from 1869-1870. United States District Attorney for the Southern District of New York, appointed by President Ulysses S. Grant, in 1870. Associate Justice of the New York State Supreme Court from 1873-1887. Presided over two trials of New York City Tammany Hall politician, William M. "Boss" Tweed, convicted in 1873 of stealing from New York City taxpayers.

DE LA MATYR, GILBERT Jul 8, 1825 Pharsalia, NY - May 17, 1892 Akron, OH
United States Representative-IN from 1879-1881. Civil War Union Army Chaplain.

FULLER (Wheaton)**, IDA B.** Sept 9, 1923 - Feb 1, 2008 Brockport, NY
Great-grandmother of 17-year old, Brittanee Marie Drexel, who disappeared April 25, 2009, during a spring break trip to Myrtle Beach, without her parents knowledge, officially declared a victim of a homicide by the FBI in 2016.

HARD, GIDEON Apr 29, 1797 Arlington, VT - Apr 27, 1885 Albion, NY
United States Representative-NY from 1833-1837.

HART, ELIZUR KIRKE Apr 8, 1841 Albion, NY - Feb 18, 1893 Albion, NY
United States Representative-NY from 1877-1879. Purchased Hemlock Island in the Thousand Islands, Jefferson County, in 1871, renamed it Hart Island.

HOLMES, CHARLES HORACE Oct 24, 1827 Albion, NY - Oct 2, 1874 Albion, NY
United States Representative-NY from 1870-1871. Elected to Congress to fill the vacancy due to the resignation of Noah Davis.

HOWARD, CHARLES WILLIS Jun 15, 1896 Albion, NY - May 1, 1966 Newfane, NY
Founded the Charles W. Howard Santa Claus School in Albion in 1937, the oldest-continuously operated Santa school in the country, now located in Midland, MI. Owned and operated Christmas Park in Albion, an attraction where Santa students could train by interacting with children. Portrayed Santa Claus in the Macy's Thanksgiving Day Parade from 1948-1965. Appeared on television in *What's My Line*, *To Tell the Truth* and *The Tonight Show*. Hired as a consultant for the movie, *Miracle on 34th Street*, in 1947.

JULIANA, JOSEPH ROBERT Oct 9, 1906 - Oct 1981 Olcott, NY
Father of author, radio host and actor, Geoffrey Giuliano, biographer of the Beatles.

MILLS, ERNEST A. 1907 NY - Nov 19, 1928 Syracuse, NY
Organist. Director of the Debutantes, an all-girl stage band at the Strand Theatre in Syracuse. Died from a broken neck suffered in a plane crash, three days earlier, near Amboy Airport. The pilot, William L. Wademan and Rose Noble, drummer for the Debutantes, survived with injuries.

PULLMAN, JAMES LEWIS Jul 26, 1800 Kent County, RI - Nov 1, 1853 Albion, NY
With **Emily Caroline Minton Pullman** (Aug 14, 1808 Auburn, NY - May 21, 1892 Albion, NY), the parents of George Mortimer Pullman, founder of the Pullman Company, maker of railway sleeping cars.

REYNOLDS, EDWIN RUTHVIN Feb 16, 1816 Fort Ann, NY - Jul 4, 1908 Albion, NY
United States Representative-NY from 1860-1861. Elected to Congress following the death of Silas M. Burroughs.

SAWYER, JOHN GILBERT Jun 5, 1825 Brandon, VT - Sept 5, 1898 Albion, NY
United States Representative-NY from 1885-1891.

MOUNT CALVARY CEMETERY
800 Pine Ridge Heritage Boulevard
Cheektowaga, NY 14215

BATT, PAUL JOSEPH May 22, 1882 Buffalo, NY - Jun 11, 1966 Buffalo, NY
Associate Justice of the New York State Supreme Court from 1943-1962. Father of Gregory Batt, hockey player and coach for Colgate University and Hamilton College.

BEER (Koch)**, FLORENCE** May 28, 1920 - Feb 1, 2014 Fairport, NY
Mother of Canadian author, Barbara Rendall.

COTTONARO, TOMMY (Thomas J.) Mar 20, 1914 Castrogiovanni, Italy - Feb 7, 2001 Niagara Falls, NY
Actor. Played the Bearded Munchkin in *The Wizard of Oz*. Appeared in small roles in *Invaders from Mars* and *The Court Jester*.

DAVIDSON, GORD (John Gordon) Aug 5, 1918 Stratford, ON, Canada - Aug 8, 2004 Buffalo, NY
Defenseman for the New York Rangers from 1942-1944. Teammate of Hall of Famers, Lynn Patrick and Bryan Hextall.

DAY, TOM (Thomas Frederick) Aug 20, 1935 Washington D.C. - Aug 21, 2000 Amherst, NY
Defensive end for the St. Louis Cardinals, Buffalo Bills and San Diego Chargers from 1960-1968. Member of the Bills' AFL championship teams in 1964 and 1965. Selected to the Pro Bowl in 1965.

DULSKI, THADDEUS JOSEPH Sept 27, 1915 Buffalo, NY - Oct 11, 1988 Buffalo, NY
United States Representative-NY from 1959-1974. Resigned from Congress, becoming a special
assistant to New York Governor, Hugh Carey.

DU PONT, MARLENE 1941 Buffalo, NY - Mar 31, 1954 Cheektowaga, NY
Student at Cleveland Hill Elementary School, Cheektowaga, killed in a fire when a furnace exploded,
killing 15 students. Her childhood boyfriend and classmate, Jackson Frank, survived, became a folk
singer and songwriter, and wrote "Marlene", released on his album, *Jackson C. Frank*, in 1965.

GRONKOWSKI, FRANK (Francis B.) 1893 Buffalo, NY - Nov 1, 1957 Buffalo, NY
Brother of Ignatius Gronkowski, United States Olympic cyclist, and the great-grandfather of Rob
Gronkowski, tight end for the New England Patriots.

HOLLING, THOMAS LESLIE Apr 23, 1889 Bad Axe, MI - Nov 25, 1966 Redington Beach, FL
Mayor of Buffalo from 1938-1942. Ceremoniously pulled the switch on Track 22, Central Terminal in
Buffalo, to signal the first regular Buffalo-to-New York run of the Empire State Express, December 7,
1941, the same day the Japanese attacked Pearl Harbor.

MADONIA, BENJAMIN P. 1902 Italy - Dec 9, 1984 Buffalo, NY
Second cousin of singer and Academy Award-winning actor, Frank Sinatra.

MUELLER, FREDERICK R. Jun 18, 1927 - May 14, 1990 Buffalo, NY
With **Irene R. Mueller** (Jan 8, 1928 - Sept 16, 2007 Buffalo, NY), the parents of actress, Chelsea Noble,
who met her husband, actor, Kirk Cameron, on the set of their television series, *Full House*.

ODRE, ANN C. Dec 25, 1923 Buffalo, NY - Mar 6, 1997 Hamburg, NY
Critically-wounded in an assassination attempt against Pope John Paul II, May 13, 1981, at St. Peter's
Square, the Vatican, while on tour, shot in the chest by Mehmet Ali Aðca, with a bullet that first passed
through the Pope. Developed a life-long bond with the Pope, who was shot four times and wounded,
later learning that both of their mothers were born in the Polish town of Wadowice.

ROSAR, BUDDY (Warren Vincent) Jul 3, 1914 Buffalo, NY - Mar 13, 1994 Rochester, NY
Catcher for the New York Yankees, Cleveland Indians, Philadelphia Athletics and Boston Red Sox
from 1939-1951. Five-time All-Star. Set a record for most consecutive games caught without an error.
Hit for the cycle for the Yankees in 1940. Member of the Yankees' 1939 and 1941 World Series
championship teams, backing up Hall of Famer, Bill Dickey.

RUSZKOWSKI, JOSEPH Sept 19, 1889 Kotuň, Poland - Dec 5, 1987 Buffalo, NY
With **Frances Albiniak Ruszkowski** (Mar 7, 1890 Janów, Poland - Aug 1976 Buffalo, NY), the
grandparents of Martha Stewart, author, publisher and television host of *Martha Stewart Living* in 1990
and founder of Martha Stewart Living Omnimedia in 1997.

RYAN, WILLIAM HENRY May 10, 1860 Hopkinton, MA - Nov 18, 1939 Buffalo, NY
United States Representative-NY from 1899-1909.

SAVIOLA, ALESSIO Oct 10, 1916 Buffalo, NY - Jan 10, 1996 Lakehurst, NJ
FBI agent. Played a key role in the arrest of Puerto Rican nationalist, Oscar Collazo, who attempted to assassinated President Harry S Truman at Blair House in Washington D.C., November 1, 1950.

SISTI, SIBBY (Sebastian Daniel) Jul 26, 1920 Buffalo, NY - Apr 24, 2006 Amherst, NY
Infielder for the Boston Bees, Boston Braves and Milwaukee Braves from 1939-1942 and 1946-1954. Appeared in the 1948 World Series for the Braves, losing to the Cleveland Indians. Coach for the expansion Seattle Pilots in 1969. Minor League Player of the Year for the Indianapolis Indians in 1946. Appeared in the Robert Redford film, *The Natural*.

WATSON, FANNY Jun 3, 1887 Rochester, NY - May 17, 1970 Albany, NY
Vaudeville singer and actress. Performed with her sister, Kitty Watson, as the Watson Sisters.

WATSON, KITTY (Catherine) Mar 14, 1886 Rochester, NY - Mar 3, 1967 Buffalo, NY
Vaudeville singer and actress. Performed with her sister, Fanny Watson, as the Watson Sisters.

MOUNT CALVARY CEMETERY
Main Street / Route 7
Oneonta, NY 13820

CALLAHAN (Welsh)**, ELIZABETH** Feb 26, 1965 Oneonta, NY - Jan 19, 2000 Wilawana, PA
Murder victim. Her husband, Casey James Callahan, serving a 12-year prison sentence in Attica State Prison, following a conviction in 2013 for a sex crime, was arrested in 2016 and charged with murder, purposely running over her with a tractor-trailer in the parking lot of a mini-mart of Route 86, Exit 59A in Athens Township. Her family had long suspected she had been murdered by her husband.

MOUNT CARMEL CEMETERY
Route 29
Johnstown, NY 12095

BURNS, GEORGE JOSEPH Nov 24, 1889 Utica, NY - Aug 15, 1966 Gloversville, NY
Outfielder for the New York Giants, Cincinnati Reds and Philadelphia Phillies from 1911-1925. Led the National League in runs scored and walks five times. Appeared in three World Series for the Giants, winning in 1921. Retired with 2,077 career hits.

MOUNT CARMEL CEMETERY
Main Mill Street
Plattsburgh, NY 12901

CONDO, JOSEPH A. 1908 - Nov 23, 1960 Plattsburgh, NY
Pharmacist. Owned and operated Condo's Pharmacy, Plattsburgh's oldest continuously-operated pharmacy. Father of Terry J. Condo, Little League baseball coach for Eric Harris in Plattsburgh in 1993, six years before he and his friend, Dylan Klebold, shot and killed 12 students, one teacher, and wounded 21 others, at Columbine High School, Littleton, CO, before taking his own life, April 20, 1999.

MOFFITT, JOHN HENRY Jan 8, 1843 Chazy, NY - Aug 14, 1926 Plattsburgh, NY
U.S. Representative-NY from 1887-1891. Civil War Medal of Honor recipient. Manager of the Syracuse Street Railway Company from 1891-1899.

MOFFITT, STEPHEN Aug 7, 1837 Clintonville, NY - Jan 3, 1904 Plattsburgh, NY
Civil War Union Army Brevet Brigadier General. Shot carrying a wounded private from the field to a hospital, Battle of Fair Oaks, lost his leg to amputation, October 27, 1864. Collector of Customs for the District of Champlain, appointed by President Ulysses S. Grant, from 1876-1880 and from 1889-1898, appointed by President Benjamin Harrison.

MOUNT HOPE CEMETERY
Fordsbush Road
Fort Plain, NY 13339

CROUSE, JACOB Mar 9, 1769 Montgomery, NY - Jul 13, 1819 Fordsbush, NY
With **Catherine Nellis Crouse** (Nov 18, 1771 Montgomery, NY - Aug 12, 1838 Fort Plain, NY), the parents of John Crouse, Syracuse banker and wholesale grocer, considered the wealthiest man in Syracuse at the time of his death in 1889. Grandparents of John J. Crouse, Mayor of Syracuse in 1876 and Syracuse businessmen, Jacob Crouse and Charles E. Crouse. Granduncle of Huntington B. Crouse, co-founder of the Crouse-Hinds Company in Syracuse.

MOUNT HOPE CEMETERY
5697 Route 12
Norwich, NY 13815

MASON, WILLIAM Sept 10, 1786 Lebanon, CT - Jan 13, 1860 Norwich, NY
United States Representative-NY from 1835-1837.

MAYDOLE, DAVID Jan 27, 1807 Seward, NY - Oct 14, 1882 Norwich, NY
Founded the David Maydole Hammer Company in Norwich. James A. Garfield, prior to his election as President, visited Norwich in 1878, received a tour of the Maydole factory, later citing Maydole as an "Element of Success" during a Washington address.

MITCHELL, HENRY 1784 Woodbury, CT - Jan 12, 1856 Norwich, NY
United States Representative-NY from 1833-1835.

PRINDLE, ELIZUR H. May 6, 1829 Newtown, CT - Oct 7, 1890 Norwich, NY
United States Representative-NY from 1871-1873.

PURDY, SMITH MEADE Jul 31, 1796 North Norwich, NY - Mar 30, 1870 Norwich, NY
United States Representative-NY from 1843-1845.

RAMSARAN (Renz), **JENNIFER L.** Apr 8, 1976 Albany, NY - Dec 11, 2012 South New Berlin, NY
Murder victim. Bludgeoned inside her home, 473 Sheff Road, by her husband, Ganesh Ramsaran, who was having an affair with her best friend and benefited from a $200,000 life insurance policy upon her death. Her body was found February 26, 2013, off Center Road in Pharsalia, NY, he was convicted and sentenced to 25 years-to-life in prison. The case was profiled on *Dateline* and *48 Hours* in 2015.

RAY, GEORGE WASHINGTON Feb 3, 1844 Otselic, NY - Jan 10, 1925 Norwich, NY
United States Representative-NY from 1883-1885 and 1891-1902.

MOUNT HOPE CEMETERY
1133 Mount Hope Avenue
Rochester, NY 14620

ADAMS, TED (George E.) 1841 Rochester, NY - Oct 26, 1894 New Durham, NJ
Semi-pro baseball player. Shortstop for the Central City Club of Syracuse in 1865 and 1867-1869.

ADLER, LEVI Oct 24, 1834 Hessen, Germany - Mar 3, 1907 Rochester, NY
With **Theresa Wile Adler** (Nov 22, 1941 Küsel, Germany - Mar 8, 1905 Rochester, NY), the grandparents of Beatrice Bakrow Kaufman, wife of Pulitzer Prize-winning playwright, George S. Kaufman, married March 15, 1917 at the Rochester Country Club.

ALDRIDGE, GEORGE WASHINGTON Nov 3, 1833 - Dec 8, 1877 Rochester, NY
Mayor of Rochester from 1873-1874. Father of George W. Aldridge Jr., Mayor of Rochester in 1894.

ALDRIDGE, GEORGE WASHINGTON Dec 28, 1856 Rochester, NY - Jun 13, 1922 Rochester, NY
Mayor of Rochester in 1894. Known as "The Boss" and "the Big Fellow." Leading political figure in

Rochester politics for 40 years. Collector of the Port of New York, appointed by his close friend, President Warren G. Harding, in 1921. Son of George W. Aldridge, Mayor of Rochester from 1873-1874.

ANDREWS, SAMUEL GEORGE Oct 16, 1796 Derby, CT - Jun 11, 1863 Rochester, NY
United States Representative-NY from 1857-1859. Mayor of Rochester in 1846 and 1850.

ANTHONY, SUSAN BROWNELL Feb 15, 1820 Adams, MA - Mar 13, 1906 Rochester, NY
Abolitionist and temperance leader. Actively campaigned for women's right to vote. The 19th Amendment to the United States Constitution, granting women over the age of 21 the right to vote, was established in 1920, fourteen years after her death. Co-authored, *The History of Women's Suffrage*, with Elizabeth Cady Stanton, Matilda Joslin Gage and Ida Husted Harper, published in six volumes, from 1881-1922. The United States Mint issued the Susan B. Anthony dollar coin in 1979.

BAKER, BENJAMIN M. Dec 27, 1807 NY - Aug 27, 1897 Rochester, NY
Owned farmland in South Park, Genesee Valley, donated to the city of Rochester in 1908, by his daughter, Francis A. Baker, for Genesee Valley Park.

BAKER, CHARLES SIMEON Feb 18, 1839 Churchville, NY - Apr 21, 1902 Washington D.C.
United States Representative-NY from 1885-1891. Fought for the Union Army during the Civil War, injured at the Battle of Bull Run.

BAKER, JOHNNY Jan 13, 1869 - Apr 22, 1931 Rochester, NY
Foster son of William F. "Buffalo Bill" Cody. Sharpshooter in *Buffalo Bill's Wild West Show* in the United States and Europe. Founded the Buffalo Bill Memorial Museum.

BARRY, PETER Mar 22, 1912 Rochester, NY - Jan 23, 1972 Rochester, NY
Mayor of Rochester from 1955-1961. Grandson of horticulturist, Patrick Barry.

BAUSCH, JOHN JACOB Jul 25, 1830 Württemberg, Germany - Feb 14, 1926 Rochester, NY
Co-founded Bausch & Lomb, Inc., with Henry Lomb, in Rochester in 1853, manufacturer of optical glass.

BEDELL, LASHONDA 1977 NY - Nov 11, 1979 Syracuse, NY
Murder victim. Beaten by her mother, Precious Bedell, in the restroom of Valle's Steak House, 2803 Erie Boulevard East in Syracuse, November 8, 1979, dying three days later from her injuries. Her mother earned her master's degree, became a teacher and wrote a book on foster care during her incarceration. She was denied clemency by Governor Mario Cuomo and his successor, George Pataki, despite the efforts of actress, Glenn Close, who befriended her in prison while shooting a documentary, though eventually released from prison, November 22, 1999, on a reduced charge of manslaughter, with the help of Onondaga County district attorney, William Fitzpatrick.

BONSTELLE (Stuart)**, JESSIE** (Laura Justine) 1871 - Oct 14, 1932 Detroit, MI
Drama coach known as "the maker of stars." Namesake of the Bonstelle Theater in Detroit. Wife of actor, Alexander Hamilton Stuart.

BOODY, AZARIAH Apr 21, 1815 Stanstead, QC, Canada - Nov 18, 1885 New York, NY
United States Representative-NY in 1853. Resigned from office in October 1853 citing "pre-existing obligations."

BOYD, THOMAS 1756 Washingtonville, PA - Sept 19, 1779 Geneseo, NY
Revolutionary War Continental Army Lieutenant. Fell into an Indian ambush, brutally and maliciously tortured. Originally buried near Little Beard's Creek, NY.

BREWSTER, HENRY COLVIN Sept 7, 1845 Rochester, NY - Jan 29, 1928 Canandaigua, NY
United States Representative-NY from 1895-1899.

BROWN, CALVIN R. 1822 NY - May 1853 Rochester, NY
Husband of medium, Leah Fox, who managed the careers of her younger sisters, Catherine and Margaretta Fox, leaders in the creation of Spiritualism, using rappings to communicate with spirits, touring New York and Ohio, holding séances for hundreds of people. Leah Fox Brown Underhill died November 1, 1890 in New York City, age 77, buried in Green-Wood Cemetery, Brooklyn. Catherine Fox Jenckyn died July 2, 1892, age 55, and Margaretta Fox Kane, March 8, 1893, age 59, buried together in Cypress Hills Cemetery, Brooklyn.

CARVER, HARTWELL 1789 Rochester, NY - Apr 16, 1875
First proposed the idea of the Transcontinental Railroad in 1849.

CHILD, JONATHAN Jan 30, 1785 NH - Oct 27, 1860 Buffalo, NY
First Mayor of Rochester, in 1834. Son-in-law of Colonel Nathaniel Rochester.

CHURCHILL, HENRY Jul 7, 1812 Stockbridge, MA - Jun 16, 1893 Rochester, NY
With **Sarah Dewey Churchill** (Apr 7, 1814 MA - Jan 25, 1888 Rochester, NY), the parents of illustrator and portrait artist, Maud Humphrey. Great-grandparents of Academy Award-winning actor, Humphrey Bogart.

CLARKE, FREEMAN Mar 22, 1809 Troy, NY - Jun 24, 1887 Rochester, NY
United States Representative-NY from 1863-1865 and 1871-1875. Vice-President of the first Republican New York State Convention in 1854.

CODY, KIT CARSON Nov 26, 1870 Lincoln, NE - Apr 20, 1876 Rochester, NY
Only son of Wild West showman, William F. "Buffalo Bill" Cody.

CODY, ORRA MAUDE Aug 13, 1872 Lincoln, NE - Oct 24, 1883 Lincoln, NE
Daughter of Wild West showman, William F. "Buffalo Bill" Cody.

COMMINS (Zodikoff)**, LENA** Aug 16, 1862 Zubarkas, Lithuania - Nov 19, 1950 Rochester, NY
Half-sister of anarchist, Emma Goldman.

COON, WILBUR BARRY Apr 3, 1870 Yates, NY - Jul 13, 1926 Rochester, NY
International shoe manufacturer.

COOPER (Lampert)**, EMMA E.** 1855 Nunda, NY - Jul 30, 1920 Pittsford, NY
Award-winning artist. President of the Women's Art Association of Canada in 1897. Wife of artist, Colin Campbell Cooper.

CRAPSEY, ADELAIDE TROWBRIDGE Sept 9, 1878 Brooklyn, NY - Oct 8, 1914 Rochester, NY
Poet. Created the cinquain form of verse. Carl Sandberg wrote the poem, *Adelaide Crapsey*, in 1918. Daughter of Rev. Algernon Sidney Crapsey.

CRAPSEY, ALGERNON SIDNEY Jun 1847 Fairmount, OH - 1927 Rochester, NY
Episcopal clergyman. Expelled from the ministry for heresy, for non-literal interpretations of the bible. Published his autobiography, *Last of the Heretics*, in 1924. Father of poet, Adelaide Crapsey.

CRONE, EDWARD REGINALD Oct 26, 1923 Rochester, NY - Apr 11, 1945 Dresden, Germany
World War II American infantry soldier. Fought in the Battle of the Bulge, captured in Ardennes, Belgium by the Germans, sent to a prison camp where he died. Inspired the "Billy Pilgrim" character in the Kurt Vonnegut novel, *Slaughterhouse Five*.

DANFORTH, HENRY GOLD Jun 14, 1854 Gates, NY - Apr 8, 1918 Rochester, NY
United States Representative-NY from 1911-1917.

DAVY, JOHN MADISON Jun 29, 1835 Ottawa, ON, Canada - Apr 21, 1909 Atlantic City, NJ
United States Representative-NY from 1875-1877. Associate Justice of the New York State Supreme Court from 1889-1905. Collector of Customs at the Port of Rochester, appointed by President Ulysses S. Grant, his close friend.

DOUGLASS, FREDERICK Feb 7, 1818 Tuckahoe Springs, MD - Feb 20, 1885 Rochester, NY
Abolitionist leader and social reformer. First influential, African-American lecturer. Published the anti-slavery paper, *North Star*, in Rochester, from 1847-1860. Advisor to President Abraham Lincoln during the Civil War.

DUNN, THOMAS BYRNE Mar 16, 1853 Providence, RI - Jul 2, 1924 Rochester, NY
United States Representative-NY from 1913-1923. Founder and President of the T.B. Dunn Company, manufacturer of perfumes and extracts. Invented the breath freshener, Sen-Sen.

ELLWANGER, GEORGE Dec 2, 1816 Württemberg, Germany - Nov 26, 1906 Rochester, NY
Horticulturist. Co-founded the Ellwanger & Barry Nursery, with Patrick Barry, in Rochester in 1840.

ELY, ALFRED Feb 15, 1815 Lyme, CT - May 18, 1892 Rochester, NY
United States Representative-NY from 1859-1863. Taken prisoner by the Confederates, witnessing the Battle of Bull Run in the Civil War, imprisoned in Richmond for six months, before he was exchanged for Confederate General Charles J. Faulkner, who was detained by the Union Army in August 1861.

ENSWORTH (Ball)**, BETSY** (Elizabeth) 1765 Granville, MA - Aug 16, 1840 Rochester, NY
2nd great-grandmother of Sir Winston Churchill, Prime Minister of Great Britain from 1940-1945 and 1951-1955. First wife of Aaron Jerome, who died April 14, 1802 in Pompey, age 37. Remarried to Dr. Azel Ensworth, died May 5, 1854 in Buffalo, age 94.

EVEREST, HIRAM BOND Apr 11, 1830 Pike, NY - Mar 5, 1913 Rochester, NY
Oil tycoon. Developed a distillation process for low-grade motor oils. Patented a steam cylinder lubricant, used in the development of high-speed machinery, in 1869.

FORD, GEORGE HENRY Dec 21, 1914 Winnipeg, MB, Canada - Dec 9, 1994 Rochester, NY
Chairman of the English Department at the University of Rochester from 1960-1972. Authority on Victorian Literature. Dickens scholar, published *Dickens and His Readers* in 1955.

FRENCH, ROBERT TIMOTHY Nov 15, 1828 Ithaca, NY - Jun 17, 1893 Rochester, NY
Founded R.T. French & Son in Rochester in 1880. His son, George Jackson French, introduced French's Mustard at the 1904 St. Louis World's Fair.

FROST (Blair)**, ELIZABETH HOLLISTER** Mar 1, 1887 Rochester, NY - Apr 9, 1958 Rochester, NY
Poet and novelist. Great-granddaughter of newspaper publisher, Thurlow Weed,

GANNETT, FRANK ERNEST Sept 15, 1876 Bristol, NY - Dec 3, 1957 Rochester, NY
Newspaper publisher. Founded the Gannett Company in 1906, establishing a major chain of daily newspapers across the United States. Unsuccessful Republican presidential candidate in 1940, losing to Wendell Wilkie.

GLAZER, ABRAHAM A. Dec 8, 1897 Lithuania - Nov 9, 1943 Rochester, NY
With **Hannah Glazer** (Jul 18, 1895 Lithuania - Feb 1980), the parents of businessman, Malcolm I. Glazer, owner of the Tampa Bay Buccaneers and the Manchester United Football Club.

GOLDBERG, MORTON Dec 17, 1916 Rochester, NY - Feb 22, 1996 Rochester, NY
National billiards champion. Nicknamed "Boston Shorty." Defeated Minnesota Fats, Willie Mosconi and Irving Crane during career.

GRAMMATICO, BENNIE (Benedicto G.) Apr 25, 1924 Rochester, NY - Nov 1, 2003 Rochester, NY
Rochester-area bandleader. Father of musician, Lou Gramm, lead singer of the rock band, Foreigner. Husband of singer, Nikki Grammatico.

GRAMMATICO (Masetta)**, NIKKI** Oct 6, 1924 - Feb 7, 2003 Rochester, NY
Big band singer. Mother of musician, Lou Gramm, lead singer of the rock band Foreigner. Wife of bandleader, Bennie Grammatico.

GRAY, MALCOLM EDWARD Sept 11, 1867 Harriston, ON, Canada - Nov 7, 1932 Rochester, NY
Owned the Rochester Can Company. Created the five-day work week for his employees, later adopted by Henry Ford and most companies throughout the United States employing skilled labor.

GREEN, SETH Mar 19, 1817 Rochester, NY - Aug 1888 Rochester, NY
Called the "Father of Fish Culture in North America." Created the Caledonia Fish Hatchery in 1864, the first of its kind in New York State.

GREENLEAF, HALBERT STEVENS Apr 12, 1847 Guilford, VT - Aug 25, 1906 Greece, NY
United States Representative-NY from 1883-1885 and 1891-1893.

HAAG, BERNHARD J. Feb 25, 1831 Germany - Aug 18, 1919 Rochester, NY
Rochester butcher on Scio Street, the Haag Block, since 1875. More than 68 years after his death, April 1988, remodelers were removing sections of the ceiling in his old butcher shop, finding body parts and limbs among the debris, belonging to an unidentified man and two women, who were murdered and dismembered shortly after their death with a hand-held meat saw.

HARD, JAMES ALBERT Jul 15, 1841 Windsor, NY - Mar 12, 1953 Rochester, NY
Last surviving Civil War Union combat veteran. Albert H. Woolson, a drummer who entered into service in the last weeks of the war, is officially the last surviving Union veteran, dying in 1956.

HARRISON, LES (Lester) Aug 20, 1904 Rochester, NY - Dec 23, 1997 Rochester, NY
Basketball Hall of Famer. Founded the Rochester Royals in 1946, now the Sacramento Kings by way of Cincinnati and Kansas City-Omaha. Head coach of the Royals from 1946-1955, leading them to five NBA division titles and the 1951 NBA Championship. Coached Hall of Famers, Red Holzman, Al Cervi, Bob Davies, Alex Hannum, Arnie Risen and Bobby Wanzer, and NFL Hall of Famer, Otto Graham and Hollywood actor, Chuck Connors.

HART, ROSWELL Aug 4, 1824 Rochester, NY - Apr 20, 1883 Rochester, NY
United States Representative-NY from 1865-1867.

HAWKES, JAMES Dec 13, 1776 Petersham, MA - Oct 2, 1865 Rochester, NY
United States Representative-NY from 1821-1823. Otsego County Sheriff from 1815-1819.

HENKLE, LEONARD 1834 OH - Sept 11, 1904 Rochester, NY
Created the Rochester Lamp. President and Manager of the Rochester Lamp Company in 1884.
Devised a system to harness the power of Niagara Falls, providing electricity to New York state.

HEYDLER, ERNST Jun 20, 1835 Prussia - Sept 26, 1882 Rochester, NY
Lutheran pastor. Founded the Lutheran Concordia Church in Rochester in 1877. Father of baseball
executive, John A. Heydler, President of the National League from 1918-1934.

HILL, CHARLES J. Apr 13, 1796 Woodbury, CT - Jul 19, 1883 Rochester, NY
Mayor of Rochester in 1842. Rochester miller, whose own brand of flour was internationally respected
for its quality.

HOLLEY, MYRON Apr 28, 1779 Salisbury, CT - Mar 4, 1841 Rochester, NY
Member of the New York Canal Commission, promoted and managed construction of the Erie Canal.

HUMPHREY, HARVEY Dec 24, 1796 Goshen, CT - May 1, 1877 Rochester, NY
With **Elizabeth Rogers Perkins Humphrey** (Dec 24, 1808 Norwich, CT - 1888 Rochester, NY), the
great-grandparents of Academy Award-winning actor, Humphrey Bogart. Grandparents of illustrator
and portrait artist, Maud Humphrey.

HUMPHREY, JOHN PERKINS Aug 3, 1836 Lansdowne, ON, Canada - 1906 Rochester, NY
With **Francis V. Churchill Humphrey** (Aug 7, 1837 Rochester, NY - May 16, 1897 New York, NY), the
grandparents of Academy Award-winning actor, Humphrey Bogart. Parents of illustrator and portrait
artist, Maud Humphrey.

HUTCHINS, CHARLES P. Sept 10, 1872 Brooklyn, NY - Dec 28, 1938 Syracuse, NY
Syracuse University football coach in 1904 and 1906. Indiana University football coach in 1910.
President of the Western Football Conference, precursor to the Big Ten Conference.

HYLAN, RAY Aug 7, 1906 - May 1983 Rochester, NY
Owned and operated Hylan Airport and the Hylan Flying School in Rochester. Donated his Boeing
F4B-4 Navy fighter, the last one of its kind, to the Smithsonian Institution, in 1960.

JACOBSTEIN, MEYER Jan 25, 1880 New York, NY - Apr 18, 1963 Rochester, NY
United States Representative-NY from 1923-1929.

KEMPSHALL, THOMAS 1796 England - Jan 14, 1865 Rochester, NY
United States Representative-NY from 1839-1841. Mayor of Rochester in 1837.

KIMBALL, WILLIAM SMITH Mar 30, 1837 - Mar 26, 1897 Rochester, NY
Founded the Kimball Tobacco Factory in Rochester, one of the world's largest tobacco product companies of its day. His Rochester home was one of only two in America designed by Louis Comfort Tiffany.

KISLINGBURY, FREDERICK FOSTER Dec 25, 1847 Ilsley, England - Jun 1, 1884 Cape Sabine
One of 25 members of the ill-fated, Greely Expedition who sailed the Arctic in July 1881, only to find themselves stranded and starving for three years. Second lieutenant to Adolphus W. Greely on the expedition, which set a record for achieving the farthest point north, toward the North Pole. Succumbed to starvation and dehydration, three weeks before seven survivors were rescued, including Greely.

LOMB, HENRY Nov 24, 1828 Burgham, Germany - Jun 13, 1908 Rochester, NY
Co-founded Bausch & Lomb, Inc., with John J. Bausch, in Rochester in 1853, manufacturer of optical glass.

LUCKEY, SAMUEL Apr 18, 1791 Rensselaerville, NY - Oct 11, 1869 Rochester, NY
Methodist Episcopal Minister. First Principal of the Genesee Wesleyan Seminary in Lima, from 1831-1836, the school moved to Syracuse in 1870 where it became Syracuse University.

MATHEWS, VINCENT Jun 29, 1766 Newburgh, NY - Aug 23, 1846 Rochester, NY
United States Representative-NY from 1809-1811.

MIKOSZ, TAMARA Dec 20, 1919 Poland - Apr 1981 Rochester, NY
Polish actress, prior to World War II. Escaped Poland following the Nazi invasion, ending her film career. Employed as an interpreter and receptionist at the George Eastman House in Rochester.

MILLENER, ALEXANDER 1761 - Mar 13, 1865 Adams Basin, NY
Drummer boy for General George Washington during the Revolutionary War.

MILLER, ABRAM CALMEN Aug 27, 1877 Russia - Sept 15, 1969 Rochester, NY
With **Hinda Rosenblum Miller** (1879 Russia - Jul 26, 1964 Rochester, NY), the parents of Mitch Miller, musical conductor, oboist, record producer and star of the 1960s NBC television program, *Sing Along with Mitch*.

MOORE, DANIEL D.T. 1820 - Jun 3, 1892 New York, NY
Mayor of Rochester from 1865-1866. Founded the agricultural magazine, *Moore's Rural New Yorker.* Accompanied the funeral train carrying President Abraham Lincoln, as it traveled through Rochester

on its way to Springfield, Lincoln's final resting place.

MORGAN, LEWIS HENRY Nov 21, 1818 Aurora, NY - Dec 17, 1881 Rochester, NY
Anthropologist. Formulated a theory of social evolution, adapted by Karl Marx and Friedrich Engels, in the development of Marxism.

MOTT, RICHARD Jul 21, 1804 Mamaroneck, NY - Jan 22, 1888 Toledo, OH
United States Representative-OH from 1855-1859. Mayor of Toledo from 1845-1846.

MYERS, JACOB H. Feb 1841 PA - Apr 1, 1920 Rochester, NY
Invented the Myers Automatic Booth, the first lever voting machine, in Lockport in 1892.

OUZER, LOUIS Mar 11, 1913 Rochester, NY - Feb 14, 2002 Rochester, NY
Photographed musicians from the 1940s to the 1980s, in black and white. Photographed Louis Armstrong, Igor Stravinsky, Count Basie, Ella Fitzgerald, Itzhak Perlman and Marion Anderson at the Eastman School of Music in Rochester. Published, *Contemporary Musicians in Photographs*, in 1979.

PATERSON (Patterson)**, THOMAS J.** 1805 Lisle, NY - 1885 Rochester, NY
United States Representative-NY from 1843-1845. Grandson of John Paterson, United States Representative-NY from 1803-1805 and Revolutionary War Continental Army General.

PAUL, CELIA 1879 Russia - Sept 16, 1938 Rochester, NY
With **Morris Paul** (1877 - Apr 28, 1953 Rochester, NY), the parents of baseball executive, Gabe Paul. Died in St. Mary's Hospital from injuries sustained in an automobile accident.

PERKINS, JAMES BRECK Nov 4, 1847 St. Croix Falls, WI - Mar 11, 1910 Washington D.C.
United States Representative-NY from 1901-1910. Chosen by the House of Representatives as a manager, for impeachment proceedings against Charles Swayne, Associate Justice of the United States District Court of the Northern District of Florida, in 1905. Wrote historical biographies, including *France in the American Revolution* and *France Under Louis XV*.

POST (Kirby)**, AMY** Dec 20, 1802 Jericho, NY - Jan 29, 1889 Rochester, NY
Abolitionist and women's rights leader. Credited with assisting the largest number of escaped slaves into Canada, from her Rochester home, shared with her husband, Isaac Post.

POST, ISAAC 1800 Westbury, NY - April 1892 Rochester, NY
Abolitionist. Close friend of Frederick Douglass. Credited with assisting the largest number of escaped slaves into Canada, from his Rochester home, shared with his wife, Amy Kirby Post. Early believer in Spiritualism, took in the Fox sisters, who communicated with spirits through rappings. Wrote the book, *Voices from the Spirit World, Being Communications from Many Spirits*, in 1852.

POTTER, HENRY SAYRE Feb 14, 1798 Galway, NY - Jan 9, 1884 Rochester, NY
First President of the Western Union Telegraph Company.

PRATT (Cleveland)**, SUSAN** Sept 26, 1784 Norwich, CT - Aug 19, 1883 Geneva, NY
Grandaunt of President Grover Cleveland and Rose Elizabeth "Libbie" Cleveland, First Lady from 1885-1886, during Cleveland's first presidency.

RAUSCHENBUSCH, WALTER Oct 4, 1861 Rochester, NY - Jul 25, 1918 Rochester, NY
Progressive Baptist Minister. Leader in the Social Gospel movement in the United States.

RITTER, FRANK H. Dec 1845 Astheim, Germany - Apr 1915 Rochester, NY
Founded the Ritter Dental Company, international manufacturer and supplier of dental equipment. Invented the modern dentist chair.

ROBINSON, CHARLES MULFORD Apr 30, 1869 Ramapo, NY - Dec 30, 1917 Albany, NY
Landscape architect. Inspired the "City Beautiful" movement. Professor of Civic Design at the University of Illinois in 1913, the first of its kind in the United States. Designed the city of Syracuse, and Los Angeles, Denver, Colorado Springs, Oakland, Omaha, Columbus, Fort Wayne and Honolulu.

ROCHESTER, NATHANIEL Feb 21, 1752 Westmoreland, VA - May 17, 1831 Rochester, NY
Revolutionary War New York Militia Colonel. Founded the city of Rochester. Father of Thomas Hart Rochester, sixth Mayor of Rochester. Father-in-law of Jonathan Child, first Mayor of Rochester.

SCHERMERHORN, ABRAHAM M. Dec 11, 1791 Schenectady, NY - Aug 22, 1855 New Haven, CT
United States Representative-NY from 1849-1953. Mayor of Rochester in 1837.

SELDEN, GEORGE BALDWIN Sept 14, 1846 Clarkson, NY - Jan 17, 1922 Rochester, NY
Automobile inventor. Filed a patent for an improved road engine for the gas-powered automobile. Son of Henry Rogers Selden, Associate Justice of the New York State Court of Appeals from 1862-1865

SELDEN, HENRY ROGERS Oct 14, 1805 Lyme, CT - Sept 18, 1885 Rochester, NY
Associate Justice of the New York State Court of Appeals from 1862-1865. Defended Susan B. Anthony, arrested for illegally voting in the 1872 election, losing the trial in 1873. Declined to accept the nomination for vice-president at the 1860 Republican Convention on the ticket of Abraham Lincoln. Father of automobile inventor, George Baldwin Selden.

SELYE, LEWIS Jul 11, 1803 Chittenango, NY - Jan 27, 1883 Rochester, NY
United States Representative-NY from 1867-1869. Founded the *Rochester Daily Chronicle* in 1868.

SHATTO (Schang)**, LILLIAN** Jun 1885 Eagle, NY - Jun 15, 1931 Rochester, NY
Sister of Wally Schang, catcher for the Philadelphia Athletics, Boston Red Sox, New York Yankees, St.

Louis Browns and Detroit Tigers from 1913-1931, winning four World Series championships, and Bobby Schang, catcher for the Pittsburgh Pirates, New York Giants and St. Louis Cardinals from 1914-1915 and 1927.

SHIPMAN, PARSON GENET Apr 18, 1799 Roxbury, CT - Jan 19, 1871 Rochester, NY
Physician, one of five brothers who became doctors. Great-grandfather of Dorothy Louise Gage, niece of author, L. Frank Baum, who used her name, "Dorothy", in his children's books, *The Wonderful Wizard of Oz*.

SIBLEY, HIRAM Feb 6, 1807 North Adams, MA - Jul 12, 1888 Rochester, NY
Co-founder and first President of the Western Union Telegraph Company. Friend of Tsar Alexander I of Russia and United States Secretary of State, William H. Seward. Instigated the United States purchase of Alaska from Russia, using a United States Government check through Western Union, not long after opening the Russian-American Telegraph route through the two countries and Canada.

SIBLEY, RUFUS A. Oct 2, 1841 Boston, MA - Mar 11, 1928 Rochester, NY
Founded Sibley's Department Store, with Alexander M. Lindsay and John Curr, in Rochester in 1868.

STEDMAN, JOHN HARRY 1843 Newport, RI - Oct 29, 1922 Rochester, NY
Invented the fuzzy pipe cleaner and the streetcar transfer. Revived the custom of placing a lighted candle in a window during the Christmas holiday season, in 1913.

STEELE, FLETCHER (John) Jun 7, 1885 Rochester, NY - Jul 16, 1971 Rochester, NY
Landscape architect from 1915-1971.

STEPHENS, FELICIA L. 1969 - Dec 26, 1989 Rochester, NY
Final victim of serial killer, Arthur John Shawcross, known as "The Genesee River Killer." Shawcross was paroled from state prison in 1987, serving 15 years for the murders of two young children in Watertown. He moved to Rochester, killing and eating the genitals of eleven Rochester-area prostitutes. He was convicted and sentenced to 250 years in state prison.

STOUT, IRA (Marion) Sept 18, 1835 Wilkes-Barre, PA - Oct 22, 1858 Rochester, NY
Bludgeoned his brother-in-law, Charles W. Littles, with a hammer, following a sensational trial covered by most of the Northeast, convicted of murder. Gained some sympathy for defending his sister, Sarah Stout Littles, from her abusive husband, though most accounts claim they shared an incestuous, brother-sister bond. Despite the support of Susan B. Anthony and Frederick Douglass to commute his death sentence, he was hanged.

STRONG (Woodbury), **MARGARET** Mar 20, 1897 Rochester, NY - Jul 15, 1969 Rochester, NY
World's largest collector of dolls, dollhouses, shells and Oriental art. Established the Margaret Woodbury Strong Museum of Fascinations in Pittsford.

STRONG, THERON RUDD Nov 7, 1802 Salisbury, CT - May 14, 1873 New York, NY
United States Representative-NY from 1839-1841. Associate Justice of the New York State Supreme Court from 1851-1859. Associate Justice of the New York State Court of Appeals in 1859.

THORPE (Cody), **ARTA LUCILLE** Dec 16, 1866 Leavenworth, KS - Jan 30, 1904 Spokane, WA
Oldest child of Wild West showman, William F. "Buffalo Bill" Cody. Mother of Arta Clara Boal and William Cody Boal, grandchildren of Buffalo Bill.

VAN DE VENTER, JOHN J. 1848 - Jan 8, 1911 Rochester, NY
Invented and manufactured the single blade pencil sharpener.

VAN VOORHIS, JOHN Oct 22, 1806 Decatur, NY - Oct 20, 1905 Rochester, NY
United States Representative-NY from 1879-1883.

VICK, JAMES Nov 13, 1818 Portsmouth, England - May 16, 1882 Rochester, NY
Horticulturist and publisher. Founded the Vick Seed Company in Rochester, importing seeds by mail-order through his seed catalogs.

WALD, LILLIAN D. Mar 10, 1867 Cincinnati, OH - Sept 1, 1940 Westport, CT
Nurse, social worker, women's rights activist and public health official. Founded the Henry Street Settlement in New York City in 1893. Named one of the 12 greatest-living American women by the *New York Times* in 1922.

WARD, HENRY AUGUSTUS Mar 9, 1834 Rochester, NY - Jul 4, 1906 Buffalo, NY
Geologist. Founded Ward's Natural Science Establishment, internationally-known provider of educational materials in science. Mounted "Jumbo" the elephant, located at the P.T. Barnum Museum at Tufts University. Jumbo's skeletal remains are located at the National Museum in Washington D.C. Stuck and killed by a car walking across a street, one of the first automobile fatalities, the other driver was charged with manslaughter. Nephew of Levi A. Ward, Mayor of Rochester from 1849-1850.

WARD, LEVI A. 1801 - Aug 6, 1881 Rochester, NY
Mayor of Rochester from 1849-1850. Uncle of geologist, Henry A. Ward.

WARFIELD, WILLIAM CAESAR Jan 22, 1920 West Helena, AR - Aug 25, 2002 Chicago, IL
Baritone singer. Known for his signature rendition of "Ol' Man River" in *Showboat*. Married operatic soprano, Leontyne Price, in 1952, separated in 1958, did not divorce until 1972.

WHIPPLE, GEORGE HOYT Aug 28, 1878 Ashland, NH - Feb 1, 1976 Rochester, NY
Awarded the Noble Prize for Physiology and Medicine in 1934.

WHITLEY, JAMES LUCIUS May 24, 1872 Rochester, NY - May 17, 1959 Rochester, NY
United States Representative-NY from 1929-1935. New York State Senator from 1918-1928.

WHITTLESEY, FREDERICK Jun 12, 1799 New Preston, CT - Sept 19, 1851 Rochester, NY
United States Representative-NY from 1831-1835. Associate Justice of the New York State Supreme
Court from 1847-1848.

WILDER, ABEL CARTER Mar 18, 1828 Mendon, MA - Dec 22, 1875 San Francisco, CA
United States Representative-KS from 1863-1865. Mayor of Rochester from 1872-1873. Published the
Morning Express and *Evening Express* in Rochester.

WILLIAMS, JOHN Jan 7, 1807 Utica, NY - Mar 26, 1875 Rochester, NY
United States Representative-NY from 1855-1857. Mayor of Rochester in 1853-1854.

ZWEIGLE, C. WILHELM 1849 - Nov 19, 1883 Rochester, NY
Founded Zweigle's Sausage Shop in Rochester in 1880, maker of the "white hot" hotdogs.

MOUNT HOPE CEMETERY
Burgoyne Road
Ticonderoga, NY 12883

BURLEIGH, HENRY GORDON Jun 2, 1832 Canaan, NH - Aug 10, 1900 Whitehall, NY
United States Representative-NY from 1883-1887. Secretary of the first Republican Convention in
New York, in 1855. Built his home in Ticonderoga in 1894, the H.G. Burleigh House, listed in the
National Register of Historic Places in 1988.

MOUNT MORRIS CEMETERY
Sand Hill Road
Mount Morris, NY 14510

HASTINGS, GEORGE Mar 13, 1807 Clinton, NY - Aug 29, 1866 Mount Morris, NY
U.S. Representative-NY from 1853-1855.

KYLE, REED W. Jun 23, 1893 Wayland, NY - Apr 1968 Mount Morris, NY
Father-in-law of John C. Prentice, co-founder of Car-Fresheners Corporation in Watertown in 1952,
with chemist, Julius "Jules" Sämann, manufacturer of Little Trees car air fresheners. Grandfather of
Grammy Award-winning musician, songwriter and producer, Mark Prentice.

MOUNT OLIVET CEMETERY
Adams Street
Frankfort, NY 13340

KILGRESS (Walsh)**, KATHRYN** Nov 16, 1916 Schuyler, NY - Oct 24, 2011 Frankfort, NY
Sister of Edward J. Walsh, head football coach at Manhasset High School, Long Island, where he coached and mentored Hall of Fame running back, Jim Brown, as well as Olympian, Jim Thorpe.

MOUNT OLIVET CEMETERY
4000 Elmwood Avenue
Kenmore, NY 14217

AILINGER, JAMES J. Jul 10, 1901 Buffalo, NY - Mar 27, 2001 Rochester, NY
Oldest-lived, former NFL player at the time of his death. Played for the Buffalo Bisons in 1924, retiring to become a dentist.

CAHILL (Russell)**, JILL** Mar 9, 1957 North Tonawanda, NY - Oct 28, 1998 Syracuse, NY
Murder victim. Mother of two, bludgeoned to near death with an aluminum baseball bat by her husband, Jeff (James F.) Cahill, in their Spafford home, April 22, 1998. He attacked again, six months later, as she drifted in and out of a coma at University Hospital in Syracuse, using false documentation to get a California laboratory to send cyanide to a company in DeWitt, disguised himself as a nurse, threw the powdered cyanide in her bed, causing her death. He was the first person in Onondaga County sentenced to death since New York State reinstated the death penalty, later commuted to life in prison.

CARROLL, SCRAPPY (John E.) Aug 27, 1860 Buffalo, NY - Nov 14, 1942 Buffalo, NY
Outfielder for the St. Paul White Caps, Buffalo Bisons and Cleveland Blues from 1884-1887.

JONES, ELMER JOHN Aug 4, 1920 Buffalo, NY - Feb 21, 1996 New Smyrna, FL
Buffalo Bisons and Detroit Lions guard and linebacker, from 1946-1948. Nicknamed "Buck." Drafted in the 2nd by the New York Giants in 1946.

MACKINNON, BOB (Robert Albert) Dec 5, 1927 Dunkirk, NY - Jul 7, 2015 Williamsville, NY
Head coach of the Spirits of St. Louis in the ABA from 1974-1975, the Buffalo Braves in 1977 and the New Jersey Nets from 1980-1981 and 1987-1988. Head coach of Canisius College from   1959-1972. Syracuse Nationals guard in 1951. Catcher in the Brooklyn Dodgers organization from 1950-1951. Inducted into the greater Buffalo Sports Hall of Fame in 1995.

MCCARTHY, JOE (Joseph Vincent) Apr 21, 1887 Philadelphia, PA - Jan 13, 1978 Buffalo, NY
Manager of the Chicago Cubs, New York Yankees and Boston Red Sox from 1926-1946 and
1948-1950. Nicknamed "Marse Joe." Won seven World Series as Yankees manager, including four
straight from 1936-1939. Lou Gehrig's manager when he removed himself from the lineup, ending his
record games played streak. Inducted into the Baseball Hall of Fame in 1957. Retired with 2,125
career wins and the highest winning percentage for any manager in history. Managed Hall of Famers,
Babe Ruth, Lou Gehrig, Joe DiMaggio, Earl Combs, Bill Dickey, Lefty Gomez. Red Ruffing, Phil
Rizzuto, Joe Gordon, Rogers Hornsby, Hack Wilson, Kiki Cuyler, Ted Williams and Bobby Doerr.

MILLER, VAN Nov 22, 1927 Dunkirk, NY - Jul 17, 2015 Buffalo, NY
Sportscaster. Play-by-play announcer for the Buffalo Bills from 1960-2004 and the Buffalo Braves of
the NBA from 1971-1977. Received the Pro Football Hall of Fame's Pete Rozelle Radio-Television
Award in 2004. Inducted into the Buffalo Bills Wall of Fame in 2014.

NILAND, CLARRISA M. Feb 15, 1910 Tonawanda, NY - Jan 25, 1996 Tonawanda, NY
Sister of Frederick William "Fritz" Niland, the inspiration for Private Ryan in the film, *Saving Private
Ryan*, and Robert Niland and Preston Niland, killed one day apart, in the Allied invasion of Europe in
1944, and Edward Niland, shot down over Burma, thought to be killed in action, spent eleven months
as a prisoner-of-war.

NILAND, JOE (Joseph P.) Oct 24, 1917 Tonawanda, NY - Feb 18, 2007 Buffalo, NY
Captain of the Canisius College basketball team from 1939-1942. Head coach of Canisius from
1947-1953. Brother of Tom Niland, LeMoyne College head basketball coach from 1948-1975. Cousin
of Frederick "Fritz" Niland, the inspiration for Private Ryan in the film, *Saving Private Ryan*, and his
brothers, Robert Niland and Preston Niland, killed in the Allied invasion of Europe in 1944, and
Edward Niland, shot down over Burma, thought to be killed in action, spent eleven months as a
prisoner-of-war. Uncle of John Beilein, head basketball coach for LeMoyne College, Canisius,
Richmond, West Virginia and Michigan.

NILAND, MICHAEL C. Jan 30, 1878 Lockport, NY - Sept 26, 1964 Tonawanda, NY
With **Augusta Witzke Niland** (1882 Tonawanda, NY - Oct 12, 1964 Tonawanda, NY), the parents of
Frederick William "Fritz" Niland, the inspiration for Private Ryan in the film, *Saving Private Ryan*, and
Robert J. Niland and Preston T. Niland, killed one day apart, in the Allied invasion of Europe in 1944,
and Edward F. Niland, shot down over Burma, thought to be killed in action, spent eleven months as a
prisoner-of-war, before his escape. Robert and Preston are buried side-by-side in the American
Cemetery, Normandy, France, Fritz died December, 1, 1983 in San Francisco, age 63, buried in Fort
Richardson National Cemetery, Alaska.

PAUL (Papa), **TOMMY** (Gaetano Alfonso) Mar 4, 1909 Buffalo, NY - Apr 28, 1991 Buffalo, NY
Professional boxer. World featherweight champion from 1932-1933.

PORTALE, RUSS (Sebastian Russell) May 21, 1914 Jamestown, NY - May 18, 2012 Wheatfield, NY
With **Josephine M. Julian Portale** (Aug 13, 1911 - Apr 23, 1999 Buffalo, NY), the parents of Carl J. Portale, publisher of *Harper's Bazaar* and *Elle*, and mentor to John F. Kennedy Jr. at *George* magazine.

ROJEK, STAN (Stanley Andrew) Apr 21, 1919 North Tonawanda, NY - Jul 9, 1997 North Tonawanda, NY
Shortstop for the Brooklyn Dodgers, Pittsburgh Pirates, St. Louis Cardinals and St. Louis Browns from 1942 and 1946-1952. Member of the Dodgers 1947 National League Pennant winning team. Shared a locker next to Jackie Robinson when he broke baseball's color barrier in 1947.

SMITH, CHARLES BENNETT Sept 14, 1870 Sardinia, NY - May 21, 1939 Wilmington, NY
United States Representative-NY from 1911-1919.

STANLEY, WINIFRED CLARE Aug 14, 1909 New York, NY - Feb 29, 1996 Kenmore, NY
United States Representative-NY from 1943-1945.

WINTRINGER (Sypnier)**, JUDITH ANN** Nov 14, 1939 Buffalo, NY - Feb 5, 2014 Buffalo, NY
Daughter of convicted pedophile, Theodore A. Sypnier, New York State's oldest prison inmate at the time of his death, December 7, 2010, age 101, at the Coxsackie Correctional Facility.

MOUNT OLIVET CEMETERY
Wood Road
Whitesboro, NY 13492

ANDERSON, IAN MACKENZIE May 29, 1938 Kirkland Lake, ON, Canada - Nov 20, 2013 Kirkland, NY
Defenseman and enforcer for the Clinton Comets of the EHL from 1965-1970. Member of three consecutive Walker Cup championship teams, including the Comets 1967-1968 team that lost only five games, the lowest total in modern hockey history. Skated over a coin on the ice, damaging his knee, ending his career. Died 11 days before his brother, minor league hockey center, Brian Anderson.

CLANCY, BILL Apr 12, 1879 Redfield, NY - Feb 10, 1948 Oriskany, NY
First baseman for the Pittsburgh Pirates in 1905. Teammate of Hall of Famers, Honus Wagner and Fred Clarke.

DOUGLAS, FRED JAMES Sept 14, 1869 Clinton, MA - Jan 1, 1949 Utica, NY
United States Representative-NY from 1937-1945. Mayor of Utica from 1922-1924.

KIEFER, JOE Jul 19, 1899 West Leyden, NY - Jul 5, 1975 Utica, NY
Pitched 15 games, losing all five of his decisions, for the Chicago White Sox and Boston Red Sox in

1920 and 1925-1926. Pitched for the White Sox one year after their "Black Sox" World Series loss to the Cincinnati Reds.

SISSON, FREDERICK JAMES Mar 31, 1879 Wells Bridge, NY - Oct 20, 1949 Washington D.C.
United States Representative-NY from 1933-1937.

TALARICO (Sgroi)**, JOSIE** (Josephine) Jul 1914 Frankfort, NY - Mar 29, 2002 New Hartford, NY
Subject of the cookbook, *Josie's Recipe Collection: From Cooks and Kitchens of Central New York*, published by her daughter, Karen Talarico, in 2004.

VAN SLYKE (Horan)**, GERTRUDE M.** Jun 20, 1926 Utica, NY - Nov 23, 2015 Syracuse, NY
Aunt of Susan Horan Kirsteins, the daughter-in-law of Mikelis Kirsteins, member of the Latvian Military Police Force used by Nazi's to murder 30,000 Jews in Latvia during World War II. He died, January 26, 1994 in Utica, before final action was taken by the United States Justice Department to deport him for his war crimes.

MOUNT PLEASANT CEMETERY
Mount Pleasant Cemetery Road
Canastota, NY 13032

BOUCHARD, JOSEPH EDWIN 1843 Lisbon, NY - Jul 20, 1879 Canastota, NY
With **Mary Lavona Tubbs Bouchard** (Apr 20, 1848 North Bay, NY - Sept 1, 1928 Canastota, NY), the great-grandparents of drummer, Albert Bouchard and bassist, Joe Bouchard, founding members of the rock band, Blue Öyster Cult.

DELANO, MILTON Aug 11, 1844 Wampsville, NY - Jan 2, 1922 Syracuse, NY
United States Representative-NY from 1887-1891.

REESE, CHAUNCEY BARNES Dec 28, 1837 Canastota, NY - Sept 22, 1870 Mobile, AL
Civil War Union Army Brevet Brigadier General. Fought in the Battle of Gettysburg in July 1863.

MOUNT PLEASANT CEMETERY
Route 5
Elbridge, NY 13060

LOFFT, SEYMOUR CHAUNCY Jul 13, 1891 NY - Feb 14, 1980 Auburn, NY
Elbridge Chief of Police from 1939-1980. Oldest active police chief in New York State at the time of his death.

MUNRO, NATHAN Mar 5, 1789 Lanesboro, MA - Jul 5, 1839 Elbridge, NY

Founded the Munro Academy, later the Munro Collegiate Institute, in Elbridge in 1835. Son of Squire Munro, early settler in the town of Elbridge. Brother of Judge David Munro, early settler in the town of Camillus. Father-in-law of John B. Burnet, namesake of Burnet Park in Syracuse.

MOUNT PLEASANT CEMETERY
Summit Street
Fairport, NY 14450

FAIRPORT FIVE ANGELS Jun 26, 2007 East Bloomfield, NY

Five young women, four of them cheerleaders, five days past their graduation from Fairport High School, were killed when their SUV veered into the lane of an oncoming tractor-trailer, bursting into flames, on Routes 5 and 20, 30 minutes south of Rochester, as the girls were heading to a parents' camp on Keuka Lake. Following behind the five girls were four more friends who witnessed the crash. Of the five victims, three were buried in Mount Pleasant Cemetery, the driver, **Bailey Elizabeth Goodman**, born October 17, 1989, **Hannah Louise Congdon**, born September 13, 1988 and **Meredith Selene McClure**, born August 22, 1989. Katherine Ciardi Shirley and Sara Marie Monnat were the other victims. A moment of silence was held for the girls by the United States House of Representatives, June 28, 2007.

MOUNT PLEASANT CEMETERY
Route 19
Houghton, NY 14744

BAKER (Shea)**, GRACE HOLDEN** Nov 6, 1923 Ottawa, ON, Canada - Apr 11, 1999 Syracuse, NY

Sister of Grammy Award-winning gospel singer, George Beverly Shea.

SHEA, ADAM JOSEPH Oct 24, 1872 Curran, ON, Canada - Nov 28, 1946 Houghton, NY

Methodist Minister. Fourth pastor of the Willett Memorial Wesleyan Methodist Church, 511 South Midler Avenue in Syracuse. With **Maude Mary Whitney Shea** (Feb 27, 1881 Merrickville, ON, Canada - Sept 1, 1971 Syracuse, NY), the parents of Grammy Award-winning gospel singer, George Beverly Shea, remembered for his performances with the Billy Graham Crusades and his rendition of "How Great Thou Art."

WRIGHT, KENNETH W. Jun 13, 1912 Syracuse, NY - Feb 16, 2003 Syracuse, NY

First admitting physician for Community General Hospital in Syracuse. Brother-in-law of Grammy Award-winning gospel singer, George Beverly Shea.

WRIGHT (Shea), **LOIS LAURA** Aug 31, 1916 Ottawa, ON, Canada - Jul 16, 2012 Syracuse, NY
Sister of Grammy Award-winning gospel singer, George Beverly Shea.

MOUNT PLEASANT CEMETERY
Park Street
Port Byron, NY 13140

BARRUS, CLARA 1864 Port Byron, NY - Apr 6, 1931 Scarsdale, NY
Physician and author. Longtime partner of naturalist, John Burroughs. Wrote the biographies, *Our Friend, John Burroughs* and *John Burroughs, Boy and Man*. Named literary executor following the death of Burroughs in 1921.

BARRUS, JOHN W. Aug 1830 Port Byron, NY - Feb 3, 1908 Port Byron, NY
With **Sarah C. Barrus** (Nov 1833 NY - Feb 7, 1908 Port Byron, NY), the parents of physician and author, Clara Barrus. Killed in an accidental fire set in his home. He turned on the draughts in the fireplace, returned to bed, only to be awakened an hour later by smoke and fire, his wife, died four days later from burns and smoke inhalation.

BUNN, MARTIN HESLOR Jun 6, 1850 Port Byron, NY - Feb 16, 1910 Syracuse, NY
With **Ida Homel Bunn** (Nov 1855 Port Byron, NY - Jun 11, 1935 Syracuse, NY), the parents of Richard Bonelli, operatic baritone, notably with the Metropolitan Opera Company.

DURGEE, THEODORE R. Aug 10, 1905 Parish, NY - Jun 10, 1973 Baldwinsville, NY
Baldwinsville educator. Namesake of Theodore R. Durgee Junior High School in Baldwinsville.

HINMAN (Blaisdell), **JENNA** Nov 22, 1987 Auburn, NY - May 5, 2014 Syracuse, NY
Fort Drum wife, died shortly after giving birth to twin girls, March 3, 2014 in Watertown, was discovered to have choriocarcinoma, a rare pregnancy-related cancer that would captivate social media and ultimately claim her life within two months.

KING, AMOS SCOTT Jan 1, 1822 Port Byron, NY - Aug 19, 1908 Port Byron, NY
Donated a bible to President-elect, Abraham Lincoln, inspired by Lincoln's farewell address to Springfield, February 11, 1861, though not the bible used for the President's inauguration, it remained as a treasured heirloom in the Lincoln family.

KING, RICHARD Nov 8, 1790 Halfmoon, NY - Apr 4, 1877 Port Byron, NY
Cayuga County homesteader. Built the first log cabin in Port Byron. Father of Amos Scott King.

PICKETT, JOHN WELCHER Sept 24, 1801 - Mar 25, 1862 Port Byron, NY
Father of sculptor, Byron M. Pickett, created the Samuel F.B. Morse statue, placed in Central Park, at 5th Avenue and 72nd Street, New York City in 1870.

RHOADES, KITTIE A. Apr 1855 Port Byron, NY - 1941 Port Byron, NY
Touring stage actress.

ROBERTS (Gregory)**, CAROL** Jun 25, 1942 Auburn, NY - Jan 24, 1997 Auburn, NY
Murder victim. Shot in the stomach by her husband, Jack Roberts, in their home, 5256 West Lake Road, town of Fleming, set fire to the house, drove to another property they owned, Howland Island Road, town of Mentz, set this house on fire and shot himself in the head.

ROBERTS, JACK (John D.) Sept 9, 1938 Auburn, NY - Jan 24, 1997 Port Byron, NY
Champion stock car race driver. Nicknamed "Fireball." Shot his wife, Carol Roberts, in her stomach, in their home, 5256 West Lake Road, town of Fleming, set fire to the house, drove to the M&M Diner in Port Byron, a diner he sold ten days prior, set the diner on fire, drove to another property they owned, Howland Island Road, town of Mentz, set this house on fire and shot himself in the head in his 1993 Cadillac, license plate, FIRE513.

SHUE (DeBottis)**, THEDA E.** 1920 Port Byron, NY - Jan 5, 1938 Fulton, NY
Murder victim. Married in 1934, age 14, to Joseph Shue, who more than three years later, distraught over their estrangement, shot her four times, stabbed her 10 more with a bayonet, threatened to kill his father-in-law, James DeBottis Sr. before turning the gun on himself.

MOUNT PLEASANT CEMETERY
Mount Pleasant Road
York, NY 14592

HAYDEN, MOSES 1786 Westfield, MA - Feb 13, 1830 Albany, NY
United States Representative-NY from 1823-1827.

MOUNT REPOSE CEMETERY
40 New Main Street
Haverstraw, NY 10927

CANIFF, MILTON ARTHUR PAUL Feb 28, 1907 Hillsboro, OH - May 3, 1988 New York, NY
Cartoonist. Created the comic strips, *Steve Canyon* and *Terry and the Pirates*. First recipient of the Cartoonist of the Year Award, in 1946.

DENOYELLES, PETER 1766 Haverstraw, NY - May 6, 1829 Haverstraw, NY
United States Representative-NY from 1813-1815.

HARRISON (Powers)**, NELL** Sept 28, 1880 Lebanon, MO - Dec 1973
Actress. Appeared in the film, *No Greater Love*, a small role in an episode of *The Honeymooners* in 1956.

HASKELL, REUBEN LOCKE Oct 5, 1878 Brooklyn, NY - Oct 2, 1971 Westwood, NJ
United States Representative-NY from 1915-1919.

LENYA (Blamauer)**, LOTTE** (Karoline) Oct 18, 1898 Vienna, Austria - Nov 27, 1981 New York, NY
Singer and actress. Won a Tony Award in 1956, the only time the award was given for an   Off-Broadway performance. Nominated for an Academy Award for *The Roman Spring of Mrs. Stone* in 1961. Appeared in the James Bond film, *From Russia with Love*. Recorded "Mack the Knife", a duet with Louis Armstrong in 1956. Wife of composer, Kurt Weill.

WEILL, KURT Mar 2, 1900 Dessau, Germany - Apr 3, 1950 New York, NY
Composer. Produced *The Threepenny Opera*, with Bertolt Brecht, which included their song, "Mack the Knife." Co-wrote "Alabama Song", "September Song" and "Lost in the Stars." Husband of singer and actress, Lotte Lenya.

MOUNT REST CEMETERY
South Lake Street / Route 19
Bergen, NY 14416

TONE, THOMAS JEFFERSON Jun 5, 1830 Bergen, NY - May 6, 1903 Bergen, NY
With **Catherine Delia Spafford Tone** (Dec 7, 1836 - Jan 7, 1916 NY), the grandparents of actor, Franchot Tone, husband of actresses, Joan Crawford, Jean Wallace, Barbara Payton and Dolores Dorn.

MOUNT VIEW CEMETERY
South Union Street / Route 16
Olean, NY 14760

BALL, WILLIAM WILSON Apr 4, 1847 East Hickory, PA - Feb 13, 1892 Olean, NY
Granduncle of Emmy Award-winning actress, Lucille Ball.

HASTINGS, JAMES FRED Apr 10, 1926 Olean, NY - Oct 24, 2014 Allegany, NY
United States Representative-NY from 1969-1976. Convicted of mail fraud in 1976, served 14 months in the United States Penitentiary, Allenwood.

HIGGINS, FRANK WAYLAND Aug 18, 1856 Rushford, NY - Feb 12, 1907 Olean, NY
Governor of New York from 1905-1907.

MARTIN, FREDERICK STANLEY Apr 25, 1794 Rutland, VT - Jun 28, 1865 Olean, NY
United States Representative-NY from 1851-1853. Postmaster of Olean from 1830-1839, appointed by President Andrew Jackson.

PORTER, TIMOTHY H. Nov 28, 1785 New Haven, CT - Dec 16, 1845 Olean, NY
United States Representative-NY from 1825-1827.

MYRTLE HILL CEMETERY
Myrtle Street
Syracuse, NY 13219

GERE, CHARLES Aug 19, 1803 Groton, CT - Nov 6, 1870 Syracuse, NY
Brother of salt manufacturer, Robert Gere and William Stanton Gere, builder of Gere Lock Farm in the town of Camillus.

HARVEY, HARRY Dec 14, 1846 England - Apr 2, 1896 Syracuse, NY
Awarded the Medal of Honor during the Civil War for capturing the Confederate flag and bearer at Waynesboro, VA in 1865.

JEROME, JAMES BISHOP Mar 12, 1788 Stockbridge, MA - Aug 8, 1852 Syracuse, NY
Cousin of Isaac Jerome, the great-grandfather of Sir Winston Churchill, Prime Minister of Great Britain from 1940-1945 and 1951-1955.

JOYCE (Tyler)**, PEARL MAY** Jul 9, 1862 Meridian, MI - Sept 16, 1886 New York, NY
New York stage actress, performed as Pearl Houghton, frequently in Syracuse as a member of the Madison Square Theater Company.

LITTLEHALES, CECIL W. 1874 Hamilton, ON, Canada - Mar 6, 1940 Syracuse, NY
Brother of concert singer and teacher, Florence T. Littlehales and concert cellist, Lillian Littlehales.

MARTINEAU, DANIEL LEROY Aug 29, 1900 Solvay, NY - Oct 25, 1961 Syracuse, NY
Suffered a heart attack, golfing at the Tecumseh Golf Club. With **Marion Alice Sidnam Martineau** (Oct 3, 1901 Solvay, NY - May 29, 1970 Syracuse, NY), the parents of Carol Martineau Baldwin, breast cancer survivor and founder of the Carol M. Baldwin Breast Cancer Research Fund, and the

grandparents of Academy Award-nominated actor, Alec Baldwin, and his acting brothers, Daniel, Billy and Steven Baldwin.

PAPWORTH, CHARLES HENRY 1868 Baldwinsville, NY - Apr 7, 1944 Syracuse, NY
Owned and operated Cash Papworth Grow-Sir, a chain of grocery stores in and around Syracuse, from 1882-1941.

PASS, JAMES Jun 1, 1856 Burslem, Staffordshire, England - Oct 30, 1913 Syracuse, NY
Founder and President of Pass & Seymour, Inc. in Syracuse, in 1890. President of the Onondaga Pottery Company from 1885-1913, founded by his father, Richard Pass. Invented a process which produced a translucent white china in 1890, winning a Medal of Honor at the Chicago World's Fair in 1893. Syracuse China first appeared on the backstamp of the their china in 1895. Namesake of the James Pass Arboretum in Syracuse.

PASS, RICHARD Oct 1824 Staffordshire, England - Jun 1880 Syracuse, NY
Founded the Onondaga Pottery Company in Syracuse in 1871. Father of James Pass, founder and President of Pass & Seymour, Inc. in Syracuse.

PERRY, OLIVER CURTIS Sept 17, 1865 Syracuse, NY - Sept 5, 1930 Dannemora, NY
Outlaw. First solo train robber in history, single-handedly holding up the *American Express Special*, September 1891, as it sped through New York State, stealing more than $78,000 in cash and jewelry. Pursued by the Pinkerton's, he was captured near Lyons, at the time, the country's most wanted man. Spent the final 49 years of his life in prison, despite several attempts to escape.

PHARIS, MILLS P. Nov 27, 1825 - Mar 2, 1892 Syracuse, NY
President of the Onondaga Pottery Company from 1890-1892. Father-in-law of Bert E. Salisbury, President of the Onondaga Pottery Company from 1913-1941. Grandfather of William R. Salisbury, President of the Onondaga Pottery Company from 1961-1971, as it transformed into Syracuse China.

NASSAU-SCHODACK CEMETERY
Chatham Street / Route 203
Nassau, NY 12123

GREGORY, HERBERT L. Oct 23, 1908 Syracuse, NY - May 2, 1966 Nassau, NY
Cousin of Walter L. Farley, best-selling author of the children's book, *The Black Stallion*.

MCCLELLAN, GEORGE Oct 10, 1856 Schodack Center, NY - Feb 20, 1927 Kinderhook, NY
United States Representative-NY from 1913-1915.

NATIONAL SHRINE OF THE JESUIT MARTYRS
Jesuit Cemetery / 136 Shrine Road
Auriesville, NY 12016

DULLES, AVERY ROBERT Aug 24, 1918 Auburn, NY - Dec 12, 2008 Bronx, NY
Roman Catholic Cardinal, selected by Pope John Paul II in 2001. First American elevated to Cardinal not to previously hold the rank of Bishop. Internationally-renowned author and lecturer. Professor of Religion and Society at Fordham University from 1988-2008. Son of John Foster Dulles, United States Secretary of State, under President Dwight D. Eisenhower. Great-grandson of John Watson Foster, United States Secretary of State, under President Benjamin Harrison. Nephew of Allen Welsh Dulles, first civilian Director of the CIA, from 1953-1961, and a member of the Warren Commission. Grandnephew of Robert Lansing, United States Secretary of State, under President Woodrow Wilson.

GOUPIL, RENE May 15, 1608 St. Martin-du-Bois, Angers, France - Sept 29, 1642 Auriesville, NY
Jesuit missionary. Canonized with Rene Goupil, John LaLonde and five others, by Pope Pius XI as "The North American Martyrs." Captured, tortured and tomahawked by the Iroquois.

JOGUES, ISAAC Jan 10, 1607 Orleans, France - Oct 18, 1646 Auriesville, NY
Jesuit missionary. Canonized with Rene Goupil, John LaLonde and five others, by Pope Pius XI as "The North American Martyrs." Clubbed and beheaded by the Mohawks as a sorcerer.

LALANDE, JEAN DE - Oct 18, 1946 Auriesville, NY
Jesuit missionary. Canonized with Rene Goupil, John LaLonde and five others, by Pope Pius XI as "The North American Martyrs." One of five founders of HIMEOBS International. Killed by the Mohawks with Isaac Jogues.

LOUGHRAN, JAMES N. Mar 22, 1940 Brooklyn, NY - Dec 23, 2006 Jersey City, NJ
President of Loyola Marymount University in Los Angeles from 1984-1991. President of St. Peter's College in Jersey City from 1995-2006. Died from injuries suffered in a fall in his home.

MCKEON, RICHARD MOORE Sept 5, 1897 Elmira, NY - Apr 27, 1983 Syracuse, NY
One of five founders of LeMoyne College in Syracuse, in 1945. Prolific writer, published in religious and secular journals.

RYAN, VINCENT B. Nov 5, 1914 Buffalo, NY - Oct 15, 2005 Bronx, NY
Founding member of the Jesuit faculty at LeMoyne College in Syracuse. Inducted into the LeMoyne College Athletic Hall of Fame in 1984.

NEW FOREST CEMETERY
2001 Oneida Street
Utica, NY 13501

CASH, DAVID Apr 14, 1917 - Nov 21, 1971 Utica, NY
Father of Dave Cash, All-Star second baseman for the Pittsburgh Pirates, Philadelphia Phillies, Montreal Expos and San Diego Padres from 1969-1980.

DODGE, SAM Dec 9, 1889 Neath, PA - Apr 5, 1966 Utica, NY
Pitched four games for the Boston Red Sox from 1921-1922.

FAIRBANK, JIM Mar 17, 1881 Deansboro, NY - Dec 27, 1955 Utica, NY
Pitched seven games for the Philadelphia Athletics, from 1903-1904, managed by Hall of Famer, Connie Mack. Teammate of Hall of Fame pitchers, Eddie Plank, Rube Waddell and Chief Bender.

KLEESPIES, JOSEPH 1836 Würzburg, Bavaria, Germany - Oct 18, 1894 Utica, NY
Owned and operated the Germania Hotel in Utica.

MILLS, WILLIE (William Grant) Aug 15, 1877 Schenevus, NY - Mar 14, 1933 Utica, NY
Pitcher for the New York Giants for two games in 1901. Father of Art Mills, pitcher for the Boston Braves from 1927-1928.

RATHBONE, JUSTUS HENRY Oct 29, 1839 Deerfield, NY - Dec 9, 1889 Lima, OH
Founded the Knights of Pythias in 1864, one of the world's oldest fraternal organizations.

NEW HAVEN CEMETERY
Route 104
New Haven, NY 13121

ALLEN (Searles)**, SUSAN K.** 1949 Oswego, NY - Sept 16, 2015 New Haven, NY
Died on what would have been the 40th birthday of her daughter, Heidi Allen, murder victim, missing since April 3, 1994 in New Haven, her body was never found.

MUNSON, AUDREY Jun 8, 1891 Mexico, NY - Feb 20, 1996 Ogdensburg, NY
Model and film actress. Known as "America's Venus" and "Miss Manhattan." Posed nude for the world's most famous sculptors and painters, a particular favorite of sculptor, Daniel Chester French, who created the Lincoln Memorial in Washington D.C. Her image can be found in statues throughout New York City, including 40 pieces owned by the Metropolitan Museum of Art, and on the Walking Liberty Half-Dollar and Mercury Head Dime coins. First actress to appear nude in films, starring in *Inspiration*, *Purity* and *The Girl o' Dreams*. Attempted suicide in 1931, following a bout of depression and confined to the Ogdensburg Psychiatric Institution for the remainder of her life.

SEARLES, SHAWNACY J. Aug 23, 1974 Oswego, NY - Jun 29, 1995 Scriba, NY
Cousin of Heidi Allen, missing since April 3, 1994 in New Haven, her body was never found. Died in a motorcycle accident, the last in a series of tragedies for the family, also losing an uncle and two aunts since Heidi Allen's disappearance.

NEW HOPE CEMETERY
Route 41A
Moravia, NY 13118

WEED, LELAND Apr 30, 1919 Grove, NY - Jun 20, 1996 Auburn, NY
Founded, owned and operated New Hope Mills, maker of pancake mix and flour, from 1947-1982.

NEW PALTZ RURAL CEMETERY
81 Plains Road
New Paltz, NY 12561

HASBROUCK, JOSIAH Mar 5, 1755 New Paltz, NY – Mar 19, 1821 Plattekill, NY
United States Representative-NY from 1803-1805 and 1817-1819. Locust Lawn, his final home, is listed as a Registered Historic Place, off Route 32, town of Gardiner.

LEFEVER, JACOB Apr 20, 1830 New Paltz, NY - Feb 4, 1905 New Paltz, NY
United States Representative-NY from 1893-1897. Father of Frank Jacob LeFever, United States Representative-NY from 1905-1907.

PATTERSON, FLOYD Jan 4, 1935 Waco, NC - May 11, 2006 New Paltz, NY
Heavyweight boxing champion from 1956-1959 and 1960-1962. Won the gold medal, middleweight class, in the 1952 Olympic Games. Knocked out Archie Moore in 1956, becoming the youngest heavyweight champion in history. First Olympic gold medal-winner to become champion. Lost to Muhammad Ali in 1972, the last fight of his career. Inducted into the International Boxing Hall of Fame in 1991.

TSCHIRKY, OSCAR Sept 28, 1866 La Chaux-de-Fonds, Switzerland - Nov 6, 1950 New Paltz, NY
Maître d'hôtel of the Waldorf-Astoria Hotel in New York City from 1893-1950. Commonly known as "Oscar of the Waldorf." Created the Waldorf Salad, the recipe making its first appearance in his book, *The Cook Book*, in 1896.

NEW WOODSTOCK CEMETERY
Route 13
New Woodstock, NY 13122

JAQUITH, HOWARD Jul 7, 1927 Syracuse, NY - Jul 6, 1998 Rochester, NY
President of Jaquith Industries in Syracuse, founded as Vega Industries in 1919.

STANTON, OLIVER Oct 16, 1780 Stonington, CT - Nov 30, 1854 New Woodstock, NY
With **Rose Underwood Stanton** (Jan 27, 1790 Stonington, CT - Dec 18, 1854 Algeria), the grandparents of L. Frank Baum, author of *The Wonderful Wizard of Oz* series of children's books.

NEWARK CEMETERY
Main Street / Route 88
Newark, NY 14513

BLACKMAR, ESBON Jun 19, 1805 Freehold, NY - Nov 19, 1957 Newark, NY
U.S. Representative-NY from 1848-1849. Elected to Congress due to the death of John M. Holley.

BROWN, EDITH S. 1912 Newark, NY - Mar 2, 1930 Newark, NY
Newark High School student musician and captain of the girls' basketball team, accepted to the University of Michigan, shot and killed by her neighbor, Clark Weinman, who claimed he shot his gun while drunk, attempting to frighten his wife into thinking he committed suicide. Grandniece of Joseph D. Senn, Associate Justice of the New York State Supreme Court.

HILL, JAMES SAMUEL 1845 Lyons, NY - Apr 10, 1865 Danville, VA
Civil War Union Army Sergeant. Prisoner-of-war, awarded the Congressional Medal of Honor in 1864. Died five days before the assassination of President Abraham Lincoln.

NEWPORT CEMETERY
7517-7527 Main Street
Newport, NY 13416

FRANCISCO, JOHN EMERSON Aug 8, 1860 - Apr 19, 1951 Newport, NY
With **Mary Ann Franklin Francisco** (1862 - 1927 Newport, NY), the grandparents of Edward J. Walsh, head football coach at Manhasset High School, Long Island, where he coached and mentored Hall of Fame running back, Jim Brown, as well as Olympian, Jim Thorpe.

WILLOUGHBY, WESTEL Nov 27, 1769 Goshen, CT - Oct 3, 1844 Newport, NY
United States Representative-NY from 1815-1817. President of the College of Physicians and Surgeons from 1812-1844, now the SUNY Upstate Medical University. Namesake of the town of Willoughby, OH.

NEWTOWN BAPTIST CHURCH CEMETERY
Farm to Market Road
Mechanicville, NY 12118

MOTT, JOHN May 4, 1806 Halfmoon, NY - Oct 7, 1846 Halfmoon, NY
With **Jane Gates Mott** (Dec 10, 1805 Halfmoon, NY - Mar 15, 1874 Gurn Spring, NY), the parents of Samuel R. Mott, founder of Mott's, Inc., maker of apple cider, juices and sauces.

NINE PARTNERS CEMETERY
Church Street
Millbrook, NY 12545

FRANCOIS, MCKINLEY H. Feb 28, 1946 - Nov 8, 1999 Poughkeepsie, NY
Father of serial killer, Kendall L. Francois, former middle school hall monitor who solicited prostitutes, strangled them, dismembered their bodies, hiding them in his home, 99 Fulton Street, Poughkeepsie, over a 22-month period, 1996-1998. He died in the Wende Correctional Facility, Alden, September 11, 2014, age 43, serving a life sentence.

TITUS, OBADIAH Jan 20, 1789 Millbrook, NY - Sept 2, 1854 Millbrook, NY
United States Representative-NY from 1837-1839.

NINEVEH PRESBYTERIAN CEMETERY
Route 7
Nineveh, NY 13813

HART, JOHNNY Feb 18, 1931 Endicott, NY - Apr 7, 2007 Nineveh, NY
Comic strip illustrator. Created the syndicated strip *B.C.* in 1958. Co-created the *Wizard of Id* in 1964, with Brant Parker. Designed the logo for the Broome County Dusters of the AHL.

NORTH BAY LAWN CEMETERY
West Lake Street
North Bay, NY 13123

LOOMIS, GEORGE WASHINGTON Feb 22, 1814 NY - Sept 6, 1889 North Bay, NY
Grandfather of Lee B. Loomis, founder of the Loomis Armored Car Service in Portland in 1925. 4th cousin of George Washington Loomis, patriarch of the Loomis Gang, brothers, Wash, Grove and Plumb Loomis, outlaws who terrorized Oneida and Madison Counties in the mid-1800s.

NORTH BRANT LAKE CEMETERY
Beaver Pond Road
Brant Lake, NY 12815

BROX (Brock)**, PATRICIA** (Kathlyn) Jun 14, 1906 - Aug 27, 1988 New York, NY
Singer. Performed with her sisters, Bobbe and Lorayne Brox, as the Brox Sisters. Appeared in the film, *The Hollywood Revue of 1929*. Performed in Irving Berlin's *Music Box Revue*, from 1921-1924, on Broadway in the Marx Brothers comedy, *The Cocoanuts*, from 1925-1926, and in the Ziegfeld Follies of 1927, with Eddie Cantor. Retired, married Robert B. Gerstenzang in 1930. Sister-in-law of composer, Jimmy Van Heusen.

BUSSE, HENRY May 19, 1889 Madgeburg, Germany - Apr 23, 1955 Memphis, TN
Jazz trumpeter. Worked with sweet bands, often with Bing Crosby. Performed with the Paul Whiteman Orchestra. Member of the house band at Chez Paree, a Chicago nightclub owned by Al Capone. Composed "Wang Wang Blues", with Gussie Mueller. Died on tour, cremated at Chapel of the Pines Crematory, Los Angeles, his ashes remained in storage until 1988, when buried next to singer, Patricia Brox, in the Gerstenzang family plot.

NORTH BROOKFIELD CEMETERY
Route 12
North Brookfield, NY 13418

LAPE, WILLARD EVERETT Jun 6, 1900 Troy, NY - Nov 23, 1974 Syracuse, NY
With **Mabel Kling Lape** (May 9, 1903 - Apr 30, 1993 East Aurora, NY), the parents of Willard E. Lape Jr., Central New York children's television host known as "Bill Everett", portrayed "Salty Sam" and "Epal" on the *Monster Movie Matinee*.

NORTH BUSH CEMETERY
1009 North Bush Road
Caroga Lake, NY 12032

DUREY, CYRUS May 16, 1864 Caroga, NY - Jan 4, 1933 Albany, NY
United States Representative-NY from 1907-1911.

NORTH CHATHAM CEMETERY
Route 32
North Chatham, NY 12132

O'HANLON (Douglas)**, VIRGINIA** (Laura) Jul 20, 1889 New York, NY - May 13, 1971 Valatie, NY
New York City schoolteacher. Wrote a letter to the *New York Sun* in 1895, asking if Santa Claus really existed. Francis Pharcellus Church, an editor at the paper, replied in his editorial with the now famous line, "Yes, Virginia, there is a Santa Claus."

TEMPLE (Douglas)**, LAURA** Mar 20, 1914 NY - Feb 12, 1998
Daughter of Virginia Douglas O'Hanlon, whose childhood letter inspired the response, "Yes, Virginia, there is a Santa Claus." Survived a house fire with her mother and children, when alerted by a neighbor shortly after children visited the house selling Christmas cards, October 27, 1965.

NORTH CUBA CEMETERY
Smith Road
Cuba, NY 14727

COLBY, NATHAN 1781 Corinth Center, VT - May 22, 1857 North Cuba, NY
With **Eunice Blood Colby** (Jan 2, 1782 West Fairlee, VT - May 15, 1862 North Cuba, NY), the great-grandparents of Laura Ingalls-Wilder, author of *Little House on the Prairie*.

INGALLS (Delano)**, MARGARET** 1775 Tolland, CT - May 6, 1836 North Cuba, NY
Great-grandmother of Laura Ingalls-Wilder, author of *Little House on the Prairie*. Her husband, Samuel W. Ingalls, died Feb 15, 1841, age 69, buried Maple Lawn Cemetery, Bolivar, NY.

NORTH ELBA CEMETERY
Old Military Road
North Elba, NY 12946

DEWEY, MELVIL (Melville Louis) Dec 10, 1851 Adams Center, NY - Dec 26, 1931 Lake Placid, FL
Librarian and educator. Created the Dewey Decimal System in 1876. Founded the Lake Placid Club, a social and recreation club, in 1895.

JEWTRAW, CHARLES May 5, 1900 Harkness, NY - Jan 26, 1996 Palm Beach, FL
United States Olympic speed skater. Won the first gold medal ever issued at the Winter Olympics, in 1924. Held the national speed skating record for 100 yards, with a time of 9.4 seconds.

WOOD, CRAIG RALPH Nov 18, 1901 Lake Placid, NY - May 7, 1968 Palm Beach, FL
Professional golfer. Won 21 PGA championships, including the Masters and U.S. Open in 1941. First golfer to lose all four majors in a playoff. Lost the 1935 Masters to Gene Sarazen's double eagle. Elected to the World Golf Hall of Fame in 2008.

NORTH GUILFORD CEMETERY
Whites Hill Road
Guilford, NY 13780

KAUFINGER, GEORGE 1934 Guilford, NY - Mar 26, 2014 Lakeland, FL
Evangilistic Minister. Author of the books, *A Gardener Weeds God's Creation* and *Wealth of a Nation*. Great-grandson of Nelson W. Aldrich, U.S. Senator-RI from 1881-1911. Nephew of Hollywood film director, writer and producer, Robert Aldrich. Grandnephew of Abby Aldrich Rockefeller, the wife of financier, John D. Rockefeller Jr., who was the son of Standard Oil co-founder, John D. Rockefeller Sr., the world's wealthiest person at the time of his death.

KAUFINGER (Aldrich)**, RUTH** Feb 2, 1912 Cranston, RI - Jan 30, 1987 Guilford, NY
Sister of Robert Aldrich, film director, writer and producer notable for *The Dirty Dozen*, *Whatever Happened to Baby Jane?*, *The Longest Yard*, *Kiss Me Deadly* and *Hush ... Hush, Sweet Charlotte*. Granddaughter of Nelson W. Aldrich, U.S. Senator-RI from 1881-1911. Cousin of Nelson A. Rockefeller, Vice-President of the United States from 1974-1977, Winthrop Rockefeller, Governor of Arkansas from 1967-1971, and David Rockefeller, the world's oldest billionaire at the time of his death, age 101, in 2017. Niece of Abby Aldrich Rockefeller, the wife of financier, John D. Rockefeller Jr., who was the son of Standard Oil co-founder, John D. Rockefeller Sr., the world's wealthiest person at the time of his death. Grandniece of Richard S. Aldrich, U.S. Representative-RI from 1923-1933.

NORTH LANSING CEMETERY
Route 34
Lansing, NY 14882

UHL, HARRY ALLEN Dec 20, 1974 Ithaca, NY - Aug 17, 2002 Cayuga, NY
Victim of a hit-and-run boat accident off Myers Point, Cayuga Lake. Floyd P. Wright, the driver of the other boat, was convicted of tampering with physical evidence and failure to stop and report a boating accident, sentenced to four years in prison. The event was featured on the Court TV *Forensic Files* episode, *Dark Waters*.

NORTH PITCHER EPISCOPAL CHURCH CEMETERY
Route 26
North Pitcher, NY 13124

MILLS, CHARLES DE BERARD Jan 15, 1821 New Hartford, NY - May 13, 1900 Syracuse, NY
Abolitionist. Husband of Harriet Ann Mills, who used their home,1072 West Genesee Street, Syracuse, as a gathering place for well-known abolitionists and temperance leaders, including Bronson Alcott, Susan B. Anthony, Ralph Waldo Emerson, Lucretia Mott and William Lloyd Garrison. Father of suffragist, Harriet May Mills. Harriet Mills died February 24, 1928 in Syracuse, age 102.

MILLS, HARRIET MAY Aug 9, 1857 Syracuse, NY - May 16, 1935 Syracuse, NY
Suffragist. Democratic leader. Candidate for New York Secretary of State in 1920, the first woman to run for state office in New York. Friend and associate of President Franklin D. Roosevelt and First Lady Eleanor Roosevelt, who would attend her funeral.

NORTH ROAD CEMETERY
North Road / Route 62
Sandy Creek, NY 13145

MUZZY, ROBERT Sept 1769 Dublin, NH - Feb 2, 1829 Sandy Creek, NY
Revolutionary War Continental Army Captain. Served under General George Washington in Burgoyne's Rebellion and General Anthony Wayne in the Battle of Fallen Timbers. Father-in-law of Betsy Elizabeth Meachem, the 3rd great-granddaughter of Myles Standish, *Mayflower* passenger, called the "hero of New England."

NORTH SCRIBA UNION CEMETERY
North Road / Route 1
Oswego, NY 13126

DICKINSON, CARL E. Jan 18, 1914 Gilboa, NY - May 2, 2009 Oswego, NY
World War II veteran. Fought on D-Day, June 6, 1944, Utah Beach, Normandy. Defended Bastogne, Belgium during Operation Market Garden. A wax figure in his likeness is displayed in a Bastogne museum, commemorating his action in the Battle of the Bulge, and is referenced in several World War II books depicting the battle.

SHOUP, CURTIS F. Jan 11, 1921 Napanoch, NY - Jan 7, 1945 Tillet, Belgium
Awarded the Medal of Honor in World War II. Namesake of the freighter, *Sgt. Curtis F. Shoup.*

NORTH STREET CEMETERY
162-178 North Street
Auburn, NY 13021

DOUBLEDAY, JANE ANN Apr 5, 1830 Auburn, NY - Jul 12, 1843 Auburn, NY
Daughter of Ulysses Freeman Doubleday, United States Representative-NY from 1831-1833 and 1835-1837. Sister of Abner Doubleday, Civil War Union Army General and historically accepted inventor of baseball, and Civil War Union Army Brevet Brigadier General, Ulysses Doubleday Jr.

HULBERT, JOHN WHITEFIELD Jun 1, 1770 Alford, MA - Oct 19, 1831 Auburn, NY
United States Representative-MA from 1814-1817.

LYNDS, ELIZABETH H. Aug 1818 Auburn, NY - Jun 19, 1824 Auburn, NY
Daughter of Captain Elam Lynds, builder and first warden of Sing Sing Prison, and warden of Auburn Prison from 1822-1824 and 1838, died January 8, 1855 in New York City, age 70. Buried with her older sister, **Julia Ann Lynds,** who died ten years earlier, October 11, 1814, also age five.

POWERS, GERSHOM Jun 11, 1789 Croydon, NH - Jun 25, 1831 Auburn, NY
United States Representative-NY from 1829-1831.

SELOVER, ISAAC ABRAHAM Sept 26, 1772 Middlesex County, NJ - Jan 13, 1843 Auburn, NY
Brother of Syche "Sophia" Selover Davison, the grandmother of John Davison Rockefeller, co-founder of Standard Oil, first American billionaire.

NORTH SYRACUSE CEMETERY
555 South Bay Road
North Syracuse, NY 13212

BEE, FRANK (Francis W.) Dec 2, 1911 Syracuse, NY - Jun 11, 1990 Syracuse, NY
With **Louise Bee** (Jan 28, 1916 Syracuse, NY - Mar 1, 1995 Liverpool, NY), the parents of Award-winning Syracuse radio DJ, Ron Bee.

BURNHAM, HELEN May 13, 1916 Earlville, NY - Feb 12, 1998 North Syracuse, NY
Onondaga County Town Justice. First female town justice in Onondaga County history, 16th in New York State history. Replaced her husband, Judge Richard Burnham, killed in a motorcycle accident in 1971. Arraigned cop-killer, Billy Blake, February 11, 1987, following the shooting death of sheriff's deputy, David Clark.

CERONE, JAMES K. Aug 11, 1954 Syracuse, NY - Feb 21, 2006 Syracuse, NY
Owned and operated JC Tech Coating in Syracuse. Former drag racer at ESTA Speedway and founder of Old School Racing. Co-owner of Cerone TV & Satellite, founded in 1928 by his grandfather, Pasquale L. Cerone. Son of James R. Cerone, owner of Cerone TV & Satellite.

CERONE, JAMES R. Jan 26, 1932 Syracuse, NY - Apr 4, 2006 Syracuse, NY
Owned and operated Cerone TV & Satellite in Syracuse, founded by his father, Pasquale L. Cerone in 1928. Senior sound engineer for the Three Rivers Inn in Phoenix, working with singers, Tony Bennett, Nat King Cole and others, during performances at the club.

COMMISSO, WILLIAM PETER 1926 Utica, NY - Oct 24, 2016 Syracuse, NY
Owned and operated Vicky's Tasty Treats in Syracuse from 1985-2001.

CONWAY, ERNEST F. Dec 9, 1874 East Syracuse, NY - Jun 26, 1964 Syracuse, NY
First Mayor of the village of North Syracuse, serving from 1925-1927.

FERGERSON, ALFRED H. Jul 3, 1921 Syracuse, NY - Jan 29, 1999 Syracuse, NY
Founded the Fergerson Funeral Home of North Syracuse in 1948.

HAFNER, JACOB Feb 12, 1906 Germany - May 29, 1991 North Syracuse, NY
Farmer and early landowner in the town of Clay. Patriarch of the Hafner family, owner and operator of Hafner's Restaurant, Hafner's Red Barn Country Store, Hafner's Ice Cream Shop and Hafner's Florist. Struck and killed by a car within sight of his property.

HINERWADEL, JOHN M. Jul 18, 1906 Syracuse, NY - May 17, 1997 Liverpool, NY
Owned and operated Hinerwadel's Grove in North Syracuse, founded by his father, John M. Hinerwadel Sr.

LANGENMAYR, DONALD KENNETH 1954 Syracuse, NY - Nov 2, 1979 Austin, TX
Three-time All-American swimmer at Auburn University. Set New York State swimming records and named All-American at Liverpool High School. Killed in an automobile accident in Texas, where he was training for the 1980 Summer Olympics in Los Angeles.

MILBACK, CHARLES 1857 - 1925 Syracuse, NY
With **Catherine Simon Milback** (Jan 1859 NY - May 10, 1935 Syracuse, NY), the great-grandparents of Alan Gratzer, drummer and founding member of the rock band, R.E.O. Speedwagon.

PRINTUP, ELMER E. Jan 1891 Syracuse, NY - Apr 19, 1938 Syracuse, NY
Semi-pro Indian baseball star. Member of the New York State Umpires Association.

TAFEL, BUD (Frederick Christian) Feb 8, 1925 Syracuse, NY - Dec 28, 1986 Syracuse, NY
Mayor of the village of North Syracuse from 1975-1979. Established the first village administrator's position in Onondaga County.

WATERHOUSE, GEORGE B. 1856 North Syracuse, NY - May 3, 1949 North Syracuse, NY
United States Army veteran, one of the last remaining to have served under General George A. Custer. Fought in the Texas and Colorado western frontier, in battles against Indians fighters.

NORTH VOLNEY CEMETERY
Hall Road / Route 4
Fulton, NY 13069

MURRAY (Vincent)**, BARBARA L.** Sept 13, 1927 Syracuse, NY - Jan 3, 1999 Syracuse, NY
Mother of convicted killer, Robin Rodney Murray, who plea bargained a sentence of 35-years-to-life for the murders of Sheila M. Small and Kyle Heifferon in Syracuse in 1984, only to recant when his mother shouted in the courtroom for him to plead innocent. He stood trial, was convicted of both murders in 1985, and sentenced to two consecutive 25-years-to life sentences.

NORTH WATERTOWN CEMETERY
811 Bradley Street
Watertown, NY 13601

BERRY, DOUGLAS J. Jul 25, 1926 NY - Sept 8, 1989 Watertown, NY
Murder victim. Coin and jewelry store owner, shot to death during a robbery by Gary Charles Evans, a serial killer known for stealing antiques and daring escapes, who jumped to his death from the Troy-Menands Bridge, crossing the Hudson River near Troy, August 14, 1998, following an escape from police custody. Evans had befriended David Berkowitz, the "Son of Sam" serial killer, while serving time at the Clinton Correctional Facility in Dannemora.

BLAKE, JACK OWEN 1962 Watertown, NY - Apr 7, 1972 Watertown, NY
First victim of serial killer, Arthur John Shawcross, known as "The Genesee River Killer." Four-months later, Shawcross raped and suffocated eight-year old, Karen Ann Hill. Following his arrest, he plea bargained a manslaughter charge with prosecutors, and served 15 years of a 25-year sentence, moved to Rochester following his parole in 1987, raped and murdered eleven women, mutilating and eating the genital flesh of his victims, found guilty and sentenced to 250 years in state prison.

NORWICH CORNERS CEMETERY
Higby Road
Frankfort, NY 13340

CHARD, FREDERICK W. Sept 21, 1883 Washington Mills, NY - Dec 20, 1966 Syracuse, NY
Owned and operated Chard's Grocery and Market in Syracuse from 1939-1966.

NOVO-DIVEEVO RUSSIAN OTHODOX CHURCH CEMETERY
100 Smith Road
Nanuet, NY 10954

CONSTANTINOVNA, VERA Apr 24, 1906 Pavlovsk, Russia - Jan 11, 2001 Valley Cottage, NY
Russian princess. Daughter of Grand Duke Konstantin Konstantinovich of Russia and Grand Duchess Yelizaveta Mavrikiyevna. Last surviving member of the Romanov family, heir to the Russian throne, since 1989. Escaped to Sweden following the Russian Revolution in 1917, with her mother, brother, Georgy Konstantinovich, niece and nephew. Great-granddaughter of Tsar Nicholas I of Russia. Second cousin of Tsar Nicholas II, last Emperor of Russia.

KONSTANTINOVICH, GEORGY May 6, 1903 St. Petersburg, Russia - Nov 7, 1938 New York, NY
Russian prince. Son of Grand Duke Konstantin Konstantinovich of Russia and Grand Duchess Yelizaveta Mavrikiyevna. Escaped to Sweden following the Russian Revolution in 1917, with his mother, sister, Vera Constantinovna, niece and nephew. Great-grandson of Tsar Nicholas I of Russia. Second cousin of Tsar Nicholas II, last Emperor of Russia.

KOWERDA, BORIS Aug 21, 1907 Vilnius, Russia - Feb 18, 1987 Hyattsville, MD
Russian assassin. Murdered Pyotr Voykov, Soviet Ambassador to Poland, in 1927, in retaliation for personally directing the assassinations of Tsar Nicholas II and the Russian Imperial Family in 1918.

SILOTI, ALEXANDER ILYICH Oct 9, 1863 Kharkiv, Ukraine, Russia - Dec 8, 1945 New York, NY
Russian composer and pianist. Student of Franz Liszt in Weimer, Germany from 1883-1886. Editor for

Peter Tchaikovsky, on the First and Second piano concertos. Cousin of composer, Sergei Rachmaninoff.

SPESSIVTSEVA, OLGA Jul 5, 1895 Rostov-on-Don, Russia - Sept 16, 1991 Valley Cottage, NY
Russian ballerina. Toured the United States with the Ballets Russes from 1916-1918. Prima ballerina, étoile, at the Paris Opera Ballet from 1924-1932.

TOLSTAYA, ALEXANDRA Jul 18, 1884 Yasnaya, Russia - Sept 26, 1979 Valley Cottage, NY
Daughter of Russian novelist, Leo Tolstoy. Awarded three St. George Medals and the rank of Colonel by the Russian government for her service in World War 1.

TOLSTOY, ILYA ANDREYEVICH Feb 3, 1903 Toptivovo, Russia - Oct 28, 1970 New York, NY
United States Army Colonel. Envoy for President Franklin D. Roosevelt in Tibet in 1942, meeting the Dalai Lama, age seven at the time. Co-founded Marineland in Florida, the world's first oceanarium. Grandson of Russian novelist, Leo Tolstoy.

TOLSTOY (Rodzianko)**, OLGA M.** Oct 27, 1911 Russia - Sept 25, 1999 NY
Wife of Vladimir M. Tolstoy, the grandson of Russian novelist, Leo Tolstoy. Daughter of Mikhail Rodzianko, Russian politician, head of the Provisional Committee of the State Duma.

TOLSTOY, VLADIMIR MIKHAYLOVICH Dec 11, 1905 Russia - Feb 6, 1988 NY
Architect. Grandson of Russian novelist, Leo Tolstoy.

YURKEVICH, VLADIMIR IVANOVICH Jun 5, 1885 Moscow, Russia - Dec 13, 1964 New York, NY
Russian Naval engineer. Designed the ocean liner, *S.S. Normandie*, built in France in 1935.

OAK GLEN CEMETERY
Main Street
Aurora, NY 13026

AVERY, DANIEL Sept 18, 1766 Groton, CT - Jan 30, 1842 Aurora, NY
United States Representative-NY from 1811-1815 and 1816-1817.

MORGAN, EDWIN BARBER May 2, 1806 Aurora, NY - Oct 13, 1881 Aurora, NY
United States Representative-NY from 1853-1859. Co-founder and first President of the Wells-Fargo Express Company. Director of the American Express Company, until his death in 1881. Brother of Christopher Morgan, United States Representative-NY from 1839-1843. Nephew of Noyes Barber, United States Representative-CT from 1821-1835.

WELLS, HENRY Dec 12, 1905 Thetford, VT - Dec 10, 1878 Glasgow, Scotland
First President of the American Express Company, co-founded with William Fargo. Unable to convince American Express to expand to California, the two men formed Wells, Fargo & Company. Established Wells College, the nation's second oldest women's college, after a long and successful banking career.

OAK HILL CEMETERY
West German Street
Herkimer, NY 13350

ABBOTT, RUTH Chittenango, NY - Jun 11, 1965 Morrisville, NY
Stage actress. Appeared on Broadway. Signed by George Jessel, playing opposite him onstage in *The Jazz Singer*, in 1926. Performed with the Frank Wilcox theatrical group. Married for a time to actor, Cleve (Morrison) Moore, the sister of actress, Colleen Moore.

DEVENDORF, IRVING ROSELL 1856 Little Falls, NY - Oct 8, 1932 Herkimer, NY
Associate Justice of the New York State Supreme Court from 1920-1925. Presided over the murder trial of Chester Gillette in 1907, made famous in the Theodore Dreiser novel, *An American Tragedy.*

GRISWOLD, GAYLORD Dec 18, 1767 Windsor, CT - Mar 1, 1809 Herkimer, NY
United States Representative-NY from 1803-1805.

MILLER, WARNER Aug 12, 1838 Hannibal, NY - Mar 21, 1918 New York, NY
United States Senator-NY from 1881-1887. Elected to the Senate due to the resignation of Thomas C. Platt in 1881.

OAK HILL CEMETERY
140 North Highland Avenue
Nyack, NY 10960

ARONSON, BORIS Oct 15, 1899 Kiev, Russia – Nov 16, 1980 New York, NY
Broadway set designer. Six-time Tony Award-winner for scenic design. Inducted into the American Theater Hall of Fame in 1979.

BERGMAN, RAY (John Raymond) Jul 15, 1891 Nyack, NY - Feb 1967 Nyack, NY
Fly fisherman. Fishing editor for *Outdoor Life* magazine. Author of the book, *Forgotten Flies*."

BROWN (Hayes)**, ESSIE** (Catherine Estelle) Jun 4, 1877 Washington D.C. - Jul 1, 1953 New York, NY
Mother of actress, Helen Hayes, one of 12 actors to win the four major entertainment awards.

Grandmother of actor, James MacArthur. Her husband, Frank V. Brown, died in 1940, age 67, buried in St. Nicholas Cemetery, Patuxent River, MD.

BROWN, WAVERLY L. Apr 10, 1936 - Oct 20, 1981 Nyack, NY
Nyack Police Department officer, first African-American hired by Nyack, in 1966. Shot and killed, with Sgt. Edward O'Grady, by the Weather Underground, a domestic terrorist group involved in the 1981 Brinks armored truck robbery of $1 million.

CORNELL, JOSEPH Dec 24, 1903 Nyack, NY - Dec 29, 1972 New York, NY
Sculptor and artist. Avant-garde filmmaker. Wrote and produced the film, *Rose Hobart*, in 1936.

DUGGAR, BENJAMIN MINGE Sept 1, 1872 Gallion, AL - Sept 10, 1956 Nyack, NY
Botanist. Vice-President of the Botanical Society of America from 1912-1914.

HART, JOSEPH JOHNSON Apr 18, 1859 Nyack, NY - Jul 13, 1926 Brooklyn, NY
United States Representative-NY from 1895-1897.

HAYES (Brown), **HELEN** Oct 10, 1900 Washington D.C. - Mar 17, 1993 Nyack, NY
Stage and film actress. Called "the First Lady of the American Theater." One of 12 actors to have won an Emmy, Grammy, Oscar and Tony Award. Appeared in the films, *A Farewell to Arms*, *The White Sister*, *Anastasia* and *Airport*. Honored with a postage stamp in 2011, and a star on the Hollywood Walk of Fame. Wife of playwright, Charles MacArthur. Mother of actor, James MacArthur.

HECHT, BEN Feb 28, 1894 New York, NY - Apr 18, 1964 New York, NY
Screenwriter, playwright and novelist. Two-time Academy Award-winner. Collaborated with Charles MacArthur on *The Front Page*, *Ladies and Gentlemen*, *Wuthering Heights* and *Twentieth Century*. Wrote the screenplays for the Alfred Hitchcock films, *Spellbound*, *Notorious* and *Rope*. Inducted into the American Theater Hall of Fame in 1983. Ghostwriter for Marilyn Monroe's autobiography, *My Story*. The 1963 film, *Gaily, Gaily* was based on his autobiography, *A Child of the Century*.

HECHT, JENNY Jul 30, 1943 New York, NY - Mar 25, 1971 North Hollywood, CA
Actress. Died from a drug overdose, shortly after finishing a small role the film, *The Jesus Trip*. Subject of the play, *The Screenwriter's Daughter*, staged in London in 2015. Daughter of screenwriter, Ben Hecht.

HOPPER, EDWARD Jul 22, 1882 Upper Nyack, NY - May 15, 1967 New York, NY
Artist. Painted modern American life, mostly in oil paintings and watercolors. His most famous work, *Nighthawks*, resides in the Art Institute of Chicago. The Museum of Modern Art in New York City houses more than 3,000 pieces of his work.

JOHNSON, ALVIN SAUNDERS Dec 18, 1874 Homer, NE - Jun 7, 1971 Upper Nyack, NY
Economist. Co-founder and first Director of the New School in New York City, in 1919.

LEIGH, WILLIAM ROBINSON Sept 23, 1866 Hedgesville, WV - Mar 11, 1955 New York, NY
Artist. Specialized in painting the American West, including the Grand Canyon and Yellowstone
National Park and the Hopi and Navajo Indians.

LEONARD, MOSES GAGE Jul 10, 1809 Stafford, CT - Mar 20, 1899 Brooklyn, NY
United States Representative-NY from 1843-1845.

LEXOW, CLARENCE Sept 16, 1852 Brooklyn, NY - Dec 31, 1910 Nyack, NY
New York State Senator from 1894-1898. Chairman of the legislative committee consolidating the five
boroughs, Manhattan, the Bronx, Queens, Brooklyn and Staten Island, forming greater New York City.

MACARTHUR, CHARLES PREVOST Nov 5, 1895 Scranton, PA - Apr 21, 1956 New York, NY
Playwright. Academy Award-winning screenwriter. Collaborated with Ben Hecht on *The Front Page*,
Ladies and Gentlemen, *Wuthering Heights* and *Twentieth Century*. Inducted into the American Theater
Hall of Fame in 1983. Husband of actress, Helen Hayes, one of 12 actors to win the four major
entertainment awards. Father of actor, James MacArthur. Brother of philanthropist, James D.
MacArthur.

MACARTHUR, JAMES GORDON Dec 8, 1937 Los Angeles, CA - Oct 28, 2010 Jacksonville, FL
Actor. Co-starred on the TV series, *Hawaii Five-0*, playing Danny "Danno" Williams. Son of actress,
Helen Hayes and playwright, Charles MacArthur. Godson of actress, Lillian Gish.

MACARTHUR, MARY Feb 16, 1930 New York, NY - Sept 22, 1949 New York, NY
Daughter of actress, Helen Hayes and playwright, Charles MacArthur. Died from a viral infection, one
month before she was to open in a new Broadway play, opposite her mother. Sister of actor, James
MacArthur.

MCCULLERS (Smith), **CARSON** Feb 19, 1917 Columbus, GA - Sept 29, 1967 Nyack, NY
Author. Wrote the novels, *The Heart is a Lonely Hunter*, *The Member of the Wedding* and *Reflections
in a Golden Eye*. Married, divorced and remarried, Reeves McCullers Jr., who tried to convince her to
commit suicide with him in a Paris hotel room, she fled, he killed himself, November 19, 1953. He is
buried there, Neuilly-sur-Seine New Communal Cemetery, Île-de-France, France.

MILLS, C. WRIGHT (Charles) Aug 28, 1916 Waco, TX - Mar 20, 1962 West Nyack, NY
Professor of Sociology at Columbia University from 1946-1962. Published the book, *The Power Elite*,
in 1956.

SAUTER, EDDIE (Edward Ernest) Dec 2, 1914 Brooklyn, NY - Apr 21, 1981 New York, NY
Composer. Jazz arranger. Played trumpet with the Red Norvo's orchestra. Arranged and composed music for Norvo, Benny Goodman, Artie Shaw, Tommy Dorsey and Woody Herman.

SIMS, ZOOT (John Haley) Oct 29, 1925 Los Angeles, CA - Mar 23, 1985 New York, NY
Saxophonist. Performed in a quartet with Al Cohn, called Al and Zoot. Performed in Woody Herman's big band, "Four Brothers" sax section. Played with Benny Goodman's band in 1943. Recorded with Chet Baker, Charlie Mingus, Quincy Jones and Phoebe Snow.

SMITH (Waters)**, MARGUERITE** Jun 4, 1890 Dublin, GA - Jun 30, 1955 Nyack, NY
Mother of author, Carson McCullers. Her husband, Lamar Smith, died August 1, 1944, Columbus, GA, age 55, buried there, Riverdale Cemetery.

STEPHENS, ABRAHAM P. Feb 18, 1796 New City, NY - Nov 25, 1859 Nyack, NY
United States Representative-NY from 1851-1853.

TOMPKINS, ARTHUR SIDNEY Aug 26, 1865 Middleburgh, NY - Jan 20 1938 Nyack, NY
United States Representative-NY from 1899-1903. Associate Justice of the New York State Supreme Court from 1906-1936.

ULLMAN, DANIEL Apr 28, 1810 Wilmington, DE - Sept 28, 1892 Nyack, NY
Civil War Union Army Major General. Commanding General of the first black troops, Corps d'Afrique, raising five regiments of African-American soldiers.

OAK HILL (COWLES) CEMETERY
Otisco Road
Tully, NY 13159

COWLES, ISAAC Mar 7, 1804 Otisco, NY - Mar 16, 1847 Otisco, NY
Struck and killed by a falling tree, working on his property. Father of Otis Baker Cowles, Onondaga County centenarian, who died from natural causes, November 6, 1933, age 101.

OAKLAWN CEMETERY
2301-2439 Pre Emption Road / Route 6
Phelps, NY 14532

KONEN, VAIL GEORGE Dec 20, 1907 Helsinki, Finland - Apr 27, 1999 Geneva, NY
Brother of Greta Konen Peck, the first wife of Academy Award-winning actor, Gregory Peck.

OAKVIEW CEMETERY
Cemetery Road
Frankfort, NY 13340

FOWLER (Jackson)**, BUD** (John W.) Mar 16, 1858 Cooperstown, NY - Feb 16, 1913
First African-American to play professional baseball before the color lines were drawn.

WALSH, EDWARD T. 1888 - Jul 7, 1948 Frankfort, NY
With **Edna Francisco Walsh** (Aug 10, 1892 - Jan 6, 1989 Frankfort, NY), the parents of Edward J.
Walsh, head football coach at Manhasset High School, Long Island, where he coached and mentored
Hall of Fame running back, Jim Brown, as well as Olympian, Jim Thorpe.

OAKWOOD CEMETERY
31 Lake Street
Chittenango, NY 13037

HANCHETT (Baum)**, MARY E.** 1826 New Woodstock, NY - 1889 Chittenango, NY
Physician. Aunt of L. Frank Baum, author of *The Wonderful Wizard of Oz* series of children's books.

HOUCK (Metcalf)**, CLARA** Aug 10, 1916 Chittenango, NY - Feb 2, 2011 Chittenango, NY
Founded Oz Fest in Chittenango in 1978, honoring *The Wizard of Oz* and its author, L. Frank Baum.
Her husband of 69 years, William Houck, died three days before her death, January 29, 2011, age 96.

LANSING, WILLIAM ESSELSTYNE Dec 29, 1821 Perryville, NY - Jul 29, 1883 Syracuse, NY
United States Representative-NY from 1861-1863 and 1871-1875. Madison County District Attorney
from 1850-1853.

PATTINSON, ELSA Sept 29, 1909 Jakobstad, Finland - Sept 7, 2005 Baldwinsville, NY
Owned and operated the Merle Norman Studio in Syracuse for 56 years.

SHELTON, FRANK (Francis) 1925 Norwich, NY - Dec 11, 2009 Chittenango, NY
Bassist for the Syracuse, Montréal and New Orleans symphony orchestras. Donated his body to the
SUNY Upstate Medical School in Syracuse following his death.

OAKWOOD CEMETERY
Oakwood Avenue
East Aurora, NY 14052

FISHER, HERMAN GUY Nov 2, 1898 Unionville, PA - Sept 26, 1975 Buffalo, NY
Founded the children's toy company, Fisher-Price, with Irving Price, his wife, Margaret Evans Price,

and Helen Schelle, in East Aurora in 1930.

HUBBARD, ELBERT GREEN Jul 19, 1882 Buffalo, NY - Nov 1970 East Aurora, NY
Managed Roycroft, an arts and crafts community in East Aurora, founded by his father, author, Elbert Hubbard Sr., from 1915-1938. His father and mother, author, Alice Moore Hubbard, both died on the *Lusitania*, torpedoed and sunk off the coast of Ireland by a German U-boat, May 7, 1915, en route to interview Kaiser Wilhelm II of Germany during World War I. Their bodies were not recovered.

HUBBARD, SANFORD 1887 Buffalo, NY - May 21, 1955 East Aurora, NY
Posed without a shirt, arms crossed, for a Grape-Nuts advertisement in 1902. Son of author, Elbert Hubbard, publisher of the Roycroft Press, and author, Alice Moore Hubbard, both died on the *Lusitania*, torpedoed and sunk off the coast of Ireland by a German U-boat, May 7, 1915, en route to interview Kaiser Wilhelm II of Germany during World War I. Their bodies were not recovered.

OAKWOOD CEMETERY
763 Portage Road
Niagara Falls, NY 14301

BOBBITT, WAYNE D. Aug 25, 1942 Vinita, OK - Aug 7, 1999 Niagara Falls, NY
With **Mary E. Biro Bobbitt** (Jan 29, 1942 Niagara Falls, NY - Jul 14, 2005 Niagara Falls, NY), the parents of John Wayne Bobbitt, who made national news, June 23, 1993, when his wife, Lorena Gallo Bobbitt, cut off his penis with a knife, as he lay sleeping in bed, drove from the house and threw it out the window of her car. She was found not guilty by reason of insanity. After an extensive search, his penis was found and reattached. He later starred in two adult movies, *John Wayne Bobbitt: Uncut* and *Frankenpenis*.

GITTINS, ROBERT HENRY Dec 14, 1869 Oswego, NY - Dec 25, 1957 Tuxedo Park, NY
United States Representative-NY from 1913-1915. Commissioner of the Niagara Falls State Park from 1918-1940. Published the *Niagara Falls Journal* from 1914-1918.

PORTER, AUGUSTUS SEYMOUR Jan 18, 1798 Canandaigua, NY - Sept 18, 1872 Niagara Falls, NY
United States Senator-MI from 1840-1845. Mayor of Detroit in 1838. Brother of Peter Buell Porter, United States Secretary of War from 1828-1829.

PORTER (Breckinridge)**, LETITIA PRESTON** Jun 22, 1786 VA - Jul 27, 1831 Black Rock, NY
Wife of Peter Buell Porter, United States Secretary of War from 1828-1829. Daughter of John Breckinridge, United States Attorney General from 1805-1806 and United States Senator-KY from 1801-1805. Aunt of Vice-President John Cabell Breckinridge.

PORTER (Breckinridge)**, MARY CABELL** Oct 12, 1826 KY - Aug 4, 1854 Niagara Falls, NY
Wife of Colonel Peter A. Porter, her first cousin, once removed. Mother of Peter A. Porter Jr., United

States Representative-NY from 1907-1909. Granddaughter of John Breckinridge, United States Attorney General from 1805-1806 and United States Senator-KY from 1801-1805. Cousin of Vice-President John Cabell Breckinridge.

PORTER, PETER BUELL Aug 14, 1773 Salisbury, CT - Mar 20, 1844 Niagara Falls, NY
United States Secretary of War from 1828-1829, under President John Quincy Adams. United States Representative-NY from 1809-1816. New York Secretary of State from 1815-1816. War of 1812 Major General. Brother of Augustus S. Porter, United States Senator-MI from 1840-1845.

PORTER, PETER AUGUSTUS Jul 17, 1827 Black Rock, NY - Jun 3, 1864 Cold Harbor, VA
Civil War Union Army Colonel. Shot six times, killed at the Battle of Cold Harbor. Grandson of Peter Buell Porter, United States Secretary of War from 1828-1829. Great-grandson of John Breckinridge, United States Attorney General from 1805-1806.

PORTER, PETER AUGUSTUS Oct 10, 1853 Niagara Falls, NY - Dec 15, 1925 Buffalo, NY
United States Representative-NY from 1907-1909. President of the village of Niagara Falls in 1878. Son of Colonel Peter A. Porter, Sr. Great-grandson of Peter Buell Porter, United States Secretary of War from 1828-1829. 2nd great-grandson of John Breckinridge, United States Attorney General from 1805-1806.

ROBINSON, JOEL R. 1809 - Jun 30, 1863 Niagara Falls, NY
Steamboat Captain. Piloted the Maid of the Mist, purchased by W.O. Buchanan in 1861, to Lake Ontario, through the Great Gorge Rapids, the whirlpool and the Devil's Hole Rapids, the lower rapids of Niagara Falls, the first person to accomplish the feat.

TAYLOR (Edson), **ANNIE** (Anna) Oct 24, 1838 Auburn, NY - Apr 29, 1929 Lockport, NY
Daredevil. First person to go over Niagara Falls in a wooden barrel and survive, October 24, 1901, her 63rd birthday, tumbled over the Horseshoe Falls on the Canadian side, a feat that lasted fifty minutes in its entirety. Married seven years to David Taylor, until his death in the Civil War.

WEBB, MATTHEW Jan 19, 1848 Dawley, Shropshire, England - July 24, 1883 Niagara Falls, NY
First person on record to swim across the English Channel, August 24-25, 1875, taking 21 hours, 45 minutes. Awarded the Stanhope Medal by the Royal Humane Society in Britain for a rescue attempt of a man overboard the Cunard Line ship, *Russia*. Author of the book, *The Art of Swimming*. Died attempting to swim through the Whirlpool Rapids on the Niagara River.

OAKWOOD CEMETERY
West Street
Nunda, NY 14517

BROOKS, MICAH May 14, 1775 Cheshire, CT - July 7, 1857 Fillmore, NY
United States Representative-NY from 1815-1817.

PECK, LUTHER CHRISTOPHER Jan 1800 CT - Feb 5, 1876 Nunda, NY
United States Representative-NY from 1837-1841.

OAKWOOD CEMETERY
1975 Baird Road
Penfield, NY 14526

BUSH, TIMOTHY Apr 1, 1766 Lebanon, CT - May 4, 1850 Rochester, NY
2nd great-grandfather of Prescott Sheldon Bush, United States Senator-CT from 1952-1963. 3rd great-grandfather of President George Herbert Walker Bush. 4th great-grandfather of President George Walker Bush, John Ellis "Jeb" Bush, Governor of Florida from 1999-2007, and entertainment reporter, Billy Bush.

DEUEL, ELLSWORTH SHAUT Aug 5, 1914 Perryville, NY - Dec 11, 2013 St. Petersburg, FL
Penfield physician. With **Lillian Marcella Ellstrom Deuel** (Mar 12, 1915 Altoona, PA - Mar 1, 1986 Prescott, AZ), the parents of actors, Peter Duel and Geoffrey Deuel.

DUEL (Deuel)**, PETER** Feb 24, 1940 Rochester, NY - Dec 31, 1971 Hollywood, CA
Hollywood actor. Starred in the TV series, *Alias Smith and Jones*, *Love on a Rooftop* and *Gidget*. Committed suicide by gunshot, following a bout with depression and alcohol. Brother of actor, Geoffrey Deuel.

OAKWOOD CEMETERY
50 101st Street
Troy, NY 12182

ALVORD, ELISHA 1773 Farmington, CT - Jul 10, 1846 Troy, NY
Salt manufacturer. First manufacturer of salt in a permanent building. First Superintendent of the Federal Salt Works. Established the largest salt business at that time, with his brother, Dioclesian Alvord. Father of Thomas Gold Alvord, Lieutenant Governor of New York from 1865-1866.

BALTIMORE, GARNET DOUGLASS Apr 15, 1859 Troy, NY - Jun 12, 1946 Troy, NY
First African-American engineer and graduate of RPI, in 1881. Designed Prospect Park in Troy.

BROWNELL, EDWIN Jun 12, 1821 Sand Lake, NY - Mar 14, 1874 Troy, NY
Uncle of Union Army Sergeant, Francis E. Brownell, awarded the Civil War's first Medal of Honor.

BULL, RICE COOK 1842 Hartford, CT - May 19, 1930 Troy, NY
Civil War Union Army veteran. Author of *Soldiering: The Civil War Diary of Rice C. Bull, 123rd New York Volunteer Infantry*, chronicling his first-hand accounts of the war.

CARR, JOSEPH BRADFORD Aug 16, 1828 Albany, NY - Feb 24, 1895 Troy, NY
Civil War Union Army Brevet Major General. New York Secretary of the State from 1880-1885.

CLUETT, E. HAROLD (Ernest) Jul 13, 1874 Troy, NY - Feb 4, 1954 Troy, NY
United States Representative-NY from 1937-1943.

CRAVER, BILL (William H.) Jun 1844 Troy, NY - Jun 17, 1901 Troy, NY
Civil War Union Army veteran. Infielder for the Troy Haymakers, Baltimore Canaries, Philadelphia White Stockings, Philadelphia Centennials, Philadelphia Athletics, New York Mutuals and Louisville Grays from 1871-1877. Led the league in triples with 13 in 1875. Expelled from major league baseball for failing to cooperate in the Louisville gambling scandal in 1877.

CUSHMAN, JOHN PAINE Mar 8, 1784 Pomfret, CT - Sept 16, 1848 Troy, NY
United States Representative-NY from 1817-1819.

DICKINSON, JOHN DEAN Jun 28, 1767 Middletown, CT - Jan 28, 1941 Troy, NY
United States Representative-NY from 1819-1823 and 1827-1831.

DRAPER, WILLIAM HENRY Jun 24, 1841 Leicester, MA - Dec 7, 1921 Troy, NY
United States Representative-NY from 1901-1913.

EATON, AMOS May 17, 1776 Chatham, NY - May 10, 1842 Troy, NY
Scientist, botanist and educator.

FILLEY, MARK (Marcus Lucius) Feb 28, 1912 Lansingburgh, NY - Jan 20, 1995 Yarmouth, ME
Pitched one game for the Washington Senators, for Hall of Fame player-manager, Joe Cronin, in 1934. Rensselaer County Family Court Judge from 1954-1971.

GREENMAN, EDWARD WHITFORD Jan 26, 1840 Berlin, NY - Aug 3, 1908 Troy, NY
United States Representative-NY from 1887-1889.

GRISWOLD, JOHN AUGUSTUS Nov 11, 1822 Nassau, NY - Oct 31, 1872 Troy, NY
United States Representative-NY from 1863-1869. Mayor of Troy in 1855.

HAYNER, FREDERICK C. Jul 30, 1922 Syracuse, NY - Jun 17, 2001 Troy, NY
World War II United States Army Air Corps veteran, from 1941-1945, popular for his
"nose art", painted caricatures on the noses of American fighter planes and bombers.

KAVANAUGH, FREDERICK W. 1871 NY - Dec 2, 1940 Waterford, NY
Chairman of the Saratoga County Republican Party from 1927-1929. Member of the New York State
Senate from 1921-1924. Owned a hotel in Cody, WY, named for his close friend, William "Buffalo Bill"
Cody. Died from a self-inflicted gunshot in the garage of his home.

KING, STEVE (Stephen F.) 1842 Troy, NY - Jul 8, 1895 Troy, NY
Outfielder for the Troy Haymakers from 1871-1872.

PAINE, JOHN Feb 12, 1793 Windsor County, VT - Feb 7, 1852 Troy, NY
First President of the Oakwood Cemetery Association in Troy. Grandfather of Lady Lilian "Lily" Warren
Price Beresford, widow of wealthy New Yorker, Louis Carré Hamersley, remarried to the Duke of
Marlborough, George Charles Spencer-Churchill, the uncle of Prime Minister Winston Churchill, and
later, Lord William Leslie de la Poer Beresford, British Army Lieutenant Colonel awarded the Victoria
Cross for service in the Anglo-Zulu War.

PATTISON, EDWARD W. Apr 29, 1932 Troy, NY - Aug 22, 1990 West Sand Lake, NY
United States Representative-NY from 1975-1979.

PHELPS, GEORGE MAY Mar 19, 1820 Watervliet, NY - May 18, 1888 Brooklyn, NY
Inventor. Telegraph instrument-maker, built most of Thomas Edison's telegraph and telephone patent
models for Western Union.

PIERSON, JOB Sept 23, 1791 Easthampton, NY - Apr 9, 1860 Troy, NY
United States Representative-NY from 1831-1835.

PRICE, CICERO Dec 2, 1805 Lancaster, KY - Nov 24, 1888 Troy, NY
United States Navy Commodore. With **Elizabeth Homer Paine Price** (Feb 17, 1828 Troy, NY - Oct 26,
1910 Troy, NY), the parents of Lady Lilian "Lily" Warren Price Beresford, widow of wealthy New Yorker,
Louis Carré Hamersley, remarried to the Duke of Marlborough, George Charles Spencer-Churchill, the
uncle of Prime Minister Winston Churchill, and later, Lord William Leslie de la Poer Beresford, British
Army Lieutenant Colonel awarded the Victoria Cross for service in the Anglo-Zulu War. She died
January 11, 1909, Dorking, Surrey, England, buried next to Lord Beresford, Clonagem Churchyard,
Curraghmore, Portlaw, County Waterford, Ireland.

REEVE, AARON BURR Oct 3, 1780 Litchfield, CT - Sept 1, 1809 Troy, NY
Attorney. Nephew of Vice-President Aaron Burr. Son of Tapping Reeve, founder of the Litchfield Law School, the first in the United States. Grandson of Aaron Burr Sr., founder and President of Princeton University from 1747-1757. Great-grandson of theologian, Jonathan Edwards Sr. Originally buried in Barker Park, Troy, reinterred in 1875

RENSHAW (Price), **LUCY JENNINGS** Aug 16, 1858 Troy, NY - Feb 23, 1896 Troy, NY
Daughter of United States Navy Commodore, Cicero Price. Sister of Lady Lilian "Lily" Warren Price Beresford, widow of wealthy New Yorker, Louis Carré Hamersley, remarried to the Duke of Marlborough, George Charles Spencer-Churchill, the uncle of Prime Minister Winston Churchill, and later, Lord William Leslie de la Poer Beresford, British Army Lieutenant Colonel awarded the Victoria Cross for service in the Anglo-Zulu War.

SAGE, RUSSELL B. Aug 4, 1816 Vernon, NY - Jul 22, 1906 Lawrence, NY
United States Representative-NY from 1853-1857. Multi-millionaire businessman. Associate of Jay Gould in the development and sale of railways in New York City. Survived an assassination attempt by Henry L. Norcross, in 1891, who was killed when his bag of dynamite exploded. Husband of philanthropist, Margaret Sage Slocum, who created a charitable foundation in his name after his death.

SLOANE, FLORENCE ADELE 1873 NY - Jan 10, 1960 New York, NY
New York City socialite. Her diary, *Maverick in Mauve*, was published by Louis Auchincloss, her granddaughter's husband. Granddaughter of William Henry Vanderbilt, the richest man in the world at the time of his death, in 1885. Great-granddaughter of Commodore Cornelius Vanderbilt. Aunt of music producer, John H. Hammond and Alice F. Hammond Goodman, the wife of jazz musician, Benny Goodman. Buried in the family plot of her first husband, James Abercrombie Burdon Jr.

TAYLOR, DEAN PARK Jan 1, 1902 Troy, NY - Oct 16, 1977 Albany, NY
United States Representative-NY from 1943-1961. Vice-President Richard M. Nixon attended his retirement celebration at the Hendrick Hudson Hotel in Troy, in 1960.

THOMAS, GEORGE HENRY Jul 31, 1816 Newsom's Depot, VA - Mar 28, 1870 San Francisco, CA
Civil War Union Army General. Nicknamed "the Rock of Chickamauga." Only general not to lose a Civil War battle. Fought for the North, despite being a native-Virginian, his family never forgave him, turned his portrait to the wall, and never spoke to him again, refusing to attend his funeral.

THURMAN, JOHN RICHARDSON Oct 6, 1814 New York, NY - Jul 24, 1854 Chester, NY
United States Representative-NY from 1849-1851. Originally interred in his family graveyard.

TIBBITS, GEORGE Jan 14, 1763 Warwick, RI - Jul 19, 1849 Troy, NY
United States Representative-NY from 1803-1805.

TIBBITS, WILLIAM BADGER Mar 31, 1837 Hoosick, NY - Feb 11, 1880 Troy, NY
Civil War Union Army Brigadier General, one of the last officers commissioned to full rank.

TOWNSEND, MARTIN INGHAM Feb 6, 1810 Hancock, MA - Mar 8, 1903 Troy, NY
United States Representative-NY from 1875-1879.

VAIL, HENRY 1782 Milbrook, NY - Jun 25, 1853 Troy, NY
United States Representative-NY from 1837-1839.

VAN SCHAICK, WILLIAM HENRY Dec 7, 1837 Troy, NY - Dec 8, 1927 Utica, NY
Captain of *The General Slocum*. Tried and convicted of criminal negligence for the fire that destroyed the steamboat on the East River, New York City, killing more than 1,000 passengers, June 15, 1904. Pardoned by President William H. Taft in 1912, serving three years of his ten-year sentence in Sing Sing Prison. His grave remained unmarked until 1999, when his grandniece placed a tombstone over his grave with his full name, dates and one word, "vindicated." Adella Martha Liebenow Wotherspoon, the youngest and last survivor of the disaster, died January 26, 2004, age 100, buried in the Wilson Memorial Church Cemetery in Watchung, NJ.

WARREN, JOSEPH MABBETT Jan 28, 1813 Troy, NY - Sept 9, 1896 Troy, NY
United States Representative-NY from 1871-1873.

WICKES, ELIPHALET Apr 1, 1769 Huntington, NY - Jun 7, 1850 Troy, NY
United States Representative-NY from 1805-1807.

WILLARD (Hart), **EMMA** Feb 23, 1787 Berlin, CT - Apr 15, 1870 Troy, NY
Women's rights activist. Founded the Emma Willard School in Troy in 1821, the first women's school of higher education.

WILSON, SAMUEL Sept 13, 1766 Arlington, MA - Jul 31, 1854 Troy, NY
Meat packer. Supplied the United States Army with beef during the War of 1812, stamping his shipments with the initials, "U.S.", earning him the moniker, "Uncle Sam", becoming a symbol of the United States.

OAKWOOD-MORNINGSIDE CEMETERY
940 Comstock Avenue
Syracuse, NY 13210

ABBOTT, SAMUEL JUNIUS Sept 18, 1833 Syracuse, NY - Mar 29, 1911 Albany, NY
Night watchman at the New York State Capitol Building. Died there in a fire, and is said to haunt the fourth floor. Haunted tours are offered every October.

ABDO, NAIF A. Mar 13, 1896 Nazareth, Palestine - Sept 14, 1976 Syracuse, NY
Owned and operated four Abdo Grocery Stores in Syracuse from 1924-1972.

ACKERMAN, C. FRED (Carl) 1873 NY - Apr 4, 1938 Syracuse, NY
Motion picture cameraman. Filmed the Boxer Rebellion in China for Biograph in 1900. Syracuse
University track & field star. Set pole vaulting records and was a member of the cycling team.

ADAMS, FOREST A. Apr 20, 1917 Lila, GA - July 24, 1991 Syracuse, NY
Founder and Pastor Emeritus of the Tucker Missionary Baptist Church in Syracuse. Marched with
Dr. Martin Luther King in Selma and Washington D.C. in the 1960's civil rights movement.

ALDRICH, BRUCE S. May 25, 1835 Scott, NY - Nov 23, 1896 Syracuse, NY
Founded the Hier & Aldrich Cigar Manufacturing Company, with John P. Hier, in 1860.

ALEXANDER, LEE May 18, 1927 New York, NY - Dec 25, 1996 Syracuse, NY
Mayor of Syracuse (D) from 1970-1985, the longest-serving mayor in the history of the city. President
of the U.S. Conference of Mayors from 1977-1978. Served six years of a ten-year
sentence in federal prison for racketeering, extortion and tax evasion, committed during his years as
mayor.

ALLEN, HENRY C. Sept 10, 1864 Newark, NJ - Aug 5, 1932 Syracuse, NY
Syracuse City engineer from 1890-1895. Surveyed New York State boundary lines between
Pennsylvania and New Jersey. Member of the Syracuse Grade Crossing Commission from
1914-1915.

ALVORD, THOMAS GOLD Dec 20, 1810 Syracuse, NY - Oct 26, 1897 Syracuse, NY
Lieutenant Governor of New York from 1865-1866. Called "Old Salt." Speaker of the New York State
Assembly in 1858, 1864 and 1879. Father-in-law of diamond expert, James A. Cheney.

AMES, FLORENCE L. 1888 MI - Dec 14, 1938 Syracuse, NY
Murder victim. Robbed of $2.35 and killed by Franklin W. Jenner in her home, 116 Stedman Street,
Syracuse, her body hidden in a neighboring house until February 16, 1939. Jenner was executed at
Sing Sing in 1940, the last Onondaga County man to be executed in New York State.

ANDREAS, LEW Feb 25, 1895 Sterling, IL - Jun 16, 1983 Syracuse, NY
Syracuse University men's basketball coach from 1924-1950. Led the 1925-26 team to the national
championship. Syracuse University head football coach from 1927-1930.

ANDREWS, CHARLES May 27, 1827 - Oct 22, 1918 Syracuse, NY
Associate Justice of the New York Court of Appeals from 1870-1892, Chief Justice from 1881-1882
and 1892-1897. Mayor of Syracuse (R) from 1861-1862. Father of William Shankland Andrews,

Associate Justice of the New York Court of Appeals. Father-in-law of novelist, Mary Raymond Shipman Andrews. Son-in-law of William H. Shankland, Associate Justice of the New York Court of Appeals.

ANDREWS, EDWARD GAYER Aug 7, 1825 New Hartford, NY - Dec 31, 1907 Brooklyn, NY
Bishop of the Methodist Episcopal Church from 1872-1904.

ANDREWS (Sessions)**, HANNAH S.** Feb 18, 1888 Englewood, NJ - Mar 17, 1961 Syracuse, NY
Wife of Paul Shipman Andrews, Assistant Attorney General of the United States. Granddaughter of Frederic Dan Huntington, first Protestant Episcopal Bishop of Central New York. Daughter-in-law of William Shankland Andrews, Associate Justice of the New York Court of Appeals and author, Mary Raymond Shipman Andrews.

ANDREWS, MARY RAYMOND SHIPMAN Apr 2, 1860 Mobile, AL - Aug 2, 1936 Albany, NY
Novelist and short story writer. Author of *The Perfect Tribute*, *His Soul Goes Marching*, *Lost Commander*, *Through the Ivory Gate* and *A Kidnapped Colony*. Wife of William Shankland Andrews, Associate Justice of the New York Court of Appeals. Daughter-in-law of Charles Andrews, Chief Justice of the New York Court of Appeals and Mayor of Syracuse from 1861-1862.

ANDREWS, PAUL SHIPMAN Aug 2, 1887 Syracuse, NY - Apr 1967 Syracuse, NY
Assistant Attorney General of the United States, under Attorney General Harlan F. Stone, in 1924. Dean Emeritus of the Syracuse University College of Law in 1927. Son of William Shankland Andrews, Associate Justice of the New York Court of Appeals and author, Mary Raymond Shipman Andrews. Grandson of Charles Andrews, Chief Justice of the New York Court of Appeals and Mayor of Syracuse from 1861-1862. Great-grandson of William H. Shankland, Associate Justice of the New York Court of Appeals.

ANDREWS, WILLIAM SHANKLAND Sept 25, 1858 Syracuse, NY - Aug 5, 1936 Albany, NY
Associate Justice of the New York State Supreme Court from 1900-1920 and New York Court of Appeals from 1917-1929, serving as Chief Justice of both courts. Presided over the libel trial brought by Albany publisher, William Barnes, against former President, Theodore Roosevelt, April 1915, in Syracuse. Husband of novelist, Mary Raymond Shipman Andrews. Son of Charles Andrews, Chief Justice of the New York Court of Appeals and Mayor of Syracuse from 1861-1862. Grandson of William H. Shankland, Associate Justice of the New York Court of Appeals.

ARCHBOLD, WILLIAM KIBBEE Jun 5, 1866 West Farmington, OH - Oct 25, 1948 Syracuse, NY
Directed the design and erection of the first steel towers used to transmit electricity from Niagara Falls to Buffalo, Rochester and Syracuse. Nephew of John D. Archbold, former President of Standard Oil and Syracuse University benefactor.

ASSMANN, FREDERICK PAUL Oct 3, 1881 Syracuse, NY - Aug 31, 1947 Hounsfield, NY
President of the Precision Castings Company in Fayetteville.

AUER, MARTIN S. Jul 21, 1918 - May 21, 1991 Syracuse, NY
New York State Senator from 1973-1985. Lost reelection in 1984 to Nancy Lorraine Hoffman by 233 votes. Died thirteen days after the death of his wife, Wilma Tucker Auer.

AVERY, MATTHEW HENRY Mar 27, 1836 Middletown, VT - Sept 1, 1881 Geneva, NY
Civil War Union Army Brevet Brigadier General. Commander of the 10th New York Cavalry.

AVERY, PARKE STEPHEN Sept 21, 1817 Groton, CT - 1898 Syracuse, NY
Salt manufacturer. Built the Parke Avery House on Park Street in Syracuse in 1850.

AYLING, CHARLES FREDERICK 1861 Syracuse, NY - Apr 13, 1941 Syracuse, NY
Syracuse attorney. Classmate of Theodore Roosevelt at Columbia University. Champion golfer, held the city league title several times. Won the National Live Bird Shoot Championship, at the Polo Grounds, New York City, in 1900 and 1901.

BABCOCK, H. FRANK (Henry) 1846 NY - Jun 4, 1931 Syracuse, NY
Civil War Union Army Corporal. Eyewitness to the assassination of President Abraham Lincoln at Ford's Theater, April 14, 1865, in attendance to watch the play, *Our American Cousin*.

BABCOCK, MALTBIE DAVENPORT Aug 3, 1858 Syracuse, NY - May 18, 1901 Naples, Italy
Presbyterian minister. Author of the hymn, "This is My Father's World."

BACON, FRANCIS EUGENE Aug 12, 1851 Fulton, NY - Feb 28, 1931 Los Angeles, CA
Co-founded the Bacon & Chappell Company in Syracuse, with Charles E. Chappell, in 1895. Father-in-law of William Groat, President of the Medical Society of New York State.

BALLARD, CLARA Aug 17, 1887 Syracuse, NY - Feb 13, 1974 Syracuse, NY
Creator and designer of clothing for young girls.

BARNES, GEORGE Oct 1, 1827 Tenterden, England - Oct 17, 1892 New York, NY
Syracuse banking executive. Early supporter of baseball in Syracuse.

BARNUM, HENRY ALANSON Sept 24, 1833 Jamesville, NY - Jan 29, 1892 New York, NY
Awarded the Medal of Honor for heroism in 1863 at Lookout Mountain, during the Civil War. Appointed Harbor Master of the Port of New York by President Benjamin Harrison.

BARNUM, JEROME DEWITT Sept 20, 1888 Syracuse, NY - Jan 16, 1965 Syracuse, NY
Publisher of the *Post-Standard* from 1915-1942.

BAUDER, RAY EMERSON 1901 Syracuse, NY - Feb 3, 1939 Syracuse, NY
Syracuse Fire Department Lieutenant. One of eight firemen killed in the Collins Block fire, the deadliest fire in the history of the Syracuse Fire Department, 225 East Genesee Street in Syracuse, when flames swept thought the building, collapsing several floors crushing the firemen under tons of debris.

BAUM, BENJAMIN WARD Jan 3, 1821 Minden, NY - Feb 14, 1887 Syracuse, NY
Pennsylvania oil magnate and banker. With **Cynthia Ann Stanton Baum** (Oct 28, 1820 New Woodstock, NY - Dec 14, 1905 Syracuse, NY), the parents of L. Frank Baum, author of *The Wonderful Wizard of Oz* series of children's books.

BAUM, DWIGHT JAMES Jun 24, 1886 Little Falls, NY - Dec 13, 1939 New York, NY
Architect. Leading figure in the development of Florida. Designed the Sarasota home of John Ringling, of the Ringling Brothers Circus. Designed Hendricks Memorial Chapel on the Syracuse University campus, Crouse Hospital in Syracuse and buildings in New York City and Sarasota. Consulting architect for *Good Housekeeping* from 1929-1930.

BAUM, HENRY CLAY Mar 3, 1859 Chittenango, NY - Aug 6, 1916 Syracuse, NY
Syracuse physician. Professor of Dermatology at the Syracuse College of Medicine. Brother of   L. Frank Baum, author of *The Wonderful Wizard of Oz* series of children's books. A yellow brick, worthy of Dorothy's ruby slippers, rests between their graves.

BAUMGRAS, PETER Jan 4, 1827 Hamburg, Germany - Oct 18, 1903 Chicago, IL
Portrait painter. Completed a portrait of President Abraham Lincoln from memory, shortly after his assassination in 1865.

BELDEN, JAMES JEROME Sept 30, 1825 Fabius, NY - Jan 1, 1904 Syracuse, NY
United States Representative-NY from 1887-1895 and 1897-1899. Mayor of Syracuse (R) from 1877-1878. Elected to Congress following Frank Hiscock's election to the United States Senate. Co-founded the contracting firm, Denison & Belden, with Henry D. Denison, in Syracuse.

BELDEN, JAMES MEAD 1852 Syracuse, NY - Sept 14, 1917 Syracuse, NY
Husband of novelist, Jessie Perry Van Zile Belden. Nephew of James J. Belden, United States Representative-NY from 1887-1895 and 1897-1899 and Mayor of Syracuse from 1877-1878.

BELDEN (Van Zile), **JESSIE PERRY** Nov 13, 1857 Troy, NY - Feb 2, 1910 New York, NY
Novelist. Author of *The King's Ward, Fate at the Door* and *Concerning the Ancestors and Descendants of Royal Denison Belden*. Wrote the short story, *Not on the Passengers List*, for *Harper's Magazine*.

BENDIXEN, HOWARD RUDOLPH Jun 26, 1895 Syracuse, NY - Jan 19, 1975 Syracuse, NY
Owned the Bendixen Tobacco Company in Syracuse, manufacturer of Yara chewing tobacco.

BENNETT, DAVID SMITH May 3, 1811 Camillus, NY - Nov 6, 1894 Buffalo, NY
United States Representative-NY from 1869-1871. Operated several grain elevators in Buffalo.
Purchased the original Dart Elevator, later destroyed by fire, replacing it with the Bennett Elevator.

BERWICK (Hofmann)**, ERNA** Nov 2, 1912 New York, NY - Jun 16, 1997 Syracuse, NY
Onondaga County Assistant District Attorney, appointed by District Attorney, Donald Mawhinney in
1942. First female district attorney in county history. Daughter of publisher, William F. Hofmann,
Syracuse Chiefs owner from 1943-1950. Sister of William F. Hofmann Jr., Syracuse Chiefs owner from
1950-1953. Wife of Theodore F. Bowes, United States Attorney for the Northern District.

BLACKWELL, CARLYLE Jan 20, 1884 Troy, NY - Jun 17, 1955 Miami, FL
Stage and silent film star. Co-produced Alfred Hitchcock's first thriller, *The Lodger*. Awarded a star on
the Hollywood Walk of Fame. Father of character actor, Carlyle Blackwell Jr.

BLODGETT, A. BURR (Andrew) 1850 Mottville, NY - Aug 19, 1910 Syracuse, NY
Superintendent of the Syracuse City School District from 1889-1910.

BLODGETT, CLEMENTS WINFIELD Feb 19, 1885 Syracuse, NY - Mar 20, 1956 Syracuse, NY
Syracuse pediatrician. Son of educator, A. Burr Blodgett. Died from first, second and third-degree
burns suffered in a fire at his home, burning trash in his fireplace, flames igniting newspapers nearby.
Deputy Fire Chief, Ernest E. Goebel, was awarded the Francis Hendricks Medal for Bravery for his
rescue attempt in the fire.

BOOKSTAVER, DANIEL Dec 19, 1828 CT - Apr 27, 1903 Syracuse, NY
Mayor of Syracuse (D) in 1863.

BOWDEN, ERNEST J. Jul 18, 1876 England - Sept 6, 1961 Syracuse, NY
Journalist. Wrote the column, "Pulpit to Pew", for the *Post-Standard* for 29 years. Husband of actress
and journalist, Ramona Baxter Bowden, the daughter of actress, Blanche Weaver.

BOWDEN (Baxter)**, RAMONA** Aug 16, 1895 New York, NY - Dec 30, 1984 Syracuse, NY
Shakespearean New York stage actress. Performed with Rudolph Valentino and Enrico Caruso.
Appeared in the film, *Little Lord Fauntleroy*, starring Mary Pickford. Religion Editor for the *Post-
Standard*. Daughter of actress, Blanche Weaver, and William D. Baxter, drama critic for the *New York
Herald-Tribune*. Wife of journalist, Ernest J. Bowden. Grandniece of suffragist, Matilda Joslyn Gage.

BOWES, THEODORE FAUS 1904 Moshannon, PA - Jan 8, 1967 Syracuse, NY
United States Attorney for the Northern District, appointed by President Dwight D. Eisenhower in
1953. Commissioner of the New York State Public Service Commission from 1961-1973, appointed by
Governor Nelson Rockefeller. Husband of Erna Hofmann Berwick, first female District Attorney in
Onondaga County history.

BOYD, ANDREW Jul 7, 1836 Dublin, Ireland - Oct 12, 1905 Syracuse, NY
Directory publisher. Published the first directory in Syracuse. National authority on President Abraham Lincoln, holding many relics and artifacts of the President, including his death bed and mattress.

BRANNOCK, CHARLES F. 1903 Syracuse, NY - Nov 22, 1992 Syracuse, NY
Invented the Brannock Shoe Device, the standard foot measuring tool for retail shops worldwide. Son of Otis C. Brannock, co-founder of the Park-Brannock Shoe Company in Syracuse.

BRANNOCK, OTIS CHARLES Nov 29, 1872 Baldwinsville, NY - Apr 4, 1962 Syracuse, NY
President of the Park-Brannock Shoe Company in Syracuse, co-founded with Ernest N. Park, in 1906. Father of inventor, Charles F. Brannock.

BRAY, WILLIAM L. Sept 19, 1865 Burnside, IL - May 25, 1953 Syracuse, NY
Head of the Syracuse University Botany Department and Dean of the Graduate School from 1918-1943. Founder of the New York State College of Forestry at Syracuse University. Namesake of Bray Hall, the oldest building on campus since 1917. Professor of Botany at the University of Texas from 1897-1907. Won a Grand Prix for his tree specimen exhibit at the 1904 Louisiana Purchase Exposition in St. Louis. Studied with Adolf Engler in Berlin, Germany, from 1896-1897.

BRAYTON, HARRY J. Oct 1, 1880 Niagara Falls, NY - Sept 20, 1939 Syracuse, NY
Onondaga County physician. Nationally respected authority on tuberculosis. Flew to Europe on the *Hindenburg*, with Syracuse newspaper publisher, Harvey D. Burrill, one year before the May 6, 1937 crash of the German zeppelin in Lakehurst, NJ.

BRESEE, STEPHEN KNOWLTON Dec 10, 1864 Newboro, ON, Canada - Mar 2, 1936 Syracuse, NY
Owned and operated Bresee Chevrolet in Syracuse. Father-in-law of Charles G. Hanna, Syracuse Mayor from 1928-1929.

BREWSTER (Baum), **MARY LOUISE** Apr 22, 1847 Cortland, NY - Nov 12, 1933 Syracuse, NY
Last surviving sibling of L. Frank Baum, author of *The Wonderful Wizard of Oz* series of children's books. Died six years before the release of the film, *The Wizard of Oz*, in 1939.

BRIGGS, CLAY STONE Jan 8, 1876 Galveston, TX - Apr 29, 1933 Washington D.C.
United States Representative-TX from 1919-1933.

BRISTOW, DAISY Sept 6, 1901 Sumter, SC - Sept 22, 1984 Syracuse, NY
Mother of Internationally-known exotic dancer, Lottie "The Body" Graves Claiborne, the former wife of Harlem Globetrotter basketball star, Reece "Goose" Tatum.

BROAD, HILDA Mar 21, 1906 Portland, OR - Mar 28, 2013 Jamesville, NY
Wife of Syracuse attorney, William L. Broad. Amateur golfer, she scored her only hole-in-one, one day

following her 80th birthday. Nanny for award-winning sportswriter, Roger Angell, while a student at Bryn Mawr College. Close friend of Julia Grant Dietz, the great-granddaughter of President Ulysses S. Grant.

BROWN, ALEXANDER T. Nov 21, 1854 Scott, NY - Jan 31, 1929 Syracuse, NY
Founded the Brown-Lipe Gear Company, now Inland Fisher Guide, with Charles E. Lipe, later added H. Winfield Chapin to form Brown-Lipe-Chapin in Syracuse, supplier of gears for General Motors. Invented the L.C. Smith shotgun and the Smith-Premier typewriter.

BROWN, JULIAN STEPHEN Mar 29, 1887 Syracuse, NY - Apr 7, 1964 Daytona Beach, FL
Automobile and boat dealer. Invented a quiet, running inboard-outboard engine for boats. Son of Alexander T. Brown, inventor and co-founder of the Brown-Lipe Gear Company.

BUNDY, WILLARD H. Oct 18, 1872 Auburn, NY - Jul 29, 1941 Syracuse, NY
Founded the W.H. Bundy Time Recorder Company in Syracuse in 1903. Son of Willard L. Bundy, inventor of the first time clock machine in Auburn in 1888.

BUNDY, WILLARD LEGRAND Dec 8, 1845 Otsego, NY - Jan 19, 1907 Syracuse, NY
Invented the first time clock machine, in Auburn, in 1888. Formed the Bundy Manufacturing Company in Binghamton, with his brother, Harlow E. Bundy, in 1889, consolidated years after his death with two additional companies, forming IBM.

BURDICK (Will)**, E. JOYCE** (Elizabeth) 1921 Syracuse, NY - Mar 10, 1965 Syracuse, NY
Society editor for the *Post-Standard*. Wife of Arnie Burdick, Sports Editor of the *Syracuse Herald-Journal* from 1956-1984. Daughter of Howard C. Will, President of the Will & Baumer Candle Company.

BURNET, JOHN BARBER Apr 14, 1818 Elbridge, NY - Jul 7, 1889 Syracuse, NY
Donated 100 acres of land, inherited from his father, Moses DeWitt Burnet, to the city of Syracuse to form Burnet Park, in 1885. Named to the first Syracuse City Council in 1848. Son-in-law of Nathan Munro, founder of the Munro Academy in Elbridge.

BURNET, MOSES DEWITT Jan 13, 1792 Syracuse, NY - Dec 29, 1876 Syracuse, NY
Early Syracuse landowner. Built the first of the James Street grand mansions in Syracuse, in the 1840s. Father of John Barber Burnet, early Syracuse landowner and councilman. Nephew of surveyor, Moses DeWitt, Revolutionary War Continental Army Major.

BURNS, WILLIS BATES May 28, 1851 Syracuse, NY - Aug 15, 1915 Syracuse, NY
Mayor of Syracuse (R) from 1886-1887.

BURRELL, PHILIP H. Jul 23, 1935 Syracuse, NY - Jan 5, 1989 New York, NY
New York City advertising and television broadcast consultant. Syracuse University student radio
personality at WOLF-AM, with Dick Clark in the 1950s.

BURRILL, HARVEY D. Dec 20, 1868 Syracuse, NY - Dec 24, 1938 Syracuse, NY
President and editor of the *Syracuse Newspapers* for 50 years. Flew to Europe on the *Hindenburg*,
with Dr. Harry J. Brayton, one year before the crash of the German zeppelin in Lakehurst, NJ, May 6,
1937.

BURT, AARON Aug 12, 1792 Westmoreland, NH - Apr 9, 1848 Jacksonville, FL
Developed the eastern area of Syracuse, with Oliver Teall and Harvey Baldwin, promoting the idea of
Syracuse as the county seat. Led the construction of the Syracuse-Utica railroad. Served three
sessions in the New York State Legislature. Named one of his sons after his friend, and future
president, Martin Van Buren. His funeral was the largest in Syracuse history at that time for a private
citizen. 3rd great-grandson of David Burt, the brother of Abigail Burt, who was the 5th great-
grandmother of President Grover Cleveland.

BURTON, BURR Apr 23, 1804 Syracuse, NY - May 4, 1865 Syracuse, NY
Salt manufacturer. Shot and killed in his home by a burglar, Henry Wilson, who confessed to the
murder in December 1865, the night before his execution, hanged in Geneseo, for a later murder
committed.

CABLE, FRANK E. Oct 14, 1858 Syracuse, NY - Mar 7, 1922 Newton Center, MA
Founded the Porter-Cable Machine Company in Syracuse, with brothers, Raymond E. Porter and
George G. Porter, in 1906.

CANNELLOS, BARBARA JOHANNA May 13, 1963 Syracuse, NY - Dec 28, 1993 Syracuse, NY
Owned and operated Cosmo's Pizza, a Syracuse University-area restaurant on Marshall Street, with
her father, George J. Cannellos and uncle, Demosthenes C. Stathis.

CANNELLOS, GEORGE JOHN Sept 13, 1925 Syracuse, NY - Jan 11, 2013 Syracuse, NY
Owned and operated Cosmo's Pizza, a Syracuse University-area restaurant on Marshall Street, from
1963-2013.

CARROLL, FRANCIS EDWARD Nov 16, 1830 Philadelphia, PA - Apr 16, 1912 Syracuse, NY
Mayor of Syracuse (D) from 1871-1872. First President of the Central City Baseball Club of Syracuse.

CARROLL (Henrici), **JEAN** (Mary) May 4, 1916 Toledo, OH - Jul 6, 1990 Liverpool, NY
Vaudeville and burlesque actress. Appeared in the films, *Dream Follies* and *Varieties on Parade*.
Daughter of actress Fern Lacey, the original *Buster Brown* in vaudeville.

CARY, BRADLEY Aug 19, 1804 Sullivan County, NY - Jan 29, 1893 Syracuse, NY
With **Matilda Phelps Cary** (Aug 12, 1806 Hebron, CT - Nov 3, 1887 Syracuse, NY), the grandparents of Sarah Huntington Sturges Fitch, the wife of Ezra H. Fitch, co-founder of Abercrombie & Fitch.

CASEY, BOB (Orrin Robinson) Jan 26, 1859 Adolphus, ON, Canada - Nov 28, 1936 Syracuse, NY
Played nine games for the Detroit Wolverines in 1882, hitting one home run with seven RBI. Teammate of Hall of Famer, Ned Hanlon. Claimed to have inspired the Ernest Thayer poem, *Casey at the Bat*, though Thayer claimed "Casey" was fictionalized.

CATON, LAWRENCE Sept 23, 1835 Syracuse, NY - Dec 22, 1905 Syracuse, NY
With **Flora Roselle Hoyt Caton** (Jul 27, 1837 Syracuse, NY - Apr 10, 1880 Gloversville, NY), the parents of Eva Caton Remington, the wife of painter and illustrator, Frederic Remington.

CHAMBERLAIN (Clere)**, ETHEL** Syracuse, NY - Oct 2, 1931 Syracuse, NY
Author and illustrator. Wrote *Omar, the Discontented Calf*, *Shoes and Ships and Sealing Wax*, *The Romance of Old Glory* and *Minnie, the Little Fish Who Lived in a Shoe*.

CHAPIN, H. WINFIELD (Henry) 1868 Oswego, NY - Nov 18, 1954 Syracuse, NY
Founded the Brown-Lipe-Chapin Company, supplier of gears for General Motors, with Alexander T. Brown and Charles E. Lipe, in Syracuse. Husband of philanthropist, Marie Chapin.

CHAPIN (Arnold)**, MARIE** 1876 - Nov 19, 1956 Palm Beach, FL
Philanthropist. First person elected life member and Honorary President of the Syracuse Symphony Association. Leading benefactor for the Syracuse University College of Fine Arts. Wife of industrialist, Henry Winfield Chapin.

CHAPPELL, CHARLES E. Sept 15, 1861 Fulton, NY - Apr 30, 1937 Syracuse, NY
Founded C.E. Chappell & Sons in Syracuse in 1924, first opened with Francis E. Bacon, as the Bacon & Chappell Company in 1895.

CHASE, FRANKLIN HENRY Sept 15, 1864 Syracuse, NY – May 24, 1940 Syracuse, NY
Syracuse city historian. Secretary of the Onondaga County Historical Society. Associate Editor of the *Syracuse Journal.* Author of the *Bibliography of Syracuse History.*

CHENEY, JAMES ALEXANDER Mar 14, 1850 Syracuse, NY - Jul 8, 1919 Syracuse, NY
Diamond expert. Employed by Joseph Frankels and Sons of New York City, the owner of the Hope Diamond from 1901-1908, entrusted to make appraisals on the diamond on several occasions. Son-in-law of Thomas Gold Alvord, Lieutenant Governor of New York from 1865-1866.

CLARK, CHARLES PARSONS Nov 26, 1822 Westhampton, MA - Jun 15, 1907 Syracuse, NY
Mayor of Syracuse (R) from 1869-1870.

CLARK, MELVILLE A. Sept 12, 1883 Syracuse, NY - Dec 11, 1953 Syracuse, NY
Founded the Clark Music Company. Invented the Clark Irish Harp. Performed two songs on the first television program in Syracuse history, December 1, 1948. Nephew of Melville Clark, founder of the Melville Clark Piano Company in DeKalb, IL. Father of physicist, Dr. Melville A. Clark, who worked on the Manhattan Project during World War II.

CLARK, MELVILLE A. Dec 19, 1921 Syracuse, NY - Nov 23, 2012 Boston, MA
MIT and NASA Physicist. During World War II, worked on atomic and hydrogen bomb design for the Manhattan Project in Los Alamos. Invented the Expressor, a keyboard synthesizer, in the 1960s. Son of Melville A. Clark, founder of the Clark Music Company.

COLLINS, GEORGE KNAPP Apr 15, 1837 Spafford, NY - Aug 2, 1931 Skaneateles, NY
Civil War Union Army Captain. Oldest member of the New York State Bar Association at the time of his death. Married **Catherine Sager Collins** (Feb 16, 1836 Guilderland, NY - Dec 24, 1928 Syracuse, NY), on June 9, 1858. Awarded first place in a contest for the longest married couple, given by Loew's State Theater in Syracuse, in September 1928. She died three months later, and buried in the gown she wore to President Theodore Roosevelt's Inaugural Ball in Washington, 1905.

COLUMBUS, STEPHEN Apr 1, 1888 Brusaw, Turkey - Oct 11, 1977 Syracuse, NY
Owned and operated the Red Star Fish Fry in Syracuse. Father of Frank K. Columbus, owner of the Public Bakery in Syracuse.

COLVIN, BENJAMIN FRANKLIN Jan 23, 1798 Cambridge, NY - Dec 16, 1861 Syracuse, NY
Patriarch of one of Syracuse's oldest families. Namesake of Colvin Street in Syracuse.

COMFORT (Manning)**, ANNA** Jan 19, 1845 Trenton, NJ - Jan 11, 1931 New York, NY
Syracuse physician. Youngest member of the first class of the New York Medical College for Women in 1865. First woman to practice medicine in Syracuse. Wife of George Fisk Comfort, founder of the Syracuse Museum of Fine Arts.

COMFORT, GEORGE FISK Sept 30, 1833 Berkshire, NY - May 5, 1910 Syracuse, NY
Founder and first Director of the Syracuse Museum of Fine Arts. Founder and first Dean of the College of Fine Arts at Syracuse University, from 1873-1893. First President of the Metropolitan Museum of Fine Arts in New York City. Husband of Dr. Anna Manning Comfort, first woman to practice medicine in Syracuse.

COMSTOCK, GEORGE FRANKLIN Aug 24, 1811 Williamston, NY - Sept 27, 1882 Syracuse, NY
Associate Justice of the New York State Court of Appeals from 1855-1861. Member of the Syracuse University board of trustees and major benefactor for the university.

COOK, JOHN F. Nov 22, 1899 Syracuse, NY - May 10, 1970 Syracuse, NY
Columnist for the *Syracuse Herald-Journal*, under the pen name "Joe Beamish."

COTTRELL, ENSIGN STOVER Aug 29, 1888 Hoosick Falls, NY - Feb 27, 1947 Syracuse, NY
Left-handed pitcher for the Pittsburgh Pirates, Chicago Cubs, Philadelphia Athletics, Boston Braves
and New York Yankees from 1911-1915, appeared in 12 games for the five teams.

COWIE, WILLIAM Oct 7, 1846 Brechin, Forfarshire, Scotland - Nov 15, 1913 Syracuse, NY
Mayor of Syracuse (R) from 1890-1891. Postmaster of Syracuse, retired September 13, 1913, two
months before his death. Published poet, admirer of Shakespeare.

COWLES, OTIS BAKER Nov 6, 1831 Otisco, NY - Aug 30, 1933 Syracuse, NY
Centenarian. Voted in 21 consecutive presidential elections, first as a Whig in 1852, then a Republican
in 1856, at the formation of the Republican Party. Enjoyed a friendship with Abraham Lincoln in the
1850s, during his short time in Alton, IL. Took his first airplane ride in 1932, age 100.

CRANE (Shaffer), **ARLINE M.** Oct 14, 1832 Montrose, PA - Apr 18, 1914 Syracuse, NY
Mother of William T. Crane, owner and operator of the W.T. Crane Piano Company, the largest music
store in Syracuse, from 1887-1927. Buried next to her daughter-in-law, Crane's first wife, **Emily A.
Silver Crane** (Jun 1866 - September 15, 1904 Syracuse, NY).

CROSIER, WILLIAM HENRY HARRISON Aug 30, 1843 Skaneateles, NY - Mar 14, 1903 NY
Awarded the Medal of Honor heroism at Peach Tree Creek, GA in 1864, during the Civil War.

CROUSE, CHARLES EDWARD Jan 31, 1850 Chittenango, NY - Jan 13, 1922 Syracuse, NY
Last survivor of six members of the Crouse family, pioneers in the grocery business in Syracuse and
Utica. Nephew of grocer and banker, John R. Crouse. Cousin of John J. Crouse, Mayor of Syracuse in
1876 and grocer, Jacob Crouse.

CROUSE, HUNTINGTON BEARD Aug 29, 1872 Fayetteville, NY - Jun 11, 1943 Syracuse, NY
Founded the Crouse-Hinds Company in Syracuse, inventor and manufacturer of the first traffic light,
with Jesse L. Hinds, in 1897. Father-in-law of Syracuse businessman, Lawrence L. Witherill.

CROUSE, JACOB Oct 22, 1824 Mindenville, NY - Nov 1, 1900 Syracuse, NY
Central New York grocer. Founded Jacob Crouse & Brothers in Syracuse, in 1869. Memorialized with
an 80-ton boulder to mark his grave, moved six miles, 900 feet per day, over the course of eight
weeks in 1904, commissioned by his son, Charles M. Crouse. Cousin of John J. Crouse, Mayor of
Syracuse in 1876. Nephew of businessman, John R. Crouse.

CROUSE, JOHN JACOB Aug 16, 1834 Syracuse, NY - Feb 10, 1886 Syracuse, NY
Mayor of Syracuse (R) in 1876. Kevin McQuain, an 18-year old Syracuse University student, was
arrested in 1988, breaking into the Crouse mausoleum as a prank, stealing his skull, boiling it in water,

cleaning it for a sculpting project in his art class. McQuain founded Skully Records after graduation. Son of businessman, John R. Crouse. Cousin of merchants, Jacob Crouse and Charles E. Crouse.

CROUSE, JOHN R. Jun 4, 1802 Mindenville, NY - Jun 25, 1889 Syracuse, NY
Syracuse wholesale grocer and banker. Wealthiest man in Syracuse at the time of his death. Built the Crouse College of Fine Arts at Syracuse University in 1889, formally the John Crouse Memorial College for Women. Father of John J. Crouse, Mayor of Syracuse in 1876. Uncle of grocers, Jacob Crouse and Charles E. Crouse.

DAILEY, JOHN PETER Dec 8, 1914 Pittston, PA - Dec 30, 1973 Syracuse, NY
Founded the Syracuse Pharmaceutical Company.

DANFORTH (Langdon)**, OLIVE** 1768 Brookfield, MA - Aug 29, 1842 Syracuse, NY
Mother of Amanda Danforth, the first white child born in Onondaga County. Daughter-in-law of Revolutionary War Continental Army veteran, Asa Danforth Sr., the second white settler of Onondaga County. Great-grandmother of Mary Elizabeth Outwater White, the wife of Andrew Dickson White, first President of Cornell University.

DARLEIGH (Burke)**, HAZEL L.** 1870 - Mar 4, 1928 Hannibal, NY
Vaudeville actress. Second wife of playwright, producer and actor, Dan Darleigh, known throughout the country for his performance of "Old St. Stebbins."

DAVIS, THOMAS TREADWELL Aug 22, 1810 Middlebury, VT - May 2, 1872 Washington D.C.
United States Representative-NY from 1863-1867. Father of Major Alexander Henry Davis, who purchased property in Syracuse in 1873, naming it Thornden Park. Grandson of Thomas Tredwell, United States Representative-NY from 1791-1795.

DEAN, ROOSEVELT T. Jul 18, 1943 Phenix City, AL - Apr 4, 2009 Syracuse, NY
Syracuse-area blues singer, guitarist and songwriter. Inducted into the Syracuse Area Music Awards Hall of Fame in 2008.

DECKER, JAMES HARRISON Aug 27, 1911 Elmira, NY - Oct 10, 1974 Syracuse, NY
Syracuse University Athletic Director from 1964-1973, succeeding Lew Andreas.

DE LIMA, PAUL Feb 4, 1881 San Paolo, Brazil - Dec 23, 1972 Syracuse, NY
Founded the Paul de Lima Coffee Company in Syracuse, in 1916.

DELLAS, JERRY Mar 15, 1896 Greece - Mar 23, 1952 Syracuse, NY
Founded the Syracuse University-area restaurant, Varsity Pizza, in 1925. Grandfather of John Dellas, co-owner of Faegan's Pub in Syracuse.

DELLAS, SPUD (Speros) Jul 6, 1923 Syracuse, NY - Dec 14, 1992 Syracuse, NY
Owned and operated the Syracuse University-area restaurant, Varsity Pizza, with his brothers, Ted Dellas and John Dellas, for 50 years, founded by their father, Jerry Dellas, in 1925. Originated the flag-turning ceremony at the restaurant following each Syracuse football win, in 1973. World War II veteran spent nine months as a German prisoner-of-war. Father of John Dellas, co-owner of Faegan's Pub in Syracuse.

DENISON, HENRY DELMATER Mar 22, 1822 Pompey, NY - Dec 19, 1882 Syracuse, NY
Co-founded the contracting firm, Denison & Belden, with James Jerome Belden, in Syracuse. Built a large portion of the Erie Canal.

DEY, DONALD M. Jun 5, 1853 Abernathy, Scotland - 1946 Syracuse, NY
Founded the Dey Brothers Department Store with his brothers, Robert Dey and James G.S. Dey, in Elmira in 1877, and Syracuse in 1883.

DEY, JAMES G. S. Jul 12, 1860 Abernathy, Scotland - Dec 12, 1925 Syracuse, NY
Founded the Dey Brothers Department Store with his brothers, Robert Dey and Donald M. Dey, in Elmira in 1877, and Syracuse in 1883. Narrowly escaped death, October 16, 1890, when the Leland Hotel caught fire, killing eight, injuring 30.

DEY, ROBERT Nov 25, 1849 Abernathy, Scotland - Aug 13, 1943 Syracuse, NY
Founded the Dey Brothers Department Store with his brothers, Donald M. Dey and James G.S. Dey, in Elmira in 1877, and Syracuse in 1883. Grandfather of Margaret Drummond Marcellus, the wife of John F. Marcellus, President of Marcellus Casket.

DEY, VIRGINIA E. Feb 22, 1917 Syracuse, NY - Feb 11, 2001 Syracuse, NY
Last direct Dey family member to work at the Dey Brothers Department Store, retiring in 1982. Daughter of Dey Brothers co-founder, Donald M. Dey.

DICKERSON, QIANA 1979 Syracuse, NY - Apr 3, 1991 Syracuse, NY
Murder victim. Reported missing, April 1991, her bones were discovered five years later, February 20, 1996, on the property of Stanley E. Grobsmith, 555 Columbus Avenue in Syracuse, by three young boys. Police searched Grobsmith's home, 227 Charles Avenue in Solvay, found her leg and torso wrapped in plastic, sealed in cardboard boxes. He hanged himself the next day, with an extension cord in a police department interview room at the Public Safety Building.

DIDAMA, HENRY DARWIN Jun 17, 1823 Perryville, NY - Oct 4, 1905 Syracuse, NY
Dean Emeritus of the College of Medicine of Syracuse University. President of the Syracuse, Onondaga, New York Central and New York State Medical Societies and New York State Medical Association. Namesake of Didama Street in Syracuse.

DILLAYE, BLANCHE (Annie) Sept 4, 1851 Syracuse, NY - Dec 31, 1931 Philadelphia, PA
Painter. First President of the Plastic Club in Philadelphia, the first women's art club, in 1897. Studied art in Paris, under Eduardo-León Garrido. Cousin of Florence Dillaye Vann, the wife of Irving G. Vann, Mayor of Syracuse in 1879.

DILLAYE, HENRY AUGUSTUS Jun 25, 1813 Plymouth, NY - Apr 18, 1889 Syracuse, NY
Father-in-law of Irving G. Vann, Mayor of Syracuse in 1879. Son-in-law of James Birdsall, United States Representative-NY from 1815-1817. Brother-in-law of William M. Fenton, Lieutenant Governor of Michigan from 1848-1852. Uncle of artist, Blanche Dillaye.

DRAKE, ERNEST W. 1871 Syracuse, NY - May 31, 1936 Syracuse, NY
Opera conductor and musical director. Known professionally as "Whitney Bennington." Worked with Anna Held, George M. Cohen and Madame Melba. Directed Lillian Russell in the stage revival of *Ermine*, in 1903.

DRAKE (Mills)**, MARIAN** Jul 24, 1902 Syracuse, NY - Dec 14, 1983 Syracuse, NY
Mother of the first set of surviving triplets born in Syracuse, two boys, one girl, May 3, 1935 at Syracuse Memorial Hospital. Three prior sets of triplets, born in Syracuse since 1900, did not survive. Direct-descendant of *Mayflower* passenger, Thomas Fuller.

DRINKWINE, WILLIAM ALFRED May 14, 1873 Syracuse, NY - Nov 6, 1931 Syracuse, NY
Founded the W.A. Drinkwine Funeral Service in Syracuse. Father of stock company actress, Gertrude Drinkwine Rich.

DRISCOLL, MICHAEL Feb 9, 1851 Syracuse, NY - Jan 19, 1929 Syracuse, NY
United States Representative-NY from 1899-1913. Member of a Congressional delegation that sailed to the Far East on a goodwill tour, led by United States Secretary of War, William Howard Taft and Alice Roosevelt, the daughter of President Theodore Roosevelt, in 1905.

DUGUID, HENRY LYMAN Dec 25, 1832 Pompey, NY - Dec 30, 1888 Tucson, AZ
Owned and operated the Duguid Saddlery Company. President of Syracuse Savings Bank from 1883-1888. Delegate to the 1884 Republican National Convention. Namesake of Duguid Park, corner of Butternut Street and Grant Boulevard, North side of Syracuse. Father-in-law of Donald M. Dey, co-founder of Dey Brothers.

DUNN, HERBERT A. Aug 21, 1893 Fabius, NY - Jan 6, 1989 Fort Lauderdale, FL
Founded Bresee Chevrolet with his father-in-law, Stephen K. Bresee, in Syracuse in 1922.

DUNNING, WILLIAM DENISON Feb 11, 1837 Whitestown, NY - Feb 8, 1918 Syracuse, NY
President of Alexander Bradley & Dunning Iron Works in Syracuse. Son-in-law of William H. Shankland, Associate Justice of the New York Court of Appeals. Uncle of William Shankland Andrews,

Associate Justice of the New York Court of Appeals

DURNEY, HELEN Aug 17, 1904 Syracuse, NY - Jun 18, 1970 Syracuse, NY
Head of the Education Department for the Syracuse Museum of Fine Arts. Employed by the Knopf
Publishing Company in New York City. Drew the pre-Disney illustrations for the children's book
Dumbo, the Flying Elephant, written by Syracuse-native, Helen Aberson and illustrated by Aberson's
first husband, Harold Pearl.

DURSTON, ALFRED HOWLETT Dec 13, 1876 Syracuse, NY - Oct 5, 1926 Syracuse, NY
President of the Durston Gear Corporation in Syracuse. Yale University football player from
1897-1899. Grandson of salt manufacturer, Parley L. Howlett. Great-grandson of Parley Howlett,
founder of Howlett Hill in Onondaga County.

DWIGHT, HENRY DALZELL 1866 Syracuse, NY - Sept 9, 1929 Flint, MI
Owned and operated the Dwight & Nye Drug Store in Syracuse, with Frederick J. Nye.

EARLL, NEHEMIAH HEZEKIAH Oct 5, 1787 Whitehall, NY - Aug 25, 1872 Mottville, NY
United States Representative-NY from 1839-1841. Onondaga County Judge, first in county history,
from 1823-1831. Superintendent of the Onondaga Salt Springs from 1831-1836. Blind later in life.
Cousin of Jonas Earll Jr., United States Representative-NY from 1827-1831.

EDGERTON (Hagadorn)**, HELENE M.** Apr 19, 1922 - Dec 29, 1994 Skaneateles, NY
Porcelain collector, whose collection of Dresden, Meissen and Sevres is exhibited at the Everson
Museum of Art in Syracuse.

EDWARDS, DANIEL MURRAY Mar 25, 1861 Johnstown, NY - May 25, 1929 Syracuse, NY
Founded E.W. Edwards and Son, with his father, Eleazer W. Edwards, in 1889. Brother of industrialist,
Oliver Murray Edwards Sr.

EDWARDS, ELEAZER WELLS Apr 17, 1838 Johnstown, NY - Nov 25, 1911 Syracuse, NY
Founded E.W. Edwards and Son, with his son, Daniel M. Edwards, in 1889. Father of industrialist,
Oliver Murray Edwards Sr.

EDWARDS, OLIVER MURRAY Oct 20, 1862 Ephratah, NY - Jul 2, 1938 Eagle Bay, NY
Founder and chairman of the O.M. Edwards Company. Invented railroad equipment for railway cars.
Son of Eleazer W. Edwards, brother of Daniel M. Edwards, co-founders of E.W. Edwards and Son.

EDWARDS, OLIVER MURRAY Dec 29, 1896 Syracuse, NY - Jan 1977 Syracuse, NY
Secretary-treasurer of the O.M. Edwards Company, founded by his father, Oliver M. Edwards Sr.
Grandson of Eleazer W. Edwards, co-founder of E.W. Edwards and Son. Son-in-law of shoemaker,
Albert Nettleton.

EGGERS, MELVIN A. Feb 21, 1916 Fort Wayne, IN - Nov 20, 1994 Syracuse, NY
Ninth Chancellor and President of Syracuse University, from 1971-1991. During his term, the Carrier Dome was built and Pam Am Flight 103 exploded over Lockerbie, Scotland, killing 270 people, including 35 Syracuse University students

ELLIS, LARRY H. May 20, 1942 - Jun 14, 2012 Syracuse, NY
Founder and pastor of God's Way Church of Jesus in Syracuse. Funk singer whose hit, "Funky Thing, Parts 1 & 2", was sampled by Jay-Z on his song, "Success." Grandson of Grammy Award-winning guitarist, Libba Cotton.

EVERSON, GILES Apr 1822 Manlius, NY - Oct 3, 1902 Syracuse, NY
Syracuse merchant. Built the Everson Building in Syracuse in 1889. Owned the Syracuse House property, downtown Syracuse, when it was sold in 1896 to build Onondaga Savings Bank.

EVERSON, HELEN S. Mar 9, 1859 Syracuse, NY - Mar 21, 1941 Syracuse, NY
Patron of the Syracuse Museum of Fine Arts. Donated $1 million to fund the museum in accordance of her will, changing the name to the Everson Museum of Art in 1942. Daughter of merchant, Giles Everson.

FALK, SAWYER Dec 9, 1898 Key West, FL - Aug 30, 1961 Paris, France
Head of the Syracuse University Drama Department from 1927-1961, which included students, Peter Falk, Suzanne Pleshette and Jerry Stiller. Directed the Mel Brooks play, *Shinbone Alley*, on Broadway in 1957.

FARMER, HARRY HAILE Jun 26, 1871 Gouverneur, NY - May 1, 1957 Syracuse, NY
Mayor of Syracuse (R) from 1920-1921.

FEARON, GEORGE RANDOLPH Mar 12, 1883 Oneida, NY - Jan 2, 1976 Naples, FL
New York State Senator from 1921-1936, President pro tempore from 1931-1932. Presented Charles Lindbergh with a set of Syracuse China, made by Onondaga Potteries, during "Lindbergh Day" in Syracuse, July 28, 1927, two months after his historic solo flight across the Atlantic Ocean.

FINDLEY, JOHN V. Feb 24, 1920 Syracuse, NY - Sept 29, 1992 Syracuse, NY
Wrote a letter to the editor of the *Post-Standard*, September 27, 1971, titled "Art or Hokum", questioning Yoko Ono's qualifications as an artist, prior to her three-week show, "This Is Not Here", at the Everson Museum of Art in Syracuse, October 9, 1971. Yoko Ono and her husband, ex-Beatle, John Lennon, wrote an amusing response to the paper on October 7th, upon their arrival at the Hotel Syracuse. John & Yoko's guests in Syracuse included fellow ex-Beatle, Ringo Starr, guitarist, Eric Clapton, poet, Allen Ginsberg, producer, Phil Spector, studio musicians, Klaus Voorman, Jim Keltner and Nicky Hopkins and anti-war protestor, Abbie Hoffman, among many other celebrities and artists.

FLINT, CHARLES W. Nov 14, 1878 Stouffville, ON, Canada - Dec 12, 1964 Binghamton, NY
Fifth Chancellor of Syracuse University, from 1922-1936.

FLOOK, WALTER E. May 6, 1915 Syracuse, NY - Jan 24, 2003 Sandy Creek, NY
Husband of Elizabeth Hofmann Flook, the great-granddaughter of Frank W. Hoffmann, founder of the Hofmann Packing Company. Acquired control of the company in 1968, with John Kachmarik, changing its name to the Hofmann Sausage Company. Coined the term, "Ball Park Frank", in the 1930s, when the plant was located on Hiawatha Boulevard, close to MacArthur Stadium, home of the Syracuse Chiefs. Father of Rusty (Walter A.) Flook, President of the Hofmann Sausage Company from 1998-2012.

FOBES, ALAN CUTLER Sept 9, 1868 Syracuse, NY - Jan 5, 1944 Syracuse, NY
Mayor of Syracuse (R) from 1904-1909. Developed Burnet Park in Syracuse. Good friend of Connie Mack, Hall of Fame owner and manager of the Philadelphia Athletics.

FOGG, PRESTON D. Apr 14, 1889 Boston, MA - Feb 23, 1969 Syracuse, NY
Quarterback and captain of the Syracuse University football team in 1911.

FORSYTH, GEORGE Dec 4, 1875 Syracuse, NY - May 20, 1953 Syracuse, NY
Engineer for the New York Central Railroad from 1896-1945. First engineer to bring the *Empire State Express* over the elevated route into Syracuse, April 24, 1936.

FRANK, CARLTON DAVID Jan 11, 1970 - Dec 2, 2010 Syracuse, NY
His final day began smoking cocaine, entering a house, 1413 West Colvin Street, stripping naked, jumping out a second floor window, managing to find his way, one-half mile to a home on the 100 block of Arlington Avenue, where he was arrested, dying in police custody. The newspaper headlines read "Naked man dies smoking cocaine, breaking into two Syracuse homes."

FRANKLIN, H. H. (Herbert) Sept 1, 1866 Lisle, NY - Apr 16, 1956 Syracuse, NY
Owned and operated the H.H. Franklin Automobile Company. Built the most successful American direct, air-cooled cars, designed by John Wilkinson, from 1902-1934. Owned the first die-casting business, coining the term "die cast." Brother of Howard L. Franklin, President of the Franklin Die Casting Corporation.

FRANKLIN, HOWARD L. Feb 5, 1857 Lisle, NY - Oct 16, 1926 Syracuse, NY
President of the Franklin Die Casting Corporation. Died from a heart attack, playing golf at the Bellevue Country Club, one month after Albert J. Will, President of the Will & Baumer Candle Company, died on the same spot, from a heart attack. Brother of H.H. Franklin, owner of the H.H. Franklin Automobile Company.

FRAZIER, GEORGE KASSON Jan 7, 1861 Syracuse, NY - Feb 5, 1913 New York, NY

Owned and managed the Syracuse Stars of the American Association in 1890, finishing in sixth place, folding at the end of the season.

FULMER, LEONARD SCOTT Aug 21, 1893 Syracuse, NY - May 17, 1967 Fayetteville, NY
Co-founded Cheplin Biological Laboratories in Syracuse, with Dr. Harry A. Cheplin, in 1932, renamed Bristol Laboratories in 1942.

GABRIELSON, FRANK Mar 13, 1910 New York, NY - Jan 24, 1980 Woodland Hills, CA
Screenwriter and playwright. Adapted *The Wizard of Oz* for the St. Louis Municipal Opera in 1942, and for a special one hour episode of *The Shirley Temple Show* in 1960.

GAGE, HENRY HILL Sept 7, 1817 Onondaga County, NY - Sept 16, 1884 Syracuse, NY
Husband of social reformer, Matilda Joslyn Gage. Father of Maud Gage Baum, the wife of L. Frank Baum, author of *The Wonderful Wizard of Oz* series of children's books. Grandfather of Dorothy Louise Gage, namesake of "Dorothy" in *The Wizard of Oz*. Uncle of actress, Blanche Weaver.

GALLUP, J. HOYT 1865 Marcellus, NY - Mar 15, 1925 Syracuse, NY
Owned and operated the J. Hoyt Paving Company in Syracuse. Supervised the laying of more pavement in Syracuse than any other person of his time.

GAMMAGE, JONNY EARL Jul 20, 1964 Syracuse, NY - Oct 12, 1995 Pittsburgh, PA
African-American motorist, pulled over during a traffic stop on Route 51, beaten and suffocated by five white police officers, John Vojtas, who was acquitted of manslaughter charges in 1996, Milton Mulholland and Michael Albert, who had their charges dropped following two mistrials, and Keith Henderson and Shawn Patterson. He was driving a Jaguar belonging to his cousin, Ray Seals, defensive end for the Pittsburgh Steelers, Tampa Bay Buccaneers and Carolina Panthers from 1989-1997.

GARDNER, GEORGE Apr 26, 1825 Derby, Derbyshire, England - Mar 23, 1893 Syracuse, NY
First Superintendent of Oakwood Cemetery, from its dedication in 1859 until 1896. Dug the first grave in the cemetery for Nellie G. Raleigh Williamson. Lived in a cottage at the cemetery where his daughter, **Lillian Oakwood Gardner** (Apr 14, 1863 Syracuse, NY - May 2, 1864 Syracuse, NY), was born, named for the cemetery, and died of scarlet fever 10 months later.

GARDNER, WALTER EDWIN Aug 7, 1849 Watertown, NY - Jul 9, 1927 Syracuse, NY
Published the *Post-Standard* from 1898-1917.

GARLAND, BENJAMIN H. Jun 10, 1895 DeKalb, TX - Jan 13, 1966 Syracuse, NY
Founded the Garland Brothers Funeral Home in 1936, the first African-American funeral parlor in Syracuse. Supervisor from the 15th Ward in Syracuse, first African-American elected, in 1961.

GARROW, ROBERT FRANCIS Mar 4, 1936 Dannemora, NY - Sept 11, 1978 Fishkill, NY
Spree killer. Convicted rapist, stabbed to death, Daniel Porter and Susan Petz in Wevertown, Daniel Domblewski in Wells, and strangled 16-year old, Alicia Hauck in Syracuse, hiding her body in Oakwood Cemetery, disclosing this information to his consul, Francis R. Belge and Frank H. Armani, who refused to divulge the location of her body, claiming attorney-client privilege. Shot and captured after eleven days on the run, following the murders in 1973. Escaped from the Fishkill Correctional Facility, September 9, 1978, when his son, Robert F. Garrow III, smuggled a gun in a bucket of fried chicken, shot to death after two days, buried near the location he hid Alicia Hauck's body in 1973. Armani wrote the book, *Privileged Information*, about the "Buried Bodies Case."

GARY, ANTWON P. Jul 12, 1979 Syracuse, NY - Jul 20, 2001 Syracuse, NY
Three-time all-city and county linebacker for Henninger High School in Syracuse, from 1995-1997, and the University of Massachusetts. Shot in the face and killed following an argument by Maximino Estrada, who was sentenced to 32 years in prison.

GAYLORD, ALBERT E. Aug 30, 1853 Syracuse, NY - May 22, 1929 Syracuse, NY
Conductor and composer. Bandmaster and orchestra leader at the Grand Opera House in Syracuse for 25 years. Husband of actress, Jeannette Gaylord.

GAYLORD, HENRY J. May 1, 1872 Syracuse, NY - Mar 28, 1955 Syracuse, NY
Founded Gaylord Brothers with his brother, Willis E. Gaylord, in Syracuse in 1896.

GAYLORD (Guy), **JEANNETTE** (Marie) May 3, 1858 England - Dec 21, 1932 Syracuse, NY
American stage actress. Appeared in stock theater companies throughout the country. Wife of conductor and composer, Albert E. Gaylord.

GEDDES, JAMES Jul 22, 1763 Carlisle, PA - Aug 19, 1838 Syracuse, NY
United States Representative-NY from 1813-1815. Salt manufacturer. Early surveyor of the city of Syracuse, appointed by Surveyor-General, Simeon DeWitt. Chief engineer of the New York canals, including the Erie Canal. Namesake of the town of Geddes on the West side of Syracuse and Geddes Street.

GEER, GEORGE HARRISON 1882 Syracuse, NY - Nov 14, 1933 Syracuse, NY
Publishing house representative. Committed suicide by carbon monoxide poisoning in his garage.

GENGE (Ryan), **BESSIE** Dec 22, 1902 Baldwinsville, NY - Jan 21, 1980 Syracuse, NY
Elected to the Syracuse Women's Bowling Association Hall of Fame in 1976.

GERE (Clark), **MARION LEMIRA** Nov 19, 1892 - Mar 8, 1977 Syracuse, NY
Local singer. Performed her own radio program in the 1930s, working with future Hollywood actor, William Lundigan. Great-granddaughter of Nathaniel Burt Searle, early settler of Onondaga Valley.

GERE, ROBERT Nov 30, 1796 Groton, CT - Dec 18, 1877 Syracuse, NY
Syracuse salt manufacturer. Assisted in the construction of the Episcopal Church in Geddes and the Salina and Liverpool locks along the Oswego Canal. Brother of William Stanton Gere, early homesteader in the town of Camillus.

GERE, WILLIAM STANTON Jul 28, 1894 Syracuse, NY - Mar 11, 1976 Syracuse, NY
Co-founded O'Brien & Gere Engineers, Inc. in Syracuse in 1944. Great-grandson of William Stanton Gere, early homesteader in the town of Camillus. 6th great grandson of William Brewster, *Mayflower* passenger, the Reverend Elder of the Pilgrim's church in Plymouth and the oldest pilgrim to have participated at the first Thanksgiving.

GILL, JOSEPH Aug 9, 1836 East Williamson, NY - Jul 14, 1924 Syracuse, NY
With **Cynthia D. Scullen Gill** (Oct 4, 1839 - Apr 19, 1897 Syracuse, NY), the parents of architect, Irving Gill, whose work is located throughout Southern California.

GOEBEL (Kyburz)**, LUCIE JENNY** Nov 11, 1903 Zurich, Switzerland - Jul 4, 1963 Syracuse, NY
Survived Japanese imprisonment in the Philippine Islands during World War II, confined in the Santo Tomas Internment Camp with her husband and two children, for 18 months before their release to home confinement. Her husband, who remained in prison, died of starvation, five days before the United States liberated the islands in 1945.

GOODELLE, WILLIAM PROVOST May 25, 1838 Tully, NY - Jun 13, 1918 Syracuse, NY
Onondaga County District Attorney, elected in 1871. Prosecuted Owen Lindsay, who killed Francis A. Colvin in Baldwinsville, December 19, 1873, winning conviction through blood evidence. Lindsay was executed, March 26, 1875.

GRAHAM, WILLIAM PRATT Nov 24, 1871 Oswego, NY - Jan 10, 1962 Syracuse, NY
Chancellor of Syracuse University from 1937-1942. First alumnus to hold the office.

GRANGER, AMOS PHELPS Jun 3, 1789 Suffield, CT - Aug 20, 1866 Syracuse, NY
United States Representative-NY from 1855-1859. War of 1812 United States Army Brigadier General. Delivered the welcoming address for Revolutionary War General, Marquis de Lafayette, on his visit to Syracuse in 1825. Cousin of Francis Granger, United States Representative-NY from 1835-1837, 1839-1841 and 1841-1843. Nephew of Gideon Granger, United States Postmaster General from 1801-1814.

GRANGER, MERTON ELWOOD Feb 8, 1882 Wayland, NY - Nov 26, 1974 Syracuse, NY
Co-founded the Syracuse Society of Architects, served as President from 1944-1945.

GREENWAY, JOHN Jan 6, 1821 England - May 28, 1887 Syracuse, NY
Owned and operated the Greenway Brewery in Syracuse from 1850-1887. Fed 20,000 people hurt by a depression, in a Clinton Square barbeque, New Year's Day, 1870.

GREGORY (Vermilyea), **MILDRED GRACE** Feb 29, 1880 Syracuse, NY - Nov 15, 1956 Syracuse, NY
Aunt of Walter L. Farley, best-selling author of the children's book, *The Black Stallion*.

GREGORY, APRIL Sept 30, 1977 Syracuse, NY - May 24, 1996 Syracuse, NY
Murder victim. Pushed violently to the floor, causing her head to split, by boyfriend, Terrence R. Evans, who claimed he put her to bed, woke up to find her dead, panicked, dismembered her body and hid her at the home he shared with his parents, 227 McKinley Avenue, next-door neighbors to April and her parents. Evans confessed to the police, November 18, 1997, leading them to her body.

GRIFFIN, JOSEPH ABBOT Dec 13, 1862 Clay, NY - Jul 9, 1937 Syracuse, NY
Chairman of the Onondaga Parks and Planning Commission. Namesake of Griffin Field, off the Onondaga Lake Parkway. President of the Hotel Syracuse from 1924-1937.

GROAT, WILLIAM AVERY Nov 9, 1876 Canastota, NY - Sept 9, 1945 Syracuse, NY
President of the Medical Society of New York in 1938. President of the Onondaga County Medical Society. Husband of Dr. Nellie Nichols Bacon Groat, the daughter of Francis E. Bacon, co-founder of Bacon & Chappell Company, with Charles E. Chappell, in 1895.

GRODAVENT, FRANK J. 1852 Syracuse, NY - Dec 15, 1941 Denver, CO
Syracuse-area architect. Designed the Onondaga Savings Bank Building, the Gridley Building and many James Street residences.

HAGGERTY, MICHAEL CHARLES 1960 Watertown, NY – Jun 30, 1974 Watertown, NY
Killed in an automobile accident. Memorialized in 1982 by his younger brother, Thomas Haggerty, a Syracuse University art student, with a 620-pound statue of a lion marking his grave. Originally buried in St. Mary's Cemetery, reinterred when the Syracuse Diocese objected to the Haggerty family placing the lion at the cemetery.

HAIGHT, JAY ALLEN Feb 3, 1878 Somerset, NY - Jul 26, 1921 Syracuse, NY
With **Lorena Root Robertson Haight** (Jun 20, 1880 Middleport, NY - Aug 31, 1968 Syracuse, NY), the parents of Angeline Haight Baysinger, the wife of Reaves H. Baysinger, Sr., head football coach for Syracuse University from 1947-1948. Grandparents of Reaves Baysinger Jr., Syracuse quarterback in 1944 and Navy from 1946-1948.

HALSTED (Palmer), **CHARLOTTE COOKE** 1866 Syracuse, NY - Jul 22, 1932 Syracuse, NY
Mother of Dr. James Addison Halsted, the third husband of Anna Eleanor Roosevelt, the daughter of President Franklin Delano Roosevelt and First Lady Eleanor Roosevelt. Died from injuries when a car

driven by her husband, Dr. Thomas Henry Halsted, lost control and plunged over an embankment in Batavia, July 2, 1935.

HALSTED (Bridgford)**, LOLA** Oct 18, 1865 - Nov 14, 1894 Syracuse, NY
Daughter of Civil War Confederate Army Major, David Benjamin Bridgford, Provost Marshal to General Thomas "Stonewall" Jackson. First wife of Dr. Thomas Henry Halsted, whose son, Dr. James A. Halsted, from his second marriage, would marry Anna Eleanor Roosevelt, the daughter of President Franklin Delano Roosevelt and First Lady Eleanor Roosevelt.

HALSTED, THOMAS HENRY Jul 8, 1865 Listowel, ON, Canada - Nov 20, 1956 LaFayette, NY
Physician. Father of Dr. James Addison Halsted, the third husband of Anna Eleanor Roosevelt, the daughter of President Franklin Delano Roosevelt and First Lady Eleanor Roosevelt. His third wife, Maida Lawrence Smyth, was the third cousin of British Army Captain, T.E. Lawrence, commonly known as "Lawrence of Arabia." She died in Delray Beach, August 1, 1982, age 78.

HANCHETT, MILTON WALDO Jul 12, 1822 Suffield, CT - Dec 28, 1904 Syracuse, NY
Inventor. Patented the first reclining dental chair in 1840. Father of Henry Granger Hanchett, concert pianist and composer.

HANNA, CHARLES GEORGE Apr 27, 1889 Syracuse, NY - Dec 16, 1942 Syracuse, NY
Mayor of Syracuse (R) from 1926-1929. Son-in-law of Stephen K. Bresee, founder of Bresee Chevrolet. Father of Virginia Hanna Ricks, his only child, arrested for murder in the death of her boyfriend, George Franklin Knapp, December 30, 1955 in Newboro, Ontario, Canada, stood trial for manslaughter and acquitted of all charges, February 17, 1956. She married four times, including Philadelphia Phillies and Syracuse Chiefs pitcher, Frank Pearce.

HARMS, FRANCIS HENRY Sept 11, 1923 St. Louis, MO - Aug 21, 1999 West Palm Beach, FL
Self-employed cable television operator and broadcaster. Operated WEZG-FM and WSOQ-AM in North Syracuse. Founded Upstate Cablevision and WNED-TV in Buffalo for PBS television.

HARRINGTON (Short)**, ANNA** 1897 Cheraw, SC - Oct 21, 1955 Syracuse, NY
Hired by Quaker Oats to portray "Aunt Jemima" in national advertisements and personal appearances, from 1935-1949.

HASKINS, JAMES P. 1812 LaFayette, NY - Jan 30, 1873 Syracuse, NY
Salt manufacturer. Purchased land owned by Zebulon Ostrom in 1854, and after his death in 1873, purchased by Major Alexander Henry Davis, who named the property, Thornden Park, later bought by the city of Syracuse in 1921, as part of City Beautiful, an urban planning movement to beautify cities throughout the country. Committed suicide, cutting his throat.

HAVEN, MELVIN Z. 1855 New Hartford, NY - Jun 23, 1931 Syracuse, NY
City Clerk and first Corporation Counsel for the city of Syracuse for Mayor James K. McGuire, from 1900-1901.

HAZARD, FREDERICK ROWLAND Jun 14, 1858 Peace Dale, RI - Feb 27, 1917 Syracuse, NY
President of the Solvay Process Company in Syracuse, succeeding his father and first President, Rowland G. Hazard II, from 1898-1917. Son-in-law of Charles Baldwin Sedgwick, United States Representative-NY from 1859-1863. Namesake of the Hazard Branch of the Onondaga County Public Library.

HEERMANS, FORBES Oct 25, 1856 Syracuse, NY - Sept 18, 1928 Syracuse, NY
Novelist. Author of *The Silent Witness*, *The Vagabond* and *Down the Santa Fe Trail*. Completed and edited the novel, *David Harum,* in 1898 under a prearranged plan with Edward Noyes Westcott, who was dying and could not finish his book.

HEID, MICHAEL Aug 8, 1881 Syracuse, NY - Aug 10, 1968 Syracuse, NY
Mayor of the village of Liverpool from 1935-1951. Participated in the dedication of the New York State Thruway, with Governor Thomas E. Dewey. Namesake of Heid Park in Liverpool. Co-owned and operated Heid's Grocery Store in Liverpool with his brother, William Heid. Brother of restaurateur, Valentine Heid.

HEID, VALENTINE A. Sept 3, 1888 Syracuse, NY - Jan 17, 1959 Liverpool, NY
Founder and owner of the hotdog restaurant, Heid's of Liverpool. Brother of Liverpool Mayor, Michael Heid, and restaurateur, William Heid.

HENDRICKS, FRANCIS J. Nov 23, 1834 Kingston, NY - Jun 9, 1920 Syracuse, NY
Mayor of Syracuse (R) from 1880-1881. New York State Senator from 1886-1891. Namesake of Hendricks Memorial Chapel on the Syracuse University campus, built through his charitable donation in 1929. Founded the Hendricks Photo Supply Company in 1860, the oldest continuing business in downtown Syracuse, until closing in 2009.

HENDRICKS, KATHRYN 1865 Kingston, NY - Feb 9, 1945 Syracuse, NY
Cousin of Francis J. Hendricks, Mayor of Syracuse from 1880-1881. Housekeeper and companion for Hendricks, following the death of his wife, Eliza Jane Hendricks, in 1912. Laid the cornerstone for Hendricks Memorial Chapel on the Syracuse University campus in 1929.

HERRING, LAYMON 1931 Sanford, FL - Mar 13, 2002 Rome, NY
Published the *Syracuse Banner*, a local newspaper for the African-American community. Died in the Mohawk Correctional Facility, serving time for the 1993 murder of his girlfriend, Patricia A. Nicklus. Fiancé of Shirley Turner Kinge, when she was found guilty of forgery, using stolen credit cards

belonging to the Harris family, a family of four murdered in Dryden, December 22, 1990 by her son, Michael Kinge.

HIER, GEORGE PHILIP Jan 20, 1826 Germany - Feb 22, 1901 Syracuse, NY
Mayor of Syracuse (R) in 1875. Brother of cigar manufacturer, John P. Hier.

HIER, JOHN PHILIP Jan 22, 1829 Germany - Feb 18, 1913 Syracuse, NY
Founded the Hier & Aldrich Cigar Manufacturing Company in Syracuse, with B.S. Aldrich, in 1860. Brother of George P. Hier, Mayor of Syracuse in 1875.

HIGHGATE, EDMONIA G. 1844 Syracuse, NY - Oct 14, 1870 Syracuse, NY
Daughter of freed slaves. Principal of a black school in Binghamton at age 19. Traveled to the South during the Civil War, establishing schools for the American Missionary Association. Died under mysterious circumstances in the home of an abortionist, Mrs. Paine, 67 East Taylor Street, during which time she was involved in an affair with John Henry Vosburg, assistant editor of the *National Quarterly Review*, whose wife was in a mental institution at the time of her death.

HINDS, JESSE LORENZO Jun 7, 1845 Binghamton, NY - Mar 9, 1928 St. Petersburg, FL
Founded the Crouse-Hinds Company in Syracuse, inventor and manufacturer of the first traffic light, with Huntington B. Crouse, in 1897.

HISCOCK, FRANK Sept 9, 1834 Pompey, NY - Jun 18, 1914 Syracuse, NY
United States Senator-NY from 1887-1893. United States Representative-NY from 1877-1887. Onondaga County District Attorney from 1860-1863. Uncle of Frank H. Hiscock, Chief Justice of the New York State Court of Appeals from 1916-1926.

HISCOCK, FRANK HARRIS Apr 16, 1856 Tully, NY - Jul 2, 1946 NY
Chief Justice of the New York State Court of Appeals from 1916-1926. Son Luther Harris Hiscock, co-founder of the Hiscock & Barclay Law Firm in Syracuse. Nephew of Frank Hiscock, United States Senator-NY from 1887-1893, and Charles Hiscock, Superintendent of the Onondaga Salt Reservation.

HISCOCK, LUTHER HARRIS May 2, 1824 Pompey, NY - Jun 7, 1867 Albany, NY
Co-founded the Hiscock & Barclay Law Firm in Syracuse. Shot to death at the New York State Convention by General George Washington Cole, making the front page of the *New York Times*, who accused him of having an affair with his wife, during his service in the Civil War. Father of Frank Harris Hiscock, Chief Justice of the New York State Court of Appeals from 1916-1926. Brother of Frank Hiscock, United States Senator-NY from 1887-1893 and Charles Hiscock, Superintendent of the Onondaga Salt Reservation.

HITCHCOCK, WILLIAM PAIGE Oct 23, 1862 NY - Oct 27, 1921 Syracuse, NY
Owned and operated the W.P. Hitchcock Wholesale Jewelry and Optical Company in Syracuse.
Unsuccessful Democratic candidate for mayor of Syracuse.

HOUGH, WILLIAM JERVIS Mar 20, 1795 Cazenovia, NY - Oct 4, 1869 Syracuse, NY
United States Representative-NY from 1845-1847.

HOVEY, ALFRED H. Feb 1812 - Aug 7, 1865 Syracuse, NY
Mayor of Syracuse (D) in 1850.

HOWARD (Teal)**, VIVIAN** May 14, 1948 Coffeyville, KS - Sept 17, 1992 Syracuse, NY
Radio personality. Hosted *The Gospel Show* on WAER-FM from 1982-1991 and *New Life Gospel* on
WOLF-AM from 1991-1992.

HOWARD, WALLIE Apr 23, 1959 Syracuse, NY - Oct 30, 1990 Syracuse, NY
Syracuse narcotics investigator. Shot and killed during an undercover drug deal, the first Syracuse
police officer killed in the line of duty since 1929. The FBI and DEA in Washington D.C. have played a
videotape at their training academies showing a dramatization of his murder as a learning tool for their
recruits.

HOWE, H. J. (Henry Joseph) Mar 4, 1840 Otisco, NY - May 30, 1916 Syracuse, NY
Founder and President of H.J. Howe Jewelers in Syracuse.

HUDSON, HENRY WADSWORTH Mar 1816 Hartford, CT - 1888 Syracuse, NY
Mayor of Hartford, CT from 1836-1840. Civil War Union Army officer.

HURST, SAMUEL Apr 28, 1814 Castle Carberry, Ireland - Jun 7, 1903 Syracuse, NY
Invented the carnival wheel amusement park ride, with James Mulholland, operated for the first time at
the New York State Fair, held on James Street in Syracuse, in 1848. George Ferris created his
version, the Ferris Wheel, for the World's Fair in Chicago in 1893. Street Commissioner of Syracuse,
under Mayors, Francis E. Carroll, William J. Wallace and Nathan F. Graves. Volunteer fireman on duty
the night of a disastrous powder explosion in Syracuse in 1848, killing 26 people. Oldest mason in the
city of Syracuse at the time of his death.

HYDE, SALEM Jun 22, 1846 Victory, NY - Apr 6, 1924 Syracuse, NY
Civic and business leader. President of Neal & Hyde, Inc., seller of dry wholesale goods.

JACKSON, MARY JEROME Apr 21, 1837 Syracuse, NY - Feb 14, 1927 Syracuse, NY
Syracuse educator. Founded the Keble School, on the current site of the Snowdon Apartments, in
1871. Died one month before her sister, Emma Jerome Jackson Lapham, the wife of drama critic, S.
Gurney Lapham. Cousin of Lady Randolph Churchill, the mother of Sir Winston Churchill, Prime

Minister of Great Britain from 1940-1945 and 1951-1955, and David Howell Jerome, Governor of Michigan from 1881-1882.

JAQUITH, DAVID H. Apr 18, 1918 Syracuse, NY - Feb 19, 1980 San Diego, CA
President and CEO of Vega Industries for twenty years. Conservative Party candidate for Governor of New York in 1962, losing to Nelson A. Rockefeller.

JEFFERY, HARLEY BRADLEY Jan 26, 1872 Syracuse, NY - Jan 19, 1954 Santa Monica, CA
Lecturer and author of spiritual counseling, healing and mysticism.

JENKINS, ARTHUR Jul 23, 1851 Buffalo, NY - 1903 Syracuse, NY
Founder and Manager of the *Syracuse Evening Herald* and *Sunday Herald*, from 1877-1903. Father of Mary Emma Jenkins, President of the *Syracuse Herald* from 1903-1957.

JENKINS, MARY EMMA May 5, 1879 Syracuse, NY - Aug 12, 1967 Syracuse, NY
President of the *Syracuse Herald* from 1903-1957, founded by her father, Arthur Jenkins, in 1877.

JENKS, CLARENCE E. Jan 10, 1918 Syracuse, NY - Dec 3, 1991 Daytona Beach, FL
Amateur radio operator. Instrumental in getting WOLF-AM on the air in Syracuse in the 1930s.

JENNEY, JULIA REGULA 1866 Syracuse, NY - Dec 21, 1947 Syracuse, NY
New York State Deputy Attorney General, under Carl Sherman, from 1923-1924, first woman to hold this office in New York State history. First woman lawyer in Syracuse. Founded the Women's Professional League of Syracuse.

JEROME, ISAAC Oct 25, 1786 Charlton, NY - Jul 19, 1866 Syracuse, NY
With **Aurora Murray Jerome** (Jan 18, 1785 Canaan, NY - Apr 6, 1867 New York, NY), the great-grandparents of Sir Winston Churchill, Prime Minister of Great Britain from 1940-1945 and 1951-1955. Grandparents of Jeanette Jerome, properly known as Lady Randolph Churchill, the wife of Sir Randolph Henry Spencer-Churchill, married in 1874 at the British Embassy in Paris.

JEROME, TIMOTHY Aug 6, 1756 Wallingford, CT - May 9, 1802 Pompey, NY
Brother of Aaron Jerome, the 2nd great-grandfather of Sir Winston Churchill, Prime Minister of Great Britain from 1940-1945 and 1951-1955.

JOHNSON, GARRISON BARRETT Jul 15, 1839 Palermo, NY - Jan 12, 1888 Boston, MA
Father of architect, James A. Johnson, partner in the firm, Esenwein & Johnson in Buffalo, with August C. Esenwein, designer of the Temple of Music for the Pan-American Exposition, the building where President William McKinley was shot, in 1901.

JOHNSTON, BARRY (William J.) 1864 Syracuse, NY - Dec 7, 1902 Philadelphia, PA
Theatrical stock company actor. Shot and killed theater actress, Kate Hassett, shooting her five times, striking twice, outside of Keith's Bijou Theatre on Eighth Street in Philadelphia, December 1, 1902, before turning the gun on himself. Claimed on his death bed that it was a planned double-suicide, though evidence pointed to a planned murder due to his jealous rage. Kate Hassett, married to Everett Beckwith, was buried in Calvary Cemetery, Aurora, IL.

JOHNSTON, GEORGE F. Mar 4, 1859 Ottawa, ON, Canada - Jan 18, 1910 Syracuse, NY
After his death, it was discovered his first marriage to Jennie Slade Johnston, in August 1879, was not dissolved, and his marriage to Arabella Ackerman Johnston, May 17, 1899 in Clayton, was not on record, nor was the name of the witness who signed the certificate, Harrison F. Williams. Neither wife remarried, both mothers of his children, and no legal matters came of the issue, though both women claimed to be his actual wife. **Jennie Slade Johnston** (Feb 23, 1860 Fairmont, NY - October 31, 1932 Syracuse, NY) is buried in Oakwood Cemetery. Arabella Johnston died January 21, 1974 in Vernon, age 93, buried in Whitelaw Cemetery, Canastota. Brother of stage actor, Barry Johnston.

KECK, HENRY Jul 15, 1873 Giessen, Germany - Apr 11, 1956 Syracuse, NY
Stained-glass artist. Owned and operated the Henry Keck Stained Glass Studio in Syracuse, from 1913-1956. Apprentice of Louis Comfort Tiffany in New York City. Constructed stained-glass windows for most Central New York churches, and others throughout the United States.

KECK, MAUDE 1884 Syracuse, NY - Mar 8, 1900 Syracuse, NY
First burial in Morningside Cemetery. Oakwood and Morningside cemeteries consolidated in 1976.

KEEP, GLENN M. Mar 1, 1886 Jennings, LA - Dec 21, 1952 Syracuse, NY
Syracuse Herald and *Syracuse Telegram* printer for 50 years. Four-term President of the Syracuse Typographical Union. Husband of Ada C. Keep, owner of Ada Keep's Restaurant in Syracuse.

KENYON, JOHN SNYDER May 5, 1843 Grosvenors Corner, NY - Feb 16, 1902 Syracuse, NY
Awarded the Medal of Honor during the Civil War for heroism, at Trenton, NC in 1862. Father-in-law of Harold McGrath, author of *The Perils of Pauline* movie serials.

KIRK, WILLIAM BURNS Jun 6, 1850 - Aug 27, 1911 Syracuse, NY
Mayor of Syracuse (D) from 1888-1889. Namesake of Kirk Park in Syracuse.

KIRKPATRICK, WILLIAM Nov 7, 1769 Zion, NJ - Sept 2, 1832 Syracuse, NY
United States Representative-NY from 1807-1809. Superintendent of the Onondaga Salt Springs in 1806 and 1810-1831. Namesake of Kirkpatrick Street in Syracuse.

KLOCK, M. CROUSE (Mabie) Apr 26, 1880 Syracuse, NY - Mar 11, 1955 Syracuse, NY
Syracuse business and civic leader. Director of the Great Lakes Steamship Company. Sold an old ship

to John Jacob Astor IV, who took it to New York via the Barge Canal. Grandson of grocer, Jacob Crouse, memorialized in Oakwood Cemetery with a gigantic boulder.

KRELL, BERT Nov 26, 1930 Syracuse, NY - May 25, 1979 Chicago, IL
Manufacturing representative for the Hawaiian Islands Products Company, based in Honolulu. Victim of the American Airlines Flight 191, DC-10 crash into an open field, shortly after takeoff from O'Hare Airport, killing all 271 onboard and two on the ground, the tenth-worst airline disaster in history, the deadliest-ever in the United States. Sheila Marie Snodgrass Charisse, the daughter-in-law of actress, Cyd Charisse, music promoter, Leonard Stogel, and two victims with Central New York ties, Carrier Corporation executive, Paul Trautmann, and Playboy Magazine managing editor and Syracuse University graduate, Sheldon Wax, died in the crash.

KRITZ, KARL Oct 18, 1906 Vienna, Austria - Dec 17, 1969 Syracuse, NY
First Musical Director of the Syracuse Symphony Orchestra, in 1961. Former conductor of the Metropolitan Opera House in New York City.

LAFLIN, ADDISON HENRY Oct 24, 1823 Lee, MA - Sept 24, 1878 Pittsfield, MA
United States Representative-NY from 1865-1871. Naval Officer at the Port of New York from 1871-1877, appointed by President Ulysses S. Grant.

LAPHAM (Jackson), **EMMA JEROME** Apr 1847 Syracuse, NY - Mar 21, 1927 Syracuse, NY
Wife of S. Gurney Lapham, drama critic for the *Syracuse Herald*. Cousin of Lady Randolph Churchill, the mother of Sir Winston Churchill, Prime Minister of Great Britain from 1940-1945 and 1951-1955, and David Howell Jerome, Governor of Michigan from 1881-1882.

LAPHAM, S. GURNEY (Smith) Jul 19, 1842 Farmington, NY - Jan 4, 1917 Syracuse, NY
Drama critic for the *Syracuse Herald*. Namesake for the Gurney Building in Syracuse, built by his son-in-law, W. Snowdon Smith. Nephew of Elbridge G. Lapham, United States Senator-NY from 1881-1885.

LARKIN, ALBERT E. Nov 18, 1872 Camillus, NY - Nov 2, 1943 Syracuse, NY
Central New York physician. Treated bandleader, John Philip Sousa, for bronchitis at the Hotel Syracuse, September 28, 1928, following two performances given by the John Philip Sousa Band at the Armory.

LAWRENCE, JAMES ROBBINS Sept 11, 1790 Norfolk, CT - Mar 21, 1874 Syracuse, NY
United States Attorney for the Northern District of New York, appointed by President Millard Fillmore in 1850. Grandson of Rev. Ammi Ruhamah Robbins, first Minister of the Norfolk Church of Christ Congregational, from 1761-1813. 4th great-grandson of William Bradford, *Mayflower* passenger and second Governor of the Plymouth Colony.

LEAVENWORTH, ELIAS WARNER Dec 20, 1803 Canaan, NY - Nov 25, 1887 Syracuse, NY
United States Representative-NY from 1875-1877. Mayor of Syracuse from 1849-1850, the second
Mayor in Syracuse history, and again from 1859-1860. Commissioner of the United States, appointed
by President Abraham Lincoln in 1861. First President of Oakwood Cemetery.

LEGETTE, LONNIE Jun 14, 1932 Lake View, SC - Feb 4, 2002 Syracuse, NY
Central New York blues singer. Performed with the band, Le Bleu. Father of Felisha Legette-Jack,
Syracuse University Hall of Fame basketball player from 1984-1989.

LEGG, BILL (William N.) Feb 15, 1931 Syracuse, NY - Jun 29, 2008 LaFayette, NY
With **May Melvin Legg** (1931 Syracuse, NY - Mar 1, 2015 Liverpool, NY), the parents of Douglas Legg,
their 8-year old son who went disappeared from their summer cabin in the Adirondacks, July 10, 1971,
after an extensive search, he was never found.

LEMP, MICHAEL Sept 1870 Germany - Mar 7, 1935 Syracuse, NY
Founded, owned and operated M. Lemp Jewelers & Silversmiths in Syracuse in 1890.

LEVEE, SPARKY (Myron) Dec 12, 1898 Russia - Feb 20, 1978 Syracuse, NY
Central New York radio and television personality for WSYR-AM and WSYR-TV. Concertmaster for the
original Syracuse Symphony Orchestra, and for the pit orchestra, opening night of the Loew's State
Theater in Syracuse, February 28, 1928. Performed on stage, supporting Jack Benny and Jean
Harlow, among others. First violinist and charter member of the current Syracuse Symphony
Orchestra in 1961.

LINCOLN, ABRAHAM Jan 1834 MD - Feb 20, 1903 Syracuse, NY
Notable for his name. Born 25 years after the birth of future president, Abraham Lincoln, and 26 years
before his election. His obituary in the Syracuse papers read "best known colored man of the city."

LIPE, CHARLES EHLE Mar 20, 1851 Syracuse, NY - Mar 17, 1895 Syracuse, NY
Founded the C.E. Lipe Company in Syracuse in 1880. Founded the Brown-Lipe Gear Company, now
Inland Fisher Guide, with Alexander T. Brown, in Syracuse. Later added, H. Winfield Chapin, to form
Brown-Lipe-Chapin, suppliers of gears for General Motors. Brother of industrialist, Willard Lipe.

LIPE, WILLARD CHARLES Oct 20, 1901 Syracuse, NY - Aug 16, 1929 Alexandria Bay, NY
Syracuse industrialist. Founded the General Aviation Company in Syracuse. Killed with his wife,
Eloise Estelle Hoyt Lipe (May 23, 1904 Syracuse, NY - Aug 16, 1929 Alexandria Bay, NY), dressed in
costume on their way to the Bum's Ball, a masquerade party held at the Thousand Island Yacht Club,
when their speedboat, *The Giggle*, piloted by Captain Ford E. Dodge, collided with a passenger boat,
The Thousand Islander, in the St. Lawrence River, between Wellesley and Cherry Islands, drowning
the couple and the captain. His body was recovered, August 22nd, his wife, three days later. Father of

Gordon Clifford Lipe, inventor of safety methods for skiers. Son of Syracuse industrialist, Willard Coughtry Lipe.

LIPE, WILLARD COUGHTRY Dec 21, 1861 Syracuse, NY - Sept 4, 1924 Syracuse, NY
Founded the Lipe-Rollway Corporation in Syracuse in 1908. Grandfather of Gordon Clifford Lipe, pioneer inventor of safety methods for skiers. Brother of industrialist, Charles E. Lipe.

LOGUEN (Logue)**, JERMAIN WESLEY** Feb 5, 1813 Cherry, TN - Sept 30, 1872 Syracuse, NY
Land owner, schoolteacher, an AME Zion minister and bishop, an abolitionist lecturer and a stationmaster of the Underground Railroad. Born to an enslaved woman and a white man, he escaped to St. Catherine's, Ontario, age 21, then to Rochester, settling in Syracuse. Helped arranged the escape of runaway slave, William "Jerry" Henry, commemorated in the Jerry Rescue Monument in Syracuse. Father of Dr. Sarah Frasier, the fourth African-American female doctor in the United States, and Amelia Loguen Douglass, the wife of Lewis Douglass, the son of social reformer, Frederick Douglass.

LONGSTREET, CORNELIUS TYLER Apr 19, 1814 Onondaga County, NY - Jul 4, 1881 Syracuse, NY
Clothing manufacturer. Commissioned James Renwick, architect of St. Patrick's Cathedral, New York City, and the Smithsonian Institution, Washington D.C., to design his home, where his family lived from 1855-1867, when he swapped residences with Alonzo Chester Yates, who renamed the home, Yates Castle, torn down in 1954 for construction of the Syracuse University Medical School.
Grandson of Onondaga County settler, Colonel Comfort Tyler. Husband of Caroline Adriance Redfield Longstreet, the daughter of publisher, Lewis H. Redfield and author, Anna Maria Redfield.

MACKAY (Cronk)**, DORIS** Mar 26, 1909 NJ - Mar 6, 1987 Syracuse, NY
Dancer and choreographer. Studied under ballet choreographer, George Balanchine, in New York City. Performed with the Royal Ballet of England. Central New York dance instructor.

MAGEE, WALTER W. May 23, 1861 Groveland, NY - May 27, 1927 Syracuse, NY
United States Representative-NY from 1915-1927.

MAITLAND (Wigglesworth)**, SYLVIA** Jul 8, 1897 Syracuse, NY - May 8, 1957 New York, NY
Grandmother of Howard B. Dean, Governor of Vermont from 1991-2003. Sister of author, Belden Wigglesworth.

MANCHESTER, WILLIAM S. Sept 6, 1830 Remsen, NY - Feb 17, 1917 Syracuse, NY
Last surviving member of a band of anti-slavery enthusiasts who freed runaway slave, William "Jerry" Henry, in 1851, commemorated by the Jerry Rescue Monument in Syracuse.

MARBLE, GEORGE BUTLER Jul 2, 1879 Arcadia, NY - Sept 21, 1950 Syracuse, NY
Founded the Marble Farms Dairy in Syracuse in 1922.

MARCELLUS, JOHN Feb 2, 1846 Schenectady, NY - Aug 27, 1941 Syracuse, NY
Founder and President of the Marcellus Casket Company. Instrumental in securing land to form Lincoln Park in Syracuse. Following the closing of Marcellus Casket in 2003, a granite marker was placed at his family gravesite reading, "Marcellus Casket Company 1872-2003."

MARLOW (Denison)**, FLORENCE S.** Apr 25, 1880 Syracuse, NY - Oct 1976 Syracuse, NY
Mother of barnstorming pilot, A. Schuyler Dunning, the husband of Academy Award-winning actress, Celeste Holm, in the mid-to-late 1940s. Buried with her second husband, John Mills Marlow, died June 22, 1958 in Syracuse, age 65.

MARSHALL, DARIUS M. May 27, 1978 Syracuse, NY - Oct 15, 2003 Staten Island, NY
Diplomatic security expert for the United Nations. Wounded, knocked unconscious by falling debris, in the September 11, 2001 terrorist attack on the World Trade Center. Two years later, one of eleven passengers killed on the Staten Island Ferry vessel, *Andrew J. Barberi*, that crashed full-speed into a concrete pier at the St. George terminal, the worst crash in the history of the ferry service. Ferry pilot, Richard Smith, attempted suicide while still on the boat and, again, later that day, convicted of manslaughter in 2006 and served 18-months for operating the ship under the influence of painkillers.

MAY, SAMUEL JOSEPH Sept 12, 1797 Boston, MA - Jul 1, 1871 Syracuse, NY
Unitarian Minister, abolitionist and reformer. President of the Syracuse Board of Education from 1867-1871. Planned the escape of runaway slave, William "Jerry" Henry, from Syracuse police, commemorated with the Jerry Rescue Monument in Syracuse. Brother of Abigail May Alcott, the wife of writer and theologian, Bronson Alcott, and the mother of Louisa May Alcott, author of the novel, *Little Women*.

MCCHESNEY, ALBERT E. Apr 17, 1848 Schaghticoke, NY - Sept 1, 1934 Syracuse, NY
Founded Hall & McChesney, Inc. in Syracuse, with Charles C. Hall, in 1878. Uncle of Francis H. McChesney, President of Hall & McChesney, Inc. from 1917-1927.

MCCHESNEY, FRANCIS HENRY Sept 8, 1867 Syracuse, NY - Nov 6, 1927 Syracuse, NY
President of Hall & McChesney, Inc. in Syracuse from 1917-1927. Nephew of Albert E. McChesney, co-founder of Hall & McChesney, Inc.

MCGRATH, HAROLD Sept 4, 1871 Syracuse, NY - Oct 30, 1932 Syracuse, NY
Novelist and short story writer. First best-selling author to write directly for movies, hired by the American Film Company to write the screenplay for *The Vengeance That Failed*, in 1912.

MCLEAN, EUGENE ECKEL Mar 6, 1821 - Jan 5, 1906 New York, NY
Civil War Confederate Army Major. Served under General Braxton Bragg and General P.G.T. Beauregard. Son-in-law of Civil War Union Army General, Edwin V. Sumner.

MCLENNAN, PETER BAILLIE Dec 3, 1850 Lyndon, NY - May 9, 1913 Rochester, NY
Associate Justice of the New York State Court of Appeals from 1898-1913. Died from injuries suffered in a fall at the Genesee Valley Clubhouse in Rochester. Father of Christina McLellan Bowers, who died, unexpectedly, on her first wedding anniversary, June 15, 1917, in Syracuse, age 29. Her husband, Spotswood D. Bowers, was the son of John M. Bowers, Chief Counsel for Theodore Roosevelt in the former President's libel trial held in Syracuse, in 1915. Grandfather of Stewart F. Hancock Jr., Associate Justice of the New York State Court of Appeals from 1986-1994. Father-in-law of Syracuse attorney, Stewart F. Hancock.

MCLENNAN, RODERICK COLLIN Mar 16, 1858 Lyndon, NY - May 15, 1919 Syracuse, NY
Graduated from the Columbia Medical School in 1886. Namesake of the McLellan Wildlife Sanctuary in Fayetteville. Brother of Peter B. McLennan, Associate Justice of the New York State Court of Appeals from 1898-1913.

MEAD, DONALD H. Dec 30, 1906 Syracuse, NY - Apr 19, 1979 Syracuse, NY
Mayor of Syracuse (R) from 1954-1957. Associate Justice of the New York State Supreme Court from 1965-1979.

MEECH, B. ABBOTT (Bradley) Mar 27, 1895 Camillus, NY - Mar 3, 1963 St. Petersburg, FL
Co-founded the Fairchild & Meech Funeral Chapel in Syracuse, with George Fairchild, in 1925.

MERRELL, G. L. (Gaius Lewis) May 14, 1843 Greene, NY - Feb 7, 1909 Syracuse, NY
Founded the Merrell-Soule Company, makers of "None Such" brand mincemeat and powdered milk, with Oscar F. Soule, in 1869.

MIRON, MURRAY S. Aug 7, 1932 Allentown, PA - Jul 26, 1995 Syracuse, NY
Professor of Psycholinguistics at Syracuse University. National expert on terrorism, consulted by the FBI and other law enforcement agencies on the Son-of-Sam case, the Unabomber and the 1993 Waco standoff with cult leader, David Koresh.

MOON, F. FRANKLIN (Frederick) Jul 30, 1880 Easton, PA - Sept 3, 1929 Syracuse, NY
Dean of the College of Environmental Science and Forestry from 1920-1929. Namesake of ESF's Moon Library on the Syracuse University campus.

MUNROE, ALLEN Mar 10, 1819 Elbridge, NY - Oct 6, 1884 Syracuse, NY
Mayor of Syracuse (R) in 1854.

MUNSON, HOWARD G. Jul 26, 1924 Claremont, NH - Oct 5, 2008 Syracuse, NY
Associate Justice of the United States District Court for the Northern District of New York from 1976-2008, appointed by President Gerald Ford. President of the Syracuse Board of Education from 1965-1973.

NETTLETON, ALBERT EUGENE Oct 29, 1850 Fulton, NY - Nov 2, 1939 Syracuse, NY
Founded the A.E. Nettleton Company in Syracuse in 1879, designer of the loafer, introduced in 1937.
President Theodore Roosevelt, Charles Lindbergh and the Wright Brothers wore Nettleton shoes.

NEWKIRK (Clemens)**, ELIZABETH** Oct 17, 1884 Amsterdam, NY - Nov 21, 1972 Syracuse, NY
Last surviving member of the family of author, Mark Twain.

NORTHRUP, ALICE E. Jul 1875 Syracuse, NY - Nov 22, 1958 Syracuse, NY
Society Editor for the *Syracuse Herald*. Daughter of Milton H. Northrup, publisher of the *Syracuse Courier*. Sister-in-law of author, explorer and war correspondent, Colonel E. Alexander Powell.

NORTHRUP, MILTON HARLOW Apr 3, 1841 Smithfield, NY - Aug 15, 1906 Syracuse, NY
Published the *Syracuse Courier*. Editor of the *Syracuse Evening News*. Postmaster of Syracuse in 1888 and 1893, appointed by President Grover Cleveland. Father of Alice E. Northrup, Society Editor for the *Syracuse Herald*. Father-in-law of author, explorer and war correspondent, Colonel E. Alexander Powell.

NOTTINGHAM, VAN VLECK Nov 25, 1814 Red Hook, NY - Jan 6, 1896 Syracuse, NY
Early settler, farmer and landowner in the town of DeWitt.

NOTTINGHAM, WILLIAM Nov 2, 1853 Syracuse, NY - Jan 23, 1921 Syracuse, NY
Donated his mansion near Syracuse University, used as the official residence for the chancellor.
Namesake of William Nottingham High School in Syracuse. Son of Van Vleck Nottingham, early settler in the town of DeWitt.

OWENS, JOSEPH F. Jun 7, 1881 Taunton, MA - Jun 16, 1970 Syracuse, NY
Founded the J.F. Owens Machinery Company in Syracuse in 1923.

OSTROM, ZEBULON Jun 10, 1786 Clinton Corners, NY - Nov 23, 1873 Syracuse, NY
Owned 76 acres of farm land, sold to salt manufacturer, James P. Haskins, in 1854, which later formed Thornden Park in Syracuse. Namesake of Ostrom Avenue in Syracuse.

PAINE, PAUL MAYO Jan 13, 1869 Troy, PA - Jul 4, 1955 Syracuse, NY
Associate Editor for the *Post-Standard* from 1899-1915. Librarian for the Syracuse Public Library from 1915-1942.

PALMER, MANNING C. Oct 30, 1830 Antwerp, NY - May 27, 1910 Syracuse, NY
Founded M.C. Palmer & Company in Syracuse. President of the American Exchange National Bank.
Sentenced to three years in Auburn Prison, following the closure and insolvency of the bank, released in August 1909, pardoned by President William H. Taft.

PAPPAS, JOHN V. Oct 20, 1920 Greece - Feb 29, 1988 Clearwater, FL
Founded, owned and operated Geddes Bakery in Syracuse, from 1957-1988.

PARK, ERNEST NATHAN Jun 26, 1874 Cardiff, NY - Nov 12, 1962 Syracuse, NY
Co-founded the Park-Brannock Shoe Company, with Otis Brannock, in 1906.

PASS, RICHARD HENRY Feb 15, 1893 Syracuse, NY - May 13, 1964 Syracuse, NY
President of the Onondaga Pottery Company. Chairman of Pass & Seymour, Inc. Son of James Pass, founder and President of Pass & Seymour, Inc. in Syracuse. Grandson of Richard Pass, founder of the Onondaga Pottery Company.

PATTEN, HADEN ADELBERT Jan 20, 1876 New Haven, NY - Apr 13, 1944 Springfield, MA
Captain of the Syracuse University football team in 1900. Nicknamed "Hoss."

PAYTON (Payette), **BOB** (George E.) Sept 9, 1942 Syracuse, NY - Aug 13, 1990 Syracuse, NY
Public television and radio broadcaster for WCNY.

PEASE, ROGER WILLIAMS May 31, 1828 Conway, MA - May 28, 1886 Syracuse, NY
First surgeon at St. Joseph's Hospital in Syracuse, from 1869-1886. Chief Medical Inspector for the Calvary Corps, Army of the Potomac, during the Civil War.

PECK, JESSE TRUESDELL Apr 4, 1911 Middlefield, NY - May 17, 1883 Syracuse, NY
Bishop of the Methodist Episcopal Church. One of four founders of Syracuse University, donated $25,000 to endow the institution in 1870. First President of the Board of Trustees of Syracuse University, from 1870-1873. President of Dickinson College from 1848-1851.

PECK, JOHN JAMES Jan 4, 1821 Manlius, NY - Apr 21, 1878 Syracuse, NY
Civil War Union Army Major General. Graduated from West Point in 1839, eighth in his class, that included Ulysses S. Grant, William B. Franklin, Samuel G. French and Franklin Gardner. First President of the New York State Life Insurance Company, from 1867-1878.

PENNOCK, STANLEY B. Jun 15, 1892 Syracuse, NY - Nov 27, 1916 Newark, NJ
Three-time All-American guard for Harvard University from 1912-1914. Inducted into the College Football Hall of Fame. Killed in an explosion at a chemical plant in New Jersey.

PETER, JOHN JOSEPH May 22, 1913 Lansing, NY - Sept 5, 2012 Jamesville, NY
Founded, owned and operated Peter's Groceries in Syracuse, in 1944, the first IGA, independent grocery store, in Syracuse. President of the New York State Grocers Association for 12 years.

PETER, JOSEPH 1946 Syracuse, NY - Nov 3, 2016 Jamesville, NY
Owned and operated Peter's Groceries in Syracuse, founded by his father, John Peter Sr., in 1944.
Syracuse University graduate. Inducted into the Syracuse Rowing Hall of Fame.

PETTY, MARY ANN Oct 4, 1818 Cazenovia, NY - Mar 7, 1912 Auburn, NY
With **Oliver Cory Petty** (Dec 30, 1813 MA - Apr 3, 1889 Syracuse, NY), the grandparents of actress,
Edna May, the top musical-comedy theatrical star in London and New York at the turn of the century,
and Adelbert P. Rich, Associate Justice of the New York State Supreme Court. 2nd   great-
grandparents of New York State Senator, George Rich Metcalf.

PHILLIPS (Danforth)**, AMANDA** Oct 14, 1789 Onondaga County, NY - Nov 1, 1831 Syracuse, NY
First white child born in Onondaga County, the daughter of Asa Danforth Jr. and Olive Langdon
Danforth. Grandmother of Mary Elizabeth Outwater White, the wife of Andrew Dickson White, first
President of Cornell University. Granddaughter of Revolutionary War Continental Army veteran, Asa
Danforth Sr., the second white settler of Onondaga County.

PIERCE (Neal)**, HARRIETT MAY** May 5, 1869 Syracuse, NY - Jun 11, 1937 Syracuse, NY
Wife of portrait painter, Thomas Mitchell Pierce. Niece of L. Frank Baum, author of *The Wonderful
Wizard of Oz* series of children's books.

PIERCE, WILLIAM KASSON May 25, 1851 Syracuse, NY - Apr 5, 1915 Washington D.C.
President of the Pierce, Butler & Pierce Manufacturing Company in Syracuse, co-founded with his
father, Sylvester P. Pierce, and brother-in-law, William A. Butler, in 1876. Entertained General Franklin
D. Grant, the son of President Ulysses S. Grant, in his Syracuse home, January 14, 1905. Committed
suicide by gunshot following the bankruptcy of his company.

POOLE, THEODORE LEWIS Apr 10, 1840 Jordan, NY - Dec 23, 1900 Syracuse, NY
United States Representative-NY from 1895-1897. United States Marshal of New York in 1899,
appointed by President William McKinley. First Director of the Bank of Syracuse. Lost his arm in the
Battle of Cold Harbor, during the Civil War.

PORTER, RAYMOND E. Nov 17, 1871 Homer, NY - Mar 18, 1954 Skaneateles, NY
Founded the Porter-Cable Machine Company in Syracuse, with his brother, George G. Porter, and
Frank E. Cable, in 1906. Editor of the *Herkimer Telegram*, covered the Chester Gillette murder case in
1907.

PORTER, RAYMOND W. Nov 16, 1888 Stillwater, MN - Jul 9, 1956 Syracuse, NY
First Vice-President of Niagara Mohawk, formally the Niagara-Hudson Power Corporation, from
1950-1956.

POWELL, ARCHIBALD CAMPBELL Jul 25, 1813 - Sept 10, 1884 Syracuse, NY
Mayor of Syracuse (R) in 1864. First Vice-President of Oakwood Cemetery in Syracuse.

POWELL, EDWARD ALEXANDER Jan 27, 1838 Shadeland, PA - Nov 19, 1925 Syracuse, NY
First President of the Syracuse Chamber of Commerce. Father of author, explorer and war
correspondent, Colonel E. Alexander Powell.

POWELL (Northrup), **JESSIE** 1876 Syracuse, NY - 1970 Washington D.C.
Wife of author, explorer and war correspondent, Colonel E. Alexander Powell. Daughter of Milton H.
Northrup, publisher of the *Syracuse Courier*. Sister of Alice E. Northrup, Society Editor for the
Syracuse Herald.

PRITCHARD, STARLING (Robert) Jul 8, 1905 Winston-Salem, NC - Jul 11, 1993 Syracuse, NY
With **Lucille Pickard Pritchard** (Sept 30, 1905 Winston-Salem, NC - Aug 13, 1987 Syracuse, NY), the
parents of Robert Starling Pritchard, the first commercially-record African American classical pianist.

QUACKENBUSH (Corkings), **ALMIRA** Feb 8, 1833 Clay, NY - Feb 18, 1925 Liverpool, NY
Twin sister of Jeremiah H. Quackenbush, recognized as the oldest twins in the United States at the
time of her death.

QUACKENBUSH, JEREMIAH H. Feb 8, 1833 Clay, NY - Oct 1, 1925 Liverpool, NY
Twin brother of Almira Quackenbush Corkings, recognized as the oldest twins in the United States at
the time of his sister's death, February 18, 1925, seven months before his own death.

RALEIGH, STUART F. Nov 27, 1918 Syracuse, NY - Oct 1, 2009 Syracuse, NY
President of General Hospital in Syracuse in the 1960s, prior to its merger with Community Hospital.
President of Memorial Hospital in Syracuse in the 1970s, prior to its merger with   Crouse-Irving
Hospital. Lost his five-year old son, David Raleigh, when he wandered off near Winnisook Lake,
Catskill Mountains, June 1959. Following an extensive search, his body was recovered four months
later, October 1959.

RANSOM, DONALD A. Oct 6, 1956 Syracuse, NY – Jul 18, 2007 Syracuse, NY
Keyboardist for the local bands, Black Lites and After FX. Syracuse Department of Public Works
employee, killed at the city's asphalt plant by a truck backing up to a fire hydrant, running him over.

REDFIELD (Treadwell), **ANNA MARIA** Jan 17, 1800 Quebec, Canada - Jun 15, 1888 Syracuse, NY
Author of the textbook, *Zoological Science, or Nature in Living Forms*, published in 1858. Wife of
publisher, Lewis H. Redfield. Mother-in-law of clothier, Cornelius Tyler Longstreet.

REDFIELD, LEWIS H. Nov 16, 1792 Killingworth, CT - Jul 14, 1882 Syracuse, NY
Pioneer publisher and printer of the *Onondaga Register* and *Syracuse Gazette*. Husband of author,
Anna Maria Redfield. Father-in-law of clothier, Cornelius Tyler Longstreet.

REDINGTON, JOHN C. O. (Calvin Owen) Aug 8, 1837 Leicester, NY - Sept 24, 1905 Syracuse, NY
Civil War Union Army Colonel. Fought at Chancellorsville and Gettysburg. Brother of Emily Ruth
Redington Montgomery, the mother of Mary Montgomery Williams Borglum, the wife of sculptor,
Gutzon Borglum, most famous for creating Mount Rushmore and Stone Mountain, near Atlanta.

REZAK, DAVID Jan 1, 1903 Nazareth, Palestine - Jan 23, 1981 Syracuse, NY
Founder and President of Silver Star Stores, Inc. Owned Rezak's Silver Star Market on the South side
of Syracuse.

RICE, EDWARD FLINT Jul 12, 1831 Pompey, NY - Dec 12, 1899 Syracuse, NY
Oldest dry goods merchant in Syracuse at the time of his death.

RIEGEL, HENRY Feb 22, 1825 Fayette, NY - May 14, 1897 Syracuse, NY
Onondaga County Judge from 1862-1883. Namesake of Riegel Street in Syracuse. Father of actor,
Charles Riegel. Grandfather of candymaker, Mary Elizabeth Evans Sharpe.

RIPOSO, MICHAEL Dec 31, 1920 Syracuse, NY - Sept 22, 1992 Syracuse, NY
Central New York pianist and big band leader. Owned a recording studio on the top floor of the
Onondaga Hotel in Syracuse. Brother of pianist, Tony Riposo, Twinkle, the Magic Piano-playing clown
on the children's television program, *The Magic Toyshop* and longtime arranger for the McGuire
Sisters.

ROBERTS, WILLIAM Nov 20, 1820 England - Jan 5, 1899 Syracuse, NY
Early settler on the South side of Syracuse. Stationmaster for the Underground Railroad. Namesake
of Roberts Avenue in Syracuse.

ROOT, AUGUSTUS I. 1833 NY - Apr 8, 1865 Appomattox, VA
Civil War Union Army officer. Killed on a reconnaissance mission, with a handful of troops, one day
before the Confederate Army surrendered at Appomattox Court House. An exhibit of his personal
effects is on display at the Appomattox Court House Museum.

ROSEMAN, EDWARD (Ernest) May 14, 1875 Terre Haute, IN - Sept 16, 1957 Syracuse, NY
Stage and silent film character actor. Appeared in the D.W. Griffith directed-films, *America* and
Running Wild, starring W.C. Fields.

RUSSELL, ARCHIMEDES Jun 13, 1840 Andover, MA - Apr 3, 1915 Syracuse, NY
Professor of Architecture at Syracuse University from 1873-1881. Designed more than 850 structures
in the Syracuse-area, including the County Court House in Columbus Circle, Crouse College on the
Syracuse University campus, Central and North High Schools, the Yates Hotel and a remodeling of
the Cathedral of the Immaculate Conception.

RUSTERHOLTZ, JEROME B. Sept 13, 1893 Erie, PA - Aug 16, 1978 Syracuse, NY
Campaigned for the construction of the New York State Thruway. Called the "Father of the Thruway"
by Governor Thomas E. Dewey at opening ceremonies in 1954.

RYDER, PHILIP S. Apr 7, 1837 Ithaca, NY - May 31, 1907 Syracuse, NY
Syracuse photographer. Known as "the Father of Professional Baseball in Syracuse." President of the
Syracuse Stars from 1876-1884.

SABINE (Lawrence), **MARGARET** Aug 26, 1818 Camillus, NY - Jun 25, 1905 Syracuse, NY
Called "Queen Victoria" for her style of dress. Daughter of James R. Lawrence, United States Attorney
for the Northern District of New York. Granddaughter of Rev. Ammi Ruhamah Robbins, first Minister of
the Norfolk Church of Christ Congregational, from 1761-1813. 5th great-granddaughter of William
Bradford, *Mayflower* passenger and second Governor of the Plymouth Colony.

SAGE (Slocum), **MARGARET OLIVIA** Sept 8, 1828 Syracuse, NY-Nov 4, 1918 New York, NY
Philanthropist. Created a foundation in the name of her late husband, Russell Sage, dedicated to
improving living and working conditions in the United States. Her total philanthropy, in life and death,
was estimated between $75 million and $85 million.

SALISBURY, BERT EUGENE May 28, 1870 Syracuse, NY - Oct 20, 1946 Syracuse, NY
President of the Onondaga Pottery Company from 1913-1941. Father of William R. Salisbury,
President of the Onondaga Pottery Company from 1961-1971. Son-in-law of Mills P. Pharis, President
of the Onondaga Pottery Company from 1890-1892.

SALISBURY, WILLIAM ROOT Jun 20, 1911 Syracuse, NY - Apr 6, 1990 Vero Beach, FL
President of Onondaga Pottery Company from 1961-1971, officially changing its name to the
Syracuse China Corporation. Son of Bert E. Salisbury, President of the Onondaga Pottery Company
from 1913-1941. Grandson of Mills P. Pharis, President of the Onondaga Pottery Company from
1890-1892.

SARGENT, WILLIS HUBBARD Oct 11, 1896 Syracuse, NY - Aug 22, 1976 Wellesley Island, NY
Member of the New York State Assembly from 1925-1933. President of the Syracuse Common
Council for one year. Member of the California State Assembly for one year.

SCHAUB, SHERRY A. Sept 20, 1968 Syracuse, NY - Oct 31, 1998 Syracuse, NY
Victim of an unsolved homicide. Single mother of five, beaten and strangled to death, her body was
found miles from her home, under the Stebbins Gulf bridge, Ransom Road in Pompey.

SCHOENECK, CHARLES A. Feb 3, 1912 Syracuse, NY - Aug 19, 1989 Syracuse, NY
New York State Assemblyman from 1954-1960. Only Syracusan to serve as New York State Majority

Leader. Senior partner of the law firm, Bond, Schoeneck & King. Nephew of Edward Schoeneck, Mayor of Syracuse from 1910-1913 and Lieutenant Governor of New York from 1915-1918.

SEDGWICK, CHARLES BALDWIN Mar 15, 1815 Pompey, NY - Feb 3, 1883 Syracuse, NY
United States Representative-NY from 1859-1863. Credited with delivering the first speech on the floor of Congress supporting the abolition of slavery. Original land owner of the Sedgwick-area of Syracuse. Grandfather of Roderick Sedgwick Burlingame, founder of the Drumlins Country Club. Father-in-law of architect, Joseph Lyman Silsbee and Frederick R. Hazard, second President of the Solvay Process Company.

SEDGWICK, PAUL J. Sept 22, 1896 Cincinnati, OH - Feb 3, 1973 Syracuse, NY
Syracuse University botanist. Pioneer in time-lapse and stereo photography, whose photographs were used by Walt Disney, among others.

SEFERLIS, GEORGIA P. Jul 28, 1940 Watertown, NY - Feb 18, 1998 Syracuse, NY
Owned and operated Georgia's Bar & Grill in Hanover Square, Syracuse, from 1986-1998.

SHANKLAND, WILLIAM HENRY Feb 20, 1804 Montgomery County, NY - Jan 1883 Cortland, NY
Associate Justice of the New York State Supreme Court in 1849 and 1857. Grandfather of William Shankland Andrews, Associate Justice of the New York State Court of Appeals. Great-grandfather of Ann Hyde Allen, the wife of author, Hervey Allen. Father-in-law of Charles Andrews, Chief Justice of the New York Court of Appeals.

SHAWKEY, BOB (James Robert) Dec 4, 1890 Sigel, PA - Dec 31, 1980 Syracuse, NY
Right-handed pitcher for the New York Yankees and Philadelphia Athletics from 1913-1927. Started and won the first game in Yankee Stadium history, April 18, 1923. Threw out the ceremonial first pitch at the remodeled Yankee Stadium in 1976. Four-time 20-game winner. Managed the Yankees in 1930. Died in Veterans Hospital, cremated at Oakwood Cemetery, his ashes were not claimed and sit in storage at the cemetery.

SHAWKEY (Weiler), **GERTRUDE K.** Feb 7, 1895 Syracuse, NY - Oct 12, 1987 Syracuse, NY
Fourth wife of New York Yankees pitcher and manager, Bob Shawkey. Shawkey's second wife, Marie Lakjer, called the "Tiger Lady" in social circles, made headlines when she shot her wealthy husband, Herbert Mason Clapp, in Philadelphia in 1910, claiming self-defense. He survived, she was not charged and the couple divorced.

SHERWOOD, CHARLES EUGENE Jan 7, 1850 Camillus, NY - Dec 5, 1943 Hamilton, NY
Leading manufacturer of pocket knives in the United States in the 1890s. Sold his business to Adolph Kastor in 1902, who created the Camillus Cutlery Company.

SILSBEE, JOSEPH LYMAN Nov 25, 1848 Salem, MA - Jan 31, 1913 Chicago, IL
Chicago-based architect. Designed the *Moving Sidewalk* for the Chicago World's Fair in 1893.
Designed the Syracuse Savings Bank and White Memorial Buildings in Syracuse. Seven of his
buildings are on the National Register of Historic Places. Son-in-law of Charles Baldwin Sedgwick,
United States Representative-NY from 1859-1863.

SIMMONS, ROY D. Sept 27, 1900 Philadelphia, PA - Aug 19, 1994 Syracuse, NY
Syracuse University lacrosse head coach from 1931-1970. Retired with a 253-130-1 record. Coached
70 All-Americans, including Pro Football Hall of Famer, Jim Brown. Won two national titles as a player
at Syracuse. Inducted into the Lacrosse Hall of Fame in 1964. Captain of the 1924 Syracuse football
team. President of the Syracuse student body in 1925. Father of Roy Simmons Jr., Syracuse
University Hall of Fame lacrosse head coach from 1971-1998.

SINGLETARY, RASHEEM 1991 Syracuse, NY - Nov 15, 2016 Emigsville, PA
Pulled over by a Pennsylvania State Trooper for a traffic stop, I-83, York County, when the trooper's
uniform was caught on the vehicle, he drove away, dragging the trooper who then shot him dead.

SKIFF, CHARLES H. Jun 14, 1858 Cicero, NY - Oct 13, 1937 Syracuse, NY
Town of Salina farmer and landowner, with his brother, George T. Skiff, from 1878-1920.

SKIFF, GEORGE T. 1861 Cicero, NY - Jul 18, 1954 Syracuse, NY
Town of Salina farmer and landowner, with his brother, Charles H. Skiff, from 1878-1920. Co-founder
and treasurer of Beak & Skiff Apple Farms. Father of Seymour N. Skiff, President and Treasurer of
Beak & Skiff Apple Farms.

SKOLER, LOUIS Apr 5, 1920 Utica, NY - Dec 25, 2008 Syracuse, NY
Professor of Architecture at Syracuse University from 1959-1991. Designed his home, 213 Scottholm
Terrace in Syracuse, listed on the National Register of Historic Places in 2010.

SLOAN (Sherman)**, MILDRED WHITE** Dec 13, 1877 Syracuse, NY - Oct 15, 1933 Syracuse, NY
Equestrienne and horse show exhibitor. Reporter for the *Syracuse Herald*. First Syracuse woman to
fly in an airplane, a five-minute flight, 600 feet above ground, piloted by Philip Orin Parmalee at the
New York State Fair, September 11, 1911. Parmalee, trained by the Wright Brothers, was killed less
than a year later, June 1, 1912, during an exhibition in Yakima, WA, age 25. Cousin of Horace White,
Governor of New York from 1910-1911. Niece of Andrew Dickson White, co-founder and first President
of Cornell University.

SMALLEY, FRANK M. Dec 10, 1848 Towanda, PA - Apr 3, 1931 Syracuse, NY
Vice-Chancellor Emeritus of Syracuse University. Coined the word "sorority" in 1882, specifically for
Gamma Phi Beta at Syracuse University, founded by Helen M. Dodge Ferguson, Frances E. Haven
Moss, Eunice Adeline Curtis and Mary A. Bingham Willoughby, in 1874.

SMITH (Lapham), **ANNIE JEROME** Jul 5, 1867 Syracuse, NY - Apr 18, 1943 Syracuse, NY
President of the Syracuse Museum of Fine Arts. Wife of Syracuse real estate magnate, W. Snowdon
Smith. Daughter of S. Gurney Lapham, drama critic for the *Syracuse Herald* and Emma Jerome
Jackson Lapham, first cousin of Lady Randolph Churchill, the mother of Sir Winston Churchill, Prime
Minister of Great Britain from 1940-1945 and 1951-1955, and David Howell Jerome, Governor of
Michigan from 1881-1882.

SMITH, BURNS LYMAN Nov 7, 1880 Syracuse, NY - Jan 14, 1941 Hollywood, CA
Founded Smith Wheel, Inc. in Syracuse. Patented the Smith Expanded Wheel in 1916. President of
Syracuse Malleable Iron Works, after the death of his uncle, W.B. Burns. Built the 42-story L.C. Smith
Building in Seattle, with his father, L.C. Smith, in 1929, at the time, the tallest building west of the
Mississippi River.

SMITH, CARROLL E. Dec 25, 1832 Syracuse, NY - Aug 21, 1903 Syracuse, NY
Publisher of the *Syracuse Daily Journal*. President of the *Associated Press* for six years. Son of
newspaper publisher, Vivus W. Smith. Grandson of Jonas Earll, United States Representative-NY from
1827-1831. Nephew of newspaper publisher, Silas F. Smith.

SMITH, CLIFFORD B. Aug 16, 1876 McKeesport, PA - Mar 6, 1962 Syracuse, NY
Stage actor. Toured the United States with the Marx Brothers and the Field and DeVoe Stock
Company.

SMITH, ELWYN LAWRENCE Jan 23, 1920 Syracuse, NY - Jul 25, 1996 Brighton, England
Grandson of Wilbert L. Smith, co-founder of Smith-Corona Typewriter, Inc. and Oliver Murray
Edwards, founder of O.M. Edwards Company. Great-grandson of Eleazer Wells Edwards, founder of
E.W. Edwards.

SMITH, HURLBUT WILLIAM Jun 22, 1865 Lisle, NY - Dec 16, 1951 Syracuse, NY
President of L.C. Smith & Corona Typewriters, Inc., co-founded with his three brothers, Lyman C.
Smith, Wilbert L. Smith and Monroe C. Smith, in 1889. Chairman of the War Memorial Commission,
presided over the construction of the War Memorial in Syracuse. After his death, his body lie in state at
the War Memorial's Memorial Hall, December 18, 1951.

SMITH, JACOB S. Nov 16, 1812 Albany, NY - Jun 22, 1881 Syracuse, NY
Syracuse businessman. Father of Emily Smith Geer, the wife of major league baseball player, Billy
Geer, later divorced, he was last heard from following an arrest for forgery in Minnesota in 1892.

SMITH, LYMAN CORNELIUS Mar 31, 1850 Torrington, CT - Nov 5, 1910 Syracuse, NY
Co-founded L.C. Smith & Corona Typewriters, Inc., with his three brothers, Wilbert L. Smith, Monroe
C. Smith and Hurlbut W. Smith, in 1889. Founded the L.C. Smith Gun Company in 1880. Wealthiest
man in Syracuse at the time of his death, worth an estimated $10 million.

SMITH, MONROE CLAYTON Apr 28, 1861 Lisle, NY - 1914 Syracuse, NY
Co-founded L.C. Smith & Corona Typewriters, Inc., with his three brothers, Lyman C. Smith, Wilbert L. Smith and Hurlbut W. Smith, in 1889.

SMITH, SILAS FRANKLIN Dec 22, 1812 Lanesboro, MA - Dec 4, 1898 Syracuse, NY
Founder and publisher of the *Syracuse Daily Journal*, first edition published, July 4, 1844. Brother of newspaper publisher, Vivus W. Smith. Uncle of newspaper publisher, Carroll E. Smith.

SMITH, THOMAS W. Nov 20, 1906 Saluda, SC - Feb 27, 1971 Syracuse, NY
President of the Addis Company in Syracuse from 1948-1971, expanding to several mall locations throughout the region.

SMITH, VIVUS WOOD Jan 27, 1804 Lanesboro, MA - Feb 7, 1881 Syracuse, NY
Publisher and Editor of the *Onondaga Journal*, later consolidated with the *Syracuse Advertiser*, publishing the first edition of the *Syracuse Standard*, September 10, 1829, the paper's name was changed to the *Syracuse Weekly Journal*, July 4, 1844. Father of newspaper publisher, Carroll E. Smith. Brother of newspaper publisher, Silas F. Smith. Son-in-law of Jonas Earll, United States Representative-NY from 1827-1831.

SMITH, WILBERT LEWIS Feb 29, 1852 Torrington, CT - Aug 28, 1937 Syracuse, NY
First President of L.C. Smith & Corona Typewriters, Inc., co-founded with his three brothers, Lyman C. Smith, Monroe C. Smith and Hurlbut W. Smith, in 1889. Co-founded the Great Lakes Steamship Company.

SMOKES, SAUNDRA J. 1954 Syracuse, NY - Aug 8, 2012 Syracuse, NY
Columnist and editorial writer for the *Post-Standard* and *Syracuse Herald-Journal*. First African-American to sit on the editorial board for the Syracuse newspapers. Cable Ace Award-winning playwright, for the video drama, *Daddy's Home*. Hosted *Saundra Speaks on Venus* on WHEN-AM.

SOULE, OSCAR FRANK Aug 22, 1834 Clay, NY - Jan 18, 1902 Pasadena, CA
Founded the Merrell-Soule Company, makers of "None Such" brand mincemeat and powdered milk, with G.L. Merrell, in 1869. Great-grandson of Cyrus Kinne, early settler and founder of Fayetteville and Manlius.

SOUTHWORTH (Keegan), **ALICE** 1904 Ogdensburg, NY - Aug 31, 1973 Skaneateles, NY
Women's Editor for the *Post-Standard* from 1942-1968. Created the annual "Women of Achievement" awards in 1951. Killed in a head-on car crash by drunk driver, Uldis Baumants, on Route 175, town of Onondaga, her husband, John Van Duyn Southworth, survived.

SOUTHWORTH, EDWARD FRANKLIN Oct 27, 1872 Boston, MA - 1940 Syracuse, NY
Founded the Iroquois Publishing Company in 1915. Husband of author, Gertrude Southworth. Son-in-law of Dr. John S. Van Duyn.

SOUTHWORTH (Van Duyn), **GERTRUDE** Mar 23, 1874 Syracuse, NY - Jul 10, 1966 Syracuse, NY
President of the Iroquois Publishing Company, founded by her husband, Edward F. Southworth, in 1915. Authored several history textbooks including, *The Story of the Empire State*. Daughter of Dr. John S. Van Duyn. Sister of Dr. Edward S. Van Duyn.

SOUTHWORTH, JOHN VAN DUYN Jun 15, 1904 Syracuse, NY - Feb 16, 1986 Syracuse, NY
Author and novelist. President of the Iroquois Publishing Company, founded by his father, Edward F. Southworth in 1915. Husband of Alice Southworth, Women's Editor for the *Post-Standard* from 1942-1968. Grandson of Dr. John S. Van Duyn.

STARK, JOHN JOSEPH Nov 6, 1884 Syracuse, NY - Apr 22, 1958 Syracuse, NY
President of the Weed-Stark Company, distributor of surgical supplies and hospital equipment. Syracuse University basketball guard in 1905. Played professionally for the Buffalo Germans and New York Celtics.

STEARNS, EDWARD CARL Jul 12, 1856 Syracuse, NY - Apr 21, 1929 Syracuse, NY
Founded E.C. Stearns & Company, the Stearns Automobile Company, the Stearns Bicycle Agency, the Stearns Steam Carriage Company and the Stearns Typewriter Company.

STEARNS, GEORGE NOBLE Sept 29, 1812 Lanesboro, MA - Jul 19, 1882 Syracuse, NY
Founded the George N. Stearns Company in Syracuse in 1860. Father of Edward C. Stearns.

STEWART, WILLIAM DAVENPORT Dec 15, 1805 - Apr 9, 1874 Syracuse, NY
Mayor of Syracuse (D) from 1865-1867.

STICKLEY, GUSTAV Mar 9, 1857 Osceola, WI - Apr 20, 1942 Syracuse, NY
Pioneer in the American arts & crafts movement. Created the Craftsman Workshops. Founded and published the *Craftsman Magazine* from 1901-1916. Brother of furniture manufacturers, Leopold Stickley and John George Stickley, co-founders of L & J.G. Stickley, Inc.

STONE, WALTER ROBINSON Sept 7, 1872 Whitesville, IN - Feb 22, 1937 Syracuse, NY
Mayor of Syracuse (R) from 1916-1920.

STREET, JACOB RICHARD Jul 1, 1860 Toronto, ON, Canada - Jul 11, 1920 Syracuse, NY
Dean of the Teacher's College at Syracuse University from 1906-1917. Professor of Education at Syracuse University from 1900-1906. Literary Editor for the *Journal of Pedagogy* from 1903-1904.

SUMNER, EDWIN VOSE Jan 30, 1797 Boston, MA - Mar 21, 1863 Syracuse, NY
Civil War Union Army General. Oldest Union commander in the field of operation. Nicknamed "Bullhead." Personally escorted President-elect, Abraham Lincoln, from his Springfield home to Washington, following his election. Led the charge, and wounded, at Cerro Gordo in the Mexican War in 1847. Acting Governor of New Mexico in 1852. Namesake of Fort Sumner, NM. Father-in-law of William W. Teall, Postmaster of Syracuse.

TAFT, ELISE HAGOPIAN Aug 15, 1906 - Dec 14, 1988 Oswego, NY
Published her autobiography, *Rebirth: The Story of an Armenian Girl Who Survived the Genocide and Found Rebirth in America*, in 1981.

TAYLOR, J. D. (James) Dec 31, 1910 Syracuse, NY - Oct 28, 1996 Jamesville, NY
Founder of the J.D. Taylor Construction Company. Built the Newhouse Communications Center at Syracuse University, designed by architect, I.M. Pei, dedicated by President Lyndon B. Johnson, August 5, 1964.

TEALL, WILLIAM WALTER Apr 23, 1818 Manlius, NY - Nov 4, 1899 Syracuse, NY
Postmaster of Syracuse, appointed by President James K. Polk in 1849. Civil War Union Army Colonel. Son of Oliver Teall, founding father of Syracuse. Son-in-law of Civil War Union Army General, Edwin Vose Sumner. Father-in-law of Charles H. Halcomb, founder of the Halcomb Steel Company in Syracuse.

TEARNEY, NY'QUEST SHYQUER 1998 Syracuse, NY - Jun 25, 2002 Boston, MA
Doused with lighter fluid, then set ablaze by a match thrown by his seven-year old brother, at the home of a relative, 338 Seymour Street in Syracuse, died three days later at Boston Shriners Hospital from his burns.

THANOS, CHRIST A. Apr 15, 1883 Greece - Jul 28, 1949 Syracuse, NY
Founded, owned and operated Thanos Import Market in the Little Italy neighborhood of Syracuse, from 1919-1949.

THOMAS, NICHOLAS May 7, 1905 Florina, Greece - Sept 2, 1989 Syracuse, NY
Owned and operated Purity Bakery in Syracuse.

TIFFANY, FRANK R. 1851 Norwich, NY - Oct 23, 1925 Syracuse, NY
Interpreter for the United States at Fort Leavenworth.

TOPLIFF, JOHN H. Dec 9, 1846 Syracuse, NY - Oct 5, 1914 St. Louis, MO
Telegraph operator. Confronted by Wyatt Earp, Deputy Sheriff of Kootenai County, ID in 1884, when he refused to send a telegram Earp demanded, attempted to run away, eventually sending the telegram when Earp threaten to "beat him to death."

TRACY, WILLIAM GARDNER Apr 7, 1842 Syracuse, NY - Dec 8, 1924 Syracuse, NY
Awarded the Medal of Honor for heroism during the Civil War at Chancellorsville, in 1863.

TRICE, LAKING DANIEL W. Mar 10, 1982 Syracuse, NY - Jul 2, 1993 Windom, MN
Drowned, visiting relatives in Minnesota. Son of Daniel W. Trice, convicted of murdering teenager, Arlene R. Tarkowski, in 1982, successfully appealed in 1984, retried, convicted again. Brother of Adrian Trice, sentenced in 2000 to 80 years in prison for slashing the face of his girlfriend, social worker and attacking two police officers.

TYLER, COMFORT Feb 22, 1764 Ashford, CT - Aug 5, 1827 Montezuma, NY
War of 1812 United States Army Colonel. Early settler of Onondaga and Cayuga Counties. Assisted in the first manufacture of salt, felled the first tree and built the first piece of turnpike road in New York State, west of Fort Stanwix. Associate of Vice-President Aaron Burr, as joint members of the New York State legislature, figuring prominently in Burr's trial for treason in 1807 when Burr was accused of attempting to form a new Republic in the Southwest. Grandfather of clothier, Cornelius Tyler Longstreet.

VADEBONCOEUR, E. R. (Edmund Robert) Feb 21, 1901 Syracuse, NY - Oct 22, 1986 Cazenovia, NY
Syracuse newspaper and radio executive. Nicknamed "Curley." President of the Newhouse Broadcasting Corporation and WSYR-AM radio. Covered General Douglas MacArthur's command in the South Pacific during World War II. Co-founded the Famous Artists Series in 1946, with Murray Bernthal and his wife, Rose Bernthal. Father of Joan Vadeboncoeur, Entertainment Editor of the *Syracuse Herald-Journal* and *Herald-American*.

VADEBONCOEUR, JOAN Mar 21, 1932 Syracuse, NY - Jan 4, 2011 Cazenovia, NY
Entertainment editor of the *Syracuse Herald-Journal* and *Herald-American*. Appeared as an extra in the 1972 film, *The Battle of the Planet of the Apes*. Daughter of E.R. "Curly" Vadeboncoeur, Syracuse newspaper and radio executive.

VALENTINE, NICHOLAS S. 1887 Syracuse, NY - Aug 2, 1956 Syracuse, NY
Last surviving brother of four, owners of the Valentino Brothers Confectionary Store in Syracuse. Condemnation Commissioner for the Onondaga Lake Parkway for eighteen years, under Joseph A. Griffin. Chairman of the civic group, returning the Syracuse Stars and International League baseball to Syracuse. Manager for the United States track & field team in the 1906 Olympic Games in Greece.

VAN BUREN, HARMON W. May 27, 1799 Mayfield, NY - Apr 24, 1887 Syracuse, NY
Son of Peter Van Buren, the first cousin of President Martin Van Buren.

VAN DUYN, EDWARD SEGUIN Aug 1872 Syracuse, NY - Feb 13, 1955 Syracuse, NY
Physician and surgeon. Founded the Planned Parenthood Center in Syracuse in 1933. World War I

United States Army Medical Corps veteran. Namesake of the Van Duyn County Home and Hospital in Syracuse. Son of Dr. John S. Van Duyn. Brother of author, Gertrude Southworth.

VAN DUYN, JOHN S. Jul 24, 1843 Kingston, NJ - Jan 15, 1934 Syracuse, NY
Only American surgeon to serve behind the fronts lines in the Civil War, Spanish-American War and World War I. Oldest-living alumnus of Princeton University, Class of 1862, at the time of his death. Namesake of Van Duyn Elementary School in Syracuse. Father of Dr. Edward S. Van Duyn and author, Gertrude Southworth. Father-in-law of publisher, Edward F. Southworth.

VANN, IRVING GOODWIN Jan 3, 1842 Ulysses, NY - Mar 22, 1921 Syracuse, NY
Mayor of Syracuse (R) in 1879. Associate Justice of the New York State Supreme Court from 1896-1912. First President of Woodlawn Cemetery in Syracuse, organized in 1878. Husband of Florence Dillaye Vann, the cousin of American artist, Blanche Dillaye.

VAN NESS, ALBERT W. Oct 21, 1873 Rochester, NY - Nov 1, 1966 Owego, NY
Syracuse University lineman and captain of the 1929 football team.

VERMILYEA, FRANKLIN C. Feb 14, 1859 Syracuse, NY - Aug 10, 1895 Syracuse, NY
With **Charlotte Edith Fisher Vermilyea** (Oct 1854 Geneva, NY - Nov 29, 1931 Syracuse, NY), the grandparents of Walter L. Farley, best-selling author of the children's book, *The Black Stallion*.

WADE, FRANK E. Oct 6, 1873 Malta Bend, MO - Mar 3, 1930 Syracuse, NY
Syracuse University head football coach from 1897-1899. Vice-President of the American Piano Company. President of the Syracuse War Chest Association. Found dead from a brain hemorrhage on a train, returning home from New York City.

WADSWORTH, HOWARD Apr 20, 1907 Syracuse, NY - Feb 2, 2006 Syracuse, NY
Founded Wadsworth-Pacific Mfg. Associates, an electronics representative firm in the 1950s, developed into a nationally-recognized company. Co-owned and operated the Wadsworth & Les Collection Agency in Syracuse.

WALDORF, PAPPY (Lynn Osbert) Oct 3, 1902 Clifton Springs, NY - Aug 15, 1981 Berkeley, CA
Syracuse University All-American tackle from 1922-1924. Head coach of Oklahoma State University from 1929-1933, Kansas State University in 1934, Northwestern University from 1935-1946 and the University of California from 1947-1956. Recruited and coached Pro Football Hall of Fame quarterback, Otto Graham, at Northwestern and Joe Kapp at California. Head of Personnel and Scouting for the San Francisco 49ers from 1957-1972. Elected to the College Football Hall of Fame in 1966. Son of Methodist Bishop, Ernest Lynn Waldorf, of Chicago.

WALLACE, WILLIAM JAMES Apr 14, 1837 Syracuse, NY - Mar 11, 1917 Jacksonville, FL
Mayor of Syracuse (R) in 1873. Associate Justice of the United States Court of Appeals for the Second Circuit from 1882-1907.

WALRATH, JOHN HENRY Oct 10, 1866 Chittenango, NY - Jun 24, 1948 Syracuse, NY
Mayor of Syracuse (D) from 1922-1925.

WARD, JOHN Oct 9, 1920 Marcellus, NY - Feb 23, 2002 Lakeland, FL
Central New York amateur golf champion. Captain of the Syracuse University golf team from 1938-1942. Set or tied eleven different course records during his career.

WASHBURN, ASAHEL CORNWALL Dec 20, 1800 Leicester, MA - Mar 23, 1883 Syracuse, NY
Congregationalist Minister. Direct-descendant of multiple *Mayflower* passengers. Granduncle of Mary Montgomery Williams Borglum, the wife of Danish-born American sculptor, Gutzon Borglum, creator of Mount Rushmore and Stone Mountain, near Atlanta. Husband of Rhoda Emma Grant, third cousin, once removed, of President Ulysses S. Grant.

WASHBURN (Grant)**, RHODA EMMA** Apr 5, 1806 Windsor, CT - Aug 29, 1890 Syracuse, NY
Third cousin, once removed, of President Ulysses S. Grant. Wife of Congregationalist Minister, Asahel Cornwall Washburn.

WEAVER (Baxter)**, BLANCHE** Apr 26, 1856 Cicero, NY - Nov 4, 1957 Syracuse, NY
Stage actress. Performed with actors, John Drew, Edwin Booth and Maurice Barrymore. Wife of William D. Baxter, drama critic for the *New York Herald-Tribune*. Mother of actress and journalist, Ramona Baxter Bowden. Niece of suffragist, Matilda Joslyn Gage. Cousin of Maud Gage Baum, the wife of L. Frank Baum, author of *The Wonderful Wizard of Oz* series of children's books.

WEAVER (Gage)**, EMMA R.** Jul 14, 1827 Onondaga County, NY - Apr 3, 1895 Syracuse, NY
Sister of Henry Hill Gage, the husband of suffragist, Matilda Joslyn Gage. With **Zebulon Weaver** (Dec 15, 1811 Morristown, NY - Mar 23, 1904 Syracuse, NY), Mother of actress, Blanche Weaver. Grandmother of actress and journalist, Ramona Baxter Bowden.

WEILER, ANTHONY, H. September 9, 1888 Syracuse, NY - June 21, 1973 Syracuse, NY
Owned and operated the A. Weiler Beauty Salon in Syracuse, founded by his father, Anton A. Weiler in 1882. Married to Gertrude K. Shawkey, prior to her marriage to New York Yankees pitcher, Bob Shawkey.

WEILER, ANTON A. 1856 Cologne, Germany - May 26, 1934 Syracuse, NY
Founded the A. Weiler Beauty Salon in Syracuse in 1882.

WELLES, BENJAMIN EMORY Feb 18, 1846 Queensbury, NY - Jan 3, 1912 Syracuse, NY
State Editor of the *Syracuse Herald*. Husband of author, Georgine Milmine.

WESTCOTT, AMOS Apr 28, 1815 - Jul 6, 1873 Syracuse, NY
Mayor of Syracuse (R) in 1860. Father of novelist, Edward Noyes Westcott.

WESTCOTT, EDWARD NOYES Sept 27, 1846 Syracuse, NY - Mar 31, 1898 Syracuse, NY
Novelist. Author of *David Harum*, published posthumously in 1898. Son of Amos Westcott, Mayor of Syracuse in 1860.

WHARTON, JOHN HERMAN Jul 2, 1889 St. Michaels, MD - Apr 2, 1921 Syracuse, NY
Dean of the College of Business Administration at Syracuse University. Shot nine times by professor, Holmes Beckwith, an instructor he recently fired, who then took his own life in his office at the university.

WHEATON, HORACE Feb 24, 1803 New Milford, CT - Jun 23, 1882 Syracuse, NY
United States Representative-NY from 1843-1847. Mayor of Syracuse from 1851-1853. Brother of Charles A. Wheaton, Central New York abolitionist and Minnesota legislator.

WHITE, HORACE Oct 7, 1865 Buffalo, NY - Nov 26, 1943 New York, NY
Governor of New York from 1910-1911. Nephew of Andrew Dickson White, co-founder and first President of Cornell University.

WHITE, HORATIO NELSON Feb 8, 1814 Middletown, NH - Jul 29, 1892 Syracuse, NY
Central New York architect. Designed the Onondaga County Courthouse and Onondaga Savings Bank in Syracuse, the Hall of Languages at Syracuse University and more than 100 churches.

WIETING, JOHN MANCHESTER Feb 8, 1817 Springfield, NY - Feb 13, 1888 Syracuse, NY
Syracuse physician. Lecturer and humorist, compared in his day to author, Mark Twain. Founded the Wieting Opera House in Syracuse.

WIGGLESWORTH, BELDEN Jun 4, 1901 New York, NY - Feb 7, 1977 Fayetteville, AR
Author and editor. Published a book of poems, *In Praise of Christmas*, in 1975, illustrated by his wife, Doris Drake Wigglesworth, who died, September 15, 1995 in Fayetteville, AR, age 89, buried there, Fairview Memorial Gardens.

WIGGLESWORTH, HENRY W. Nov 2, 1866 Belfast, Ireland - Mar 19, 1945 Luzerne, Switzerland
Father of author, Belden Wigglesworth. Great-grandfather of Howard B. Dean, Governor of Vermont from 1991-2003.

WIGGLESWORTH (Belden), **OLIVE G.** Jun 5, 1874 Syracuse, NY - Apr 26, 1909 Syracuse, NY
Mother of author, Belden Wigglesworth. Great-grandmother of Howard B. Dean, Governor of Vermont from 1991-2003. Niece of James Jerome Belden, United States Representative-NY from 1887-1895 and 1897-1899 and Mayor of Syracuse from 1877-1878.

WILKINSON (May), **CHARLOTTE COFFIN** Apr 24, 1833 Scituate, MA - Aug 3, 1909 Briarcliff, NY
Wife of banker, Alfred Wilkinson. Entertained authors, Charles Dickens and Wilkie Collins, in their James Street home in Syracuse. Daughter of Unitarian Minister and abolitionist, Samuel J. May. Cousin of Louisa May Alcott, author of the novel, *Little Women*.

WILKINSON, JOHN Sept 30, 1798 Troy, NY - Sept 19, 1862 Syracuse, NY
Founding father of the city of Syracuse, taking its name from the Italian city, Siracusa, due to some similarities, both cities had salt water springs and an area to the north, called Salina. First postmaster and resident lawyer in Syracuse. President of the New York Central Railroad. Grandfather of automobile engineer and inventor, John Wilkinson.

WILKINSON, JOHN Feb 11, 1868 Syracuse, NY - Dec 25, 1934 Syracuse, NY
Automobile engineer for the H.H. Franklin Car Company. Invented an air-cooled engine and an air compressor self-starter. Grandson of John Wilkinson, founder of the city of Syracuse.

WILL, ALBERT JOHN Jun 8, 1866 Syracuse, NY - Sept 17, 1926 Syracuse, NY
President and General Manager of the Will & Baumer Candle Company. Died of a heart attack, golfing at the Bellevue Country Club, four years to the day and close to the same hour as his brother, Anthony Will Jr., who died playing golf at the Onondaga Golf and Country Club. Son of candlemaker, Anthony Will Sr. Brother of Louis Will, Mayor of Syracuse from 1914-1915. Half-brother of Theodore C. Eckermann, President of Will & Baumer.

WILL, ANTHONY Feb 14, 1864 Syracuse, NY - Sept 17, 1922 Syracuse, NY
President of the Will & Baumer Candle Company. Died of a heart attack, golfing at the Onondaga Golf and Country Club. Son of candlemaker, Anthony Will Sr. Brother of Louis Will, Mayor of Syracuse from 1914-1915 and Albert J. Will, president of Will & Baumer. Half-brother of Theodore C. Eckermann, President of Will & Baumer.

WILL, LOUIS E. Nov 13, 1857 Syracuse, NY - Jul 15, 1932 Syracuse, NY
Mayor of Syracuse from 1914-1915. Only Progressive Party Mayor in Syracuse history. Son of candlemaker, Anthony Will Sr. Brother of Will & Baumer Candle Company Presidents, Anthony Will Jr., Albert J. Will and half-brother of Theodore C. Eckermann.

WILLIAMS (Bell), **ANNAMAE** Jul 16, 1931 MS - Aug 26, 1996 Syracuse, NY
Civil rights and local community activist. Spent thirty years assisting low-income families in Syracuse.

WILLIAMSON (Raleigh), **NELLIE G.** Jun 11, 1838 Cicero, NY - Nov 6, 1859 Syracuse, NY
First internment in Oakwood Cemetery, section 5, lot 52, listed in the cemetery burial roster as
internment #1.

WILLISTON, CHARLES FERRE Jun 3, 1816 Springfield, MA - Sept 22, 1896 Syracuse, NY
Mayor of Syracuse (D) from 1856-1857. First Mayor of Syracuse reelected to office.

WILTSE, HOOKS (George) Sept 7, 1880 Hamilton, NY - Jan 21, 1959 Long Beach, NY
Pitcher for the New York Giants and Brooklyn Tip-Tops from 1904-1915. Teamed with Hall of Famer,
Christy Mathewson, to form one of the top lefty-righty pitching duos of their time. Pitched a ten-inning
no-hitter in 1908, losing a perfect game when he hit the Phillies pitcher, the 27th batter of the game.
20-game winner in 1908 and 1909. Filled in, playing first base in the 1913 World Series, preserving a
Mathewson shutout with several outstanding defensive plays. Brother of Lew "Snake" Wiltse, pitcher
for four teams from 1901-1903.

WINTON, WILLIAM Dec 7, 1805 - Mar 19, 1871 Syracuse, NY
Mayor of Syracuse (D) in 1858.

WITHERILL, LAWRENCE L. Aug 16, 1897 Syracuse, NY - Sept 14, 1977 Cazenovia, NY
President of L.A. Witherill from 1928-1948, founded by his father, Liston A. Witherill. Son-in-law of
Huntington B. Crouse, co-founder of the Crouse-Hinds Company.

WITHERILL, LISTON AMES Oct 28, 1857 Union, NY - Oct 10, 1923 Syracuse, NY
Founded L.A. Witherill in Syracuse in 1898.

WOODRUFF, JASON COOPER Mar 11, 1800 - Jul 16, 1878 Syracuse, NY
Mayor of Syracuse (D) in 1852.

WOODWORTH, CHARLES T. Sept 11, 1893 Rochester, NY - Dec 1, 1988 Syracuse, NY
Founded the Woodworth Brick & Tile Company in Syracuse in 1933.

WOODWORTH (Eckhoff), **FLORENCE** Mar 9, 1900 Brooklyn, NY - Aug 22, 2005 Syracuse, NY
Unmarried until age 75, she married 82-year old widower, Charles T. Woodworth, founder of the
Woodworth Brick & Tile Company, and moved into the Hotel Syracuse, rooms 3041 and 3042 on the
fifth floor, the last person to live in the hotel before it closed, May 28, 2004.

WORDEN, STANLEY ELMORE Jun 13, 1905 Syracuse, NY - Dec 18, 1994 Syracuse, NY
Stained-glass artist. His work appears in churches in 51 New York State counties and 37 states.
Director of the Henry Keck Stained Glass Stuido in Syracuse, following the death of founder, Henry
Keck, in 1956.

OGDENSBURG CEMETERY
811 Montgomery Street
Ogdensburg, NY 13669

AVERELL, WILLIAM Nov 23, 1821 Ogdensburg, NY - Feb 28, 1897 Ogdensburg, NY
With **Mary Lawrence Williamson Averell** (Feb 11, 1829 Elizabeth, NJ - Jul 1, 1876 Ogdensburg, NY), the parents of Mary Williamson Averell Harriman, the wife of railroad tycoon, Edward H. Harriman. Grandparents of W. Averell Harriman, Governor of New York from 1955-1958, and Cornelia Averell Harriman Gerry, the wife of thoroughbred race horse owner and breeder, Robert L. Gerry.

CURTIS, NEWTON MARTIN May 21, 1835 De Peyster, NY - Jan 10, 1910 New York, NY
United States Representative-NY from 1891-1897. Civil War Union Army Brigadier General. Awarded the Congressional Medal of Honor for his service in the war. Author of *From Bull Run to Chancellorsville*. Son of Samuel Ryan Curtis, Civil War Union Army General and United States Representative-IA from 1857-1861.

FINE, JOHN Aug 26, 1794 New York, NY - Jan 4, 1867 Ogdensburg, NY
United States Representative-NY from 1839-1841.

JAMES, AMAZIAH BAILEY Jul 1, 1812 Stephentown, NY - Jul 6, 1883 Ogdensburg, NY
United States Representative-NY from 1877-1881.

KING, PRESTON Oct 14, 1806 Ogdensburg, NY - Nov 12, 1865 New York, NY
United States Senator-NY from 1857-1863. United States Representative-NY from 1843-1847 and 1849-1853. Founded the *St. Lawrence Republican* newspaper. Committed suicide, tying a bag of bullets around his neck, jumping from a ferryboat into New York Harbor.

MALBY, GEORGE ROLAND Sept 16, 1857 Canton, NY - Jul 5, 1912 New York, NY
United States Representative-NY from 1907-1912. Died during his third term in office.

MASON, BURTON JAMES Apr 3, 1880 De Peyster, NY - Mar 3, 1945 Ogdensburg, NY
With **Ena G. Evans Mason** (1885 – Mar 20, 1968 Albany, NY), the parents of Edwyn E. Mason, New York State Senator and Assemblyman from 1953-1978.

PERKINS, BISHOP Sept 5, 1787 Becket, MA - Nov 20, 1866 Ogdensburg, NY
United States Representative-NY from 1853-1855.

SEYMOUR, EUGENE FORD Apr 15, 1870 Morristown, NJ - Apr 5, 1966 Los Angeles, CA
With **Sophie Mildred Bower Seymour** (July 13, 1886 Kemptville, ON, Canada - April 15, 1974 Los Angeles, CA), the grandparents of Academy Award-winning actress, Jane Fonda, and actor/writer, Peter Fonda, and the great-grandparents of actress, Bridget Fonda.

SEYMOUR, FORD DEVILLARS Aug 15, 1906 Ogdensburg, NY - Feb 15, 1985 Los Angeles, CA
Uncle of Academy Award-winning actress, Jane Fonda and actor/writer, Peter Fonda. Brother of Frances Ford Seymour, the first wife of Academy Award-winning actor, Henry Fonda.

SEYMOUR, FRANCES FORD Apr 14 1908 Brockville, ON, Canada - Apr 14, 1950 Beacon, NY
Mother of Academy Award-winning actress, Jane Fonda and actor/writer, Peter Fonda. Grandmother of actress, Bridget Fonda. Widow of New York City millionaire, George Tuttle Brokaw, the first husband of journalist, Clare Boothe Luce. Remarried September 16, 1936, to Academy Award-winning actor, Henry Fonda. Committed suicide, slicing her throat with a razor, days after Fonda asked for a divorce.

SEYMOUR, GEORGE DEVILLARS May 13, 1821 Ogdensburg, NY - Nov 11, 1892 Ogdensburg, NY
With **Frances Gabrielle Ford Seymour** (Jun 9, 1827 Morristown, NJ - Jan 18, 1898 Ogdensburg, NY), the great-grandparents of Academy Award-winning actress, Jane Fonda and actor/writer, Peter Fonda, and the 2nd great-grandparents of actress, Bridget Fonda.

SHERMAN, SOCRATES NORTON Jan 22, 1801 Barre, VT - Feb 1, 1873 Ogdensburg, NY
United States Representative-NY from 1861-1863.

OLD AMENIA BURYING GROUND
Mygatt Road
Amenia, NY 12501

BRONSON, JOHN Apr 23, 1701 Waterbury, CT - Nov 9, 1785 Amenia, NY
With **Comfort Baldwin Bronson** (- Aug 29, 1773 Amenia, NY), the 2nd great-grandparents of Louisa May Alcott, author of *Little Women*.

OLD MILITARY CEMETERY
Dodge Avenue
Sackets Harbor, NY 13685

COVINGTON, LEONARD WAILES Oct 30, 1768 Aquasco, MD - Nov 14, 1813 Guilderland, NY
United States Representative-NY from 1805-1807. War of 1812 United States Army Brigadier General. Mortally wounded in the Battle of Crysler's Farm.

PIKE, ZEBULON MONTGOMERY Jan 5, 1779 Trenton, NJ - Apr 27, 1813 Toronto, ON, Canada
War of 1812 United States Army General. Explored much of the Southwest portion of the United States, including the headwaters of the Mississippi River. Discovered Pike's Peak in Colorado. Namesake of Pike Counties in Kentucky, Ohio, Illinois and Alabama. Killed by a flying rock from an exploding British ammunition store.

OLD MOUNT IDA CEMETERY
Pawling Avenue
Troy, NY 12180

BIRD, JOHN Nov 22, 1768 Litchfield, CT - Feb 2, 1806 Troy, NY
United States Representative-NY from 1799-1801.

BROWNELL, BENJIMAN Jun 18, 1771 - May 15, 1826 Troy, NY
With **Huldah Bullock Brownell** (Aug 10, 1767 Sand Lake, NY - Aug 4, 1813 Troy, NY), the grandparents of Civil War Union Army Sergeant, Francis Edwin Brownell, awarded the first Medal of Honor in the Civil War for killing James Jackson, the proprietor of Marshall House in Alexandria who shot and killed Elmer E. Ellsworth attempting to capture the Confederate flag, the first Union officer killed in the Civil War.

SEYMOUR, DAVID LOWREY Dec 2, 1803 Wethersfield, CT - Oct 11, 1867 Lanesborough, MA
United States Representative-NY from 1843-1845 and 1851-1853.

WHITE, HENRY E. Apr 1, 1837 - Jul 15, 1837 Troy, NY
Infant son of Dr. Russell J. White and Helena Anne Boynton White, the grandparents of actor, Vincent Price.

OLD PRESBYTERIAN CEMETERY
Plainville Road
Lysander, NY 13094

KENNEDY, SARAH ANN Apr 11, 1818 Lysander, NY - May 31, 1840 Lysander, NY
Died two days after being thrown from her carriage, her horse had broken free, returning home from purchasing her wedding bonnet, for her wedding in the days ahead, to Willard H. Downer.

OLD READING CEMETERY
Church Street
Reading Center, NY 14876

BACON, ELIJAH Apr 9, 1760 Dedham, MA - Dec 10, 1851 Reading Center, NY
3rd great-grandfather of Elizabeth Bacon Fitzgerald, the wife of Edmund B. Fitzgerald, an insurance executive and namesake of the Great Lakes freighter, *SS Edmund Fitzgerald*. 4th great-grandfather of baseball executive, Edmund Bacon Fitzgerald, co-founder of the Milwaukee Brewers in 1970.

OLD SCHOOL BAPTIST CHURCH CEMETERY
Peraglie Road
Jefferson, NY 12093

WHITE, ALFRED S. Mar 7, 1809 - Sept 29, 1892 Richmondville, NY
With **Julia A. Snyder White** (May 17, 1813 - Sept 23, 1903 Richmondville, NY), the parents of Mero L. White Tanner, the wife of James R. Tanner, Civil War Union Army Corporal, who lost both legs in the Second Battle of Bull Run, and was present at the deathbed of President Abraham Lincoln, serving as stenographer, recording the events. Died October 2, 1927, age 83, buried in Arlington National Cemetery, with his wife and three children.

OLD SOUTHEAST CHURCH CEMETERY
1601 Route 22
Brewster, NY 10509

CROSBY, JOHN 1794 - Nov 1820 Brewster, NY
Father of poet, lyricist, composer and hymnist, Fanny Crosby. 3rd great-grandson of Thomas Crosby II, the 8th great-grandfather of Academy Award-winning actor and singer, Bing Crosby and 9th great-grandfather of singer, David Crosby.

FOSTER (Larson), **SUSANNA** (Suzanne) Dec 6, 1924 Chicago, IL - Jan 17, 2009 Englewood, NJ
Actress. Operatic soprano. Starred as Christine in the 1943 remake of *The Phantom of the Opera*. Husband of actor, Wilbur "Wib" Evans. Gave birth to her second son, Philip Evans, in London, delivered by John Peel, Queen Elizabeth's personal doctor, who also delivered Prince Charles and Princess Anne.

OLD STONE FORT CEMETERY
Fort Road
Schoharie, NY 12157

SWART, PETER Jul 5, 1752 Schoharie, NY - Nov 3, 1829 Schoharie, NY
United States Representative-NY from 1807-1809.

WILLIAMS, DAVID Oct 21, 1754 Tarrytown, NY - Aug 2, 1931 Schoharie, NY
Revolutionary War New York State Militiaman. Captured Major John André, with John Paulding and David Williams, discovering documents of his secret meeting with General Benedict Arnold, prior to the execution of their treasonous plan. André was hanged, and General George Washington awarded the three militiamen the Fidelity Medallion. Van Wart died, May 23, 1828 in Elmsford, age, 69, buried there, Old Reformed Dutch Churchyard.

OLD TABERG CEMETERY
Taberg-Florence Road
Taberg, NY 13471

MORTON, BENJAMIN W. 1763 MA - Dec 14, 1851 Taberg, NY
With **Hannah Dexter Morton** (Dec 5, 1770 Athol, MA - Oct 10, 1848 Taberg, NY), the 4th great-grandparents of actress and model, Raquel Welch, and the 5th great-grandparents of actress Tahnee Welch.

MORTON, JONATHAN 1765 MA - Mar 8, 1853 Taberg, NY
Brother of Benjamin W. Morton, the 4th great-grandfather of actress and model, Raquel Welch.

OLD VAN CORTLANDTVILLE CEMETERY
Locust Avenue
Van Cortlandtville, NY 10567

PAULDING, JOHN Oct 16, 1758 Peekskill, NY - Feb 18, 1818 Staatsburg, NY
Revolutionary War New York State Militiaman. Captured Major John André, with Isaac Van Wart and David Williams, discovering documents of his secret meeting with General Benedict Arnold, prior to the execution of their treasonous plan. André was hanged, and General George Washington awarded the three militiamen the Fidelity Medallion. Van Wart died, May 23, 1828 in Elmsford, age, 69, buried there, Old Reformed Dutch Churchyard.

OLDEN-BARNEVELD CEMETERY
Mapledale Road
Barneveld, NY 13304

VAN DER KEMP, FRANCOIS ADRIAAN May 4, 1752 the Netherlands - Sept 7, 1829 Barneveld, NY
Leader of the Dutch political uprising, the Patriottentijd. Moved to New York State in 1788, settled in Constantia, founded the Agricultural Society for the Western District of New York. Corresponded regularly with John Adams, Benjamin Franklin, George Washington and Thomas Jefferson. Named the most scholarly man in the country by New York Governor, Dewitt Clinton.

WOOLSEY, MELANCTHON LLOYD May 8, 1758 Queens Village, NY - Jun 29, 1819 Trenton, NY
Revolutionary War Continental Army Lieutenant. Major General in the New York Militia. Military aide to
New York Governor, George Clinton. Died in Trenton, en route to Sackets Harbor to visit his son, United
States Navy Commodore, Melancthon Taylor Woolsey.

WOOLSEY, MELANCTHON TAYLOR Jun 5, 1780 Plattsburgh, NY - May 18, 1838 Utica, NY
United States Navy Commodore. Supervised the construction of the *U.S.S. Oneida* in 1808, the United
States' first warship on the Great Lakes, put to use during the War of 1812.

OLDSVILLE CEMETERY
Ward Road
Hammond, NY 13646

ALGUIRE, TIMOTHY D. October 26, 1954 Massena, NY - Nov 15, 2016 Massena, NY
Owned and operated Triple A Service Center, Massena. Killed riding a lawn tractor, mowing a lawn in
Brasher Falls, when his mower ran over a cable dog leash attached to a deck post, the cable wrapped
around the mower's blades breaking the post, the post falling and striking him in the head.

OLIVET CEMETERY
Craig Road / Route 58
Pavilion, NY 14525

WRIGHT, HENRY M. 1870 Wyoming County, NY - Jul 12, 1934 Pavilion, NY
Working in his barn, Keller Road, smothered to death under a pile of hay that collapsed upon him.

ONEIDA CASTLE CEMETERY
East 2nd Street
Oneida, NY 13421

JENKINS, TIMOTHY Jan 29, 1799 Worcester, MA - Dec 24, 1859 Oneida, NY
U.S. Representative-NY from 1845-1849 and 1851-1853.

MORGAN, WATER D. Sept 6, 1928 Franklin Springs, NY - Sept 24, 2016 Verona, NY
Minor league hockey player for the senior league's Clinton Comets.

ONEIDA COMMUNITY CEMETERY
Kenwood Avenue
Oneida, NY 13421

MILLER, KENNETH HAYES Mar 11, 1876 Kenwood, NY - Jan 1, 1952 New York, NY
Painter, based on Fourteenth Street in New York City. One of the first artists to have his work represented in the Museum of Modern Art, founded in New York City in 1929.

NOYES, JOHN HUMPHREY Sept 3, 1811 Brattleboro, VT - Apr 13, 1886 Niagara Falls, ON, Canada
Utopian socialist. Founded Oneida Community, a religious commune, in 1848. Coined the term "free love."

NOYES, P. B. (Pierrepont Burt) Aug 18, 1870 Kenwood, NY - Apr 15, 1959 Oneida, NY
President of Oneida Limited, maker of stainless steel tableware. Son of John Humphrey Noyes, founder of Oneida Community. Published the science fiction novel, *The Pallid Giant: A Tale of Yesterday and Tomorrow*, in 1927.

ONEIDA NATION BURIAL GROUNDS
North Lake Road / Route 15
Oneida, NY 13421

HALBRITTER-WILLIAMS (Winder)**, GLORIA** Dec 25, 1925 Nedrow, NY - Aug 18, 2016 Nedrow, NY
Designed the official seal of the Oneida Indian Nation. Mother of Ray Halbritter, CEO of Oneida Nation Enterprises who negotiated a gaming license with Governor Mario Cuomo to build the Turning Stone Resort Casino in Verona, 1993.

SHENANDOAH (Skenandoa)**, DANIEL** 1812 Oneida, NY - 1891 Oneida Castle, NY
Oneida Indian Nation Chief. Great-grandson of Oneida Indian Chief, Daniel Skenandoa.

ONEONTA PLAINS CEMETERY
Oneida Street
Oneonta, NY 13820

BOCKES, GEORGE LESLIE Jan 14, 1874 Skaneateles, NY - Apr 27, 1940 Oneonta, NY
New York State Assemblyman. Otsego County Judge. Namesake of the George L. Bockes Memorial Forest, town of Hartwick, Otsego County, for his work in conservation.

CONROW (Burdick)**, JESSIE** Jul 16, 1894 Davenport, NY - Nov 23, 2002 Oneonta, NY
With **Clyde Conrow** (Jun 24, 1895 Jefferson, NY - Aug 5, 1958 Oneonta, NY), the grandparents of singer/songwriter, Jerry Jeff Walker, most remembered for his song, "Mr. Bojangles." Died at the age of 108.

CROSBY, MELVIN R. Sept 30, 1920 Oneonta, NY - Mar 2, 2006 Oneonta, NY
With **Alma Conrow Crosby** (Jan 19, 1920 Oneonta, NY - Jul 25, 2011 Oneonta, NY), the parents of singer/songwriter, Jerry Jeff Walker, most remembered for his song, "Mr. Bojangles."

FOWLER, DICK Mar 30, 1921 Toronto, ON, Canada - May 22, 1972 Oneonta, NY
Starting pitcher for the Philadelphia Athletics, managed by Hall of Famer, Connie Mack and Jimmie Dykes, from 1941-1942 and 1945-1952. Won 15 games in 1948 and 1949. Led the National League in losses with 16 in 1946. Served in the Royal Canadian Infantry during World War II.

MASKER, WILLIAM E. Jan 28, 1949 Oneonta, NY - Jan 11, 1953 Oneonta, NY
Headline read, "Boy Who Lived on Bananas is Dead." Suffered from a congenital disease of the pancreas preventing his body from digesting most foods, he would eat 3-4 bananas a day until he died from pneumonia, two weeks shy of his fourth birthday.

ONONDAGA NATION NEW CEMETERY
Route 11A
Nedrow, NY 13120

BIG TREE, CHIEF JOHN (Isaac Johnny John) Jun 2, 1877 Nedrow, NY - Jul 6, 1967 Nedrow, NY
Iroquois Chief. Called the "greatest Indian film star of all-time." Appeared in more than 100 films. Posed for artist, James Fraser, for the profile of the Indian Head nickel in 1912, actually a composite of three American Indians, his contribution is reflected from the nose up. Grandson of Seneca Chief, Red Jacket.

LAZORE, ANGUS J. Oct 12, 1897 Syracuse, NY - Aug 5, 1967 Syracuse, NY
Secretary for the Six Nations Confederacy. Player, coach and manager of the Syracuse Red Devils lacrosse team.

LYONS, LOREN D. Apr 16, 1941 Nedrow, NY - Oct 2, 1991 Syracuse, NY
Brother of Oren Lyons, Chief of the Onondaga Nation Indians. Nephew of Leon Shenandoah, Chief of the Iroquois Confederacy. Amateur drummer, played with Count Basie's band at the New York State Fair. Attacked by six men, near the Gifford Street Rescue Mission, robbed of a bottle of wine and his shoes, then thrown into Onondaga Creek, under the Fabius Street overpass, where he drowned.

PRINTUP, MOSE 1882 Syracuse, NY - Apr 24, 1938 Syracuse, NY
Died five days after the death of his cousin, Indian baseball star and umpire, Elmer Printup.

SHENANDOAH, LEON May 18, 1915 Nedrow, NY - Jul 22, 1996 Syracuse, NY
Chief of the Iroquois Confederacy. Holder of the title "Tadadaho." Spiritual and political spokesman of the Grand Council of Chiefs, governing the Haudenosaunee, the Six Nations Confederacy. Uncle of Oren Lyons, Chief of the Onondaga Nation Indians.

WATERMAN, PAUL Nov 15, 1922 Nedrow, NY - Aug 25, 2002 Syracuse, NY
Chief of the Onondaga Nation Indians from 1967-2002. Influenced museums and collectors to return thousands of skeletal remains and burial artifacts to the Iroquois and other American Indian tribes.

ONONDAGA NATION OLD CEMETERY
Route 11A
Nedrow, NY 13120

HALBRITTER, ARTHUR RAY Jan 8, 1926 Nedrow, NY - Jun 8, 1962 Syracuse, NY
Father of Ray Halbritter, CEO of Oneida Nation Enterprises who negotiated a gaming license with Governor Mario Cuomo to build the Turning Stone Resort Casino in Verona, 1993.

WINDER (Cornelius)**, MARY** Apr 27, 1898 Nedrow, NY - Jun 11, 1954 Syracuse, NY
Wrote politicians and government officials for more than 30 years fighting to recover thousands of acres of land guaranteed to the Oneida Indian Nation through the 1794 Treaty of Canandaigua. Grandmother of Ray Halbritter, CEO of Oneida Nation Enterprises including the Turning Stone Resort Casino, Verona.

WINDER (Beauvais)**, JANICE** May 26, 1929 Oka, QB, Canada - Jun 25, 1976 Nedrow, NY
Killed in a trailer fire with her brother-in-law, Samuel Winder, West Road, Oneida Nation, the Oneida City Fire Department did not respond to their call sparking an FBI investigation. Aunt of Ray Halbritter, CEO of Oneida Nation Enterprises including the Turning Stone Resort Casino, Verona.

WINDER, SAMUEL Feb 2, 1928 Nedrow, NY - Jun 25, 1976 Nedrow, NY
Killed in a trailer fire with his sister-in-law, Janice Beauvais Winder, West Road, Oneida Nation, the Oneida City Fire Department did not respond to their call sparking an FBI investigation. Uncle of Ray Halbritter, CEO of Oneida Nation Enterprises including the Turning Stone Resort Casino, Verona.

ONONDAGA VALLEY CEMETERY

2500 Valley Drive
Syracuse, NY 13207

BARTELS, HERMAN Apr 15, 1853 Richtenberg, Prussia - Aug 1, 1910 Syracuse, NY
Owned and operated the Bartels Brewing Company in Syracuse and Wilkes-Barre. Convicted of arson from the burning of the Fanning Malt House in Syracuse in 1906. Twice jumped bail, fled to Canada, returned and sentenced in 1908.

BEERS (Fredenburg), **NANCY J.** Apr 29, 1937 Syracuse, NY - Aug 22, 2008 Syracuse, NY
Breeder of American Staffordshire terriers. Owned and operated X-Pert Beers' Cherry Valley Kennels in Pompey, with her husband, Edward K. Beers, died November 14, 1999, age 64.

CHRISTOPHER, JAMES Dec 15, 1915 Syracuse, NY - Nov 14, 2006 Mooresville, NC
Founded Allied Industrial Laundry in Solvay in 1953.

CLIFT, CHARLES E. Sept 8, 1926 - Mar 30, 2006 Millbrook, AL
First Director of the Burnet Park Zoo in Syracuse. Founded the Fantastic Animal Land in Tully. Director of the Santa Ana Zoo in California and the Montgomery Zoo in Alabama.

COLE, GEORGE E. 1854 Otisco, NY - Oct 26, 1913 Syracuse, NY
London Metropolitan policeman. Provided an escort for Queen Victoria and Prince Albert.

CORNELIUS, ELI May 4, 1916 Canada - Jan 10, 1987 Canastota, NY
Upstate New York Lacrosse Hall of Famer. Played for the Onondaga Athletic League from 1948-1954. Close friend and assistant of Syracuse University lacrosse coach, Roy Simmons Jr. Known for his stick-making abilities, he was buried with a miniature lacrosse stick.

CORNELL, B. EMMETT 1870 Fulton, NY - Dec 26, 1934 Syracuse, NY
Founder and president of the Cornell Bus Lines from 1922-1933.

DANFORTH, ASA Jul 25, 1846 Worcester, MA - Sept 2, 1818 Onondaga County, NY
Second white settler of Onondaga County, resided in Onondaga Hollow. Revolutionary War New York Militia Major-General. New York State Senator from 1802-1805. Father of Canadian highway engineer, Asa Danforth Jr. Grandfather of Amanda Danforth, the first white child born in Onondaga County. Originally buried in Old Arsenal Cemetery in Syracuse, removed to the family plot of his son-in-law, Thaddeus M. Wood.

DAVOLI, JOSEPH Apr 28, 1941 Syracuse, NY - Apr 15, 1995 Syracuse, NY
Central New York attorney. Partner of the law firm, Davoli, McMahon and Kublick. Father of Hollywood film actor, Andrew Davoli.

FORMAN, JOSEPH Pleasant Valley, NY - Jan 15, 1824 Syracuse, NY
Father of Judge Joshua Forman, founder and first President of the village of Syracuse.

FREEMAN, CLAUDE C. Jun 22, 1937 Saranac Lake, NY - Jan 15, 2012 Syracuse, NY
Artist. Known for his pencil drawings of Adirondack landscapes. Professor Emeritus at SUNY/ESF for fifty years.

GATEWOOD, LITTLE WILLIE (Deacon) Aug 4, 1937 Auburn, AL - May 28, 2013 Syracuse, NY
Syracuse musician. Fronted the R&B band, the Fabulous Tornatoes, from 1966-1972. Released the singles, "The Camel" in 1969, and "Little Bitty Baby" in 1973.

GEORGIADE, GEORGE 1935 New York, NY - Jan 27, 2015 Syracuse, NY
Syracuse Police Department Lieutenant. Accused Syracuse Mayor, Lee Alexander and Chief of Police, Thomas Sardino, of waging a campaign of dirty tricks against political enemies in 1983. Following a six month investigation, an Onondaga County grand jury did not return an indictment. Brother of actor, Nicholas Georgiade, co-star of *The Untouchables*.

HALL, GEORGE May 12, 1770 New Haven, CT - Mar 20, 1840 Syracuse, NY
United States Representative-NY from 1819-1821.

HAWKINS, CLIFFORD D. Apr 14, 1896 Syracuse, NY - Oct 25, 1980 Nedrow, NY
Founded Green Hills Farms Groceries in Syracuse.

HECK, CHARLES E. Jul 3, 1925 Connellsville, PA - Jun 15, 2002 Syracuse, NY
Father of Michael Heck, Grant Junior High School student in Syracuse whose Hancock Airport bathroom stall scribble, "April 20, 1965 Mike Heck + Salena Bennett" inspired Allen Ginsberg's poem, *Graffiti 12th Cubicle Men's Room Syracuse Airport*, included in his award-winning book of poems, *The Fall of America*, in 1972.

HELMS, BILL Jan 7, 1894 Syracuse, NY - Dec 3, 1957 Syracuse, NY
Owned and operated the fast food, fish-fry restaurant, Bill's Inn, located at various locations in Onondaga Valley in Syracuse, founded in 1921.

HITCHINGS, HORACE KING Nov 1889 NY - Nov 28, 1950 Syracuse, NY
Apple grower. Owned and operated Hitchings Fruit Farm in South Onondaga. Committed suicide by shotgun in his office at the farm.

HORR, BILL (Marquis Franklin) May 2, 1880 Munnsville, NY - Jul 1, 1955 Syracuse, NY
Syracuse University offensive tackle from 1905-1908. Selected to the Walter Camp All-American team in 1908, the first Syracuse player to be honored. Intercollegiate track & field champion with 14 medals

on discus and hammer throw. Member of the 1908 United States Olympic Track & Field Team, winning a silver and bronze medal. Defeated Jim Thorpe in discus throw in 1908. Purdue University and Syracuse University offensive line coach from 1911-1923.

LAWITTS, WILLIAM Jun 10, 1924 Syracuse, NY - Mar 2, 2001 Syracuse, NY
Founded, owned and operated Durston's newsstand, named for the Durston Apartments on Warren Street in Syracuse, for 40 years.

MCGUIRE (Pearsall)**, PEARL** Jul 1882 St. Louis, MO - Mar 2, 1961 Syracuse, NY
Postmistress of Nedrow from 1941-1951. Women's Director of the New York State Fair from 1939-1941. Close associate of First Lady Eleanor Roosevelt and Harriet May Mills. Wife of Edward S. McGuire, the brother of James K. McGuire, Mayor of Syracuse from 1896-1901.

MEACHEM, THOMAS GOLDSBROUGH Apr 3, 1878 Syracuse, NY - Aug 18, 1928 New York, NY
Founded the Meachem Gear Company in Syracuse in 1919. Son of Syracuse businessman, Thomas W. Meachem.

MEACHEM, THOMAS WILLIAM Jun 7, 1849 East Bloomfield, NY - Oct 1920 Syracuse, NY
Syracuse businessman. Delegate from New York to the Democratic National Convention in 1912, 1916 and 1920. Namesake of the Thomas W. Meachem Elementary School in Syracuse. Father of Thomas G. Meachem, founder of the Meachem Gear Company in Syracuse.

MUIR, DOUGLAS A. Aug 4, 1917 Syracuse, NY - Sept 22, 1987 Syracuse, NY
With **Mary E. McGrath Muir** (Mar 10, 1919 Utica, NY - Apr 30, 2009 Syracuse, NY), the grandparents of journalist, David Muir, anchor of *ABC World News Tonight* and *20/20* and WTVH-TV in Syracuse from 1995-2000.

MURPHY, EDWARD F. Dec 14, 1916 Jamesville, WI - Feb 10, 1991 Syracuse, NY
Central New York radio and television broadcaster. WSYR-AM announcer. Voted the most popular-area DJ in 1947. Hosted the first live television series in Central New York, in 1952. Host   of *Hollywood Matinee* and *Dialing for Dollars*.

NELSON, LINDA A. Jun 15, 1958 Inglewood, CA - Feb 27, 1984 Syracuse, NY
Associate Editor of *Women's Day Magazine* in New York City.

NICHOLS, ALTON Nov 19, 1916 Syracuse, NY - Feb 24, 2009 Syracuse, NY
Married 84-year old Betty Hall, December 11, 2007 in Syracuse, making headlines when they were forced to live apart due to housing and medical rules at the care facility where they were living. Following an outpouring of support, they were reunited ten months later at the Loretto Geriatric Center in Syracuse.

O'BRIEN, JIM (James L.) Mar 26, 1943 Syracuse, NY - Apr 30, 2005 North Syracuse, NY
Syracuse disc jockey for WNDR-AM and WNTQ-FM from 1961-1995. Known as the "King of the DJ's" and "Dean of the Dawn."

OSTRANDER, WARREN E. Mar 7, 1901 Syracuse, NY - Feb 13, 1988 Syracuse, NY
Last surviving firefighter who fought the Collins Block fire at 225 East Genesee Street in Syracuse on February 3, 1939, the deadliest in the history of the Syracuse Fire Department, killing eight firefighters.

PIETROMONICA (Russo), **CATHERINE E.** Jul 16, 1925 Naples, Italy - Mar 26, 2004 Syracuse, NY
Second cousin of Academy Award-winning actress, Sophia Loren, related through Sophia Loren's mother, Romilda Villani.

ROLLINS, ROXIE ELWIN Nov 3, 1901 Hastings, ON, Canada - Mar 11, 1968 Syracuse, NY
Owned and operated the Seneca Dairy on South Salina Street in Syracuse from 1933-1953. Husband of Kathleen Hayes Rollins Snavely, the longest-lived person born in the history of Ireland at the time of her death in 2015.

SMITH, WILFORD M. Aug 7, 1918 Burke, NY - Dec 15, 1990 Syracuse, NY
World War II Army veteran. One of the first American GI's to enter the Dachau concentration camp, April 29, 1945, liberating prisoners following Germany's defeat.

SNAVELY (Hayes), **KATHLEEN** Feb 16, 1902 Feakle, Clare, Ireland - July 6, 2015 Syracuse, NY
Died at age 113 years and 140 days, the longest-lived person born in the history of Ireland. She was the sixteenth oldest person in the world at the time of her death. Traveled to Syracuse as a 19-year old immigrant in 1921, where she remained the rest of her life.

SOUTHWORTH, HAROLD CLAYTON 1905 St. Regis Falls, NY - May 7, 1963 Syracuse, NY
Brooklyn Dodgers baseball scout. Father of Bob Southworth, baseball coach for Corcoran High School, Syracuse, from 1965-2015, winning 700 games.

WARD, RENE WELLINGTON Mar 1, 1893 Solvay, NY - Jun 17, 1969 Syracuse, NY
Called the "Solvay Bad Man" for his lifelong criminal career consisting of burglaries, grand larceny and numerous jailbreaks, including the Onondaga Penitentiary in Jamesville, the Saratoga County Jail, and the Clinton Correctional Facility in Dannemora.

WEBSTER, EPHRAIM 1762 Hampstead, NH - 1824 Tonawanda, NY
Revolutionary War veteran, joining the Continental Army at age 15. First white settler in Onondaga County, known as Webster's Landing. Opened the first trading post. Married an Onondaga Indian maiden. Negotiated treaties between the Onondagas and the United States Government. Grandfather of Tahtoho, Chief of the Onondaga Indian tribe until age 71.

WELLS, ALFRED F. 1909 Syracuse, NY - Dec 7, 1941 Oahu, HI
United States Navy Machinist's Mate 1st Class. Killed in the Japanese attack on Pearl Harbor, December 7, 1941, serving aboard the *U.S.S. Oklahoma*, capsizing after absorbing nine torpedo hits, resulting in 429 casualties. Originally buried with other unidentified sailors at the Punchbowl, the National Memorial Cemetery of the Pacific, Honolulu, his remains were positively identified in 2015, reburied the following year.

WILEY, RUBY NELL Mar 31, 1948 Apopka, FL - Jul 14, 2002 Syracuse, NY
Mother of Nicholas Lee Wiley, Central New York serial killer, convicted of murdering three women, Lottie Thompson, Hannah Finnerty and Tammy Passineau, in 2004, three months after his release from prison for sexual assault and battery.

WILLIAMS, CHARLES Oct 5, 1955 Syracuse, NY - Dec 11, 2010 Syracuse, NY
Found dead in a snowbank behind St. James Church, shirtless and covered in five-feet of snow, by police officers investigating an armed robbery on South Salina Street. Police suspect he died of natural causes and had been there for days.

WOOD, THADDEUS MEAD Mar 9, 1772 Lenox, MA - Jan 10, 1836 Onondaga County, NY
War of 1812 New York Militia Major-General. First attorney in Onondaga County. Son-in-law of General Asa Danforth, second white settler of Onondaga County.

ONTARIO CENTER CEMETERY
Ridge Road
Ontario, NY 14519

CHURCH (Davis)**, SARAH** 1779 CT - Jun 1841 Ontario, NY
Grandmother of newspaper editors, William Conant Church and Francis Pharcellus Church, an editor at the *New York Sun*, who received a letter from eight-year old, Virginia O'Hanlon, in 1895 asking if there was really a Santa Claus. He replied in an editorial with his now famous line, "Yes, Virginia, there is a Santa Claus."

ORAN CEMETERY
Oran Station Road
Oran, NY 13125

FINN, SHERWOOD May 18, 1930 Syracuse, NY - May 3, 2005 Fayetteville, NY
Central New York real estate magnate. Owned the Longley Jones Management Corporation with E. Carlyle Smith, turning the residential sales company into a commercial sales and leasing corporation.

OSWEGATCHIE CEMETERY
597 Oswegatchie Road
Oswegatchie, NY 13670

POTTER, FREDERICK B. 1857 - Feb 28, 1942 Star Lake, NY
Dodge City cowboy, acquaintance of Buffalo Bill, Calamity Jane and Wild Bill Hickok.

OULEOUT CEMETERY
Route 28
Franklin, NY 13775

HINE, LEWIS WICKES Sept 26, 1874 Oshkosh, WI - Nov 3, 1940 Hastings-on-Hudson, NY
Documentary photographer. Photographed immigrants arriving to America at Ellis Island and the construction of the Empire State Building in New York City. Staff investigator and photographer for the National Child Labor Committee in 1908.

OUR LADY OF ANGELS CEMETERY
Route 18
Whitehall, NY 12887

INGALLS, JOYCE ELAINE Jan 14, 1950 Charleston, SC - Aug 5, 2015 Burbank, CA
Actress. Appeared in the films, *Lethal Weapon 4* and *Paradise Alley*. Model with the Ford Modeling Agency. Named in divorce proceedings by Sasha Stallone, filed against her husband, Sylvester Stallone, following their publicized affair in 1978. Wife of television producer, Darrell Fetty.

LAPIERRE, WILLIAM Mar 8, 1872 Keeseville, NY - Jun 23, 1952 Whitehall, NY
With **Agnes Harvey LaPierre** (Jun 1872 Chazy, NY - 1952 Whitehall, NY), the great-grandparents of Wayne LaPierre, Executive Director of the National Rifle Association.

ST. CLAIRE, EBBA (Edward Joseph) Aug 5, 1921 Whitehall, NY - Aug 22, 1982 Whitehall, NY
Catcher for the Boston Braves, Milwaukee Braves and New York Giants from 1951-1954. Father of Randy St. Claire, pitcher for the Montreal Expos, Cincinnati Reds, Minnesota Twins, Atlanta Braves and Toronto Blue Jays from 1884-1992 and 1994.

OUR LADY OF HELP CHRISTIANS CEMETERY
48 Cemetery Avenue
Albany, NY 12204

CRAUGH, JOSEPH PATRICK Mar 19, 1893 Penn Yan, NY - Dec 9, 1969 Utica, NY
Chairman of the Utica Mutual Insurance Corporation. Held several statewide offices in New York. Head of the Yates County Democratic Party in 1927. Defeated by John Taber in the 1928 and 1930 elections for United States House of Representatives-NY, 36th Congressional District. Taber held that seat from 1923-1963.

OUR LADY OF PEACE CEMETERY
Oswego Road
Clay, NY 13041

GARDNER, MARSHALL L. Jun 30, 1938 Port Washington, NY - Jul 2, 2005 Syracuse, NY
Owned and operated the Celebrity Den Restaurant in Syracuse for twenty years.

HAMLIN (Martin)**, SHIRLEY ANNE** Aug 3, 1937 Syracuse, NY - Mar 27, 2017 Phoenix, NY
Kissed a broken statue of Saint Ann as an 11-year old child, causing tears to flow from the eyes of the statue and continue to do so for many years. Her mother's statue had fallen from her windowsill, April 3, 1949, on Hawley Avenue in Syracuse. Her story made news around the world, her local Roman Catholic church calling it a "phenomenon."

HOLOHAN, JOHN D. Apr 19, 1921 Cohoes, NY - Mar 2, 2007 Syracuse, NY
Father of Pete Holohan, wide receiver for Notre Dame from 1977-1981 and the San Diego Chargers, Los Angeles Rams, Kansas City Chiefs and Cleveland Browns from 1981-1992.

LAPORTA, LUKE L. Jul 9, 1924 Jamaica (Queens), NY - Nov 19, 2013 Syracuse, NY
Created the first Little League in Central New York. Chairman of Little League, Inc., from 1983-2013. Inducted into the Syracuse Sports Hall of Fame in 1990.

MORRIS, SHEENA LEE Aug 1, 1986 Syracuse, NY - Jan 1, 2009 Bradenton Beach, FL
Found dead in her shower at the Imperial House Condominiums outside of Tampa, hanging by a dog leash, ruled a suicide. Her parents, not satisfied with the medical examiner's ruling, appeared on *Dr. Phil* and hired famed forensic pathologist, Dr. Michael Baden, to perform a second autopsy, July 21, 2010. No evidence of homicide was found.

NAVE, CHRISTOPHER P. Jul 29, 1932 Syracuse, NY - Jan 28, 2006 Syracuse, NY
Owned and operated the Karmelkorn Shoppe in Syracuse.

RAO, SAM (Salvatore) 1931 Alì Superiore, Sicily, Italy - Dec 5, 2016 Baldwinsville, NY
Owned and operated Willowbrook Construction and Rao Custom Homes in Syracuse.

RUSSO, VINCENT J. Feb 18, 1928 Syracuse, NY - Jan 21, 2011 Syracuse, NY
Struck head-on by a drunk driver, Michael J. Iannettoni, who had four prior convictions for DWI and was awaiting sentencing for a fifth, on his way to Sunday Mass, January 9, 2011, Buckley Road, Liverpool, died 12 days later from his injuries. Sponsored by New York State Senator, John DeFrancisco, "Vince's Law", toughening penalties for drunk drivers with multiple offenses, passed legislation in 2014. Iannettoni died August 18, 2012, in Auburn Correctional Facility, age 60, buried in Woodlawn Cemetery in Syracuse.

WATSON, JENNI-LYN MARIE Feb 24, 1990 Syracuse, NY - Nov 19, 2010 Liverpool, NY
Murder victim. Dance major, studying ballet, at Mercyhurst College in Erie, PA, reported missing while home on Thanksgiving break, sparking a weeklong search and national coverage. Her body was found, November 27th, buried in Hamlin Marsh in Clay Central Park, off Wetzel Road, a few miles from her home, 7406 Donegal Lane in Liverpool. Her ex-boyfriend, Steven Pieper, charged with her murder later that same day, was sentenced to 23 years-to-life in prison.

OUR LADY OF VICTORY BASILICA
767 Ridge Road
Lackawanna, NY 14218

BAKER, NELSON HENRY Feb 16, 1842 Buffalo, NY - Jul 29, 1936 Lackawanna, NY
Roman Catholic priest. "Padre of the Poor." Designated Venerable by Pope Benedict XVI in 2011. Named Buffalo's most influential citizen of the 20th Century. Originally buried in Holy Cross Cemetery in Lackawanna, removed to the Basilica in 1999.

OWASCO RURAL CEMETERY
East Lake Road / Route 38A
Owasco, NY 13130

CASTOR (Daniels), **STACEY R.** Jul 24, 1967 Clay, NY - Jun 11, 2016 Bedford Hills, NY
"Black Widow" murderer, killed her husbands, Michael E. Wallace and David W. Castor with anti-freeze, then attempted to kill her daughter, Ashley Wallace, to cover up her crimes. Sentenced to 51 1/2 years in prison, following a nationally-televised trial, died there, Bedford Hills Correctional Facility for Women. Subject of an ABC *20/20* special and an episode of *Forensic Files*.

DANIELS, GERALD W. Jul 26, 1941 Syracuse, NY - Feb 27, 2002 Syracuse, NY
Father of Stacey Castor, "Black Widow" murderer, who killed her husbands, Michael E. Wallace and David W. Castor, then attempted to kill her daughter, Ashley Wallace, to cover up the crimes. Hospitalized with a lung ailment, he was due to be released, his daughter brought him a can of soda to drink, he died and she had him cremated.

JENKS, GEORGE CHARLES Apr 13, 1850 London, England - Sept 12, 1929 Owasco, NY
Novelist, playwright and journalist. Wrote for the dime-novel series, *Diamond Dick* and *Nick Carter*, for *Street & Smith*.

WALLACE MICHAEL E. Sept 16, 1961 Auburn, NY - Jan 11, 2000 Weedsport, NY
Murder victim. Originally thought to have died from a heart attack, his body was exhumed in 2007, autopsied, and changed to homicide, due to antifreeze poisoning. His widow, Stacey R. Daniels Castor, was charged with the attempted murder of her daughter, Ashley Wallace, in an attempt to blame his murder, as well as the death of her second husband, David W. Castor, on her daughter. She was charged with the poisoning deaths of both husbands in a case that gained national attention as the "Black Widow" murders. Following a nationally-televised trial, she was sentenced to 51 1/2 years in prison. Both husbands were originally buried in the same burial plot, David W. Castor, was removed by his son in 2016.

OWL'S NEST CEMETERY
Route 9L
Lake George, NY 12845

EGGLESTON, EDWARD Dec 10, 1837 Vevey, IN - Sept 3, 1902 Lake George, NY
Author and historian. Wrote the novel, *The Hoosier Schoolmaster*, in 1871. Brother of author, George Cary Eggleston. Died at his estate, Owl's Nest, buried there next to his wife, Elizabeth Goodsmith Eggleston, died January 27, 1890 in Lake George, age 61.

OXBOW PRESBYTERIAN CHURCH CEMETERY
Church Road
Oxbow, NY 13671

BENTON, ABNER May 16, 1786 Hampshire, MA - Feb 6, 1845 Oxbow, NY
First physician and Postmaster of Oxbow. First surgeon to practice antiseptic methods. Father of Civil War Union Army Colonel, Zebulon H. Benton. Father-in-law of Caroline Bonaparte Benton, daughter of Joseph Bonaparte, King of Spain.

BONAPARTE (Benton)**, CAROLINE CHARLOTTE** 1822 NJ - Dec 25, 1890 Richfield Springs, NY
Daughter of Joseph Bonaparte, King of Spain, and his American-born mistress, Annette Savage.
Niece of Napoleon Bonaparte I, Emperor of France and Louis Bonaparte, King of Holland. Cousin of
Napoleon III, Emperor of France. Wife of Civil War Union Army Colonel, Zebulon Howell Benton.

PALATINE BRIDGE CEMETERY
Carmen Court
Palatine Bridge, NY 13428

WAGNER, WEBSTER Oct 2, 1817 Palatine Bridge, NY - Jan 13, 1882 Bronx, NY
Founded the Wagner Sleeping Car Company in Buffalo. Invented the sleeping car and parlor car on
trains. Member of the New York State Senate from 1872-1882. Killed in the Spuyten Duyvil train
accident in the Bronx.

PALENTOWN CEMETERY
Palentown Road
Kerhonkson, NY 12446

BATES, PEG LEG (Clayton) Oct 11, 1907 Fountain Inn, SC - Dec 6, 1998 Fountain Inn, SC
Tap Dancer. Lost his leg in a cotton gin accident, age 12. Appeared on *The Ed Sullivan Show* twenty
times. Owned and operated the Peg Leg Bates Country Club in Kerhonkson from 1951-1987, the first
black owner of a resort in the Catskill Mountains. Namesake of the Clayton Peg Leg Bates Memorial
Highway in Ulster County.

PALMYRA CEMETERY
272 Vienna Street
Palmyra, NY 14522

BUTTERFIELD, MARTIN Dec 8, 1790 Westmoreland, NH - Aug 6, 1866 Palmyra, NY
United States Representative-NY from 1859-1861.

HALL, AMBROSE Aug 29, 1774 Lanesborough, MA - Oct 14, 1827 Palmyra, NY
With **Clarissa Wilcox Hall** (Sept 30, 1796 Palmyra, NY - Jul 17, 1827 Palmyra, NY), the grandparents of
Jeanette Jerome, properly known as Lady Randolph Churchill, wife of Sir Randolph Henry Spencer-
Churchill, married in 1874 at the British Embassy in Paris. Great-grandparents of Sir Winston
Churchill, Prime Minister of Great Britain from 1940-1945 and 1951-1955.

SAMPSON, JAMES 1813 Ireland - 1881 Palmyra, NY
Father of United States Navy Admiral, William Thomas Sampson.

SAMPSON (Aldrich), **MARGARET SEXTON** Oct 31, 1842 Palmyra, NY - Jan 16, 1878 Annapolis, MD
First wife of United States Navy Admiral, William Thomas Sampson.

WALKER, CHARLES CHRISTOPHER Jun 27, 1824 Drewsville, NH - Jan 26, 1888 Corning, NY
United States Representative-NY from 1875-1877.

PARK VIEW CEMETERY
40 Fehr Avenue
Schenectady, NY 12304

BAKER, W. R. G. (Walter) Nov 30, 1892 Lockport, NY - Oct 30, 1960 Syracuse, NY
Radio and television pioneer. Vice-President of General Electric, responsible for the development of
Electronics Parkway in Syracuse.

GRABOWSKI, JOHNNY (John Patrick) Jan 7, 1900 Ware, MA - May 23, 1946 Albany, NY
Backup catcher for the Chicago White Sox, New York Yankees and Detroit Tigers from 1924-1929 and
1931. Member of the Yankees' Murderer's Row World Series championship team in 1927. Died from
burns suffered in a house fire.

PARMA UNION CEMETERY
Parma Union Cemetery
Parma, NY 14468

GIANGREGORIO BROTHERS Jun 11, 2016 Castile, NY
Brothers, **Dylan J. Giangregorio**, born January 14, 2007, and **Preston D. Giangregorio**, born May 26.
2010, from Brockport, drowned at Letchworth State Park when they fell over the 70-foot Lower Falls
after entering the water above the falls, off-trail. Five others survived, including three children. Two adults
supervising the five children, Chad Staley and Tyler Jennings, were charged with second-degree
manslaughter for criminally negligent homicide.

PAWLING CEMETERY
Route 22
Pawling, NY 12564

DE LAURENTIIS, FEDERICO Feb 28, 1955 - Jul 15, 1981 King Salmon, Alaska
Producer. Son of Academy Award-winning producer, Dino de Laurentiis and actress, Silvana Mangano. Brother of actress, Veronica de Laurentiis, and producer, Raffaella de Laurentiis. Uncle of chef and Food Network host, Giada de Laurentiis. Killed in a mid-air collision of two airplanes, filming a nature documentary.

DEWEY, THOMAS EDMUND Mar 24, 1902 Owosso, MI - Mar 16, 1971 Miami, FL
Governor of New York from 1943-1954. Republican candidate for president in 1944, losing to Franklin D. Roosevelt, and in 1948, upset by Harry S Truman, incorrectly predicted as the winner by the *Chicago Daily Tribune* headline "Dewey Defeats Truman." Manhattan District Attorney from 1938-1941. Prosecuted Lucky Luciano and Dutch Schultz. Namesake of the New York State Thruway.

GWINN, RALPH WALDO Mar 29, 1844 Noblesville, IN - Mar 27, 1962 Delray Beach, FL
United States Representative-NY from 1945-1959.

MANGANO, ROY (Rocco) Jul 1, 1927 Rome, Italy - Mar 6, 1991
Italian film actor. Brother of actress, Silvana Mangano. Uncle of actress, Veronica de Laurentiis, and producer, Raffaella de Laurentiis.

MANGANO (de Laurentiis), **SILVANA** Apr 21, 1930 Rome, Italy - Dec 16, 1989 Madrid, Spain
Italian film actress. Appeared in the films, *Bitter Rice, The Tempest, Barabbas* and *Dune.* Wife of Academy Award-winning producer, Dino de Laurentiis, from 1949-1988. Mother of actress, Veronica de Laurentiis, and producer, Raffaella de Laurentiis. Grandmother of chef and Food Network Host, Giada de Laurentiis.

TOFFEY, JOHN JAMES Jun 1, 1844 Pawling, NY - Mar 13, 1911 Pawling, NY
Civil War Union Army First Lieutenant. Award the Medal of Honor in 1897. Nephew of John Lorimer Worden, Commander of the *U.S.S. Monitor* in the Civil War. Brother of Daniel Toffey, Captain's Clerk on the *U.S.S. Monitor.*

WORDEN, JOHN LORIMER Mar 12, 1818 Mount Pleasant, NY - Oct 18, 1897 Washington D.C.
United States Navy Rear Admiral. Commanded the *U.S.S. Monitor* in the Battle of Hampton Roads in the Civil War, against the Confederate vessel, *C.S.S. Virginia*, rebuilt from the *U.S.S. Merrimack*, the first-ever battle between ironclad steamships.

PEACEDALE CEMETERY
Dale Avenue
Highland Falls, NY 10928

BIGELOW, JOHN Nov 25, 1817 Malden-on-Hudson, NY - Dec 19, 1911 New York, NY
American Envoy to the Court of Napoleon III in France, appointed by President Abraham Lincoln in 1861. Co-owned and edited the *New York Evening Post*. Published *The Autobiography of Benjamin Franklin* in 1868.

FAUROT, JOSEPH A. Oct 14, 1872 NY - Nov 20, 1942 St. Albans (Queens), NY
New York City Police Department Deputy Commissioner. First police detective to use fingerprints to identify a criminal and first to obtain a conviction using fingerprint evidence.

PECKS CEMETERY
Hall Road
Oswego, NY 13126

VINCENT, SHERMAN M. Nov 13, 1901 Rochester, NY - Apr 18, 1974 Anaheim, CA
With **Naomi Myra Sikes Weller** (Jan 9, 1908 Volney, NY - Sept 18, 1997 Buena Park, CA), the grandparents of convicted killer, Robin Rodney Murray, who plea bargained a sentence of 35-years-to-life for the murders of Sheila M. Small and Kyle Heifferon in Syracuse in 1984, only to recant when his mother, Barbara L. Vincent Murray, shouted in the courtroom for him to plead innocent. He stood trial, was convicted of both murders in 1985, and sentenced to two consecutive 25-years-to life sentences.

PENDERGAST CEMETERY
River Road
Phoenix, NY 13135

PENDERGAST, HANK (Henry James) Oct 23, 1883 Phoenix, NY - Mar 30, 1957 Syracuse, NY
New York State trapshooting expert. Won the National Champion of Champions in 1929.

PERRY FAMILY CEMETERY
Wuetherich Road
Rome, NY 13440

PERRY, GEORGE HAZARD Jan 4, 1757 South Kingston, RI - Feb 22, 1825 Lee, NY
Uncle of United States Navy Commodore, Oliver Hazard Perry, hero of the Battle of Lake Erie, defeating the British in 1813, United States Naval Commodore, Matthew C. Perry, and their older sister, Mary Perry Coulter Benneman Black, born April 27, 1769, died May 20, 1888 in Story County, IA, age 119, which, if verified, would make her among the oldest-lived people in history.

PERRYVILLE CEMETERY
Siebenbaum Road
Canastota, NY 13032

DEUEL, JACOB BETTINGER Nov 16, 1887 Piqua, OH - May 31, 1950 Rochester, NY
Rochester-area physician, specialized in radiology. With **Norma Shaut Hill Deuel** (Jan 22, 1889 NY - Feb 9, 1981 Penfield, NY), the grandparents of actors, Peter Duel and Geoffrey Deuel.

PETERBORO VILLAGE CEMETERY
Oxbow Road
Peterboro, NY 13134

ARMOUR, PRESTON Aug 1793 - Apr 25, 1879 Munnsville, NY
Uncle of Philip D. Armour and Herman O. Armour, co-founders of Armour & Company, a meatpacking business, in Chicago in 1867.

FRANK (Ward)**, EMMA MAY** Nov 27, 1928 Munnsville, NY - Oct 2, 1988 Munnsville, NY
Only sister of the "Ward Boys", four brothers, Delbert, Lyman, Roscoe and Bill, who lived together on a farm in Madison County, made famous in the award-winning documentary, *Brother's Keeper*, in 1992, chronicling Delbert's nationally-covered trial in the death of his brother, Lyman, and his subsequent acquittal. None of her brothers married or had children, she had eight children with her husband, Charles A. Frank.

MILLER (Smith)**, ELIZABETH** Sept 20, 1822 NY - May 22, 1911 Peterboro, NY
Woman's rights activist known for the bloomers she wore as a catalyst for dress reform. Used her Peterboro home as a station in the Underground Railroad. Daughter of Gerrit Smith, United States Representative-NY from 1853-1854.

SMITH, GERRIT Mar 6, 1797 Utica, NY - Dec 28, 1874 New York, NY
United States Representative-NY from 1853-1854. Leading abolitionist, philanthropist and social reformer of his day. Financial supporter of abolitionist, John Brown. Unsuccessful candidate for president in 1848, 1856 and 1860. Founded the Church of Peterboro in 1843. Son of Peter Smith, namesake of Peterboro. Father of suffragist, Elizabeth Miller Smith. Great-grandson of Petrus Smith, whose Tappan farm was the site of the hanging of Major John André, executed as a spy during the Revolutionary War. Cousin of social reformer, Elizabeth Cady Stanton.

SMITH (Fitzhugh)**, NANCY** (Ann Carroll) Jan 11, 1805 Hagerstown, MD - Mar 6, 1875 Peterboro, NY
Wife of Gerrit Smith, United States Representative-NY from 1853-1854. Mother of suffragist, Elizabeth Smith Miller. Daughter of Colonel William F. Fitzhugh, a founding father of Rochester.

SMITH, PETER   Nov 15, 1768 Tappan, NY - Apr 15, 1837 Schenectady, NY
Early settler of Madison County. Namesake of the hamlet of Peterboro. Fur trader and partner of John Jacob Astor. Grandson of Petrus Smith, whose Tappan farm was the site of the hanging of Major John André, executed as a spy during the Revolutionary War. Father of Gerrit Smith, United States Representative-NY from 1853-1854. Grandfather of suffragist, Elizabeth Miller Smith.

STONE, ASAHEL CLAUDE 1805 Nelson, NY - 1866 Peterboro, NY
New York State Senator. Father of Josephine Stone Baum, the wife of Adam Clarke Baum, L. Frank Baum, author of *The Wonderful Wizard of Oz* series of children's books.

PHOENIX PIONEER CEMETERY
Main Street / Route 57
Phoenix, NY 13135

OLMSTED, TIMOTHY Nov 12, 1759 Hartford, CT - Aug 15, 1848 Whitesboro, NY
Teacher and composer of sacred music. Revolutionary War veteran. Fifer and member of the Connecticut regimental band of music.

PHOENIX RURAL CEMETERY
Chestnut Street
Phoenix, NY 13135

DILLON, EMERSON JAMES Feb 3, 1902 Marcellus, NY - Feb 6, 1971 Syracuse, NY
World War II United States Naval Commander in the Pacific. Health officer for the town of Schroeppel. Namesake of the Emerson J. Dillon Jr. High School in Phoenix. Father of Emerson J. Dillon Jr., New York State trooper fatally killed in 1974.

DILLON, EMERSON JAMES May 26, 1936 Syracuse, NY - Oct 24, 1974 Canastota, NY
New York State trooper. Stopped a speeding vehicle on the New York State Thruway, unaware the two occupants were fleeing the scene of an armed robbery, shot and killed following an exchange of gunfire. Son of Dr. Emerson J. Dillon Sr., health officer for the town of Schroeppel.

SWEET, THADDEUS C. Nov 16, 1872 Phoenix, NY - May 1, 1928 Whitney Point, NY
United States Representative-NY from 1923-1928. Elected to Congress due to the death of Luther Wright Mott. Speaker of the New York State Assembly from 1914-1920. President of the Sweet Paper Manufacturing Company. First sitting congressman to be killed in an airplane crash.

WILLIAMS, GLENN W. Sept 9, 1903 Mount Carmel, PA - Apr 6, 1975 Clay, NY
News Director at WNDR-AM from 1951-1958 and 1963-1971 and WSEN-FM from 1959-1962. Called the "Dean of Central New York broadcasters."

PIERREPONT HILL CEMETERY
Clare Town Line-Pierrepont Center Road / Route 24
Canton, NY 13617

BACHELLER, SAMUEL - Nov 10, 1830 Canton, NY
With **Sally Sanford Bacheller** (- Sept 5, 1874 Canton, NY), the grandparents of novelist and journalist, Irving Bacheller.

MERRITT, EDWIN ALBERT Jul 25, 1860 Pierrepont, NY - Dec 4, 1914 Potsdam, NY
U.S. Representative-NY from 1912-1914, elected due to the death of George R. Malby, died before the end of his first term. Son of Civil War Union Army Brigadier General, Edwin A. Merritt.

MERRITT, EDWIN ATKINS Feb 26, 1828 Sudbury, VT - Dec 26, 1916 Potsdam, NY
Civil War Union Army Brigadier General. United States Consul General in London from 1881-1885. Represented New York at the second inauguration of President Abraham Lincoln. Father of Edwin A. Merritt Jr., U.S. Representative-NY from 1912-1914.

PINE BANK CEMETERY
Wells Curtice Road
Canandaigua, NY 14424

STILES, ANSON ROSE Sept 9, 1797 Canandaigua, NY - Mar 14, 1861 Canandaigua, NY
Brother of Philemon Stiles, the great-grandfather of Academy Award-winning actor, Humphrey Bogart.

STILES, STEPHEN Oct 12, 1828 Canandaigua, NY - Nov 10, 1888 Canandaigua, NY
Granduncle of Academy Award-winning actor, Humphrey Bogart.

Milton Keynes UK
Ingram Content Group UK Ltd.
UKHW021130060923
428126UK00009B/191